by the Catalyst Staff

with a Foreword by Bess Myerson

Also from Catalyst:

Marketing Yourself: The Catalyst Women's Guide to Successful Resumes and Interviews

Career Option Series for Undergraduate Women

The Education Opportunity Series

The Career Opportunity Series

Self-Guidance Series

The Resume Preparation Manual: A Step-by-Step Guide for Women

Creating Change for College Women

How to Go to Work When Your Husband Is Against It, Your Children Aren't Old Enough, and There's Nothing You Can Do Anyhow by Susan S. Gillotti, Felice N. Schwartz and Margaret H. Schifter

What to Do

The Catalyst Career Guide for Women in the '80s

with the Rest of Your Life

A TOUCHSTONE BOOK
Published by Simon and Schuster
NEW YORK

First Touchstone Edition, 1981
Published by Simon & Schuster, Inc.
Simon & Schuster Building
Rockefeller Center
1230 Avenue of the Americas
New York, New York 10020

TOUCHSTONE and colophon are registered trademarks of Simon & Schuster, Inc.

Designed by Jeanne Joudry

Manufactured in the United States of America

2 3 4 5 6 7 8 9 10

3 4 5 6 7 8 9 10 Pbk.

Library of Congress Cataloging in Publication Data

Main entry under title:
What to do with the rest of your life.
  (A Touchstone book)
  1. Vocational guidance for women—United States.
I. Catalyst, inc.
HD6058.W38   1981   650.1'4'024042   81-9037
ISBN 0-671-25070-1   AACR2
ISBN 0-671-25071-X Pbk.

Permission to reprint excerpts from the following is gratefully acknowledged:

Health Careers 1975–76: A Directory of Career Information and Training for New York State by Glynn Rudich. Copyright 1975 by United Hospital Fund. Reprinted by permission of United Hospital Fund of New York.
"Health Careers Calendar" reprinted from *Health Careers Guidebook,* U.S. Department of Labor in *Career World* magazine, Vol. 3, No. 6, February 1975. Reprinted by permission of *Career World* magazine, Curriculum Innovations, Inc. Highwood, IL 60040.
Modified material from *A Report to the President and the Congress on the Status of Health Profession's Personnel in the United States,* August 1978, United States Department of Health, Education and Welfare.
Dentistry—A Changing Profession, revised, 1975 edition by the American Dental Association. Copyright by the American Dental Association. Reprinted by permission.
Material by Vivian Guilfoy, director of the Boston YWCA's program, Nontraditional Occupations for Women.
"Safety Tip for Operating Engineers" from *June 1972 Convention Proceedings* of the International Union of Operating Engineers. Reprinted courtesy of the International Union of Operating Engineers.

Dedication

*To those women who will be
the vanguard of the future,
meeting rewarding challenges,
making impressive contributions,
leading full lives, and
aspiring to ever-greater successes.*

Acknowledgments

Catalyst gives warm thanks to the corporations who provided the funding that enabled us to undertake the research and writing of this book. Their generous support for this effort clearly demonstrates their commitment to the full integration of women into the workforce in a manner that is mutually productive and equitable for both women and employers.

New York Life Insurance Company
  contributed funding for Guide I: *A Guide to Planning Your Career*

Pfizer, Inc.
  contributed funding for Guide II: *A Guide to Health Careers*

International Business Machines Corporation
  contributed funding for Guide III: *A Guide to Science and Engineering Careers*

Davis Polk & Wardwell
  contributed funding for Guide IV: *A Guide to Law and Government Careers*

American Telephone and Telegraph Company
  contributed funding for Guide V: *A Guide to Skilled Trades Careers*

Xerox Corporation, General Motors Corporation, Philip Morris, Inc., John Hancock Mutual Life Insurance Company, Citibank, N.A., the Western Electric Fund, and *Continental Illinois National Bank and Trust Company*
  contributed funding for Guide VI: *A Guide to Business Careers*

Contents

172294

10   CONTENTS

GUIDE IV   A GUIDE TO GOVERNMENT AND LAW CAREERS

Foreword

Ready, Get Set—and make sure you know where and how to Go.

That's the concept which Catalyst has developed and is delivering with skill and dedication to all women—and with practical guidance to those women who may have started off on the wrong foot, or not even reached the starting line at all—in the race toward the increasing opportunities today.

Catalyst embodies an important truth—that even an idea whose time has come, especially one that has come to us too slowly and too spottily, needs all the help it can get to stay alive and grow.

Lip service to equality is all around us in abundance, and too often it only camouflages the stale, stubborn myths of our society, which are so deeply rooted that they provide a hard-core resistance even to the most sweeping changes in the social climate.

The evidence of the hardiness of these myths is the continuing double standard in our lives, more subtle perhaps but still continuing in career and professional opportunities, in legal protections, in political participation, in artistic and scientific recognition and advancement, in the businesses and trades that have "traditionally" been closed to women, and in the choices of lifestyles in home, family and community.

Catalyst knows a closed door when it sees one, and its efforts have helped to open many closed doors, and to open wider those in which only a symbolic foot has been wedged.

But the concept of Catalyst embodies another truth, equally important—that even an open door might as well be a closed door for women who don't know where to go to find it, or who lack the required skills and sense of direction to move through the door and up to the highest level of their potential.

That truth is the most challenging for women, because its battleground is not society in general, as in the case of the first truth, but the awareness and understanding and initiative of each woman herself. Ignorance, or inertia, or indecision, are not the best roadmaps for any woman who

19

wants to go from here to there. They are the negative qualities which can turn hard-won opportunities into easily lost futures. Women who don't know where to go in pursuit of career, or what to do if they find one within reach, aren't really going anywhere, or at least not as far in the right direction for them.

Enter Catalyst.

Catalyst was born before "Women's Lib" became a headline in our national vocabulary, when the Equal Rights Amendment was just a gleam in any state legislature's eye, and for almost two decades it has been doing effectively what its perceptive organizers foresaw as an urgent and growing need: helping women find their way to career opportunities, and guiding them toward career advancement.

Despite the achievements of Catalyst and others who are dedicated to whittling away the social and economic inequities based on sex, the hugeness of the task is reflected in the fact that even today, with realized opportunities for women seeming to accumulate all around us, women are significantly represented in only twenty of the 480 major occupations —and scarcely if at all represented in the other 460 career categories, all of which have been "traditionally" male, and many of which offer exceptional opportunities for those women who are not only willing but ready and able to make the most of them.

"Ready and able"—those are the operative words whose definition leaps off every page of the new book by the editors of Catalyst.

What to Do with the Rest of Your Life is complete and clear step-by-step information for women who want to find themselves and find careers in which they can serve with dignity, fulfillment and reward.

It's a no-nonsense book. No wringing of hands, no lofty philosophizing that misses the practical point—which is, which always is, where are the promising careers happening and how can I make them happen for me?

Catalyst shakes up some old theories, and brushes aside some stale misconceptions and goes right to the source to dig up the facts. It tells a woman how she must honestly evaluate her own potential and be able to select the career which can best respond to that potential. It emphasizes the skills and education which a woman must acquire to move into and then move ahead in whatever career she chooses. It spells out what steps to take and what missteps to avoid. It defines the pluses and minuses of careers, through expert analysis, and also through interviews— unusually candid—with women who are already in those careers or now preparing for them.

And they've put it all in a challenging book.

The challenge is now in your hands.

Bess Myerson

Catalyst: What It Is, Why We Wrote This Book

Catalyst: Something that brings about a change, that initiates a reaction and enables it to take place. Catalyst, the national nonprofit organization dedicated exclusively to women and their careers, has been creating a climate for change since it was founded in 1962 by Felice N. Schwartz, its president, and five college presidents. With the goal of expanding career opportunities for women, Catalyst has a comprehensive national program that:

- informs women, employers, counselors, educators, legislators, and the media about issues of common interest through its specialized information center, open to the public
- offers career information and guidance to women at all stages of their careers through its more than 150 publications
- provides counseling to nearly a million women through its network of more than 200 resource centers nationwide
- helps corporate women progress in their careers, and helps employers respond to their needs through its programs for employers
- offers corporations outstanding women candidates for corporate directorships and assists them with their search through its Corporate Board Resource

Catalyst's current priorities include addressing the needs in particular of the two-career family, the undergraduate woman, and the upwardly mobile woman. Our role is to facilitate the growing partnership of employers and women by helping women plan their careers and by helping business and industry develop the talent and leadership they need.

Catalyst designed this book to promote the constructive integration of women into all areas of the workforce, especially those which have been traditionally male and in which opportunities for women are expanding.

This book will help women who are planning their futures, seeking jobs for the first time, changing careers, or returning to the job market.

Although 50 percent of all women are now in the labor force, most women work in traditional, low-paying "female" occupations. Of 480 major occupations, working women are concentrated in only 20. But the best opportunities for women today are in the other 460, the fields in which they have been seriously underrepresented. The more technical and thus more traditionally "male" the field, the better the promise for women. For that reason Catalyst has chosen to emphasize in this book the areas of health, science and engineering, skilled trades, law and government, and business, areas that offer women the greatest opportunities for a responsible, well-paying career.

Forward motion in the cooperative venture of employers and women is irreversible. The need for skilled management and creative talent in the years ahead is tremendous. Women can help corporations compete in the world market, a necessity in today's global society. Technological advances have freed women from the burdens of household responsibility, and corporations cannot afford to waste the vital resource of women's talents. The opportunities for both women and corporations have never been greater.

(Catalyst's national headquarters are at 14 East 60 Street, New York, New York 10022.)

Contributors

The staff of Catalyst conceived and executed the research, writing and editing of this book.

The publications staff included Carol A. Day, vice-president, director of publications and managing editor; Larayne Ewald, editor and researcher; Maria Muniz, editor; and Dana L. Topping, assistant. Contributing writers included, for "A Guide to Planning Your Career," Dr. Esther E. Diamond and the publications staff of Catalyst; for "A Guide to Health Careers," Sharon Whitney with Edmund Day; for "A Guide to Science and Engineering Careers," Avima Ruder with Edmund Day; for both "A Guide to Skilled Trades Careers" and "A Guide to Law and Government Careers," Priscilla Claman; for "A Guide to Business Careers," Priscilla Claman with Edmund Day and Jacqueline Thompson.

Contributing editors were Catherine Calvert for "A Guide to Planning Your Career"; Edmund Day and Timothy Bay for "A Guide to Science and Engineering Careers"; Dorothy McKinnon and Faye Ran for "A Guide to Business Careers." Susan Richner and Kate Rohrbach assisted the editors.

The publications staff of Catalyst gives special thanks to Felice N. Schwartz, president of Catalyst, and to Jeannine Green, Catalyst's executive vice-president, for their help. The entire Catalyst staff made important contributions. Without their assistance this project could not have been completed. Reviewers, advisers, and experts we consulted, too numerous to include by name, were outstanding in their support. Finally, we thank the more than 1,000 women working in the different fields who openly share their experiences and their expertise with the readers through us. For many of us their enthusiasm and encouragement was the most rewarding aspect of the project, a reward that we know the reader will also experience.

Introduction

Suddenly you have been discovered. The working (or soon to be working) woman, you are now in the spotlight as the subject of countless books, magazine columns, newspaper articles, movies, theses, soap operas, radio and television shows and commercials—the target of a veritable media blitz! Analyzed, observed, described, classified, criticized, pressured, and even encouraged, you are today's superwoman.

The working woman *is* news, but she's certainly not new. Women have always worked—because they have had to and because they wanted to. What *is* new is the changing work world of women. Legal and social advances have combined to create a new climate, and you now have more opportunities to create a satisfying worklife. This book will help you take advantage of the new climate. You will find out how to change your life through work that takes full advantage of your abilities and interests and that contributes to a sense of fulfillment, and to a fuller pocketbook. In short, you will discover how to plan and begin your career, perhaps the major part of the rest of your life.

Career—what does it mean to you? A 9-to-5 necessity, or a satisfying and meaningful life experience? A challenge, or something that occupies your time? A career can be anything *you* want it to be, if you are willing to spend the time and effort to develop the skills needed to plan and manage it.

It's surprising how many people are willing to spend more time choosing a stereo or car than formulating a career plan. It's not surprising therefore how many of these same people are unhappy with their choices. Since you will spend a great part of your life on the job, planning your career necessarily implies planning your life. And since your career decisions will affect your life-style and the health and happiness of you and your family, it is even more imperative that you make well-informed choices, using utmost care to develop your own personal career (and life) plan.

Career planning is built on career awareness—knowledge of your options, skills, and motivations. In turn, career awareness depends on

25

self-awareness. You must know yourself before you can make intelligent decisions for yourself. That's what the first part of this book is all about. First you'll take a closer look at the changing world of you, including all those things you need to know to make informed choices—your needs, skills, interests, values, and characteristic ways of behaving.

You will also begin to explore career options and learn how to make decisions, set goals, and design your own plan of action for achieving those goals. You will then learn how to go about getting a job: how to write a resume, conduct interviews, find job leads and follow them up, and put your best self forward.

If you are feeling overwhelmed, don't worry! You will receive a great deal of help and support as you go through this process. Our carefully designed exercises and activities will help you organize and clarify your thoughts and feelings about work and yourself. Writing down such information will help you convert generalities into specifics, let you see what you've forgotten, and help you establish some priorities. As you get to know yourself and the world of work better, many things will begin to fall into place. You will see patterns of experiences, abilities, personal qualities, and values that will help you determine your future course.

You will also be receiving the help of the hundreds of women and employment experts we talked with to prepare this book. You will read the words of working women pursuing careers in health, science and engineering, law and government, skilled trades, and business. Once you have learned how to plan your career and are equipped to deal with the realities of getting a job, any job, you will read about promising careers in these areas and find out how to find and get the one that's right for you. Whether or not you will work may no longer be a subject for debate. What you choose to do and how you do it is the present challenge. It's a most exciting one for society and women in general but, more importantly, for you yourself, today's new woman.

How to Use This Book as a Tool for Planning Your Future

This book is an action guide, a tool to help you help yourself to plan and begin your career.

You will be using a notebook as you work through the exercises and checklists of Guide I, the section on planning your career. Follow the step-by-step instructions as you work through these important activities. You may also want to go back to your notebook and add to these exercises once you have completed the rest of the book. Another suggestion is to read the first section on career planning as you also read through the other parts of the book on specific career areas. Reading both types of material—self-assessment and career information—at the same time may help put your knowledge of self into the larger perspective of the world of work.

The boxed sections that highlight various points made throughout the book will give you more insight. Although you may think you need facts and just the facts, you will find the advice of the women we profile in each career chapter stimulating and thought-provoking. We don't expect you to score yourself, but the quiz on women "firsts" in each field is fun and eye-opening to those who may have thought that men have been the only leaders. And the short historical snapshots of outstanding women, the Note from the Past sections, emphasize women's important role throughout the ages.

Use this book to begin the lifelong work that is required to produce a continually satisfying career experience. The resource sections listing organizations to consult and publications to read will help you find more information on the career area that is your target. It's extremely important to work through the book on your own and to use it as a *beginning*. It's your head start. The commitment you bring to this effort and the way you carry through on your plans will help you identify and get what you want. Success begins here.

Guide I

A Guide to Planning Your Career

Funding for this Guide was provided by New York Life Insurance Company.

CHAPTER 1:

WHAT'S IT ALL ABOUT?

The Changing World of Work

Women now comprise over 42 percent of the U.S. labor force. As a working woman, you live in a world very different from that of your grandmother, mother, or even perhaps that of an older sister. More and more women are working outside the home for longer periods of time and in a wider variety of occupational roles. Families with double wage-earners are no longer an exception; for many families a woman may be the primary or sole source of income.

Increasingly women are considering it "natural" to work; their jobs are no longer considered "secondary," but rather a logical expression of their individual goals and aspirations. The longer lifespan, increased control over reproduction, and concentration of childbearing and rearing into a shorter period of the life cycle introduce new possibilities for women.

Let's take a closer look at how these and other important changes affect you.

- *Legal Protection.* Laws protect your rights in many new ways, not as they did earlier when the law's "protection" limited women's opportunities for entry, advancement, and growth into occupations and fields in which men predominated. Previously women could not, for example, work the same number of hours as men, and they could not perform tasks considered dangerous for them (but not for men), such as lifting heavy objects or working in a mine or on a construction site. Today, however, as a woman you cannot be discriminated against in vocational and technical education; you cannot be barred from admission to schools or classes on the basis of sex by an institution receiving federal support; nor can you be discriminated against in employment because of race, religion, sex, or national origin. Also, employers now are required by law to take Affirmative Action, or active steps, to find women and place them in jobs in which they are underrepresented.

• *More Women in the Labor Force.* By mid-1977, according to the Department of Labor, 40 million women were in the labor force—about 41 percent of the country's entire labor force. For a sense of how dramatic the increase has been, consider these figures supplied by the National Commission on Women and Work: The number of women holding jobs has grown from 18 million in 1950 to 42.1 million in July 1978, a 129 percent increase. In addition, the number of working mothers has increased more than tenfold since the period preceding World War II.

• *More Women in Jobs That Used to Be "For Men Only."* Increasing numbers of women have been entering careers that traditionally have been dominated by men. The most dramatic shift, according to the Census Bureau, has been the large influx of women into the skilled trades. In the early 1970s almost half a million women were working in the skilled trades as craft and related workers. This figure represents an 80 percent increase over 1960—twice that for women in all occupations, and 8 times that for men in the skilled trades. In some occupations not only the percentage but the actual numerical increases for women exceeded those for men. The number of women carpenters, for example, grew from about 3,300 to approximately 11,000. The number of women electricians more than tripled; women auto mechanics increased from about 2,300 to 11,000; women painters went from about 6,400 to nearly 13,400. Other notable increases were made by machinists, compositors, and typesetters.

In predominantly male professions for the same 10-year period, the number of women lawyers more than doubled, the number of women physicians increased from about 16,000 to nearly 26,000, and the number of women dentists rose from about 1,900 to more than 3,100. Women in engineering showed one of the most dramatic increases— from about 7,000 to approximately 19,600—more than 4½ times the increase rate for men.

In traditionally male sales occupations, women insurance agents and brokers increased from about 35,300 to nearly 56,600, women real estate agents from about 46,100 to 83,600, women stock and bond sales agents from 2,100 to 8,900.

In managerial occupations, the number of women bank officers and financial managers rose from 2,100 to a whopping 54,500. Women sales managers, other than those in retail trades, went from 100 to 8,700.

A number of other nontraditional occupations showed substantial rates of growth for women, among them mail carrier, guard, police officer, bartender, and bus driver.

• *Women Helping Women.* The growing consciousness of women and their organizing into a variety of pressure groups have been powerful political forces for change, both legislative and social. Women in almost every major career field have organized to assist each other; witness the Association for Women in Science, Women in Construction, the Coalition of Labor Union Women, International Association for Personnel Women, and many other organizations. Formally and informally, women are helping each other—by sharing job leads, recommending other women for boards of directors, critiquing resumes, and serving as mentors to other women.

These advances are obviously great ones for women as a group, and the statistics prove it. But how do they affect *you* as an individual worker? For one thing, your career options are now practically limitless. For the first time you can really sit down and ask, "What do *I* want to be?" and if the answer is sheet-metal worker or plumber or doctor or scientist, it's *ok!*

In addition, if someone tries illegally to prevent you from becoming what you choose to be, there are places you can turn to for legal help and redress. The law is now working for you, not against you. And perhaps most importantly, you are not alone! You will find that you will get both moral and concrete support from other women, in groups and individually.

What these changes won't do is magically open the right doors for you. Specifically, you must be aware of your options, be appropriately qualified, and know where the jobs are and how to get them.

QUIZ

Do you know which of the following statements are myths and which are truths—or half truths? Try to answer on your own; then check the answers on the following page to see how you did.

1. Women who get married won't really have to work; their husbands will take care of them.
2. Most women work just for pin money.
3. Women work only until they have children; then they stay at home.
4. There is more job turnover among women workers than among men workers.
5. Women are out sick more often than men.
6. Women are more particular than men about the surroundings in which they work.
7. Women prefer not to work for other women.
8. Men prefer not to work for women.
9. Women are more content than men with jobs that don't challenge them intellectually.

10. Women are less concerned than men with getting ahead on the job.
11. In two-career families it's generally the man's career that is given more weight in decisions affecting both partners' careers.
12. Many women work so that they can avoid doing household chores.
13. The earnings gap between men and women is widening.
14. Women today get equal pay for equal work.
15. Women work in all occupations in which men are employed.
16. Men are better suited than women for certain kinds of jobs.
17. The more education a woman has, the more likely she is to work.

Quiz Answers

Here are the answers to the True and False statements that you quizzed yourself on. Compare your answers with these. How well did you do?

1. *False.* This is the famous Cinderella myth, still common among high school girls. It doesn't take long, however, for reality to register: More than 50 percent of the women in the labor force are married, and the percentage in the work force of the 25-to-34 age group — most of whom are married, are living with their husbands, and have children at home — is increasing rapidly. Many women at home go back to work when their children reach school age because it often takes two incomes to provide children with the many advantages parents want to give them. Divorce, a husband's illness, and widowhood are other possibilities ignored by the Cinderella myth.
2. *False.* The Federal Women's Program of the United States Civil Service Commission refers to this point of view as the "cake winner fallacy: men are bread winners, women are cake winners." While women may work for other reasons, such as self-fulfillment, most women work because of economic need.
3. *Another myth.* According to the Department of Labor, over half of the married women with children between ages 6 and 17 are in the labor force. The Civil Service Commission reports a return rate of more than two-thirds of the women on maternity leave from federal jobs.
4. High turnover rates are true of all employees — men and women — who are under 25, in low-income jobs, particularly clerical jobs. Since women make up a large part of this group, in actual numbers their turnover rate exceeds that of men. At professional levels the difference is much less, according to a federal study.
5. The national average for sick leave for women is 5.9 days; for men, 5.2 days. The difference is insignificant.
6. A University of Michigan study shows that while women exhibit somewhat more concern than men about the physical aspects of the work environment, a challenging job is far more important and women are not about to trade it for better working conditions.

7,8. Studies reported by the Department of Labor show that women have no preference in the matter and that most men who don't want to work for a woman
supervisor have never worked for one. In one study, where at least three-fourths
of male and female executives surveyed had worked with women managers, their
evaluation of women in management was favorable. Those who reacted unfavor-
ably displayed a traditional/cultural bias about other questions as well.

9. *False.* The University of Michigan study cited earlier indicates that women are
just as eager as men to have a job they find challenging and that uses their
abilities.

10. *False.* The number of women entering management training programs and taking
advantage of a great variety of opportunities to upgrade their qualifications label
this statement as undeniably a myth.

11. Unfortunately, there is a great deal of truth to this statement. In a *Psychology
Today* survey, 65 percent of the males and only 9 percent of the females responding said their careers were given more weight. About 33 percent of the females
but less than 16 percent of the males said that equal weight was given to both
careers.

12. If women work to get away from household chores, many of them must be sadly
disillusioned. The same *Psychology Today* survey found that women still do most
of the grocery shopping, cleaning, cooking, and clearing away after meals. One
bright note, however: younger women were more likely to report equal sharing of
homemaking responsibilities.

13. This statement is clearly *not a myth.* In 1955 women's median annual earnings
were 64 percent of men's. By 1975 this percentage had shrunk to approximately
59 percent.

14. This statement might be considered half-truth, half-myth. The law decrees that
women should get equal pay for equal work, but there are many jobs — especially
at the managerial and professional levels — in which the term "equal work" is
difficult to define. Women in these jobs consequently are often notoriously under-
paid.

15. *True.* Women work in all occupations in which men are employed. They are not,
however, employed in nearly the same proportions. In some occupations, for
example, as few as 3 percent of the workers are women. Most women are
employed in a very narrow range of low-status, low-paying, dead-end occupations.

16. *False.* This myth is one of the most persistent of all myths about women and
work. A Labor Department study using the General Aptitude Test Battery (GATB)
should help lay it to rest. The study found that in two of the seven areas important
in the skilled trades there were no sex differences; women excelled in four of the
areas, and men excelled in one. The authors of the study noted that in most cases
the differences would be of little practical significance.

17. *True.* The likelihood of a woman working increases with the amount of education
she has. For one thing, the more education a woman has, the greater the number
of options available to her. For another, the more education she has the more
reluctant she is to let it go to waste.

A Career Development Glossary

To help you clarify what we mean when we refer to a job, occupation, career, or self-concept, here are some definitions to keep in mind.

Job: The specific occupation in which a person works or in which the work is performed, such as a job as a clerk for a certain bank, as a chemist for a certain company, or as a construction worker on a particular site.

Occupation: A specific work role or kind of work activity, such as teacher, chemist, engineer, or bricklayer, without reference to the particular location or situation in which the work is performed.

Career: A pattern of related work or occupational sequences. The pattern might be one in which the person pursues the same occupation throughout his or her life, even though changes of employer or specific work situations might be involved. The pattern might also be one in which the person moves upward within a field, starting out as a proofreader for a publishing company, for example, and moving to editorial assistant, copy editor, assistant editor, associate editor, and finally senior editor, or perhaps, the head of a publishing company. Still another type of career pattern might involve a series of occupations that seem unrelated but each of which builds on important strengths and learning acquired in the preceding occupations. The pattern that emerges is one of increasing responsibility and "generalist" skills, which are important in leadership roles in many businesses, industries, and community and government organizations.

Self-concept: The way in which we view ourselves, including our perceptions of the ways in which others see us.

The Career Development Process—What the Experts Have to Say

Career development is not something that you are beginning now. Whether you realized it or not, you began the process when you were very young, for career development is the lifelong process of becoming aware of the world in which we live (including the world of work), and of experiencing work-related activities, developing interests and values, increasing our self-knowledge, investigating careers, and making a series of educational and career choices.

Every expert seems to have a theory about the process; many of these theories are complicated and some are boring. Few are mutually exclusive. Before taking a closer look at your own career development thus far, it may be helpful to see how the experts view the process. Their theories can help you analyze your own decision-making abilities and aid you in developing a more holistic approach to career development.

Most psychologists use the term career development to express their belief that thinking, planning, and making decisions about careers is a continuous, lifelong process. Both psychologist Donald Super and economist and manpower expert Eli Ginzberg view the process as a systematic one that progresses through distinct stages of human development. Basically, the process begins with fantasy choices made in early childhood and continues with the exploration of interests and capacities and the making of tentative choices. Throughout the process, a person tries to bring those choices in line with realistic opportunity, based on his or her abilities and the potential for securing proper training. Both Ginzberg and Super agree that the process results in a compromise between an individual's abilities, interests, and opportunities, and existing social factors, job requirements, and realistic potential.

Super stresses that a person's occupational choice is largely determined by his or her self-concept. The development of a self-concept culminates in choosing an occupation according to the kind of person you believe yourself to be, and the way you perceive your abilities, values, preferences.

Similarly, Dr. John L. Holland believes that choosing an occupation is an expression of one's personality. According to his theory, making a good occupational choice means matching your personality to an occupation that suits it. Along these lines, he has keyed over 400 occupations to six personality types and environments. For instance, he defines *realistic* occupations as those which emphasize concreteness and primary dealings with things rather than people or ideas. Realistic occupations include the skilled trades, many technical occupations, and some service occupations.

Career choice is not made within a vacuum, and theories such as Dr. Anne Roe's take this fact into account. She stresses the quality of early child-parent relationships, which affect the development of the child's interests and, in turn, adult occupational choices. Warm, loving relationships, she believes, lead to orientation toward persons in life generally and in career choice; cold, rejecting relationships lead to nonperson orientation and career choices, scientists being a prime example of the latter orientation.

Something to keep in mind, however, is that these occupational choice theories were based on, and framed for, white, middle-class American men. The central notion of these theories is that a person can thoroughly explore *all* the possibilities, giving equal and full consideration to all his or her interests and inclinations. Then he or she is free to compromise and make a career decision. However, women are subject to other crucial factors that affect their choice of occupation in a somewhat different way than men. Sociologists Shirley Angrist, Elizabeth M. Almquist, and

Samuel H. Osipow and his colleagues have studied these factors. A major theme that emerges from their work is that sex-role socialization greatly colors a woman's career choice. Women's early socialization and the sex-segregated structure of the labor force combine to place major limitations on women, resulting in their perceiving only a narrow range of alternatives.

According to this school of thought, women are not so free to explore all their alternatives because they are conditioned by a "feminine" socialization to prefer, and enter, a limited number of occupations. Little girls have been traditionally reared to be passive, nurturing, helpful, and subservient. As women, they extend this self-concept to their role as workers, and this factor in turn affects which occupations they will choose. Those occupational fields which are largely male-dominated may be seen as masculine, or best suited to men and therefore "unsuitable" for women. Most women (even college-educated women) choose occupations that are predominantly female. As Angrist and Almquist point out, these occupations are those which are most attuned to their motherhood/family/domestic orientation and can be seen as an extension of their nurturing and helping functions.

Since the occupational structure parallels family structure to a great extent, women tend to avoid competitive situations that require initiative, and they often settle for positions of subservience.

Osipow points out that other factors such as parental models, husband's attitude and support, and timing and age of children, can combine to either help or hinder a woman's career choice.

Almquist and Angrist recognize too that role models can be crucial to a woman's career development and choice. Women can more easily perceive themselves in careers when those around them act as influential models, demonstrating that occupation is an important personal commitment. This influence is particularly significant when the role model is a woman because then the model more clearly illustrates that a woman can play more than one central life role, for instance, both mother and doctor.

Implications of the Career Development Process for You

Please remember that these career development theories are all only theories; some may be applicable to you, while others may be completely off target. However, you must keep in mind two important things as you go through this book and the process of planning your career. First, career development is a lifelong process. And you are not really a novice at it, although you may feel like one.

Second, as a woman, special factors have affected your past decisions and may affect your future ones. These factors include early sex-role socialization, lack or presence of role models, and family and friends' attitudes. The career choice you make at any point is largely determined by many of the choices you've made earlier in your life, whether or not they have been intentional. In turn these choices were partly determined by all the influences mentioned above. For example, if you chose when you were a child to play with a doll rather than a mechanical toy, your choice probably reflected the way your parents felt about what was appropriate behavior for girls as opposed to that for boys. Lack of the kinds of play experiences that are typical and acceptable for boys has influenced many girls to reject comparable learning experiences—in math or science, for instance—throughout their school years. Similarly, career decisions are often limited by default, based on many earlier decisions such as what games to play, what to read, what courses to take, what hobbies to pursue, and even what friends to choose.

Career decisions, then, do not just involve matching your abilities and interests to existing job requirements, although that step is, of course, part of the process. You have to consider all the variables that are components of career decisions, even if, right now, you don't feel ready to make any major decisions about work.

One way that can help you consider all the variables involved in career decisions is to start to keep a record of some of the things you already know about yourself and about work. The next two parts of this chapter will help you do just that by preparing your personal biography and recalling your early impressions about work.

Some words of warning:

1. Our exercises are not meant to analyze *you*—you are meant to analyze *them*. They will not tell you what you can or cannot do, or tell you how good or bad a person you are. They will simply provide you with information useful in assessing where you stand with regard to a career and then formulating a plan of action. It's up to you to extract the information and make sense of it for yourself.

2. Career and life planning do not happen overnight. Be patient; do not jump to conclusions hastily or prematurely. You cannot sit down for an hour or a day and expect *Bingo!*: Instant Career Plan. The process will take hard work and effort on your part, in addition to a substantial investment of time. It's a growing and building process that involves acquiring information and putting the pieces together. Therefore plan to work hard.

3. Don't feel that you are locked into making one irreversible career plan. A recent *Psychology Today* survey of 23,000 workers revealed that two-thirds expected to change jobs within the next five years. Their reasons were many, including money, benefits, need for growing and learning opportunities, and the need to use talents to the fullest. One hopes that all people grow and change; so will you and your goals and plans. What you want now may not be what you want or need 10 or even

2 years from now. But it's important to establish a *direction* for yourself. Otherwise you may find yourself drifting in the crowd and never doing what you *want* or *could* do.

Your Notebook

An important part of this discovery process includes keeping a notebook, both to record your responses to the various exercises and to enter your own notes, observations, and comments as you go through the process of self-assessment, career exploration, and decision making. (A three-ring binder with dividers and plenty of paper is best.) This notebook will serve as a very personal kind of journal. From time to time you may want to share or discuss aspects of it with family or close friends, or you may choose to keep it entirely private. In either case, you will find it a valuable resource that you will want to go back to again and again, reviewing what you've written, reassessing it, and making changes as you acquire new information and gain new insights.

A convenient way to use this book with your notebook is to make photocopies of the various exercises suggested and to put them in your notebook so that you will have a total record, in one place, of the process of exploration, discovery, and decision making. For some exercises, you may want to enter only a summary of what you feel is the most important information or insight you derived. (You'll also find that it's best to find a quiet place to work and think, where you'll be uninterrupted.)

If you think this process sounds like work, we warned you, it is! But it is also a very exciting process of discovery. However, even precise step-by-step instructions, the most thorough exercises, and the advice of leading experts won't work if you don't. So plan to invest time and effort, starting now.

Your Personal Biography

Suppose someone asked you for a short biography of your life, including educational experience, work experience, significant achievements, and hobbies, in just 10 minutes. Could you do it? Many people find it very difficult to talk about a subject that should be very close to them—themselves!

The first exercise in your notebook will be to develop a personal biography, part of your self-assessment. Your aim is to write down as much information as possible about yourself, your abilities, skills, interests, education, and so on. This biography is *your* personal inventory; so be sure to include everything, no matter how obvious a given aspect of your history may seem. Complete each item without thinking about what you *ought* to write. Take into consideration everything you have done at home, in the community, at school, and other places, including paying jobs or volunteer work. Be as specific as possible. Don't worry about form or phrasing; this is an exploratory exercise, not a thesis.

In filling out your personal biography you may find it useful to talk to your friends, family, and former business associates. They can often help you to remember important information that you might otherwise overlook.

PERSONAL BIOGRAPHY

Name: _____

Place and date of birth: _____

Current address: _____

Father's name and occupation: _____

_____

Mother's name and occupation: _____

_____

If married, husband's name and occupation: _____

_____

Children's name(s) and age(s): _____

_____

_____

1. Education

High School				Yr. Grad.
College	Yr. Grad. or # Credits	Degree	Major	Minor
Graduate or Professional School	Yr. Grad. or # Credits	Degree	Major	Minor
Other (describe)				

During your education, which subjects did you like best?

_____   _____

_____   _____

Why?

_____

_____

_____

Which subjects did you like least?

_____   _____

_____   _____

Why?

_____

_____

_____

Were your grades best in your major? _____ Yes _____ No   If no, explain:

_____

_____

Have you taken (or are you now taking) any extension, adult education, or other courses? _____ Yes _____ No   If so, what are they, and why did you become interested in them?

_____

_____

_____

_____

_____

Would you now be interested in further training or specialized courses to help in your career? _____ Yes _____ No   Comments:

_____

_____

Describe your extracurricular activities while in school and underline the ones that still interest you.

_____

_____

_____

_____

_____

_____

_____

_____

What three achievements in school made you most proud?

1 _____

2 _____

3 _____

2. Jobs

On the next page—in the column marked Chronology—fill in one line for each year that you worked at a specific job, even if it was unpaid work. Begin with the most recent year you worked and list backward, year by year, to a maximum of 10 years. If your job experience in recent years has been brief or nonexistent, include some of your earlier paid or nonpaid work.

Fill in the organization, title, and salary for each year worked, even though some of the lines might be identical or very similar. And be sure to include all jobs (full- or part-time), even if they do not represent your current field of interest. If you were a housewife for some or all of these years and did not have outside work, see if you can translate this experience into work-related terms. If you are a recent or near graduate, be sure to indicate all your summer jobs and any part-time work you had during your school years. After each job, list the reason why your employment was terminated, whether you quit, were fired, or were promoted.

CHRONOLOGY

Year	Organization	Title Activity	Salary	Reason for Termination

Look over your chronology and list what you think were the most significant achievements of your work history.

_____

_____

_____

_____

_____

Did you ever feel discriminated against on the job because of your age, sex, or ethnic background? List any instances and the jobs during which they occurred.

_____

_____

_____

3. Membership In Organizations—Past and Present

List civic, political, cultural, feminist, professional, and social groups of every kind: esoteric, intellectual, exercise, community, etc. Briefly note the degree of your involvement in each activity.

Organization	How You Are/Were Involved
1 _____	_____
2 _____	_____
3 _____	_____
4 _____	_____

5 _____   _____

_____

6 _____   _____

_____

4. Miscellaneous

List the people you feel have been most influential in your life and why.

_____

_____

_____

List the one thing you like the best about yourself and why.

_____

_____

_____

List any books you have read and enjoyed within the past year.

_____

_____

_____

List any hobbies that you actively engage in (include any sports activities).

_____

_____

_____

Now that you've completed your personal biography, review it. How do you feel about it? It's more impressive than you thought it would be, isn't it?

The information you've gathered here will not only be helpful in getting a clearer picture of where you've been and where you're going, but it will come in handy when you have to write a resume.

Your Early Impressions of Work

As a child, early impressions of your world and the people in it were very important in your development. Children internalize these early impressions, which ultimately color and influence the way a child thinks and feels.

Your exposure to the working world began very early—long before your first school days. This early exposure included the way your family members and others around you viewed and valued their work; it also included the ways society divided the work roles of men and women.

Try to recall some of your early impressions about work and think about how these impressions might have shaped your own attitudes toward various kinds of work and work roles. Recalling these thoughts and feelings will help you discover how your own first perceptions influenced your later career development, and thus you will increase the store of self-knowledge essential for wise decision making.

Divide your impressions into the three broad categories of family; school; and movies, books, and TV. Some questions you can ask yourself to get your thoughts flowing are listed below. As you begin to recall your impressions, you will probably think of other questions and impressions. Write them all down in your notebook. Don't worry about style or grammar, just let your memory drift and explore, recording anything that comes to you.

Family:

> —What did your father do? How did he feel about his job?
> —How did you feel about your father's occupation? Were you proud of him?
> —Did your mother work outside the home? If so, why?
> —Was her income needed to support the family?
> —How did your mother feel about her job? How did you feel about it?
> —How did your father feel about her working? Was he accepting, encouraging, critical?
> —If your mother was a housewife, how did you and your family view the work she performed in the home? Did you view it as "work" or just simply her obligation?
> —Did you ever visit your mother's or father's place of work? What do you remember about it?

Think of other relatives' occupations. What were your impressions of their roles as workers? Was there any individual you particularly admired? Why?

School:

—Did you view your teachers as workers or simply a kind of substitute mother/father?

—What did the other children around you want to be when they grew up?

—How marked was the difference between what little girls and little boys wanted to be?

—How did your textbooks portray male and female workers?

—Did the images conform to conventional sex-role stereotypes?

Movies, Books, TV:

—Try to remember the way workers, especially women, were portrayed by the media. What kinds of work were women portrayed doing? What about men?

—Did any fictional movie, television, or literary figure ever make you think you wanted to do what he or she did? What did he or she do? What attracted you to the occupation?

Also jot down any impressions gained from observing workers in your neighborhood and community. Can you think of ways in which these impressions might have influenced your early interests, decisions about courses, and other factors that might in turn influence your occupational choice? Think about your present attitudes about work and work roles, and try to trace them back to their beginnings. Have your attitudes changed greatly or are they basically the ones you had as a child?

Find a quiet place and time to relax and think about your responses. This type of reflection will also be important and necessary in the next chapter, in which you will discover more about yourself.

CHAPTER 2

LOOKING AT YOUR INTERESTS, VALUES, ACHIEVEMENTS, ABILITIES

It sounds trite, but the best advice about getting a step ahead with your career plans is to know yourself. How? You've already started: By preparing your Personal Biography and thinking about your early impressions of work, you have begun to get to know yourself better. Your notebook and the exercises and activities suggested in this chapter will help you to continue to do just that—to look at yourself honestly and to assemble a picture of yourself that takes into account your past, your present, and your dreams and goals for the future.

The next step? Do the exercises and activities presented here, recording the results in your notebook. You will gain in self-awareness, coming to know yourself realistically and thoroughly. You will explore your personal characteristics and needs, your values, interests, abilities, and accomplishments. And you will get to know other things about yourself that you may not have realized were true before you started reading this book.

This process can be fun and exciting, uncovering a you that you didn't know existed. As Richard Bolles, author of *What Color Is Your Parachute?*, has said, "Life is a continuum, with a steady continuing core, no matter how the basic units or building blocks may need to be rearranged. . . . Therefore, we need to look back, and see when we were (and are) enjoying life—and precisely what activities we were doing at that moment, what skills or talents we were employing, what kinds of tasks we were dealing with, what kinds of accomplishments were being done, and precisely what it was that was 'turning us on.' " Use the exercises in this chapter to help you do just that.

Remember: there are no right or wrong answers. This process is personal and private; so be honest with yourself as you record your findings in your notebook.

Getting to Know Yourself Exercises: 1. Assessing Your Interests

Your interests are simply your likes and dislikes, your preferences for or rejection of a wide variety of things, based largely on your own needs, values, and experiences. You can obtain information about your interests in three principal ways.

- Look at your expressed interests, or what you think or say interests you. (However, this information is not always reliable, because of possible misconceptions about what is involved in any particular activity or occupation. Young people, for example, often express interest in activities or occupations that seem glamorous to them—such as astronautics or medicine or physics—without really knowing what's involved.)
- Analyze your manifested or demonstrated interests, or the kinds of activities you have become involved in and enjoy.
- Measure your interests, using an interest inventory. (You may have taken one or more of these inventories in school.) Of the two principal types, one compares your preferences for activities in broad, general fields with those of others in your age group. In this category are the Kuder Preference Records and the Kuder General Interest Survey, Holland's Self-Directed Search and his Vocational Preference Inventory, and the Ohio Vocational Interest Survey. The second type of inventory compares your preferences with those of satisfied workers in a number of occupations. The Strong-Campbell Interest Inventory, a revision of the Strong Vocational Interest Blank, and the Kuder Occupational Interest Survey are examples of this type. (Some YWCAs, career counseling centers, and career advisory groups offer testing services like these.)

Whether or not you have ever taken a formal inventory of your interests, it's important to review your interests and see how they fit in with your emerging career plans. Think back over your hobbies, school courses, past jobs, etc. Using your notebook, make two lists: one of at least a dozen activities you really enjoy and another of about the same number of activities you absolutely detest. Next to each item on each list indicate what one or two key things about each activity make it so appealing or unappealing to you.

Now you're ready to classify your interests—to look for hidden patterns. There are many ways to classify interests. Kuder classifies interests as outdoor, mechanical, scientific, persuasive, artistic, musical, social service, and computational. John Holland classifies them in accordance with the personality/environment theory described earlier: realistic, investigative, artistic, social, enterprising, and clerical. The government's *Dictionary of Occupational Titles* classifies them on the basis of five pairs of factors; a positive preference for one factor implies rejection of the other factor in the pair, as shown below:

1. Situations involving a preference for activities dealing with things and objects.

   vs.

6. Situations involving a preference for activities concerned with people and the communication of ideas.

2. Situations involving a preference for activities involving business contact with people.

   vs.

7. Situations involving a preference for activities of a scientific and technical nature.

3. Situations involving a preference for activities of a routine, concrete, organized nature.

   vs.

8. Situations involving a preference for activities of an abstract and creative nature.

4. Situations involving a preference for working for people for their presumed good, as in the social welfare sense, or for dealing with people and language in social situations.

   vs.

9. Situations involving a preference for activities that are nonsocial in nature, and are carried on in relation to processes, machines, and techniques.

5. Situations involving a preference for activities resulting in prestige or the esteem of others.

   vs.

10. Situations involving a preference for activities resulting in tangible, productive satisfaction.

Now go back over the activities you've listed in your notebook, looking for patterns. What interests keep appearing?

Have you found any surprises in your interest profile, or is it much what you expected it to be? If your interests have changed over the years, chances are that you've expanded your horizons and discovered new activities that you enjoy. There was a time when your interests were expected to stabilize by late adolescence, when young people (generally males) were expected to make career decisions and stick with them, consequently, new interests did not have a chance to develop. Current theories of career development and social acceptance of career shifts and multiple careers greatly decrease the emphasis on the stability of interests.

Now put the information you have just compiled about your own interests to work for you. Using your notebook, relate your interests to your past experiences and to the work you think you would like to do in the future. For example:

In the past, I always enjoyed _____

_____

_____

but I greatly disliked _____

_____

_____

In a job, I think I would enjoy most _____

_____

_____

I know I would hate to _____

_____

_____

Add whatever additional comments occur to you. Think about your interests as you go through the rest of the suggested activities in this book. Note the things you like to do and those you dislike, adding them to what you have noted here.

Getting to Know Yourself Exercises: 2. Assessing Your Work Values

Most people, men and women alike, work for economic reasons; they need to support themselves or other members of their families. Working can provide more rewards than just a paycheck, however, and most of us work for a variety of reasons. In fact, most people say that even if they didn't need the money, they would continue to work.

Work values is a term that psychologist Donald Super defines as the goals that motivate people to work, the satisfactions they seek in their jobs (intrinsic values) or the outcomes or concomitants of their jobs (extrinsic values). Researchers in human behavior have defined values in many ways, and they have identified different sets of values. Most of these definitions of values, however, and most of the sets of values have much in common. Some have defined values as deep, enduring beliefs that guide our behavior and what we seek in life. Others have defined them to mean those qualities which we consider intrinsically desirable apart from a given situation.

Your interests embody your values, but they are not synonymous with them. For example, scientific interest might incorporate the values of pursuit of knowledge and reason and intellectual stimulation. Artistic interest might incorporate the values of beauty and harmony.

Values also reflect needs—for example, if fame is one of your values, you probably have a need for recognition and admiration. If leadership is one of your values, you probably have a need to dominate others.

Do the exercise that follows to help you begin to clarify your motivations for working. The statements are divided into categories representing 13 work values. (Other kinds of values, like valuing spiritual experiences or close family relationships, also have an effect—for example, on the kinds of work environments you might prefer. Consider them when analyzing these other values.) As you read through the statements, check each one that you feel is very important to you. You will begin to see a pattern in your reasons for wanting to work.

Recognition (getting respect, prestige, social approval)
__ I want to have my work recognized and valued by others.
__ I want to work only for a firmly established, well-known institution whose name people recognize.
__ I would settle for almost any job so that I could say I was working.
__ I want a job that is somewhat glamorous in the eyes of others.
__ The current social pressure on women to work has strongly affected me.
__ Promotions are important to me.

Achievement (attaining mastery of a field; self-advancement; growth)
__ I enjoy seeing the results of my efforts.
__ I like to work on long-range projects, toward broad and important goals.
__ It is important to me that my work lead to better opportunities.
__ I am most satisfied when I can apply myself thoroughly to a task, doing it well.
__ I am most satisfied when I have a chance to learn from what I do.
__ I am unhappy if I feel that I am wasting and frittering away my time.

Dominance (exercising leadership; directing; having power, influence over others)
__ I like to use my leadership abilities.
__ I enjoy planning and organizing a program or activity.
__ I feel good about myself when I am responsible for large enterprises.
__ I get a feeling of satisfaction from directing and supervising other people's work.
__ I enjoy having others come to me for advice and ideas.
__ I enjoy making presentations to convince others of a product or an idea.

Social Welfare (doing something that has meaning for others; working for society or another person's benefit)
__ I would be happiest working in a service organization.
__ I prefer working for a not-for-profit organization or in a service role in a commercial enterprise.

___ I like to do a good and useful job anywhere I'm needed.
___ My primary interest in a job involves helping people and doing things to help make a better world.
___ Doing work that gives me a chance to help many people in need is important to me.
___ I want to use my energies and abilities to help make the world a better place to live in.

Self-expression (working in an area particularly suited to the development of one's abilities)
___ I like to test myself to confirm my sense of who I really am.
___ I have a feeling that I could really develop my abilities in the right work.
___ I feel that a lot of my natural talent is being wasted without the opportunities I would have on a job.
___ Being able to express myself is important to me.
___ I like the opportunity to try out some of my own ideas.
___ I think I have an original outlook that I would like to bring to a job.

Money (gaining in socioeconomic status; meeting material needs of others)
___ I must base my job decisions on the amount of salary and fringe benefits offered.
___ I can't afford to take a job at a low salary to get a start in work I really want.
___ I think that I would tend to measure my worth as an employee according to my salary.
___ It is important to me to have as high an income as possible.
___ Getting money and material things is very important to me.
___ I think that those whose opinions I value will measure my worth according to my salary.

Moral Values (behaving in a way consistent with some moral code)
___ I am ashamed of not using what I've learned.
___ Depending on others for economic support makes me feel inadequate or lazy.
___ I believe that work builds character.
___ After several days of leisure, I feel guilty about useful work I might have done.
___ To me work is important as a kind of service to humankind.
___ Service gives me pleasure.

Independence (being free from supervision and restriction; "standing on one's own feet")
___ I need to feel that I can depend on myself for a decent living wage.
___ I want to have some part of my life that is independent of my family and others close to me.
___ I think I am more dependent on my children and their lives than is good for me.
___ I just like the feeling of being independent.

___ I feel my family would be better off if I were less dependent on them.
___ I like to do things on my own, without having a lot of orders and directions.

Creativity (contributing new ideas; being original and inventive)
___ I prefer thinking of new hypotheses for research to replicating what has already been done.
___ I have musical, artistic, scientific, or writing talent that I would like to develop and use in my job.
___ I don't want to waste my problem-solving ability.
___ I like to come up with a new way to handle an old problem or implement a more efficient approach or technique.
___ I like to tackle problems that others prefer to avoid.
___ I like to try out original solutions rather than rely on conventional tactics and established procedures.

Challenge (handling difficult or complex work)
___ Easy work bores me.
___ Hard work stimulates me.
___ If there is a difficult problem, I have an urge to tackle it.
___ The work world seems to offer me the satisfaction of solving tough problems.
___ Without challenges I feel unused and unfulfilled.
___ I like to work on assignments that require real learning and effort.

Interpersonal Relations (being with companions, other employees, colleagues)
___ I want more opportunity to be with people who share my interests.
___ The isolation of being at home is depressing.
___ I need the feeling of being part of a group or a working team.
___ I feel best when I'm with other people.
___ I think that a career would enrich my life with interesting friends.
___ I am lonely now that my children have grown up.

Variety (preferring diverse activities, "changes of scenery")
___ I think I need a career so that I can get away from the house some of the time.
___ I enjoy a variety of activities, rather than just a single area of concentration.
___ I get bored seeing the same people and doing the same things all the time.
___ I feel that a job would give me the variety of contacts with other people that I don't find in my neighborhood or among my friends.
___ I'm always looking for new things to do and new ways of doing familiar things.
___ I love change and variety; they make me feel alive.

Stimulation (finding a stimulating activity)
___ I need activity outside of my home to keep life interesting.
___ I like to be doing something new all the time.
___ I need a sense of accomplishment at the end of my day.

___ I have too much time on my hands.
___ I envy my husband's/partner's career and interaction with people.
___ I wish I could organize my life around interesting and constructive projects.

Now that you have completed the first part of the exercise, go back and add up the number of checks you have marked in each category. Then, on a separate page, write the category names in descending order based on the number of checks. Your list might look something like this:

Achievement:	6
Money:	5
Self-expression:	3

If you have rated money only 2, for example, and self-expression received a total of 6, that should tell you much about yourself, your values, and your eventual career choice. Look at your list and concentrate on the three work motivations that have highest scores. Were you aware, before this exercise, of how much these things matter to you? Look next at the three lowest. Do these tell you more about yourself? Notice whether you have many low or many high areas and recognize what that means about the level of your overall motivation to work. Pay attention also to the categories on your list that fall in the middle range; they may represent wishes and inclinations that are growing and becoming more important to you.

Getting to Know Yourself Exercises: 3. Assessing Your Achievements, Accomplishments, and Demonstrated Abilities

Your values and interests are important in your long-range career plans, but you need the corresponding abilities, as demonstrated by your achievements, to make full use of them in a career. Interests are frequently confused with abilities. It is not unusual for someone to look at his or her interest inventory results and say, "This tells me what I can be." While we tend to enjoy doing those things we do well, psychologists and career counselors have established little relationship between interests and abilities. People with high literary interest, for example, are not necessarily capable of producing a novel, a poem, or a play. They may simply enjoy reading literature.

Abilities, achievements, and aptitudes were once thought to be completely separate qualities. Today, however, as educational psychologist Robert L. Thorndike points out, educators are a great deal less certain that there is a real distinction. The terms abilities, skills, and aptitudes are used almost interchangeably, although some educators still define

ability and aptitudes as the *capacity* to do something, skills a
onstration of that capacity, and achievements as actual *accomplishments*. Tests of achievement, for example, are generally designed to
show how much in-depth learning of specific curriculum content the
student has accomplished. So-called aptitude tests, on the other hand,
attempt to test your broader understanding of concepts and processes.

The Department of Labor's *Dictionary of Occupational Titles* (DOT)
defines aptitudes as "the specific skills and abilities required of an individual in order to learn or perform adequately a task or job duty." Following is the DOT list of aptitudes. The list represents only one of a
number of classification schemes.

Intelligence. General learning ability. The ability to "catch on" or understand instructions and underlying principles. Ability to reason and
make judgments. Closely related to doing well in school.

Verbal. Ability to understand meanings of words and ideas associated
with them, and to use them effectively. To comprehend language, to
understand relationships between words, and to understand meanings
of whole sentences and paragraphs. To present information or ideas
clearly.

Numerical. Ability to perform arithmetic operations quickly and accurately.

Spatial. Ability to comprehend forms in space and understand relationships of plane and solid objects. May be used in such tasks as blueprint
reading and in solving geometry problems. Frequently described as the
ability to "visualize" objects of two or three dimensions, or to think
visually of geometric forms.

Form Perception. Ability to perceive pertinent detail in objects or in
pictorial or graphic material. To make visual comparisons and discrimi-
nations and see slight differences in shapes and shadings of figures and
widths and lengths of lines.

Clerical Perception. Ability to perceive pertinent detail in verbal or
tabular material. To observe differences in copy, to proofread words and
numbers, and to avoid perceptual errors in arithmetic computation.

Motor Coordination. Ability to coordinate eyes and hands or fingers
rapidly and accurately in making precise movements with speed. Ability to make a movement response accurately and quickly.

Finger Dexterity. Ability to move the fingers and manipulate small objects with the fingers rapidly or accurately.

Manual Dexterity. Ability to move the hands easily and skillfully. To
work with the hands in placing and turning motions.

Eye-Hand-Foot Coordination. Ability to move the hand and foot coordinately with each other in accordance with visual stimuli.

Color Discrimination. Ability to perceive or recognize similarities or differences in colors, or in shades or other values of the same color; to identify a particular color, or to recognize harmonious or contrasting color combinations, or to match colors accurately.

Whatever distinction, if any, may truly exist among your abilities, aptitudes, skills, and achievements, prospective employers will be interested mainly in what you have accomplished, as demonstrated by the various types of experience you have had, paid and unpaid. Evaluating your experience as objectively as possible will add new dimensions to the complex and slowly emerging picture that is uniquely you.

If you have not worked outside your home for some years—or if you have never done so—it may be difficult for you to be realistic about what you have to offer a prospective employer. You may overestimate your abilities, but more typically you will underestimate them. It's important to remind yourself that you may have used—or may be using now—a valuable skill without receiving pay for doing so. As a matter of fact, a revised standard application form for federal job-seekers permits women who have been out of the labor force for a while to list political, social, or charitable work performed on a volunteer basis. In some cases, this work is counted as work experience.

On the other hand, one can overestimate the knowledge required for keeping adequate financial records for a household or for a community organization; the quality and variety of administrative skills which serve for a short-term project in political or philanthropic activities are not necessarily sufficient for an ongoing institutional program. You must also take into account the fact that many fields have developed rapidly in recent years; the competency of 5 or 10 years ago may be inadequate now without "refresher" courses or additional training.

But remember, too, that if your prospective employer recognizes your innate ability, your professional attitude and your interest, your initial performance on the job will probably be received with patience and helpfulness. Your employer will be interested in your ultimate productivity, and if he or she senses in you the potential for quality contribution to the work situation, the employer will want to help you regain and extend your former capabilities.

To help you review your achievements, think about the various activities in which you've participated in the past. How often did you do each of them, and how recently? How well did you perform them? How much did you enjoy them? In your notebook list a minimum of five specific events (personal, school, community, or work) that you feel represented accomplishments, and don't worry if they aren't earthshaking.

It will be easier if you use an action verb like the ones listed below to begin each sentence.

designed	established	sold	presented
researched	analyzed	expanded	organized
trained	invented	developed	negotiated
supervised	directed	planned	administered
contracted	reduced costs	managed	conducted
improved	wrote	created	prepared
implemented			

Now, go back and indicate for each event when you were involved in the activity—was it 10 years ago, 2 years ago, currently or very recently?

The next step is to analyze the achievements you've just listed. Consider them one by one and then list the skills, knowledge, or personal attributes that you think enabled you to accomplish each task. Think about your personality as well as your specific skills and abilities. Traits that affect your accomplishments might include willingness to work hard, patience, ability to handle people, sales ability, organizing ability, knowledge of antiques, ability to sketch, logical thinking, dynamic presentation, or virtually any other skill or capability. List anything you can think of that contributed to your success in each achievement. Here's an example:

Achievement: *Increased number of volunteers at local hospital by more than 25%.*

Skills, knowledge, and personal traits required to achieve this: *organizational skills, sales ability, capacity to motivate people, good public speaker, hard work, ability to overcome resistance.*

Next, review the results. What skills show up most frequently? Select the four or five that are repeated most often and list them in your notebook in order of frequency.

In looking over your accomplishments, don't compare yourself with "superwoman" stories. Increasingly these days, the media are commenting on and describing in detail brilliant, talented women who are "making it" in the business or entertainment world. This kind of news story can be a source of both encouragement and discouragement. On the one hand, you may be excited by the possibilities opening up for you; on the other, as you compare yourself to glamorous, successful women whose hobbies are car racing and ballet, who have risen to fame as nuclear physicists or editors in chief of major magazines, and who are described in terms like "eager for challenge" and "unintimidated by difficult obstacles," you may feel like a big zero. But remember: your own satisfaction is the most important yardstick by which to measure your accomplishments.

You may not recall all your achievements the first time around. Once you have listed what you do recall, however, you will probably find yourself remembering additional things you have accomplished. Ask members of your family or your close friends to review your list—both to get their perceptions of your achievements or accomplishments and to help you add items that you may have forgotten. And, who knows? Tomorrow or the next day you might try your hand at something you have never done before. If you spend a significant amount of time on it —for example, holding a community office, or building a new desk for your study, or sculpting or painting—you will certainly want to add it to your list.

Getting to Know Yourself Exercises: 4. Assessing Your Personal Characteristics

Taking stock of your personal characteristics is another essential step in the search for self-knowledge. Certain characteristics seem to be essential in almost all kinds of work. For example, being responsible, efficient, resourceful, flexible, cooperative, objective, and sensible is basic to a professional attitude toward work and necessary for success in almost any job.

On the other hand, some personal characteristics are very important in some occupations and less so or not at all in others. In fact, certain characteristics that are desirable in some occupations may actually be undesirable in others. For example, being a loner may be a desirable characteristic for a scientist involved in long hours of laboratory research, but it's not particularly desirable for a worker on a construction team.

Here is a list of personal characteristics that, in different combinations, are important in various occupations. Mark each characteristic as it applies to you—H for high, or very strong, A for average, and L for low or very weak. Later, as you explore various occupations in depth and find out about the personal characteristics associated with them, you will find it helpful to refer to your self-ratings on this list.

You may find it useful to make several copies of this list and to ask one or more friends or family members to rate you. You can then see yourself as others see you and compare their perceptions of you with your perceptions of yourself. (An extra plus: Involving your family in your career exploration and planning will also help make them your allies and a continuing source of support.)

Be sure to look back at the previous exercise to see which traits you listed as used in accomplishments.

CHECKLIST

✓ Active	__ Enterprising	__ Open-minded
✓ Accurate	✓ Enthusiastic	__ Opportunistic
__ Adaptable	__ Fair-minded	__ Optimistic
__ Adventurous	__ Farsighted	__ Organized
✓ Affectionate	__ Firm	__ Original
✓ Aggressive	__ Flexible	__ Outgoing
✓ Alert	__ Forceful	__ Painstaking
✓ Ambitious	__ Formal	__ Patient
__ Artistic	__ Frank	__ Peaceable
✓ Assertive	✓ Friendly	__ Persevering
__ Attractive	✓ Fun-loving	__ Pleasant
✓ Bold	✓ Generous	__ Poised
__ Broad-minded	✓ Gentle	__ Polite
✓ Businesslike	✓ Good-natured	__ Popular
✓ Calm	✓ Happy-go-lucky	__ Practical
✓ Capable	✓ Healthy	__ Precise
✓ Careful	__ Helpful	__ Progressive
✓ Cautious	✓ Honest	__ Prudent
✓ Cheerful	__ Humorous	__ Purposeful
✓ Clear-thinking	__ Idealistic	__ Quick
__ Clever	__ Imaginative	__ Quiet
✓ Competent	✓ Independent	__ Rational
✓ Competitive	✓ Individualistic	__ Realistic
✓ Confident	__ Industrious	__ Reasonable
✓ Conscientious	✓ Inflexible	__ Reflective
✓ Conservative	__ Informal	__ Relaxed
✓ Considerate	✓ Ingenious	__ Reliable
✓ Cooperative	✓ Intellectual	__ Reserved
✓ Courageous	✓ Intelligent	__ Resourceful
__ Creative	__ Inventive	__ Responsible
✓ Curious	✓ Kind	__ Retiring
__ Daring	__ Leisurely	__ Robust
✓ Deliberate	__ Light-hearted	__ Self-confident
✓ Democratic	✓ Likable	__ Self-controlled
✓ Dependable	✓ Logical	__ Sensible
✓ Determined	✓ Loyal	__ Sensitive
✓ Dignified	✓ Mature	__ Serious
✓ Discreet	✓ Methodical	__ Sharp-witted
__ Dominant	__ Meticulous	__ Sincere
__ Eager	__ Mild	__ Sociable
__ Easy-going	✓ Moderate	__ Spontaneous
✓ Efficient	__ Modest	✓ Spunky
✓ Emotional	__ Natural	✓ Stable
__ Energetic	✓ Obliging	✓ Steady

__ Strong	__ Trusting	(Write in and rate below
__ Strong-minded	__ Trustworthy	any additional words that
__ Sympathetic	__ Unaffected	you believe describe you.)
__ Tactful	__ Unassuming	
__ Teachable	__ Understanding	__
__ Tenacious	__ Uninhibited	__
__ Thorough	__ Verbal	__
__ Thoughtful	__ Versatile	__
__ Tolerant	__ Warm	__
__ Tough	__ Wholesome	__

Go back and look over the list. Select those eight or ten traits you think describe you best. List them in your notebook.

Putting It All Together

Little by little, you've put together a many-faceted picture of yourself. Nobody else has precisely the same combination of qualities. Women you know may do some things better than you or have qualities that you wish you had, but there are most likely other things that you do better and qualities that they and others admire in you and wish they had.

Look back at how you have evaluated various aspects of yourself. What do your personal characteristics, your interests, your values, your accomplishments, and your education add up to? What patterns do they form? Which of your qualities would you like to use in your work? Are there things you would like to change about yourself?

Arrange a page in your notebook to resemble the following arrangement, allowing plenty of room under each heading, to help you synthesize the information you will need to answer these questions.

Instructions: Write under each column first, what interests, values, etc. you want to use in your work; second, what you would like to develop in relation to those interests, values, etc.; and third, what plans you have (or should have) to take some action to develop those interests, values, etc.

Now that you've recorded these discoveries in your notebook, review them and repeat the exercises and update your findings at frequent intervals. The next step is to look at the world around you and the career options that it offers.

	I would like to use these things in my work:	I would like to develop these things about myself (specify in what way, e.g. be more outgoing)	I plan to . . . (indicate what you will do to develop each thing you have established as being important to you; answer where appropriate; some categories may not apply):
My interests [Example:	writing	learn magazine writing style	enroll in a class after work; read more good magazines]
My work values			
My achievements, accomplishments, experience			
My personal characteristics			

63

CHAPTER 3

LOOKING AT CAREER OPTIONS

By reading and working through the preceding pages of this book, you've engaged in plenty of introspection, including some focused self-exploration, self-assessment, and soul searching. Thus far you have given most of your attention to your private world—what you dream of, need, want, are, and could become. This is an appropriate place to start but not an adequate place to stop. Now it's time to look at reality, both within society and in your community, as well as within the individual career fields you may be considering.

Stretch Your Mind

Expand your thinking about careers. At this point in your life there are two important reasons for doing so. First, like many people you may be going through life with a limited awareness of the career possibilities that exist for you; or you may be locking yourself into a fixed direction that may now be out of date, based heavily on a traditional or too-limited view of yourself. Right now is an ideal time for exploration, whether you are still in school, planning to go back to work, or even working. Now is the time to investigate or even try out the multiple possibilities that may be right for you.

The second reason for stretching your thinking about career options is related to the concept of "building blocks." Your experience, knowledge, and skills are your basic building blocks; they form the base on which career choices and careers are constructed. Like any carefully built structure, the broader and the sounder the base, the more likelihood there is of there being the freedom and the ability that is necessary to construct whatever you want. So if you expand your thinking about careers now, without waiting for someone to give you the answers (which doesn't happen anyway), you'll be able to begin to test your

64

interests and talents with selected educational preparation, school and community activities, and work experience (especially with summer or part-time jobs if you're still in school; with temporary or volunteer work if you're trying out careers). Every time you actively expose yourself to a new discipline or add expertise to familiar activities, you strengthen your career base and you reinforce the building blocks of your future.

What are the new career opportunities that are opening for women like you? Some career experts estimate that there are 40,000 different jobs in the United States. In the pages that follow, you will find a broad overview of career fields. As you examine the listings, use both a free-wheeling imagination and a realistic awareness of who you are. Within every one of these fields you will find many specific positions that represent a variety of additional options, but you can postpone sorting out these specific choices for some later time when your need to define your direction is more urgent. Now is the time to broaden your horizons, narrowing them only enough to keep them in line with your interests, personality, and talents.

If you haven't given much thought to career interests and inclinations, think seriously about each broad area listed. Try to eliminate ones that seem unsuitable and identify ones that seem to be viable possibilities, worth further exploration. If, on the other hand, you have made some choices in career direction, push your preconceptions aside for the moment to consider each of the career fields. As you read through the list, jot down in your notebook titles of either fields or positions that interest you. Don't worry about the number or variety of items that attract you; your ultimate choosing is better put off to that time when you know you've considered *all* your options.

At a Glance: Careers in Business, Science and Engineering, Health, Law and Government, and Skilled Trades

Business

Goods, money, people—these three factors dominate business today. Business in turn dominates our nation's system of free enterprise. What is business? It is profit directed; it includes all economic and commercial activities; it provides the goods and services necessary to maintain a nation's standard of living.

You can maintain a personal standard of living by making business your business—by pursuing a career in one of the business fields described in this book—business economics, management, marketing, public relations, advertising, retailing, insurance, finance, banking, personnel, production, accounting, data processing, business law, and small business. Business careers like these are available in every industry.

And certain business knowledge and skills are required in the other career fields of science and engineering, health, law and government, and skilled trades. Many business jobs are in high demand.

Science and Engineering

Does the thought of science and engineering careers conjure pictures of lonely laboratories and field sites? Those are only two of the many work settings of today's scientists. Jobs in science and engineering can be found in academia, industry, government, publishing, law, health care —everywhere new technology is needed for developing new products, testing new ideas, and solving old problems in new ways. From creating new brands of toothpaste to developing life-saving surgical equipment to testing auto-safety devices to discovering new solar systems, the work of scientists and engineers is as diverse and eclectic as the world in which we live.

Competition is great, and the skills needed are very specialized in these fields, but more and more women are facing the challenges. They are beginning to pursue these careers in greater numbers—as mathematicians, astronomers, physicists, chemists, biologists, biochemists, geologists, oceanographers, meteorologists, paleontologists, and all types of engineers.

Health

The prospects for women in health careers, especially medicine, are more favorable today than at any other time in the past 100 years, evidenced especially by the increased enrollment of women in medical schools. The employment outlook in all the health fields is very encouraging.

Under the umbrella of "health care" or "health services" are literally hundreds of occupations and professions, varying widely in requirements and responsibilities but united in the common aim of preventing and treating illness. Some of those fields demand lengthy and rigorous training but others may be entered by a relatively short preparatory route. Careers in medicine, dentistry, nursing specialties, optometry, chiropractic, podiatry, pharmacy, therapy specialties, medical technology, health care administration, and biostatistics are available to women who want to pursue a future in health fields.

Law and Government

Political decisions, government services, and the law of the land affect us all many times a day. The radio station that wakes you is regulated by a government agency, the Federal Communications Commission; the water you use to make your morning coffee is supplied by the munici-

WORK OPTIONS YOU MIGHT NEED OR WANT TO CONSIDER

Not everyone is able to—or even likes—to work a traditional 9-to-5 schedule, and increasing numbers of companies are experimenting with varied approaches to organizing their employees' working time. More flexibility might be just what you need in your work day, with time organized to suit your family's schedule or your own peak periods of energy. Some of these plans take a full-scale commitment from your employers; others you might be able to work out on an individual basis.

Flexitime. With this plan, companies require their employees to put in a certain number of hours on the job each week, arranged, however, to suit themselves. "Core hours" in the middle of the day require attendance from everyone. But you can arrive and leave when you want to, accumulating extra hours to use in a half-day off or simply arranging your schedule to beat the morning rush. More autonomy and choice have resulted in a rise in production, reduced absenteeism, and more efficient use of time spent on the job at companies that try flexitime.

Job Sharing. When two people share one permanent, full-time position—its responsibilities, its hours, its salary—they've been able to open up rewarding careers for themselves. By working half a day each or splitting the week between them, they often enhance their effectiveness on the job by their increased concentration and more efficient use of time. City planners, teachers, school psychiatrists, and many other professionals have convinced their employers that two are very definitely worth the price of one. Less tardiness, less absenteeism, fewer incidents of job fatigue, and lower job turnover result from these increasingly satisfied employees. For more information, write or phone:

New Ways to Work
457 Kingsley Avenue
Palo Alto, California 94301

or

Job Sharers
P.O. Box 1542
Arlington, Virginia 22210

Part-Time Work. Many part-time jobs are limited in scope, but some women have been able to develop good part-time jobs from work they once held full time. An employer might agree to give a good employee the freedom to work at home two days a week, or scale down a full-time job into a part-time one.

Free-lancing. Sometimes setting your own hours, pace, and tasks is the greatest luxury—or biggest necessity. Free-lancing from home can mean more work, for you must not only complete your tasks but constantly drum up new business; balance this aspect against the freedom of being your own boss, allotting your days as you will or must. The range of freelance jobs available is so wide—from the humdrum one of typing to such glamorous jobs as a photographer or writer to one woman's success as a creative cake designer — that there is no one right way to set up shop. It is easiest, however, to think of free-lancing as setting up your own business, with yourself as the product. This arrangement means that you'll have to deal with questions of financial soundness, time allocation, marketing, and deadlines, but the rewards will be all yours. And free-lancing may be facilitated, in any business, when you leave a full-time job to do it, for you will have built up work habits and contacts that can help you succeed.

---

pality in which you live; the speed at which you drive your car is determined by state law. We are all surrounded by government and governed by law.

The administration of government and the practice of law require the services of more than 13 million Americans. All levels of government employ a spectrum of people in a variety of fields—legislators, administrators, engineers, personnel specialists, social workers, urban planners, teachers, law enforcement officials, clerical personnel, lawyers, nutritionists, and a multitude of others, including opportunities to pursue a political position at the local, state, or national level.

Skilled Trades

Apprentice, journeyman, master skilled trade worker—this is now the career route of an increasing number of women throughout the country. In industry, construction, government, and on their own, women are training for and practicing skilled trades, learning the rewards and challenges of working in nontraditional fields. They're discovering that they can do the jobs well and that the work is in many cases more involving, higher paying, and more suited to them than traditional women's jobs they may have held.

Carpentry, electricity, masonry, painting and papering, operating engineering, and welding are among the fields women are pursuing. The demands on these pioneering women are great, but they're successfully proving themselves every day on the job and are becoming more and more recognized by their employers and the public at large as valuable skilled workers who are willing and prepared to meet the challenges of the jobs, and anxious to reap the rewards as well.

Etc., Etc., Etc.

You probably have noticed that the fields and positions listed in the preceding pages are in no way all-inclusive. Expand this list by thinking of careers of your neighbors, relatives, acquaintances, or most admired public persons, and by recalling some profiles of successful individuals you have read in current magazines or newspapers. In your notebook include these other areas that you might want to consider, such as forestry, photography, ranching—any area that has a claim to your interest, disposition, or talents.

Levels and Environments

Thus far, your primary attention has been directed toward career fields, with some secondary reference to positions within these fields. But there are two other dimensions to the world of careers that you will wish to consider: levels and environments.

Women haven't had opportunities to work at the upper levels of most career fields, and many of them haven't aspired to do so in the past. You can now seek a higher level position—an administrative role, a professional role, a managerial role, a significant role as entrepreneur—if you choose to do so. Within the professions, you can choose, too, one of the more prestigious—and financially rewarding—roles; that is, you can select litigation or corporate law as well as the traditionally "feminine" family court work, or you can choose surgery or ophthalmology as well as pediatrics.

The opportunity to train for such roles is increasingly available to you, and the chance to move upward on the ladder of responsibility and authority and independence is expanding. Do you want such roles?

This question of the level of your career is part of the spread of options that confront you. It isn't axiomatic that a woman aspire to the highest career levels, but she should know that her aspirations can be as high—or low—as she chooses. It may take time, in certain fields, to reach high-level career roles, but there is no longer any reason for a woman to turn away from any natural ambition she feels.

The other area in which every woman has options is one of environment—the setting or the enterprise in which she chooses to work. For example, she can be an accountant employed by a large industry or working as an Internal Revenue agent, teaching at a university, working as a private practitioner, functioning as part of a large accounting firm, or doing or supervising the accounting activities of a complex medical center. Many other fields offer a comparable range of environments—industry, education, government, public institutions, private practice, or entrepreneurship.

As you consider specific career fields that seem of interest to you, be aware of these alternatives and gauge the ones that appear to fit your nature and interests. There are special characteristics to the divergent environments—varying degrees of work pressure, different kinds of work associates, different time commitments, different settings such as

ɔry, outdoors, office—and different institutional arrangements of
hy and peer relationships. Any one—or all—of these factors is
likely to affect how happy you are in your work and how satisfied you
feel about your career and private life.

Exploring Options

Sources of Occupational Information

You now have a basic list of occupations that you want to find out more
about. Where and how can you find this additional information?

In addition to the detailed information about each career field presented in this book, there are two other very important sources of occupational information to help you.

The first is the *Occupational Outlook Handbook* (OOH), published
biannually by the United States Department of Labor's Bureau of Labor
Statistics. The OOH gives up-to-date information about the nature of the
work; where the jobs are found; specific duties, requirements, and qualifications; salary ranges; anticipated growth; ways to enter; chances for
advancement; work settings; and other information necessary to
thoughtful career investigation. This basic guidebook describes several
hundred of the most frequently found occupations arranged in 13 clusters of related occupations. It also includes 36 industry "statements,"
grouped according to major divisions in the economy. Each statement
provides information about jobs in the industry, training requirements,
and earnings potential. The OOH is available at many libraries and
career counseling centers, regional offices of the Department of Labor
or for $8.00 from the United States Government Printing Office, Super-
intendent of Documents, Washington, D.C. 20402.

The other major source of information is the *Dictionary of Occupational Titles* (DOT), referred to earlier, which is now in its fourth edition. The DOT lists and defines occupations alphabetically, and indexes
at the back of the book also categorize them by industry and occupational
group. There are 20,000 occupational or job titles listed (some occupations are known by more than one job title). Each definition includes
statements about the training time, aptitudes, interests, temperaments,
physical demands, working conditions, work performed, and industry
associated with the occupation. It is available in libraries and through
regional offices of the Department of Labor (check your phone directory
under United States Government) for $12.

In addition, look into the career pamphlets produced by professional
and business organizations. These publications often describe career
paths, work functions, and the future opportunities, in addition to outlining education requirements and specific positions. These pamphlets
vary in quality; the best are excellent, honest descriptions, and the worst

GETTING HELP FROM COUNSELORS

You may find you'd like to talk to a counselor about your plans: you can bounce ideas off her, ask about alternatives you might never have thought about, have her help you interpret all the information you've gathered about yourself and various occupations. Places where you can look for such help finding or selecting a counselor include:

—American Personnel and Guidance Association
5203 Leesburg Pike
Falls Church, Virginia 22041

Its *Directory of Approved Counseling Services* is available for reference in libraries or may be ordered direct from the association for $4.50 prepaid.

—Jewish Vocational Services or YWCAs
—State employment service offices
—College, community college, and continuing education career counseling centers, many of which offer their services, generally for a fee, to nonstudents
—Women's resource centers of various kinds, including the Catalyst Network centers throughout the country
—Corporation counseling programs
—Executive search organizations
—Private employment agencies (though most of these do not include counseling as one of their priorities)

Make your selection of a counselor very carefully, almost as if you were choosing a doctor, especially if you find a service that involves a substantial fee. Here are some things to look for:

• The counselor should have had adequate training for the job. In some states school and college counselors are certified or licensed. Private counselors are not required to be, although professional counselors may move from school or college counseling into private practice.
• The counselor should know about current occupational trends, requirements, and related information.
• Materials in the counseling office should be current. Facts about employment outlook, training requirements, and earnings may be obsolete and misleading if they are more than five years old.
• Occupational information should not be recruitment material for a particular company.
• If you are being tested, make sure the tests are reputable and appropriate for the purposes for which they are being given. Be sure that the tests are appropriate for use with women and free from sex bias, or at least that the interpretive

materials provide help in interpreting women's scores where the scores may simply reflect the way women have been brought up.
• Find a counselor or service that follows a policy free from sex bias and is dedicated to helping you find a job based on your abilities, interests, qualifications, and goals.
• Purely practical factors might affect your decision — distance from your home and convenience of arrangements, fees, hours, and days when services are available, and whether you can stop in with questions later. Try to find some recommendations by other professional groups or women who have used the service.

---

are poor, self-serving promotional pieces. If possible, ask for the guidance of a librarian or counselor in identifying quality publications.

If you can find trade magazines or professional journals for each of the fields you're considering, browse through them, read a few articles, and consider how interested you are in the content of each one. Take advantage of every opportunity to talk with friends, former employers, teachers, or family about each of the career possibilities you are considering. They may provide you with information and insights that will help you narrow down too wide-ranging choices or expand too limited awareness of options. Remember, however, that sometimes those who seem to know you best—because they've known you longest—may recognize in you only what they wish to recognize, ignoring your potential in other areas that may not fit in with their fixed perception of you.

Write for information from any women's caucus or association connected with a career field about which you are curious. A growing number of such groups are eager and willing to help you think through your opportunities and discover your rights. Names and addresses of these groups frequently appear in professional journals and trade magazines that you can find in your library. If you can't locate the references in these publications, for a current listing of these groups, check in some of the popular women's magazines or write or phone:

American Association of University Women
Higher Education Office
2401 Virginia Avenue NW
Washington, D.C. 20036

Both the *Encyclopedia of Associations,* a standard library reference book, and the listings in the OOH will also give you names and addresses of more groups and associations to write to for information.

If your college or community has a women's center, take advantage of it by using its information resources of books, career pamphlets, and informed staff or attending its career-oriented workshops or lectures and

COMPUTER GUIDANCE SYSTEMS

If you'd like a personalized hand with your career choices but are not willing or able to track down a counselor, try one of the computer-assisted occupational information systems available now. These systems vary greatly in quality; though some provide such minimal and general information that they're virtually useless, others can be of real service. Here are some of the better systems:

- *System of Interactive Guidance (SIGI)*. SIGI helps you sort through your values and their relative importance. You ask the computer for a list of occupations that meet your value requirements—for example, working on the East Coast, working for a small company—and then ask more information about its subsequent suggestions. You can work on predicting the chances of success in preparing for the occupation, plan ways to qualify for entry, and make decisions based on combinations of rewards and risks.
- *DISCOVER*. The DISCOVER College%Adult System lets you talk back to the computer as it encourages you to think about your values in relation to jobs, puts you through a variety of decision-making steps and exercises, introduces you to the ways in which the world of work is organized, lets you browse among different occupations, and gives you solid information about them. The last report helps you narrow down your list of possibilities to a final choice and a few backups. An important part of the computer's report is to point out discrepancies between the information you may have given and your goals.
- *Career Information System (CIS)*. This Oregon program delivers information rather than analysis. Current job material, suggested reading matter, and cassettes of occupational interviews, as well as sources for training are part of this service to schools and social agencies.
- *Computer-Based Educational Opportunity Center*. This free service to New Yorkers helps users learn about and enroll in post-secondary and adult education programs. Mobile computer terminals are available for your use at street fairs, community and church events, block parties, and such. Find out if a similar center or service is available in your city.

---

talking with counselors or others who are concerned with women's career options.

Interviewing for Information

One of the best ways to get information about what actually happens on a job in your career field is to talk to others who are currently working in that field. Most business and professional people find it flattering that you are interested in what they do and will be pleased to spend some time with you discussing their work. If you don't know anyone who is working in your field, ask your professors, your family, and your friends to suggest someone.

Don't neglect this approach to getting information just because you do not have an entree to an appropriate professional, although it's obviously easier if you know someone. For example, if photography is your career field, check the Yellow Pages for local photographers and call one "cold," explaining that you're interested in a career in photography and would like to discuss his or her work. If publishing is your career choice, and you're not in New York City, where most of the major publishers are located, you can often get helpful information from someone in a related field—an editor on your local paper, for example. If possible try to talk to a woman who has achieved success, as she will be able to describe any special problems she has encountered.

Prepare carefully for these "interviews for information" so that you will be sure to get answers to your most important questions without wasting the busy professional's time. In your notebook make a list of things you are interested in knowing more about. Among the questions to ask are:

- —What do you do in your work?
- —How did you get started in the field?
- —What steps did you take to get where you are now?
- —What entry-level jobs are best for learning as much as possible?
- —What salary can one expect at the entry level?
- —What is the typical career path for advancement based on performance?
- —What do you like best about your job?
- —What do you like least about it?
- —Are there any special considerations for women embarking on a career in the field?
- —If you could start all over again today in launching your career, what steps would you take?

Listen carefully to the professional's advice and summarize the important points in the career options section of your notebook. The professional may also be willing to suggest colleagues who might agree to talk with you as well. Often these information interviews yield a wealth of valuable data and provide insight that only a working professional has. Follow up all interviews for information with a thank-you letter, and send a copy of it to the person who recommended the professional to you.

An Insider's Look at a Company

Many companies offer guide-conducted tours to interested persons. Call and ask for one in the companies for which you might like to work. Since these tours are often designed for stockholders, your guide will probably have detailed information about the workings of the firm. You will also have a chance to observe the day-to-day working environment, and by letting your guide know of your interest in the field, she can probably arrange for you to speak with a professional within the firm or give you the name of someone to contact with your questions. For a tour of a smaller company, try making an appointment through the receptionist for someone to show you around. Some of the valuable things you might discover include:

—Many areas of a working environment you might not be exposed to when first entering a job—executive suites, conference rooms, etc.
—The logistics of how the firm is set up; the tour may provide you with some incentive for your possible future with the company.
—Job opportunities in a large firm that you might not have been aware of—creative research and media workrooms, for example.
—Impressive things the company has done to enhance the working environment, providing a company lunchroom, auditorium, interior plantings, and art exhibits, etc.

Keeping Track of All Your New Information

As you're discovering, much valuable information is available about careers and specific job opportunities. Don't let it slip through your fingers by counting on your memory to record it all. For each of the careers on your list, make your own basic information sheet. The following is an example of one. Few people will need answers to exactly the same set of questions; so add to or eliminate from the sheet as appropriate for you.

SAMPLE INFORMATION SHEET

OCCUPATION _____

1. Main duties/tasks:

2. Education/training required:

3. Occupational environment or setting (physical and social):

4. Range of earnings:

5. Personal characteristics required:

6. Future projected employment:

7. Levels (entry and higher):

8. Opportunities for advancement:

Now examine each of the occupations you have collected information about to see how they fit in with your own needs, characteristics, values, etc. (You might want to look back over your profile from the previous chapter to remind yourself.) Here are some questions to ask yourself about each (make up a second sheet for each occupation, and write down your answers):

—Would this work be satisfying to me?
—Would it tap my best talents?
—Could I do this work well?
—Does it fit in with my motivations for work?
—Does it suit my personality?
—Would I like the life-style that tends to go along with this kind of work?
—Will this kind of work fit in with my long-range hopes for myself?
—Does it offer me opportunities to move up or move to another related field?
—Am I willing and able to invest the time and money to get the training and education needed?
—What do I like most about this occupation?
—What do I like least?
—Additional comments/summary

From your responses and the information you have collected you probably have already eliminated several occupations. Sort the remaining occupations into two stacks:

1. Occupations I would like to consider.
2. Occupations about which I am uncertain.

You have now finished one more important stage in the planning process. Now it's time to move on and find out more about the decision-making process.

CHAPTER 4

PUTTING IT ALL TOGETHER—

Decisions, Goals, Plans

*"Would you tell me, please, which way I
ought to go from here?"
"That depends a good deal on where you
want to get to," said the Cat.
"I don't much care where—" said Alice.
"Then it doesn't matter which way you go,"
said the Cat.
"—so long as I get somewhere," Alice
added as an explanation.
"Oh, you're sure to do that," said the
Cat, "if you only walk long enough."*
—Alice in Wonderland

Alice quite obviously has not yet formulated her career plan effectively.
"Walking long enough" will probably only get her sore feet. Like Alice,
you're not likely to get anywhere if you don't care where you're going.
To get somewhere, you must set up a direction for yourself, which means
making some decisions.

Making decisions and setting and implementing goals are not things
of which you should be afraid. You make decisions all day every day.
You make some decisions automatically, for example, the decisions to
make your bed in the morning and to wash your hair at night. And you
make other decisions, ones that require a little thought but not much
deliberation—what clothes to wear, where to have lunch, or what program to watch on television. Some decisions you make require somewhat more thought and perhaps some consultation with others, for
example, whom to invite to a small dinner party when space limitations
dictate that you invite only eight from among a wide circle of friends.

And there are other decisions you make, highly critical ones that require in-depth investigation on your part—deciding on a college major, or which of two houses to buy, or which career to pursue.

A survey by *Psychology Today* in 1978 indicated that almost 40 percent of the readers questioned were pursuing an occupation that they had come to by chance, without much planning or thought; only 23 percent were working in an occupation of their choice!

These results shouldn't be too surprising to us, for many people avoid making conscious decisions. Like Alice, they drift with the tide, hoping to get somewhere. Others greatly prefer to let someone else decide for them. Still others try very hard to decide but let themselves be immobilized by too many alternatives until they are victims of a decision-making paralysis. Any one person may use one or another of these approaches (or non-approaches) to decision making, depending on the magnitude and complexity of the decision. The more important and far-ranging the decision, however, the more critical it is for the decision maker to be aware of and weigh all the relevant factors and possible outcomes.

Before you begin to make a decision, take heed of these guidelines:

1. Make sure you've done your homework and fully explored all your options. You can't make an intelligent decision unless you have something from which to choose. Be sure you've done the exercises in the previous chapters; otherwise you may find yourself coming to decisions prematurely and without all the relevant information.

2. Don't worry about making one *final* decision. Very few decisions are irreversible. People mature and change; goals change also. Don't feel guilty about changing your goals: they must adapt to a changing *you!*

3. Remember: Decision making is a skill that can be learned. If you feel unsure about your present decision-making ability, you can learn to improve it.

4. Don't be afraid to take the first step. You will be stuck in the mud indefinitely unless you act.

Logical Decision Making

Decision making is a logical procedure that involves these basic steps. In making a decision, you:

1. Define the object of the decision and set a goal.
2. Explore and evaluate resources.
3. State your alternatives.
4. Evaluate the possible outcomes and risks of each alternative.
5. Make tradeoffs and then the final decision.

Making a decision is not as complicated as you might think. Actually, you go through these same steps for all kinds of decisions every day. For instance, take a look at this hypothetical situation. Barbara Ellis is over-weight and very unhappy about it. She doesn't like the way she looks and feels, and so she has decided to lose weight. Let's see how she would follow the five basic steps of decision making to reach her goal.

1. Defining the object and setting the goal.
   Decision: "I want to lose weight. My goal is 20 pounds in the next month."

2. Exploring and evaluating resources.
   "I will need the cooperation of my family and friends as well as some sort of diet plan to help me reduce. My resources include great will-power, and a strong desire to feel better."

3. Stating alternatives.
   a. "I can go on a crash diet and systematically starve myself and lose weight rapidly."
   b. "I can go to a doctor for some counseling and medication."
   c. "I can change my eating habits and begin an exercise program."
   d. "I can join a weight-reducing club."
   e. "I can go away to a weight-reduction spa or clinic for a week or more."

4. Evaluating possible outcomes and risks of each alternative.
   a. "A crash diet will subject me to great hunger pangs and may not be good for my health. I may also gain the weight back immediately after I start to eat again."
   b. "Medication may help me lose the weight initially, but it won't keep the weight off. Besides, I don't want to take pills."
   c. "This plan will take the longest, but the alteration of my eating habits will help me keep the weight off permanently; the exercise will keep my body in shape.
   d. "A club might help me lose weight, but it will cost extra money and I'm not sure I have the time to attend the weekly meeting."
   e. "A week at a spa would definitely help me lose weight, but it's also an extra expense; plus it would mean I'd have to be away from my family for at least a week."

5. Making tradeoffs, and the final decision.
   "I must rank my alternatives and make tradeoffs, considering all the possible outcomes and risks. Alternative c (combination of diet and exercise) might take longer, but it will help me to lose weight and keep it off, with the least amount of risk and expenditure. However, if it's too difficult to achieve my 20-pound goal that way, I may join a weight-reduction club. I've made my final decision; yet I've kept my options open.

Think about the decisions you've made today. Pick one and fill in the following chart. It's likely that you followed the five basic steps of decision making.

My decision: _____

My goal: _____

Alternatives: **Possible Outcomes:**   **Risks:**
_____

_____

_____

_____

Tradeoffs and final decision:_____

_____

_____

Before applying the decision-making process to your own career decisions, take a closer look at each of the steps.

Step One: Defining Your Decisions and Setting Goals

The most difficult part of decision making is probably defining just what it is you're deciding! Deciding which career you want to pursue is a critical decision, since all your subsequent decisions will be based on this first one. Your starting point must be a clear one.

Go back and look at your notebook list of "Occupations I would like to consider," and "Occupations about which I am uncertain." Now try to merge your expanded knowledge of yourself with your extended awareness of career possibilities so that you can make a list of all the career fields that you'd like to explore in depth.

Fill out a chart like the following one and keep it in your notebook.

Occupation:_____

Work Factors	Your Value			
	Poor	Fair	Good	Excellent
Ability to acquire training and/or education				
Work environment				
Growth potential				
Salary potential				
Job security				
"Fringe" benefits				
Prestige and reputation				
*				
*				

*Add any other factors that may be of importance to *you*.

Setting Goals. Many people get stuck in the decision-making process at the point at which they must set goals. A goal is not a decision—it's simply a statement of what you *want* (and often, *when* you want it). The most important thing to remember about goal setting is: BE SPECIFIC! If you're vague and nonspecific about what you want, you won't have the slightest idea of how to get it.

You can only act after all your self-awareness and career-awareness have been translated into a clear statement of your goal, one that allows you to formulate the specific actions or alternatives necessary to attain your goal. For instance, a statement such as "I want to pursue a career in science," is the object of your *decision* to pursue a career. However, a statement such as "I want to be a research and development scientist in a government lab" is the *goal* of your decision.

Write down your goals, to examine them more closely and to focus them in case they aren't specific enough. Set a time limit for yourself too; time limitations help clarify your intentions further and are a good way of measuring progress.

Step Two: Exploring and Evaluating Resources

You've already explored and evaluated many resources, but now it's time to explore which specific resources you have at hand and which ones you'll need to achieve your particular goal. For instance, check any educational or technical training requirements that may be necessary for your goal. Look at the financial picture: Do you have the money you need to achieve your goal? If not, where can you get it? Explore any arrangements you may have to make about your family. For instance, if your goal will involve being in school for part of the day, explore what arrangements you could make for your children's care. Analyze the uniqueness of your specific situation. Be as concrete and specific as possible.

Step Three: Stating Alternatives

All decision making requires that you have at least *some* information about alternatives. If you have no alternatives, you obviously have no decision to make.

The more complex and important the decision, the greater your need for information about the various alternatives. You need to know what kind of information is relevant, if it's available, and how to get it. Suppose, for example, you are planning a vacation; the alternatives you are considering include camping in the mountains, going to the seashore, and taking a trip abroad. What would you consider in trying to arrive at a decision? You would probably have to know about available accommodations and what they cost, distance from home, how you would get there and back, available activities for you and those who might accompany you, and so on.

The same process applies to career alternatives. Sometimes the information you need lies deep within yourself and is accessible only through persistent self-searching and reassessment, as in the case of your needs, goals, and values. At other times the information must be sought from objective sources; you'll need to consult books, government publications, and possibly individuals who are knowledgeable about the various fields of work and the occupations and requirements within them. Much of the time you will need to use both kinds of information to produce yet another kind—possible outcomes and risks inherent in each alternative you are considering.

Step Four: Evaluating Possible Outcomes and Risks of Each Alternative

Most critical decisions representing a turning point in our lives—for example, whether or not to get married, attend college, live away from home—are more complicated than deciding on a vacation. Rarely do you have a choice between a situation that is perfect and one that is flawed; the appropriate decision is usually not obvious. Sometimes you are faced with two equally attractive alternatives. More likely, though, when critical decisions are involved, you must make a choice between two or more less-than-perfect situations. Weighing and comparing the advantages and disadvantages of each require some expert juggling.

Taking Risks. Just as people differ in their general approach to decision-making, they differ in the amount of risk they are consciously willing to take. Some adopt the gambler's philosophy, staking everything on the long shot and hoping for the most desired outcome, even though the probability of its occurrence is minimal. Others prefer to play it safe, choosing the alternative that involves the least amount of risk, even though the outcomes or consequences might not be very desirable. Still others weigh all the alternatives, calculate the levels of risk involved, and make their choices on the basis of which alternative will provide the maximum gain for the least amount of risk.

While risk-taking attitudes are largely a matter of personality, the most cautious as well as the most adventuresome person can benefit greatly by carefully weighing alternatives and the risks they involve. Ask yourself: Is the outcome I hope for worth the risk? If the outcome is important enough—if it involves values that are critical to your self-concept and chosen life-style or to the welfare of those close to you—you may decide that a greater risk than you would ordinarily take is worthwhile. How great a risk? Only you can judge. But you should be able to evaluate the degree of risk involved in various alternatives, and you should be aware of the tradeoffs you can make.

Keep in mind, too, that although you do have control over the decisions you make, you don't have control over the outcomes or consequences. Rarely, if ever, can we predict an outcome with certainty. Anyone who's ever played the stock market or listened to the weather forecast knows that. A recession sets in, unforeseen by even the top economists; a corporation goes bankrupt or moves its operations to another city; certain technological innovations make much of your training unnecessary and/or even useless—these are the types of circumstances that could dramatically affect your plans. The more information you have, however, the greater the probability of your predicting accurately, and the less the risk.

Here's a chance for you to try your hand at evaluating alternatives and risks:

Alternative 1, Company A. Suppose Company A, a relatively new firm, offers you an exciting, creative job in a field in which you are very interested. The job would give you a chance to use your abilities, be involved in major decisions, and advance as the company grows. You would, however, be under a great deal of pressure and would be expected to work long hours; and since the company is small and new, in a highly competitive field, its future is somewhat precarious. Even if it survives, because it is so new there is a possibility that it will go through a number of changes in management and policy as it grows.

Alternative 2, Company B. Suppose you have also been offered a job by Company B, a well-established company with an excellent reputation. You would have security and a good benefits program working for this firm. Again, the work would be in a field in which you are interested and you would probably be able to advance, but advancement would be much more slow than in Company A. Also, because of Company B's highly structured organizational setup, you would be less involved in decision making, and you would have less of a chance to initiate your own ideas and follow them through.

Obviously, if you could combine the challenge of Company A with the stability of Company B, you would have no problem. But to decide between these two alternatives, you must figure out the outcomes and risks involved in both, including the possibility that Company A *might* succeed. Using the following chart as a guide, list the possible outcomes, both positive and negative, of each alternative in your notebook.

Job A—Possible Outcomes	Important to have	Doesn't matter	Important not to have
1. _____			
2. _____			
3. _____			
4. _____			
5. _____			
6. _____			
7. _____			

Job B—Possible Outcomes	Important to have	Doesn't matter	Important not to have
1. _____			
2. _____			
3. _____			
4. _____			
5. _____			
6. _____			
7. _____			

List as many outcomes as you can. Check the first column if the outcome you list is important for you to have in a job, the second column if it doesn't matter one way or another, and the third if the outcome represents a value or characteristic that you definitely *don't* want in a job.

Use this same chart to evaluate all kinds of alternatives. After you have really explored your alternatives and become aware of possible outcomes and risks, you will be prepared to make tradeoffs and your final decision.

Step Five: Making Tradeoffs and the Final Decision

Every decision you make involves a compromise. Of necessity you must select one particular course of action or option over another. You must rank your alternatives and choose the one that best enables you to reach your desired goal. To do so, you must make tradeoffs, exchanging some of the things you want in a job for others you want even more; compromising and accepting some things you don't like to gain something you want very much. Trading-off is something you do every day of your life, for example, giving up a chance to see a play you really want to see in order to stay home and finish a term paper or giving up a dessert you love in order to keep your weight down. You may have to go through the trading-off process a number of times before you are really satisfied that you have made a good decision.

Go back to our hypothetical companies A and B and put yourself in that situation again. What tradeoffs can you make? For example, if you rate the opportunity to be creative and the need for security equally high, how much are you willing to pare down the one to have the other? Go through each of the choices until you can see more clearly which ones represent more gains than losses for you.

Keeping Your Options Open

Making a decision shouldn't mean closing off all other options. Some options, of course, are more difficult to keep open than others. Your options to go into medicine or engineering, for example, will be less viable if in high school and college you decided to take only the minimum amount of math and science. It may be very difficult later to make up for those earlier decisions and consequent lack of preparation, but it is not impossible *if* you are willing to spend the time and work hard.

Periodically, you may want to reassess your situation to see if the direction you have chosen is still the one in which you want to go. As you grow in skill and self-confidence in an occupation, you may want to move into another occupation or field that will give you room for even more growth. You may want to combine school with work to broaden your range of options, enabling you to move more easily into a higher

That "Gut" Feeling

"Gut" feelings—everybody has them now and then. You make an important decision based on a very careful evaluation of all the alternatives available and, afterward, you're plagued by a gnawing feeling of dissatisfaction and unhappiness deep inside you. That feeling may be a signal that in spite of all your careful thinking and meticulous weighing of the pros and cons, you may be making a mistake.

Such feelings can be an important factor in your decision making. By no means should they be the governing factor, but neither should you ignore them. Don't wait uneasily to see how things work out; as soon as you receive the signal that something may be wrong, reevaluate your decision.

Analyze the reasons underlying your concerns and think about what you can do to overcome them, for example, talking things over with a member of your family, a trusted friend, or a counselor. Sometimes others can help you get a new perspective on a situation.

Even if a decision doesn't work out, you won't be stuck with the consequences forever. You may lose time in attaining a long-range goal, but it is within your power to consider new alternatives and make new choices. All around you are people who have successfully changed college majors, schools, jobs, careers, places of residence, lifestyles, and life partners when their earlier choices didn't work out. Very few decisions are totally irreversible.

The important thing to remember is that you can make "gut" feelings work *for* you!

---

level of responsibility or into other fields where you can make better use of your expanded skills.

Continuing your education, even after you have decided and embarked on a career, is one of the surest ways to keep your options open and ensure that they will keep expanding. In most fields the more education you acquire, the better your chances are for advancement or for lateral mobility into new areas.

Keep in mind too, that none of your education or work experience is ever really wasted. Everything you learn contributes in some way to your total repertoire of knowledge and skills—and to your own personal satisfaction.

Planning and Implementing Your Plans

Now you must formulate a plan of action for achieving all your goals. Think of the word *action;* you must come up with a list of concrete and specific steps, plus an estimate of the amount of time each step will take. It's important to write your plan down in your notebook and review it periodically. For one thing, plans tend to be much more logical and efficient when written. Plus, writing down your planned steps will give you a handy timetable against which to assess your progress and planning ahead gives you a greater sense of security and a better chance to control your own life.

Remember: You cannot jump immediately from your starting point to your final goal. Many intermediate steps along the way must be taken. Be as specific as possible about what each step involves before you begin acting on it.

You might, for example, decide to finish all the educational requirements necessary *before* taking a job. In that case find out about programs that give credit for experience or credit by examination. For example, you can obtain credit toward a college degree at many colleges through the College Entrance Examination Board's College-Level Examination Program (CLEP), in which you demonstrate in an examination the extent of the knowledge you have obtained in different content areas through work, home study, and various other ways. A comparable program, the American College Testing Program (ACT) Proficiency Examination Program (PEP), has a similar examination. You might also want to investigate a relatively new development in colleges—the weekend college, which gives those who cannot attend during the week or at night a chance to work for a degree. Many of these programs are open both to students who have had some college and those who have had none. Another possibility is a college-level cooperative work-study program, in which study in any one of a number of professional fields is combined with work experience in the field of study. Or you might want to try the route from volunteer to paid work, possibly combined with appropriate course work.

You can, on the other hand, take an entry-level job in a field in which you are interested and think you might be happy and try to work your way up. On-the-job training, tuition-reimbursement programs sponsored by the company, and taking courses at night will help you move on to a higher level. For example:

- In engineering you might start out as a tracer, with experience and further training become a senior drafter, and eventually—if you earn a bachelor's degree along the way—become an engineer.
- In law you might begin as a legal secretary, take courses at a community college or four-year college that will qualify you as a paralegal specialist, and eventually, after additional college work and graduation from law school, you can become a practicing lawyer.

These examples are only an indication of the many steps you can take. Whatever you finally decide to do, take the time to write down your plans and the steps you must take to reach your goal. Your record in your notebook of your own personal plan will help keep you motivated *and* keep you moving.

OK, you've finally decided what you want to do and approximately when you want to do it. The next step is learning how to market yourself and your skills to get the job you want.

CHAPTER 5

YOU HAVE THE SKILLS—

Now Get the Job

The working world—it can seem pretty impenetrable when you're on the outside looking in. How *do* you find the job you want, with an employer you'd like to work for, people you want to work with, at the right salary? And once you've found such a job, how do you actually get it?

The job hunt process is never easy, and there are no magic tricks guaranteed to get you job offers. In today's job market competition for good jobs is tough; so you'll need to do some careful planning and preparation if you're going to be successful at the job of finding a job.

You already have a head start: a clear idea of your skills, interests, values, and needs. However, before you actually start looking for an employer, you must learn how to "market" what you have to offer. Some good news: you can learn proven techniques that will make this process easier.

One word of advice before you start: it's absolutely essential that you be organized. Buy an accordion file (the cardboard type with pockets) and set up your personal job-hunt filing system. Include such things as articles you've clipped, information about potential employers, carbon copies of *everything* you send out, records of interviews, and notes from conversations about job leads. You may think you'll remember these things, but you won't. And if you don't already have an appointment calendar, get one in which to note interviews, when and to whom you've sent your resume, follow-up details, etc. Make sure it has plenty of space in the back for names, addresses, and phone numbers of contacts. Keeping an adequate supply of stationery, envelopes, and stamps on hand will also help you approach your search in the businesslike way it deserves.

Once you have everything in order and are ready to jump into the fray, don't panic. There's more work ahead, but the payoff is a job that fits your requirements. What's next includes writing a good resume and cover letter, learning how to interview for a job, and starting the search for actual leads through such avenues as campus placement, want ads, and employment services.

Your Resume

Your resume is a one-page advertisement for yourself. Its long-range purpose is to get you a job, but its more immediate purpose is to get you an *interview*. The resume is the first (but one hopes not the only) chance you have to sell your employer on your capabilities. That paper has to come alive to show your skills, experience, and accomplishments in 250 words or less.

You can organize your resume in several ways to tell different stories; you make the choice according to what you need to emphasize or downplay. There is no one "right" resume style; each person should tailor her resume to her own needs. (There are, however, lots of "wrong" resumes —sloppily typed, disorganized, or vaguely written ones. Such resumes almost automatically cancel you out, since employers figure that if you do such a poor job for yourself, you'll do a poor job for them.) Most resumes should be neatly printed on one page of 8½-by-11 paper. Beyond that, you might choose one of these common resume formats: the chronological resume, the functional resume, or the combination resume.

Chronological Resume

The resume form that you and interviewers are probably most familiar with is the chronological resume. In this type of resume you list your experience in chronological order, starting with your most recent job, which generally receives the most emphasis. You'll find this resume easiest to prepare, and a good way to display the steady employment record of someone who hasn't done much job hopping. However, a chronological resume can put undesirable emphasis on job areas or employment gaps you may want to minimize. It can also make it difficult to spotlight your areas of greatest skill.

Functional Resume

A good way to highlight your qualifications without emphasizing specific dates is by using the format of the functional resume. This resume is especially useful if you've interrupted your career for a few years or want to downplay certain things you feel can be best handled in an interview. With it you can demonstrate professional growth or certain in-demand skills you may possess. If you're making a career change, you can use it to illustrate those portions of your previous experience which are applicable to a new job. However, many employers are suspicious of this style; they may ask to see additional work-history information.

Combination Resume

Another option is the form of resume that is a combination of the functional and the chronological types. In this form, company names and dates are included in a separate section, after job functions are listed. This resume may be the best solution, as long as it is very attractively laid out and succinctly written so that the employer doesn't lose interest before the end.

Don'ts of Resume Writing

Whatever resume form is most appropriate to present your experience (you may decide to try all three, selecting a different one according to each job opportunity), certain things do not belong on *any* resume:

- Anything that doesn't contribute to getting you an interview; i.e., names and ages of your children, hobbies that have nothing to do with your job target, your astrological sign, etc.
- Your job objective. Listing this item may limit your range of possibilities, unless you're willing to redo the resume for each job position. Instead, mention your prospective position in your cover letter.
- Blots, typos, wavy margins, and handwritten corrections or additions.

The First Draft

Writing your resume takes several tries and increasingly refined drafts. Look over the personal biography and achievements lists you've already worked on for skills and abilities you'd like to highlight. Then rough out your first draft. Keep these guidelines in mind:

- Use the minimum number of words necessary. Avoid introductory phrases such as "My duties included" or "I was in charge of."
- Use action words like *designed, improved, supervised, conducted,* and *prepared.*
- Where appropriate, include expressions that show the employer you know the field, e.g., specific jargon related to the job.
- Avoid extraneous information. You'll dilute your key selling points if you try to convey too many ideas at once.
- Break up long ideas into short, clearly written sentences or phrases.

CHRONOLOGICAL RESUME

Roberta Simon
415 High Street
Portland, Oregon 97208
(503) 710-4183

Staff Assistant

WORK EXPERIENCE

1971 - Present

Staff Assistant to chairman,
Department of Sociology
University of Oregon

Responsible for smooth day-to-day running of
department of 15 persons.

—Prepare university and government surveys and
  reports.
—Prepare agenda and faculty meeting minutes.
—Authorize expenditures of $175,000 budget.
—Analyze quantity audits, projections, and financial
  statements.
—Interpret and apply university and government
  policies.

1969– 1971

Assistant to chairman of Math Department, Portland
State University

—Carried out administrative policies of section—
  processed payroll, coordinated work schedules,
  ordered supplies and equipment.
—Scheduled meetings and appointments.

1968– 1969

Secretary/editor, *Journal of Applied Math*

—Directed day-to-day journal operation.
—Handled all general queries with authors.
—Served as liaison between authors and publisher.
—Prepared statistics, agenda, and minutes of editors'
  meetings.

EDUCATION

BA Portland State University, 1968. Humanities
major. Honor student.

THE FUNCTIONAL RESUME

Roberta Simon
415 High Street
Portland, Oregon 97208
(503) 710-4183

MAJOR WORK EXPERIENCE

Research

Developed university and government surveys and reports for sociology department of major university. Researched background material for articles appearing in major national mathematics journal.

Financial Analysis

Analyzed quantity audits, projections, and financial statements of university department. Authorized expenditures of $175,000 budget.

Editing

Directed day-to-day operations of national mathematics journal. Handled all general queries with authors and served as liaison between authors and publisher.

Administration and Management

Responsible for smooth running of 15-person department. Prepared minutes and agenda for faculty and editorial meetings. Carried out administrative policies of section—processed payroll, coordinated work schedules, ordered supplies and equipment. Interpreted and applied university and government policy.

EDUCATION

BA Portland State University, 1968.
Humanities major. Honor student.

COMBINATION RESUME

Roberta Simon
415 High Street
Portland, Oregon 97208
(503) 710-4183

RESEARCH

Developed university and government surveys and reports for sociology department of major university. Researched background material for articles appearing in major national mathematics journal.

EDITING

Directed day-to-day operations of the *Journal of Applied Math.* Handled all general queries with authors and served as liaison between authors and publisher.

FINANCIAL
ANALYSIS

Analyzed quantity audits, projections, and financial statements of university department. Authorized expenditures of $175,000 budget.

ADMINISTRATION
AND MANAGEMENT

Responsible for smooth running of 15-person department. Prepared minutes and agenda for faculty and editorial meetings. Carried out administrative policies of section: processed payroll, coordinated work schedules, ordered supplies and equipment. Interpreted and applied university and government policy.

1971– Present:

Staff assistant to chairman, Department of Sociology, University of Oregon

1969– 1971:

Assistant to chairman of Math Department, Portland State University

1968– 1969:

Secretary/editor, *Journal of Applied Math*

EDUCATION

BA Portland State University, 1968. Humanities major. Honor student.

- Whenever possible list accomplishments rather than just describing duties. Start out with key benefits you can offer the employer, like: "Saved the company $100,000," or "Designed a better system."

The Final Draft

Once you have written your first draft, review, edit, and rewrite it until you are satisfied. Go through this process as many times as necessary. Then retype your resume, following these tips:

- Single space your resume and keep the total length to a page or two. (One page is preferable.)
- Retain an attractive amount of white space. Leave at least 1-inch margins; double space between paragraphs; allow at least 1 inch at the top and bottom of the page.

- Keep paragraphs short—no more than 8 to 10 lines.
- Emphasize each new category of information with a heading (e.g., Education, Work Experience) in such a way that readers can quickly find the specific information they seek.
- Avoid unnecessary and obvious captions, such as "Name" and "Address."

Test Marketing

After preparing and typing your final draft, you're ready to test-market the resume. Begin by reading it critically to yourself; then show it to friends and colleagues who might pick up things you miss. Keep in mind that the purpose of the resume is to get you an interview. Now, rate yourself (and have your readers rate you), using the following checklist:

___ Overall appearance. (Do you want to read it?)
___ Layout. (Does it look professional? Is it well typed and printed, with adequate margins, etc.? Do the key sales points stand out?)
___ Length. (Could it tell the same story if it were shortened?)
___ Relevance. (Has extraneous material been eliminated?)
___ Writing style. (Is it easy to get a picture of your qualifications?)
___ Action orientation. (Do sentences and paragraphs begin with action verbs?)
___ Specificity. (Does it avoid generalities and focus on specific information about experience, projects, products, etc.?)
___ Accomplishments. (Are your accomplishments and problem-solving skills emphasized?)
___ Completeness. (Is all the important information covered?)

Once you have critiqued the resume yourself, try to find someone to review it who has had some experience in the business or professional world. Since many people are afraid to be too critical, be prepared with specific questions: "Do I give enough information about my most recent position?" "Is it too long?" "Would *you* want to interview me based on this resume?"

After making final revisions, have the resume typed and printed. If you don't have access to a top-quality typewriter with a clean ribbon, go to a professional typing service. It's worth it. And the expense of having 100 copies printed on good-quality paper is nominal when you consider the benefits of a well-presented resume. Store the typed original in a sealed flat envelope in your file in case you need it for reprinting.

Your Cover Letter

Every resume you send out should be accompanied by an individualized typed letter. This cover letter is your chance to make a special impression. Use it to pinpoint your skills and experiences, relating them to the particular job you seek.

In addition, slant your cover letter toward each potential employer. Whenever possible, research the employing organization before you write the letter. Read annual reports and product brochures, contact people in the organization, or, if you have a good understanding of the field, simply ask yourself what kinds of problems this particular employer might be facing. Finally, call the switchboard to find out the name and title of the person most likely to do the interviewing. Address your letter to that person.

COVER LETTER

415 High Street
Portland, Oregon 97208
(503) 710-8976

December 2, 1977

Dr. John Callan
Department of Mathematics
University of Illinois
Champaign-Urbana, Illinois 50987

Dear Dr. Callan:

Dr. Eugene Simmons of the University of Oregon told me recently that you are planning to expand the personnel of the University of Illinois Mathematics Department and to begin publishing a new journal of mathematics in the fall.

As secretary/editor of the *Journal of Applied Math*, I worked daily with authors, publisher, and printer, overseeing production and layout of this quarterly. Our circulation rose steadily after I designed a direct-mail campaign to mathematics departments all over the country.

In addition to this experience, I have had seven years' experience as assistant to the chairmen of two different university departments. Administrative work, budgeting and financial projections, and supervising support staff were all part of my responsibilities.

I plan to be in Champaign-Urbana early next month, and I would like to meet you January 5 or 6 for an interview. I'll call you to inquire when you'll be available.

Yours truly,

Roberta Simon

The letter needn't be long—normally not more than three or four paragraphs. But be sure to close with a request for an interview. Suggest a specific time or reason, such as "I would like to stop by with some samples of my work. Could we meet briefly next Thursday afternoon?" or "I will call your office to discuss a possible interview date."

Keep track in your appointment calendar of each resume and cover letter you send out, and note the date you plan to follow up. Also, be sure to file the carbon copy of each letter.

Your Interview

Your resume and cover letter were successful—you've landed an interview. The employer wants to know more about you; you, the "interviewee," want to know more about the employer and the specific job.

If you're nervous (most interviewees are), keep in mind that an interview is really an exchange of information on both sides, not a hot seat for an innocent job seeker. The goal of the interviewer is not to trip you up or embarrass you; he or she wants to determine whether you have the qualifications and the potential to do a specific job well.

Preparing for an interview involves being ready to answer the interviewer's questions and to ask some of your own. You should have mastered your background material almost as if you were to be tested on it. Go back over the information you've collected about the industry and the particular company. If it's scanty and your library doesn't have details, call or write the organization's public relations division and ask for copies of annual reports, corporate brochures, promotional materials, and the house organ. You cannot know too much about your prospective employer. Interviewers *expect* you to be sufficiently well informed to ask pertinent questions and discuss the company and job opportunities intelligently.

Be prepared to explain more about the information on your resume. Go back over the self-appraisal section in your notebook, looking for your strengths and accomplishments. Think of ways to relate them to the position for which you're being interviewed. You can prepare an index card, a sort of "crib sheet," of the major points you wish to make, and take it along to study as you wait—but don't read from it in the interview!

Practicing before you walk in can make all the difference for your peace of mind. If friends are also looking for jobs, meet a few times to take turns playing interviewer/interviewee.

Make sure you've got everything you're planning to wear before the day of the interview so you don't frazzle yourself in hunting. And allow enough time to get to the appointment a little early. These extra minutes will give you a chance to check out where you might be working, as well as to catch your breath and collect yourself. Punctuality counts. And appearance *does* matter. If you err on the conservative side when it comes to dress you won't go far wrong.

When you arrive for your interview, you may be asked to fill out an application for employment. Follow instructions and fill out the entire form, even if you feel the questions have been answered by your resume. If some inquiries are not applicable to you, use the abbreviation NA rather than leaving the question unanswered. You can refer to your resume for details such as dates and job descriptions; in fact, you should bring along an extra resume for this purpose, or in case the employer has misplaced the one you sent. Other things to bring: your Social Security card, a typewritten list of your references and their addresses and telephone numbers, samples of your work if appropriate or your portfolio, letters of recommendation you may already have.

What actually happens during the interview is not only up to the interviewer. It's also your responsibility. Many interviewers ask a series of structured questions; others rely on you to tell them what you can do. Being asked to "Tell me about yourself" is a golden opportunity to talk about your assets and accomplishments. If you are asked to discuss mistakes you've made or your worst habits, you can also turn the interview to your advantage. Answer questions quickly and intelligently, but if a particular question requires some thought, say so. It's perfectly all right to say, "I have never considered that aspect in those terms" if you're thrown a curve ball. Make sure you've tried to bring up all your strong points. Boast a little, but avoid sounding too cocky or conceited!

Your own questions about the company and the work environment shouldn't lead the interviewer to think you're afraid of work or are turned off by the position or the company. Your initial interview is not the time to focus on what the company can do for you. There's time for that once you've interested them to such an extent that they're wooing *you*. In addition, salary specifics really shouldn't be negotiated at this first meeting. If you're asked what you expect as a starting salary, don't state a flat amount. Indicate a range that is acceptable and in line with what your experience—or lack of it—has led you to expect. Leave yourself some bargaining room.

Finally, know when it's time to leave. Most interviews are less than an hour, some as short as 20 minutes. If you feel the interviewer is drawing the session to a close, don't talk on and on. Before you leave, ask if there's any additional information you should provide, thank the interviewer for the opportunity to discuss the company and the job, and ask when you can expect to hear from the firm. If, by some flash of good fortune, you are offered the job on the spot, you're perfectly justified in asking for a few days to think about it.

After the interview, you need time to think about all you've heard. You also need to spend some time with your notebook. For each interview, use a separate sheet of paper to record details about the job and the employer, areas of your interviewing technique you need to improve, points you think you handled effectively that you can repeat in the next attempt, etc.

If you are interested in the job, send a note to the interviewer immediately to thank her or him for spending time with you. It's a chance to reiterate your interest in the job and to remind the firm who (among the herd of applicants) you are. Add that you're willing to meet further or to furnish any additional information that might be needed.

If you are not interested in the job but are offered it, express your refusal without sounding too negative. Life is long, and you may want to work with that company later in your career. Again, a brief thank-you letter to the interviewer is appropriate.

If you receive an offer you are willing to accept—don't dither. Call the employer promptly with your decision, and find out exactly when, where, and to whom you should report for your first day on the job. Follow with a letter expressing your enthusiasm and eagerness to join the organization.

Your Job Search

Now that you have a good resume and are ready to interview, where and how do you actually look for a job?

Studies show most women land their jobs by direct application to the employer; answering local newspaper ads and asking friends for help are the next two most effective approaches. (See chart.) Obviously, you can't just mail out a few hundred copies of your resume and wait to be discovered. You have to *make* yourself lucky. You must pursue obvious and not-so-obvious possibilities. Here are some of the sources for job leads you might not have considered. Try every one you can.

People

Friends, relatives, counselors, instructors—all those people you meet daily—can be a great help. Talk about your job search to anyone who'll listen. If it's someone who doesn't know you well, mention any pertinent information that sets you apart from most applicants—a 4.0 average, a lifetime interest in medicine, etc.

Even if the people you speak with don't know of any specific job openings, they do know other people. Try the stepping stone method: If you want a job in graphic design but you only know people in business, ask a friend for an introduction to the graphic arts director at her company. Many people are flattered and pleased to be able to help if you approach them in the right way. And someday you can return the favor. Be sure to thank them—in writing if possible—for any help.

METHODS USED BY WOMEN AND MEN TO LOOK FOR WORK AND METHOD BY WHICH CURRENT JOB WAS OBTAINED, JANUARY 1973

Method	Percent who used each method		Method used to get job	
	Women	Men	Women	Men
Total jobseekers (thousands)	4,688	5,749	4,688	5,749
Percent	[1]	[1]	100.0	100.0
Applied directly to employer	64.4	67.3	34.6	35.1
Asked friends:				
About jobs where they work	47.2	53.8	10.7	13.8
About jobs elsewhere	36.6	45.9	4.8	6.2
Asked relatives:				
About jobs where they work	25.1	31.0	5.1	6.9
About jobs elsewhere	23.9	30.1	1.7	2.7
Answered newspaper ads:				
Local	47.5	44.6	14.5	10.3
Nonlocal	8.6	14.2	1.1	1.4
Private employment agency	22.4	19.9	7.9	3.8
State employment service	29.2	37.1	5.2	5.0
School placement office	13.0	12.0	2.8	3.1
Civil Service test	15.2	15.4	2.8	1.6
Asked teacher or professor	11.8	9.2	1.6	1.2
Went to place where employers come to pick up people	0.7	2.0	0.2	0.1
Placed ads in newspapers:				
Local	1.4	1.7	0.4	0.1
Nonlocal	0.2	0.7	—	[2]
Answered ads in professional or trade journals	2.6	6.7	0.3	0.5
Union hiring hall	1.1	9.9	0.1	2.6
Contacted local organization	5.7	5.5	0.9	0.7
Placed ads in professional or trade journals	0.4	0.8	[2]	—
Other	11.5	11.9	5.3	5.1

[1]Because some respondents indicated the use of more than one method, the sum of the components exceeds 100 percent.

[2]Less than 0.05 percent.

U.S. Working Women: A Databook. U.S. Dept. of Labor Bureau of Labor Statistics, 1977.

State Employment Services

More than 2,400 public employment service offices provide four basic services—job information, employment counseling, referral to job training, and job placement. The counselors often know the general job climate in their localities, as well as what kinds of workers are employed and by whom, wages that are paid, and hiring requirements. Job Information Service units permit job seekers to select their own jobs from a computerized listing of job opportunities in the area. And it's free. To find the office nearest you, look in the telephone directory under the name of your state, or call your mayor's office and ask for the appropriate referral.

Placement Centers at Educational Institutions

Competition for interviews is becoming so intense that staying in close contact with your school's placement office is vital. These offices often house fine career libraries and provide practical help as well as lists of available jobs. For example, the alumnae placement center may offer specific suggestions about potential employers you may never have considered or give you the names and addresses of former students who are successful in your field to contact for advice or leads. Even if it is located outside your geographic area, the office may be able to provide you with a letter of introduction to a local placement officer.

Campus Recruitment

All sorts of employers recruit on campus—hotel chains, stores, oil companies—and usually they stipulate the types of people they want to interview and what sorts of positions are available. If participating in campus recruitment isn't possible for you, contact those companies directly. The *College Placement Annual* is a good directory to these and other corporations. It is available in college libraries and guidance offices or for $5 from

College Placement Council
P.O. Box 2263
Bethlehem, Pennsylvania 18001

Publications and Public Libraries

The "Help Wanted" column is an obvious starting place, but the help a paper can give you doesn't end in the want ads. Job opportunities can be spread throughout the newspaper. Scan the back issues of the major dailies in the areas in which you would consider working. Check regional editions of such papers as *The Wall Street Journal*. Watch for industry trends or information that could result in jobs that are not yet

TIPS FOR YOUR FIRST JOB: WHAT EMPLOYERS EXPECT

You've got the job—now how do you keep it? Surprisingly, many more people are fired because of poor work habits than because of inability to do the work that's expected of them. From the beginning, treat your work life seriously. In general, your success will be related to your willingness to do more than is actually required, to your continuing improvement in your assigned tasks, and to your good judgment. Remember to:

—Do your job competently. However pleasant you are, if your work is unsatisfactory, you will be discharged.
—Develop interest in your job, and show it.
—Be prompt and attend regularly.
—Dress for the job. Employers do notice how you look, and it's good for your own self-esteem to be ready for business. Indifference to dress often goes along with indifference to a job.
—Accept criticism and suggestions gratefully, even if they're not given very tactfully.
—Be cheerful, but know the time and the place for humor.

Getting along with your fellow employees is important, not only to make your workday pleasant, but to ensure that you'll all work together effectively. They'll expect you to like them, to participate in the department, to know when to mind your own business, and to be loyal to them.

If you do for some reason feel as if you might be up for a firing, don't just sit and wait for a summons from the boss. Confront the situation professionally. Ask for an evaluation of your work, and for help in pinpointing where you need improvement. Too many bosses find dealing with such personnel problems so difficult that they let employees drift in ignorance of their true feelings. It's up to you to find out both how you're doing and how to do it better. And after all, if your worst suspicions are true, it's easier to start looking for another job while you still have one.

---

available, like articles and columns that announce new products, personnel changes, business expansion, or newly funded projects.

Professional journals and trade publications, many of which you're already reading to keep up with the newest trends in your field, can also give you job leads. As with newspapers, don't just look at classified or display advertisements. Scan the personnel change announcements, reports on new products, etc. You could even contact the editor or author of a piece you particularly like and ask for advice.

Consider placing an advertisement for yourself in any of the previously discussed publications. If you can't find a specialist in your field for advice on the best way to phrase it, be sure to look at other similar ads. As you look them over, pretend you're an employer. Which ads make *you* want to find out more about that person? If you do place an ad for yourself, be prepared for responses from employment agencies— they'll know you're looking.

Even the telephone directory can be a goldmine of help. (Larger public libraries often have out-of-town phone directories as well as out-of-town newspapers, if you're thinking of making a geographic move.) You can use the white pages listings in dictionary fashion, checking key words in a field to see if there is a local association that could lead you to information or job possibilities. The yellow pages section is a ready source for names and addresses of firms, nonprofit organizations, and commercial employment agencies by category.

While you're at the library, be sure to take advantage of all its other sources of information. For example, there are a number of directories that list names, addresses, type, and size of companies, as well as the names and titles of key executives. Depending on your field, check: *Dun and Bradstreet's Million Dollar Directory; Standard and Poor's Directory of Directors; National Advertising Register; Thomas' Register of American Manufacturers;* the *Museum Directory; Hospital Directory;* and *Foundation Directory;* and *Literary Market Place.* There's even a *Directory of Directories,* which lists names and publishers' addresses for directories in almost every field. The *Encyclopedia of Associations* is a similar guide to approximately 500 professional organizations.

Not-for-Profit Agencies

Professional organizations, government agencies, unions, and other groups sometimes provide placement services. Women's resource centers, such as the more than 160 in Catalyst's National Network, offer counseling and placement services too. (Write Catalyst national headquarters, 14 East 60th Street, New York, New York 10022, for an up-to-date list.) Other not-for-profit places to consult are local YWCA, NOW, and Urban League offices.

Personal Applications

Making personal unsolicited applications by sending out your resumes and cover letters is your direct-mail campaign—a blitz of any and every organization that might be interested in what you have to offer. Try to find out who your immediate supervisor or department head would be if you were hired; then direct your letter and resume to that person, rather than to a nameless person in the personnel department. If that's not possible, call to find out the name of the head of personnel and address your letter to him or her directly.

Commercial Employment Agencies

Employment agencies are a last resort, for many are not worth the fees they charge. Some are reliable and helpful; especially worth investigating are ones that specialize in your particular field. Here's a good idea on how to find out which agencies to contact: call or visit a major employer in your field, introduce yourself as someone gathering career information, and ask its personnel recruiters which agencies they find useful. When dealing with an agency, be *sure* to find out the fee scale and who pays—the applicant or the employer. Before signing *anything,* ask to take home the documents and read them in peace. It's even a good idea to ask someone else to check them over with you to make sure you're getting what you're paying for.

SETTING THE STAGE FOR MOVING UP AND ON

Here are a few techniques that will help you in a climb toward the top.

Get involved in the activities of your work group. Polish your skills in dealing with people—that's the very core of a manager's job. And the friends you make now may help you later.

Strive to be as good at your job as you can. There's something to learn everywhere, and showing that you can be responsible, even at a beginner's level, will help you make a good reputation for yourself. Learn about the jobs of the people around you, too.

Once you've mastered your own particular skill, begin to get ready for the next job you've targeted. If that effort involves special training after work or preparing for examinations, then the time and energy you invest will pay off later. You have already spent some time thinking about what goals are most appealing to you, what your career path should be. But don't stop now; keep it up. Talk to other people in your company and field to make sure you have a realistic sense of what the steps are for working toward what you want. This is also a good time to begin building the network of friends and acquaintances in other companies who can help you—and whom you can help—with tips and job leads as your careers develop.

Always show initiative and a sense of responsibility, not only for your own job, but for the progress of the company. Every job is improvable; share your ideas with those who can implement them.

Most careers involve some switching among companies; so always keep your eyes open for what's available elsewhere. Many promotions come when you change employers.

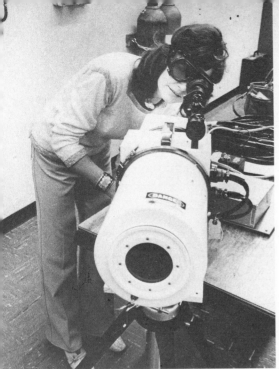

BETTYE LANE

FREDA LEINWAND

GUIDE II **A Guide to Health Careers**

Funding for this Guide was provided by Pfizer, Inc.

FREDA LEINWAND

CHAPTER 1

HEALTH CARE—

Number-One Area of Employment

Right now more than 4½ million people are employed in the field of
health care in the United States. This figure is expected to reach 6 million by the 1980s, which will make health care the number-one area of
employment in the country—providing more jobs and more kinds of jobs
than any other field. The number and diversity of these job opportunities
make it an excellent career for women, but these two factors are only
part of the story.

The field is a naturally attractive one to many women. The concepts of
caring and of helping, implicit in health care, are familiar ones to
women. Some of the great heroines in history—Florence Nightingale,
Clara Barton, Edith Cavell, Jane Addams, Margaret Sanger, Sister Ken-
ney, and Helen Taussig, to name a few—were engaged either directly
in health care services or in closely related fields. Generally, women are
seriously concerned over how much they can contribute to society and
to themselves in terms of job satisfaction. Most health care salaries are
competitive with those in other fields; some are very high. What other
field of endeavor can offer such rich returns in the deep, personal satisfaction one person can derive from helping another? Health care workers take pride in being skilled members of a team that provides highly
valued services to the community.

The relatively few areas where women have encountered some difficulty and resistance in the past (as medical doctors, for instance) are
opening up at both training and employment levels. In occupations such
as nursing, medical technology, and occupational and physical therapy,
the majority of workers are women, and the increasing demand in these
areas will continue to make them good career opportunities for women.
Additionally, newly emerging occupations, such as physician's assistant

109

and emergency medical technician, promise to offer equal opportunity to women.

The American "health services industry," as it is known, is the outgrowth of a health care system that was still in its infancy as late as 1893, when the first modern American medical school was founded at Johns Hopkins University in Baltimore. Its faculty consisted of four physicians.

Mid-19th-century health care was not significantly better than that of the colonial period when the practice of medicine was more of a "cottage industry" than a real system of professional, scientific treatment for the sick and injured. Consider the great reliance on homemade "cure-alls" or "patent medicines" whose primary ingredients were alcohol and/or opium derivatives, and the lack of knowledge of such basics as antiseptics and bacterial and viral infections. Many "medical practitioners" were outright charlatans and hucksters; even the best were poorly trained by today's standards. Many hospitals and charitable institutions for the needy provided only a quarantined, out-of-sight place for people to die. Surgery consisted mainly of amputations, too often followed by infection and death.

Nurses also were poorly qualified as health practitioners. Although nursing is traced back to the earliest civilizations, formal training in modern methods owes much to Florence Nightingale, who brought about many reforms in the education of nurses. The New England Hospital for Women and Children in Boston graduated the first class of trained nurses in the United States in 1872, and the first college nursing curriculum was established at the University of Minnesota in 1909.

Two developments of the past 75 years, the continually increasing expenditures for health services and the huge expansion in employment in the health sector, have created our modern American health service industry. This "industry" comprises labor, capital, and goods and services, just as any other industry, although we tend not to think of health services in this way. The human element of disease and suffering, and their treatment and relief, tends to dominate our conception of health care.

The more than 4½ million people employed in the health service industry work in more than 200 types of jobs related to more than 50 major health care occupations. Of the 71 industries recognized by the United States Bureau of the Census, health services ranked second in 1970 with 4,345,668 persons, representing a 69 percent increase in manpower over the preceding decade and employing 4.8 percent of the nation's total workforce. Physicians numbered approximately 350,000, or 1 physician for every 562 people in the United States. Yet only 1 in 5 health professionals is a physician, and among all health care workers only 1 in 14.

The trend in expenditures for health services has been one of rapid expansion. Although estimates of the total "cost" of the American health

QUIZ

Here's a quiz to test your knowledge of the history of women in the health professions. Don't be discouraged if you don't know all the answers.

Do you know . . .

1. Who received the first medical degree conferred on a woman in modern times?
2. Who was the first woman to earn a dental degree and the first to be admitted to a state dental association?
3. What health pioneer said, "It's six times safer to be a soldier in the trenches of France than to be born a baby in the United States"?
4. Who was the first black woman to receive a degree as a trained nurse?
5. What celebrated physician was known among her 11th-century contemporaries as *Magistra Operis* — consummate practitioner?
6. What Greek woman became a physician despite a law that on pain of death forbade a woman to study or practice medicine?
7. What noted physician and medical researcher has been called the "Curie of America"?

QUIZ ANSWERS

Here are the answers to the quiz. How well did you do?

1. A pioneer in preventive medicine, sanitation, and public health, *Elizabeth Blackwell* (1821– 1910) was rejected by at least 15 medical schools before she was accepted at Geneva Medical College, where she graduated at the head of her class.
2. Although not the first woman to practice dentistry, *Lucy Hobbs Taylor* (1833– 1910) recorded a professional first for women when, after years of struggle and rebuffs, she received the first dental degree granted to a woman.
3. Physician *Sara Josephine Baker* (1873– 1945) pioneered in public health work and education. She devoted her life to improving the health of children.
4. A graduate of the New England Hospital for Women and Children, *Mary Eliza Mahoney*'s (1845– 1926) excellent record paved the way for other black women to become nurses in spite of the rigid discriminatory practices prevalent in most nursing schools at the time.
5. Educated at the famous Salerno medical school in Italy, *Trotula Platearius* (11th century) was a brilliant physician and educator, and the author of a much-celebrated book on obstetrics and gynecology.
6. *Agnodice* (ca. 300 B.C.) wore male clothing in order to study medicine. However, when it became known that she was a woman, the women of Athens pleaded so

eloquently for her life that the magistrates enacted a new law enabling women to study and practice medicine.
7. *Florence Sabin* (1871–1953) has been called the "Curie of America" for her extensive medical research and her pioneer work in the study of tuberculosis.

---

system vary, they range between $150 billion and $175 billion, or up to 8.5 percent of the gross national product in 1977. As a percentage of the gross national product, health care expenditures increased by approximately 80 percent in the 25 years from 1950 to 1975; the consumer price index for medical care increased about 125 percent over the same period, compared with an increase of only about 61 percent for the economy as a whole.

The greatest increases for health care expenditures have been in hospital costs. The average rate per day for a patient in a hospital has risen from approximately $15 in 1950 to $175. Manpower has grown from an average of 178 workers per hospital to more than 325 per 100 patients. Hospital construction coupled with expensive new technologies has necessitated a proportionately large increase in capital expenditures. This trend has many causes, some of which are discussed below, and many ramifications, the most significant for the purpose of this Guide being that, especially for skilled nonphysician medical workers, the prospects for continuing expansion in employment are very good.

Interest in Health

In the first three-quarters of this century three broad interests have had the most influence on the growth and direction of health care: (1) the professionalism and strong self-interest of some of the medical profession, (2) the demand for quality care by a determined public, and (3) the politicizing of the health care issue and the growing concern of lawmakers for more efficient organization and effective management of health care. Controversy exists over what seem to be the conflicting interests of the parties involved, and adoption by Congress of a major comprehensive health services plan would widely influence health care financing, taxation, and distribution of health monies, as well as the organization and geographical allocation of the pool of skilled medical resources available, the health-team concept of medical care, decentralization and mobilization of services now provided only in hospitals, computerization and specialization/technicalization, and even patients' rights to information, choice of type and manner of treatment, etc.

In 1910 Abraham Flexner's report on medical education emphasized the need to develop and adhere to criteria that define the standards of professional conduct. The discrediting of diploma mills and the medical profession's self-regulating credentialing procedures have ensured that the direction of health care aims has continued to be high. Problems such as the overconcentration in certain areas of the country of doctors, nurses, and other skilled medical workers while other regions needing these professionals are without them, and questions such as disproportionately high rates of elective surgery for certain specialties, for example, will continue to vex the health care system until a national policy has been legislated.

An ever-greater dissemination of information through the media to a larger and better-informed public has created a demand for health care services, expressed through consumer advocacy groups and health legislation lobbying. Voters are responding to outcries against nursing home abuses, Medicaid fraud, and misuse of public funds, and soaring costs for health care. One lobby, the 1977 National Women's Conference, has offered specific recommendations on health care. It proposed training and research programs for the needs of the disabled; broader insurance benefits to include preventive health services, home support services, and comprehensive mental health care; outreach programs for victims of hazardous drug therapy; alcohol and drug abuse research and treatment centers for women; representation of women on all federal, state, and private health policy and planning bodies; and a network of community-based, low-cost reproductive health services. As these suggested programs are put into effect, additional trained health care personnel will be needed to run them.

The reasons for the current activity by many interest groups are numerous and complex. A mixture of for-profit, not-for-profit, and government-financed endeavors, the health services industry has areas of overlapping coverage that waste money and resources as well as areas of inadequate coverage. The salaries of many hospital employees, skilled and nonskilled, have long been below what they should have been, and now the compensating increases look large. New technology is expensive to invent and to implement, as are the many new and more frequently administered diagnostic tests; longer lifespans mean more people in need of critical and constant medical attention in old age. And, across the board, inflation has added another large chunk to expenses.

From the enactment of Social Security to the Medicare and Medicaid programs, the Hill-Burton Act that made funds available for hospital construction, the Emergency Medical Systems Act of 1973, and the Health Maintenance Organization Act of 1973 that gave federal backing to the establishment of prepaid group health organizations, Congress has influenced the organization and planning of our health care system. A majority of the citizens believe that at least *some* changes *must* be made, de facto changes recognized, and a greater degree of planning and improvement in the prevention of disease and the quality of care realized over the next several years.

Three possibilities being considered that would give major impetus and new direction to our health care system in the next 25 years are (1) in the area of money: federally funded comprehensive health care services and/or insurance for all Americans; (2) in the area of quality of care: a system based, not on a single physician caring for patients on an individual fee-for-service basis (the recent historical model), but on a physician team serving members of a prepaid group and supported by highly skilled nurses and technicians having more responsibility than they do now for care, treatment, and testing that do not require the particular expertise of a physician; and (3) in the area of prevention: emphasis throughout the health care system on preventing sickness and disease, with special attention given to environmental and occupational factors.

Where the Jobs Are

The opportunities for a career in the health care field are excellent and will continue to expand. There's a place in this vital and challenging field for all kinds of people performing all kinds of tasks. Health occupations offer women mobility, status, and good salaries as well as nourishment for the mind and heart. And breakthroughs in medical science and technology are creating new jobs in every area of the field. The range of places to work is almost as varied as the types of jobs. In planning for your employment as a health worker you will want to consider the following settings—they are the major centers of health services.

Hospitals are the most familiar health care facility. The more than 7,000 hospitals in this country vary in size from small rural hospitals to huge urban institutions. Some hospitals are privately financed, others are supported by the community or the state, and still others operate in connection with universities as training centers for students of all aspects of medicine. Many hospitals are engaged in research programs, sponsor health education programs for the community, and provide preventive medical services. Doctors and nurses are the most visible members of the hospital staff; but their effectiveness is dependent on the services of other departments, such as pharmacy, laboratories, radiology, housekeeping, and general administration—each of which requires a variety of special skills.

Nursing homes and extended-care centers provide care for the chronically ill and aged. An increasing population of citizens over 65, greater general affluence, and new welfare and insurance benefits have combined to create a rising demand for such facilities. Nursing homes provide services that range from skilled professional care to the purely custodial. In addition to doctors and nurses, they require the services of nurses' aides, food service workers, maintenance staff, clerical help, and rehabilitation and recreation employees.

Community health departments are the official health arm of a city or county. Vigilantly concerned with the health of the community as a whole, the community health office monitors pollution, provides inoculations, and strives to control communicable diseases. It also operates maternity and child welfare clinics and dispenses health information. Jobs are here for doctors, dentists, nurses, nutritionists, veterinarians, statisticians, and administrative personnel, depending on the size of the department.

Voluntary health agencies represent special areas of interest. Among the largest and best known of the thousands of these agencies dedicated to the task of focusing public attention on a special aspect of the medical field are the American Cancer Society, the National Tuberculosis and Respiratory Disease Association, and the American Heart Association. These agencies encourage professional education and research, and organize fund-raising drives to provide essential financial support in their special fields. They employ administrative specialists, public health educators, statisticians, public information experts, and often fund raisers. The larger associations also support staffs of medical specialists, public health nurses, and social workers.

Business and industry offer health services to employees. Many corporations maintain clinics or medical offices to organize health programs and to provide medical care. These centers employ doctors and nurses on a full-time or part-time basis, and, depending on the size and needs of the company, additional professionals such as dentists, psychiatrists, nutritionists, x-ray technicians, physical therapists, and occupational health workers.

Schools are concerned with preventive and protective health care for pupils. The main purpose of school health programs is to maintain a safe, healthful environment. The health office is responsible for making sure that immunization regulations are followed. It also administers sight and hearing tests and provides health education. The school nurse is the most familiar person in this picture; but doctors, dentists, dental hygienists, dietitians, psychologists, social workers, and mental health specialists are often involved. Many thousands of health professionals are also employed as instructors in colleges and universities to prepare students to work in the health professions.

Mental health centers care for and educate the community. Psychiatric clinics and public education programs are the main responsibilities of these facilities. In addition to psychiatrists, psychiatric nurses, social workers, and psychologists, they employ other specialists, such as occupational therapists and mental health workers.

Rehabilitation centers serve the disabled. The responsibility of the rehabilitation center is to help persons disabled by accident or illness to assume or resume roles as functioning, participating members of society. The broad spectrum of experts whose skills can help the handicapped to lead productive lives includes doctors, rehabilitation counselors, nurses, orthopedists, prosthetics experts, and physical therapists.

Research centers expand the horizons of health care. These specialized laboratories are located chiefly in university schools of medicine, dentistry, osteopathy, public health, pharmacy, nursing, and veterinary medicine and in drug companies. Medical research is funded by the government as well as public sectors including large foundations and voluntary health agencies, and private organizations. In recent years the annual cost of government-sponsored medical research has been close to $3 billion, of which approximately two-thirds has been provided by the Federal Government. The United States Public Health Service in Washington, D.C., supports its own laboratories and also provides grants for projects conducted elsewhere. Research centers employ highly trained scientific specialists, such as biochemists, bacteriologists, physicians, biologists, and physicists, as well as armies of laboratory technicians.

Doctors' offices are usually the first stop for medical care. A doctor's office may be a private one or part of a group practice or clinic. The services of the doctor or dentist, nurses, and other skilled professionals are backed up by laboratory technicians, clerical workers, secretaries, and receptionists. This category includes many of the major places where health jobs are located.

How This Guide Is Organized

The specific career fields in health care covered here are presented in the next five chapters, the last being a summary of the education and training demands and available financial aid programs for health care study.

Chaper 2 of this Guide to Health Careers covers health services and hospital administration careers. Health and public health administrators manage institutions, organizations, programs, and services within the health delivery system. Although only a few women are presently top administrators of hospitals, many women serve at the midmanagement level and more than a few are making their way to the top of the field. Women trained in hospital administration are necessary to every health program, large or small. Hospitals are not the only employers; administrators are needed in schools, government agencies, nursing homes, clinics, and other health care settings.

In Chapter 3 careers in medicine are presented, including medical doctors, osteopaths, and dentists, plus a discussion of podiatry and optometry careers. The primary emphasis is on the physician, usually the most highly trained and credentialed health care worker. The woman doctor's career options are numerous: she may engage in general practice or concentrate on a specialty. Whatever her choice, the medical profession offers rich rewards (not only monetary ones) to make up for the heavy demand on her time and energy.

Chapter 4 describes nursing careers, including nurses, nurse practitioners, and midwives. Specialization is a trend in nursing, but the best-known nursing career remains that of the hospital-based RN, or registered nurse, the person who has primary responsibility for the daily care of patients, usually under the supervision of staff physicians. Ample opportunities for nurses exist in all health care settings.

Therapists are discussed in Chapter 5, with attention given to physical, occupational, art, music, dance and recreation therapy. Although all these therapies use distinct types of treatment and highly specialized techniques and have different training requirements, they share the goal of helping those with health-related problems to overcome or deal with handicaps. The outlook for all types of therapists is favorable.

In Chapter 6 a variety of health occupations is presented—biostatistician, medical laboratory technologist, medical writer and copywriter, pharmacist, photographer, illustrator, health records administrator, inhalation specialist, etc. Each of these health-related occupations is very different from the others, but all offer growth and variety in addition to the challenge and reward of helping others.

The last chapter, Chapter 7, summarizes the educational requirements and routes to follow to become educated, credentialed, certified, registered, and licensed in health care careers. How to get admitted to medical school is given special attention.

CHAPTER 2

HEALTH PLANNING AND ADMINISTRATION

In 1752 Benjamin Franklin and Dr. Thomas Bond established the Pennsylvania Hospital in Philadelphia. Early hospitals such as this one were actually boardinghouses for the indigent and places where people went to die.

Institutionalized health care has come a long way since 1752. Hospitals and health facilities have developed and grown from a few boardinghouses to thousands of complex, multiservice institutions. In 1873, 200 hospitals were in operation in the United States. Today the 7,000 hospitals and thousands of health-related facilities constitute a huge multibillion-dollar industry.

A critical issue facing the health industry is coordinating this vast and growing number of resources into an efficient system that will provide the best possible care for the greatest number of people. The evolution of the health industry and changing attitudes about how health care is and should be delivered have made good management essential to the economic survival and operating efficiency of the modern health care system. This in turn has led to an increasing reliance on the managerial and policy-making skills of the health planner and administrator.

In 1934 the first graduate program in hospital administration was introduced at the University of Chicago. Today more than three dozen graduate school programs in the United States teach planning and administration. Such programs are also in South America, Europe, Australia, and Africa.

Health planners and administrators are responsible for formulating and implementing the policies and plans that run our modern health care system. The primary distinction between planners and administrators is one of emphasis. Planners are generally involved in policy design; administrators are generally concerned with policy implementation. For instance, a health planner might decide where to locate a community drug abuse treatment clinic and arrange the types of services it will provide. An administrator might be the director of the center and be responsible for ensuring that the clinic and health team work effectively in the best interest of the community.

There is considerable overlap between the functions of planners and administrators. A planner must always keep in mind the managerial implications and possible consequences of her decisions; a plan is worthless if it can't be implemented by management. A good administrator should also be a partner in the formulation of long-range planning efforts to ensure the continuing efficient operation of any facility.

Although both planner and administrator can be involved in policy making, an administrator's policy making is generally limited to her own health facility or institution. The complexity and scope of her policies are therefore largely determined by the nature and size of the health unit. A health planner, however, can be involved in policy planning that may affect an entire district, community, or nation, and her decisions may be more complex and far-reaching.

Planning, Administration, and Women

Generally speaking, health planning and administration have been men's fields. Women who have ranked in hospital administration have traditionally been nuns, nurses, and the occasional woman doctor. In the broader field of health care planning and administration there have been such figures as Eliza Chapell Porter, director of the Chicago Sanitary Commission during the Civil War. Mrs. Porter collected and disbursed food, medical dressings, and other supplies for use at military hospitals; she recruited nurses and established a special diet kitchen for convalescents.

In 1907 Jane Addams of Hull House in Chicago addressed the American Hospital Association on "The Layman's View of Hospital Work Among the Poor." Ms. Addams called herself a layman, but her vision and dedication were of a very high order. As volunteer work gains the recognition and legitimacy it deserves, more women will be remembered for their organizational and administrative capabilities.

Today women in administrative positions are usually employed as assistant administrators, but the picture is gradually improving. In New York, for instance, several nonmedical women are already serving as deputy hospital directors in state hospitals. The question is no longer whether women will rise in health planning and administration, but *when*.

Where the Jobs Are—Administration

The largest consumer of management services is the *hospital*, and more health care administrators are employed in hospitals than in any other setting. With services to patients becoming ever more varied and complex, the hospital provides employment for many kinds of administrators.

The chief hospital administrator is responsible for everything and everyone at the hospital. She is concerned, not only with patient care, but with all facets of the hospital's operation. The administrator directs and coordinates all the activities and departments within the hospital, from dietary and housekeeping services to communications. In a small facility she personally supervises the activities of each department; in a larger facility her staff of administrative assistants keep her informed about daily operations. Depending on the size of the institution, a chief administrator may be responsible for more than 30 departments.

The administrator may supervise additional special services such as a community blood bank, a poison control or suicide prevention center, and services for the handicapped, besides supervising and facilitating the services of the medical staff.

In a small hospital even the public relations and financial aspects of a hospital's operation may be her responsibility, and she and her assistants prepare budgets, hire and train personnel, and purchase supplies and equipment. In a large institution the chief administrator supervises specialists heading the various departments within central administration, such as budget and finance, personnel, or accounting. Medical record libraries, pharmacies, and in some cases a research department also need supervision.

Obviously, an administrator must be able to make decisions concerning every facet of hospital service; moreover, she must sometimes make decisions that are controversial. One woman with 10 years' experience described the unique nature of decision making in a health care setting: "People who work in the health field value decisions arrived at democratically. Problems arise, however, when people don't understand what the term democratic means. It doesn't mean that everyone has equal responsibility in decision making.

"Your input comes from your knowledge base, which has to be evaluated by the person ultimately in charge, such as the director of the institution. There has to be someone who makes a final decision based on everybody's contribution. If this process is clearly understood, people can feel they are legitimately part of the decision making, and not that there is only an illusion of democracy."

Many types of facilities offer health care, and administrators can be found in a large variety of settings.

FACTS AND FIGURES

- About 160,000 persons worked as health services administrators in 1976.
- Most worked in health facilities, including hospitals (which employed about half), nursing and other personal care homes, and in health management firms that provide administrative services to health facilities at a specified contract price.
- Some worked for government agencies, including state and local health departments, the United States Public Health Service, in Veterans Administration and Armed Forces hospitals and clinics, and voluntary health agencies that conduct research and provide care and treatment for victims of particular diseases or physical impairments.
- In 1976 the chief administrators in hospitals with up to 199 beds averaged $25,500; some, in larger hospitals, earned over $45,000.
- Most administrators in voluntary health agencies earned between $15,000 and $30,000 in 1976.
- In 1977 the average salary paid administrators of federal hospitals was $26,700. Recent recipients of master's degrees in health administration starting work in VA hospitals earned $14,097.

The United States Public Health Service and some state and local *community health departments* sponsor hospitals and clinics; environmental health agencies, which generate research and statistics on air quality and water pollution; centers for health information and education, including counseling services; and health-related community action programs.

Linda Breslin is one of eight chiefs of service at a state mental hospital complex. She's in charge of an inpatient unit offering a full range of professional services, an outpatient unit that includes a day hospital and individual and group therapy, a staff of eight at an adult home, and a community education program. Ms. Breslin has a master's degree in social work and was an experienced therapist when she began her administrative career as a social work supervisor. According to a colleague, she is "fast, bright, focused, and tough."

It's not unusual for a top administrator in a specialized health care setting such as a mental hospital to be a trained clinician who learned administration on the job. Ms. Breslin does not deal with the financial end of running the hospital. If she should ever wish to leave clinical work altogether and go into straight staff administration, she anticipates getting additional training in business administration, including fund raising and finance.

Voluntary health agencies and *social service organizations* consist of more than candystripers and telethons. The Red Cross, renowned for its overseas services, runs a domestic blood program. The Cerebral Palsy and Muscular Dystrophy Associations provide day camps and a host of other services. Other groups operate adoption centers, halfway houses, and such shelters as the Hearts Ease Home for Girls. Volunteer agencies identify and study special problems; they provide financial support for research and professional education.

Arleen Bregman works in volunteer services. With a bachelor's degree in foreign languages and no definite career plans, Ms. Bregman was hired as program coordinator for a suburban office of the Muscular Dystrophy Association. Her outgoing nature and assertiveness made her a valuable employee. She says that many such entry-level opportunities are readily available in the voluntary sector.

Ms. Bregman served as a jill-of-all-trades in her job as program coordinator, as do many workers in small offices. She organized fundraising programs and public health education seminars, kept account books, wrote public service announcements and press releases, and produced a half-hour local radio show on health care topics. Captivated by her work, she returned to school for a master's degree in public health education, which led to her transfer to an urban office of the association at twice her former salary.

Other career opportunities in the private sector are in *long-term care facilities*, including nursing homes, which will be hiring many more health care workers in the coming years. As with volunteer health agencies and service organizations, you can become a volunteer at any age and explore an area before committing yourself to it.

Service provided to protect and maintain the health of workers in business and industry is called *occupational health*. Many businesses and corporations contract group health plans that offer a wide range of clinical services; some companies run their own clinics. The world's largest department store, Macy's, has its own team of physicians and health workers who have to be hired, assigned, paid, and kept supplied with technical goods and services.

Group practices have to be managed, as do *home health services*. Jobs in *rehabilitation* are of all kinds—in drug abuse clinics and in physical-therapy institutes, in managing programs for the mentally handicapped, and in research.

A health care administrator in an academic setting may seek funds and develop a brand-new program, such as the one Dr. Mary Ann Ells, former dean of the College of Nursing at the University of Maine, set up. (Dr. Ells, RN, MS, PhD, was the first woman dean of a college in the University of Maine system.) Dr. Ells was instrumental in establishing a pediatric nurse practitioner training program. Her objectives were to build a program for specialized training, place certified practitioners in jobs in rural parts of the state, as well as help physicians and traditionally trained nurses to understand and deal with nurses in an independent role. Dr. Ells also worked to amend the state Nursing Practice Act to include nurse practitioners; the state legislature approved the amendment in 1974.

Dr. Ells is one of a small number of registered nurses with extensive graduate school education in public health and administration. Many employment opportunities are open for women with her combination of clinical and academic experience. There are many routes to follow, however, in seeking a career in health administration.

Skills and Qualifications

A wide range of skills is required to be a good administrator. Personal traits vary, but every administrator should have a profound understanding of human relations and ability. Diplomacy, tact, and good communications skills are essential since the administrator must deal, not only with patients, but with boards of directors, hospital trustees, community representatives, union representatives, doctors, staff workers, families of patients, and perhaps the media.

A thorough grounding in personnel policies and, in some cases, skill in collective bargaining are also very important. An administrator must have the ability to accept and evaluate information from many sources.

As one deputy administrator says, to understand good administrative work, "you have to know how to maneuver." Patience and farsightedness are other qualities she says are necessary for a career in health administration: "You have to be able to tolerate the frustrations that come from outside the institution—from funding sources, from people over whom you have very little control. The best defense against the difficulties of day-to-day work is having an overall vision. If, for instance, you're really committed to providing preventive health care for the neighborhood your clinic serves, then you can cope with the setbacks and resistance you meet in setting up parent education and parent effectiveness training programs. And if you're 'willful,' you'll win."

Human relations are only one area of an administrator's job. Skill in financial management, including budgeting, economics, and data processing, is also necessary.

Health Planning

Planners often work in the same places as administrators—in the planning or research division of a hospital, in a community health center or other health facility, for voluntary agencies or private research organizations, and in government agencies responsible for planning the nation's health care delivery.

Planners must have a generalist's perspective as well as the analytical skill to assess a problem correctly and to develop a workable solution. Increasingly, planners are being required to master the tools and techniques of quantitative analysis that will enable them to anticipate more accurately the possible outcomes and practical consequences of a decision and to prepare policies accordingly. Positions in planning also require good research skills. A modern health planner may be involved in projects such as drafting a plan for national health insurance, formulating plans for controlling environmental pollution, deciding where to locate a community health facility and arranging which services it will provide, or encouraging and motivating physicians to work in rural areas where there is a doctor shortage.

Some planners combine academic work with consulting for government or private agencies.

Getting There—Training

Varied programs in health planning and administration are currently found in schools of public health, business and management, medical schools and in programs on public policy or policy science.

A bachelor's degree in administration may get you an entry-level or midmanagement position. However, federal and professional-association job guidelines are increasingly calling for a graduate degree as a requisite for midmanagement positions. A master's degree is necessary for advancement into top-level management positions; a PhD is necessary for teaching and research positions.

Participation in a formal educational program develops the wide range of skills needed by a good planner or administrator. Courses in natural science, psychology, sociology, statistics, accounting, and economics are desirable. The curricula of the various programs reflect the emphasis of each particular school or department. For instance, business school programs emphasize management skills, while a public policy program stresses analytical and quantitative skills. Since there is no standard first-year curriculum for the different programs, you can choose one that emphasizes your particular area of interest. It really is necessary to "shop around" and read program catalogues carefully. You should also ask what kinds of jobs were obtained by previous graduates; the answers will help clue you in to the particular emphasis of a program.

Master's degree programs generally last two years. The academic portion of the program combines work in both managerial and quantitative techniques. Courses may include organizational structure, sociopolitical processes, statistics, analytical methods, and economic theory. Specific health-related courses will acquaint the student with the huge mosaic of institutions, agencies, and programs that make up the modern health care system. A thesis or special project is often required and you may have to pass a comprehensive examination.

Many programs include a period of supervised administrative residency in a hospital or other health facility. During this residency, which may last only a summer or an entire year, the student gains insight into the operation and organization of a health facility. She works closely with department heads, attends staff and board meetings, and in the process acquires a good understanding of the complexities of internal management. During her residency a student may also make important contacts that will help her in obtaining a future position. As one graduate program dean says, "People have connections, and if your work is good, their connections will open doors for you." Most graduate programs will also assist you with job counseling and placement.

Persons entering the field of health planning and administration usually begin at midmanagement level as assistants or perhaps in a small institution as directors of particular departments. As their skills and talents are refined and demonstrated and as they gain more experience, upper-level management positions will be open to them.

No certification, registration, or licensure is usually required, although the American Psychological Association will certify mental health administrators.

BASIC RESOURCES

For more information on careers in health planning and administration, and for a list of accredited educational programs, write:

American Academy of Health Administration
P.O. Box 5518
Texarcana, Texas 75503

American College of Hospital Administration
840 North Lake Shore Drive
Chicago, Illinois 60611

American Health Planning Association
2560 Huntington Avenue (Suite 305)
Alexandria, Virginia 22303

Association of University Programs in Health Administration
1 Dupont Circle NW (Suite 420)
Washington, DC 20036

GETTING IN, MOVING UP: HEALTH PLANNING AND ADMINISTRATION

College graduates generally start in entry-level or midmanagement positions whether in hospitals or community action programs. Many employment opportunities are available, especially for women with both clinical and academic experience. However, most of the top administrative positions in hospitals are still held by men.

Maxine Jobe, Hospital Policy Planner

Two years out of school, Maxine Jobe is director of policy analysis at a medical center connected with a hospital, medical school, and university. Her work includes analysis of legislation and programs, policy writing, statement writing, and interacting with department heads and physicians.

"When I was in college and looking around for a career, although I was attracted to business-type operations, the for-profit sector was not that appealing to me. I guess I was very much a child of the 60s; I was wary of working for some huge business conglomerate. Health care seemed different; sure it is a business, but it is also a little more 'humane.' So I earned an undergraduate degree in history, then went to a graduate school for a master's degree in business administration with a specialization in health care management."

Prerequisites for her graduate degree included courses in accounting, economics, statistics, calculus, and introduction to business management. Ms. Jobe picked up in summer school the math she lacked so she could concentrate on business management of health care at the beginning of the program. "I chose the MBA because it is a marketable degree leading to a wide range of job possibilities. I think the business degree puts you one step ahead.

"Someone said he thought what is needed for this job is intellectual organization and the ability to penetrate confusion and come up with clarity. I strive for that, and I believe my background in history and having written so many papers have been a great help."

Business school provided more than a degree. Ms. Jobe made contacts there that led to her first job. "My position was line administrator in a hospital ward. To advance, you go from department head to assistant administrator to associate administrator, and eventually administrator of the hospital, although it is very rare for a woman to achieve that. However, I discovered that the line job just didn't interest me."

When she decided to make a change, those same business school contacts helped her get her present position. "This is a staff job, which means I am not involved in the day-to-day operation of the hospital, although what I do serves the hospital and various divisions within it. My day has a lot of variety, which makes it a good job for me."

Ms. Jobe doesn't do a lot of paperwork in the traditional sense, but has stacks of mail to read through every morning. "I go through the *Federal Register* and scan all the trade publications and all the general informational handouts a hospital gets. What I'm looking for is anything that might pertain to us.

"As federal or state regulations come out, I do an analysis to see how they will affect the medical center and what it will take to comply with them. I also analyze operational policies: how we're staffing the operating room, what our admission policies are, and so on.

"I'm almost always working at some kind of project that calls for writing skills. I write a lot of policy statements, which means meeting with the people involved, helping them clarify and enunciate their objectives, and developing with them a policy statement. Sometimes I work with an individual, sometimes with a committee. Right now we're trying to put together an in-house physician's newsletter, and I'm writing an article on the medical staff appointment system for it.

"Today I'll also meet with a department chairman who is presenting a study to the board of trustees on suicides within the psychiatric unit and the presence or absence of attending physicians at the time of the suicides. I'll help him put together his background material and develop a format for his presentation.

"I spend a considerable amount of time meeting with people. Three hours yesterday were spent discussing a special inspection and survey that takes place in three months. Today I'm meeting key people to discuss how we can better organize the staff within the medical center.

"I'll also spend time today working on charges for the various medical committees, coming up with goal proposals and preparing for a meeting next week with each of the chairmen. I'll prepare a memorandum for the medical staff on changes in the state health code on reimbursement for hospital stays and how we'll have to start selecting and questioning these stays. And tomorrow I have a meeting with the chairman of the medical board about reorganizing the board.

"At a working lunch today I and other staff are meeting with the policy analysis unit from another institution to exchange ideas.

"If it's necessary, I prefer to stay late rather than take work home. This is such an active environment to work in, with lights on all night long, that I never feel beleaguered if I'm here past dinnertime. My husband doesn't mind either because he's also career oriented and a hard worker, so my job is very compatible with my private life. Usually we get the month of August together in Maine, but that doesn't always work out.

Free time is not always under your control. For instance, we moved this summer and I anticipated having lots of time to fix up our new place. Summers are generally very quiet, because many physicians go away in August, but a big batch of new regulations came out at the end of July and I was here deciphering them until 10 o'clock every night in August."

Ms. Jobe feels confident about her qualifications as an administrator: "If the administrator can give physicians something they can't get themselves, then she has something marketable. And that's why I think a business background is so important. Physicians hate to get bogged down by paperwork and budgeting—after all, it really takes time away from their work as *doctors*. I can offer help with those and other administrative and business practices, and leave them with more time for practicing *medicine*."

At present she is a bit skeptical about going all the way to the top. "A university medical center like this is a big system, and there's a lot to learn. If my work is good and if it catches the attention of the right people, I could conceivably reach positions where I have more and more responsibility.

"But only three or four women have ever made it to the number-one position in a hospital hierarchy in the United States. Most of the ones who go fairly far usually have a male mentor clearing the way. My plans are to live in the present—we don't expect to have children any time soon—and then make a new-phase career plan when I've really mastered this position. In other words, I'm not letting my ambition get ahead of my expertise!"

CHAPTER 3

DOCTORS

Medical doctors, osteopaths, dentists, optometrists, and podiatrists are all graduates of doctoral programs. Of the various occupations, MDs and osteopaths (DOs) are seen most frequently as primary care physicians with MDs claiming the practice of the mainstream of contemporary health care.

The rewards of the profession include prestige and personal satisfaction as well as financial remuneration. According to recent public opinion polls, the most respected members of American society are medical doctors. And according to statistical surveys, doctors earn the highest average per capita income of all workers. Although between 1950 and 1976 the number of practicing physicians increased by 70 percent, there is a perennial and serious doctor shortage in many areas of the country.

Getting into medical school is a tough proposition for both men and women. Doctors go through an education and training period that is costly, long, and rigorous. Dedication is a basic requirement. Those who succeed have an aptitude for self-discipline and delayed gratification. Once in practice, many doctors work very long days and nights, frequently on call. Another drawback: Among all professionals, doctors incur the highest rates of alcoholism and suicide.

Although almost 90 percent of all doctors are male, the proportion of women applicants accepted by medical schools is rising sharply, and gains are visible in terms of total enrollment. In 1977 women made up 25 percent of the first-year class in medical school—the largest number of women seeking careers in medicine since the turn of the century. This was a big shift for the United States, which has a smaller percentage of female doctors than any country in the world except Spain, South Vietnam, and Madagascar.

The struggle has been a long one. Women were the first healers and midwives, and healing was an art passed on from mother to daughter.

129

However, the advent of institutionalized medicine made women's participation in the medical profession difficult, if not impossible.

In 1847 Elizabeth Blackwell was admitted to Geneva Medical College after having been rejected by at least 15 medical schools. In 1849, when she graduated at the head of her class and became the first woman in the United States to receive a medical degree, Dr. Blackwell initiated a struggle against masculine skepticism and establishment opposition that continues even now.

Mary Edwards Walker, the first known accredited female physician and surgeon in the United States, graduated from Syracuse Medical College in 1855. She served in the Union Army and spent four months in a Confederate prison until she was exchanged "man for man" with a Southern major. Dr. Walker was awarded the medal of honor. Later, dressed in top hat, trousers, and tails, she lectured on feminist topics.

The courage and unconventionalism of both Elizabeth Blackwell and Mary Walker were a *faca noma,* however. Very few 19th-century American women gained admission to the halls of science and formal study of the healing arts. It was deemed improper and a violation of decency for women to study the human body in close association with men.

The doors of most hospitals and medical schools were closed also to blacks, Jews, and other minorities, especially in Boston, the heart of the medical establishment. But adversity seemed to make women strong in Boston, and female doctors who went elsewhere to earn their diplomas returned to find support there for building their own hospitals and faculties of medicine. These institutions provided medical training to many women in the late 19th and early 20th centuries.

When women were finally admitted to previously all-male schools, the female-only schools and hospitals were gradually closed or absorbed by other institutions. During both World Wars more women were admitted to medical schools when male enrollment fell. Their participation, however, was viewed as a necessity not a right; once their tuition dollars were no longer needed, they were again excluded. The present reversal of that policy is to a great extent a consequence of Title IX of the 1964 Civil Rights Act and the women's movement in general.

In the 1930s and 40s the image of "lady doctors" was tweedy, sensibly shod, and asexual. Women doctors were concentrated in typically "female" fields such as pediatrics and gynecology. In the 1950s women doctors were required to be superwomen. Women practicing today who became doctors then tell the story:

"I worked after school, studied every night and all weekend, and adopted a four-hour-a-night sleep schedule that has been my habit ever since."

"I married a doctor; my first child was born Christmas day. I'd been working in a small hospital and was back at work in a week."

"I worked right up to my daughter's birth. I was giving a transfusion just two hours before she was born—I'd been in labor 18 hours by then."

FACTS AND FIGURES: MDs

- About 360,000 physicians were professionally active in the United States in 1976.
- Of the 9 out of 10 who provided patient care services, nearly 215,000 had office practices; more than 94,000 others worked as residents or full-time staff in hospitals. The remainder taught or performed administrative or research duties.
- In 1976 about 15 percent of the physicians who provided patient care were general practitioners; most specialized in one of the 34 fields for which there is graduate training.
- The largest specialties are internal medicine, general surgery, obstetrics and gynecology, psychiatry, pediatrics, radiology, anesthesiology, ophthalmology, pathology, and orthopedic surgery. Family practice, which emphasizes general medicine, is the most rapidly growing specialty.
- Northeastern states have the highest ratio of physicians to population, Southern states the lowest. Many remote and rural areas are without MDs.
- Salaries of medical school graduates serving as residents in hospitals vary, but earnings of $12,000 to $13,000 are common; many hospitals also provide full or partial room, board, and other maintenance allowances.
- During the first year or two of independent practice, some physicians may earn little more than the minimum needed to pay expenses; but earnings rise rapidly as their practice develops.
- The net income of physicians who provided patient care averaged almost $54,000 in 1976. Self-employed physicians usually earn more than those in salaried positions; specialists usually earn considerably more than primary care practitioners.
- In 1977 graduates who had completed an approved three-year residency but had no other work experience could expect to start working at a VA hospital for about $27,000 to $31,500. Full-time workers could expect another $5,500 to $5,800 in other cash benefits or "special" payments.

"My husband and I established practice together. We worked about a 10-hour day, then spent time with the children and gardening. I enjoyed canning, and I made most of our clothes, too."

One of these superwomen suggests that they were like "immigrants in a strange land, trying to get perfect marks so as not to be sent back to the old country."

Today the rising number of women in medicine provides an opportunity to create a new image. Women live, study, and work in an increasingly supportive atmosphere. Shared-schedule residencies are available, child care co-ops are rare but may be formed, and some mates are more open to sharing household responsibilities. Women find it easier to share and face problems instead of denying them; they are increasingly supporting each other—in groups and individually. But medical school and postdoctoral training are still, for both women and men, rigorous tests complete with their own occupational hazards.

For instance, studying pathology and observing the course of real-life disease can bring on the student symptom syndrome. Medical students, interns, and residents are subject to imagining they exhibit the symptoms of the diseases they are studying. One student of neurology developed a "focal seizure," a thumb twitch in her left hand. She spoke to a resident in brain surgery who said, "It looks like a tumor in the right lobe. We may have to operate." She went for a second opinion to the chief of service, who said, "You're drinking too much coffee." When she rotated into pediatrics, the twitch went away.

Institutionalized Sexism

Women in medical training may face what may amount to an identity crisis. Medical students in general have traditionally been viewed by staff and faculty members as inferior and inept. The men's-club atmosphere of training institutions has helped to sanction disregard for women. Dialogue in many surgeries is characteristically crude, and jokes are often made at the expense of women. The *Playboy*-style "nudie" slides of female anatomy that have illustrated medical school lectures over the years add to the situation. In this environment the student may be expected to be tolerant or even appreciative of the "wit."

Sexism can take many forms. Not all women are ideological feminists, yet some older male faculty members often insist on labeling them all as "women's libbers" while at the same time denying that the term is pejorative. Some use a more subtle approach such as addressing a woman as "Ms." instead of "Doctor." In some cases women have been totally ignored in class and on rounds; often no lockers or adequate changing facilities are provided for them.

Women respond to institutionalized sexism in different ways. Some cope by denying that it exists; they think that women who "react" are immature or are asking for special favors. Women who know their minds and speak them are sometimes called overly sensitive or hysterical. They can expect one day to see a professor throw up his hands and wearily repeat Freud's question, "What does woman want?"

Although the picture has been bleak, it is improving and will continue to do so. The women's movement has done much to call public and government attention to the problems of women students. Federal regulations have also had a decided impact. Medical schools are heavily dependent on federal funding—Affirmative Action requirements plus the threatened loss of funds have done much to "enlighten" many administrators. The medical profession itself is developing a "healthier" and fairer attitude, and women are gaining increasing acceptance and encouragement in every area of the profession. Even patients' attitudes are changing. Some patients may still insist on having a male doctor, but many others are equally determined to be treated by a woman. For the most part, women in medical institutions support each other; their rising numbers will go a long way toward reversing the traditional hostility to women in medical practice.

Also, *all* women in *all* schools do not suffer the same degree of discrimination. Even women who have been unsettled by anti-women attitudes can name male colleagues and professors who are sensitive and considerate. More and more men and women are finding it easier to deal with each other as doctors and colleagues—and friends.

Although sexual discrimination has not yet disappeared from the medical profession, there is every hope that it eventually will. Women students, however, should be prepared to encounter some forms of sexism in the still male-dominated medical institutions; preparing yourself will make it that much easier to cope. Talk to male and female students in the schools you are considering and get their advice. It helps to know what to expect. A strong sense of self and a positive attitude about your abilities and rights will help you and your fellow students.

If present enrollment trends continue into the 80s, the woman doctor will be the rule, not the exception. As long as women continue to support each other and make their voices heard, they have everything to gain and nothing to lose.

The Rigors of a Medical Education

Medical education is undergoing widespread reevaluation, and the general structure of programs as well as specific course work varies from institution to institution. However, one unvarying fact remains—a doc-

---

"ATTENTION, STUDENTS . . ."

A doctor's education is in most cases long and costly. Many people have to seek grants and loans from the Federal Government, private foundations, or medical associations. (For more financial aid information, see Chapter 7.) In any case, a doctor's projected earnings generally cover loan repayments.

Before considering medical school in a foreign country, investigate all the hazards involved. Americans rejected by United States medical schools are strongly discouraged from studying medicine abroad. It is important to find out what special examinations are required to practice in the United States after graduation from a foreign medical school. A personal interview with someone who has studied medicine abroad can be valuable.

---

tor is expected to learn hundreds of thousands of facts during the course of her career. A medical student gets a good head start on this "quota" during her first two years of medical school when courses require a great deal of memorization. Traditionally a first-year student takes such basic science courses as anatomy, biochemistry, physiology, and perhaps some behavioral sciences. Courses commonly offered during the second year include pathology, pharmacology, microbiology, physical diagnosis, and lab procedures as well as introductions to certain specialty fields.

The last two years of school are spent in clinical study, during which students rotate through clerkships in specialties—pediatrics, internal medicine, surgery, obstetrics–gynecology, psychiatry, etc.—and get direct clinical experience and contact with patients in hospitals and outpatient wards. It is then that a student may discover she doesn't like psychiatry, for instance, but is very interested in internal medicine, perhaps particularly gastroenterology. (Almost all MDs and a smaller percentage of DOs go on to specialize after medical school.)

A relatively new and major trend in medical education is to integrate lecture and lab learning with clinical experience at a much earlier point than in the traditional sequence. Many students now get some patient contact before the last two years of school.

State board licensing examinations are generally taken during the senior year of medical school; the National Board of Medical Examiners also gives an examination which is taken in medical school and is accepted by most states. Physicians licensed in one state can obtain a license to practice in many other states without further examination; however, reciprocity is not universal, and another examination may be necessary.

Medical students must take Parts 1 and 2 of the exam given by the National Board of Medical Examiners while still in medical school. Part 3 is taken after the MD degree has been granted and a doctor has completed six months of residency in an approved hospital. Certification (after examination and completion of residency) in a particular specialty is also granted by 20 examining and certifying boards approved by the American Board of Medical Specialties. Depending on the specialty and where it is practiced, continuing education credits may be required to maintain and update licensing qualifications.

Graduate training in hospitals was traditionally offered in two steps. One year consisted of general or rotating internships including work in different specialties or a straight internship in one specialty. The next step was a residency that provided advanced experience in a chosen area of specialization. As doctors began to specialize earlier in their careers, the rotating internship was phased out and straight internships in a chosen specialty became the preferred route.

Recent changes in postdoctoral education, however, have meant that,

GETTING IN, MOVING UP: DOCTOR OF MEDICINE

After graduation from medical school with a Medical Doctor (MD) degree, the doctor receives her graduate training as a resident on the staff of a hospital. Residencies generally take three to five years; some specialties may take as long as seven or eight. A resident is eligible, after licensing, to practice at the end of her first year of residency.

Career opportunities range from positions at Veterans Administration hospitals to group practice, from psychiatry to family practice of general medicine. Physician shortages exist in many parts of the country.

---

as of 1975, MD graduates begin residencies immediately after completing medical school, bypassing the internship altogether. In other words, the internship has now become the first year of residency. (DOs are still required to complete a one-year internship. Additional training is needed to specialize.)

Residents form the house staff of a hospital. They are supervised by a chief resident who in turn is supervised by the faculty member in charge of that specialty. More than 20 possible specialization areas are open for a resident.

During the residency, a young doctor *quickly* learns what *being* a doctor means. As one woman put it, "So many horrendous things are happening that you have to grow up and cope in a hurry. You're only in your mid-20s and you've only seen a few patients at this point in your career, and here you are thrust into the pit."

Life in a hospital can be hectic and exhausting. Another woman doctor recalled her days as an intern in the emergency room (ER): "For one month I worked 24 on/24 off, seven days a week in ER. Maybe around 3:00 or 4:00 AM I'd find a cot (never clean—there was a joke that you were going to get a lint infection if you lay down) and get 20 or 30 minutes of sleep. Cases ranged from light to heavyweight, with some people using the ER like a doctor's office for ordinary complaints. You'd take care of acute business on the spot—sewing, patching, slinging. Serious emergencies ranged from acute pulmonary edema, stroke, heart attack, shock, GI [gastrointestinal] bleeding, asthma attacks to drug overdose. When you got off a shift, you were either tired enough to sleep standing up or too tired to sleep at all."

The residency training period varies in length, but is generally three to five years, with some specialties and subspecialties taking as long as seven or eight. A resident becomes eligible to practice medicine after her first year of residency.

SHARING A RESIDENCY: ONE WAY TO COPE

A handicap for women seeking postgraduate medical training has been the need to cope with the heavy demands of a residency program and at the same time keep a home intact. Women with small children have been especially pressed—help is hard to find, and for some there is the guilt of being an absent mother. Shared-schedule residency training positions in which two people share one job, with each receiving half the salary plus appropriate credit toward specialty certification, is one innovative solution.

A number of hospitals have agreed to this kind of arrangement, and more will follow suit as the Federal Government now requires that all institutions receiving federal assistance make available "a reasonable number" of such positions in internal medicine, family practice, obstetrics—gynecology, and pediatrics; similar programs are also open to doctors of osteopathy.

Most women have elected to do half-time residencies for only a year or two, but a woman (or a man) could conceivably take six years to complete a standard three-year stint. Federal legislation does not stipulate the sex of the physician or call for an accounting of the time not spent in the program. Directors of residency training programs generally expect that the shared residency will be used for the purpose for which it was designed: to allow residents with family responsibilities to spend more time with their families.

Doctors who are parents can seek flexible residencies, which take a little longer to complete. For instance, a part-time residency program was introduced in 1962 at the New York Medical College with the needs of physician mothers specifically in mind. The program takes nine months a year and four years instead of three to complete.

An individual may have to design such a program for herself and find a program director willing to cooperate; but the general approach is legal and is approved by the Liaison Committee on Graduate Medical Education. And more and more institutions are developing such programs.

Doctors are salaried during the period of residency, according to a sliding scale based on the year of training. "By the time students reach residency training," one doctor says, "they've climbed far enough up the ladder to earn a little respect, a little time off, and a semblance of human life."

Training to Become an Osteopath

A minimum of three years of college is required for admission to an accredited osteopathic hospital; a baccalaureate degree is preferred. You

DOs VS. MDs

A doctor's primary concern is the treatment and prevention of human illness, disease, or injury. To this end, she may be engaged in general practice, specialized treatment, teaching, or research. The two types of physicians are the MD (Doctor of Medicine) and the DO (Doctor of Osteopathy). Both MDs and DOs acquire almost identical training and use scientifically accepted methods of medical diagnosis and treatment. The difference is basically one of philosophy; DOs pay special attention to the effects of the musculoskeletal system on the entire body, and place added emphasis on the relationship between body structure and organic functioning. DOs may also use structural diagnosis and manipulative therapy along with other traditional forms of diagnosis and treatment. A larger number of DOs than MDs presently go into primary care. DOs practice and preach holistic medical care, and they maintain the right to be different.

The 14 osteopathic colleges graduate about 1,000 new DOs each year. This number is soon expected to reach 1,400. The 124 medical schools in this country graduate approximately 16,000 MDs annually.

must have taken at least one year each of English, biology or zoology, inorganic and organic chemistry, and physics. Applicants for admission usually take the New Medical College Admission Test (New MCAT).

Four years at an osteopathic college leads to the degree of Doctor of Osteopathy (DO). Graduates generally do a one-year internship after graduation. Certification in various specialties may require additional

FACTS AND FIGURES: DOs

- About 15,000 osteopathic physicians practiced in the United States in 1976.
- Almost 85 percent were in private practice; a small number had full-time salaried positions in osteopathic hospitals and colleges, private industry, or government agencies.
- Most osteopaths are "family doctors" who engage in general practice; in 1976 about 25 percent were practicing in specialties.
- More than half of all osteopathic general practitioners are located in towns and cities of fewer than 50,000 people; specialists practice mainly in large cities.
- Incomes usually rise markedly after the first few years of practice; in 1974 the average income of osteopathic general practitioners was $31,000.

GETTING IN, MOVING UP: OSTEOPATHY

Osteopathic graduates generally complete a one-year internship. Most osteopaths are in private general practice. Those who specialize usually practice in large cities.

postgraduate training. All states require successful completion of licensing examinations.

Specializing

In the past the popular specialties for women have been pediatrics, psychiatry, internal medicine, family practice, anesthesiology, pathology, obstetrics and gynecology, and radiology.

Psychiatrists are particularly in demand. In 1970 it was estimated that 19 million Americans suffered from mental illness and of these 2 million were seriously ill. As the population has grown, so have the figures. Now, despite about 28,000 psychiatrists, a shortage of 10,000 psychiatrists is anticipated by 1980.

According to a young psychiatrist at a state hospital, "The world is headed toward such complication that if you don't know how to deal with it, you're going to sink. Values are shaken, styles are worn out, and people are lost and terrified. At the interpersonal level, conflict identification and resolution—the guts and blood of many relationships, including work—must be learned.

"Psychiatrists also have to help establish preventive medicine. They should be committed to helping people find ways to feel good about themselves. Self-esteem leads people to take care."

Other needs in medical care are for inner-city practitioners in large urban areas and for physicians from racial minorities. Dr. June Christmas, a black who is Commissioner of the Department of Mental Health, Mental Retardation, and Alcoholism for New York City, addresses both problems:

"In New York City, with a large concentration of physicians, there was a ratio of 237 physicians to 100,000 inhabitants in 1970. In nonwhite areas, the ratio was as low as 33 per 100,000.

"For many inner cities the only alternative to the overcrowded, impersonal public hospital ER may be the 'Medicaid mill' with its frequent practice of unnecessary x-rays, laboratory tests, and examinations, as well as its financial abuses."

AREAS OF SPECIALIZATION FOR MDs

The following are the *areas of specialization* recognized for Board Certification. After a licensed physician has completed a hospital residency program of a specified number of years, he or she is eligible to sit for the Board exams in his or her specialty. (The length of residency training is given in parentheses after the description.)

Anesthesiology—Administration of drugs or gases that cause complete loss of sensation. (2)

Colon and Rectal Surgery—Surgery which specializes in the disorders or diseases of the lower digestive tract, the colon, and the rectum. [Also called proctology.] (5)

Dermatology—Science of the skin and its diseases. (3)

Family Practice—Specialization in general or family practice. (3)

Internal Medicine—Specialization in diseases or injuries to the body that do not require surgery. (3)

Neurosurgery—Diagnosis and surgical treatment of brain, spinal cord, and nerve disorders. (4)

Nuclear Medicine—Treatment of diseases, especially cancer, with the use of radioisotopic substances.

Obstetrics and Gynecology—Deals with pregnancy, childbirth, and diseases of the female body, particularly of the genital, urinary, and rectal organs. (3)

Orthopedic Surgery—Surgical prevention and correction of deformities. (4)

Otolaryngology—The science dealing with the diseases of the ear, nose, and throat. (4)

Pathology—The specialty that deals with diagnosing abnormalities in tissue removed at operations and postmortem examinations. (4)

Pediatrics—Specialization in children's diseases. (2)

Physical Medicine and Rehabilitation—Science of restoring use of muscles that have been impaired owing to accident, illness, or birth. (3)

Plastic Surgery—Cosmetic and restorative surgery. (5)

Preventive Medicine—Community and public health specialization. (2)

Psychiatry and Neurology—The mind and its diseases, and the nervous system and its diseases are subjects of specialization. (3)

Radiology—Use of x-ray and other forms of ionizing radiation in the diagnosis and treatment of disease. (3)

Surgery—Involves operative procedures for correction of deformities and defects, repair of injuries, and treatment of diseases. (4)

Urology—Diagnosis and treatment of diseases and disorders of the kidneys, bladder, ureters, urethra, and the male reproductive organs. (4)

—Health Careers 1975–1976: A Directory of Career Information and Training for New York State, United Hospital Fund, 1975, second printing 1976, pp. 61–63. Used with permission of the United Hospital Fund.

Minority groups constitute nearly one-fifth of the nation's population, but only 1 out of 15 medical students is black, Mexican American, Native American, or Puerto Rican, according to Dr. Christmas. Women and men from these groups need to be supported and encouraged to enter careers in health care.

Nationwide, the physician shortage is not over, and national health insurance would create a sharp increase in the demand for medical services. Too few physicians locate in rural areas and the maldistribution of specialists is acute. While more internists are needed in Alaska, more pediatricians in South Dakota, and more obstetrician–gynecologists in Wyoming, many Eastern states have an abundance of these specialists. Despite evidence of a surplus of surgeons nationally, Mississippi has relatively few. And it goes without saying that too few doctors are women—a situation that we can hope will be remedied in the near future.

Dentists

The demand for dentists far outweighs the supply. American mouths contain an estimated 800 million unfilled cavities, and only half of all adults see a dentist more than once a year. The *Journal of Dental Education* has estimated that nearly 65 percent of poor children in the United States have never seen a dentist. However, people are becoming increasingly aware of the necessity of regular dental care in preventing and controlling diseases. The expansion of dental health insurance programs will make it easier for more people to afford care and will result in even greater need for dental practitioners.

In 1976 in the United States a smaller number of women were in dentistry (1.9 percent) than in any other health profession. In other parts of the world dentistry attracts a high percentage of women: in Scandi-

FACTS AND FIGURES: DENTISTS

- About 112,000 dentists were at work in the United States in 1976.
- Of these 9 out of 10 were in private practice; approximately 5,000 served as commissioned officers in the Armed Forces; about 1,400 worked in other federal jobs, chiefly in VA hospitals and clinics and for the Public Health Service. Roughly 4 percent taught in dental schools, did research, or administered dental health programs full time.
- Most dentists are general practitioners; about 10 percent specialize.
- During the first year or two of practice, dentists often earn little more than the minimum needed to cover expenses, but earnings usually rise rapidly as their practice develops. Specialists generally earn more than general practitioners. Average income of dentists in 1976: about $39,500. New graduates of dental schools who went to work for the Federal Government in 1977 started at $17,056.

navia 25 to 30 percent of dentists are women; in Eastern Europe and the USSR, the percentage soars to 80 percent.

Dr. Jean C. Campbell is a fellow of the American College of Dentistry. She has published widely, has a private practice, conducts research, and is a spokeswoman for the American Dental Association (ADA):

"I've been to conferences in Japan and in the USSR, where many women dentists participate. But in this country I've talked to people who say they've never seen a woman dentist before. When they stop and think about it, however, they seem to really like the idea of being treated by a woman."

Dentistry is an attractive career for a married woman with children; she can set up an office at home and choose her own hours. The equipment needed for a private practice is impressive (and expensive), but it can be contained in a relatively small space. Also, since the practice of dentistry entails few emergency calls, a private practitioner can easily establish office hours to coincide with the hours her husband is at work and her children in school.

The ADA is encouraging women to enter dentistry by making people like Dr. Campbell more visible to the public. The association also states that women are needed to participate in group practices and to assume leadership in community dentistry programs.

A number of women are entering dentistry as a second career. Dr. Doris J. Stiefel of the University of Washington School of Dentistry respects these students, many of whom are in their mid-30s: "I'm very much impressed with the caliber of women who have gone back to school to become dentists. They're highly motivated and do very well. At our school even women with children manage very well."

Since 1972 the number of women dental students has doubled, and 800 women were enrolled in dental schools in 1977. In 1966 there were only 50!

Dental School

Lack of role models has not been the sole factor deterring women from entering dentistry. Like medical schools, dental schools have had formal and informal quota systems designed to protect the male monopoly, although, in general, women have reported less discrimination in dental schools than in medical schools.

Dental students pursue a four-year program leading to a DDS (Doctor of Dental Surgery) or a DMD (Doctor of Dental Medicine); the terms are synonymous. Curriculum varies among dental schools, but it is generally divided into three broad areas. Usually, most of the first year and much of the second are devoted to the basic sciences—anatomy, biochemistry, embryology, histology, pathology, pharmacology, and physiology. The second broad area includes the clinical sciences—diagnosis, treatment, and dental materials—generally taken during the last two years. Finally, the dental student learns to apply the dental sciences to the *practice* of dentistry, taking courses such as business management, professional ethics, patient psychology, and community health. Social science courses are distributed throughout the study sequence in some curricula.

Traditionally the basic lab courses have been concentrated in the first two years of school, with the last two years reserved for clinical training. However, a new trend in dental education integrates theory and clinical practice earlier in the curriculum.

Licensing examinations are given by state boards of dentistry, but the test given by the National Board of Dental Examiners is often accepted

---

GETTING IN, MOVING UP: DENTISTRY

Many women are entering dentistry as a second career. Whether they are seeking a first career or a second, women are needed to participate in group practice and in community dentistry programs.

---

as a substitute for the written part of the state exam. National Board examinations are in two sections, with Part 1 taken after completion of two years of dental study and Part 2 in the spring of the final year. Delaware also requires dental school graduates to serve one year of hospital internship. A dental license awarded by one jurisdiction permits the recipient to practice only within that jurisdiction.

In some states a dentist cannot be licensed as a "specialist" without two or three years of graduate education, several years of specialized experience, and successful completion of a special state examination.

The ADA recognizes 60 schools of dentistry in the continental United States and Puerto Rico and another 10 in Canada. Most schools are in the Eastern states or on the West Coast, but programs are being established at the Universities of Colorado and Mississippi and at Oral Roberts University in Oklahoma. Tuition and costs averaged $5,000 a year in 1977, but more than half of all students receive loans or subsidies from their dental schools, the government, or private sources. Inflation continues to drive tuition and costs upward.

Dental Practice

More than 91 percent of active dentists are engaged in some kind of private practice. The general practitioner performs a variety of services including examining teeth for cavities, taking radiographs (x-rays), filling cavities, extracting teeth, and designing and fitting dentures, bridges, and other appliances. Dentists are also licensed to prescribe medications and administer injections.

About 10 percent of all graduates go on to specialize, which generally requires a minimum of two years of postdoctoral training and practice. A residency program in a hospital is often required.

Many options are open to the dental graduate. For instance, dentists connected with volunteer services have opportunities to travel. The Peace Corps still seeks technicians and health professionals, including dentists, and Dental Health International looks for 90-day volunteers to work in developing nations. At several schools (one is the University of Washington) the student affairs office places short-term volunteers in Central America, Ecuador, Israel, and Africa. Health teams work in mobile units and at regional hospitals.

Dental research can also be a very exciting and rewarding field. New frontiers in research include development of techniques for transplanting natural teeth and studies into the cause of cleft palate and cleft lip, which afflict 7,000 babies each year. Studies under way in immunology could lead to prevention of tooth decay and discovery of the causes of other oral diseases, including cancers. Government and education are additional sources of employment, and employment opportunities in general are expected to be very good through the mid-1980s.

EIGHT AREAS OF SPECIALIZATION RECOGNIZED BY THE AMERICAN DENTAL ASSOCIATION

Dental Public Health — The control and prevention of dental disease and the promotion of oral health through organized community efforts. It is that form of dental practice which treats the community as a patient, rather than the individual.

Endodontics — Deals with the causes, diagnoses, prevention and treatment of diseases of the pulp and other dental tissues which affect the vitality of teeth.

Oral Pathology — Concerned with the nature of diseases of the mouth, through study of their causes, processes, and effects. As diagnostician, the oral pathologist does not necessarily treat the diseases directly, but may provide counsel and guidance to other specialists who do provide treatment.

Oral Surgery — Includes a broad scope of diagnostic, operative, and related services dealing with diseases, injuries, and defects in the jaws and associated structures.

Orthodontics — Science of tooth and oral structure development. The orthodontist treats problems related to irregular dental development, missing teeth, and other abnormalities in order to establish normal functioning and appearance.

Pedodontics — Treatment of children, adolescents, and young adults whose dental development is not complete.

Periodontology — Science of diseases which affect the oral mucous membranes as well as other structures which surround and support the teeth. Periodontology may be considered as a clinical projection of oral pathology to include treatment of the conditions named above.

Prosthodontics — Science and art of replacing missing natural teeth and associated structures with fixed or removable substitutes.

—*Dentistry—A Changing Profession,* Revised, 1975. p. 16. Copyright by the American Dental Association. Reprinted by permission.

Dentistry is a promising field that offers personal fulfillment and financial security for women. As one woman dentist assured us, "I'll never give it up; I love it!"

Optometrists

Half the people in the United States need eye care, and optometrists provide most of it. The demand for optometric service is growing so rapidly that the American Optometric Association has estimated that 18,000 additional optometrists will be needed by 1990. The increase in the number of women entering schools of optometry is reflected in the total enrollment (approximately 15 percent in 1978), but not yet in the number of graduates and people working in the field. Today 5 percent of the nation's 19,700 optometrists are women.

Optometrists examine eyes and related structures for vision problems, disease, and other abnormal conditions. They provide treatment by prescribing ophthalmic lenses, contact lenses, or other optical aids, and provide vision therapy when needed. They test for depth and color perception and the ability to focus and coordinate the eyes. Optometrists also detect systemic diseases such as glaucoma and cataracts. If eye disease or injury is diagnosed, the optometrist will send the patient to an ophthalmologist (eye physician) for treatment or surgery. In some states such as New Jersey, Delaware, and West Virginia, optometrists can prescribe and use drugs for diagnosis and treatment.

Optometrists conduct research and can specialize in work with the aged, children, or the partially sighted. They may take continuing education courses in such skills as the fitting and adjustment of contact lenses—a particularly lucrative field.

To gain the Doctor of Optometry (OD) degree, students in a four-year college of optometry study the basic behavioral and social sciences and receive comprehensive training in vision care. Optometric study includes courses in ocular anatomy, ocular pathology, physiological optics, and the geometry of light. A minimum of two years of preprofessional college work—including mathematics, physics, chemistry, and biology or zoology—is a prerequisite to professional study. (Most entering students have a baccalaureate degree.) Graduates must take state licensing examinations.

More than 63 percent of all optometrists are engaged in private practice. Many are also involved in group practice, research, teaching, community and public health, as well as Armed Forces health programs. The profession is particularly attractive to women since the hours are generally flexible with many opportunities for part-time work.

GETTING IN, MOVING UP: OPTOMETRY

Flexible hours and opportunities for part-time work make a career in optometry attractive to many women. Demand for optometric services is growing rapidly, and more than half of all optometrists are in private practice.

Podiatrists

In 1974, 6 percent of the nation's 7,500 practicing podiatrists were women. Podiatrists are health professionals who deal with the examination, diagnosis, treatment, and prevention of diseases and disorders of the human foot. Podiatrists perform surgery, fit corrective devices, and prescribe drugs and physical therapy.

A minimum of two years of preprofessional college work is required for admission to colleges of podiatric medicine. (Most students, however, have a baccalaureate degree.) Preprofessional work should include courses in English, biology or zoology, organic and inorganic chemistry, and physics. Beginning in 1978 all students are required to take the New Medical College Admission Test (New MCAT) as an entrance requirement.

Doctors of Podiatric Medicine (DPMs) are graduates of a four-year course of study. The first two years are largely devoted to class and laboratory work in the basic medical sciences. The last two years emphasize clinical science and experience and include courses in general diagnostic procedures, therapeutic procedures, orthotics, prosthetics, and operative podiatry. Residency programs are available. Specialization requires additional study and includes children's foot disorders, foot surgery, and conditions affecting the elderly.

To practice, a state license is necessary. Most podiatrists engage in private or group practice. Some serve on hospital staffs, in community clinics, as teachers and researchers, and in government and Armed Services health programs. Employment opportunities continue to look favorable through the mid-1980s.

Dr. Louise Cousins, Medical Doctor

Most students do not find medical school easy, and Dr. Louise Cousins was not an exception. "Being a woman definitely made it harder," recalls

---

GETTING IN, MOVING UP: PODIATRY

Employment opportunities continue to be favorable. Most podiatrists engage in private or group practice. Many specialize in such fields as children's foot disorders and foot surgery. For those interested in geriatrics, specialization in foot disorders of the elderly is a profitable field.

Dr. Cousins, now doctor of internal medicine with additional training and a subspecialization in gastroenterology. "It was most obvious when we female graduates applied for internships. No matter how high your class standing or how impressive your medical school, women were often seen as 'second rate' by those who were offering internships. I also experienced the adversities common to all medical students—male or female—including conflicts with hospital chiefs of service."

Another issue Dr. Cousins had to confront was the emphasis on academic medicine. "Private practice was very much looked down on, and we were made to feel that the only worthwhile pursuits were teaching and research. Anyone who didn't qualify as a professor was thought to have sold herself down the river. It wasn't until my last year, in my last rotation, that I finally worked with a physician I could identify with. I went to him on the last day and said, 'Doctor M., it's very hard for me to tell you this and I'm very embarrassed, but I just want you to know that after all these years, I finally found a doctor I want to be like.'

"It was very hard to elude brainwashing, and when I finally decided *not* to stay in academic medicine but to enter private practice, as I had originally intended, I was still very apologetic. When I went to the chief of service and told him my plans, he laughed and said, 'Well, doctors are what we're supposed to be training.'"

Moving to the Southwest, where she opened her practice, had been a lifelong desire. To set up her practice, Dr. Cousins had to get admitting privileges at the local hospital for her patients. In return she signed a contract requiring her to contribute six hours a week at the hospital's free clinic, a fairly standard agreement.

"This area is such an attractive place to live that we are overrun with doctors. Of course, I knew that when I came, so I expected things to get off the ground slowly. My financial picture was severe at first—I almost had to close my doors after just three months. Fortunately, a very competent accountant showed me how to limp through this period.

"As an internist, I see people with high blood pressure, diabetes, peptic ulcer, liver disease, pulmonary insufficiency, obesity—that kind of thing. I see adolescents and adults. We have an interesting cross section of the population here: Spanish people from the valley, outlandish hippies, extremely wealthy people, interesting artistic and intellectual people, cowboys, ranchers, people from the scientific community—and just one hospital to serve them.

"A typical case for me would be someone, perhaps a woman, with a gastrointestinal complaint. She comes in with abdominal pain and reports having vomited blood for two days. I'll put her in the hospital; probably look down her throat with an endoscope to help identify the source of the bleeding. It will probably be a peptic ulcer. I'll treat her in the hospital for a few days, stabilize her and teach her how to live with an ulcer, and see her again in a couple of weeks.

"The work is very demanding. Sometimes situations arise that you're not formally trained to handle: interpersonal relationships with difficult patients; psychophysiological problems, where people are really mentally disturbed but are blaming bodily conditions. These things are difficult and wearing on all physicians. With a straightforward problem—the patient has hepatitis, he turned yellow, he's vomiting, he doesn't feel well—with that, we know where we're at. I think I use up more energy on difficult interpersonal care than I do on a bleeding ulcer or a critically ill patient, where it's just a matter of doing what you know you have to do.

"Of course a whole day of routine stuff can be very boring. Like irritable bowels. I do a *lot* of irritable bowels, and that isn't too exciting. Of course you don't want *every* case to be a diagnostic enigma, where you have to pull out every book on your shelf and refer to the literature and call five other physicians; but such cases can be a real challenge to me as a doctor.

"I personally would find it difficult having a family, but women I went through school with seem to cope all right. I'm told that the prejudices against women are weakening or at least being suppressed. And it's getting easier to combine a medical practice with outside interests. Specialties like pathology, radiology, anesthesiology, and psychiatry, for example, offer a woman a reasonably regulated life with flexibility and time for herself.

"It was tough getting where I am today, but I really like to take care of people. I've had a great deal of illness in my own life and have been neglected and often not received good medical care. I think it's so terribly important for somebody who is ill to have a concerned, interested, involved physician who will help solve that patient's problem and support him or her in the future. I get a lot of gratification out of playing that role."

Dr. Julie Kiefer, Dentist

Julie Kiefer, DDS, is a young woman who set up her own dental practice a few years ago in a small Western city. She's a highly motivated person and with a lot of hard work, sound planning, and a willingness to take risks, Dr. Kiefer has achieved the professional goal she's had since childhood. "I was interested in becoming a dentist from the sixth grade on, and somehow I kept my resolution. Guidance counselors would say to me, 'Don't you think you'd better have an alternative, dear?' But *I* didn't think so!"

Dr. Kiefer has always enjoyed working with her hands and has done woodcraft, needlepoint, leather craft, sculpture, and so on. She remembers going to the dentist often as a child and being "fascinated by all the intricacies of what the dentist was doing: I was frightened to death but fascinated by the *handicraft* of the whole thing.

"Before I entered dental school, I had met only one woman dentist, a lady in my hometown who had become a pedodontist [a specialist in child dentistry] at age 65. She was a fantastic dentist. My brother had been hit in the mouth, and she diagnosed potential abscesses and sent him to an endodontist for root-canal therapy, which prevented serious infection. In other words, she was attentive and anticipated complications. She was also very nice, but I can't say I was motivated only by her. I was motivated by what people in the profession *did*—by their work, not their personalities.

"The extraordinary part of this profession—as opposed to, for example, medicine—is that you're dealing with tiny, tiny areas. It's so intricate and everything is so little—nerves, roots, everything! For instance, surgery in the mouth. It's practically all microscopic work."

Dr. Kiefer's ability to do painstaking, skilled work with her hands was a real plus when it came to getting into dental school. The Dental Admission Test (an entrance requirement) includes several hours of manual dexterity testing. "You're also given a written exam and a psychological test.

"If I were characterizing dental school, I would have to say that what they do is mold you into a dentist. As far as dentistry goes, you're not to have any ideas of your own, because dentistry is such an exacting field. One of the aims of dental education is to train you to be a perfectionist. A student can work and work at something, and it can be very nice, and the professor will say, 'This is no good,' just because a tiny detail needs redoing. He'll throw your work away and tell you to start over. That is upsetting, but you get used to it because they're really just training you to do work that is completely and exactly right at all times."

Other attributes Dr. Kiefer cites as necessary to make it through dental school are physical stamina, perseverance, and good study habits. "You also need the ability to say to yourself, 'Just a little bit more, just a little bit more,' and keep that up for about four years!"

It wasn't easy. In addition to taking out loans—"Loans are easy to get, you just sign your name and owe a lot of money"—she worked part time while going to dental school full time. "The way I did it was to get a BS in dental hygiene first. Then I worked part time, cleaning teeth and doing lab work for the professors." But Dr. Kiefer doesn't recommend working while studying: "Dental school is hard, and they usually discourage anyone from trying to work, even part time."

Dr. Kiefer was one of only three women in a class of 105, but she says she didn't feel handicapped.

Many of her dental school classmates entered group practices with other dentists or established partnerships after graduation, but Dr. Kiefer wanted to make it on her own. "I built this practice by putting out my shingle, sweeping the floor, and taking anybody who walked through the door, as well as lots of emergency referrals from the ADA. Patients do your word-of-mouth advertising; one tells another." She also took out more loans.

"I do a lot of endodontics and root-canal treatments. I get referrals on these and probably do as many as a specialist. But basically I do full-mouth reconstructions. This is for people who come in with a whole mouth of bad teeth. They need root-canal treatment, periodontal treatment for the gums, dental surgery, the whole bit. So I'm into all these aspects of it—rebuilding the whole mouth."

On a typical workday, after coffee, she lines up the day's work, puts on her gown, and sees the first patient. From then on, she's busy the whole day. Between patients, she's back in the laboratory "doing the handicraft part of the profession, the carving of wax patterns and the crowns." She doesn't schedule herself a lunch hour but takes it if she has time.

Dr. Kiefer also feels fortunate because her dental assistant (who is also her receptionist and secretary) is willing to work long hours with her. "She came about two months after I started my practice. She had no knowledge of dental assisting at all, but I trained her on the job while she took correspondence courses. She has since graduated from a state university, is now a state-registered dental assistant, and ranks as an honor student as far as the state boards are concerned.

"I have a small office at this point, but I'm going to expand. I always go to school, constantly keeping abreast of things. This means 50 to 60 hours a year of postgraduate work. I also read a stack of journals. Recently I've scheduled time for vacations—I've traveled; but right now I'm very happy at home."At this point her debts are almost paid off, and Dr. Kiefer has a busy and interesting practice. "If a young woman wanted to go into this profession, I'd give her every encouragement. I've never been sorry!"

BASIC RESOURCES

For more information on medical careers write or phone:

Medicine —General

American Medical Association
Council on Medical Education
535 North Dearborn Street
Chicago, Illinois 60610

American Medical Women's Association
1740 Broadway
New York, New York 10019

Association of American Medical Colleges
1 Dupont Circle NW
Washington, D.C. 20036

Dentistry

American Association of Dental Schools
1625 Massachusetts Avenue NW
Washington, D.C. 20036

American Dental Association
211 East Chicago Avenue
Chicago, Illinois 60611

Association of American Women Dentists
435 North Michigan Avenue
Chicago, Illinois 60611

Optometry

American Optometric Association
7000 Chippewa Street
St. Louis, Missouri 63119

Osteopathy

American Association of Colleges of Osteopathic Medicine
4720 Montgomery Lane
Bethesda, Maryland 20014

American Osteopathic Association
212 East Ohio Street
Chicago, Illinois 60611

Podiatry

American Podiatry Association
20 Chevy Chase Circle NW
Washington, D.C. 20015

THIS CALENDAR gives you a quick check on how many years of education, after high school, you should count on for the representative health occupations listed here. The lines and symbols show what is customary—some people take only minimum required training; many take more.

●   Requires no special training.

▬■■■■■■■■■■   Entails an apprenticeship, special course, or on-the-job training.

▬▬▬▬▬▬▬   Requires special training in college, in a hospital or special school, or in a professional school after 1 to 4 years of college.

○   Though the line shows the minimum period to qualify, more preprofessional years in college lengthen the total training time.

☐   First square means one can get a junior professional job after college. Subsequent squares indicate that more study—to or beyond the master's or doctor's degree—as well as experience   is usually needed for advancement.

▬▬▬▬■■■■■   Requires special training of varying periods of time.

YEARS OF EDUCATION AND TRAINING BEYOND HIGH SCHOOL FOR CAREERS IN SELECTED HEALTH OCCUPATIONS

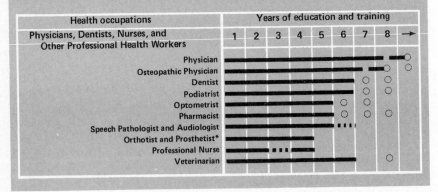

Health occupations	Years of education and training
Physicians, Dentists, Nurses, and Other Professional Health Workers	1 2 3 4 5 6 7 8 →
Physician	
Osteopathic Physician	
Dentist	
Podiatrist	
Optometrist	
Pharmacist	
Speech Pathologist and Audiologist	
Orthotist and Prosthetist*	
Professional Nurse	
Veterinarian	

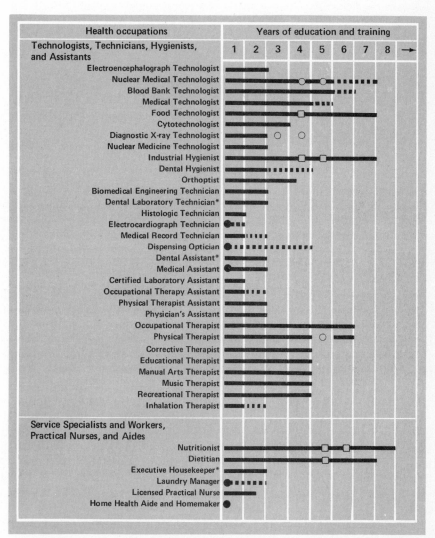

*In certain areas, 1 to 4 years of apprenticeship, a special course, or on-the-job training are acceptable in lieu of formal training. Beginning in 1980, orthotists and prosthetists will be required to have a B.S. in the field.

Reprinted from HEALTH CAREERS GUIDEBOOK, U.S. Labor Dept.

CHAPTER 4

NURSES

Nurses are by far the largest group of professionals employed within the vast health care industry. Each year, more than 180,000 nurses enter the labor force on a full- or part-time basis. Employment of nurses, from aides to administrators, is projected at 1.2 million by 1985—an increase of half over the number employed in 1974. Many factors—including a growing population, an increased percentage of older people, and more health insurance and health maintenance programs—are responsible for the rising need.

Nursing practice is moving toward more independence, more specialization, and increased community outreach. One new trend is the revival of a valuable vocation: midwifery. Also new is the increasing number of nurse specialists working as certified primary health care practitioners.

Changing attitudes within the nursing profession are altering the health care environment. Many nursing leaders believe that sexism, as well as racism, stands in the way of women realizing their full professional potential. The physician/nurse relationship in health care (from which other health workers take their cue) has evolved over the years to the point where nurses are generally seen as the doctor's technical assistants. The relationship is too often characterized by medical authoritarianism on one hand and nursing deference on the other. Today, however, many nurses find this role inappropriate. Physicians-in-charge are being viewed more as colleagues than as unapproachable authority figures.

The professional consequences of these attitudes are important. Viewing the nurse as technician and physician's "go-fer" can detract from the development of the nurse's patient orientation. The primary role of nursing includes caring, helping, comforting, and guiding; although some nurses wish to work strictly as technicians, many now feel that role should not be arbitrarily assigned to *all* nurses.

Some educators believe that ideally the clinical concerns of both doc-

FACTS AND FIGURES

- About 960,000 persons worked as registered nurses in 1976; roughly one-third worked part time.
- Roughly three-fourths worked in hospitals, nursing homes, and related institutions.
- About 65,000 worked as community health nurses in government agencies, schools, visiting nurse associations and clinics.
- Nurse educators in nursing schools accounted for approximately 33,000.
- Another 20,000 worked as occupational health nurses in industry.
- About 100,000 worked in the offices of physicians or other practitioners, or as private-duty nurses hired directly by patients.
- In 1976 the average salary for RNs employed in hospitals was $11,280; industrial nurses averaged $240 a week. Federally employed nurses earned an average of $15,500 in 1977.

tor and nurse should overlap, with the whole health care team strengthened by a spirit of interdependence. Trust and mutual decision making then become essential. How to achieve this quiet revolution in attitudes while providing the best possible care for patients is a developing and continuing issue in the nursing world.

Whether one leans toward a progressive nursing ideology or holds a more traditional view of the nursing role, the profession offers many opportunities. Projections are that there will be room for many kinds of nurses in the growing health care industry. Job descriptions distinguish kinds of nurses according to function; individual training and, of course, personal capabilities further distinguish one nurse from another.

The most highly skilled member of the profession is the registered nurse, or RN. The extent of the care she provides can vary considerably, according to her degree of education and specialized training.

More nurses are employed in hospitals than in any other health care setting. In the hospital environment, the RN, under the supervision of staff physicians, is the person who has primary responsibility for the daily care of patients. She administers medication, changes surgical dressings, assists with blood transfusions and intravenous treatment, and is often charged with the responsibility of explaining to a patient and his or her family what future regimen of care may be required. The natural line of promotion in hospital nursing is from general-duty nurse to head nurse to supervisor, and finally director of nursing services.

Within the hospital, nurses in intensive care units work under the

CHANGING IMAGES IN NURSING

Most of us have grown up with an image of Florence Nightingale as the "lady with a lamp," the ministering angel who tended the sick and wounded during the Crimean War. However, there was another side to Florence Nightingale, a side usually hidden by the conventional stereotype: she was a rabble rouser. She tackled the government and took it to court, causing sanitary codes to be enacted where there had been none. Feigning ladylike helplessness, Florence Nightingale was often able to manipulate men to speak for her and take action that she, as a woman, was unable to take. She stepped on egos and established order whenever it was in the interest of a healthy society.

Florence Nightingale became a nurse over the objections of her wealthy family at a time when hospitals were generally squalid and unsanitary institutions, and nursing largely attracted ladies of questionable virtue. Singlehandedly, she changed the way nursing was to be practiced in the future, and she fought to establish nursing as a respectable and independent profession. Still, her "angelic" nature has been the prevalent model in nursing education, and nurses have generally been persuaded to fashion themselves in her most passive image.

Many nurses, however, are dedicated to setting history straight. In 1973, at a convention of the National Organization for Women (NOW), 30 nurses who recognized a link between feminism and the changing roles in nursing organized a task force called Nurses NOW. Today, there are pocket groups in the Northeast and on the West Coast, working at changing the image of nursing for the public and for nurses themselves.

Nurses NOW is not seen as a competitor to existing professional organizations; rather it is viewed as a complement. One of its goals is to improve nurses' self-confidence and professionalism in bureaucratic, male-dominated medical institutions. A second goal is to help nurses create change from within. "Nurses must learn how to strategize, organize, and negotiate," says one young nursing leader.

Other groups like Nurses Coalition for Action in Politics and Nurses for Political Action, both arms of the American Nurses Association, are working to encourage nurses to take a more active part in government affairs and to organize for more effective political action. As the delivery and nature of medical care is changing, nurses are fighting for increased responsibility and status, and to be involved in long-range health policy and planning. From giving traditional bedside service to opening private practices, nurses are working to expand their opportunities as professionals.

---

most unrelenting stress. All their patients are in crisis, suffering from cardiac arrests, lung collapses, bleeding ulcers, thyroid "storms," and similar events.

"Sometimes I have nightmares about dialysis," says one veteran intensive care nurse. "How fast can I get the tubing in? The patient will die if I fumble."

How does it feel to see people dying? Many nurses try to hide their tears or depression under small talk about the latest movie or the terrible food in the cafeteria. Patients' families may misunderstand and think the nurses are frivolous and don't care about what's happening. But nurses must fight to keep their personal feelings and professionalism in balance; sometimes they join together in therapy groups to vent their emotions and renew strength. Not all nurses are suited for the demands of intensive care service.

Registered nursing has its own clinical specialties such as pediatrics, obstetrics, psychiatry, rehabilitation, and surgery; usually specialties require advanced courses of study. The obstetrical nurse, for example, must complete a graduate program leading to a master's degree, which also qualifies her for a teaching position.

Nurse-Midwife

One clinical specialty that is being enthusiastically revived is midwifery. A midwife is an RN who has followed a further organized pro-

---

NOTE FROM THE PAST:

Adah B. Samuels Thoms and Other Distinguished Minority Nurses

Adah B. Samuels Thoms (1863– 1943), a determined young woman from Virginia, was a graduate of two separate nursing programs in New York City, including the then newly accredited Lincoln Hospital school of nursing. In 1905 she became supervisor of the Lincoln Hospital surgical nursing division and shortly afterward acting director of the training school. It was not then the custom to promote a black to a top position, but Ms. Thoms ran the program for a number of years.

She helped organize the National Association of Colored Graduate Nurses in 1908 and later served as its president. The organization's goals were to combat discrimination within and outside the nursing profession, develop leadership among black nurses, and advance professional standards.

Another distinguished minority woman in nursing was Major Lorette S. Jendritza, an American Indian who was born in 1920. She was a member of the Air Force Nurse Corps and operating room supervisor at the Air Force Academy Hospital. Bertha Sanchez, a native of the Philippines, was nursing director of Project Concern in Vietnam in the late 1960s; she was publicly cited for her exceptional service.

gram of study and clinical experience that qualifies her to care for mothers and babies throughout the entire maternity cycle (including delivery), as long as the pregnancy remains "normal."

Nurse-midwives are devoted to the idea of family-centered care, and they encourage husbands to be part of maternity education and the birth process. Many midwives also believe in prepared childbirth and teach classes in Lamaze ("natural" birth) techniques and help women to use breathing exercises during labor. The nurse-midwife is a caring member of the health team, and her touch can provide the security a mother needs.

Training programs for a nurse-midwife can run from eight months to two years and qualify nurses for certification by the American College of Nurse-Midwives (ACNM).

Nurse Practitioner

Gaining popular acceptance is the specialty of nurse practitioner. The nurse practitioner is a registered nurse who has had one to two years' advanced training preparing her to function independently with a caseload of clients and their families. A nurse practitioner can take a health history, give a physical examination, keep and maintain patient records, provide preventive care by monitoring diet and nutrition, and provide symptomatic treatment as well as render emergency care.

"While nurses have been performing the functions indicated by the name 'nurse practitioner' for some time, the name itself is only about a dozen years old. Such nurses have only now begun to receive professional and legal recognition for their services," says Evelyn K. Tomes, chair of nursing education at Meharry Medical College in Nashville, Tennessee. "Some nurse practitioners have now hung out their own shingles, but that's kind of rare and depends on what the state nursing practice act permits.

"Nurse practitioners work in public health departments, outpatient units of mental hospitals, neighborhood health centers, rural health centers, health maintenance organizations, and as visiting nurses with inner-city caseloads. What we're currently singling out as nurse-practitioner training will become more and more incorporated into general nurses' training, and more and more options will be open to the graduate nurse."

Other Alternatives for RNs

Ample employment opportunities for RNs are offered by public health services, aimed at the care of the sick, and preventive medical services

GETTING IN, MOVING UP: REGISTERED NURSING

After certification, an RN can work as a general-duty nurse in a hospital, contract to do private duty either in a hospital or at home, or work in a doctor's office, among other career possibilities. A master's degree is often required for supervisory and administrative positions as well as in teaching and in research. Two increasingly popular specialties are nurse-midwife and nurse practitioner.

that employ nurses to go into homes, schools, public clinics, and industry. The private-duty RN contracts independently to provide bedside care for patients at home or in a hospital. Registered nurses perform vital services in doctors' and dentists' offices; others serve in the military forces or with governmental agencies in the United States and abroad. Many nurses also teach at schools of professional and practical nursing, as well as at colleges and universities that offer preparatory courses in nursing and related fields.

Licensed Practical Nursing

Licensed practical nursing (LPN) is a field especially attractive to women reentering the labor market and to young people searching for meaningful work. Licensed practical, or vocational, nurses perform a large share of the direct patient care in health facilities, usually under the supervision of an RN or physician. In a hospital setting, her work will include taking and recording temperature, blood pressure, pulse, and respiration rate. She will also dress wounds and observe patients.

GETTING IN, MOVING UP: LICENSED PRACTICAL NURSING

The need for LPNs is so great that vacancies in training programs are hard to find. Because the educational requirements are more readily met than those for becoming a registered nurse, the field is especially attractive to women reentering the labor market.

Since the LPN is so directly involved with a patient, she is in an excellent position to observe any unusual or adverse reactions to medication or treatment and report them to a physician or RN. An LPN may also give alcohol rubs, massages, and apply compresses. She often sterilizes and assembles equipment such as catheters and tracheotomy tubes.

In addition to hospital service, LPNs can also work in places such as nursing homes, public health centers, doctors' offices, and can also contract to work as private-duty nurses in a patient's home.

Getting There—Education

LPNs. Practical nursing education programs require a high school diploma, are generally 12 to 18 months long, and include classroom study and clinical practice and supervision. Full-time attendance is required. Because it is well known that thousands of practical nurses are hired each year, the training programs are well filled; applicants should research more than one program and plan ahead for admission. After completing the training program, the student must take a state board licensing exam.

RNs. Most registered nurses receive two to five years' education. This education may include associate degree programs at two-year community and junior colleges and graduation from three-year hospital diploma schools (both being deemphasized by the American Nurses Association as not fully preparing the student); college baccalaureate degree programs in four- and five-year programs at universities (if you have a diploma or an associate degree in nursing, you may transfer credits toward a bachelor's degree); and master's degree programs at graduate school or study for certification within specialties. In the mid-60s the American Nurses Association (ANA) endorsed the four-year baccalaureate degree as the basic educational level for professional nurses. Therefore the longer programs offered by colleges and universities are growing in number and size, while those requiring less preparation, attached to hospitals, are declining.

A master's degree is often required for supervisory and administrative positions as well as for jobs in nursing education, public health nursing, clinical specialization, and research. Most graduate programs combine study of a clinical area, such as medical–surgical nursing, with study of a functional activity such as teaching, supervision, or consultation. Other continuing education programs are available for nurses who wish to broaden their spheres of practice or become specialists such as physicians' assistants, midwives, or family nurse practitioners.

Graduates of all three types of nursing programs are eligible to take the state licensing examination required for practice. The examination takes two days and is given by all state boards of nursing at least once a year. To practice in another state you must meet the requirements of that state, but it is usually not necessary to take another examination.

Hospital diploma schools traditionally provide board and lodging in exchange for students' labor in the wards, but in college programs nursing students live much like other students. In one program at the University of Maryland, for instance, students spend their first two years at the sprawling College Park campus, taking prenursing science courses along with general education requirements. In their junior and senior years they attend the university's professional school complex in downtown Baltimore for nursing course work and hospital "laboratory" experience.

Nursing students in baccalaureate programs study anatomy, physiology, and microbiology. Their elective courses include health care and politics, nursing in the social order, and emotions and the life cycle. While enrolled in a baccalaureate program, one may decide to go into administration, research, consultation, or teaching; a BS degree is needed for graduate study in these fields.

The general education offered at hospital schools varies; a wider course selection is usually available at schools associated with colleges and universities. But hospital school graduates, like baccalaureate degree nurses, can seek additional training for certification in a specialty —obstetrics, pediatrics, psychiatry, geriatrics, surgery, anesthesiology, or midwifery, for example. Credits can later be transferred to baccalaureate programs toward a BS degree.

Employment Variation from Area to Area

Although projections for nursing jobs are very good, a nursing license does not automatically open doors everywhere. In financially embattled urban centers there may be a freeze on health care jobs in the public sector, despite the need for more workers. Public and private institutions in a given area may have filled their quota of workers and anticipate few people retiring or leaving their jobs for other reasons. However, at the same time, another locale may be crying for help.

Employment opportunities in nursing are expected to be especially good in Southern states and inner-city locations where money is available. If a prospective nursing student has no desire to relocate, she should check with a local nursing association or vocational counselor at a community college about job prospects in her locale. (Perhaps an allied occupation, such as medical technology or health administration, would be a better choice.)

Seattle-Tacoma is an area with a large supply of professional nurses. Shana Fouts, a young woman from Walla Walla, found herself "wait-listed" at the University of Washington School of Nursing after completing her prenursing requirements. After waiting a year for her number to be called in the lottery system and still determined to have a career in nursing, she enrolled in another college program, a less prestigious one but good. After graduation she faced her next test: a tight job market.

"I really prepared myself for interviews," Ms. Fouts says. "When I was in school, I saved articles from nursing magazines that told about questions interviewers would ask and also helped you develop useful questions of your own. You've got to be aggressive if you're serious about getting a job here."

Her hard work and planning paid off. She landed three job interviews after graduation and was soon employed as a staff nurse at a small Scandinavian American hospital north of Seattle. Her plans are to acquire some solid experience, then look into further educational possibilities that might lead to more independence from the hospital milieu.

Susan Campbell, Nurse-Midwife

To Susan Campbell, being a nurse-midwife means more than just a 9-to-5 job. Babies really determine the work schedule, and a nurse-midwife may count on working a more than 40-hour week. The special nature of the job demands equally special qualities in a nurse.

"The nurse-midwife must be willing to give that extra care, that extra time and effort," says Ms. Campbell, "because babies can come at any hour of the day or night. The nurse needs to have compassion, interest, and involvement, but she also must be confident of her judgment. She must be able to make clinical decisions based on scientific knowledge and be able to go ahead and do what's needed."

Most nurse-midwives, like Ms. Campbell, work in a hospital environment, and the demand for their services is growing. Ms. Campbell explains, "There are not nearly enough such practitioners. Requests for help come from Florida to California to Alaska to Maine, as well as from overseas. If I weren't so involved here, I could have a mission abroad in a minute."

Originally a city person, Ms. Campbell received her training in rural nursing and nurse-midwifery in Kentucky. She recognized a need for her services in Appalachia and worked at a district nursing service there for several years. She then helped set up a midwife service at the nearby hospital, where she is now one of four nurses in the midwife program.

"Our population here is mainly low income," Ms. Campbell says; "lots of unemployment, lots of people on welfare. As a district nurse-midwife, I got to know whole families. I did prenatal and postpartum care; and I did some home deliveries, although most people preferred to come to the hospital. I went into the homes to visit postpartums and to help the mothers assess their health practices. There are many teen-age

THE THRILL OF IT ALL: NURSING

"I feel like I have real job security—nurses are always needed and I like knowing that I have a skill that will always be in demand."

"As a nurse-midwife, I've witnessed many, many births, but each time I see one, I still get an emotional high. It's really a miracle."

"Being a nurse practitioner really gives me a great sense of independence—and that's very important to me."

mothers here, and a lot of our counseling deals with diet, nutrition, and hygiene."

Ms. Campbell and her partners in the district nursing service offered a plan of total health care to pregnant women and their families that took them right into the community. They tried to visit every family in the area, letting them know that care was available. They assured every woman that, as Ms. Campbell puts it, "we were interested in her as a person, and in her welfare as well as that of her child. We made it clear we were there to support her, not to take away her authority but to strengthen it."

If a woman wants her support, the nurse-midwife's first task might be analysis of the family diet.

"We ask the family to recall what they ate the previous day," she says. "Then we have to find out who does the cooking. New families just getting started often live with parents and the mother or mother-in-law might be the one doing the cooking. If, for instance, the prenatal woman needs more protein in her diet and much less salt, and the mother of the household cooks with lard and uses a 5-pound bag of salt a month, we have to convince the family to change this habit."

A nurse-midwife follows a patient in her progress through the entire maternity cycle (including delivery), giving classes and individual instruction on the actual birth process as well as on relaxation and breathing techniques. She shows pictures of a fetus to the mother and lets her listen to the heartbeat of her own unborn child and, Ms. Campbell points out, tries "to involve the father in the process so that he becomes an important person, too, because it's not just the mother but the whole family that's involved in childbirth."

Ms. Campbell's hospital offers a woman a "home-type birth." The patient has a private room, and her husband or whoever she wishes can be with her during the delivery. The other children in the family are also free to visit her and the new baby. "It enhances the family's responsibility to one another and its cohesiveness," Ms. Campbell claims.

In a normal pregnancy (which occurs 90 to 95 percent of the time) an obstetrician will see the patient once early in the pregnancy and again during the late stages to make sure that everything is progressing as it should. A midwife stays with the patient throughout labor. The hospital does use medications and local anesthesia, but Ms. Campbell quickly points out, "We don't knock a woman out. She becomes a participant, and the center of the procedure. We seek a slow, controlled delivery, and that takes the woman's cooperation and that of the person who's there to support her."

Nurse-midwives are so well educated in the birth process that they can easily recognize abnormal symptoms, the signal to call in a physician. "The nurse-midwife is not an independent practitioner," Ms. Campbell says. "She must have the support of a physician as a backup; if trouble comes she knows she can call and the doctor will come. But she also must be able to institute treatment before the physician arrives. Here's an example: If a postpartum mother is hemorrhaging and it will take 10 to 15 minutes for the doctor to get there, the nurse-midwife must have the fortitude to go ahead and remove the placenta if that's what's

---

THE DAILY GRIND: NURSING

"It can get really hectic; in emergency situations you have to think on your feet and your decisions have to be right because a person's life is on the line."

"Dealing with the terminally ill is very emotionally trying. Controlling your own grief is extremely difficult, but you must both for your sake and for the sake of patients and their families."

"Some doctors still cling to an old-fashioned image of a nurse as a glorified servant-in-white. That can take away a lot of your initiative and undermine your sense of professionalism."

---

called for. You have to enter the uterus with your hand and remove the placenta manually or else the patient may bleed to death."

After the birth a nurse-midwife helps the patient during her three- or four-day hospital stay, teaching her to care for the infant and deal with the family when she and the child return home. After the mother is discharged, a nurse-midwife will see her at home or in the clinic within 48 hours. Care, including help in family planning if it is desired, continues for from six weeks to one year after the birth.

For nurses like Susan Campbell the long hours and erratic work schedules are not a problem. "Midwifery school, the educational process, is sometimes difficult," she recalls, "but it's very much worth it."

BASIC RESOURCES

For more information about nursing careers, write or phone:

Nursing

    American Nurses Association
    Coordinator of Undergraduate Programs
    Department of Nursing Education
    2420 Pershing Road
    Kansas City, Missouri 64108

    National Student Nurses Association
    10 Columbus Circle
    New York, New York 10019

Licensed Practical Nursing

    National Association for Practical Nurse Education and Service
    122 East 42d Street
    New York, New York 10017

Nurse-Midwifery

    American College of Nurse Midwives
    1000 Vermont Avenue NW (Suite 1210)
    Washington, D.C. 20005

CHAPTER 5

HEALTH THERAPY

Rehabilitation and restoration are central aspects of health care. Persons disabled by injury or illness, victims of birth defects or physical or mental handicaps, all need special care and rehabilitation. Although the entire health team plays an important part in the rehabilitative process, these patients especially need the specific knowledge and skills of trained therapists. Therapists cover a wide range of skills; those who will be discussed in this chapter can generally be described as "hands-on" people. They deal in direct patient contact or in motivating individuals and groups to action.

Physical therapists apply specific exercises and treatments to patients to restore them to the fullest possible level of physical and mental activity and mobility. *Occupational therapists* instruct patients in skills and crafts to help build strength, coordination, self-confidence, and in many cases to prepare them to return to work. *Music, dance, art,* and *recreation therapists* combine knowledge of psychology with the techniques of artistic expression and recreation to facilitate communication and rehabilitation.

The factor that serves to link all these health professionals is a genuine concern for the emotional and physical well-being of others. Therapists seek to minimize the disabilities of patients while at the same time encouraging and helping them to reach their full potential. It takes great dedication in addition to special training to be an effective and caring therapist.

Physical Therapy

Whether administering to the banged-up football hero or treating the disabled stroke victim, physical therapists (PTs) apply physical treatments to restore their patients to health.

A typical physical therapy agenda includes the use of exercise, mechanical apparatus, and massage as well as applications of heat, cold, light, water, or electricity to treat patients suffering from muscle, nerve, joint, and bone diseases or from general disability. PTs also teach disabled persons how to use and care for braces, crutches, and artificial limbs, and instruct family members on how to continue or supplement treatment of the patient at home. Very often, a PT must be able to help a disabled person to accept and to adjust to a physical handicap.

"There's an old stereotype of the physical therapist as weightlifter—but you don't have to be big and burly. It's not a matter of strength so much as knowledge of body mechanics that counts," says one young woman of average size and an excellent physical therapist.

An ability to communicate effectively and work well with others is also essential in physical therapy. In institutional settings, the physical therapist is most often part of a health care team. At a rehabilitation institute, for instance, she may work with a social worker, occupational therapist, psychologist, nurse, and speech therapist. All these professionals must be able to integrate their skills and interact well with each other to best serve a patient.

A physical therapist tests and evaluates the individual's range of mobility and strength, and with the concurrence of the primary physician, draws up a program with a specific therapeutic objective. For instance, in treating a form of arthritis called rheumatoid spondylitis, the therapist seeks to strengthen spinal muscles and increase breathing capacity, obtain normal positioning of the spinal column, and relieve symptoms. To achieve this she works with posture training, recommends adequate rest,

---

FACTS AND FIGURES: PHYSICAL THERAPISTS

- About 25,000 persons worked as licensed physical therapists in 1976.
- Most worked in hospitals; others worked for nursing homes, rehabilitation centers or schools for crippled children, physicians' offices, clinics, public health agencies, or research organizations. A few served as consultants in government and voluntary agencies or as members of the Armed Forces.
- Starting salaries for new graduates averaged $11,200 in 1976; experienced therapists, $14,000.
- Beginning therapists employed by the Veterans Administration earned starting salaries of $10,473 in 1977; the average salary paid by the VA to therapists was $15,700. Supervisory therapists may earn more than $20,000.

GETTING IN, MOVING UP: PHYSICAL THERAPY

The physical therapist is generally part of a health care team. A bachelor's degree combined with graduate training in physical therapy leads to a certificate or a master's in PT. Interest is growing in Shiatsu and T'ai Ch'i Chu'an as alternatives to traditional techniques such as hydrotherapy, electrotherapy, massage, and exercise. With increasing public recognition of the importance of rehabilitation, employment opportunities both public and private are growing.

defines which physical activities should be avoided, and shows how to adapt beds and other furniture for maximum therapeutic value.

A physical therapist also has to be aware of the interaction between her special skills and the more personal, human aspects of disability and illness. Linda Wolf is a physical therapist in her first year of clinical work at a rehabilitation institute in New Jersey. As she sees it, "the major prerequisite for this work is being able to deal with people. You have to like people and have a lot of patience."

Training

You can take several routes toward a career in physical therapy:

- Four years at a college with an undergraduate program approved by the American Physical Therapy Association with a major in PT.
- A bachelor's degree in a related field that includes specific science requirements, plus a 12- to 16-month concentrated program leading to a certificate in PT.
- A bachelor's degree in another field—for instance, psychology or biology—plus a master's degree in PT.

Some schools provide a one- or two-year program for students who have completed some college, or junior-senior programs to which a student can transfer from another institution. For admission to such programs, you should include in your college courses English, mathematics, psychology, and several credits—including laboratory courses—in biology, chemistry, and physics.

PT training combines many hours of clinical practice with academic coursework in anatomy, physiology, psychology, principles of administration and medicine, and various therapy techniques—including hydrotherapy, electrotherapy, and massage. A student also learns how the therapist functions within the context of the total health care system, which includes not only the patient but the patient's family and the community. Interest is growing in alternative modes of therapy, especially Shiatsu, a form of Japanese massage, and a Chinese exercise system called T'ai Ch'i Chu'an.

Preparation for a master's degree generally takes two years and includes courses similar to those in the undergraduate program plus instruction and training in teaching, research, and administration. Part-time study is more feasible in master's degree programs than in others because many of them are designed for people who work.

All states require licensing or registration (which permits use of that coveted "R" with professional designations) to practice physical therapy on a professional level. State examinations are given at least once a year, and you must comply with the legal requirements of the state in which you wish to practice.

Linda Krasilovsky, clinical coordinator and instructor in physical therapy at Ithaca College in Ithaca, New York, notes that many physical therapists return to school after a few years of field experience at hospitals or rehabilitation centers after graduation. "We're trying to get away from being generalists and to go into specialty areas. Physical therapy is a competitive field, and you've got to set yourself apart from the rest in a way. If you want to put in the extra time, you can go into teaching or into pediatrics or whatever specialty you want. Specialization is available if you're willing to work for it." Going back to school may mean taking part in a continuing education program rather than attending classes full time. Courses are given in such areas as cardiopulmonary therapy, muscular dystrophy, and cerebral palsy, or on such new techniques as biofeedback to monitor patients.

The majority of physical therapists—approximately 80 percent—work in hospitals and nursing homes. Others are employed by rehabilitation centers, schools, doctors' offices, and public health agencies; some are entrepreneurs who set up therapy centers at places such as hot springs, and a number of therapists open their own offices and engage in private practice, taking referrals from physicians who by law must prescribe the treatment. Most people in private practice are male (as are most of those with master's degrees), but women still dominate the profession over all—about 75 percent of physical therapists are women. The availability of part-time employment makes this field an especially attractive one for women.

Because of increasing public recognition of the importance of rehabilitation, the need for physical therapists is rapidly growing. For women who have the right combination of skill and caring, physical therapy can be a very rewarding career.

Occupational Therapy

Teaching skills and imagination are among the primary requisites for a career as an occupational therapist (OT). By planning a combination of recreational, vocational, educational, and creative activities the occupational therapist helps patients who have suffered mental or physical illness or a disability again lead a normal life.

Occupational therapists work with patients of all ages. They may specialize in preschool or early-childhood programs for exceptional children, or they may work exclusively with the cerebral palsied. OTs may work with the elderly, helping them to adapt to the tasks of daily living despite diminished strength or impaired mobility. Therapists may also work with patients with artificial limbs, helping them achieve normal skills, or children with learning disabilities, helping them manage the demands of a school curriculum.

The range of possibilities in the services provided by the occupational therapist is really limited only by her imagination and ingenuity. She may use arts and crafts, or concentrate on teaching a child to use an artificial leg; she may give typing lessons to an injured mechanic who must regain his manual dexterity, or teach a partially paralyzed housewife one-handed housework techniques. Both the physical and mental recovery of a patient are the occupational therapist's concern, and to this end she will design activity that will best meet a patient's needs.

An OT's responsibilities include making evaluations of patients' behavior, abilities, and likes and dislikes in order to plan the most suitable program or activity. The work is very creative, but it also requires a good amount of patience because the sick or disabled are easily discouraged by what they view as slow progress or clumsiness in their efforts. An occupational therapist must try to overcome these psychological setbacks and help her patients keep trying until they are successful.

GETTING IN, MOVING UP: OCCUPATIONAL THERAPY

Almost 90 percent of occupational therapists are women. Bachelor's degrees, certificates of proficiency, master's degrees, and PhDs are all available in this field. Teaching, research, and high-level administrative positions generally require a PhD. Both full- and part-time employment opportunities are increasing.

Work and Training

OT is a field dominated by women—approximately 90 percent are women. The largest single employer of occupational therapists has been government hospitals, but increasing opportunities can now be found in private hospitals, rehabilitation centers, halfway houses, community centers, homes and camps for the handicapped, and also in private homes as part of home-visit programs.

One may become eligible to be a registered occupational therapist (OTR) through a four-year college program that includes six to nine months' clinical training. For those who have earned a bachelor's degree before enrolling in a program of OT training, there is an advanced-standing course of 18–20 months divided between academic and clinical work. Several universities also offer master's degree programs in OT; a master's is recommended for persons aiming at research, teaching, or administrative posts. Courses may include art, psychology, journalism, and sociology, as well as physiology and orthopedics. Students also learn practical problem-solving techniques, such as how to teach patients to feed themselves, how to adapt equipment to an individual's particular needs, and how to evaluate muscle strength, coordination, and range of motion, and how to do sensory testing.

Some graduate programs for students with a degree in another field may be less than two years and often offer a certificate of proficiency. Teaching, research, and high-level administrative positions generally require a PhD.

The American Occupational Therapy Association administers a national registration examination to graduates of any of the above programs. Successful completion of the exam entitles graduates to use the designation registered occupational therapist (OTR).

Like physical therapists, OTs are expected to be increasingly in demand as more home services and comprehensive community health centers are established; although the demand for full-time workers in this field is great, an OTR can arrange to work on a part-time basis either with private patients or in a community facility.

Arts Therapy—Music, Art, and Dance

The expressive therapies—music, dance, and art—are devoted to facilitating communication through primarily nonverbal means. Effective arts therapists are artists themselves; in addition, they are trained in the social sciences and have clinical experience in therapy.

Arts therapists have specific objectives beyond the general idea of "expressing yourself" and adapt their techniques to different clinical situations. They work with a wide range of individuals who have emotional or affective disorders, as well as with the general population in health maintenance. Professionals whose work has always been esteemed by patients, they are now being recognized and supported within the health care system. Most arts therapists are women, but efforts are being made to encourage more men to enter the various disciplines.

Music Therapy

"Music hath charms to soothe . . ." may be a comforting observation, but it's not the entire picture in music therapy. "Music can be used to excite a range of feelings—even to provoke stress. It can be used to make someone feel angry and to express anger in an acceptable way. Music isn't just the great esoteric presentation in therapies. It can be used in many ways," asserts Carol Hampton Bitcon, director of adolescent social development at Fairview State Hospital in California.

The stereotype of an arts therapist as a buoyant Little Mary Sunshine is a very limited view of the personality required for this kind of work. As Ms. Bitcon says, "The leader [therapist] is a model and others imitate. If she shows only a few emotions, she's giving a very limited repertoire to the participants. Many times when you come into a group, you have to go into neutral so others will have the choice of going into a low or a high feeling. If you're all bubbly, people are likely to follow you instead of expressing how they really feel.

"The creative process must be truly a part of the individual. It isn't something to be put on for the duration of a session. A serious demeanor is as much a part of creativity as joy."

Music therapists rely on a variety of activities—including group ensembles using folk or traditional instruments, choruses, rhythmic activities, and individual instruction—to enhance a person's self-understanding and help a patient adapt to society. Ms. Bitcon works with developmentally disabled young people, the retarded, autistic, deaf, blind, or cerebral palsied. In work with groups she sometimes uses a combination of instruments and chanting.

"We use a musical method called Orff-Schulwerk [O-S], which has been adapted clinically so that elemental music making becomes a tool of socialization. For instance, an activity in O-S would be a group co-authoring a composition on a theme of names: Who are you? Each person would have a turn with an instrument in expressing who he or she is; then there would be group chanting and the next person would take up the instrument. You would be taking a turn, having everyone give you attention; you would share your composition, and then turn your attention to others. The whole process is geared toward success—a successful experience with music. It's ego building."

Another goal in work with the mentally ill or developmentally disabled is teaching them to combine their emotional feelings with the correct physical expressions of those feelings. For example, such patients may say that they're angry and at the same time smile. The therapist may say, "Show us how you feel on the instrument [drums, xylophone, etc.]. And also show us how you feel on your face. If you're mad, let us know you're mad. If you're happy, let us know what those feelings are."

Research has been done on music therapy with the deaf, and there is a curriculum in use for such work. Its goals are improved social skills and sensory enjoyment for the deaf person. (Deaf people perceive rhythmic vibrations, and some residual reception of sound may exist.) In music therapy, deaf participants sit on a wooden floor near instruments that give strong vibrations. "Signing," or manual communication, is incorporated with rhythms. With the vibrations as a model, the patients strive for improved voice inflections (high/low, loud/soft) and correspondingly appropriate facial expressions.

Music therapists work in counseling services, nursing homes, and recreation and rehabilitation facilities, as well as in mental health and retardation centers. Although registration is not required for many jobs in the field, most employers prefer certified therapists who are qualified to train others on staff, such as nurses, social workers, or aides.

To qualify for registration with the National Association of Music Therapists (NAMT), one must generally have an undergraduate degree in music (a BM, BA, or BME including courses in music therapy, psychology, sociology, biological science, and general education), along with a six-month clinical internship. Someone who already has an undergraduate degree can take required coursework and do the internship as a graduate student assistant. Registration may not be required for certain jobs in the field. Certain universities offer a master's degree in music therapy.

The NAMT cannot predict employment trends, but people in the field believe that prospects are encouraging. The field is relatively new, and

---

GETTING IN, MOVING UP: MUSIC THERAPY

A BM, BA, or BME in music therapy is required. Registration may not be required but is preferred by most employers. Employment opportunities include work with the deaf as well as with the mentally ill or developmentally handicapped.

---

the potential for advancement is good. Newly funded programs in the arts for the handicapped, as well as jobs as activity coordinators, employ music, dance, art, recreation, and occupational therapists. Arts therapists and interns are also being increasingly used in local special education programs.

Dance Therapy

Just as music therapists are engaged in much more than filling time with a pleasing occupation, so dance therapists have objectives in diagnosis, intervention, and treatment. According to the American Dance Therapy Association, "Dance therapy is distinguished from other utilizations of dance which may be recreational or educational in nature, by its focus on the nonverbal aspects of behavior and its use of movement as the process for intervention."

Dance therapy is a form of psychotherapy that uses both rhythmic form and basic dance movement and is particularly effective for patients who have difficulties with verbal communication. Its application is becoming more widespread, but other health professionals are sometimes ignorant of its clinical orientation. One dance therapist describes a typical situation this way: "Our little group was 30 minutes into the session —and I felt that one of our members was on the brink of declaring himself in a much more bold, physical way—when the doctor peered through the door and walked in and cheerfully joined our circle, collapsing everything that had been built up.

THE DAILY GRIND: DANCE THERAPIST

"The profession is relatively new and still developing. As a result, finding a job can be difficult."

"Sometimes a therapist can get really frustrated if she sees that a patient is making little progress. You know that it takes time, but sometimes you wish you could just snap your fingers and make a person well."

"It's discouraging sometimes when you come across a person who doesn't seem to take your skill seriously. Some don't understand the hard work and study necessary to become a dance therapist."

THE THRILL OF IT ALL: DANCE THERAPIST

"If I can help a withdrawn child come out of her shell through movement and dance, I feel I've done something important."

"It's such a creative profession. Dance is creative in and of itself, but you have to be particularly innovative in the therapeutic setting."

"I have always been interested in science and medicine, and I've had training in dance since the age of 4. Becoming a dance therapist has enabled me to combine several interests that I love."

"The doctor was very embarrassed and apologetic after learning that it had been an inappropriate thing to do. Some doctors think dance therapy is as casual as the patients' social dancing hour. Often in their psychiatric training doctors are not given even one hour's introduction to other forms of mental health care."

Dance therapists, like music therapists, are also models for affective behavior. Claire Schmais, coordinator of the master's degree program at Hunter College in New York City, describes what can happen in a session:

"First of all, let me say we're rather existential; we have to deal moment to moment. We can't go in with a rigid preconception of what to do. In other words, we have knowledge of manic-depressives, but when we come to an individual we have to look at him in his particular way of being manic-depressive.

"If the person is very withdrawn, depressed, the first thing I have to do is meet him at the energy level he's at. I can't come in all cheery and tra la la—that would put him right off. I have to connect in movement in a way that lets that patient know that I know how he feels, how it is to be depressed; but I also have to let him know through my actions that I know how to free myself from that feeling."

Ms. Schmais therefore encourages mature, experienced dancers to enter the field. "This is not a field for someone who has not danced; it's not for someone who has just taken one or two courses. A woman going into this career has to feel dance as a primary mode of expression. And she needs a breadth of experience. For this reason I like to see women enter the field who are moving into a second career—people who have had life experience, who have been in the world, and who have been on their own. A number of older women who have had careers in dance—doing their own choreography and performing—go into dance therapy and do very well. Life experience is very, very helpful."

Dance therapists work in all the settings that other therapists work in, and when qualified some engage in private practice. Wynelle Delaney, an adjunctive assistant professor at Texas Women's University at Houston, has a private practice. She does diagnostic evaluations with children and teaches adult "well groups."

"A lot of what I do is not necessarily therapy; it's more like health maintenance. I believe health care is moving more toward this holistic approach. The traditional way said, 'You see people according to what is wrong with them.' That's the pathological, medical model: 'There's something wrong that has to be fixed.' What's coming more and more is, rather than waiting until people become sick, knowledge is applied to prevention and health maintenance.

"This is what I'm seeking with the adults in my classes. I don't have a therapy contract with them, although they get therapeutic experiences. We're there to explore and become self-aware, to get in touch with ourselves—with our strengths and weaknesses—working with the mind, the body, and spiritual awareness, in health maintenance. We learn to keep ourselves functioning well and to take most of the responsibility for our own health maintenance."

A baccalaureate degree in dance or dance therapy coupled with clinical training generally form the requirements for certification as a dance therapist. Admission to master's programs in dance therapy usually requires an undergraduate degree in dance or dance therapy or the equivalent extracurricular dance experience. Graduate study includes training in dance therapy, group dynamics, psychology, and movement behavior as well as a clinical internship with a practicing dance therapist.

GETTING IN, MOVING UP: DANCE THERAPY

Dance therapy is a rewarding field for mature experienced dancers. A baccalaureate degree in dance, dance therapy or education is needed; a master's degree is recommended. However, a strong background in dance combined with a degree in a related field plus dance therapy training and clinical experience may be sufficient. Registered dance therapists may engage in private practice or supervise other dance therapists.

If an individual has a particularly strong dance background, a bachelor's or master's degree in a related field such as psychology, special education, or dance, supplemented with dance therapy training and supervised clinical internship, may be sufficient.

The American Dance Therapy Association (ADTA) establishes specific professional standards as prerequisites to ADTA registration. Only those with registry certification may use the designation dance therapist registered (DTR). Registered dance therapists may engage in private practice and supervise other dance therapists. For entry-level positions in public or private hospitals and agencies, registration is not required.

Art Therapy

Just as in music and dance therapies, professionalism in art is a requisite to being an able art therapist. As one art therapist says, "I really think a person has to be a practicing artist to do art therapy. Knowing techniques doesn't substitute for what you learn by spending time alone in a studio making art and struggling with discovery, confronting your own inner self."

Art therapy, like music and dance, focuses on process, not on product, and is used primarily in the treatment of psychiatric disorders. Therapists work with the emotionally disturbed, physically handicapped, neurologically impaired, or socially deprived. Art therapists may be found in programs for acute alcoholics, in maximum-security prison psychiatric wards, or as consultants in school curriculum and program development.

Natasha Mayers is a working artist in Maine. She taught in the Peace Corps and at a free school before plunging full time into batik, then welded sculptures, did drawings, and, for the past few years, painted. She was awarded a scholarship at the Skowhegan School of Art and presently works one day a week at the Augusta Mental Health Institute.

"Just about every artist I know in the state who works in art therapy has created his or her own job. My first job here was at a prison. I went there and said, 'Do you have an art course here?' When they said they didn't, I said, 'Hire me.' I didn't set a salary figure, I just said I wanted to teach one or two days a week. The authorities found the money to pay me; but after I left, the next person hired was told to find his own funding." She also recently wrote a grant proposal for the state mental hospital to hire a poet, a theater person, a dancer, and an artist for one year. The proposal was approved by the Arts and Humanities Council and the Mental Health Commission.

Ms. Mayer's principal interest as a therapist is in encouraging the individual in personal expression and in sharing whatever communication may come out of the process. She considers this private communication and only infrequently reports to the staff of the hospital, which seems to be satisfactory to them.

GETTING IN, MOVING UP: ART THERAPY

To be able to interpret a patient's art as a means of nonverbal communication, an art therapist must be trained in psychological theory as well as in therapeutic and artistic techniques. Art therapists generally have an undergraduate degree in art, art education, or psychology; a master's degree is recommended.

Art therapy is a very young field that looks highly promising for women with the talent and motivation to make it a rewarding profession.

Other therapists may deal more with diagnostics. Trained diagnosticians, through analysis of a work of art, can describe the artist's illness, and state of mind and whether a self-destructive or psychotic episode is possible. They'll share this information with others responsible for patient care.

Art therapists work in a wide variety of settings including mental health clinics, prisons, drug rehabilitation centers, research centers, and nursing homes. A four-year undergraduate program in art therapy, art, art education, or psychology is generally combined with clinical experience. A master's degree is recommended, though it may not be necessary for employment. The preferred route to a Master of Art, Master of Professional Studies, or Master of Creative Art degree is to follow the BA with a two-year graduate program in art therapy. An alternative is a master's degree program in art education or psychology plus clinical training in art therapy.

The American Art Therapy Association has set up a series of educational and clinical requirements as prerequisites to taking the National Qualifying Art Therapy Examination; these include a graduate school degree in art or social science and 2,000 hours of supervised experience. Successful candidates may use the designation registered art therapist (ATR). Registration may not be necessary for employment.

Recreation Therapy

Today greater emphasis is being placed on the importance of recreation in rehabilitation. Recreation therapists, usually under the supervision of a psychiatrist, plan and conduct recreational programs—for instance, in drama, athletics, arts and crafts, social dancing, gardening, or camping —that will have a specific value for patients who are physically handicapped, mentally ill, socially maladjusted, or developmentally disabled, or for "well groups," such as senior citizens.

GETTING IN, MOVING UP: RECREATION THERAPY

Recognition of the value of recreational therapy is growing, but the field remains one of the less well paid. A degree in recreational therapy or recreational leadership is recommended; a master's degree may be necessary, particularly for supervisory positions.

A recreation therapist might organize an institutional newspaper, take a group to the movies, or create a soap-bubble-blowing spree for people who need deep-breathing exercise. Good recreation therapists are sensitive to the people they're working with and adapt to the needs of the moment. The emphasis is always on social participation rather than on competition.

Recreation therapists are sometimes involved in work very much like that of trained occupational therapists. Rebekah Blaine is director of Independent Living, a pilot program for the elderly in Mayfield, Kentucky. Ms. Blaine's concern is to find ways that will allow the aging to live at home as long as possible.

Ms. Blaine has a master's degree in recreational therapeutics, which is necessary for administration, research, teaching, and training others. A four-year undergraduate program in recreational therapy or recreational leadership is recommended. Women with undergraduate degrees in related disciplines can take a graduate training program, one to two years in length, combining coursework with clinical experience. A master's degree is necessary for some positions.

Though most recreation therapists work in institutional settings such as hospitals and prisons, they are also employed by nursing homes, halfway houses, rehabilitation centers for the physically handicapped, and schools for the blind.

Recreation therapy is not an especially well-paid field. As with music, dance, and art, its status depends very much on the particular institution. However, the professionalism of the workers is becoming more and more appreciated, and education about the nature of the therapies is opening up attitudes and doors.

For registration information consult the National Therapeutic Recreation Society.

Sandy Bernstein, Physical Therapist

Her job as a physical therapist at a rehabilitation center in the Northeast is Sandy Bernstein's first. "I work in adult rehabilitation, with people who've had strokes or limbs amputated, who have spinal cord injuries and are paralyzed, or who have broken legs and have been in casts a long time. These patients live at the rehabilitation center for the duration of their therapy. They're no longer acutely ill, and now it's a matter of getting them back on their feet so they can go home.

"Mostly I work with a middle-age or geriatric population. My caseload includes about 10 patients whom I see twice a day for about 40 minutes each. I usually work with two people at a time.

"When someone comes in who has had a stroke, the first thing I do is look at his or her chart and review the medical history to get an idea of what the patient can do. Then I test for physical strength and range of motion, using a universal grading system. With the patient seated in a wheelchair or lying on a mat table, I will, for instance, ask him or her to raise a knee to the chest; or I will hold one arm and ask the patient to raise it above his or her head. From such movements I can estimate strength.

"I will evaluate how well someone can transfer from a wheelchair to the table; how well he or she can ambulate. With a lower-extremity amputee, I evaluate the strength of the residual limb and work toward building it up enough so that the person can wear a prosthesis, or artificial limb. Stump muscles have to be strong enough for the person to move the limb. When I have determined the patient's weaknesses, I set up a program to build up deficient areas. My aim is to get the person as independent as possible.

"Many modalities are used here. The techniques include using hot and cold packs and several different kinds of equipment—a shortwave diathermal machine, traction devices, whirlpool baths, and ultrasound. But basically in rehab you train patients to walk at parallel bars and use dumbbells and sandbags for building strength. For instance, you may put a sandbag on a patient's leg and have him lift it, which increases strength. Or you have him work with overhead weighted pulleys."

She is "moderately strong," claims Ms. Bernstein, "and only about average size, but I expect I'll get a lot stronger. My roommate says my biceps are going to grow! However, size isn't really that important. With proper body mechanics a smaller person can learn how to handle people just as well as a larger person can, and we would both need some help transferring an individual who's 6 feet tall and partially paralyzed.

"For instance, a person who has had a stroke and is paralyzed on one side sometimes leans heavily to the paralyzed side when he or she stands up to transfer to the table from a wheelchair. You have to be prepared to counteract this. Or when you're trying to get such a patient to walk again the patient may need to lean heavily on you because his or her muscles are weak."

Ms. Bernstein says she's really a physically oriented person. She swims a couple of nights a week and hikes as much as possible. She doesn't often stay out late during the week; as she explains, "by Friday night I'm really tired. But I'm getting used to it!"

When asked how much autonomy physical therapists have, Ms. Bernstein replied, "Most departments of physical therapy have a physiatrist or other medical doctor in charge. If this doctor is a person who respects other people's knowledge and skills, then you will probably be permitted to use a fair amount of initiative. The doctor is usually involved in consultation, examining the patient and ordering general types of treatment—exercise or ambulation or gait training [walk, trot, run]. The therapist is permitted to use her judgment and proceed as she thinks best. The doctor reviews the patient's progress every few days. Of course, what the doctor says is the last word. In a private practice of physical therapy (more women should try this career option because it's more lucrative), you have more independence, although you still must work according to a doctor's prescription."

According to Ms. Bernstein, "This field tends to bring out assertiveness. You may start off quiet or shy, but you have to be able to communicate and you learn to do it. Communication is a matter of trying to get the patients to do things, to motivate them to do physical tasks that may be painful or boring not for you but for themselves. You have to understand that each patient is different and each has individual problems. You won't be happy as a physical therapist if you're not interested in people.

"Meeting so many people is one thing I really enjoy about my work. They're basically very friendly and appreciative of what you're doing. It's great when you can help someone to walk again and to be able to go home! What's frustrating is working with terminally ill patients. You know you can help them a little bit but you can't really put them back together. You have to learn how to overcome your feelings and give people support without going overboard."

What originally turned her on to physical therapy, Ms. Bernstein recalls, "was the Easter Seal telethons I saw as a child—that and being a candystriper at a rehabilitation institute near my high school. I still hope and plan to work with children who have cerebral palsy. Those jobs are pretty hard to come by, though. It's a Catch-22—they want people with experience, and if you don't get the job, you don't get the experience!"

Physical therapy, like many health care vocations, is becoming increasingly specialized. Most physical therapists get clinical experience in hospitals or rehabilitation centers before going into a specialization. To become fully qualified for work with handicapped children, Ms. Bernstein will need additional academic and on-the-job training; but because the job market is very competitive in urban centers, she plans to stay in her present job for now.

"Meanwhile," she says, "I take weekend courses in pediatrics and cerebral palsy therapy. I spent three summers as a counselor at a camp for handicapped children, so I know I like working with them. I'm also quite realistic about the situation. The progress of such children is very slow—you can work with them for years and see no more than a minimal change.

"I think one reason I'm looking forward to working with children is that you have to be especially creative; you have to think up games and motivate them with different means. Anyway, I have my application in at several places and plan to keep reminding them of my interest!"

BASIC RESOURCES

For more information about therapy careers, write or phone:

Physical Therapy

> American Physical Therapy Association
> 1156 15th Street NW
> Washington, D.C. 20005

> National Association of Physical Therapy
> 7738 Mount Vernon
> Lemon Grove, California 92045

Occupational Therapy

> American Occupational Therapy Association
> 6000 Executive Boulevard (Suite 200)
> Rockville, Maryland 20852

Music, Art, and Dance Therapy

> American Art Therapy Association
> P.O. Box 11604
> Pittsburgh, Pennsylvania 15228

> American Dance Therapy Association
> 2000 Century Plaza (Suite 230)
> Columbia, Maryland 21044

> National Association for Music Therapy, Inc.
> P.O. Box 610
> Lawrence, Kansas 66044

Recreation Therapy

National Therapeutic Recreation Society
% National Recreation and Parks Association
1601 North Kent Street
Arlington, Virginia 22209

CHAPTER 6

A VARIETY OF HEALTH CARE OCCUPATIONS

The large and still growing health care industry includes many more occupations than those that immediately spring to mind like doctor, nurse, or dentist. Specializations are being developed that have not yet been officially delineated, and the scope and emphasis of many vocations are changing according to the demands of increasingly critical health care consumers. More significantly, these allied health occupations are becoming more and more important as the concept of a teamwork approach to health care delivery becomes prevalent.

The ranks of a variety of these health care occupations are increasingly being filled by women. Several of these occupations require direct patient contact, but most are limited in this respect. All these occupations are vital to the effectiveness and quality of contemporary health care.

In addition to the therapists described in the preceding chapter, health care occupations include pharmacists, respiratory specialists, medical laboratory workers (technologists, technicians, and assistants), medical record administrators, and biostatistics and communications specialists (writers, illustrators, and photographers).

Pharmacy

Americans make about 5 billion trips to the pharmacy each year—and it takes a lot of pharmacists to fill all those prescriptions! Of the approximately 120,000 licensed pharmacists in the United States, more than 25,000 are women—a number anticipated to become even larger in the near future. Women are now more than one-third of all pharmacy students.

184

A pharmacy career can provide a woman, not only with a diverse and challenging professional opportunity, but also with plenty of opportunity for part-time work, as well as substantial financial rewards.

The pharmacist's most obvious function is to dispense prescriptions. In the past, a pharmacist mixed ingredients by hand to form powders, tablets, capsules, and ointments, and the mortar and pestle became the readily recognizable tools of the trade. A pharmacist had to be extremely precise at *all* times since a little too much of a certain ingredient might cost a person his or her life.

Today, however, compounding is only a very small part of a pharmacist's practice, since most drugs are now manufactured in the form in which they are to be used. The modern pharmacist is seen more as a specialist in the science of drugs, and she must understand the use, composition, manufacture, and properties of thousands of drugs as well as their effects on the body. A pharmacist must also know how to test all these medications for strength and purity. Increasingly the pharmacist is being viewed by physicians and dentists as an adviser who is available for current information about drugs, their activity and availability.

Pharmacists work in many settings—hospitals, community drug stores, long-term care facilities, community health clinics, pharmaceutical companies, etc. The Federal Government employs many pharmacists in agencies such as the Public Health Service, Drug Enforcement Ad-

---

FACTS AND FIGURES: PHARMACISTS

- About 120,000 persons worked as licensed pharmacists in 1976.
- Of the more than 90,000 who worked in community pharmacies, more than two-fifths owned their own pharmacies.
- Most of the remaining 30,000 worked for hospitals, pharmaceutical manufacturers, and wholesalers.
- Some were employed by the Federal Government, chiefly in VA hospitals and clinics and the Public Health Service.
- Most towns have at least one pharmacy with one pharmacist or more in attendance. Most pharmacists, however, practice in or near cities and in states with the largest populations.
- Starting salaries for pharmacists generally range from $14,000 to $17,000. In 1975 the average annual starting salary in hospitals and medical centers was $14,600.
- In 1977 the minimum entrance salary in federal agencies for pharmacy graduates with a bachelor's degree was $11,523; most, however, qualified for starting salaries of $14,079.

---

ministration, Food and Drug Administration (FDA), and many other agencies of the Department of Health, Education, and Welfare (HEW).

Hospitals and community drugstores are the largest employers of pharmacists. In hospitals and clinics, pharmacists dispense prescriptions and frequently advise the medical staff on the selection and effect of drugs. The pharmacist is considered one of the principal authorities on the use of medications.

In 1976 more than two-fifths of all pharmacists owned their own pharmacies. In community pharmacies or drugstores pharmacists dispense prescription drugs and are available to consumers for guidance on their proper use; they also sell other health-related items. Many pharmacists handle nonpharmaceutical merchandise such as cosmetics, toys, and stationery supplies. They may also need to hire and supervise personnel. The combination of general merchandise and health-related services requires entrepreneurial know-how as well as pharmaceutical skills. A pharmacist must keep not only general prescription records but detailed records of all legally controlled drugs (stimulants, depressants, etc.) received and dispensed. Some pharmacists use minicomputers to aid in record keeping.

Other Options

For women with "cloak and dagger" instincts, a job as a government pharmaceutical inspector may be an interesting option. These inspectors enforce legal standards where drugs are manufactured. The Food and Drug Administration employs the largest number of drug inspectors; the Drug Enforcement Administration, the FBI, the Internal Revenue Service, and the Commerce Department are other government agencies that employ drug "sleuths." A job as a drug inspector with the FDA can provide a woman with a good opportunity for travel; she will be given thorough training in checking, analysis, and enforcement procedures before being sent out on assignment.

Drug manufacturers are another source of employment. Pharmacists there may work on drug research and development, quality control, or sales. In general, employment trends for pharmacists look favorable through the mid-1980s, with the profession expanding approximately 16.4 percent each year.

Training

There are 72 accredited colleges of pharmacy in the United States. Most pharmacists are graduates of five-year college programs that lead to a Bachelor of Science (BS) or Bachelor of Pharmacy (B Pharm) degree. About a third of the colleges offer six-year advanced degree programs that lead to a Doctor of Pharmacy (Pharm D) degree, which is slightly

GETTING IN, MOVING UP: PHARMACY

Employment opportunities in this lucrative field range from community drugstores, pharmaceutical companies, and hospitals to federal health, food, and drug enforcement agencies. Advanced degrees are necessary for teaching, research, and high-level administrative work. All states require licensure.

---

more prestigious. Any of these degrees qualifies a person for licensure. The several education routes that can be taken include:

- A five-year program at an accredited college of pharmacy leads to a Bachelor of Science degree.
- Two years of preprofessional study at an accredited college or university (including chemistry, organic chemistry, biology, physics, math, economics and social science) plus three years at a college of pharmacy leads to a BS degree.
- A doctoral program consisting of two years of preprofessional study and four years of professional study at a college of pharmacy leads to the PhD degree.

Advanced degrees are necessary for teaching, research, and high-level administrative work. The Pharmacy College Admission Test (PCAT) is usually recommended for admission to colleges of pharmacy.

A license to practice is required in all states—this means passing a state board examination and usually having a specified amount (generally at least six months) of supervised experience or internship under the supervision of a registered pharmacist. Internships are generally served in hospitals or community pharmacies. Most states have reciprocal licensing agreements and many pharmacists are licensed to practice in more than one state.

Specializations in pharmacy include: pharmacology (study of the effects of drugs on the body), pharmaceutical chemistry (study of the physical and chemical properties of drugs in dosage form), pharmacognosy (study of drugs derived from plant or animal sources), hospital pharmacy, clinical pharmacy, and pharmacy administration. A PhD degree is necessary for teaching, advanced research, and administrative work.

Respiratory Therapy

One of the fastest-growing health professions is that of the respiratory specialist, also called respiratory therapist. The respiratory therapist is one of the key people to respond to a hospital emergency room (ER) call.

When this spine-chilling alert summons the cardiopulmonary arrest team, it includes a respiratory therapist who will manage the resuscitation equipment used to save a heart-attack victim's life. Work in the ER is intense; if the patient's breathing stops for longer than three to five minutes, there is little chance of recovery without brain damage. A life is on the line.

Respiratory therapists work with oxygen masks, catheters, nebulizers, monitors, vaporizers, breathing devices, and aerosol medications. Their objective is to assure that the patient receives an adequate oxygen supply along with proper elimination of carbon dioxide from the system. Respiratory therapists work in the ER, at the patient's bedside, and in operating rooms. ER is the most dramatic setting for many of the critical situations requiring inhalation therapy; these include treatment for heart failure, stroke, drowning, head injuries, and drug poisoning.

"I'm 34," says Marcia Flynt, a respiratory therapist who works at an inner-city ER in Chicago, "and I've been doing this work for six years. People wonder how I stay cool, but I don't think I deserve credit for it. I'm a person who by nature enjoys working under pressure and with intense concentration. Besides, you adapt to the work through experience.

"I still go out in the ambulance once in a while when we're short-handed, but that's unusual. I'm being groomed for a supervisor's job, and I need to stay here to coordinate things. A lot can happen at once, and we want to give our utmost to every situation."

Besides emergency aid, respiratory workers give selective care on a day-to-day basis. They work with people who have chronic asthma and emphysema, a disease that has grown to near epidemic proportions. They contribute to diagnostic procedures in the laboratory by obtaining lung secretions for cancer detection; and they employ new techniques in treating gangrene, carbon monoxide poisoning, tetanus, and other disorders. They may also instruct and supervise other members of the respiratory therapy department.

Half the workers in this profession are women, and most are certified members of the American Registry of Respiratory Therapists.

The two basic options that lead to a career as a respiratory therapist are:

GETTING IN, MOVING UP: RESPIRATORY THERAPY

Associate and bachelor's degrees in respiratory therapy are available. The field is one of the fastest-growing in the health professions, and half of the workers in it are women.

• Completion of a two-year AMA-approved respiratory therapy program at a hospital or community or junior college [hospital programs generally lead to a certificate of completion; community and junior college programs lead to an Associate in Applied Science (AAS) degree].
• Completion of a four-year program combining college curriculum and specialized training in respiratory therapy that leads to a Bachelor of Science (BS) degree.

The National Board for Respiratory Therapy of the ARRT administers a qualifying examination. The written section is taken after graduation; the clinical section is taken after completion of one year of clinical experience. Candidates who pass the exam may use the designation registered respiratory therapist (RRT). Registration is recommended since it may be a prerequisite for employment.

Medical Laboratory Work

When considering occupations in medical laboratory work, it's possible to get lost in a maze of titles. In a simple hierarchy according to levels of responsibility from the top down, the chief of a laboratory service is a medical doctor with the title pathologist. Directly under the pathologist is the medical technologist; next, the medical laboratory technician, and finally the clinical laboratory assistant. All medical laboratory workers

---

FACTS AND FIGURES: MEDICAL LABORATORY WORK

• About 240,000 persons worked as medical laboratory workers (technologists, technicians, and assistants) in 1976.
• Most worked in hospital laboratories. Others worked in independent laboratories, physician's offices, clinics, public health agencies, pharmaceutical firms, and research institutions.
• VA hospitals and laboratories employed about 2,400 medical technologists and 2,000 medical laboratory technicians and assistants in 1976. Others worked for the Armed Forces and the Public Health Service.
• Starting salaries for medical technologists in hospitals and medical centers averaged $10,600 in 1976, according to a survey conducted by the University of Texas Medical Branch.
• The Federal Government paid newly graduated medical technologists with bachelor's degrees starting salaries of $9,303 in 1977; those with experience, superior academic achievement, or a year of graduate study entered at $11,523.

GETTING IN, MOVING UP: MEDICAL TECHNOLOGY

A vital contributor to the effectiveness of health care, the medical technologist has little public contact although her knowledge and skills may determine the therapeutic decisions of doctors. Certification gives employment preference in large hospitals and research laboratories.

are engaged in analyzing human tissues, blood, and other body fluids, using such precision instruments as microscopes and automatic analyzers. About 80 percent of the workers are women.

Medical Technologists

The medical technologist operates behind the scenes as one of health care's most valuable, but least visible workers—she is the detective of medicine. With her scientific knowledge and laboratory skills, she can perform complex diagnostic tests—chemical, microscopic, electronic, and bacteriological—to track down disease, parasites, or undesirable matter in body fluids and tissues. Using sophisticated techniques, she can, for example, examine blood for cholesterol or leukemia. Medical technologists know the theories behind the tests they perform and can

THE DAILY GRIND: MEDICAL TECHNOLOGIST

"Sometimes the pathologist gets all the glory in this department, although the lab workers are really doing the nitty-gritty work."

"When the blood supply gets really low (it sometimes does), I begin to worry that if there's a real medical emergency, we may not be able to meet the demand."

"There are times I get bogged down with a lot of supervisory paperwork and I'd rather be doing more hands-on work."

recognize when a test result does not correlate with a diagnosis or prescribed procedure. Physicians have great respect for their knowledge; the astuteness of a technologist can mean life or death to a patient.

Technologists in small laboratories supervise and perform many types of tests; those working in large laboratories tend to specialize in fields such as blood banking, microbiology, and nuclear medicine. Blood-bank technologists, for instance, complete a special certification program that covers a range of topics from red-cell freezing and human genetics to bone marrow transplant and transfusion with "cross-match-incompatible" blood.

Three years of college with 16 semester hours of biology and chemistry (with one course in organic or biochemistry, plus a course in mathematics) are required. One year of clinical training in a hospital laboratory educational program in medical technology approved by the Committee on Allied Health Education and Accreditation of the AMA is needed. Upon completion, a student receives a BS degree from the college and generally a certificate from the hospital. College graduates who wish to be certified must complete the 12-month program in an accredited school of medical technology. Advanced work leading to the master's degree (which may be needed for teaching or research positions) is available at a growing number of universities.

Graduates of approved programs are eligible to take the national examination administered by the Board of Registry of the American Society of Clinical Pathologists. Successful completion gives certification with the professional designation MT(ASCP) and employment preference in large hospitals and research labs.

THE THRILL OF IT ALL: MEDICAL TECHNOLOGIST

"Through a microscope, I see worlds that many people never even dream of—it's fascinating."

"I perform a function that is central and essential in the hospital and to the care of a patient; that's important to me."

"The profession is always changing—I take a lot of continuing education courses to keep up with all the innovations. It's exciting."

Laboratory technology is considered a career-ladder profession with many possibilities for continuing education and advancement on the job.

Medical Laboratory Technicians

A medical laboratory technician's broad background enables her independently to perform routine tests and analyze their results and to conduct special tests and diagnoses—for instance, in clinical chemistry, hematology, urinalysis, microbiology, blood banking, and serology—under a technologist's supervision.

Laboratory technicians may have general training or be specialized. The most familiar specializations are those of the histologic technician, who cuts and processes microthin sections of body tissue for examination by the pathologist; and the cytotechnologist, who screens cell samples for malignant and benign tumorous cells. Chris Hickel describes what she does as a cytotechnologist:

"Once the tissue sample is spread on a slide, fixed with alcohol, and stained with dye, I put it under the microscope, where it's magnified 100 times. I look for abnormalities in size, shape, color, and other cellular characteristics. If everything looks normal, the test is negative. But if there are abnormalities, there may be a malignancy; I must then make an initial diagnosis of the problem on the basis of my knowledge of the patient's medical history.

"After my analysis has been completed, the laboratory supervisor also views the sample, and then the pathologist makes the final diagnosis. This diagnosis can mean the difference between a followup test for the patient a few months later, a request for an immediate biopsy, or plans for radiation therapy or surgery."

Several options leading to a career as a medical laboratory technician are approved by the AMA:

- A two-year program which includes supervised clinical experience and leads to an Associate in Applied Science (AAS) degree.
- An AAS degree program with specific science courses plus a 12-month medical laboratory techniques program.
- An AAS degree program with specific science courses in addition to five years of acceptable laboratory experience. The lab experience must be within seven years immediately preceding the date of application for board examination.

Candidates who have completed an approved program are eligible to take the national examination administered by the American Society of Clinical Pathologists (ASCP). Successful candidates may use the designation medical laboratory technician (MLT). Certification may be necessary for employment in some states and is recommended. Some states

GETTING IN, MOVING UP: MEDICAL LABORATORY TECHNICIAN

Holders of an Associate of Applied Science degree are eligible for certification, which may be necessary for employment in some states. Some states require licensing.

---

also require state licensing examinations as a prerequisite to employment.

Clinical Laboratory Assistants

Clinical laboratory assistants, or certified laboratory assistants, are also an integral part of the laboratory team. They prepare slides, stains, and cultures, and generally lay the groundwork for technical procedures to be performed by others. The assistants are charged with one or more specific tasks such as collecting blood specimens, grouping and typing blood, and analyzing blood and other body fluids. Clinical laboratory assistants are usually graduates of 12-month educational programs, most of which are found in hospitals.

In addition to hospitals and commercial laboratories, job opportunities for medical laboratory workers can be found at health maintenance organizations, pharmaceutical companies, public health departments, and in group health practices.

Medical Record Administration

Results of laboratory tests are just one kind of data entered on a patient's medical record. Other information includes medical history, reports of physical examinations, x-ray findings, pulmonary-function tests, cardiogram tracings, and reports by nurses, physicians, and therapists, and even diet orders. Such records are used for the diagnosis and treatment of illness, as evidence for legal forms and insurance claims, and as a source of data for research and planning. Those responsible for the storage and utilization of these records are medical record administrators, also called medical record librarians. These health care workers are part of the hospital or institutional management staff and are well-paid professionals in growing demand.

Medical record administrators must know how to apply the latest technology of information retrieval and storage, including microfilm, teledata systems, and computers. They are required to analyze record content to compile statistics for the medical staff and hospital administration. They must be able to oversee a department of workers, including medical record technicians, transcriptionists, and clerks.

Basically the programs that lead to a career as a medical records administrator are of two types:

- A four-year college course culminates in a bachelor's degree in medical record science or administration. If you have two or more years of college, you can often enter a medical record administration program at the junior-year level.
- Four years of college with a major in another subject, plus a one-year program, leads to certification in medical record science. Certificate programs are open to students with three years of college. Some affiliated colleges or universities grant a baccalaureate degree to students who complete their fourth college year in an accredited hospital certificate program.

Graduates of degree or certificate programs are eligible to take the national examination given annually by the American Medical Record Association. Those who pass become registered record administrators (RRA). Registration is recommended; it may be required for employment and/or advancement.

Science studies important to medical records work include anatomy, physiology, fundamentals of medical science, medical terminology, and medical record science. Hospital organization and administration, health law, statistics, and data processing are management studies often required for medical record work.

Medical record technicians assist the administrators. The technicians code diseases, operations, and special therapies according to recognized classification systems and enter the codes on medical records. Analyzing records and cross-indexing information are a major part of a technician's job. A technician also types reports, compiles statistics, and reviews records for completeness. She may supervise clerical personnel, work

---

GETTING IN, MOVING UP: MEDICAL RECORD ADMINISTRATION

Graduates of degree or certificate programs are eligible for registration, which is recommended and which may be necessary for employment and/or advancement. Medical record administrators are part of hospital or institutional management staff and are well-paid professionals in growing demand.

GETTING IN, MOVING UP: BIOSTATISTICS

Although no licensing, certification, or registration is required and even an undergraduate degree in an unrelated subject plus some statistical or math background can get you an entry-level job, the higher the degree, the better the starting salary.

---

with a research team, or direct the record department in a small hospital or nursing home. The work requires an Associate of Applied Science degree earned at a community or four-year college or a one to two-year certificate program at a vocational-technical school or hospital.

A medical record clerk, another important member of the medical record team, usually trains on the job and may work under supervision in a large medical record department—typing, filing, and copying statistics; or as the only record person in a small institution, such as a nursing home, where there is personal contact with the patients as well as with other staff members.

Biostatistics

Biostatisticians use math and statistics in a medical context. They plan and conduct surveys and experiments for basic research on morbidity and mortality and on the effectiveness of preventive measures and im-

---

THE DAILY GRIND: BIOSTATISTICIAN

"At times the work is really boring. A lot of the paper and pencil stuff—the preliminaries—can be tedious, though essential."

"I find myself thinking of everything in terms of numbers—sometimes they threaten to overwhelm me."

"It's a very demanding job; your brain is always working—you operate almost like a minicomputer. Sometimes I'm afraid I'll burn out!"

munization techniques. Biostatisticians in analytical work interpret data and summarize findings in tables, charts, and written reports.

Most biostatisticians are employed in government and public-health organizations, although they also work in industry and as private consultants. Biostatisticians must complete four years of college with a major in statistics, physical or biological sciences, or engineering. Master's degree programs in this specialty can be entered with an undergraduate degree in an unrelated subject if you have some statistics or math background or course work. In general, the higher the degree, the better the starting pay. The average salary in biostatistics is higher than that in any other nonsupervisory job.

Required subjects for statistics majors are mathematics through integral calculus, statistical methods, and probability theory. Courses in computer use and technique are helpful. For those with the aptitude, biostatistics is an excellent career. A PhD is necessary for teaching and advanced research.

No licensure, certification or registration is required.

Medical Advertising and Reporting

With health care products, services, and educational programs rapidly expanding, there is also a growing need for specialized communicators and technicians to produce all forms of medical communications. Journals, textbooks, newspapers, films, filmstrips, audiotapes and videotapes, and articles and magazines for the lay public must keep up with the information explosion.

THE THRILL OF IT ALL: BIOSTATISTICIAN

"I get a lot of chances to work on really innovative projects, and I like that challenge."

"I've always been good with numbers and at science, and this way, I've been able to combine and use my best skills."

"It's great when I can manipulate numbers to come up with facts that were previously hidden or unknown. I feel like I've done something really important."

Barbara Robin Slonevsky, vice-president of Creative Annex, a medical print and graphics company in New York City, describes the "bread and butter" of medical advertising and sources of material for medical reporting:

"Advertising and promotion include ads in medical journals, direct-mail promotions that go to physicians, and sales promotions—detailed descriptions of products that salespeople use when they go to a doctor's office.

"Postgraduate courses at medical schools, continuing education courses at universities, monographs [technical papers] published by professional societies, conferences, symposiums, etc., are all grist for the communications mill.

"Medical news publications differ from medical journals in that news articles do not go into depth on a topic; they are like summaries of papers that have been delivered at meetings."

A medical writer's background ideally includes both journalism and medical science education. A staff writer working for a pharmaceutical company or at a public health agency will perform many of the same tasks: writing and editing pamphlets, booklets, and brochures; preparing annual reports, speeches, and lectures; writing news releases; preparing scientific exhibits; and possibly writing scripts for audiovisual programs.

A staff writer must be a team worker, able to deal with senior editors, printers, illustrators, and graphic artists, and willing to accept criticism as well as deliver it tactfully. She must deal accurately with details, keep up to date by reading current literature and attending conferences and technical meetings, and, of course, enjoy writing and dealing with words.

Four-year college programs in medical journalism are offered at the Universities of Illinois, Missouri, Oklahoma, and Texas. Also, two-year programs in technical writing are offered at many community colleges and vocational–technical schools.

Medical Illustration

Accomplished in drawing, painting, and modeling, a medical illustrator must also be familiar with typography, layout, and design. Using extensive artistic talents and scientific knowledge, she can reduce a complicated idea to a simple diagram or a schematic concept. She is especially proficient at drawing from life—a live operation may be her subject.

Some medical illustrators work for publishing and pharmaceutical companies, designing brochures or illustrating medical texts. Most work for large teaching hospitals and research centers; many are employed by large universities with medical schools.

Illustrators use a variety of media to produce drawings or sculptural models of the normal human anatomy as well as pathological body structures. They also prepare graphs and charts, and illustrate articles in

GETTING IN, MOVING UP: MEDICAL ILLUSTRATION

Some medical illustrators work for publishers and pharmaceutical companies, but most are employed in hospitals and research centers. Although college degrees are recommended, no registration or licensure is required.

medical and scientific journals and textbooks; some produce exhibits and visual aids for classrooms and lectures.

Although creativity is important to all artists, accuracy is the most important factor to the medical illustrator since her work is very often used for teaching. To get work, an illustrator needs a varied portfolio to demonstrate her capabilities, whether seeking admission to a training program or a job.

Two to four years of college with courses in art and basic sciences such as anatomy, histology, physics, and zoology are recommended. Very few students are admitted each year to the seven accredited university schools of medical illustration which give certificates of completion, a bachelor's or a master's degree. A medical illustration career demands a talent for perseverance and self-promotion as well as great interest and skill in art.

No certification, registration, or licensure is required.

Biomedical Photography

Skill in the use of both still and motion picture cameras is required of the biomedical or biological photographer. She must often do live shootings—for instance, a heart transplant—and be adept at functioning within the medical setting without disturbing or endangering the patient or medical team.

The biomedical photographer uses all sorts of photographic techniques. For instance, time-lapse photography can provide a detailed analysis of microscopic life, perhaps of chromosomes dividing within a cell. Many photographers will also take photographs of hospital events for the public relations department. Some create educational filmstrips, slide shows, and documentaries and animated films for public and commercial television.

Associate and Bachelor of Science degrees in biomedical photography are available. The options that lead to a career as a biomedical photographer include:

GETTING IN, MOVING UP: BIOMEDICAL PHOTOGRAPHY

For women with photographic skills and an interest in medicine and science, this field offers many job opportunities ranging from working with medical personnel in a hospital to preparing documentaries for public and commercial television.

- A two-year course leading to an Associate in Applied Science degree in biomedical photography.
- A four-year Bachelor of Science degree program in biomedical photography.
- Two years of college including specific science courses plus two years of study at a school of commercial photography or two years' experience as a commercial photographer.
- Two years of college as a prerequisite to an apprenticeship or on-the-job training in a medical center, hospital, or research facility.

The Biological Photographic Association administers a certification examination. Successful candidates may use the designation registered biological photographer (RBP). Generally, registration is not necessary for employment.

Anne Cotter, Pharmacist

A pharmacist who owns and runs her own community practice in an Ohio suburb, Anne Cotter says she likes her job "enormously. . . . My mother had a drygoods store, and I grew up working there on Saturdays, helping with inventory, and so on. It never occurred to me that I *wouldn't* set up my own business some day."

After she completed her formal education, Ms. Cotter worked as a pharmacist for 10 years in chain drugstores. If she hadn't been attracted to community pharmacy, Ms. Cotter thinks she "would have still followed my love for chemistry and stayed in pharmacy. I could have gone into pharmaceutical chemistry, medicinal chemistry, or biochemistry. But I enjoy the people part of my work as much as the science."

When she decided the time was right to go into business for herself, Ms. Cotter hired a drug consulting agency "to tell me what kind of business I could expect in this location. When they determined that it was a good venture, I applied for a federal loan and made a down payment. At first I ran the business by myself. Then, because it was too much for one pharmacist to handle, I asked my husband—he's also a pharmacist but he was working elsewhere—to join me.

"We fill prescriptions, but we also sell health-related items, such as trusses and ace bandages and beanbag weights for physical therapy, plus the usual drugstore items like magazines and chewing gum."

The major part of her day, Ms. Cotter says, "is spent in what some colleges of pharmacy are now calling 'office practice.' This means being available to answer customers' questions about their prescriptions and checking to be sure it's OK for them to take a certain medication. We keep patient medication profiles, and we counsel people on aspects of health care.

"When someone comes into the store, prescription in hand, my first task is to find out if the person is a regular customer and has a drug profile in our files. After determining whether the prescription is compatible with any other medications the person may be taking or with allergies or other known medical idiosyncracies he or she may have, I then fill it as written, type out a label, and make an entry in the medical file.

"Most prescriptions today are filled from stock; that is, they are in ready-to-use form—tablet, ointment, drops, or whatever. We do concoct some ointments and preparations, usually for dermatologists who are trying different things for skin treatments."

Ms. Cotter is always available to answer her customers' questions. Should a medication be taken before or after a meal? What foods if any should be avoided? and so on. She tries to counsel the patient on how to take the drug for its most effective use.

Then, as she details her daily responsibilities, Ms. Cotter says, "I also spend part of the day conversing with physicians in the area about a new product or recommended types of treatment. Pharmacists are very knowledgeable about new drugs and their specifics, and physicians—at least in this part of Ohio—frequently rely on us for information, to supplement manufacturers' promotion material." (Manufacturers' detail men, as they are known, are frequently pharmacists themselves.)

"There's considerable paperwork," Ms. Cotter explains. "All prescriptions must be recorded and kept on file. Narcotics prescribed must be reported to a federal agency at the end of each month. Third-party intervention—prescriptions paid for by union benefits, welfare, or insurance companies—also involves a lot of paperwork."

Knowledge of laws, she points out, is necessary "because pharmacy is heavily regulated by federal, state, and local laws and regulations. You have to know what you're allowed to do and what not, how many of such-and-such kind of pill may be dispensed at one time, which prescriptions you can take over the phone, and so on."

Ms. Cotter and her husband divide duties. She says that "it's a lot easier sharing the responsibility. We also have a very reliable housekeeper. I have never felt that we deprived our children of anything, including time. I think we've learned to make good use of our time together so that we don't spend it doing meaningless things, and the children seem to be all the better for it—there's no overcoddling or overprotecting. They are free when they get home from school to spend time alone, and each of them is capable of putting a meal on the table."

Keeping up with new developments is essential. "Continuing education for pharmacists is required by law in only a few states at this time. Nevertheless, it's still very important to read trade and professional journals and literature, as well as to attend lectures, seminars, and training sessions. For example, a seminar is coming up in a couple of weeks on what considerations a pharmacist should use when selecting an over-the-counter preparation for a cough, cold, or allergy. It will be given in two two-hour sessions, and I'll arrange to have the store pay for one of us to attend."

Ms. Cotter advises future pharmacists: "First you have to believe that drugs serve a good purpose in life and are part of total health care, regardless of what particular line of pharmacological practice you follow —manufacturing, research, drug sales, hospital work, or community pharmacy. As to what line to choose, your personality helps determine that. If you don't enjoy dealing with people face to face, the retail end of running a business may not be for you. Also if you do not want the day-in and day-out responsibility of running a business, working for a chain or in a hospital practice might be better.

"Plenty of jobs are around for people who are willing to relocate. Naturally, some areas are saturated—for instance, cities that have two or three colleges of pharmacy—but there seem to be jobs for everyone, especially if you're willing to go a short distance out of the metropolitan areas."

"As for me," Ms. Cotter happily proclaims, "it's a very comfortable way of life. I know my customers, and I feel very useful and connected with the community. I really have a very pleasing practice."

BASIC RESOURCES

For more information on the careers discussed in this chapter, write or phone:

Respiratory/Inhalation Therapy

American Association for Respiratory Therapy
7411 Hines Place
Dallas, Texas 75235

Laboratory Technologists, Technicians, and Assistants

> American Medical Technologists
> 710 Higgins Road
> Park Ridge, Illinois 60068

> American Society for Medical Technology
> 5555 West Loop South (Suite 200)
> Bellaire, Texas 77401

Medical Record Administration

> American Medical Record Association
> John Hancock Center (Suite 1850)
> Chicago, Illinois 60611

Biostatistics

> American Statistical Association
> 806 15th Street NW (Suite 640)
> Washington, D.C. 20005

> Biometric Society
> P.O. Box 269, Benjamin Franklin Station
> Washington, D.C. 20044

Communications (Writing, Photography, Illustration, etc.)

> American Medical Writers Association
> 5272 River Road (Suite 290)
> Bethesda, Maryland 20016

> Health Sciences Communications Association
> P.O. Box 79
> Millbrae, California 94030

Pharmacy

> American Association of Colleges of Pharmacy
> Office of Student Affairs
> 4630 Montgomery Avenue (Suite 201)
> Bethesda, Maryland 20014

> American Pharmaceutical Association
> 2215 Constitution Avenue NW
> Washington, D.C. 20037

Education for Allied Health Centers

Department of Allied Health Evaluation
American Medical Association
535 North Dearborn Street
Chicago, Illinois 60610

CHAPTER 7

EDUCATION AND TRAINING

Deciding which health career you'd really like to enter is only the first step. As a prospective health care professional, you must consider many factors. For students entering vocational training programs, careful evaluation of a program is essential since future employment will greatly depend on the type and quality of training received. For students applying to professional school, admissions requirements and tests must be dealt with. How to finance an education is a problem that all students will face.

In this chapter you'll find hints on how to evaluate training programs and apply to professional schools, as well as the basics of financial aid. And for those of you who are still unsure about which health career to pursue, the discussion on volunteering will give you some ideas on how to get additional exposure to many health professions.

Medical and Dental Schools

Deciding to go to medical or dental school is one thing; getting in is another. You'll have to contend with course requirements, letters of recommendation, entrance exams, and a good deal of soul searching. These barriers are not insurmountable, but the competition is keen. It takes a lot of plain hard work and perseverance just to gain admission. The following basic details about entrance exams and admissions requirements will help prepare you.

Medical School

Say MCAT to any premed student, and chances are you will inspire total terror. The New Medical College Admission Test (New MCAT) is administered twice a year (May and October) in colleges around the country. It is usually taken first during the spring of the junior year in college. When you register to take the test, you must indicate the schools to which you want your scores sent. Therefore, you must decide which medical schools you are interested in attending *before* you take the MCAT.

Instituted in the spring of 1977, the New MCAT is a day-long exam, with both morning and afternoon sessions. It is divided into four sub-tests: reading skills, quantitative skills, science knowledge, and scientific problems.

The MCAT is simply a method of supplying schools with a standardized measure of academic ability and achievement that can be compared on a nationwide basis. As with most standardized testing, the importance placed on MCAT scores varies from school to school. Generally, medical schools place the most emphasis on college grades, especially in science courses. Letters of recommendation, particularly from your college premedical committee, and personal interviews also play important roles. Because of the large number of applications they receive each year, medical schools are becoming increasingly selective in granting personal interviews. If you are invited for an interview, you can assume that the school is seriously considering you.

Medical schools have very high admissions requirements, which of course vary among the schools. You may find yourself applying to from 10 to 15 (or more) schools. The percentage of students actually admitted is small compared to the total number of applications received. Since

---

MORE MEDICAL SCHOOL INFORMATION

The Association of American Medical Colleges (AAMC) publishes *Medical School Requirements: USA and Canada*. This guide contains an alphabetical listing of all accredited medical schools in the United States and Canada, as well as information on tuition, admissions requirements, factors schools consider in selecting candidates, and other useful information. It is revised annually.

Your college premed office can probably loan you a copy. Or you can purchase one for $5 by writing:

Association of American Medical Colleges
Attention: Memberships and Subscriptions
1 Dupont Circle NW
Washington, D.C. 20036

AMERICAN MEDICAL COLLEGE APPLICATION SERVICE

The Association of American Medical Colleges has set up a nonprofit centralized application processing service for applications to medical schools. Called the American Medical College Application Service (AMCAS), it offers the convenience of allowing you to submit only one set of application materials and transcripts regardless of the number of AMCAS schools to which you apply. If you are applying to any of the more than 80 AMCAS schools, you simply fill out a master form, which will be sent along with your MCAT scores and college grades to whichever AMCAS school(s) you indi-cate. (AMCAS does not, however, duplicate recommendations, which must be sent directly to each school.)

Although AMCAS is convenient, it has two drawbacks: expense and limited partici-pation. The cost is $10 for one school and increases $5 for each additional school until the fifth one; after the fifth school, each additional school costs $10. Although most state universities are registered with AMCAS, many schools (including Harvard, Boston, New York University, Johns Hopkins, and Yale) are not. You must apply directly to any non-AMCAS school.

For more information, registration forms, and a list of AMCAS schools, see your premedical adviser or write or phone:

American Medical College Application Service
c/o Association of American Medical Colleges
1 Dupont Circle NW (Suite 200)
Washington, D.C. 20036

competition for admission is intense, it stands to reason that the better qualified you are, the better your chances will be.

Undergraduate preparation is extremely important. Most medical schools require a bachelor's degree, although some accept three years of college if minimum course requirements have been met. Regardless of your major, you *must* take at least one year each of organic chemistry, inorganic chemistry, general biology or zoology, general physics, and English. Physics may be deferred until your senior year since you won't be tested on it in the MCAT. Some schools consider it "desirable" to take some advanced science courses, and it may be advisable for you to do so. Mathematics, social science, and liberal arts courses are also help-ful since the emphasis now is on a broad educational background rather than the strictly scientific material that is covered in medical school itself.

Extracurricular activities do not play a decisive role in the admissions decision. However, experience in a hospital volunteer program, college

FOR STUDENTS OF OSTEOPATHY

The American Association of Colleges of Osteopathic Medicine has established a centralized application service (AACOMAS) similar to the AMCAS medical and dental school service.

For more information, write or phone:

American Association of Colleges of Osteopathic Medicine
Director, Department of Educational Services
5720 Montgomery Lane (Suite 609)
Washington, D.C. 20014

---

premed society, scientific research project, etc., can provide you with valuable experience, good sources for letters of recommendation, and that little "extra" that may help your chances.

Your college premed adviser can help you plan your course sequence and suggest medical schools. Your adviser is also a good source of information about the MCAT. You can obtain an MCAT information booklet listing test centers, sample questions, and a registration form by writing:

MCAT Registration
American College Testing Program
P.O. Box 414
Iowa City, Iowa 52240

Dental School

The dental equivalent of the MCAT, the Dental Admission Test (DAT) is administered twice a year (October and April) in colleges throughout the country. As with the MCAT, the DAT is generally taken at least once during the spring of the junior year in college (many students take it twice—in October and April). When you register to take the test, you must indicate the schools to which you'd like your scores sent.

The DAT is a day-long exam that is divided into five areas: natural science (biology and both inorganic and organic chemistry), reading comprehension (dental and basic science), verbal ability, quantitative ability, and the Perceptual Motor Ability Test (PMAT), which consists of two- and three-dimensional problem solving.

Schools place varying degrees of emphasis on DAT scores. However, for all schools, the DAT scores are only one factor in evaluating the admission potential of a candidate. As with medical school admission,

DENTAL SCHOOL APPLICATION SERVICE

The American Association of Dental Schools Application Service (AADSAS) acts as a clearinghouse for students applying to dental schools. Implemented in 1972, this service provides a student with the opportunity of applying to any of its subscriber schools by submitting one standardized application and one transcript. The fee is $30 for the first school and $5 for each additional school. Currently 45 of the 58 American dental schools subscribe to this service. You must apply directly to any nonregistered school.

For more information, see your predental adviser or write or phone:

American Association of Dental Schools
Application Service
P.O. Box 4000
Iowa City, Iowa 52240

letters of recommendation and personal interviews may play important roles. Generally, most emphasis is placed on a strong undergraduate academic record.

The competition for admission to dental school is tough and getting tougher. Dental schools receive a large volume of applications, and only a small percentage of applicants can be admitted. In addition, dental schools have become increasingly selective in granting personal interviews.

An overwhelming majority of students entering dental school have a bachelor's degree, although some schools will accept three, in some cases even two, years of college if the necessary course requirements have been met. Regardless of your major, you must take a minimum of one year each of English, organic chemistry, inorganic chemistry, biology or zoology, and physics. (Physics is not included on the DAT and may be deferred until your senior year.) Dental college emphasis is strongly shifting toward the production of patient-oriented, broadly educated health professionals, and the inclusion of behavioral and social sciences as well as liberal arts courses in your undergraduate curriculum is important. Some advanced science courses may also be desirable, as well as extracurricular activities such as volunteering in a dental clinic or working on a scientific research project.

The DDS (Doctor of Dental Surgery) and DMD (Doctor of Dental Medicine) require three, three and a half, or four years of dental school. Further specialization generally requires a minimum of two years of advanced study.

"ATTENTION, DENTAL STUDENTS . . ."

The American Association of Dental Schools publishes the guide *Admission Requirements of US and Canadian Dental Schools,* which contains details about requirements for application and admission to accredited dental schools. It also includes general career information, sources of financial aid, explanation of dental curricula, costs of education at each school, and more.

Most college predental offices have this volume on file for students to consult. It can also be purchased for $7.50 by writing:

American Association of Dental Schools
1625 Massachusetts Avenue NW
Washington, D.C. 20036

Caution: Some borderline premed students view dentistry as an alternate career and apply simultaneously for admission to both dental and medical schools. Medical and dental schools do not look kindly on students using dental school admission as a lever for getting into medical school later. In general, dental colleges find that students who have had their hearts set on a medical career and use dentistry as a fallback are less happy as students and professionals. Dental schools generally would rather have applicants who have been consistently "predental" rather than "disappointed doctors." However, they are also aware that many successful dental practitioners were former premedical students. There is no hard and fast policy, but you can be certain that your application will come under very strict and careful scrutiny if you are in this position.

Your college predental adviser can help you plan your course sequence as well as give you valuable advice and information about dentistry and the DAT. You can also receive information and a registration form for the DAT by writing:

American Dental Association
Division of Educational Measurements
211 East Chicago Avenue
Chicago, Illinois 60611

Evaluating Vocational Training Programs for Health Careers

When deciding to pursue a career in any field, be sure you know as much as possible about where *you* are going. Explore your occupational

ALLIED HEALTH EDUCATION DIRECTORY

If you are considering a career in an allied health field, a very valuable source book is the *Allied Health Education Directory,* published by the American Medical Association (AMA). This annual publication provides a complete listing of AMA-accredited training programs in allied medical education. It also contains statistical data and information on the accreditation process as well as a listing of 23 occupations, including job descriptions, education essentials, and other important information.

The 530-page directory is available for $10; write:

American Medical Association
Order Unit
535 North Dearborn Street
Chicago, Illinois 60610

goals and the availability of future jobs; then, find the educational program that fits your specific goal. It is necessary to be cautious especially when considering vocational training programs. Don't underestimate the importance of choosing the academic route that will best meet the requirements of the job and prepare you for the licensing, certification, or registration regulations that may be essential to your future employment.

Visit the schools that interest you. Most schools will send you information about specific programs so that you can get an idea of what they have to offer before you schedule your visit. When evaluating and selecting a vocational school, start with the most important question—Is the school accredited? Also inquire whether the school provides clinical training or is affiliated with a hospital. Does the school have a placement or career counseling service? How successful has it been at placing graduates? How large are classes? The more questions you ask, the more you will know about the school.

Training programs are not limited to vocational institutions. Graduate schools at universities are often broader in scope than their names imply. For instance, a school of medicine may also include a department of nursing education, school of dental science, and educational programs for dental hygienists and public health administrators. If a school doesn't have what you're looking for, it's a good bet that someone in the admissions office can steer you in the right direction.

Information about the necessary academic requirements and listings of training programs that meet the standards of a specific profession can

VOLUNTEERING AND CAREER EXPLORATION

Reading is a fine way to get an overall view of the health professions, but an excellent way to get some first-hand exposure is through hospital volunteer work.

People of all ages and from all walks of life volunteer to work in hospitals. Many students find hospital volunteering a valuable means of exploring career possibilities, for it provides a chance to work within a structured health care setting and become at least somewhat familiar with or accustomed to the discipline, pressure, and emotional and physical demands made on workers in all the health professions.

Volunteer assignments supplement various hospital staff jobs. Depending on your interests and skills and/or the available openings, as a volunteer you may work in the patients' library or the gift shop, you may spend your time visiting and reading to or translating for patients, or you may help out in the rehabilitation wards. The possibilities are numerous.

You will usually be expected to devote three to four hours one day a week to the hospital and to take your job *seriously.* As a volunteer, you will be instructed in hospital rules, regulations, and ethics as well as given any specific training you may need for your assignment. The hospital will be investing valuable staff time in this orientation and training; volunteering is not something to be taken lightly. (You might consider drawing up a "contract" between you and your supervisor which specifies your hours, exact duties, responsibilities, and job description.)

Volunteering is also not a training program or a direct lever for future employment in a hospital or other health care facility. In fields other than health care, volunteering might be a stepping stone to paid employment, but the nature of health care makes this possibility unrealistic. Practically every health care occupation requires some formal educational preparation and/or training—without it, employment is virtually impossible. Volunteering is not an adequate substitute. Volunteering, however, can acquaint you with the large numbers and varieties of jobs and skills involved in running a hospital and providing effective patient care. Volunteering may lead you to decide definitely on a health career, or it may convince you that it is not for you.

If you would like to be a hospital volunteer, contact the director of volunteer services at the hospital in which you would like to work. Volunteers also work in social agencies, community centers, and mental health centers. If you have time or a particular skill to donate to an organization, but don't know how to start, try the Yellow Pages under "Organizations," or "Associations," or specific subject headings relating to public services. Sometimes, local libraries carry listings of volunteer opportunities or can provide you with information on how to find a volunteer assignment in your community. Your community may have its own volunteer placement bureau. You can also contact the national volunteer associations that sponsor a great many types of programs in different areas and fields. Two good sources of information are:

ACTION
806 Connecticut Avenue NW
Washington, D.C. 20006

Association of Junior Leagues of America, Inc.
825 Third Avenue
New York, New York 10022

---

be obtained by writing to the various professional societies listed at the end of each chapter of this Guide.

Public health departments, both local and federal, can also inform you about approved training programs. Write to your Regional Medical Program Coordinator (check your phone directory under United States Government—HEW, Department of; or write the Public Health Service, 200 Independence Avenue SW, Washington, D.C. 20201) for Public Health Service Publication 75, "Directory of State, Territorial, and Regional Health Authorities."

Caution: Check the job market and future employment projections *before* acquiring specific training. Employment opportunities will vary according to geographical location, local financial resources, and a number of other variables. Some training institutions have had difficulty placing all their graduates. For instance, those who invest time and money in training as paraprofessionals and physicians' assistants sometimes find that these jobs are not available in their geographical areas or, in some cases, are not legally sanctioned. A state employment service, hospital association, or health manpower agency will be able to advise you about your local employment situation.

Dollars and Sense—Ins and Outs of Financial Aid

Even before you've gotten over the hurdles of college entrance exams, program evaluation, and admissions officers, and later when you've *finally* been accepted into professional or vocational school, you'll find yourself asking, "How do I pay for all this?" (This question is usually accompanied by a tremor in the voice and an expression of panic on the face.) Faced with apparently astronomical fees for tuition, books, and living expenses, many students begin to feel that while they have just won the battle, they may lose the war!

The costs of obtaining a medical or dental education are high and steadily soaring. Though this trend is unfortunately expected to continue, the high cost of education should not deter you from a career in

FEDERAL AND PROFESSIONAL ORGANIZATION AID SOURCES

Federal Programs

Armed Forces Health Professions Scholarship Program. (Medicine, dentistry, osteopathy, optometry, pharmacy, podiatry, and veterinary medicine.) Pays tuition and supplies money for books and fees, plus a monthly stipend. Recipients are obligated to serve a year of active duty in the Armed Forces for each year they participate in the program. A minimum of two years of service is required.

Health Resources Administration. (Grants-in-aid for nursing students.) Grants include aid to students in diploma, associate, or baccalaureate degree programs. Aid is also available for professional nurses studying for their doctorate degree and to those who are preparing for teaching, supervisory, or clinical specialty positions.

United States Public Health Service. Program similar to that offered by the Armed Forces (see above). Does not provide money for books and fees, but monthly stipend is larger.

Health Professions Student Loan Program. (Medicine, dentistry, osteopathy, optometry, pharmacy, podiatry, and veterinary medicine.) Students can borrow a maximum of $3,500 a year; 3 percent interest on unpaid balance begins at time loan becomes repayable, which is one year after graduation or termination of full-time study. Repayment may be extended over a 10-year period. Note: If a borrower agrees to serve at least two years in a physician-shortage area, the government will pay 60 percent of the outstanding principal and interest on any education loan. It will pay an additional 25 percent of the balance for a third year of such service. A similar loan program is available for nursing students.

Guaranteed Student Loan Program. Up to $2,500 may be borrowed from a bank or savings and loan association. Loans are guaranteed by the Federal Government; repayment begins within a year after graduation or termination of studies.

---

health service. Numerous sources of financial aid are available. Be assured that very few people can meet such costs without turning to outside assistance; more than half of all students currently enrolled in medical or dental school receive aid from scholarship and loan programs. (Other financial sources include gifts and loans from family and friends, or student's own earnings.)

Professional school curricula are very demanding; therefore, students are strongly advised *not* to work during the first two years of school

Professional Associations

American Association for Inhalation Therapy. This group administers the Mead Johnson Fellowships for advanced education in inhalation therapy. Five awards of $500 are given annually.

American Association of Medical Assistants. Students may borrow up to $300 interest-free. Repayment may be extended over a two-year period. Note: Payments are returned in full if a student works for two years in the field of medical assisting after graduation.

American Fund for Dental Education. The Guaranteed Loan Program for undergraduates provides up to $3,000 a year for a four-year program and up to $3,500 per year for a three-year program; graduate students may borrow up to $3,000 a year (maximum of $12,000). Interest of 8 percent must be paid annually while a student is in school. Repayment begins four months after graduation or termination of studies and may be extended over a 10 year period.

American Medical Association. The AMA Education and Research Foundation Student Loan Guarantee Program provides up to $1,500 a fiscal year with a maximum allowable sum of $10,000 over a seven-year period. Applicants must be medical students, interns, or residents enrolled in full-time study/training and must show evidence of financial need. Loans become payable after medical training is completed or interrupted.

American Medical Record Association. A loan fund is available for students in medical record librarian and medical record technician programs. Students in library programs can borrow up to $1,500; students in technician programs, up to $500. A 3 percent interest charge on the unpaid balance begins the second year after graduation. The interest is 4 percent the third year after graduation and thereafter. Repayment may be extended over a four-year period.

American Osteopathic Association. Each year 25 awards of $1,500 are given to entering osteopathic students.

National Association of American Business Clubs. A number of scholarships are awarded annually to students of physical, occupational, speech, and hearing therapy in AMA-approved schools.

Information Sources

For more information on these and other programs, see your financial aid officer or write:

Federal Programs

Bureau of Health Manpower
Public Health Service Scholarship Program
Student Assistance Branch
9000 Rockville Pike
Bethesda, Maryland 20014

Department of Health, Education, and Welfare
Health Resources Administration
Nursing Student Loan Program
Division of Nursing
Bethesda, Maryland 20014

Armed Forces Programs

American Osteopathic Association
Air Force and Navy Scholarships
Director, Washington Office
Cafritz Building (Suite 1009)
1625 I Street NW
Washington, DC 20006

Department of the Air Force
HQ ATC/RSOSR
Randolph AFB, Texas 78148

Department of the Army
(DASG-PTP)
Washington, D.C. 20314

Department of the Navy
(Code 3174)
Bureau of Medicine and Surgery
Washington, D.C. 20372

Allied Health Professions

American Association for Inhalation Therapy
Research and Education Fund Committee
3554 Ninth Street
Riverside, California 92501

American Association of Medical Assistants
AMA Endowment
200 East Ohio Street
Chicago, Illinois 60611

American Medical Record Association
Foundation of Record Education
875 North Michigan Avenue (Suite 1850)
Chicago, Illinois 60611

National Association of American Business Clubs
Scholarship Program Committee
P.O. Box 5127
High Point, North Carolina 27262

Medicine, Dentistry, Osteopathy

American Association of Dental Schools
1625 Massachusetts Avenue NW
Washington, D.C. 20036

American Dental Association
Division of Educational Measurements
1625 Massachusetts Avenue NW
Washington, D.C. 20036

American Fund for Dental Education
211 East Chicago Avenue (Suite 1630)
Chicago, Illinois 60611

American Medical Association
Medical Scholarship and Loan Program
535 North Dearborn Street
Chicago, Illinois 60610

American Osteopathic Association
Office of Education
212 East Ohio Street
Chicago, Illinois 60611

General

Graduate and Professional School Financial Aid Service
P.O. Box 2614
Princeton, New Jersey 08540

---

when most, if not all, time is spent preparing for or attending lectures and labs. Many students work during the summer; some also are able to work during the last two years of school.

Scholarships and loans are granted primarily by individual schools and the Federal Government. Your school's financial aid office can sug-

FINANCIAL AID FOR MINORITY STUDENTS

Many agencies and foundations are working in the health fields to provide resource materials, career information, and financial aid to needy minority students. Here are just a few of them:

American Fund for Dental Education. This group sponsors Dental Scholarships for Undergraduate Disadvantaged Minority Students, including in particular blacks, Mexican Americans, American Indians, and Puerto Ricans. Write or phone:

> American Fund for Dental Education
> 211 East Chicago Avenue
> Chicago, Illinois 60611

Aspira of America. This national Puerto Rican self-help organization has a "Health Careers Program" that provides counseling and financial assistance to students entering the health professions. For more information, write or phone:

> Aspira of America
> 22 East 54th Street
> New York, New York 10022

National Chicano Health Organization. Information and services are provided to Chicano students pursuing careers in the health professions. Write:

> National Chicano Health Organization
> 827 Sherman Street
> Denver, Colorado 80204

National Medical Association. Resource materials on the field of health care for minorities are offered in addition to a financial aid program for disadvantaged students. For more details, write or phone:

> National Medical Association
> 2109 E Street NW
> Washington, D.C. 20037

National Medical Fellowships. Financial awards are granted to first- and second-year medical students from minority groups underrepresented in the profession. Contact:

> National Medical Fellowships
> 3935 Elm Street
> Downers Grove, Illinois 60515

Robert Wood Johnson Foundation. Financial assistance for women and minority students (in particular from rural areas) who are interested in the medical and dental fields is provided. Contact:

Robert Wood Johnson Foundation
Forrestal Center
P.O. Box 2316
Princeton, New Jersey 08540

Additional information on scholarships, fellowships, grants and loans can be obtained from the *College Blue Book* (Macmillan Information, New York, New York,
1977), available for reference in most college libraries and/or financial aid offices.
Additional information can also be obtained by writing:

Association of American Medical Colleges
Minority Student Opportunities in
U.S. Medical Schools
1 Dupont Circle NW
Washington, D.C. 20036

---

gest additional outside sources such as professional or philanthropic
organizations and other unexpected sources of aid, as well as offer information on government loans. If you can demonstrate need, you can receive funds from more than one source; be sure, however, to report to
each potential source all monies you have already been awarded.

Although many professional schools have their own scholarship or
tuition remission programs, these monies are scarce and usually go to
only the neediest students; therefore, many students turn to government
aid programs which offer scholarships, grants, and loans. These pro-

---

WHERE TO FIND OUT MORE

Library reference books can be very helpful. Resource books with chapters on health
personnel include the *Medical and Health Information Directory* (Gale Research Company, Detroit, Michigan, 1977). You can also get helpful pamphlets and periodical
newsletters free of charge from both professional organizations and government agencies. For instance, you can ask to receive the monthly *Allied Health Education Newsletter* and the 100-page booklet titled *Education for Allied Health Careers* from the
Department of Allied Health Evaluation of the American Medical Association (535
North Dearborn Street, Chicago, Illinois 60610), and the *Health Resources News* from
the Bureau of Health Resources Administration (Parklawn Building, Rockwell, Maryland
20852).

grams are quite comprehensive and attractive, and aid is more easily attainable from them than from school funds.

A variety of financial aid programs including scholarships, grants, work-study programs and loans is available for students in the allied health fields. Professional associations for the individual fields are good sources of financial aid and/or information. Many government loan and scholarship programs also include the allied health professions.

Many state governments also provide good financial aid, but these programs vary from state to state. For information on programs available in a particular state, write to the Superintendent of Higher Education in that state. Most libraries have directories of government agencies and officials listing their addresses.

Lending institutions and banks also provide educational loans that do not come under federal supervision. These loans don't offer the same

---

MORE HELP WANTED?

The organizations listed throughout this Guide are all sources of information on their fields. Some provide brief bibliographies of materials about careers, whereas others offer free or inexpensive pamphlets.

You might also find the following publications helpful. Since you probably won't find them in your corner bookstore, we have included current price and ordering information. Keep in mind that availability and prices change. (If ordering, you should specify "current issue" and request a list of other related publications.) You might try to get them first through your local public library—it's a good (and free) source of information. If it doesn't have the material in its collection, it can usually borrow them for you from another library through interlibrary loan systems; some libraries will even order materials at your request.

Career Information

Barron's Guide to Medical, Dental, and Allied Health Science Careers, 3rd revised edition. Dr. Saul Wischnitzer. 1977. (Available for $4.95 from Barron's Educational Series, Inc., 113 Crossways Park Drive, Woodbury, New York 11797.)
Careers in Medicine for the New Woman, Carol Jochnowitz. New York: Franklin Watts, 1978; $6.90 hardcover.
A Guide to Health Careers for Minorities, Women, Rural Youth, 1977. (Single copy free from National Health Council, 1740 Broadway, New York, New York 10019.)
Introduction to the Health Professions, 2nd edition. Edited by Anne S. Allen. St. Louis: C. V. Mosby Company, 1976.

On the Health Scene. Mary Lou Lambing and Mary Frances King. New York: Springer Publishing Co., 1976.

Thirteen Nurses What They Say... undated (Single copy free from National Student Nurses' Association, 10 Columbus Circle [Room 2330], New York, New York 10019.)

What Is a Nurse-Midwife? (Available for 25 cents from American College of Nurse-Midwives, 1012 14th Street NW [Suite 801], Washington, D.C. 20005.)

"Why would a girl go into medicine?" Medical Education in the United States: A Guide for Women. 1974. Margaret A. Campbell. (Available for $3.95 from Feminist Press, Clearinghouse on Women's Studies, P.O. Box 334, Old Westbury, New York 11568.)

Women and the Health Professions

Complaints and Disorders, the Sexual Politics of Sickness. Barbara Ehrenreich and Dierdre English. 1973. (Available for $2.50 from Feminist Press, P.O. Box 334, Old Westbury, New York 11568.)

Dance Therapy: Narrative Case Histories of Therapy Sessions with Six Patients. Helen Lefco. Chicago: Nelson-Hall Company, 1974; $9.95 hardcover.

Doctors Wanted. No Women Need Apply. Sexual Barriers in the Medical Profession, 1835–1975. Mary Roth Walsh. New Haven: Yale University Press, 1977; $15 hardcover.

Expanding Horizons for Nurses. Bonnie Bullough and Vern Bullough, editors. New York: Springer Publishing Company, 1976; $9.95 ppr.

A History of Women in Medicine from Earliest Days to the Early 19th Century. 1977 reprint of 1938 edition. Kate Hurd-Meade. New York: AMS Press; $49 hardcover.

Opening the Medical Profession to Women. Autobiographical Sketches. Elizabeth Blackwell. 1977. (Available for $4.75 from Schocken Books, 200 Madison Avenue, New York, New York 10016.)

Witches, Midwives, and Nurses: A History of Women Healers. Barbara Ehrenreich and Deirdre English. 1972. (Available for $1.95 from Feminist Press, P.O. Box 334, Old Westbury, New York 11568.)

Woman Doctor. The Internship of a Modern Woman. Florence Haseltine and Yvonne Yaw. Boston: Houghton Mifflin Company, 1976; $8.95 hardcover.

Bibliographies

Careers in Health and Medicine — Career Source Bibliography, Vol. 6, No. 4, November 1977. (Available for 75 cents from American Personnel and Guidance Association, 1607 New Hampshire Avenue NW, Washington, D.C. 20009.)

Health Manpower. An Annotated Bibliography, rev. edition. Barbara I. Bloom. 1976. (Available for $4.50 [$3.60 members] from American Hospital Association, 840 North Lake Shore Drive, Chicago, Illinois 60611.)

easy repayment plans as government loans; however, they can be a good source of aid. Shop around to make sure you get the best available plan.

A sampling of aid programs currently available follows, including a brief bibliography of some financial aid literature as well as program organization addresses. One final word—the price is high but *not* impossible. There are no easy answers or guides to tell you how to get financial aid. But that doesn't mean that money isn't available. The money *is* there —somewhere. You must work hard to find it. There are innumerable ways to finance an education; success depends largely on thorough research and your own initiative and perseverance. Start *early,* familiarize yourself with all the plans and requirements—plan ahead.

BASIC RESOURCES: FINANCIAL AID

Barron's Guide to Medical, Dental and Allied Health Sciences Careers, revised edition. Dr. Saul Wischnitzer. 1977. (Available for $4.95 from Barron's Educational Series, Inc., 113 Crossways Park Drive, Woodbury, New York 11797.)

College Blue Book, library reference. New York: Macmillan Information, 1977.

Helping Hands: A Selected Bibliography of Financial Aid for Health Careers. (Available for $1 from the American Medical Association, 535 North Dearborn Street, Chicago, Illinois 60610.)

Need a Lift? (Available for 50 cents from the American Legion Educational and Scholarship Program, Indianapolis, Indiana 46206.)

Where to Get Health Career Information. (Free from the National Health Council, 1740 Broadway, New York, New York 10019.)

The following publications are available from the Health Resources Administration (HRA):

How Health Professions Students Finance Their Education, DHEW Publication (HRA) 74-13

How to Pay for Your Health Career Education, DHEW Publication (HRA) 74-8

How to Pay for Your Health Career Education: A Guide for Minority Students, DHEW Publication (HRA) 74-8

To obtain the HRA publications listed above write:

Health Resources Administration
Information Office
NIH Building 31, Room 5B-63
9000 Rockville Pike
Bethesda, Maryland 20014

Allied Health Professions: Special Project Grants. (Available from Department of Health, Education, and Welfare, Public Health Service, National Institutes of Health, Bethesda, Maryland 20014.)

Directory of Financial Aids for Women, library reference. Gail Ann Schlachter. Los Angeles, California: Reference Service Press, 1978.

Guide to NIH Programs and Awards. (Available from National Institutes of Health, Division of Research Grants, Westwood Building, 5333 Westbard Avenue, Bethesda, Maryland 20016.)

HEW Fact Sheet: Five Federal Financial Aid Programs, Publication (OE) 75-17907. (Available from Department of Health, Education, and Welfare, Office of Education, Washington, D.C. 20202.)

For Women Only

Several scholarship and loan programs have eligibility requirements that limit them to women. Here are a few:

American Medical Women's Association. Loans of up to $500 are given to women medical students toward payments of tuition fees and expenses. Interest is 4 percent and begins six months after graduation or termination of studies. Address inquiries to:

> American Medical Women's Association
> Chairman, Scholarship Loan Committee
> 1740 Broadway
> New York, New York 10019

Association of American Women Dentists. The Gillette Hayden Memorial program provides loans of up to $2,000 to assist women dental students in completing their education. Applicants must be third- or fourth-year students and must demonstrate financial need. Contact:

> Association of American Women Dentists
> 435 North Michigan Avenue (Suite 1717)
> Chicago, Illinois 60611

Association of University Women. Several programs are sponsored by this group. Contact:

> American Association of University Women
> Fellowships Office
> 2401 Virginia Avenue NW
> Washington, D.C. 20037

Maternity Center Association. The Hazel Corbin Assistance Fund scholarship provides funds for RNs enrolled in approved nurse-midwife programs who plan to use their skills clinically. Awards are generally in the form of monthly stipends; maximum $200 monthly. Contact:

Maternity Center Association
48 East 92d Street
New York, New York 10028

Women's Medical Association of the City of New York. Women physicians from any country are eligible to apply for the Mary Putnam Jacobi fellowship, which provides funds for postgraduate medical education, research, or clinical investigation. Contact:

Women's Medical Association of the City of New York
Chairman, MPJF Committee
1300 York Avenue
New York, New York 10021

An excellent source of information of financial aids available to women in all fields is the *Directory of Financial Aids for Women* by Gail Ann Schlachter (Reference Service Press, Los Angeles, California, 1978). It contains a listing of scholarships, fellowships, loans, grants, internships, and awards and prizes designated primarily or exclusively for women. It also lists women's credit unions, sources of state educational benefits, and reference sources on financial aid. Check your college library or women's center for this reference volume.

COMPENDIUM OF HEALTH CARE CAREERS

(The following list of careers is not meant to be exhaustive but rather to give you an idea of the range of career options in these fields and the practical, on-the-job applications.)

Ambulance Attendant. Accompanies and assists ambulance driver on calls, assisting in lifting patient onto wheeled cart or stretcher and into and out of ambulance; renders some first aid. May be required to have Red Cross first-aid training certificate.

Art Therapist. Plans and conducts art therapy programs in public and private institutions to rehabilitate mentally ill and physically disabled. Directs and organizes such activities as adapted sports, dramatics, social activities, and arts and crafts; reports findings to other members of treatment team and counsels on patient's response.

Audiologist. Specializes in diagnostic evaluation of hearing; prevention, habilitative and rehabilitative services for auditory problems; and research related to hearing and attendant disorders. May work in public schools; also in colleges and universities, clinics, research centers, hospitals. States may require a master's degree or its equivalent; some require teaching certificate for work in public schools. Licensure may be required for audiologists working outside schools. Job prospects competitive but favorable. Average starting salary for MA degree holders working for Federal Government in 1977: $14,097; higher outside government.

Audiometrist. Administers audiometric screening and threshold tests, generally pure-tone air conduction, to individuals or groups, under supervision of audiologist, otologist, or otolaryngologist. Fits earphones on subject and provides instructions on procedures to be followed; adjusts equipment controls and records responses.

Blood Bank Credit Clerk. Reviews and verifies applications for blood credit for members of blood donor groups; informs hospital of result of verification; answers inquiries regarding blood credit from patients, donor groups, hospitals, health insurance organizations.

Central Supply Supervisor. Directs activities of personnel in hospital central supply room to furnish sterile and nonsterile supplies and equipment for patient use. May be required to hold registered nurse license.

Centrifuge Operator. Tends centrifuges which extract plasma from whole blood. Marks each plasma bottle with blood group; stores filled bottles in freezer.

Cephalometric Analyst. Traces head x-rays and illustrates cosmetic result of proposed orthodontic treatment.

Chemistry Technologist. Performs qualitative and quantitative chemical analyses of body fluids and exudates, following instructions, to provide information for diagnoses and treatments. Tests specimens for sugar and albumin and for various chemicals, drugs, and poisons.

Communications Coordinator. Coordinates hospital telephone communications systems. Confers with hospital personnel to determine requirements for switchboards, public address systems, and extension telephones, etc. Writes instruction and procedure manuals for switchboard operators and trainees. May prepare records and reports for management.

Corrective Therapist. Provides medically prescribed program of physical exercises and activities designed to prevent muscular deterioration resulting from long convalescence or inactivity due to chronic illness. Utilizes any or combination of resistive, assistive, or free-movement exercises, utilizing bars or hydrogymnastics. Instructs patients in use, function, and care of braces, crutches, and canes, and in use of manually controlled vehicles. Directs blind persons in foot travel. Prepares progress reports.

Cytotechnologist. Stains, mounts, and studies human cells to determine pathology. Executes variety of laboratory tests and analyzes to confirm findings. Reports information to *pathologist*. One-year training program and two to four years of college.

Dental Assistant. Works with dentist in examining and treating patients; prepares materials for impressions and restorations; exposes radiographs and processes dental x-rays. Provides oral health instructions and sterilizes instruments. Duties do not require dentist's professional knowledge and skill. Works in private dental offices, dental schools, hospital dental departments, state and local health departments, or private clinics; also as federal employee. Most learn their skills on the job, others in post-high school programs. Some become practicing dental hygienists. Employment opportunities expected to be highly favorable through mid-1980s. Salaries depend on education and experience, geographic location, and duties.

Dental Hygienist. Performs preventive and therapeutic services under dentist's supervision; provides oral health education in clinics and to public. Responsibilities vary, according to state law where employed. Many work part time; most work in private dental offices. Must be licensed. Candidates must be graduates of an accredited dental hygiene school and pass written and clinical exams. Competition is keen for dental hygiene school; applicants must have completed high school. Employment opportunities for dental hygienists expected to be good through mid-1980s. Earnings vary; full-time employees in private offices averaged $12,900 in 1976.

Dental Laboratory Technician. Makes dentures, fabricates metal or porcelain crowns and inlays to restore teeth, and makes dental orthodontic appliances. Follows instructions of dentist; uses impressions made by dentist of a patient's mouth. Trainees in beginning jobs usually mix and pour plaster into casts and molds; with experience, go on to more difficult work. No formal education needed, though training programs exist; on-the-job training lasts four to five years. Most work in commercial laboratories; others in dental offices, hospitals, and for Federal Government. May become certified dental technician by passing written and practical exams. Job opportunities should be excellent through mid-1980s. Salaries averaged $9,400 for two to five years' experience in 1976. Highest salaries paid to ceramics specialists.

Dentist. Examines teeth and other mouth tissues to diagnose and treat diseases or abnormalities; takes x-rays, fills cavities, straightens teeth, and treats gum diseases. Works with patients and in laboratories. About 10 percent are specialists. Requirements: graduate of approved dental school, passed written exam, licensed to practice. Dentistry requires manual skills and dexterity, good visual memory. Earnings high for established practice: average income in 1976, $39,500. Practices established most easily in small towns, where dentists become well known and competition may be less intense.

Endodontist. Examines, diagnoses, and treats diseases of nerve, pulp, and other dental tissues affecting vitality of teeth. Treats infected root-canal and related tissues; may remove pathologic tissue by surgery. Treats and realigns or reinserts teeth. Bleaches discolored teeth to restore appearance.

Oral Pathologist. Examines and diagnoses tumors and lesions of mouth. Examines mouth tissues using microscope and other laboratory equipment. Sends reports of diagnosis to referring dental practitioner.

Oral Surgeon. Performs surgery on mouth and jaws. Extracts teeth; removes tumors and other abnormal growths. Corrects abnormal jaw relations by mandibular or maxillary revision. Sets jaw fractures. May treat patients in hospital.

Orthodontist. Prevents, diagnoses, and corrects deviations from normal that occur in growth, development, and position of teeth and other dental-facial structures. Designs intra- and extra-oral appliances to alter position and relationship of teeth and jaws. Fabricates appliances such as space maintainers, retainers, bite plates, arch wires, and head caps.

Periodontist. Treats inflammatory and destructive diseases of investing and supporting tissue of teeth. Cleans and polishes teeth, corrects occlusions, and performs operations. Follows up treatment to ensure maintenance of restored function and to determine that oral health practices are followed.

Pedodontist. Treats children's teeth. Treats primary and immature teeth and constructs and places bridges, dentures, and appliances.

Prosthodontist. Restores and maintains oral functions. Records positions of jaws; replaces missing teeth and associated oral structures with substitutions to improve mastication, speech, and appearance. Corrects natural and acquired deformation of mouth and jaws, using various appliances and instruments.

Public Health Dentist. Participates in planning, organizing, and maintaining dental health programs of public health agencies. Analyzes dental needs of community. Provides clinical and laboratory dental care and services. Conducts field trials of new dental equipment, methods, and procedures. Provides lab and technical aid to private practitioners, such as surveying office x-ray machines for excess radiation.

Dialysis Technician. Sets up and operates artificial kidney machine for dialysis treatment of patients with kidney disorders or failure. Assembles machine parts; mixes solutions; positions patient. Takes and records blood pressure readings and performs matrocrit and clotting-time tests on patients. Cleans and sterilizes kidney machine and reusable containers. Makes parts such as connectors and shunts; may assist with surgical insertion of shunts into vein and artery of patient's arm or leg.

Dietitians

Clinical Dietitian. Plans and directs preparation and service of diets prescribed by physician to meet nutritional needs of patients in hospitals, nursing homes, or clinics. Instructs patients and their families on requirements and importance of diets.

Community Dietitian. Plans, organizes, coordinates, and evaluates nutritional component of health care services for an organization.

Consultant Dietitian. Advises and assists personnel in public and private establishments, health-related facilities, child-care centers, and schools on food service systems and nutritional care of clients.

Diet Clerk. Compiles dietary information for kitchen personnel on preparation of foods for hospital patients.

Dietetic Technician. Provides services in assigned areas of food service management, teaches principles of food and nutrition, and provides dietary counseling, under direction of dietitian.

Research Dietitian. Conducts nutritional research to expand knowledge of one or more phases of dietetics. Research may be in nutrition science and education, food management, or food service systems and equipment; also in how body uses food. Usually employed in medical centers or education facilities, but may work in community health programs.

General Notes: More than one-half work in hospitals, nursing homes, and clinics, including about 1,100 in Veterans Administration and the United States Public Health Service. Colleges, universities, and school systems employ a large number of dietitians as teachers or in food service systems. Most of the rest work for health-related agencies, in restaurants or cafeterias, and for large companies that provide food service for their employees. Requirements: Bachelor's degree, preferably with a major in foods and nutrition or institution management. For professional recognition (registered dietitian), postgraduate dietetic internship or approved trainee program. Employment opportunities, full time or part time, for qualified dietitians expected to be good through mid-1980s. Starting salaries for hospital dietitians averaged $11,300 in 1976; for experienced dietitians, between $13,900 and $25,300.

Electrocardiograph (EKG) Technician. Applies electrodes to patient and manipulates switches of electrocardiograph machine to take heartbeat tracings, recognizing and correcting any technical error; conducts other tests such as vectorcardiograms, stress testing, pulse readings, Holter monitoring and scanning, and echocardiography (ultrasound). Most work in cardiology departments of large hospitals; others work part time in small general hospitals, or full or part time in clinics and doctors' offices. Usually trained on the job; training lasts from three to six months for basic EKG tests and up to one year for more complex tests. Job prospects favorable through mid-1980s. Starting salaries averaged $6,900 a year in 1976; experienced technicians earned as much as $13,700.

Electroencephalographic (EEG) Technologist and Technician. Investigate and record the electrical activity of the brain for diagnosis of various brain diseases by neurologists. Technologists and technicians operate electroencephalography machinery. Technicians take patients' medical history, help patients relax before the test, and help in choosing the appropriate kinds of instrument controls and electrodes. Technologists also perform these functions, but have a more thorough knowledge of all aspects of EEG work. They can also repair equipment and act as immediate supervisors of technicians. Technologists often have administrative duties such as managing the laboratory, keeping records, scheduling appointments, and ordering supplies. Both work primarily in neurology departments of hospitals; also in private offices of neurologists and neurosurgeons. Most technicians trained on the job, though advances in medical technology will require more academic training. Standards for technicians and technologists recommend one to two years of preparation, and training programs may be carried on in hospitals, colleges, junior colleges, and medical schools. Job prospects expected to be good in future. Starting salaries of EEG technicians in hospitals and medical centers averaged $7,800 in 1976; technologists earned

$1,000 to $2,000 more. Federal Government salaries were lower in both cases.

Emergency Medical Services Coordinator. Directs medical emergency service program, including coordinating activities of persons involved in rescue and transportation of accident or catastrophe victims and others requiring emergency medical assistance. Arranges for emergency medical facilities, staff, communications networks, and vehicles. Keeps records; coordinates activities of personnel; runs training programs for ambulance and rescue personnel. Encourages public interest in first-aid training in schools and community organizations. Prepares reports of progress, problems; plans for the future.

Emergency Medical Technician. Administers first-aid treatment and transports sick or injured persons to medical facility, working as member of emergency medical team. Two other types of emergency medical technicians are EMT-paramedics and EMT-dispatchers. Paramedics may administer drugs and use more complex equipment. Dispatchers receive and process calls for emergency medical assistance. Many EMTs work as volunteers on rescue squads; others are trained employees of police and fire departments and private ambulance companies. Standard 81-hour training course required for all EMTs is offered by police, fire, and health departments, in hospitals, and as a special course in medical schools, colleges, and universities. Applicants must be 18 years old, have a high school diploma or equivalent, and driver's license. Job prospects very good in future, with more full-time positions. Starting salaries for training program graduates were between $7,500 and $9,000 in 1976.

Executive Housekeeper, Medical Services. Directs institutional housekeeping program to ensure clean, orderly, and attractive conditions. Plans work schedules, inspects and evaluates physical condition of establishment, and submits recommendations for repairs to management. Periodically inventories supplies and equipment. Directs departmental training programs and hiring. Writes reports for management.

Health Physicist. Devises and directs research, training, and monitoring programs to protect plant and laboratory personnel from radiation hazards. Sets inspection standards, safe work methods, and decontamination procedures; tests surrounding areas to ensure that radiation is not in excess of permissible standards. Conducts research; advises public authorities on dealing with radiation hazards.

Hospital Admissions Clerk. Interviews incoming patient or representative and records information required for admission; assigns patient to room and explains hospital regulations. May compile data for occupancy or census records. May store patients' valuables; may arrange for diet choices, telephone, or television.

Industrial Hygienist. Conducts health program in industrial plant or governmental organization to recognize, eliminate, and control occupational health hazards and diseases. Collects samples of dusts, gases, vapors, and other potentially dangerous materials for analysis. Investigates adequacy of ventilation, exhaust equipment, lighting, and other conditions which may affect employee health, comfort, or efficiency. Prepares reports; instructs employees on occupational health.

Industrial Therapist. Arranges salaried, productive employment in actual work environment for mentally ill patients, to enable patients to perform medically prescribed work activities and to motivate and prepare patients to resume employment outside hospital environment. Evaluates progress.

Inhalation Therapist. Administers respiratory therapy care and life support to patients with deficiencies and abnormalities of cardiopulmonary system, under supervision of physician and by prescription. Most work in hospitals, in respiratory therapy, anesthesiology, or pulmonary medicine departments. Formal training is stressed; approved program in respiratory therapy may last 18 months to four years. Respiratory therapists with a certificate of completion from an AMA-approved therapist training program, 62 hours of college credit, and one year of postgraduate experience are eligible to apply for registration by the National Board for Respiratory Therapy. Those with an approved training program degree and one year of experience may apply for examination for the certified respiratory therapy technician credential. Job prospects expected to be good through mid-1980s. Starting salaries in hospitals and medical centers averaged $9,900 in 1976; top salaries ranged as high as $17,600.

Insurance Clerk. Verifies hospitalization insurance coverage, computes patients' benefits, and compiles itemized hospital bills. Answers patients' questions regarding statements and insurance coverage.

Laboratory Assistant, Blood and Plasma Performs routine laboratory tests related to processing whole blood and blood components. Observes thermostats on storage units, inspects blood units returned from hospitals to determine whether plasma can be salvaged. Cleans and maintains laboratory equipment and laboratory. Performs related clerical duties.

Licensed Practical Nurse. Cares for ill, injured, convalescent, and handicapped persons in hospitals, clinics, private homes, sanitariums, and similar institutions. Works under direction of physicians and registered nurses. Provides hospital bedside care, such as taking and recording temperatures and blood pressures, changing dressings, administering some medicines, and helping patients with bathing and other personal hygiene. Also assists in the delivery, care, and feeding of infants. Some work in specialized units or operate sophisticated equipment. Training programs usually last one year. All states require licensing; applicants must complete approved instruction course and pass written exam. Job prospects expected to be very good through mid-1980s. Average starting salaries in hospitals were $9,100 in 1976; federal salaries slightly lower.

Manual Arts Therapist. Instructs patients in prescribed manual arts activities to prevent anatomical and physiological deconditioning, and to assist in maintaining, improving, or developing work skills. Teaches activities such as woodworking, photography, metalworking, agriculture, electricity, and graphic arts. Prepares reports of patient's adjustment to aid physicians in evaluating patient's progress and ability to meet physical and mental demands of employment.

Medical Laboratory Technician. Performs routine tests in medical laboratory for use in treatment and diagnosis of disease. May work in several areas or specialize. Requirements: Two years of postsecondary training in junior or four-year college or university, Armed Forces, or vocational/technical school. Job prospects favorable through mid-1980s; starting salaries averaged $8,700 in 1976.

Medical Physicist. Applies knowledge and methodology of science and physics to all aspects of medicine, to address problems related to diagnosis and treatment of human diseases. Advises and consults with physicians in treatment and diagnosis programs. Plans, directs, and participates in supporting programs to ensure effective and safe use of radiation and radionuclides in human beings by physicians. Teaches principles of medical physics to physicians, students, and technologists. Conducts research in remedial procedures and acts as consultant in education and research.

Medical Record Administrator. Plans, develops, and administers medical systems for hospital, clinic, health care center, or similar facility, to meet standards of accrediting and regulatory agencies. Size and type of institution affect duties and amount of responsibility. Most work in hospitals. Preparation for career offered in specialized programs in colleges and universities, most lasting four years and leading to bachelor's degree in medical record administration. One-year certificate programs also available to those with bachelor's degree. Job prospects good through mid-1980s. Salaries vary, with average starting salary $12,312 in 1976; federal salaries lower on average.

Medical Record Technician. Compiles and maintains medical records of hospital and clinic patients. Transcribes medical data; analyzes and codes information; files; keeps registries and abstracts. In small hospitals, plans and administers medical records systems, a job held by medical record administrators in large hospitals. Works in hospitals, clinics, nursing homes, community health centers, governmental agencies, consulting firms, health maintenance organizations, insurance companies. Requirements: generally two-year associate degree from an accredited college and passage of accreditation exam. Usually seeking eventual supervisory position. Job prospects very good through mid-1980s; salaries vary greatly. In 1976 median salary was $11,000.

Medical Technologist. Performs chemical, microscopic, serologic, hematologic, immunohematologic, parasitic, and bacteriologic tests to provide data for use in treatment and diagnosis of disease; makes cultures; types and cross-matches blood samples. In small laboratories, performs many types of tests; in large labs, specializes. May make independent judgments; some do research, develop lab techniques, teach, and perform administrative duties. Requirements: four years of postsecondary school training from accredited school or hospital. Job prospects favorable through mid-1980s. Salaries vary; starting salaries in hospitals and medical centers averaged $10,600 in 1976.

Microbiology Technologist. Cultivates, isolates, and assists in identifying bacteria and other microorganisms, and performs various bacteriological tests. Receives human or animal body materials from autopsy or diagnostic cases, or collects specimens directly from patients. Examines for evidence of diseases or parasites.

Music Therapist. Plans, organizes, and directs music activities and learning experiences as part of care and treatment of patients to influence behavioral changes leading to increased experience and comprehension of self and environment. Joins with other members of rehabilitation team in planning music activities designed to meet patients' needs, such as solo or group singing, rhythmic and other creative music activities, music listening, playing in bands or orchestras, or attending concerts. Instructs patients; studies and analyzes patients' reactions to various experiences, and prepares reports describing symptoms indicative of progress or regression. Submits periodic reports to treatment team or physician.

Nuclear Medical Technologist. Prepares, administers, and measures radioactive isotopes in therapeutic, diagnostic, and tracer studies, utilizing variety of radioisotope equipment. Attends to patients and their records; assists physician in use of scanning devices. Responsible for storage of radioactive material and disposal of radioactive wastes. Requirements: registration as a medical technologist, radiologic technologist, or RN; at least three years of training in college or medical school. Training program lasts one year, then eligible for certification exam.

Nursing Aide, Orderly, Attendant. Answer patients' bell calls and deliver messages; serve meals, feed patients; may also give massages, take temperatures, and assist patients in getting out of bed and walking. Duties depend on policies of institution, type of patient being cared for, and capacities of the aide, orderly, or attendant. Work in hospitals, nursing homes, and other facilities; generally trained on the job. Opportunities for promotion limited without further training. For licensing, applicants need one year of specialized training. Job prospects expected to be good through mid-1980s; salaries are low, with starting salaries for nursing aides in 1977 averaging $125 to $145 a week in Veterans Administration hospitals; substantially lower earnings in nursing homes and related facilities than in hospitals.

Occupational Therapist. Plans, organizes, and conducts occupational therapy program in hospital, institution, or community setting to facilitate rehabilitation of mentally, physically, or emotionally handicapped. Evaluates capacities and skills, sets goals; may work alongside physician, physical therapist, vocational counselor, and other specialists. Works in hospitals, rehab centers, nursing homes, schools, and other centers. Requirements: degree or certification in occupational therapy from accredited school. May take certification exam for registration. Recent graduates usually begin as staff therapists; advancement possible to supervisory or administrative positions. Job prospects expected to be very good in future, due to public interest in rehabilitation and success of established occupational therapy programs. Starting salaries in hospitals averaged $12,000 in 1976. Experienced therapists earned as much as $17,000; some administrators, $25,000 to $30,000.

Occupational Therapy Aide. Orders supplies, prepares work materials, helps maintain tools and equipment. Keeps records on patients, prepares clinical notes, and performs other clerical duties. Works in same locations as assistants, but most often in hospitals. Trained on the job; training time depends on duties. Employment opportunities expected to be good in future. Beginning salaries in 1976 were about $6,200.

Occupational Therapy Assistant. Works under supervision of professional occupational therapists to help rehabilitate physically and mentally disabled patients. Helps plan and implement programs of educational, vocational, and recreational activities that strengthen patients' muscle power, increase motion and coordination, and develop self-sufficiency in overcoming disabilities. Almost half work in hospitals; others in nursing homes, schools for the handicapped and mentally retarded, rehabilitation centers, special workshops, outpatient clinics. A small number are in Armed Forces. One-year junior and community college programs and two-year college programs award associate degrees; graduates take proficiency examinations and receive title of certified occupational therapy assistant. Employment opportunities expected to be favorable, if competitive, through the mid-1980s. In 1976, annual salaries ranged from $7,500 to $9,000 for inexperienced assistants; for experienced occupational assistants, from $8,500 to $12,000.

Optometric Assistant. Performs general office/clerical work, measures patients for correct glasses, helps patients with exercises for eye coordination, inserts lenses in frames, repairs frames, and cleans and cares for instruments. Works in private practice for optometrist; usually trained on the job. One- and two-year formal training programs available. Job prospects good through mid-1980s; many opportunities for part-time work. Salaries ranged from $100 to $160 a week in 1976, depending on training and experience.

Optometrist. Examines eyes for vision problems, diseases, and other abnormal conditions. Tests for proper depth and color perception and ability to focus and coordinate eyes. Prescribes lenses and treatment, supplies eyeglasses, and fits and adjusts contact lenses. May specialize.

Most work in private practice or partnership; some in specialized hospitals or eye clinics or act as consultants to health advisory committees or remedial reading programs. Requirements: Doctor of Optometry degree, state board exam and license. Four-year degree program is competitive—only 12 schools accredited in 1976. Favorable employment outlook. Salaries averaged $33,000 for experienced in 1977.

Orientation Therapist for Blind. Assists newly blinded patients to achieve personal adjustment and maximum independence through training in techniques of daily living. Trains patients to orient to physical surroundings and to travel alone, and to attend to such personal needs as eating, grooming, dressing, and using dial telephone. Instructs patients in handicrafts such as leatherworking or weaving to improve sense of touch. Teaches patients to read and write Braille. Instructs patients in group activities such as swimming or dancing to increase capacity for social participation. Prepares progress reports.

Orthoptist. Aids persons with correctable focusing defects to develop and use binocular vision. Measures visual acuity. focusing ability, and eye motor movement. Aids patient to move, focus, and coordinate eyes to aid in vision development. Improves patients' visual skills, near-visual discrimination, and depth perception, using developmental glasses and prisms. Instructs adult patients or parents of young patients in utilization of corrective measures at home.

Orthotist. Provides care to patients with disabling conditions of limbs and spine by fitting and preparing devices known as orthoses, under direction of and in consultation with physician. Examines and evaluates patients' orthotic needs and formulates design of orthosis. Selects materials and takes measurements. Performs fitting, evaluates orthosis on patient, and makes adjustments to assure fit, function, cosmesis, and quality of work. Instructs patient on orthosis use. Maintains patient records. May supervise orthotic personnel in research and development activities or lecture to colleagues. May perform functions of prosthetist and be designated orthotist/prosthetist.

Osteopath. Diagnoses, prescribes for, and treats disease, relying upon accepted medical and surgical modalities; and when deemed beneficial, treats with manipulative therapy. May practice any medical and surgical specialties. Most are family doctors with general practice; in 1976, 25 percent specialized. To obtain license to practice must be graduate of an approved school and pass a state board exam. Educational requirements include three years of college plus four-year graduate program. After graduation nearly all serve one-year internship. Salaries usually rise significantly after first few years of practice.

Pharmacist. Compounds and dispenses medications, following prescriptions issued by physician, dentist, or other authorized medical practitioner. Many work in community pharmacies; of these, more than two-fifths own their pharmacies. Others work for hospitals, pharmaceutical companies, and wholesalers. Often community and hospital pharmacists do consulting work for nursing homes and other health facilities. License required; candidate must be graduate of an accredited pharmacy college, pass state board exam and usually have practical experience. Job prospects favorable through mid-1980s, with some competition expected. Salaries start at $14,000 to $17,000, with experienced pharmacists often earning considerably more.

Pharmacy Clerk. Mixes pharmaceutical preparations under direction of pharmacist; prepares inventory and orders supplies; labels preparations; cleans equipment; computes charges.

Physiatrist. Specializes in clinical and diagnostic use of physical agents and exercises to provide physiotherapy for physical, mental, and occupational rehabilitation. Prescribes and administers treatment such as light therapy, diathermy, electrosurgery, thermotherapy, cryotherapy, iontophonesis, and kinesitherapy. Instructs physical therapist and other personnel in nature and duration or dosage of treatment. Recommends occupational therapy activities for patients with extended convalescent periods or whose disability requires change of occupation.

Physical Therapist. Plans and administers medically prescribed physical therapy program for patients to restore function, relieve pain, and prevent disability following disease, injury, or loss of body part. Works at hospital, rehabilitation center, nursing home, health agency, or in private practice. All states require license; applicants must have degree or certificate from an accredited physical therapy educational program and have passed a state board exam. Opportunities for advancement better with a graduate degree and some clinical experience. Job prospects expected to be competitive through the mid-1980s, with best opportunities in rural and suburban areas. Starting salaries averaged $11,200 in 1976.

Physical Therapy Assistant and Aide. Work under supervision of professional physical therapists to rehabilitate disabled. Help test patients' capabilities; use therapy equipment; help strengthen muscles and instruct on use of artificial limbs. Aide cares for and assembles treatment equipment; performs clerical duties. Works in hospitals, clinics, rehabilitation centers, nursing homes. Assistant must be graduate of approved degree program and licensed. Job prospects expected to be excellent through mid-1980s. Weekly starting salaries in 1976 about $116 for aides, $170 for assistants.

Physicians and Surgeons. Traditional program consists of four years of postgraduate study. After completing core course in the basic medical sciences, students continue clinical study in a clerkship. Except Arkansas and Georgia, states determine licensing under standards of National Board exams. Exam consists of three parts, including basic multiple-choice medical sciences exam (can be taken after second year of medical school); clinical sciences exam (taken near end of senior year); and a test of clinical competence (taken after passing first two parts, gaining an MD degree, and serving an approved hospital internship or residency for at least six months). Certification awarded after first full year of internship or residency.

Internships are of two types. Mixed internships provide training in two to three fields, with concentration in one. Straight internships specialize in a single area. Internship year is fast becoming first year of residency, which generally follows. Residencies are conducted in the area of specialization and their length varies.

Allergist–Immunologist. Diagnoses and treats diseases and conditions with allergic or immunologic causes. Examines patient, records history. Analyzes reports and test results and prescribes treatment for asthma, dermatological disorders, connective tissue syndromes, etc. Refers patient to consultant services when necessary.

Anesthesiologist. Administers anesthetics during surgical, obstetric, and other medical procedures. Records condition of patient before, during, and after anesthesia. May instruct medical students in administration of anesthesia and signs of complication or reactions which may require emergency measures.

Cardiologist. Treats diseases of heart and its functions. Examines patient, prescribes medications, and suggests diet and exercise programs. Refers patient to a surgeon specializing in cardiac cases when necessary. May research anatomy and diseases characteristic of heart.

Dermatologist. Diagnoses and treats human skin diseases. Examines skin, takes blood samples, and makes chemical and biological analyses from a variety of tests to identify and treat diseases. Prescribes treatment for problems including abscesses, skin injuries, cysts, birthmarks, and scars. Three-year residency required.

Family Practitioner. Provides comprehensive medical services for family members, regardless of age or sex, on a continuing basis. Examines patients and keeps history. Diagnoses illnesses; prescribes treatments; inoculates against disease. Refers patient to medical specialist when necessary. Requirements: three- to four-year graduate medical program; three-year residency. Must pass state board exam and be licensed. Salaries high; depend on experience, duties, geographical location.

Flight Surgeon. Examines physical condition of flight personnel and studies effects of high-altitude flying. Helps personnel acclimate to high-altitude conditions and low-pressure chambers. Observes response in blood pressure, pulse, respiration, and body temperature to determine physical fitness.

General Practitioner. Attends to a variety of medical cases in general practice. Examines patients, conducts tests, and administers treatments. Inoculates and vaccinates against disease. May conduct physical exams for insurance company applicants or provide health care to passengers or crew aboard ship. Primarily office practices. Requirements: three- to four-year graduate program in medicine. Most states also require a one-year internship or residency. Must pass state board exam and be licensed. Salaries high; depend on experience, duties, geographical location.

Gynecologist. Diagnoses and treats diseases and disorders of female genital, urinary, and rectal organs. Examines patient, using physical and radiological examination findings, laboratory tests, and patients' statements. Prescribes medication or appropriate exercise or hygiene, and performs surgery as needed. May care for patient during pregnancy or deliver babies. Three-year residency.

Internist. Diagnoses and treats disease and injuries of internal organ systems. Examines patient for symptoms of organic or congenital disorders and determines extent of injury or disorder using x-rays, blood tests, electrocardiograph, etc. Prescribes medicine and recommends exercise and dietary program. Refers patient to appropriate specialist when necessary.

Neurologist. Diagnoses and treats organic diseases and disorders of nervous system. Studies results of chemical, microscopic, biological and bacteriological analyses of blood and cerebrospinal fluid to determine nature and extent of disease or disorder. Orders, and studies results of, electroencephalograms or x-rays to detect abnormalities of brain waves or indications of abnormalities of brain structure. Advises on treatment by neurosurgeon when indicated; prescribes and administers drugs and treatments. Three-year residency.

Obstetrician. Treats women during prenatal, natal, and postnatal periods. Examines patient, determines need for modified diet and physical activities, and prescribes medication or surgery if indicated. Delivers infant and cares for mother following childbirth. Performs cesarean section or other surgical procedure; may treat patients for diseases of generative organs. Three-year residency.

Ophthalmologist. Diagnoses and treats diseases and injuries of eyes. Performs various tests to determine vision loss or extent of injury, prescribes and administers medications, and performs surgery when necessary. Directs remedial activities to aid in regaining vision or to utilize remaining sight.

Otolaryngologist. Diagnoses and treats diseases of ear, nose, and throat. Performs tests to determine extent of loss of hearing due to aural or other injury, and speech loss due to diseases or injuries of larynx. Performs surgery as indicated. May specialize. Four-year residency.

Pathologist. Studies nature, cause, and development of diseases, and structural and functional changes caused by them. Also studies effects of drugs on genetic types. Often specializes (forensic pathology, neuropathology). Acts as consultant to other doctors; performs autopsies. May work in medical school, hospital, clinic, medical examiner's office, or research institute. Four-year residency.

Pediatrician. Plans and carries out medical care program for children from birth through adolescence to aid in mental and physical growth and development. Examines patient, prescribes and administers medications and immunizations, and performs variety of other duties. Two-year residency.

Podiatrist. Diagnoses and treats foot diseases and deformities; performs surgery, fits corrective devices, and prescribes drugs, physical therapy, and proper shoes. May specialize in foot surgery, bone disorders, or geriatrics. Works mainly in large cities; for hospitals, medical colleges, other podiatrists, or Federal Government. All states require graduation from accredited school of podiatric medicine, passage of written and oral proficiency examination, and license to practice. A few states require one-year residency. Job prospects favorable through mid-1980s, especially in hospitals, extended-care facilities, public health programs. Salaries rise with established practice; average income exceeded $42,000 in 1976.

Proctologist. Diagnoses and treats diseases and disorders of anus, rectum, and colon. Diagnosis uses patient medical history, instrumental inspection of rectum and colon, x-ray photography, and evaluation of laboratory test results. May perform surgery for removal or repair of parts, or prescribe medications. Five-year residency.

Psychiatrist. Studies, diagnoses, and treats mental, emotional, and behavioral disorders. Organizes data concerning patient's family, personal history, and onset of symptoms. May consult with other sources such as general-duty nurse or psychiatric social worker. Orders laboratory and other special diagnostic tests and evaluates data. Formulates treatment program. May use somatic, group, or milieu therapy and variety of psychotherapeutic methods and medications. Three-year residency.

Radiologist. Diagnoses and treats diseases by using x-rays and radioactive substances, examining internal structures and functions of organ systems. Treats benign and malignant internal and external growths by exposure to radiation from x-rays, high-energy sources, and natural and manmade radio-isotopes directed at or implanted in affected areas. May specialize in diagnostic radiology or radiation therapy. Three-year residency.

Surgeon. Performs surgery to correct deformities, repair injuries, prevent diseases, and improve function. Performs operations using a variety of surgical instruments and employing established surgical techniques appropriate for specific procedures. May specialize as neurosurgeon, plastic surgeon, or orthopedic surgeon. Four-year residency.

Urologist. Diagnoses and treats diseases and disorders of genitourinary tract. Examines patient with x-ray, fluoroscope, catheter, cytoscope, radiation emanation tube, and similar equipment. Performs surgery and prescribes medication. Four-year residency.

Veterinarian. Concerned with diagnosis, prevention, and treatment of animal disorders; includes occupations in veterinary bacteriology, epidemiology, virology, pathology, and pharmacology. Helps prevent outbreak and spread of animal diseases, many of which can be transmitted to humans. Treats animals on farms, in clinics, and in hospitals. May specialize in small animals or pets, or health and breeding of farm animals. May inspect meat, poultry, and other foods for government. Most work in private practice; practice varies according to geographic location. Requirements: Doctor of Veterinary Medicine from accredited college, written and oral board exams. Job prospects expected to be favorable through mid-1980s. Salaries in private practice vary; average salary for federal employees: $24,300 in 1977.

Prosthetist. Provides care to patients with partial or total absence of limb by planning fabrication of, writing specifications for, and fitting devices known as prostheses under guidance of and in consultation with physician. Examines and evaluates prosthetic needs in relation to disease entity and functional loss. Formulates design of prosthesis and selects materials and components. Performs fitting, evaluates patient, and makes adjustments to ensure fit, function, comfort, and workmanship. Instructs on prosthesis use. May supervise assistants, laboratory research and developmental activities; performs functions of orthotist.

Public Health Educator. Plans, organizes, and directs health education programs for group and community needs. Conducts community surveys and joins with other health specialists and civic groups to ascertain health needs and goals. Develops and maintains cooperation between public, civic, professional, and voluntary agencies. Prepares and disseminates educational and informational materials. Promotes health discussions in schools, industry, and community agencies.

Radiologic Technologist. Applies roentgen rays and radioactive measures to patients for diagnostic and therapeutic purposes; x-rays used for bone fractures, ulcers, blood clots, lung disease, brain tumors, etc. Works under supervision of radiologists. Three specialties: x-ray technology, nuclear medicine technology, radiation therapy. Requirements: formal education in x-ray technology; programs last from two to four years. Written examination leads to registration with American Registry of Radiologic Technologists. Job prospects very good through mid-1980s; starting salaries averaged $9,000 in 1976.

Recreational Therapist. Plans, organizes, and directs medically approved recreation program for patients in hospitals and other institutions. Uses activities such as adapted sports, dramatics, social activities, and arts and crafts in accordance with patients' capabilities, needs, and interests. Prepares reports for patients' physicians or treatment teams, describing responses.

Registered Nurses

Community Health Nurse. Instructs individuals and families in health education and disease prevention in community health agency, clinic, home, or school; gives periodic care as prescribed by physician; works with community leaders, teachers, physicians.

Nurse Anesthetist. Administers intravenous, spinal, and other anesthetics to render patients insensible to pain during surgical operations, deliveries, or other medical and dental procedures. Positions patient and administers prescribed anesthetic, regulating flow of gases or injecting fluids intravenously or rectally. Observes reaction to anesthesia, periodically counting pulse and respiration, taking blood pressure, and noting skin color and dilation of pupils. Administers oxygen or initiates other emergency measures to prevent surgical shock, asphyxiation, or other adverse conditions. Informs physician of patient's condition during anesthesia. May give postoperative care as needed.

Nurse Consultant. Advises hospitals, schools of nursing, industrial organizations, and public health groups on nursing activities and health services. Reviews and suggests changes in nursing organization and administrative procedures. Analyzes nursing techniques and recommends modifications. Aids schools in planning nursing curricula, and hospitals and public health nursing services in developing and carrying out staff education programs. Assists in developing guides and manuals for nursing services, prepares data for articles and lectures, participates in surveys and research.

Nurse Educator. Demonstrates and teaches patient care in classroom and clinic to nursing students and instructs students in principles and application of physical, biological, and psychological subjects related to nursing. Also conducts continuing education courses for registered nurses, practical nurses, and nursing assistants.

Nurse-Midwife. Provides medical care and treatment to obstetrical patients under supervision of obstetrician, delivers babies, and instructs patients in prenatal and postnatal health practices.

Nurse Practitioner. Provides general medical care and treatment to assigned patients in facilities such as clinics, health centers, or public health agency, working with physician. Performs services such as physical examinations that traditionally have been handled by physicians. Requirements: Registered nurse with advanced training.

Nursing Service Director. Administers hospital nursing program to maintain standards of patient care and advises medical staff, department heads, and administrator of hospital on nursing service. Recommends new or revised policies, interprets policies to staff and community groups, promotes good working relationships with community agencies and other hospital departments. Assists in budget preparation, performs personnel management functions, and appoints professional and auxiliary nursing staff. Initiates studies of effectiveness in relation to objectives and costs. Participates in community health programs. May assist nursing schools with curricular problems.

Occupational Health Nurse. Provides nursing service to employees or personnel who become ill or suffer an accident on premises of store, factory, or other establishment. Treats minor injuries and illnesses, provides for the needed nursing care, arranges for further medical care if necessary, and offers health counseling.

Office Nurse. Cares for and treats patients in office, as directed by physician. May perform routine laboratory work.

School Nurse. Plans policies, standards, and objectives of school health program in cooperation with medical authority and administrative school personnel. Reviews findings of medical examinations to evaluate health status of pupils and progress of program. Instructs classes in child care, first aid, and home nursing, and establishes emergency nursing procedures. Cooperates with school personnel in identifying and meeting social, emotional, and physical needs of schoolchildren. Administers immunizations and maintains health records of students.

General Outlook: Opportunities good for part-time work; most work in hospitals, nursing homes, and related institutions. License required; must be graduate of an approved school of nursing and pass written state exam. Diploma, baccalaureate, and associate degree programs prepare for licensing. Diploma programs usually require three years of training conducted by hospitals and independent schools; degree programs usually require four years in college or university. Associate degree programs in junior and community colleges require approximately two years of nursing education. Other programs provide licensed practical nurses with the training necessary to become RNs while they continue to work part time. Employment opportunities favorable through mid-1980s. Starting salaries for RNs in hospitals in 1976 averaged $11,820; nursing homes paid slightly less.

Rehabilitation Services Coordinator. Plans, administers, and directs operation of health therapy programs such as physical, occupational, recreational, educational, music, and manual arts. Consults with medical and professional staff and other personnel to plan and coordinate patient and management objectives. Conducts staff conferences, plans training programs, analyzes operating costs and budget, coordinates research projects; may do consultant work.

Sanitarian. Plans, develops, and executes environmental health program. Works with schools or other groups, sets standards and enforces regulations concerned with food processing and serving, collection and disposal of solid wastes, sewage treatment and disposal, plumbing, noise ventilation, air pollution, radiation, etc. of recreational areas, hospitals, and other institutions. Confers with government, community, civil defense, and private organizations.

Speech Pathologist. Specializes in diagnosis and treatment of speech and language problems, and engages in scientific study of human communication. May work in public schools, colleges and universities, clinics, research centers, hospitals. State may require master's degree or equivalent; some require teaching certificate for work in public schools. Licensure may be required for work outside schools. Job prospects competitive, but favorable. Average federal starting salary for MA degree holders was $14,097 in 1977; salaries outside government were higher.

Surgical Technician. Performs any combination of following tasks before, during, and after operation: Washes, shaves, and sterilizes operative area of patient; places equipment and supplies in operating room according to surgeon's directions, and arranges instruments as specified by general-duty nurse; maintains fluids for use during operation; adjusts lights and other equipment; cleans room. May assist in administering blood, plasma, or other injections and transfusions. May hand surgeon instruments during operation. Most are trained in vocational/technical schools, hospitals, and community and junior colleges; training programs last from nine months to one year; some junior college programs last two years and lead to an associate degree. Some on-the-job training. Association of Operating Room Technicians awards certificate to those who pass examination. Job prospects good through mid-1980s. Average starting salary was $7,400 in 1976.

Tissue Technologist. Cuts, stains, prepares, and mounts tissues for examination by pathologist. Prepares specimen by freezing; bone specimens by decalcifying. Prepares and maintains paraffin, reagents, and other solutions and stains, according to standard formulas. May assist pathologist in autopsy.

Ultrasound Technologist. Operates ultrasound diagnostic equipment to produce two-dimensional ultrasonic pattern and positive pictures of internal organs, for use by professional personnel in diagnosis of diseases, study of malfunction of organs, and prenatal examination of fetus and placenta. Selects equipment according to specifications of investigation. Explains process to patient and instructs and assists patient in assuming position required for exposure to ultrasonic waves. Adjusts controls, observes, and removes recorder strip printout to obtain permanent record of internal examination. Discusses test results with department supervisor or personnel.

Ward Clerk. Prepares and compiles records in hospital nursing unit, such as obstetrics, pediatrics, or surgery. Copies information from nurses' records onto patient medical records. Records diet information. Prepares discharge notice. Handles messages to patients and medical staff. Directs visitors; distributes mail, newspapers, and flowers to patients. May assist in dressing and feeding patient. May keep record of absences and hours worked by unit personnel.

Ward-Service Supervisor. Supervises and coordinates activities of workers engaged in clerical and patient transport duties of patient care unit. Schedules work hours, trains new employees, and evaluates performance. Inventories equipment and supplies and prepares purchase orders and requisitions for supplies or repair services. Inventories and stores patient's personal articles. Checks records of patient admissions, transfers, discharges, surgery, or tests to ensure completion of forms and signatures. Performs other duties as necessary.

X-Ray Developing Machine Operator. Tends equipment that develops, fixes image, and dries x-ray plates.

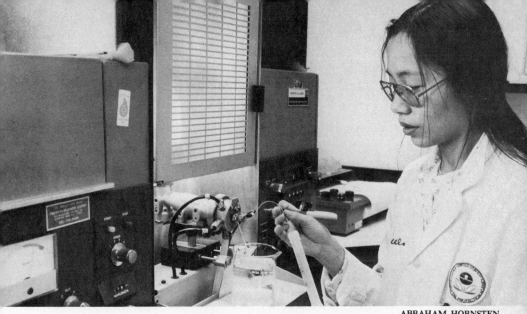

ABRAHAM HORNSTEN

Guide III A Guide to Science and Engineering Careers

Funding for this Guide was provided by
International Business Machines
Corporation.

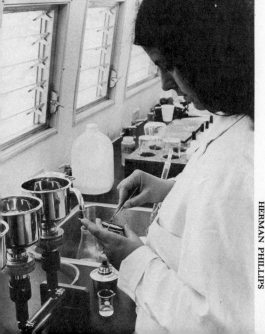

HERMAN PHILLIPS

CHAPTER 1

SCIENCE AND ENGINEERING —

The Endeavors, the Careers

What do you think of when you picture a scientist? A small, whiskered old man muttering in a foreign accent, lost amid bottles of bubbling liquids? Or maybe a gangly guy with a crew cut and bow tie, chalk all over his rumpled suit, lecturing excitedly to a group of semicomatose students? The modern scientist doesn't usually fit those old stereotypes. One of the biggest differences is that the scientist many of us picture is more frequently now a woman.

The Scientific Method

The methodology of science is our definition of science: knowledge arrived at through a specific method. This sets no limits on knowledge but tells us only that a method exists that can discover a certain kind of knowledge. This method has proved so fruitful that its truths are rapidly altering our most fundamental concepts, beliefs, and perhaps the very way our minds function. The scientific principle of internal combustion led to the invention and use of faster modes of transportation and altered our experience of time and space. The mathematics of Einstein (1879–1955) and others led to telecommunications networks that may someday eliminate the need for personal transportation as machines produce for us, computers fix the machines, and video phones keep us in constant communication with each other. Science fiction perhaps, but what of consciousness-altering chemicals in our foods, electromicrographic brain surgery, computerized biostatistical information on all humanity?

As recently as the beginning of the 19th century, science was knowledge, not a skill. It was a study, not practical preparation for a livelihood. Now, however, science has grown into a broad and expanding occupa-

247

tional field. Modern industrial and technological innovations have engendered new scientific fields and problems. The modern scientist may be involved in "pure" research or in solving problems in environmental pollution and urban planning. Private industry spends many millions on research and development, and government conducts organized research on a large scale.

Scientists are bringing us by quantum jumps from the 20th into the 21st century and a world of technological wizardry: space colonization, genetic engineering, laser technology, computers programmed to think like humans.

It is a problematic future. So much hangs in the balance—the threats posed by inadequate distribution of food resources, the hazards of radiation, and the destruction of the environment. Scientists and engineers, our technological workforce, are wrestling with these problems in the laboratory, helping to shape our future.

The breakneck pace of scientific achievement in the postwar period has not kept pace, however, with a new fact of economic life: the growing interest among women to join the ranks of science. Historically women have been second-class citizens in science, for the most part working without proper credit and often in the shadow of men. From this *de facto* segregation arises the notion of science as something alien to women's experience and talents.

A new generation of women is beginning to make its way into the marketplace. Changes in attitude, set in motion by the women's movement, have provided the momentum for expanding ambitions. Meanwhile the scientific establishment is slowly coming out of its social isolation to confront a world of rising expectations and falling stereotypes.

Certainly in numbers, women are still a small percentage of the total workforce in science and engineering. Their numbers, however, are increasing in a nearly geometric progression: The proportion of women within the science labor force has increased from 8 percent in 1969 to roughly 14 percent in 1974. For the past 50 years, 1 in every 40 PhDs in physics has been held by a woman, while 1 in every 250 engineering PhDs has been awarded to a female.

At present women have not really made their presence felt strongly in the scientific community; their numbers are still comparatively small and their leverage limited. But a new generation of career women will put themselves into the mainstream by the simple weight of their numbers. Many more women are enrolling in science and engineering courses in college, earning degrees, and preparing for careers in the profession. A recent study showed that between 1966 and 1974 the overall number of women enrolling in four-year colleges and universities rose from 38.2 percent of female high school graduates to 44.2 percent. But the percentage of women majoring in scientific and engineering

QUIZ

Women in science have been competing with their male colleagues for a long time. Many of them finished first in the race to introduce a new concept or innovation. To get off to a good start, here's a quiz on "firsts." Don't be discouraged if you get stumped.

Do you know . . .

1. Who was the first person to use a female mannequin to teach the delivery of a fetus?
2. Who first publicized the dangers of DDT?
3. Who was the first inventor of the cotton gin? (Hint: It wasn't Eli Whitney!)
4. Who was America's "First Lady of Engineering"?
5. What woman received a medal from the King of Denmark for discovering the first telescopic comet?
6. Who was the first woman to win a Nobel Prize and the first person to win it twice?
7. Who was the first woman mathematician of note, and an inventor and teacher of philosophy as well?
8. What woman was France's first mining engineer and an expert on mineral resources?

Quiz Answers

1. In 1759 midwife *Angelique du Coudray* (1712– 89), who used a mannequin to teach the delivery of a fetus, was sent on a tour of hospitals to teach more than 4,000 students her method.

2. Marine biologist and conservationist *Rachel Carson* (1907– 64) was denounced by the manufacturers of DDT and similar substances when she alerted the public to the dangers of chemical control of pests and insects.

3. Eli Whitney took credit, but American social reformer *Catherine L. Greene* (1755– 1814) developed the *method* for building the cotton gin. It was unthinkable at that time for a woman to apply for a patent; so Whitney, who actually built the machine after Ms. Greene helped give him the opportunity to do so, was credited with the invention.

4. *Lillian Moller Gilbreth* (1878– 1972), a pioneer in industrial engineering, was America's "First Lady of Engineering." She was instrumental in developing the concept of scientific management in industry.

5. America's first woman astronomer, *Maria Mitchell* (1818– 89), received a medal from the King of Denmark for discovering "Mrs. Mitchell's Comet" in 1847.

6. *Marie Curie* (1867–1931), the most famous of women scientists, received her first Nobel Prize in physics in 1903 and her second in chemistry in 1911; she was the first person to receive two Nobel Prizes.

7. *Hypatia* (370–415), the first woman mathematician of note, was also an inventor of the astrolabe as well as many other instruments still in use. She was assassinated by an angry Alexandrian mob for her defiance of Christian theology and her teaching of pagan philosophy.

8. *Baroness de Beausoleil* (b. 1610) wrote on the science of mining and achieved great reputation for investigating the mineral resources of France.

---

subjects increased three times faster than the overall enrollment of women. The change on the graduate level is even more striking. The number of women earning doctoral degrees in science and engineering rose from 744 in 1966 to 2,590 in 1974.

Employment Realities

Despite legal leverage the employment picture facing the future female scientist is not promising. The second half of the 50s and the early part of the 60s were the boom years for the scientific–industrial establishment. The electronics industry flourished. Research in private institutions and academia, fueled by expansive government and private funding, went into high gear. The late 60s, however, saw a downturn in the economy. By the recession of 1970, the whole machinery of scientific research went into a holding pattern. Money became scarce in academia, and PhDs suddenly found themselves adrift in a buyer's market.

In 1968, 62 percent of women scientists were employed by educational institutions, but by 1974 the proportion had declined to 26 percent. On the other hand, the proportion of women scientists working in business and industry more than doubled between 1964 and 1974. A larger share of women worked for federal, state, and local governments in 1974 than in 1968.

"Increases in the participation of women have been more rapid than have positive changes in opportunity during the past five years," notes Betty M. Vetter of the Scientific Manpower Commission. One notable case is that of engineering, as she pointed out in a paper given before the 1976 annual meeting of the American Association for the Advancement of Science (AAAS): "Because women engineers are still so rare the heightened awareness of employers to the sexist discrimination of the past has brought real opportunity to new women engineering graduates

PHYSICAL, LIFE, EARTH—THE ORGANIZATION OF SCIENCE, PLUS ENGINEERING

The natural sciences can be divided into three broad categories: *physical sciences,* including mathematics, physics, astronomy and chemistry; *life sciences,* including all aspects of biology and biochemistry; and *earth sciences,* for example, geology, paleontology, oceanography, and meteorology. We use these categories in this Guide to divide the standard career areas, although the lines of demarcation are blurred. Nuclear chemists and nuclear physicists deal with the same phenomena. Researchers trained as chemists work on biochemical problems, as do biologists. Some paleontologists are interested in the geological aspects of their work, others in the biology of fossil species. The work of oceanographers and marine biologists overlaps. And some mathematicians claim that pure mathematics is numerical logic, more properly a branch of philosophy than of science.

Engineering puts the laws of science to practical use, applying knowledge of the properties of matter and energy to construction, machinery, and products. Chemical engineers, for instance, develop new chemicals and materials and design equipment to produce them. Mechanical engineers focus on heat and power and the machines that provide them. Civil engineering, which began as public works during the Roman era —roads, bridges, aqueducts—now includes building support-system design. Electrical engineers deal with all types of electrical systems in buildings and machines, automobiles, and airplanes. Other engineering specialists concentrate on water supply, sewage disposal, nuclear power, energy conservation . . . problems and challenges of our technological society.

---

in the past few years." Nevertheless, at present women make up an unimpressive 1.5 percent of the engineering population.

Discrimination, Dr. Vetter comments in her paper, still plays a role in both the daily life and overall status of women in science. Even without the problems of a shaky economy, she remarks, women scientists have had more difficulty "finding employment than have men with comparable education and experience." They also, she asserts, "find it more difficult to advance." A sampling of 1977 science graduates conducted by the National Science Foundation a year after their graduation adds weight to her words. Roughly 1.5 percent of the males were still looking for full-time jobs in science in contrast to 6.5 percent of the white female graduates.

Discrimination emerges in salary figures, although here, too, the gap is closing. For example, at educational institutions the median salary paid to male scientists in 1976 exceeded that paid to women by nearly $1,000 ($17,294 to $16,430). (Black women, however, fare much better in this respect. The median salary for a black woman in academia was $18,375, an edge of almost $2,000.)

The field of science is still permeated with a masculine mystique, which affects women at every level of their careers. "Not only is the field defined as male by virtue of its membership, it is defined as male in relation to its methodology, its thought, indeed its goals," wrote distinguished physicist and biologist Evelyn Fox Keller. "To the extent that analytic thought is conceived as male thought, to the extent that we characterize the natural sciences as the 'hard sciences,' to the extent that the procedure of science is to 'attack' problems, and its goal to 'conquer' or master nature, a woman in science must in some ways feel alien."

Society has hardly encouraged women to pursue careers in science. From childhood women are brought up to feel that science is not relevant to their future and are nudged toward more conventional interests. Parents provide their young sons with puzzles, science kits, reference materials, intellectual stimuli to feed their scientific curiosity. Young girls, however, usually miss out on that kind of encouragement. They are also indoctrinated with the idea that they should not compete with boys. Studies have shown that many women with a real talent for science instead enter occupations such as social work, law, nursing, or else become math or science teachers.

The upshot is a gap between girls and boys in their understanding of science, a discrepancy that grows during the high school years. One 1972–73 study revealed that girls' knowledge of science trailed that of boys'. The gap widened from 2 to 3 percent among 9-year-olds to 6 percent by the age of 17.

Occupational stereotypes have been broken down by the women's movement. Girls are now looking at science and math with a different set of values and expectations. In 1957, 42 percent of the boys questioned in a National Science Foundation survey said that they were seriously considering a career in science or engineering, while only 23 percent of the girls shared that goal. In 1975, 57 percent of the boys were weighing a career in these fields, compared to 42 percent of the girls.

Science Education

What kind of preparation should the future woman scientist look for in school? A comprehensive science background is essential, with mathematics the common denominator for every scientific or engineering specialty. Without four years of high school math—more if possible—a science major in college will find herself hard pressed to keep pace with her fellow students. High school chemistry and physics are, of course, basic. And do not overlook English, as well as other languages. "So much of science is teamwork. If you can't communicate your ideas and opinions, what good are they?" comments one biochemist.

Most female scientists recommend an undergraduate major in the student's chosen field or one closely related. It may be better to concentrate on basic science and specialize later. For example, a potential astronomer might major in physics to prepare, not only for graduate work in astronomy, but also for a job in industry as an engineer, should that become necessary.

"Go to the best undergraduate school you can," advises a physicist. "You'll be in a better position to find a good job or get into a top graduate school." Graduates of top schools have an easier time finding jobs because the school itself lends prestige: professors at such schools are more likely to have a network of contacts at other universities and in government and industry. "Check out professors in your field beforehand. This is important for undergraduates and essential for graduate school," suggests a biologist. "Bibliographies of scientific abstracts at your library will tell you if he or she has published recently, how often and where. Someone who's not producing papers is more likely to be out of the research mainstream. His name won't carry as much weight. That can hurt later when you need recommendations for graduate school or employment."

Women's colleges have proved better incubators of scientific talent than their coed counterparts. Twice as many graduates of women's colleges as those from co-educational schools go on to earn PhDs in science. Perhaps one explanation is that the student at a women's college is more likely to come under the influence of a female teacher, who can become a role model and mentor. A supportive teacher can be critical to a young woman's drive for success; her encouragement can help offset some of the setbacks her protégée will encounter in the professional world. Science students at any school should ask for help from the teachers who can support them through their studies.

Getting Help on the Job

Once in the working world, the female scientist finds herself thrown into a society where men control the power, dominate the thinking, and usually make the rules—to their own best interests.

A woman's upward progress may in part depend on the sponsorship of a mentor. Senior scientists need to be persuaded to hire an unknown junior, to allow an apprentice to work independently in the laboratory or with colleagues. Senior colleagues can help young associates get results published and secure research funds. Such collaboration may lead to eventual recognition for the associate.

This system can work to the disadvantage of women because some scientists have misgivings about sponsoring women associates. They may assume that a woman's commitment to science may be over-shadowed by her private and domestic life, or—however unjustifiably —that a woman's financial dependence on a job may be less than that of a man. Because of these assumptions they may be unwilling to help underwrite the career of a woman associate.

Not all scientists and engineers have adjusted to the different career patterns and working styles of female co-workers. For one thing, many scientists expect to pay a high personal price for success, routinely putting in long hours in the laboratory, letting research take precedence over their personal lives. They are suspicious of colleagues—many of them women—who do not easily fit into this pattern. They may be uneasy around women who are dedicated and capable yet must put limits on their work because of domestic responsibilities. They are not used to dealing with colleagues who may have to take a leave of absence at some time because of childbirth and rearing. These elitist attitudes are dissipating as more and more women successfully juggle domestic and professional lives and achieve recognition in their fields.

SCIENCE CAREERS: A NOTE ON GETTING (AND STAYING) THERE

The complexity and problems of our modern world have created careers based exclusively on science. As available scientific knowledge accrues in a vast repository of scholarly journals and technical reports, the various sciences have become increasingly specialized. The modern scientist is now caught between the need to specialize in order to make a significant contribution in some area and the need to maintain a broad base of knowledge.

Just as science as a career has become increasingly complex, it also has become increasingly broad. Scientists may work indoors or out, alone or as part of a research team, with their hands or strictly with their heads.

Science education never ends; as a practicing member of the scientific community, you must continually keep abreast of developments in your field as well as others. Your academic work is not an end in itself but rather a means by which you prepare for your career. Financially, an advanced degree is a sound investment; the higher your degree, the more you will advance. A BS or MS may get you a position doing some basic research, but a PhD is essential for college teaching and advanced research.

Since your investment in a science career will be a considerable one, you should do some serious thinking before you decide to take the plunge.

NEW CAREER OPPORTUNITIES FOR THE FUTURE—GEOLOGY, ASTRONOMY, BIOCHEMISTRY

As science becomes more highly specialized and more far-reaching in its scope, new opportunities develop in various fields.

For example, growing energy needs coupled with environmental concerns have generated a real demand for scientists and engineers. Women geoscientists are "being actively recruited, hired, and promoted by employers, particularly the energy companies," one recent report noted. These women, the study continued, are moving into employment areas offering good salaries and job mobility.

In the past decade we have become increasingly aware of our intergalactic connection. Astronomers throughout the world search the heavens for chemical clues to help us understand our origins on earth. Cosmology, interstellar chemistry, exobiology are all spinoffs of this rapidly growing field of study. Astronomy, like engineering, is a field that has surprisingly few women. The percentage of PhDs awarded to women in astronomy fell from a high of 27 percent in the 20s to 6 percent in the late 60s and 70s. Perhaps we will see this trend reversed, as more women become part of the scientific foray beyond earth's atmosphere.

Another frontier, on a different scale, is opening in biochemistry. Today biochemists are involved in a wide range of research that promises to have an important bearing on life in the future: They are probing into the mysteries of DNA, the building blocks of life, studying and analyzing the internal mechanisms that control the process of aging, isolating the various chemicals in the brain that affect behavior and synthesizing them artificially. Path-breaking work like this will call for a new generation of scientific researchers.

Their historic isolation from the scientific mainstream works against women in other ways. Since they are not members of the "club," women may not have access to an informal but valuable system of "contacts" who can help their advancement. They may miss important channels of communication lying outside the boundaries of the laboratory and scientific periodicals.

However, women in the profession are creating their own support system. For example, in recent years groups of women scientists, acting spontaneously and often without formal organization, have been assisting women in industry and academia. They have been encouraging women students to pursue science careers and working within the profession to break down social and institutional barriers that hinder women's progress.

Women are on the verge of making the breakthrough. By their achievements they have overturned longstanding myths. They have proved that men do not have an innate superiority in math and science ability; that women do have the temperament, persistence, and dedication to succeed in this rigorous field, and that scientists can combine a family life with a profession.

By sheer numbers women are becoming assimilated into the scientific community. They are achieving an acceptance long overdue, acquiring power that is due them, and making a larger—perhaps fateful—contribution to the brave new world of technology that is evolving. Women now working as scientists and engineers are paving the way for you to follow in their path—whether you want to be a chemist, paleontologist, zoologist, or mechanical engineer.

CHAPTER 2

PHYSICAL SCIENCES —
Mathematics, Physics, Astronomy, Chemistry

The sciences referred to as physical sciences involve the efforts of physicists, chemists, astronomers, and mathematicians, and all those who work in specialties in each of these fields. A *physicist* may study activity within an atom, something neither she nor anyone can observe directly. A *chemist* may devote decades to figuring out the exact structure of a molecule as complicated as a labyrinth yet so small that several billion billion (10^{18}) could be mailed for the cost of a first-class stamp. An *astronomer* may gaze at light that has been streaking toward our solar system for thousands of years. A *mathematician* may work with only paper, pencil, and her own intelligence to conceive and prove abstract theorems. No matter which of the physical sciences a person specializes in, she deals with fundamental laws of matter and energy and space, the atomic and subatomic building blocks of stars and starfish and the processes that keep them running.

Mathematics and Mathematicians

Mathematics is the language of science. Scientific ideas are expressed mathematically. Theoreticians—or pure mathematicians as they are sometimes called—are the creative artists of the field and often work in research institutes or at universities. They explore abstract mathematical problems without regard to practical application. Applied mathematicians, on the other hand, develop solutions to practical problems, which do not, of course, exclude theoretical approaches. Since math is the universal language of science, applied mathematicians are employed in jobs in all the natural and social sciences.

GETTING IN, MOVING UP: MATHEMATICS

An advanced degree is needed to begin most trading or research careers in math, but with a bachelor's degree you can expect to get a job performing computations for senior mathematicians or grappling with some of the less advanced problems in applied mathematics. Another option would be to get a position as a research assistant while earning an advanced degree. Because of the extensive reliance on computers in mathematics today, you will need to learn at least the fundamentals of computer programming and operation. Indeed, many of the more than 26,000 annual math graduates (at all levels) turn to related fields such as computer work and statistics, fields in which many new openings occur each year.

FACTS AND FIGURES: MATHEMATICIANS

- About 38,000 persons worked as mathematicians in 1976.
- Roughly three-fourths of them worked in colleges and universities, most as teachers but some mainly in research and development with few or no teaching duties.
- Most other mathematicians worked in private industry (primarily the aerospace, communications, machinery, and electrical equipment industries) and government. (Most federally employed mathematicians were in the Department of Defense and the National Aeronautics and Space Administration.)
- Mathematicians work in all states but nearly half are employed in California, New York, Massachusetts, Pennsylvania, Illinois, Maryland, and New Jersey.
- Average starting salaries in 1976: $11,500 with bachelor's, $14,300 with master's, above $20,000 with PhD (most with some experience).
- Starting federal salaries in 1977: $9,303 or $11,523 (depending on college records) with bachelor's and no experience, $14,097 or $17,056 (depending on college grades) with master's, $17,056 or $20,442 with PhD. Average salary for all federally employed mathematicians was $23,100.
- Employment trends and prospects: Average annual openings projected through 1985: 1,550. Keen competition is expected, especially for those seeking teaching positions in colleges and universities. Women with advanced degrees in applied mathematics will have a less difficult time finding satisfactory employment.

In addition to analysis, mathematics includes the fields of geometry, which deals with the properties of space; topology, which extends geometry into the fourth—and higher—dimensions; and various branches of algebra.

Physics and Physicists

Like mathematics, physics is one of the primary physical sciences, and physicists use mathematics to express the relationship between energy and matter and to describe the forces and laws of nature. Some physicists are primarily theoreticians; others focus their attention on experimental work. However, whether they teach at a university or conduct experiments in industry, most physicists are engaged in research.

Physics specialists concentrate on particular states of matter, changes of state, and matter–matter and matter–energy relationships. Theoretical physics attempts to describe *all* natural phenomena in mathematical form. Solid-state physicists study the physical properties of solids; plasma physicists investigate highly ionized gases. Acoustics is the branch of physics concerned with the production, transmission, and effects of sound; optics deals with visible light and other electromagnetic rays, which can be considered as particles or as waves of energy. Other physicists focus on heat, electricity, or magnetism, or their interactions; mechanics, the way a physical system behaves after interaction with its environment; and fluids, a control technology using fluids instead of mechanical parts to sense, control, and process information. (A carpen-

---

GETTING IN, MOVING UP: PHYSICS

In college, a future physicist should provide herself with a solid background in all aspects of physics before beginning to specialize. If a job in her specialty fails to materialize, she will still have a broad spectrum of employment possibilities.

Graduate work in physics is virtually a must even for most entry-level jobs, and definitely so for promotion. With a bachelor's degree you may qualify for some research positions in industry, performing routine lab assignments, for example. Instrument companies sometimes hire BAs and train them as technical salespeople. Other possibilities are computer programming or systems analysis, since a strong math background is essential for a physicist. Graduate physicists almost invariably go into research or research and teaching.

---

ter's level and a fever thermometer both employ fluid dynamic phenomena.) Atomic physicists study the structure of the atom and its elementary particles—electrons, protons, and neutrons; and scientists have been finding more and more of these infinitesimal bits of matter—muons, mesons, for example—whose existence can be confirmed only by observing the effects they produce on each other. Nuclear physicists are most interested in the internal structures and behavior of the atomic nucleus.

Phyllis Eisenberg, Physicist

"Physics is a frontier science," Phyllis Eisenberg remarks. "It wasn't studied quantitatively before because the equipment—electron microscopes, particle accelerators, and such—didn't exist. We may be on the way now to understanding basic interactions of matter and energy."

FACTS AND FIGURES: PHYSICISTS

- About 48,000 people worked as physicists in 1976.
- Nearly 1 out of 3 worked in private industry, mostly in companies manufacturing chemicals, electrical equipment, and aircraft and missiles.
- Nearly half worked in colleges and universities, teaching or doing research.
- About 8,000 were in federal jobs, mostly in the Departments of Defense and Commerce.
- More than one-third worked in California, New York, or Massachusetts, especially in heavily industrialized areas and university communities.
- Average starting salaries in 1976 in manufacturing industries: $12,000 with a bachelor's, $13,000 with a master's, and $19,000 with a PhD.
- Starting salaries in the federal agencies in 1976: $9,303 or $11,523, depending on college grades, with a bachelor's, $11,523 or $14,097 with a master's, $17,056 or $20,442 with a PhD. Average salary for all federally employed physicists in 1977 was $23,850.
- Average starting salaries for college and university faculties in 1976: $10,800 with a master's and $12,800 with a PhD.
- Employment trends and prospects: Average annual openings projected through 1985: 1,700. Employment is expected to grow faster than the average for all occupations. Employment opportunities are good over all, but with keen competition for teaching positions in colleges and universities.

Dr. Eisenberg's own interest in physics began early. "I made a conscious decision as a youngster to find out how things work on a microscopic scale. A *Scientific American* article I read as a college freshman guided me to a lab project in experimental optics. And my adviser was convinced I could succeed as a physicist."

A long-standing curiosity about fundamental principles led Dr. Eisenberg to research in solid-state physics at a California electronics lab. Along the way she taught high school physics after getting her BA, went back to school for a PhD, married, and taught in universities for years. Widowed over five years ago at the age of 50, Dr. Eisenberg moved to "Silicon Valley" (so called for the number of electronic firms clustered there) near San Francisco.

"My work is all research, and very fruitful right now. The best use of my talents is to pursue problems in the lab, not to direct other people's research." Dr. Eisenberg's work is similar in technique to basic research as practiced in universities and government labs except that their range of questions studied is not completely open to her. "I'm investigating the optical properties of thin films with two or more components, and the electrochromic changes in color and other properties under certain conditions, for example, in an electrical field." Dr. Eisenberg explains, "There might be a commercial application in display devices."

In the lab, Dr. Eisenberg spends a lot of time setting up and performing tests, directing the work of her technical assistants—she wishes she had more help—and farming out problems in x-ray and electron microscopy. "You learn to use the resources and talents of other people to solve your problems." Part of her day is spent communicating with colleagues, "taking advantage of their good ideas," on her research, attending and occasionally giving seminars, and talking with the frequent visitors to the lab. She must also regularly read scientific journals and prepare papers and talks on her work. Now that her children are on their own, she may spend 12 hours a day in the lab for weeks at a time. "Of course, like many scientists, I'd like to discover an earth-shaking fundamental principle," remarks Dr. Eisenberg. Her more modest long-range goal, however, is to establish a permanent professional reputation as a good physicist.

"Female physicists have perhaps too much visibility," notes Dr. Eisenberg. (Only 7 percent of BA and MA physicists are women, and less than 3 percent of the PhDs.) "There's a certain amount of masculine ribbing you have to take with good grace." She compares the comments by male colleagues to the rings of Saturn: "Individually insignificant dust particles—the remarks—make a very real aggregate." To eliminate such problems, Dr. Eisenberg thinks there ought to be more women in physics. She recommends that interested high school students take "every scrap of math, all other science courses, and a machine shop, carpentry, or car repair course to get used to working with your hands."

Anyone who's taken those courses and done well has a much better chance of acceptance at any college."

Dr. Eisenberg herself went from a high school where girls were barred from shop classes to a women's college "where everyone supported my career goals—they do have a professional interest in encouraging women scientists." In graduate school some congenial male fellow students included her in discussions and some hostile male professors didn't. Her thesis adviser was unable to place her as a postdoctoral fellow because "physicists at other universities didn't want women in their labs." In job seeking, she feels she encountered definite discrimination in hiring practices, pay scales, and advancement. A "disproportionate number" of the women scientists in her lab were laid off during a cutback a year ago: "It wasn't just 'last hired, first fired'—one woman had 10 years' seniority." Although there are problems for women in such a predominantly male field, Dr. Eisenberg feels that the rewards are worth it and she encourages women to take on the challenge. "Only when there are substantial numbers of women physicists will these problems disappear."

Astronomy and Astronomers

Astronomy is the study of the arrangement and distribution of the stars. All astronomy is concerned with celestial bodies and the observation and interpretation of the spectrum of radiation from long-wave low-frequency radio to very-short-wave high-frequency cosmic rays anywhere in the universe.

Astronomers spend more time analyzing data collected at observatories than stargazing, and theoreticians may visit observatories only rarely. Astronomy may actually be the most theoretical of all the sciences.

An astrophysicist studies the physical properties of stars, meteors, and planets—luminosity, size, mass, density, color—their chemical elements, origins, and "lives." She may investigate the evolution, structure, and internal motion of galaxies. X-ray astronomy has existed only since

---

GETTING IN, MOVING UP: ASTRONOMY

A bachelor's degree, but preferably a master's, is necessary for even an entry-level position as an assistant. A PhD is a prerequisite for anyone with career ambitions.

FACTS AND FIGURES: ASTRONOMERS

- About 2,000 persons worked as astronomers in 1976.
- Most worked in colleges and universities; others in observatories operated by universities, not-for-profit institutions, and the Federal Government.
- Of the approximately 600 astronomers in federal agencies in 1976, most worked for the National Aeronautics and Space Administration and others for the Department of Defense.
- A few astronomers work in museums or planetariums, others work for firms in the aerospace field.
- Starting federal salaries in 1977: $9,303 or $11,523, depending on college grades, with a bachelor's, $11,523 or $14,097 with a master's, and $17,056 or $20,442 with a PhD. Average annual salary in 1977 for federally employed astronomers and space scientists was $25,100.
- Employment trends and prospects: Average annual openings projected through 1985: 30. Employment is expected to grow more slowly than average for all occupations because the funds available for basic research in astronomy are not expected to increase enough to create many new positions. There will be keen competition as the number of degrees granted in astronomy probably will exceed the number of job openings.

1962, when astronomers discovered the first x-ray source besides the sun. X-ray astronomers study the evidence of black holes and clusters or superclusters of galaxies. Some astronomers work in research labs analyzing meteorites and moon rocks (they might be called astropetrologists) while others design experiments for spacecraft to confirm or disprove the existence of life elsewhere in our solar system, galaxy, and universe. The Viking missions to Mars carried several biology experiments; the Voyagers carry a message to possible intelligent life in outer space, a message that may be received and understood in a million years —or never.

In addition to optical telescopes, astronomers use radiotelescopes and x-ray and ultraviolet satellites to capture information that may be coming toward the earth. Some astronomers work with engineers, designing satellite- and earth-based instruments. The space program has produced much advanced technology, especially miniaturized equipment. Besides imaginative and exciting theories about the past, present, and future of the universe, astronomers may ultimately provide practical answers to questions about new energy sources for the future.

THE THRILL OF IT ALL: ASTRONOMERS

"You try to make every minute at the telescope count — it's an incredibly exciting time."

"When I look up at the stars, I don't see how I could not be an astronomer."

"Astronomy is more ethereal, appeals more to the imagination than some other disciplines."

Getting There—Education

The majority of astronomers teach or conduct research; at many universities they are expected to double as physics or math instructors.

High school students interested in taking astronomy should look for summer intern programs at planetariums, observatories, or universities, especially those with women astronomers on the faculty. In college a degree in physics with options in astronomy is the most realistic choice. You must take lots of physics even if you are an astronomy major because the disciplines are drawing so close that there is the possibility of their eventual synthesis. And you'll need a reading knowledge of two foreign

THE DAILY GRIND: ASTRONOMERS

"You need stamina to stay up all night, watching and evaluating and deciding what to do."

"A good sense of self-confidence is important. Women are sometimes treated as curiosities and not taken seriously."

"You may be away from home on assignments and observations for weeks or even months. It's very disruptive of family life."

languages, German and French or Russian. Even classical solar-system astronomy and orbit calculations now involve computer work, so training in computers, electronics, and lab work is good preparation for an industry job. A PhD is a prerequisite for almost every direct astronomy career, but with a bachelor's or master's degree you might begin your career as a telescope or instrumentation assistant at an observatory, or as a teacher not involved in research. Other job opportunities exist at planetariums and in the aerospace industry.

It is important to attend the best possible college with an astronomy faculty (who can provide advice and letters of recommendation). Don't be shy. Ask questions, knock on doors. You must develop courage and confidence. Don't take no for an answer.

Chemistry and Chemists

Chemistry deals with the properties and transformations of materials, and the laws that govern the combination of elements. This enormous field has been extensively subdivided: for example, inorganic chemists study elements and compounds other than those of carbon; organic chemists deal with the more than 1 million carbon compounds. The distinction derives from a 19th-century belief that substances made by plants and animals were somehow "vital" and different from substances made in a laboratory—a view that was maintained until the nitrogenous compound urea was synthesized; chemists now know that there is no difference between synthetic and "natural" compounds with the same elements and structure. Physical chemists observe natural phenomena and record their observations. Thermochemists study the effects of heat on states of matter; photochemists, the effects of light; piezochemists,

---

GETTING IN, MOVING UP: CHEMISTRY

The chemistry job market has improved since the early 70s, although it's not so good as in the early 60s. New government regulations by such agencies as the Environmental Protection Agency and Food and Drug Administration require chemists for enforcement. Drug and food companies, regulated by the government, need chemists, too—especially at the BA level. A BA, however, is not sufficient for research or academic positions; such positions—and promotions in general—require a PhD.

FACTS AND FIGURES: CHEMISTS

- Nearly 150,000 persons worked as chemists in 1976.
- Of these about three-fifths were in private industry, almost half of them in chemical manufacturing; others worked for manufacturers of food, scientific instruments, petroleum, paper, and electrical equipment.
- Colleges and universities employed about 25,000 chemists in 1976.
- Approximately 25,000 chemists worked for state and local governments (mainly in health and agriculture) and for federal agencies (chiefly the Departments of Defense, Agriculture, Interior, and Health, Education, and Welfare).
- About half of all chemists worked in New York, New Jersey, Ohio, Pennsylvania, Illinois, and California.
- Average starting salaries in 1976 in private industry: $11,500 with a bachelor's, $13,600 with a master's, $18,700 with a PhD.
- Starting salaries in 1977 for federally employed chemists: $9,303 or $11,523, depending on college grades, with a bachelor's, $14,097 with two years' graduate study, and $17,056 or $20,442 with a PhD. Average salary for all federally employed chemists was $19,900 in 1977.
- In colleges and universities the average 1977 salary with a master's was $17,000 and $21,000 with a PhD.
- Employment trends and prospects: Average annual openings projected through 1985: 6,400. Opportunities are good for graduates at all degree levels. An increased demand for plastics, synthetic fibers, drugs, and fertilizers, in addition to activities in health care, pollution control, and energy will contribute to the need for additional chemists.

the effects of mechanical forces; and electrochemists, the effects of electrical forces.

Analytical chemists try to determine the chemical composition of substances. Until the mid-20th century they could take molecules apart only piece by piece and then try to reassemble them. Now crystallographers can determine the structures of crystals by studying the geometric patterns made when x-rays are diffracted (bent) by atoms in the crystals. Spectroscopers can measure the relative masses of charged atoms to furnish a substance's molecular weight. By looking at the patterns made by electromagnetic rays passing through a substance, they can determine its elements, their arrangement, and the bonds between them. Stereochemists analyze the structure and geometry of molecules.

Radiation and nuclear chemists study how individual atoms and subatomic particles behave during chemical reactions. Polymer chemists

THE THRILL OF IT ALL: CHEMISTS

"A chemist needs insatiable curiosity. She should also be ambidextrous!"

"A chemist can be as creative as an artist. When you see the structure you've put together it's beautiful and fun."

"A background in chemistry opens up all kinds of areas; there are all kinds of things one can do."

investigate substances with long molecules, especially those made of repeating units, such as rubber, nylons, and plastics. Biochemists work with the proteins, nucleic acids, and other chemicals that form the structural and functional units of living, or once living, organisms. (Their field is discussed, along with biology, in the next chapter.)

Getting There—Education

High school students interested in a career in chemistry should take math, chemistry, and physics. English is also important: good reading

THE DAILY GRIND: CHEMISTS

"An education in science gets out of date quickly unless you keep up with new developments in the profession."

"Over half the faculty wouldn't take women as research assistants. Some male graduate students were against my being awarded a special stipend for being an outstanding research assistant."

"To solve problems you must correlate a sea of mud of data."

comprehension is necessary to help absorb and digest the information in all the books and journals you must keep up with, and communication skills are needed in effectively presenting your ideas orally and in scholarly reports. The National Science Foundation sponsors programs for high school students interested in chemistry careers. Many government agencies offer summer internships, and some colleges provide summer lab jobs to high school students. When applying to colleges, choose schools accredited by the American Chemical Society.

With a bachelor's degree you can begin a career in chemistry analyzing or testing products or assisting senior chemists. However, most research and college teaching positions require advanced degrees. Some companies will sponsor promising employees during their graduate work, often at least financing tuition.

BASIC RESOURCES

Among the professional societies that are information sources for careers in the physical sciences are:

American Astronomical Society
211 FitzRandolph Road
Princeton, New Jersey 08540

American Chemical Society
1155 16th Street NW
Washington, D.C. 20036

American Institute of Physics
335 East 45th Street
New York, New York 10017

American Association of Physics Teachers
335 East 45th Street
New York, New York 10017

Manufacturing Chemist's Association
1825 Connecticut Avenue NW
Washington, D.C. 20009

CHAPTER 3

LIFE SCIENCES —

Biology, Biochemistry

Life scientists of many sorts call themselves biologists, but the majority are better classified by the type of organism they study. Botanists, for example, study plant life, zoologists study animal life, and microbiologists investigate microscopic organisms such as bacteria, viruses, and molds. All these subdivisions, like wheels within wheels, encompass further specialties.

A life scientist may scrutinize the eaters and the eaten—interactions among the animals and plants of an ocean or desert. Or she may focus on a particular one-celled organism or even on one process within that organism. An ecologist's work may take her to muggy tropical islands or gale-swept tundras. A biochemist may spend her working days—and sometimes nights—in a well-organized, air-conditioned laboratory. Whatever she does and wherever she works, a life scientist will be involved with fundamental questions about living things: How do they differ from the soil, air, and water around them? How do they cope with different or changing environments? What makes them grow and reproduce and die? What makes them think?

This focus on living organisms is the chief difference between life scientists and physical or earth scientists. However, many biological disciplines overlap or merge with the work of social and physical scientists and even engineers.

Ethologists, for example, observe animal behavior and are sometimes called animal psychologists. A biochemist studying the behavior and chemical nature of living things may work alongside an organic chemist investigating the structures of biologically derived chemicals such as hormones and proteins—or one person may do both kinds of research. A paleobiologist studies fossils and other remains of long-dead animals and plants; but so does a paleontologist, who is considered a geologist.

FACTS AND FIGURES: LIFE SCIENTISTS

- Approximately 205,000 persons worked as life scientists in 1976; about 100,000 as biological scientists, 65,000 as medical scientists, and 40,000 as agricultural scientists.
- Nearly three-fifths worked in teaching and research jobs at colleges or universities, and large numbers of medical investigators worked in medical schools and hospitals.
- In 1976 about 40,000 life scientists were in private industry, mostly in pharmaceutical, industrial chemical, and food processing industries.
- State agricultural colleges and agricultural experiment stations employ sizable numbers of specialists in agronomy, horticulture, animal husbandry, entomology, and related areas.
- About 18,000 life scientists worked for the Federal Government in 1976—more than half for the Department of Agriculture, others for the Department of the Interior and the National Institutes of Health.
- State and local governments employed roughly 22,000 life scientists.
- Approximately 6,000 life scientists worked for not-for-profit research organizations and foundations; a few were self-employed.
- Employment is concentrated in some metropolitan areas (e.g., nearly 6 percent of all agricultural and biological scientists work in the Washington, D.C., area), but life scientists are distributed fairly evenly throughout the United States.
- Average starting salaries in 1976 in private industry: $10,900 with a bachelor's in agricultural science, $10,200 with a bachelor's in biological science.
- Starting federal salaries in 1977: $9,303 or $11,523, depending on college grades, with a bachelor's, $11,523 or $14,097 with a master's, $17,056 or $20,442 with a PhD. Average salary for federally employed agricultural and biological scientists in 1976 was $21,600.
- Employment trends and prospects: Average annual openings projected through 1985: 10,700. Opportunities are good for those with advanced degrees because of increased activities in medical research and environmental protection. Although those with lesser degrees may face competition, they may become research assistants or laboratory technologists or enter the health care field.

Biophysicists use math and physics to understand the functions of human and animal bodies and those of plants. They have helped design cardiac pacemakers, a combination of biology and engineering.

In 1976 in the United States 205,000 people worked as life scientists. About three-fifths of them worked for colleges and universities. The Federal Government employed 18,000 life scientists, about half in the

Department of Agriculture. Approximately 40,000 other life scientists worked in private industry.

The nearly 20,000 women who attended graduate school in the mid-70s were a sizable minority—about 30 percent—of all life sciences graduate students. Of the 123,000 life scientists working for colleges and universities, 20 percent are women. More than 80,000 new graduates each year compete for only 16,000 jobs. The Scientific Manpower Commission, which projects these same figures through 1985, notes, however, that the oversupply of life scientists will not be nearly as large as the surplus of social science and humanities graduates.

Biology and Biologists

The vast territory of biology can be divided roughly into botany, the study of plants; zoology, the study of animals; and microbiology, the study of protozoa and other microorganisms.

Botanists may devote themselves exclusively to mosses (inbryology), mushrooms or other fungi (mycology), trees (dendrology), or to other subdivisions. Zoologists may concentrate on birds (ornithology), insects (entomology), snakes (herpetology), or on other orders, classes, or phyla. Parasitologists explore the complex life cycles of worms and leeches.

Other biologists—anatomists and embryologists, for example—compare structures, such as skeletons, or processes, such as growth and development. Or they may apply genetics, physiology, or pathology to investigations of plant or animal heredity, function, or disease. Others are systemists or taxonomists, who classify species and search for new ones. Ecologists are concerned with the interactions of organisms and their environments.

What biologists do and where they work are as varied as their specialties. Marine biologists like Dixie Lee Ray (a biology professor and Washington State governor from 1977 to 1981) collect data during cruises on oceanographic vessels and later analyze the data in their labs. Limnologists like Ruth Patrick (winner of the $150,000 Tyler Ecology Prize and head of a 70-member department at the Academy of Natural Sciences in Philadelphia) may be found thigh-deep in a river, taking water samples to study pollution levels and set clean-water standards. Ethologists like Jane Goodall study animals in their natural habitat. Dr. Goodall has spent much of the past 15 years—with time out to start and finish college and get a doctorate—living near Lake Tanganyika in Africa among baboons and chimpanzees.

Other biologists conduct research in laboratories, teach college and high school classes, or work in museums of natural history, national and state parks, or in wildlife preserves. The careers of the pharmacologists, toxologists, cytologists, histologists, and immunologists parallel those of

GETTING IN, MOVING UP: BIOLOGY

In this getting-overcrowded field, many temporary jobs are available with the National Park or Forest services for high school biology majors. Such work would be good preparation for a career with the Environmental Protection Agency, for example. A BS is needed for entry-level jobs in industry, where career opportunities may be better than in academic fields. For advanced research work, especially in health-related fields, many specialists have an MD degree.

biochemists. Many specialists have MDs instead of, or in addition to, advanced degrees in biology. They may work for the National Institutes of Health or other government agencies, or at hospitals and medical research centers.

Getting There—Education

High school students interested in biology careers should enjoy chemistry, math, and physics. Many biologists advise students not to major in biology if it is the only science they like since the field is getting so overcrowded. High school students may be able to find summer jobs in wildlife centers or working for the National Forest or Park services, which hire thousands of people for temporary jobs each year. Participation in science fairs and science essay contests is part of good preparation.

College majors in biology should make an effort to meet and get to know faculty members in the life sciences departments. A faculty member who knows you can help make the difference in your admission to graduate school, your being hired for a summer job, or even your employment after you earn your degree. With so many premedical, predental, and other professional majors taking biology, even senior-level courses at large universities may have several hundred people enrolled.

A biology BA/BS can become a lab technician or high school teacher. She may work in industry, where career opportunities for a BS or MS may be more promising than those for a PhD in academia. An outdoor type might enjoy work as a forester or park biologist, an environmental inspector or monitor for the Environmental Protection Agency, or a fisheries biologist, perhaps specializing in aquaculture (sea farming).

Lorraine Benjamin, Biologist

"On a collecting cruise the work is physically hard and intellectually demanding. That's why I love it!" says Lorraine Benjamin, a research assistant at an Atlantic Coast oceanographic institute. As part of a research team headed by a senior scientist, she goes out three or four times a year on a special oceanographic vessel to collect samples from sea floor to surface. The rest of the year Ms. Benjamin works in the lab, analyzing the specimens gathered on these trips.

On nearly every trip the vessel drags surface tows that pick up the midocean plankton Ms. Benjamin's research group is studying. The complicated scheduling of ocean research projects is coordinated by the institute computer.

"Almost all scientists get 'shiptime grants' included in their research funds," Ms. Benjamin remarks. "Sometimes two researchers go out together if their work doesn't conflict." One might be a biologist studying the adaptations of a genus of water striders, the only known open ocean

---

NOTE FROM THE PAST

Abbess Hildegarde

During the Middle Ages Europe's most learned women were found in the convents. Nuns received a superior education and were not burdened by the responsibilities of home and family.

One of the most remarkable of these women was Abbess Hildegarde of Bingen. Called "the Sybil of the Rhine" and "the Marvel of Germany," St. Hildegarde provided the most scientifically valuable record of medical knowledge and natural science in the Middle Ages. She corresponded with all the highest representatives of church and state; no woman in the Middle Ages had greater influence. One of Abbess Hildegarde's most extensive works is her *Physica,* nine books treating minerals, plants, birds, fishes, insects, and quadrupeds. (The book on plants has 230 chapters!) The work was so important that several editions had already been printed as early as the 16th century.

St. Hildegarde's interests were encyclopedic, and she wrote many books on pathology, physiology, and therapeutics. Although for religious reasons her knowledge of anatomy was largely conjectural and far from accurate, it was said that all who went to her came away cured.

---

insects, and the other might be a geologist analyzing the mineral composition of ocean floor rocks.

Not all researchers work in midocean. One of Ms. Benjamin's colleagues studies dinoflagellates (the "red tide" organisms) at Cape Hatteras, the Florida keys, Taiwan, and Hong Kong; she also has them sent to her from around the world.

Ms. Benjamin grew up near the Atlantic Ocean and was "always interested" in biology, especially marine biology. In high school she took every science course offered and entered every science fair. Even so, she says she "crept into the career very gradually. The atmosphere at my college in the early 60s was very traditional. I was not encouraged to go for a doctorate, though I should have been on the basis of my performance. An MA was supposedly 'enough' for a woman. I always had the feeling that things going on around me weren't fair, but since I had no contact with other women in the same situation, I mistakenly thought I might be the one who was wrong."

After getting her MA in biology and science education, Ms. Benjamin taught for several years in the South at a traditional college, where, as she recalls, "the youngest *female* instructor automatically took minutes at department meetings. A man and I helped with electronmicroscopy for a senior professor who had definite ideas about sex roles: I did all the preparations; my male colleague took all the photographs!" There Ms. Benjamin supervised an honors tutorial course in freshman biology, designed lab experiments and programmed instruction with film loops and slides, wrote a lab manual and a study guide, and prepared a reading list. Despite all her hard work, as a lecturer she was not a full faculty member. Ms. Benjamin regrets that "I had no vote in faculty meetings and no voice in policy or curriculum—not even for the course I ran."

After she married a fellow biologist, Ms. Benjamin moved to the Atlantic Coast. She has been working in her present job at the institute for several years. "I took a month off when my son was born. He's in nursery school now and my husband, who is in graduate school, arranges his schedule to care for our child. When my husband has earned his PhD, I might go back to school and get mine."

Changes in plankton physiology and their biochemical constituents are the focus of Ms. Benjamin's research. She describes her current job as "almost 100 percent research," although she advises graduate students, helps her senior scientist teach a course every other year, and trains postdoctoral fellows working in the lab. "Eventually I'd like to do more teaching after I have built up a good research reputation so that I can avoid teaching general biology to freshmen again," Ms. Benjamin comments. "Pure research can be ego-shattering when a hypothesis fails and all your emotional eggs are in one basket. Teaching can be an important and vital component of a career, especially working with graduate students. When someone's been working for you for three or four years, you see that person grow scientifically. It's tremendously satisfying to realize what you've done for a student, how you've helped establish him or her in a career."

Ms. Benjamin is also in charge of overseeing the institute's Affirmative Action program. She speaks to high school and college students and sets up job training programs and summer institutes for minority and women students and teachers from schools with a high percentage of minority enrollment. "As a black, I can be highly effective," Ms. Benjamin states with some satisfaction, "in recruiting both minorities and women to this fascinating field."

Biochemistry and Biochemists

Biochemists study the behavior and chemical nature of living things. Their laboratory research may be in genetics, molecular biology, or agriculture. Experiments made by biochemist Martha Chase (with Alfred Hershey) showed that four-fifths of viral DNA (deoxyribonucleic acid, the genetic material) entered an infected bacterium while four-fifths of viral proteins were left out, proving that DNA rather than protein had to be what genes were made of. Biochemist Barbara McClintock mapped (determined gene order on) corn chromosomes. Her work was useful for genetics in general and also for the knowledge it provided on how corn development is controlled—and might be changed to improve agricultural varieties.

Biochemists may try to develop microorganisms that can grow on petroleum and help clean up oil spills or can provide abundant high-protein food for humans and animals. By analyzing food values, biochemists can develop more nutritious foods. Gladys Emerson studied the body's needs for B-complex vitamins and vitamin E and the deficiencies that may occur if those needs are not met.

Metabolism, photosynthesis, and enzyme activity are other fields of investigation for biochemists. Gerty Cori, who with her husband, Carl, and B. A. Houssau won a Nobel Prize in 1947, traced the catalysis or breakdown of glycogen, the energy-providing substance animal enzymes make from blood sugar for storage in muscle tissue. When muscles work, glycogen is converted to lactic acid and then, through the complex Cori cycle involving several body organs and numerous enzymes, back into glycogen.

The demand for biochemists, especially in biomedical research, will continue in the future, but colleges and universities may intensify the competition by turning out more new graduates than are needed. A young woman with a BA or BS in biology or chemistry might find employment as a lab technician, working under the supervision of a doctor of biochemistry. Although she may be an important participant in original research projects, without an advanced degree, her chances of doing self-guided research will be very small.

Because so many women scientists are biochemists, entry-level jobs are as accessible to well-qualified women as men. The administrative hierarchy in academia, industry, and government is still male dominated, but that may change as men at the top retire and a substantial percentage of those moving up the ladders are women.

BA or BS biochemists work in industry or government as research assistants doing testing and analysis. Drug companies also employ biochemists, hoping that some will find useful new compounds (as did Rachel Brown and Elizabeth Hazen, who discovered the fungicide nystatin). Government biochemists (like Frances Kelsey, who, by insisting on more pre-licensing testing of thalidomide, prevented possibly thousands of birth defects) test new drug products, food additives, and other chemicals. Some biochemists go into business for themselves and start their own diagnostic labs.

Getting There—Education

A strong high school background in math and sciences is essential for the future biochemist. English is also important; lab work is done by teams who must be able to communicate their ideas informally and in committee meetings and departmental seminars. Research scientists spend a lot of time writing proposals for grants and papers for scientific journals.

A course in lab or medical technology enables a high school graduate to start working in a lab while taking college courses. Lab experience can help the new college graduate seeking a job. PhDs are often hired as lab technicians, not for their possible creative insights, but because they know how to operate complex lab equipment and need less training. They can bridge the gap between theoretical and practical knowledge. With lab experience behind her a BA would have similar training and thus an advantage for such work. Biochemistry students generally major in biology and minor in chemistry or vice versa. Prospective biochemists should also take college math and physics courses.

GETTING IN, MOVING UP: BIOCHEMISTRY

Although entry-level jobs are readily available for women, climbing the career ladder remains more difficult for women than for men. And such advancement is all but impossible without a PhD. Some biochemists set up their own diagnostic lab services.

FACTS AND FIGURES: BIOCHEMISTS

- About 12,700 biochemists were employed in 1976.
- Nearly half of all biochemists work for colleges and universities.
- About two-thirds of all biochemists work in basic and applied research.
- More than one-fourth of all biochemists are employed in private industry, mainly by manufacturers of drugs, cosmetics, and insecticides.
- Of biochemists working for federal, state, or local governments, most do health and agricultural research for federal agencies.
- Not-for-profit research institutes and foundations also employ biochemists, and a few self-employed biochemists act as consultants.
- According to a 1976 survey by the American Chemical Society, salaries for experienced biochemists averaged $18,000 with a bachelor's, $19,000 with a master's, and $26,000 with a PhD.
- Employment trends and prospects: Average annual openings projected through 1985: 800. Employment is expected to grow faster than average for all occupations. Favorable opportunities exist for those with advanced degrees because of increased activities in medical research and environmental protection.

Advancement to independent research and administrative posts is all but impossible without a doctorate. Getting a PhD can be less expensive, however, than getting a bachelor's degree. Many graduate students receive monthly stipends of $300 to $400, plus free tuition, on teaching assistantships or research grants during the three, four, or more years it takes to get a PhD. Postdoctoral fellowships are also available. Graduate students specialize in some aspect of biochemistry or apply biochemical techniques to study genetics, development, or metabolism in plants or animals. As biology becomes more analytical and less descriptive, biochemistry plays an increasingly larger role in every biological discipline.

BASIC RESOURCES

For information on careers in various of the life sciences contact:

American Institute of Biological Science
1401 Wilson Boulevard
Arlington, Virginia 22209

American Association of Zoological Parks and Aquariums
Oglesbay Park
Wheeling, West Virginia 26003

American Society for Horticultural Science
National Center for American Horticulture
Mt. Vernon, Virginia 22121

American Society of Zoologists
P.O. Box 2739
California Lutheran College
Thousand Oaks, California 91360

Farm Credit Administration
Washington, D.C. 20578

Society of American Foresters
5400 Grosvenor Lane
Washington, D.C. 20014

Soil Society of America
677 South Segre Road
Madison, Wisconsin 53711

United States Department of Agriculture
Forest Service
Washington, D.C. 20250

United States Department of Agriculture
Office of Personnel
Washington, D.C. 20250

Two interesting publications on agricultural careers are:

Careers in Agriculture and Natural Resources —Agriculture, available from the National Association of State Universities and Land-Grant Colleges (Dupont Circle NW [Suite 710], Washington, D.C. 20036).
Careers in Agronomy, available from the American Society of Agronomy, Inc. (677 Segoe Road, Madison, Wisconsin 53711).

CHAPTER 4

EARTH SCIENCES —

Geology, Oceanography, Meteorology, Paleontology

The four "elements" noted by the ancient Greeks—water, earth, fire, and air—are the province of earth scientists. Oceanography, geology, paleontology, and meteorology began as descriptive sciences, recording the effects of quiet inlet waters on grains of sand as well as the cataclysmic aftermaths of earthquakes. Within the past century, scientists have become more analytical—learning how pressure, light, heat, and acidity mold and move earth, water, and air.

An oceanographer may spend weeks at sea on a research vessel, investigating currents or mapping the ocean floor with echo sounders. A geologist may collect sample rocks in the field or evaluate their mineral content and origin in a laboratory. Paleontologists search for fossils on field trips and later study them in laboratories. Meteorologists predict the weather by analyzing precipitation from drizzles to blizzards or its absence, for example, or by studying the upper atmosphere.

Whatever her speciality and wherever she practices it, an earth scientist applies the laws of physics and chemistry to the titanic forces that create mountains and volcanoes, winds and waves. The work of earth and life scientists intertwines. Paleontologists study the petrified remains or traces of plant and animal life. Soils, the concern of geologists, result as much from the activity and decay of animals and plants as from the crumbling of bedrock. The distribution of oceanic life can tell an oceanographer much about water temperatures and currents. Biology even influences the weather; for instance, topsoil without a cover of vegetation that blows off in a wind storm may create dust clouds that affect the regional degree of sunlight and thus the local temperatures. Earth scientists rely on the quantitative methods of physics and chemistry to examine oceanic, continental, and atmospheric phenomena. And

279

engineers work with earth scientists to design and build the instruments needed for research.

Geology and Geologists

Geology is a wide-ranging field with many subspecialties. Petrologists investigate the composition of rocks and their origin; mineralogists do the same for minerals, including gems. Other specialists concern themselves with processes: Geochemists, for example, study the chemical composition of rocks and minerals and the chemical changes affecting them. Geomorphologists study the shape of the earth's surface and its alteration by such forces as erosion and glaciation. Volcanologists study the origin of igneous rocks and the life cycles of volcanoes. Sedimentologists explore the deposition of sedimentary rocks.

Geophysicists investigate the size, shape, interior, surface, and atmosphere of the earth. They measure electrical, gravitational, and magnetic forces produced by the earth and the effects of solar radiation. Seismologists study the vibrations caused by earthquakes and such human activities as underground drilling and nuclear tests, and measure the effects of those vibrations on subterranean formations. Hydrologists examine the distribution, circulation, and physical properties of surface and underground water.

Practical applications of geology include petroleum geology, finding and retrieving oil and natural gas; economic geology, locating mineral resources; and engineering geology, using geological knowledge in the construction of roads, dams, and buildings, particularly in floodplains and areas of earthquake activity. Medical geologists study the beneficial and harmful effects of minerals on the human body. For instance, geologists are trying to determine why asbestos is a carcinogen and a general health hazard, while other minerals that are similar chemically but dif-

GETTING IN, MOVING UP: GEOLOGIST

Although a master's degree is sufficient for advancement into management in industry, a PhD is needed by anyone planning on doing research or teaching at a university. Employment opportunities are good for geophysicists in oil and other resource industries. Medical geologists are benefiting from the current interest in health and environment.

ferent physically—the "federal fibers" now regulated by the same rules governing asbestos—seem to pose no threat to health.

Getting There—Education

All geologists now need a solid background in math and science because geology has moved from a descriptive to a quantitative science. A combined BA with a major in geology and math, physics or chemistry is most useful. Many new BAs are hired by oil companies and trained in exploration.

In geology, unlike some other scientific fields, many students work in industry between degrees. A company may pay the tuition for an MA program. If not, pay your own way; an MA in geology is the minimum requirement for a professional rating, and it provides enough training for

FACTS AND FIGURES: GEOLOGISTS

- More than 34,000 people worked as geologists in 1976.
- Of these, more than three-fifths were in private industry, mostly petroleum companies but also mining and quarrying concerns. Some were employed by construction firms; others were independent consultants to industry and government.
- More than 2,000 geologists are employed by the Federal Government. Two-thirds work for the Department of the Interior in the United States Geological Survey, Bureau of Mines, and Bureau of Reclamation. State agencies also employ geologists.
- About 9,500 work at colleges and universities.
- Geologists also work for not-for-profit research institutions and museums.
- Employment is concentrated in states with large oil and mineral deposits. Almost two-thirds work in Texas, California, Louisiana, Colorado, and Oklahoma.
- According to a survey by the College Placement Council, in early 1977 graduates with master's degrees in geology and related geological sciences received average starting salaries of $14,900.
- Starting federal salaries in 1977 were $9,303 or $11,523, depending on college grades, with a bachelor's; $11,523 or $14,097 with a master's; $17,056 or $20,442 with a PhD. The average salary for geologists was above $25,000.
- Employment trends and prospects: Average annual openings projected through 1985: 1,300. Employment is expected to increase faster than average for all occupations because of the demand for petroleum and minerals. Employment opportunities are good for bachelor's degree holders; very good for those with advanced degrees.

you to move upward. In industry an MA or MS is considered sufficient academic background for a geologist to get into management.

Some observers believe the PhD market in geology is being glutted and only those who are planning to do research or teach in universities should study for a PhD. Most geology departments require an MA for admission to a PhD program. The average geologist gets a PhD at age 30 or so.

Gloria Vaughn, Geologist

"I liked the promise of field work and outdoor life, and the challenges to the mind that geology presented," Dr. Gloria Vaughn remembers. With the encouragement of her geologist husband she switched from a chemistry major to geology, a change of fields she says she has "never regretted, although my professional commitment has caused havoc in my personal life. At the beginning of my marriage I accepted the traditional role of wife; but trying to handle the tremendous amount of work in my career, as well as all a wife's chores, was too exhausting.

"Graduate school offered intellectual challenge and a sense of discovery in my courses," Dr. Vaughn recalls, "despite the fact that some unsympathetic male professors made it the most painful three years of my life. Until my thesis adviser twisted his arm, the graduate adviser wouldn't sign a form for me to enter the PhD program." Years earlier a woman had had a fellowship and dropped it to get married; she became his permanent excuse for discriminating against women. Sex discrimination was also revealed in a "series of assumptions and innuendos, but only a few professors were openly hostile."

Field work attracted her to geology, but Dr. Vaughn at first avoided field-oriented problems "on the advice of my major professor. He said I should make myself acceptable as a women geologist by working in the lab." Women geologists are concentrated in mineralogy and petrology, detailed laboratory analysis of mineral and rock composition. When Dr. Vaughn got her PhD in the late 60s, she encountered "blatant discrimination." "The oil companies told me outright they wouldn't hire women because 'they get pregnant and quit. It takes two years to train them and that's as long as they last.' " Mandatory Affirmative Action programs for government-funded work have caused at least an official reversal of this attitude, however, and now oil companies are actively seeking women geologists. (One of Dr. Vaughn's former students, a woman in her mid-20s with a geology BA, heads a four-member uranium exploration team in Colorado, for example.)

Dr. Vaughn is currently the only woman in a large state university geology department. Her work is half teaching—everything from freshman geology with biweekly field trips to graduate seminars—and half research. Right now she is investigating mineral processing and separation: "A flotation process is used to separate minerals, but a certain amount is always lost. I'm trying to isolate and analyze the material lost to determine if it is always the same type of material and to see if there are certain mineralogical differences between it and the material that is retained."

Like many academic geologists, Dr. Vaughn has done some free-lance consultant work during the summers. She is currently debating whether to remain as one of the 50 or so women geologists on American faculties. "There are so few role models for woman students," she laments; "I hate to take one away by getting a job elsewhere." Nevertheless, she is considering the higher salaries and shorter hours found in industrial and government research. "In academia you have two full-time jobs, teaching and research. And you're constantly competing with other teachers for graduate students and grants."

Working for an oil company wouldn't necessarily mean that Dr. Vaughn would have to give up basic research. One oil company geological research program "discovered some of the most important rules and laws—all purely theoretical—of structural geology."

Dr. Vaughn sees a great future in geology for herself and other women. "It's an expanding field with expanding exploration for mineral resources and energy sources, environmental studies such as evaluations of the strength of the land for structures and waste disposal, medical studies of toxic and cancer-causing minerals. As long as the environment and the exploration and conservation of natural resources remain important, geologists will be needed."

Whether or not she continues to teach, Dr. Vaughn expects to pursue her research. "The earth is very complex, and in earth science you must know a lot before you can become creative. You accumulate that knowledge as you mature. Creative scientists—and I hope I am one—continue to be creative throughout their lives."

Oceanography and Oceanographers

Oceans cover nearly three-fourths of the earth's surface. The study of their boundaries and their contents is carried out at sea and along seacoasts by oceanographers. These scientists use special cameras, bathyscapes, and bathyspheres built to withstand tremendous undersea water pressures; sonar instruments; computers to analyze data; and a variety of other sophisticated measuring and recording devices.

Physical oceanographers study ocean temperature and density, the transmission of sound and light in water, and water movement as tides, currents, and waves. Geographical oceanographers investigate sea-floor sediments, mineral nodules on the sea floor, rocks and topography; and

GETTING IN, MOVING UP: OCEANOGRAPHY

A PhD is necessary for most jobs other than technician, especially because of the keen competition in the field. An undergraduate college major in geology, biology, math, chemistry, or physics will give you the background you'll need for graduate work. Pick one of these sciences to specialize in and learn as much about the ocean as you can. Continue with the same field in graduate school and learn more about the ocean.

Work at a coastal laboratory and experience on board boats and ships is a definite plus for an aspiring oceanographer.

they map the ocean-floor mountains that are as high as those on the continents and valleys that are much deeper. Chemical oceanographers assay the chemical composition of ocean water and chemical reactions in the ocean. Biological oceanographers (marine biologists) are interested in oceanic plant and animal life. Oceanographic technicians, who

FACTS AND FIGURES: OCEANOGRAPHERS

- About 2,700 persons worked as oceanographers in 1976.
- More than one-fourth of these were employed by the Federal Government (e.g., the Navy and the National Oceanic and Atmospheric Administration).
- About half worked in colleges and universities.
- Some oceanographers work in private industry; a few for fishery laboratories of state and local governments.
- Most work in states that border on the oceans (4 out of 10 in California, Maryland, and Virginia).
- Starting federal salaries in 1977 were $9,303 or $11,523, depending on college grades, with a bachelor's, $11,523 or $14,097 with a master's, $17,056 or $20,442 with a PhD. Average salary for experienced federally employed oceanographers was $23,800.
- Employment trends and prospects: Average annual openings projected through 1985: 100. Applicants are likely to face strong competition. Those with PhD degrees should find favorable opportunities but those with less education may be limited to routine analytical work as research assistants or technicians.

THE THRILL OF IT ALL: OCEANOGRAPHERS

*"Those long trips to sea may disrupt family life,
but from what I hear, the reunions are marvelous.
For years women have waited for their men to return
from sea; a little reciprocity is long overdue."*

*"I love the ocean, and learning about it and
studying and analyzing its properties has never
diminished in the slightest my emotional attachment
to the sight and sound of endless waves rolling in."*

may be high school or junior college graduates, work as divers, aides, or instrumentation assistants.

Meteorology and Meteorologists

Meteorology encompasses a broad spectrum of jobs, from operations (forecasting) to research. Some women with children have found the odd hours of the graveyard (after midnight) shift in operations difficult (a forecaster must work 24 hours a day) but most have persevered.

THE DAILY GRIND: OCEANOGRAPHERS

*"Women never went to sea — it's untraditional.
It's also considered unlucky by some superstitious
people to have women on ships."*

*"Ocean trips may last for months, with rough,
dangerous weather, long hours of exhausting
work, and separation from family and friends."*

*"The competition is very stiff. There are so
few jobs."*

GETTING IN, MOVING UP: METEOROLOGY

Meteorologists can find work in any branch of the armed services, with movie companies on location, with commodities markets or in agribusiness, or with government agencies concerned with the environment. The aviation industry relies more and more on up-to-the-minute meteorological reports from the scientists it employs.

Future meteorologists need to study as much math as possible in high school, as well as physics, English, and foreign languages. Practice describing complex events in a logical way. It will train you to *observe*— not just see—and understand. Undergraduates may major in meteorology or in a related field, such as physics.

FACTS AND FIGURES: METEOROLOGISTS

- About 5,500 persons worked as meteorologists in 1976; additional thousands in the Armed Forces did forecasting and other meteorological work.
- More than 1,800 meteorologists worked for the National Oceanic and Atmospheric Administration and more than 200 for the Department of Defense.
- Almost 2,000 were in private industry—several hundred worked for commercial airlines; others for private weather consulting firms, companies that design and manufacture meteorological instruments, and firms in aerospace, insurance, engineering, utilities, radio and television, among others.
- More than 1,300 worked for colleges and universities.
- Nearly one-fifth of all meteorologists live in California and Maryland; one-tenth work in the Washington, D.C., area.
- Starting federal salaries in 1977 were $9,303 or $11,523, depending on college grades, for a bachelor's and no experience; $11,523 or $14,097 for a master's; $17,056 or $20,442 for a PhD. Average salary for federally employed meteorologists was $24,500.
- Airline meteorologists' salaries ranged from $16,000 to $24,000 in 1976, depending on experience.
- Employment trends and prospects: Average annual openings projected through 1985: 200. Favorable opportunities exist in industry, weather consulting firms, radio and television, government, and colleges and universities.

GETTING IN, MOVING UP: PALEONTOLOGY

Paleontology is not a large field. Since the academic and museum job market is very tight, an aspiring paleontologist might spend her high school or college summer vacations as a volunteer in a natural history museum or on a dig. Nothing is guaranteed, but these unpaid apprenticeships could lead to paid positions after college. A specialization in paleontology is usually delayed until graduate school, after earning a BA in geology or biology. Curricula tend to be somewhat flexible; in paleontology it is said you learn more by experience than from formal courses.

Paleontology and Paleontologists

Special fields in paleontology/paleobiology range from dendrochronology, the study of past climates through their effects on tree ring growth, to pollen analysis, the study of ancient pollen deposits.

Museum and university paleontologists spend much time in the field; better-paid oil company researchers may rarely leave their air-conditioned labs. Oil companies hire paleontologists and other geologists in two categories: MS and PhD "professionals" and "nonprofessional" BA/BS laboratory technicians who are well paid but have little opportunity for advancement.

For research in paleontology a large collection of reference fossils is essential. Many paleontologists work in museums housing such collections rather than in an academic setting. Like university faculty, museum curators must publish articles on their research to maintain their professional standing.

BASIC RESOURCES

For information on earth science careers, write or phone:

American Congress on Surveying and Mapping
733 15th Street NW
Washington, D.C. 20005

American Geological Institute
5205 Leesburg Pike
Falls Church, Virginia 22041

Association of American Geographers
1710 16th Street NW
Washington, D.C. 20009

National Council for Geographic Education
115 North Marion Street
Oak Park, Illinois 60301

CHAPTER 5

ENGINEERING CAREERS

The stereotypical portrait of the engineer in hard hat and overalls, with a sheaf of blueprints, a slide rule, and a plumb line says nothing about gender; but if it were to be painted in oils rather than words, the chances are good that almost all Americans would picture a male. In actuality if all the engineers in the United States were to sit for a group portrait, they *would* be overwhelmingly male. Until quite recently the stereotype and the reality reinforced each other to the extent that young women seldom thought of entering engineering or were discouraged when they did think of it, because it was a "man's field." Thus it remained a "man's field."

However, that pattern appears to be due for some very rapid and long overdue alterations. The barriers have been falling, and an environment once inhospitable toward women is becoming far more inviting. Greater professional commitment and higher career aspirations on the part of large numbers of women are combining with increased acceptance and recruitment on the part of educators and employers. And so the chain is at last breaking.

Engineering is an amazingly rich field that offers abundant opportunities. No other profession has as many diverse specialties and applications, and few professions offer its challenges, financial rewards, and opportunities to make a contribution. America's more than 2 million engineers constitute the second-largest professional group in the country (exceeded only by teachers), and engineering is by far the single largest occupation for men. It is also one of the most common routes to management positions in industry, and it can be entered with only a bachelor's degree. Engineering also has taken on broader horizons and new social dimensions as applied technology is marshaled to deal with environmental and energy problems, urban blight, traffic congestion, and inadequate health care delivery. Add to all this an excellent employment outlook for the foreseeable future, and you realize why engineering is an attractive field for women.

NOTE FROM THE PAST

Ellen Swallow Richards

A pioneer in the field of sanitary engineering, Ellen Swallow Richards (1842–1911), was the first woman admitted to the Massachusetts Institute of Technology. She was accepted without charge as a special student so that the president of the institute could say she was not a "real" student if the trustees or other students complained. Because the heads of the various departments did not want to see a woman receive the DS in chemistry, Ellen Richards never received her doctorate. Nevertheless, she continued to work at MIT and established the Woman's Laboratory, which offered training in chemical analysis, industrial chemistry, mineralogy, and biology. Ms. Richards also set up a correspondence school for women; she wrote to each of the science students, advising them on health and finance.

Ellen Richards was instrumental in establishing MIT's program in sanitary engineering, the first in any university. For 27 years she taught air, water, and sewage analysis, and many of her pupils went on to become leaders in public sanitation.

One description of the engineer's role puts it this way: "The basic distinction between the linked professions of science and engineering lies in their goals. The scientist aims to discover new knowledge, whether useful or not, while the engineer strives to put knowledge, old or new, to work efficiently for the needs of mankind."*

Engineers turn dreams into reality. They build culverts and computers; design satellites and sewage systems; bring warmth or coolness, water, and light to many who assume that the flick of a switch or twist of a faucet does the job. Many scientific discoveries were made possible in this century because engineers built the reflecting telescopes, electron-microscopes, cyclotrons, and other devices that enabled scientists to observe, often for the first time with any accuracy, distant stars or viruses or elusive atoms. Much of an engineer's work is hidden and unnoticed —except when it happens to go wrong.

The attributes common to all engineers, whether they are involved in aerospace or agriculture, in undersea exploration or mass surface transit, are the desire and ability to solve problems—problems that arise from the daily needs and contingencies of living or the more exotic problems associated with advancing frontiers of knowledge. By applying mathematics, science, and technology to the materials and forces of nature,

---

* *Life Science Library, Engineer,* by Joe McCarthy and Clifford C. Furnas. Alexandria, Virginia: Time-Life Books, 1966, p. 9.

FACTS AND FIGURES: ENGINEERS

- More than 1.1 million persons worked as engineers in 1976.
- Approximately half worked in manufacturing industries (chemicals, electrical and electronic equipment, aircraft and parts, machinery, scientific instruments, primary metals, fabricated metal products, and motor vehicles); more than 340,000 in non-manufacturing industries (mainly construction, public utilities, engineering and architectural services, and business management consulting services).
- Colleges and universities employed about 45,000 in research and teaching jobs.
- Federal, state, and local governments employed about 150,000, of whom more than half were federal employees (mostly in the Departments of Defense, Agriculture, Interior, Transportation, and the National Aeronautics and Space Administration). Most engineers in state and local government agencies worked in highway and public works departments.
- Engineers are employed in every state, in small cities and large, and in rural areas. Some branches are concentrated in particular industries and geographic areas.
- According to the College Placement Council, the average starting salary in 1976 in private industry for engineers with a bachelor's degree and no experience was $14,800, almost $16,500 for a master's degree and no experience, and above $21,000 for a PhD.
- Starting federal salaries in 1977 were $9,303 or $11,523, depending on college grades, for a bachelor's degree with no experience, $11,523 or $14,097 with a master's, $17,056 or $20,442 with a PhD. Average salary for experienced federally employed engineers was $25,900.
- In 1976, for a 9-month academic college year, faculty members with 5 years' experience beyond the bachelor's degree received about $15,150; those with 18 to 20 years' experience beyond the bachelor's degree, about $21,150.
- Employment trends and prospects: Average annual openings projected through 1985: 52,500. Employment is expected to grow faster than average for all occupations. Opportunities for engineering school graduates will be very good as supply is likely to fall short of demand. Many openings also will be filled by upgraded technicians and graduates in related fields.

---

engineers design useful equipment and labor-saving devices for industry and home; invent and develop new processes, systems, fibers, and computers; investigate a wide range of phenomena leading to the conservation of natural resources; and expand our technological capabilities in increasingly elaborate and imaginative directions.

It is not just a matter of building a better mousetrap for less; engineering is a pragmatic and methodical way of reducing abstract theory to tangible and serviceable fact.

IS ENGINEERING FOR YOU?

Should *you* consider an engineering career? Evaluate your interests and abilities by asking yourself the following questions:

- Do I have an aptitude for math and science?
- Am I curious about how things work and how to make them work better?
- Do I think logically and analytically?
- Am I patient, persistent, and determined to see things through?
- Do I like to work as a member of a team?
- Do I seek practical solutions to problems?
- Do I have the ability to visualize shape, size, function, color, and motion?

If you answer yes to these questions, you already possess some of the qualities essential to being a good engineer. As an engineer you will probably be required to work with other engineers to solve a particular problem. Frequently, the more complex engineering jobs are tackled by technicians, scientists, and engineers in a project group; thus the ability to work well with others is essential. Stability and objectivity are characteristics that enhance any scientific endeavor and are necessary prerequisites to engineering as well.

Specialties and Subdivisions

Within the many specialties in engineering are countless subdivisions. Technology has grown so pervasive and complex that each facet of an

EDUCATION FOR ENGINEERING

Engineering, unlike the sciences, does not require a graduate degree for most positions in government or private industry. However, students interested in college teaching or university or industrial research usually go on to get MS and PhD degrees. More and more students now seek work experience before beginning graduate study. Some graduate schools prefer that a student work before beginning graduate study.

For more information on education, financial aid, and finding work, consult Chapter 7 of this Guide.

engineering problem demands a specific type of training and expertise. In this chapter, we take a closer look at four main engineering areas: chemical, civil, electrical, and mechanical. But these are just four of the 25 specialties and their 85 subdivisions recognized in engineering.

For a keen appreciation of the impressive scope of professional engineering activities, read the Sunday want ads in any major newspaper. As an aerospace engineer, you might test space-age materials for the National Aeronautics and Space Administration or help design a more efficient wing configuration for a commercial aircraft manufacturer. An agricultural engineer might grow high-protein plants in multistory greenhouses, a biomedical engineer might supervise patient-monitoring systems for a hospital, an industrial engineer might accelerate the food distribution patterns for a supermarket chain. There are also sonar installation engineers, optical instrumentation engineers, quality control engineers, and crystal engineers, as well as ceramic engineers and petroleum engineers.

Within each engineering specialty numerous functions must be performed: administration, research and development, design, sales, consulting, construction, installation, production and quality control, teaching and training. Thus an engineer can accommodate her interests and abilities, not only in terms of the specific field she chooses (e.g.,

Licensing

All 50 states and the District of Columbia require a professional license for engineers who offer their services to the public or whose work affects life, health, or property. A license for any kind of engineering work is becoming more of a necessity every year. Licensing prerequisites include an engineering degree from an accredited school, a minimum of four or more years of satisfactory engineering experience and a passing grade on a two-day written state examination. The first part of the exam, usually taken in the senior year of college, covers fundamentals; the second part is offered after several years on the job.

Some specializations have additional licensing requirements. For example, structural engineers in California, who must certify the soundness and earthquake resistance of buildings, bridges, and highways, first become licensed civil engineers, then work three more years and must pass a 16-hour written exam.

Information on licensing is available from:

National Council of Engineering Examiners
P.O. Box 752
Clemson, South Carolina 29631

mining, textiles, or hydraulics), but also in terms of the orientation within that area she subsequently decides to pursue (e.g., research, technical writing, or field supervision).

An engineer has a wide choice of work environments. She may spend her time at the drafting board or computer terminal or laboratory workbench. Or she may clamber around the catwalks of an oil rig or sewage processing plant. Wherever human endeavor is aimed at improving our living conditions or extending our ability to cope with conditions beneath the sea or in outer space, an engineer—or more likely a team of engineers—is on the job. Engineers work at construction sites, at desks; in major cities, in small towns; for local governments, for federal agencies, for foreign countries; in remote outposts or giant urban industrial plants.

Chemical Engineering and Engineers

Chemical engineering is a large and diversified branch that applies chemical, physical, and engineering principles to manufacturing processes in which materials undergo chemical change.

For years chemical engineering was the most popular specialty among women, and today these engineers are among the most highly paid in the profession. One successful woman engineer who received her degree in chemical engineering recalls that when she was in college the only place she could envision "girls really being accepted" was in a laboratory. Many women have chosen this specialty for similar reasons,

FACTS AND FIGURES: CHEMICAL ENGINEERS

- About 50,000 persons worked as chemical engineers in 1976.
- Most of them were in manufacturing industries, mainly those producing chemicals, petroleum, and related products.
- Some worked in government agencies or taught and did research at colleges or universities.
- A small number worked for independent research institutes and engineering consulting firms, or as independent consulting engineers.
- Employment trends and prospects: Average annual openings projected through 1985: 1,850. Employment is expected to grow faster than average for all occupations in response to industrial expansion, particularly in the chemicals industry.

but their careers have shown that chemical engineers, whether women or men, can branch out in many different directions.

Chemical engineers may specialize in oxidation, polymerization, plastics or rubber, pollution control or liquid rocket fuels, etc. They are often involved with determining the most efficient manufacturing process possible, which involves a working knowledge also of mechanical and electrical engineering.

Stephanie Ellis, Chemical Engineer

"Engineering is an interesting mental exercise, but that's not all," comments Stephanie Ellis; "it's also problem oriented and productive. When you get an answer, you can accomplish a lot."

Only four years out of college, Ms. Ellis works as a troubleshooter for a Texas oil refinery. She calculates process controls and optimal refinery operations in her office but may spend several days in a row in the plant working around pumps carrying slurry heated to 110 degrees, gathering data, or just checking up on operations. Her irregular work schedule, sometimes eight hours on duty and eight off, might be a problem, she thinks, if she had a husband or children.

In the refinery she hasn't found it hard to get along with the male blue-collar workers. "They gave me a chance to prove myself. Once I did, they accepted me as an engineer and the person in charge." Her college experience at a technical institute with 99 percent male enrollment was good preparation.

"I was interested in majoring in chemistry and decided to spend one year at the institute to see if I liked the field," she recalls. "I was impressed by the outlook and intentions of people in chemical engineering, so I switched majors and stayed put until graduation." There were a few initial social and physical discomforts in college. Ms. Ellis felt "a bit on display," and one building where she had a three-hour lab course had no women's washroom, but her academic performance won her acceptance by faculty and fellow students.

Her present job offers good potential for advancement. (The president of her corporation started his career in the same job she now holds.) Ms. Ellis's personal long-term goal is "management of a technically oriented company—this one or another. The problem will be that most technical managers want to work problems for their staffs instead of letting staff members do it. I'll probably be no exception. But it's good for managers to keep up with changes in the technical end."

Chemical engineers tend to specialize within one field, Ms. Ellis has found, some concentrating on certain kinds of chemicals (for example, petroleum products, coal tar derivatives, or plant alkaloids), others on equipment design (such as heat exchangers of distillation pumps used in all types of chemical engineering: oil, coal, tar, fertilizer, food, and other chemicals). Continuing emphasis on the energy field keeps chemical engineers in strong demand. "The job outlook is amazing," says Ms. Ellis. "People with a BS in chemical engineering—even with a C-minus average—are being offered $16,000 a year." Potential chemical engineers should be good in math, science, and, she says, "have a good English background for reading, like to work with machines, and not mind getting greasy or dirty." Over 9 percent of working chemical engineers are now women and Ms. Ellis thinks there should be more.

Civil Engineering and Engineers

Civil engineering, the oldest branch of the engineering profession, relates to the physical needs of a city or community. Traditional examples are the building of roads and bridges, but today the field encompasses complex societal problems including water and air quality and transportation systems. Civil engineers are involved in many subspecialties—structural, hydraulic, wastewater, transportation and urban planning, and soil mechanics. Related categories are architectural and environmental engineering.

Civil engineers supervise projects, help design airfields and harbors, inspect bridges, and develop new sewage systems. Their work is perhaps more visible to the average citizen than that of any other engineering field. The majority are employed by federal, state, and local governments, and the construction industry, although large numbers are employed by consulting engineering and architectural firms.

Elizabeth Eng, Civil Engineer

"I was interested in art and math, and thought I might go into architecture. Civil engineering seemed more practical to me and my family, so I started in that instead. Now I'm glad I did!"

Elizabeth Eng is a civil engineer specializing in soils research. Her involvement with a project begins with writing proposals and continues until construction is complete on the highway, dam, bridge, or building. Between these stages she does site exploration, investigates soil dynamics, and plans the foundation design and earth dams needed. "Earthwork constructions need a geotechnical person on site all the time to advise on soil mechanics and other problems," Ms. Eng explains. "Once the job is under way, I take a junior engineer, one who's still learning and getting experience, out to stay on site."

These construction sites are located in California, where her company is headquartered, and around the United States and in South America

FACTS AND FIGURES: CIVIL ENGINEERS

- About 155,000 civil engineers were employed in 1976.
- Most worked for federal, state, or local governments or in the construction industry. Many worked for consulting engineering and architectural firms or as independent consulting engineers; others for public utilities, railroads, educational institutions, and manufacturing industries.
- Civil engineers work in all areas of the country, usually in or near major industrial and commercial centers. They often work at construction sites, sometimes in remote areas or in foreign countries. In some jobs they must often move from place to place to work on different projects.
- Employment trends and prospects: Average annual openings projected through 1985: 9,300. Employment is expected to increase faster than average for all occupations as a result of growing needs for housing, industrial buildings, electric power-generating plants, and transportation systems. Work on environmental pollution and energy self-sufficiency will also result in openings.
- Average starting salaries in 1976: $13,764, depending on educational background and experience.

---

and Africa. "I get extra pay for work outside the country. My husband and children are quite understanding, but I usually have only one or two days' notice before leaving for Brazil or Nigeria or wherever. I have to keep my passport current and my shots up to date."

Earthquake engineering, one of Ms. Eng's interests, has applications in such unlikely-seeming places as Dayton, Ohio, and Boston, Massachusetts, as well as near California's San Andreas fault. In California, a structural engineer from the state structural safety enforcement agency reviews all public facility construction plans, approves or rejects the designs, and works in the field to make sure that private contractors, architects, and engineering firms meet earthquake safety standards.

Ms. Eng worked up till the day each of her children was born, then took a six-month leave of absence but "keeping in touch with the state of the art—and with office gossip." She also kept up her activities with the Society of Women Engineers, working with high school girls, "trying to get them to take more math." These professional activities outside work are "enjoyable and introduce me to present fellow women engineers and I hope some future ones." If her leaves of absence had been more extensive, say, two years or more, Ms. Eng thinks she might have had to take review courses before reemployment.

Another option for mothers of small children is part-time or temporary work in job shops that hire engineers (especially industrial, mechanical, and electrical engineers) by the hour to do design work. Some engineers —usually well established and older, less likely to be the mothers of small children—work on their own as freelance consultants.

Two possible avenues for Ms. Eng's career development are freelance work as a consultant with her own business or working with her present company or another large firm, gradually moving from technical expert to project manager to administrator. An MS has enough educational background for a well-paid job as a technical expert.

Future engineers should be interested in science, physics, and the environment and should realistically assess their goals. "For some engineers it's just a job. To others, engineering is a career, a hobby, and intellectual recreation," Ms. Eng notes. "Recognize what you want to be. Some types are more analytical. Others, such as construction or civil engineers, are more creative. To me, seeing my design come to life—I can go out and see and touch it and say, 'It's mine'—is a profound satisfaction. Engineering is anything but theoretical. You know when you've blown it or when you've succeeded."

Electrical Engineering and Engineers

Electrical and electronics engineers today make up the largest group within the profession and are in great demand by business and industry. All the equipment used in generating or distributing electrical energy, from power plants to toaster ovens, requires their services. The fast-growing area of electronics needs these engineers to work with high-speed computers, semiconductors, microminiatured components, and other advanced technology.

The demand for electrical and electronic engineers greatly exceeds the supply; perhaps that is one reason why this field was selected by more female engineering undergraduates in 1972 than any other speciality. The field is highly diversified: electrical engineers concentrate their experience in specific areas such as communications equipment; electronic apparatus such as television, radar, and computers; electric motors and generators; and electrical appliances of all kinds. Electrical engineers are needed extensively by industry and business.

Sheila Eberhardt, Electrical Engineer

"My *male* high school counselor told me to become a high school science teacher," Sheila Eberhardt recalls, "but my *female* high school science teachers urged me to go into physics!" Her family, especially

FACTS AND FIGURES: ELECTRICAL ENGINEERS

- About 300,000 electrical engineers were employed in 1976.
- Most of them worked for manufacturers of electrical and electronic equipment, aircraft and parts, business machines, and professional and scientific equipment.
- Many worked for telephone, telegraph, and electric light and power companies.
- Large numbers of electrical engineers are employed by government agencies and by colleges and universities.
- Others work for construction firms, for engineering consultants, or as independent consulting engineers.
- Employment trends and prospects: Average annual openings projected through 1985: 12,200. Employment is expected to increase faster than average for all occupations. Growing demand for computers, communications, and electric power-generating equipment, military and consumer electronic goods, and increased research and development in nuclear power generation will spur demand.

her engineer father, supported her decision midway through college to switch from physics to a "more down-to-earth" electrical engineering major.

After college in New England she and four other new graduates got jobs in a local communications company research lab. "The three men were put on the graduate studies program. They got three days a week off the first year and two days a week off the second year to get their master's degrees—at full pay, of course," Ms. Eberhardt remembers. "The woman and I were told we could take a few hours off a week—without pay—to attend classes. It took three years for me to get my master's in information science." Ms. Eberhardt then moved to the Washington, D.C., area and a position as a communications and computer engineer.

"I do research in the transmission of signals, especially digital information from computer to computer—teaching computers to talk to each other." She has designed special-purpose computers to switch process data and correct errors—the electronic equivalent of an old-fashioned switchboard operator.

As the assistant manager of her research and development group, Ms. Eberhardt takes part in hiring. "In hardware [machines], the men claim women are physically incapable of handling the work, although field work for engineers consists of overseeing others' work. not tightening bolts or opening valves. So most of the women engineers in the company work for me in software [designs and programs]. I've also been hiring minority men. It's good for the white males to look around and see people practicing engineering who don't look like stereotypical engineers."

Ms. Eberhardt sometimes thinks of starting her own company to combine her expertise in electronics with her after-hours interest in music, but she isn't sure she wants "the hassle" of running her own company. Another alternative is moving into management, "possibly in a smaller company where I could have a manager's salary and power and still continue my technical work," she speculates.

What's it like for a woman engineer among all the men in the field? Ms. Eberhardt was the only woman in her class in undergraduate school, and she remembers that "no one wanted to do homework with a girl, so I worked on my own. If there had been even three or four other women, I wouldn't have had to bear such a stigma." But times have changed: "The women in school now will be in the workforce in five years, and as more women enter, women engineers will become more and more accepted. Which is great because women have a lot to offer—and to gain —in this type of job."

Mechanical Engineering and Engineers

Mechanical engineers make up the second-largest subgroup within the profession and the broadest in its range of activity. Mechanical engineers design and develop machines which produce power—engines,

---

FACTS AND FIGURES: MECHANICAL ENGINEERS

- About 200,000 mechanical engineers were employed in 1976.
- Almost three-fourths were in manufacturing—mainly in the primary and fabricated metals, machinery, transportation equipment, and electrical equipment industries.
- Others worked for government agencies, educational institutions, and consulting engineering firms.
- Employment trends and prospects: Average annual openings projected through 1985: 7,900. Employment is expected to increase faster than average for all occupations, because of the growing demand for industrial machinery and machine tools and increasing complexity of industrial machinery and processes.
- Average starting salaries in 1976: $14,964.

turbines, and reactors—and machines which use power—refrigeration and air-conditioning equipment, elevators, machine tools, and steel rolling mills. Some mechanical engineers work in marine applications; others in the automotive industries. Some specialize in machinery for a special material such as rubber; others in hydraulics or instrumentation.

Margaret Bauer, Mechanical Engineer

"Technology is at the hub of almost anything that goes on. Engineers have to be aware of economics and finance and do the best job at the least expense," explains Dr. Margaret Bauer. "Scientists doing research on grants can afford to be no less aware of financial problems."

Dr. Bauer has done both. After getting her PhD in mechanical engineering, she taught and did research in the Midwest in "solar energy fluid mechanics problems, trying to figure out ways to store energy for power plants or home nighttime use. I found some government grants available but only for basic research, not applications. I liked teaching, but teaching at a major university you have to be a showman and hustle for grant money. You really don't get to do much research yourself. And even if you do, it's hard to do research, teach, and find money—and do them all well."

Dr. Bauer now heads up a mechanical systems group designing heating, ventilating, air-conditioning, and fire protection systems for federal buildings. She is in charge of 10 mechanical engineers, in addition to draftspeople and clerks. She assigns work, makes sure deadlines are met,

---

ATTENTION, HIGH SCHOOL STUDENTS INTERESTED IN ENGINEERING

General Motors Institute (GMI) in Flint, Michigan, offers an excellent opportunity for students to prepare for engineering careers. GMI is a private, five-year, fully accredited college owned and supported by General Motors Corporation. The institute's cooperative plan enables its students to combine academic study with work assignments in a sponsoring General Motors unit. For more information on this opportunity to learn and earn, write:

General Motors Institute
1700 West 3d Avenue
Flint, Michigan 48502

---

and checks budgets. She reviews designs by outside consultants and by her staff, and for some projects she designs her own systems. "If problems develop while the mechanical systems are being put in, I may go out and take a look. And I do make the final inspection after construction," Dr. Bauer explains. "But like 95 percent of engineers, I work in an office, not in the field."

High school preparation for a career in mechanical engineering should include math, chemistry, physics, mechanical drawing (if it's offered), and shop courses. Dr. Bauer's high school mechanical drawing courses landed her a job as a draftswoman, which she held for several years while going to school at night. Dr. Bauer advises against specializing too soon in college. "There is a good market for engineering jobs now, but demands change. When people are highly specialized—for example, aerospace engineers—they can't move into another area. Nuclear engineers have only a few companies they can work for. Now, with energy

---

OTHER SPECIALTIES WITHIN ENGINEERING

Aeronautical engineers design planes, helicopters, and other aircraft, including air-cushion vehicles that "float" a few inches off the land or water. *Astronautical engineers* are concerned with spacecraft; avionics specialists deal with the electrical systems of air- and spacecraft. *Industrial engineers* analyze the human and material components of manufacturing and try to organize them efficiently.

Agricultural engineers focus their attention on improving farm tools and machinery, conserving soil and water, controlling pests, and streamlining food processing and distribution. Pacemakers, artificial kidney machines, and other devices contributing to modern health care are the province of *biomedical engineers. Ceramic engineers* design and build nonmetallic products; for example, the new smooth stovetop cooking surfaces. *Mining, metallurgical,* and *petroleum engineers* devise equipment and methods for extracting minerals, oil, and gas from the earth, refining or purifying them, and converting them into useful products.

Environmental engineers work to prevent or control environmental health hazards; fields of specialization include sanitation, air pollution, industrial hygiene, public health, and radiological health.

Nuclear engineers combine scientific knowledge of nuclear reactions and radiation with engineering principles to produce heat, power, and special nuclear products such as the radioisotopes used extensively in biological and biomedical research. *Material science engineers* try to relate such properties of materials as tensile strength, flexibility, and ductility to their molecular structures.

conservation in the news, refrigeration and heating are important. Keep your options open so you'll be able to move around and broaden your experience. You may change your mind in a few years—don't box yourself into one field.

"Career planning is important. Love of the technical work may cause problems if you are tied to the technical ladder and don't get any management background. Twenty years later, it's too late."

Young women planning families should not avoid engineering because they may have to drop out. Dr. Bauer feels that "an engineering BS is a good background for a job, even in a business office, and even without graduate school." Since many if not most mothers of young children *will* wind up working even if they hadn't planned to, "you might as well choose a career with top options." Dr. Bauer and her husband, a math professor who supports her professional goals, moved South to further her career, and his has not been set back. They each commute 30 miles a day to work—in opposite directions.

"One more thing: A lot of women seem to think engineering means not being able to work with people," Dr. Bauer adds. "Lots of women want to be doctors and extend the lifespan, but what good will that be if everyone is freezing? Engineering deals constructively with problems everyone faces."

BASIC RESOURCES

For career information in the fields listed, contact:

Agriculture Engineering

> American Society of Agricultural Engineers
> 2950 Niles Road
> St. Joseph, Michigan 49085

Biomedical Engineering

> Alliance for Engineering in Medicine and Biology
> 4405 East-West Highway (Suite 404)
> Bethesda, Maryland 20014

> Biomedical Engineering Society
> P.O. Box 2399
> Culver City, California 90130

Ceramic Engineering

American Ceramic Society, Inc.
65 Ceramic Drive
Columbus, Ohio 43214

Chemical Engineering

American Chemical Society
1155 16th Street NW
Washington, D.C. 20036

Manufacturing Chemists Association, Inc.
1825 Connecticut Avenue NW
Washington, D.C. 20009

Civil Engineering

Engineering Manpower Commission of the Engineers' Joint Council
345 East 47th Street
New York, New York 10017

Engineers' Council for Professional Development
345 East 47th Street
New York, New York 10017

National Society of Professional Engineers
2029 K Street
Washington, D.C. 20006

Extractive and Metallurgical Industries

American Institute of Mining, Metallurgical, and Petroleum Engineers
345 East 47th Street
New York, New York 10017

American Powder Metallurgy Institute
201 East 42d Street
New York, New York 10017

American Society of Metals
Coordinator for Career Development
Metals Park, Ohio 44073

Engineers' Council for Professional Development
345 East 47th Street
New York, New York 10017

Louisiana Technical University
Department of Petroleum Engineering
Ruston, Louisiana 71270

National Coal Association
Educational Division
1130 17th Street NW
Washington, D.C. 20036

Industrial Engineering

American Institute of Industrial Engineers
25 Technology Park/Atlanta
Norcross, Georgia 30092

Mechanical Engineering

American Society of Mechanical Engineers
345 East 47th Street
New York, New York 10017

Nuclear Engineering

United States Energy Research and Development Administration
Washington, D.C. 20545

Safety Engineering

American Society of Safety Engineers
850 Busse Highway
Park Ridge, Illinois 60068

Tool and Equipment Designing and Drafting

American Institute for Design and Drafting
3119 Price Road
Bartlesville, Oklahoma 74003

International Association of Machinists and Aerospace Workers
1300 Connecticut Avenue NW
Washington, D.C. 20036

International Federation of Professional and Technical Engineers
1126 16th Street NW
Washington, D.C. 20036

National Machine Tool Builders Association
2139 Wisconsin Avenue NW
Washington, D.C. 20007

CHAPTER 6

A VARIETY OF OCCUPATIONS RELATED TO SCIENCE AND ENGINEERING

The tight job market for scientists, the long years of preparation needed to earn a PhD, the intense competition for grant money—these drawbacks dissuade some very qualified people from pursuing a career that uses their knowledge and flair for scientific and technical endeavor. If you are interested in and want to be involved in science and engineering as part of your work, should you give up just because you don't want to join the ranks of doctoral candidates and face the rigors of academic life? The answer is *No*. You can find a job that capitalizes on your interest in the world of science and yet spares you the long years of preparation and the drawbacks of pursuing a career as a professional scientist or engineer.

Many jobs demand knowledge of scientific principles and skills—technician, research assistant, librarian, science editor or writer, even management jobs in business and patent and environmental law careers. The applications of science and engineering are all around us and so are careers that involve these developments of modern society. Women with interest and skills in these fields can find employment that uses their scientific bent.

Significant contributions to scientific progress can be made by technicians without advanced degrees, even without BAs, and by writers and editors who help scientists communicate their ideas. Science librarians must understand what kind of information library users are looking for. And patent and environmental lawyers specialize in the legal aspects of scientific discoveries and the impact of science and technology on all of us and on our environment.

Research and Research Assistants

Research assistants (also called science technicians), with or without BAs, work everywhere scientists and engineers are employed—in museums, academia, industry, and government. Opportunities for rapid or extensive advancement without graduate degrees are uncommon, but learning on the job can replace formal training. Also, many firms subsidize professional training for their employees. Frequently, universities permit their employees to take courses free of charge during work hours. The Armed Forces, which employ many technicians, also provide on-the-job educational opportunities. In addition to working in offices and laboratories, biology technicians work for zoos or botanical gardens, chemists as environmental monitors for government agencies, life and earth scientists as aides or guides in national and local parks and preserves.

In many jobs at this level, little expertise is presumed or required, and the necessary skills either don't become obsolete quickly or are simple enough to be learned rapidly. Therefore, technical assistants returning to work after a hiatus might find jobs more easily than those who were employed at more advanced levels. Another bonus: Some technicians can arrange curtailed working hours while their children are of school age.

More than 700,000 persons are employed as technical research assistants or science technicians. Many begin work with a two-year associate degree in science technology. Generally, employers prefer some specialized training since technicians are needed in areas as diverse as aeronautics, air-conditioning and heating, chemistry, electronics, instrumentation design, and biomedical lab work. For some technicians, this specialization requirement may include returning to school for a higher degree.

Some 475,000 science technicians work in private industry, about 160,000 in various government agencies, the rest at educational institutions and nonprofit organizations. Training programs are given by schools of technology, technical institutes, and two-year colleges.

Mary Frances Appleton, Technical Assistant

"My job is to help the curator do his work most effectively," explains Mary Frances Appleton, technical assistant in a museum of natural history. "I help with the research, maintain the collection in invertebrate paleontology—this involves keeping the catalog up to date and making, or pointing out the need for, any necessary repairs—proofread reports and journal articles my supervisor writes, and even do some research of my own."

With a BA in biology and "no desire right now to go to graduate school," Ms. Appleton thinks her job has more pluses than minuses. "It's true that I work under someone else's direction and that his needs take priority, but except for emergencies or deadlines, I have almost complete freedom in organizing my own workweek. Not being in charge means I don't have to worry about 'publishing or perishing,' getting grants for my research, or supervising other people. I'm more or less left alone to do my own work, and it's work that I enjoy doing."

For the general laboratory project, Ms. Appleton's duties include prying fossils out of rocks. "On an average dig, half the fossils found are embedded in the matrix—rock—and can't be removed. The rocks are shipped here to the lab, and I try to pick out the bone by using sand abrasion, acid etching, or pins and needles. If I can't pry it out completely, at least I can try to bring the bone into relief." Working with the curator, she may piece together parts of the fossil. (Whole-skeleton assembly is done by the exhibition department.)

The museum where Ms. Appleton works houses some of the world's finest collections of skeletons, skins, dried flowers and insects, and shells, representing hundreds of thousands of animal and plant species, all of which are available for employee research projects. Ms. Appleton's current private project is mostly bibliographic: "I'm analyzing all the published papers, and unpublished ones if we have copies of them, on a group of horselike South American marsupials, the proterotheres. These animals rapidly became extinct about 2 million years ago when the Isthmus of Panama rose and thus created a land bridge over which North American mammal species invaded South America. By comparing the literature and also studying the fossils here, I hope to be able to present a complete and unified picture of proterothere evolution and extinction."

Ms. Appleton does not feel that her museum colleagues, most of whom have PhDs, treat her as an inferior. "Certainly I could be replaced by another technician. But the job itself—the work that I do—is important, and everyone here recognizes that fact."

Now in her early 20s and recently married, Ms. Appleton claims that she has "no ambitious career goals. I realize my job is a dead end, but that absolutely doesn't bother me—the work itself is so varied. If it gets boring after a few years, I'll find something else to do. Right now I really enjoy the work I do."

Patent and Environmental Law and Lawyers

Opportunities for women in law are very good, and those for women lawyers who have a science or engineering background are excellent. The combination of law and science is an especially appropriate one for the practice of patent law. Patent applications, trademark disputes, patent infringement cases—the primary work of the patent lawyer—all require a good grasp of the technical aspects of the product or design. A background in science puts the patent lawyer a step ahead of others in her field. And law can provide the solution for the woman who wants a career in science without the headaches of academic life.

Lawyers involved with science often practice environmental law, some working for government agencies, others on behalf of citizen environmental groups. Some major law firms permit their partners and associates to spend a certain amount of time in public service work. The increase in recent years of government regulations about the use and misuse of the environment has brought a corresponding increase in legal cases involving the environment—and both sides in these cases need lawyers who understand science as well as legal matters.

(Legal careers are fully described in Guide to Government and Law Careers.)

Science Communications Occupations

Science generates lots of words on paper, and scientists and engineers have been known to have problems expressing their ideas clearly and coherently for the nonscientific reader. Specialists in making technical subjects comprehensible to the layman, science writers and editors are employed by newspapers, magazines, science journals, and book companies, and even by television and radio stations. Large universities and medical centers also need staff writers to prepare news releases and technical reports. Corporations employ science and technical writers, too; for example, to write computer and other equipment manuals and sales brochures.

THE THRILL OF IT ALL: SCIENCE WRITERS AND EDITORS

"The communication of scientific ideas can have as great an impact on scientific progress as the ideas themselves. We science writers and editors bridge the gap between scientists and the general public."

"I realized I could never teach high school science—being a technical writer is a much better career for me and still uses my knowledge of science."

"I have to be very well informed on new developments in science, but I find it very interesting. It keeps me on my feet—always learning new things."

THE DAILY GRIND: SCIENCE WRITING AND EDITING

*"Free-lancing is a good solution for me, but
the pay scales and lack of job security make
it something I wouldn't recommend to everyone."*

*"Deadlines are the bane of my life.
Everything seems to come all at once."*

*"Research is not my first love, writing is.
I hate tracking down facts that I know are
true just to validate them, but it's something
that must be done."*

Opportunities in science communications also include technical translation, which requires fluency in at least two languages as well as technical expertise, and working as a science librarian, with an undergraduate degree in a scientific field and a Master of Library Science (MLS) degree.

Some graduate library schools, such as that at the University of Illinois in Urbana, offer special programs in librarianship for science majors on computer applications, operations research, and reference service to library patrons. Qualified librarians without formal science backgrounds sometimes become science specialists, but it is virtually impossible to become a librarian without an LS degree.

BASIC RESOURCES: RESEARCH AND ENGINEERING TECHNICIANS

The following organizations are good sources for career information.

Engineer's Council for Professional Development
345 East 47th Street
New York, New York 10017

International Chemical Worker's Union
1659 West Market Street
Akron, Ohio 44313

National Association of Trade and Technical Schools
Accrediting Commission
2021 L Street NW
Washington, D.C. 20036

CHAPTER 7

GETTING PREPARED —

Education and Training

Science Education, Financial Aid, and Employment

Should you follow in the path of the women scientists interviewed for this book? Of course, not everyone should pursue a career in science, not even every undergraduate science major. But everyone is a *potential* career scientist. As such, carefully evaluate your interests and abilities.

Although 20 years ago it may have been relatively easy for an average student to be assured a place in graduate school, not to mention financial aid and subsequent employment, competition is now much keener and money is at a premium. Since financial support and subsequent employment cannot be taken for granted, your decisions about a career in science must be made with maximum guidance and exploration of yourself and your alternatives.

Before you decide to apply for further schooling, take time to identify your career goals and assess your individual needs and abilities. Ask yourself some basic questions:

—Can I work at one thing for long hours at a time?
—Are my observations accurate and detailed?
—Do I work just as well in a group as I do alone?
—Are my mathematical skills good, or can I learn to make them good?
—Can I analyze new facts and figures logically and coordinate them with my previously acquired knowledge?
—Do I deal well with both abstract concepts and concrete principles?
—Am I patient?

Accuracy, patience, self-reliance, stamina—all these qualities and more are essential if you are considering a career as a scientist. Mathematical skill is necessary for basic investigation in any branch of science. Perseverance is a prerequisite since failure, not success, may be the rule, and an experiment may have to be repeated many times before it is considered successful. You must also be able to endure the small, monotonous, yet essential tasks required for most testing and measuring tasks. Although you may be involved in an independent research project, many present-day science problems require multidisciplinary solutions. Teamwork requires time, patience, and coordination to be successful; you must be able to work effectively as part of a group.

As a scientist you must also be imaginative and receptive to new ideas, even though they may challenge long-accepted beliefs. A questioning attitude is the trademark of every good scientist. In addition, you must be willing to invest a good amount of time in your education. As a future scientist, you will be required to spend many years in study. It will take from three to five years after your undergraduate work just to get your PhD, and so you must set your sights to the future.

Graduate School

Having determined that your interest is genuine and you have the necessary stamina and abilities, what about graduate school?

Entrance requirements will vary significantly among the many graduate schools offering advanced degrees in science. The more prestigious, well-established universities can be more selective in their admissions policies. A general rule is that you should have at least a 3.0 (out of a possible 4.0) undergraduate scholastic average to do graduate work.

Some schools may require that you take the Graduate Record Examination, which is designed to measure educational background and general scholastic ability. The GRE, as it is known, is divided into two parts —an aptitude section and an achievement section. Although many academicians question the value of this and other standardized testing as an accurate measure of knowledge, the GRE can provide you and the university with some idea of your ability to tackle graduate school.

If your grade point average is below 3.0, almost all graduate departments will require you to take the GRE. It is also advisable to take it if you are a better-than-average student and intend to apply for a national fellowship. A very good score on the GRE will increase your chances of getting one.

Knowledge of one or more foreign languages is important to a scientist and is usually a requirement for a PhD candidate. Scientists and engineers frequently need to read important articles and papers published in a foreign language or to travel abroad in connection with teaching, research, or training. Ideally, language training should start while you are still an undergraduate student.

As a graduate student you will be expected to complete successfully a prescribed set of courses and pass both written and oral predoctoral examinations. Traditionally a PhD must pass a written exam in two foreign languages, usually German and French or Russian. Your significant accomplishment as a graduate student, however, is your PhD dissertation, an original and scientific research contribution in your chosen field.

Which Graduate School?

Choosing a graduate school is an important step, one to be taken carefully. In making your decision, take into account the overall excellence of a university, but even more importantly, explore the quality of the intellectual atmosphere and the facilities offered by the particular department you are interested in. Talk to faculty members who are involved in scientific areas or projects of interest to you (eventually you will pick one of them as your research adviser). It is also important to talk to students already enrolled in the department to get their reactions and opinions.

Although the quality of a graduate school isn't easily measured, several factors will give you some indication:

—What is the publication record of the faculty?
—How many are members of the National Academy of Science, National Science Foundation, or are similarly honored Fellows?
—How many PhDs did the department grant during the previous academic year?
—What projects are faculty and students currently undertaking?
—How much money is available for research equipment, supplies, fellowships, or research and teaching assistantships?
—How up to date is their laboratory equipment?
—What is the faculty–student ratio?

The answers to these questions will help you to evaluate the university and the department.

Don't forget to consider personal preferences. For instance, would you prefer a large cosmopolitan university or a smaller, more personal institution that may not have the staff or equipment of a larger university? Write to the universities you are interested in and request descriptive brochures, newsletters, fellowship announcements, and any other available information. If possible, schedule a personal visit to some of the universities and visit their laboratories.

Money Matters—Financial Aid

All right, so you think you have a scientific "temperament" and you've chosen your graduate school. Now how do you pay for it?

Financial aid is available from a variety of sources, including federal and state governments; national, state, and local organizations; business and industrial firms; philanthropic individuals and educational institutions.

Most financial aid is awarded on the basis of demonstrated need, usually computed according to this formula:

> Cost of education *minus* parental contribution *minus* student contribution (summer savings, personal assets) *equals* financial need.

Financial aid comes in various forms. Research and teaching assistantships available to graduate students provide a stipend, a small amount of money for living expenses. Your university will also probably have its own scholarship and fellowship program. Outstanding students who have done exceptionally well as undergraduates and who have very good scores on the GRE may qualify for very competitive federally sponsored fellowships.

A major source of fellowships is the National Science Foundation (NSF). A federal agency founded in 1950, the NSF helps formulate government scientific policies, correlates research activities within government, and encourages the spread of scientific information. Its funding activities are largely devoted to research grants, expansion of scientific facilities, and study fellowships. In 1978 the NSF offered 490 fellowships for graduate education in science.

Your department and university fellowship or financial aid office can give you detailed information about university and federal fellowship and scholarship programs.

Work—Getting It

Having invested time, money, and work to earn your PhD, what do you do with it? You have several options: work in industry, government, or academia. Only *you* know what you are best suited for.

As a rule, industry and government salaries are higher than academic salaries. However, don't make the mistake of thinking that you'll work 15 years in industry, make some money, and then retire to a life of "academic bliss." The transition from industrial to academic employment can rarely be made. As an industrial scientist, you will work within

FOR WOMEN ONLY—GRANTS, FELLOWSHIPS, LOANS

A number of grants, loans, and scholarships are reserved for women. Here are a few:

Business and Professional Women's Foundation
2012 Massachusetts Avenue NW
Washington, D.C. 20036

Sponsors a Loan Fund for Women in Graduate Engineering studies. Loans up to $2,000 for tuition and fees for graduate-level training in engineering.

Graduate Women in Science
c/o Dr. Margaret Stone, President
L. H. Bailey Hortorium
Cornell University
Ithaca, New York 14853

Sponsors the Eloise Gerry Fellowship Fund for research in science by women.

Graduate Women in Science
c/o Dr. Evelyn Murrill
1109 117th Street (Apt. 4)
Kansas City, Missouri 64131

Provides grants-in-aid for research projects in mathematical, physical, and biological sciences at both the predoctoral and postdoctoral levels.

Zonta International
Marion Dudley, Public Relations Director
59 East Van Buren Street
Chicago, Illinois 60605

Sponsors the Amelia Earhart Fellowship awards given to women for advanced study and research in aerospace science.

American Association of University Women
    Educational Foundation
Fellowship Office
2401 Virginia Avenue NW
Washington, D.C. 20037

Sponsors the Annie J. Cannon Award in Astronomy for research in astronomy. Usually awarded to women under 35 who have earned a doctorate. Also sponsors:

—Marie Curie Fellowship in radiology, physics, and chemistry
—Sarah Berliner Fellowship in physics, chemistry, and biology
—Ida H. Hyde Fellowship in euthenics and eugenics

Danforth Foundation
Director of Graduate Fellowships for Women
607 North Grand Boulevard
St. Louis, Missouri 63103

Sponsors fellowships for women who want to teach but whose academic careers have been interrupted by raising a family, illness, or other circumstances.

For more information about fellowships, grants, and awards, consult the *Annual Register of Grant Support* (Marquis Academic Media).

---

a restrictive environment that allows for very little publication of research findings under your own name; a concern may permit publication only in its name. Unless you are outstanding in your field and are recognized as such by your peers, your chances of obtaining a position at a top academic institution will be small.

Other considerations are also important before deciding whether to teach or to work in industry or government. As an academician you must devote time to *both* teaching and research, and both are equally important *and* demanding. A professor must teach and advise undergraduates and be available for consultation. He supervises graduate students and is involved in guiding their thesis research. As a professor, you are responsible for carrying out your own research and are expected to participate in the academic affairs and service work of your department and the university.

Academic positions are as a rule accessible to only the very competitive, and universities almost never actively recruit or advertise available faculty positions. Recommending for hiring is principally by word of mouth; therefore it helps to have contacts. Take the initiative: contact department chairmen and send your resume.

Some universities use the services of national professional societies that match employment opportunities with applicants. Seek out and join the societies appropriate to your field.

Manufacturing and industrial employers are the most active recruiters. Among the areas of good employment prospects are chemicals and drugs, metals and metal products, tire and rubber products, aerospace and engineering, electrical machinery.

An industrial scientist works in research and development, R and D.

FUNDING YOUR WORK

You'll need to know how to get money even after your education aid problems are over. As a scientist/researcher, you must quickly learn the ins and outs of applying for grants and fellowships to finance your projects, especially when working for an academic institution or consulting firm. Grant support is a multibillion dollar enterprise, and the competition for available funds is fierce. When looking for money for a project, consult the *Annual Register of Grant Support* (Marquis Academic Media). This valuable book tells you the basics of preparing and writing grant proposals, and even more important, lists many grant sources (government, private foundations, unions, etc.) for every academic discipline. The science listing is comprehensive, covering such topics as type, purpose and duration of the grant; amount of funding available; eligibility requirements; number of applicants; deadlines; addresses.

This insider's volume is available at most college libraries and fellowship or financial aid centers. Many consulting firms use it to guide them in their search for project money and have it on hand for their employees. In science and engineering the scramble for project funds is never-ending; so make yourself as adept as you can at the grantsmanship game.

Research groups in industry may work on design or on solving any technical problems arising out of product development and manufacture. An R and D scientist must be a good team worker. R and D projects often take as long as seven or more years to complete and public recognition of your work will be small or nonexistent. You must exhibit great restraint in discussing your work with scientists outside your company to avoid being "scooped" by a competitor.

An industrial scientist works for a profit-making organization and is expected to make a return on the company's investment in her. Consequently, research must continue in a money-making direction or it will be discontinued. An academician can be more independent and can plan and execute research on a more individual basis.

Most graduating students who seek jobs in industry find them through on-campus industrial recruiters. Your departmental office or college placement office can tell you which recruiters are on campus or when they will be.

Before World War II, most scientists were employed by private industry. Now an increasing number are finding employment within federal research labs and administrative agencies. A great deal of scientific research is carried on by a multitude of federal departments. You may work in a national laboratory or in federally funded R and D centers in fields such as environmental science, forestry, plant genetics, and physics, to name just a few. Government salaries are competitive with industrial compensation scales.

A scientist working within the government will usually find excellent laboratory facilities and wide opportunities for research and publication. However, she may also feel the effects of administrative delays, bureaucratic red tape, and political manipulation more than in other areas of employment.

Relatively few scientists are employed in research institutes and not-for-profit organizations. Salary levels fall between those of industry and government, but job security cannot be guaranteed. You must quickly develop an expertise in applying for the grants that will enable these institutions to keep you on as a salaried employee; the competition is keen.

As a scientist, don't overlook the opportunity to extend your scientific training to other areas of employment. For instance, combining a chemistry background with knowledge of art history and training in conservation techniques could lead to a career in art conservation. Your science training would be useful in science writing and publishing—someone has to write and edit all those textbooks and scientific magazines! Other

---

PROFESSIONAL SCIENCE AND ENGINEERING ORGANIZATIONS— HOW THEY CAN HELP YOU

Professional organizations offer a variety of services to students and job hunters. Basically, they exist to promote the interests of workers in specific occupational fields and to educate students and new workers in career possibilities. Many of these associations provide career aids and brochures, and frequently they offer prizes and awards for excellence to professionals in the field. Most publish scientific journals and magazines, some of which include employment advertising.

Scholarship and financial aids to students involved in research are also offered by many of the groups, and some sponsor courses, seminars, and workshops. Although some professional organizations are strictly honorary, many offer career counseling or placement services to those outside their ranks. They can be very valuable sources of information and support during a job hunt. Frequently your contacts with others in your field are your most important assets when looking for a job. Even the listing on your resume of the professional organizations you belong to cannot be overlooked as a factor that can give you a competitive edge.

Most societies offer full and student membership to qualified applicants. Two representative examples of professional associations in the field of science are the American

Chemical Society (ACS), 1155 16th Street NW, Washington, D.C. 20036, and the Association of Women in Science (AWIS), 1346 Connecticut Avenue NW, Room 1122, Washington, D.C. 20036.

Over 100 years old, the ACS operates an employment clearing house, which matches resumes on file with specific job openings throughout the country. As an added service, the society arranges on-the-spot interviews between members and prospective employers at ACS national meetings. Openings are advertised in the society's *Chemical and Engineering News,* sent free to members. (Nearly 20 journals are published by the ACS to supply its members with news and developments in every field of chemistry.) In addition, an unemployed member of the society may have 50 copies of her resume printed by the ACS without charge. College seniors who have completed at least three-fourths of their chemistry degree requirements qualify for ACS associate membership; full membership requires at least a bachelor's degree in chemistry.

Formed in 1971, the AWIS sponsors a wide range of career development programs to promote equal opportunities for women in science. Among its major activities are an employment service for members and an educational foundation that awards scholarship and incentive money to students. The triweekly *AWIS Job Bulletin* is free on request to members. Among AWIS's current projects is the Registry of Women in Science in North America and Hawaii, intended to serve as a resource for employers, associations, advisory committees, and editorial boards. The Registry will list 20,000 women scientists.

For a comprehensive listing of professional organizations, look in your library for the *Career Guide to Professional Associations: A Directory of Organizations by Occupational Field* (Cranston, Rhode Island: Carroll Press, 1976). It lists organizations by profession and tells what services they provide. Also consult the *Encyclopedia of Associations* (Detroit, Michigan: Gale Research Company, 1978), a basic research tool available in most libraries.

The "Basic Resources" boxes of this Guide also offer brief listings of the professional societies for many disciplines.

---

areas of employment include forensics, museums, patent law, computers —use a little initiative and imagination. You'll be surprised how many careers you could actually consider with a background in science.

For more information on the material covered in this chapter, check your library for *Graduate School in the Sciences: Entrance, Survival, and Careers.* (A Wiley-Interscience Press book, it is currently out of print but it is still found in many libraries.) It will tell you just about everything you want to know about graduate school for science study— and then some.

Engineering Education, Financial Aid, and Employment Training for Engineers

Most undergraduate programs in engineering are four or five years long. For the first year or two they share a common core curriculum, including math, physics, chemistry, humanities, social sciences, and communication skills.

During the first two years or so, students are generally given an overview of the fields within engineering to help in choosing a specialization in their sophomore or junior year. Among the five-year programs are some which offer a bachelor's degree, others that award a master's degree, and still others that supply the graduate with a double bachelor's degree—in engineering and in liberal arts.

Many educational programs include a period of cooperative education in which the student obtains first-hand experience in actual job situations through alternating periods of study and work. Students are usually placed in a job after a minimum of one year of schooling. Because of this practical work experience in a real engineering setting, graduates of cooperative programs are especially sought after by employers.

Some specialties, such as nuclear engineering and biomedical engineering, require a master's degree. After earning a bachelor's degree many engineers seek experience working as an engineer before deciding which area of graduate work, if any, they wish to pursue. Work experience gives them the necessary knowledge about themselves, their work, and available options so that they can make an informed decision. In many cases employers help pay for graduate schooling; thus many engineers have found that working first really pays off.

Money Matters—Financial Aid

Financial aid for engineering students is offered by various institutions and organizations and is usually awarded on the basis of demonstrated financial need. Most schools have their own fellowship and scholarship funds. The Federal Government also offers a variety of aid programs. Many social and professional organizations offer scholarships and loans for students who are members or in fields of interest to the organizations. Additional sources of aid are local clubs, fraternal organizations, veterans associations, youth groups, and religious organizations. Your college financial aid office can give you the most complete information on what money is available. Make every effort to visit the financial aid officer at your present or prospective institution and explore all possible sources of aid.

Work—Getting It

Engineering is a wide-open field. Engineers function in a variety of roles and in many areas such as manufacturing, construction, business, education, government, and health care, to name just a few.

Two-thirds of all engineers are employed by private industry. The armed services are the largest federal employer of engineers. Engineering positions are also available in state and local governments, although these areas have experienced cutbacks in recent years. Engineers are also employed by colleges and universities in teaching and research positions and some work as independent consultants or owners and operators of private businesses.

Most technical institutes and colleges have placement offices that help students contact prospective employers, including federal agencies, industrial firms, and consulting engineering organizations. Many industries send campus recruiters to colleges to describe job openings and opportunities and to arrange interviews with interested new graduates. Don't ignore them in your job search. Take advantage of all that's offered you on campus.

Ads in professional technical journals such as the *Engineering News-Record* are other good sources of job information. Federal, state, city, and county civil service boards will give you the details about engineering opportunities working for government.

In any job search, be sure to follow the guidelines for writing resumes, interviewing (for both jobs and information), and job hunting described in the Guide to Planning Your Career.

All signs point to the 80s and beyond as being an exciting time for women scientists and engineers, a time when their ranks will increase dramatically, causing an equally dramatic increase in their acceptance by male colleagues. (This trend is already evident in the life sciences.) In the early Renaissance, huge sections of every map were marked Terra Incognita (unknown lands) and intrepid pioneers set off to explore them. Today's unknown lands are the frontiers of science; today's adventurers, the women and men who explore the secrets of the atom, the universe, and life itself. The challenges are great ones, but the rewards match them.

MORE HELP WANTED?

The organizations listed in the "Basic Resources" sections in this Guide are all sources of information on the fields they represent. For example, some provide brief bibliographies of materials about careers, whereas others have free or inexpensive pamphlets available.

You will also find the following publications helpful. Since they probably are not carried by most bookstores, we have included current price and ordering information. Keep in mind that availability and prices change. (If ordering, you might also specify "current issue" and request a list of other related publications.) Try to get these materials first through your local public library—it's a good (and free) source of information. If it doesn't have what you need in its collection, it can usually borrow for you from another library through interlibrary loan systems; some libraries will even order materials at your request.

Career Information

Career Guide: For Future Minority and Women Scientists. Yolanda S. George and Joanne Williams. 1977. (Single copy free from Yolanda S. George, University of California, Lawrence Livermore Laboratory, P.O. Box 808, Livermore, California 94550.)

Careers for Women in Mathematics. Association for Women in Mathematics (undated). 7 pp. (Available from Association for Women in Mathematics, c/o Wellesley College, Wellesley, Massachusetts 02181. Single copy free, but send self-addressed, stamped envelope.)

Federal Career Directory (1976–1977): A Guide for College Students. U.S. Civil Service Commission. (Available for $3.45 from Superintendent of Documents, U.S. Government Printing Office, Washington, D.C. 20402.)

I'm Madly in Love with Electricity and Other Comments About Their Work by Women in Science and Engineering. Nancy Kreinberg. 1977. (Available for $2 from Lawrence Hall of Science, University of California, Berkeley, California 94720; Attn: Careers.)

Space for Women: Perspectives on Careers in Science. Derived from The Earth in Cosmos: Space for Women, A Symposium for Women on Careers in Astronomy, Astrophysics, and Earth and Planetary Sciences, held October 1975. (Single copy free from Smithsonian Astrophysical Observatory, Center for Astrophysics, 60 Garden Street, Harvard University, Cambridge, Massachusetts 02138.)

Why Not Be a Technical Writer? Women's Bureau, U.S. Department of Labor. Leaflet 47 (rev.), 1971. (Available for 50 cents from Superintendent of Documents, U.S. Government Printing Office, Washington, D.C. 20402.)

Women in Physics. American Physical Society, Committee on the Status of Women in

Physics. (undated). (Single copy free from American Physical Society, Committee on the Status of Women in Physics, 335 East 45th Street, New York, New York 10017.)

Women in Science and Technology: Careers for Today and Tomorrow. American College Testing Program. 1976. (Available for $1.50 from American College Testing, P.O. Box 168, Iowa City, Iowa 52240.)

Womengineer. Sara Jane Neustadtl, 1974. (Available for 25 cents from Engineer's Council for Professional Development, 345 East 47th Street, New York, New York 10017.)

Women, Science and Engineering

Covert Discrimination and Women in the Sciences. AAAS Selected Symposia Series. Edited by Judith Ramaley, 1978. (Available for $12.50 plus 50¢ postage and handling from Westview Press, 5500 Central Avenue, Boulder, Colorado 80302.)

The Double Bind: The Price of Being a Minority Woman in Science. Report of a Conference of Minority Women Scientists, Airlie House, Warrenton, Virginia. Shirley Mahaley Malcom, Paula Quick Hall, and Janet Welsh Brown. 1976. (Available for $3 from American Association for the Advancement of Science, Office of Opportunities in Science, 1776 Massachusetts Avenue NW, Washington, D.C. 20036.)

Mathematics and Sex. John Ernest, 1976. (Single copy free from Prof. John Ernest, Mathematics Department, University of California, Santa Barbara, California 93106.)

A Profile of the Woman Engineer. Prepared by the 1974–75 Statistics and the 1975–76 Publications Committees of the Society of Women Engineers (undated). (Single copy free from Society of Women Engineers, 345 East 47th Street, New York, New York 10017.)

Sexism and Science. Evelyn Reed. New York: Pathfinder Press, 1978; $12, hardcover.

Successful Women in the Sciences: An Analysis of Determinants. Edited by Ruth B. Kundsin. *Annals of the New York Academy of Sciences,* vol. 208 (1973). (Available for $30 from Scholarly Reprints, 1 Park Avenue, New York, New York 10016.)

Women and Minorities in Science and Engineering. National Science Foundation. 1977. (Available for 75 cents from Superintendent of Documents, U.S. Government Printing Office, Washington, D.C. 20402.)

Women in Engineering—Beyond Recruitment. Proceedings of Conference held June 22–25, 1975, at Cornell University. Edited by Mary Diederich Ott and Nancy A. Reese (undated). (Available for $2 from Division of Basic Studies, College of Engineering, 170 Olin Hall, Cornell University, Ithaca, New York 14853.)

Women in Engineering: Bridging the Gap Between Society and Technology. Proceedings of an Engineering Foundation Conference held July 12–16, 1971, at New England College, Henniker, New Hampshire. Edited by George Bugliarello, Vivian Cardwell, Olive Salembier, and Winifred White (undated). (Available for $2 from Vivian Cardwell, Assistant to the Dean, College of Engineering, University of Illinois Chicago Circle, P.O. Box 4348, Chicago, Illinois 60680.)

Women in Geology. Proceedings of First Northeastern Women Geoscientists Conference held April 26–27, 1976, at St. Lawrence University, Canton, New York.

Edited by Susan D. Halsey, Barbara McCaslin, Wendy L. Carey, and William D. Romey. 1976. (Available for $2.50 from Ash Lad Press, P.O. Box 396, Canton, New York 13617.)

Women in Science: A Man's World. Impact of Science on Society, vol. XXV, No. 2 (April–June 1975). (Available for $4 from Unipub, P.O. Box 433, Murray Hill Station, New York, New York 10016. Limited availability.)

Women and the Scientific Professions: The MIT Symposium on American Women in Science and Engineering. Edited by Jacquelyn A. Mattfeld and Carol G. Van Aken. Cambridge, Massachusetts: MIT Press, 1965. (1976 hardcover reprint edition available for $16.50 from Greenwood Press, 51 Riverside Avenue, Westport, Connecticut 06880.)

Women in Science and Technology. A Report on Workshop on Women in Science and Technology held May 21–23, 1973, at MIT. Prepared by Edith Ruina (undated). 39 pp. (Available for $2.50 from MIT Press, 28 Carleton Street, Cambridge, Massachusetts 02142.)

Bibliographies

Bibliography on Women: With Special Emphasis on Their Roles in Science and Society. Audrey B. Davis. 1974. (Available for $3.95 plus 50¢ postage and handling from Science History Publications, 156 Fifth Avenue, New York, New York 10010.)

Science and Engineering Careers: A Bibliography. Eleanor Babco. 1974. (Available for $2 from Scientific Manpower Commission, 1776 Massachusetts Avenue NW, Washington, D.C. 20036.)

Women in Engineering: A Bibliography on Their Progress and Prospects. Christy Roysdon. 1975. (Single copy free from Christy Roysdon, Mart Science and Engineering Library, Building 8, Lehigh University, Bethlehem, Pennsylvania 18015.)

Women in the Sciences. LC Science Tracer Bullet, TB76-2. Constance Carter. March 1976. (Single copy free from Reference Section, Science and Technology Division, Library of Congress, 10 First Street SE, Washington, D.C. 20504.)

Women in Science Bibliography. Hinda Levin and Donald D. Thompson. (undated). (Single copy free from Donald D. Thompson, Mary Baldwin College, Staunton, Virginia 24401.)

COMPENDIUM OF SCIENCE AND ENGINEERING CAREERS

(The following list of careers is not meant to be exhaustive but rather to give you an idea of the range of career options in these fields and the practical, on-the-job applications of the area of scientific study.)

Agricultural Engineer. Designs agricultural machinery and equipment, develops methods of production and distribution for agricultural products. Also works in natural resource preservation. Most work for manufacturers and distributors of farm equipment, electric utility companies; a few are federal employees, mainly in Department of Agriculture. Employment expected to grow through mid-1980s. Average starting salaries for federal employees in 1977 between $9,303 and $11,523. Average salary for engineer with 20 years of experience $26,000 in 1976.

Agronomist. Plant specialist working to improve quality and quantity of crop production. Analyzes soil, develops new growth procedures, and helps in control of disease, weeds, and pests. Experiments to determine efficient ways of planting, cultivating, and harvesting crops such as grains, cotton, and tobacco. Also studies climate effects on crops. Some work in university research labs, others for industrial concerns. Average starting salaries with a bachelor's degree between $9,000 and $12,000 in 1976, $11,000 to $14,000 with a master's, $15,000 to $20,000 with a PhD.

Astronomer. Studies universe, using physics and mathematics, to explain origins and behavior of solar system and distant galaxies. Uses large telescopes, radiotelescopes, and other instruments to detect electromagnetic radiation from distant sources. Usually specializes in branch of astronomy, such as instruments and techniques, sun, solar system, or evolution of stars. Almost all do research or teach in colleges or universities. May also work in observatories or for Federal Government, design astronomical instruments, or do consulting work. Astronomy is smallest branch of physical sciences; only 2,000 astronomers employed in 1976, 600 of them by Federal Government. Most astronomers have PhD. Salaries relatively high: doctoral federal employees started at $17,056 to $20,442 in 1977, those with bachelor's at $9,303 to $11,523.

Biomedical Engineer. Uses engineering in health science professions. Many study engineering aspects of man and animals; others design medical instruments such as pacemakers, artificial hearts and kidneys, and lasers for surgery, or design and build systems for laboratory or hospital procedures. Specialized biomedical training must be accompanied by training in major engineering field (mechanical, electrical, chemical, or industrial). Most teach and do research in colleges and universities. Others work in industry, sales, and federal and state agencies. Average starting salaries in industry in 1976 were $14,800 for bachelor's degree, $16,500 for master's, and above $21,000 for PhD.

Ceramic Engineer. Uses clay, silicates, and other nonmetallic minerals to make products such as spark plugs, glass, cement, bricks, and dishes. Most specialize: manufacturing and developing heat-resistant materials or working with glass or structural materials like bricks, for example. May be researchers, designers and testers, or administrators of production. About 6 percent in sales and service occupations; most work in manufacturing industries. Employment opportunities good, particularly in nuclear energy and defense programs. Entering industrial salaries averaged $14,000 in 1976, $14,500 with bachelor's degree and up to five years' experience, $15,800 with master's degree, $19,000 with PhD.

Chemical Engineer. Applies chemical and engineering science to the design, construction, operation, and improvement of chemical processes. Lab techniques developed may be applied to large-scale production processes in industry, where most are employed. Industrial positions also in sales and customer service, market research, plant management, and technical writing. Conducts research to determine process success or to investigate principles such as heat transfer or distillation. Employment outlook highly favorable, particularly in industry, as technological advances enlarge production of industrial chemicals. Entering salaries in 1976 averaged $15,300 with bachelor's degree and no experience. Average earnings with between 12 and 13 years of experience: $25,150 in 1974.

Chemist. Develops new substances and improves existing ones for almost any use. More than one-half work in research and development. Some work in technical marketing and sales, others teach in colleges and universities. Often specialize in such subfields as analytical chemistry, organic chemistry, biochemistry. Entering salaries in 1976 averaged $21,000 with a bachelor's degree, $22,000 with a master's, $25,800 with PhD.

Civil Engineer. Works in planning, construction, and maintenance of roads, tunnels, bridges, airports, harbors, water supply and sewage systems, and buildings. Oldest branch of engineering profession, civil engineers are primarily designers and supervisors, overseeing technical details of construction. Hold administrative jobs ranging from construction site supervisor to city engineer to top-level executive. Specialties include structural, hydraulic, environmental, and geotechnical engineering. Of the nearly 155,000 employed in 1976, most worked in federal, state, and local government agencies or for construction companies; others in private consulting firms, public utilities, and manufacturing. Often required to travel. Average starting salaries in 1976 about $13,764, depending on educational background and experience.

Drafter. Draws plans showing exact specifications and dimensions of building project which are used by engineers, architects, scientists, and designers; determines strength, quantity, quality, and cost of materials. Final drawings include detailed view of project from every side. Drafters are classified by the type of work: *Senior drafters* produce scale drawings, *detailers* draw separate parts and give measurements, *checkers* watch for errors, and *tracers* make minor corrections and trace drawings for reproduction. Nearly all work in private industry. Trained in technical institutes and two-year programs elsewhere. Senior drafters averaged $15,300 in private industry in 1976.

Environmental Analyst. Performs research to develop methods of controlling environmental pollution. Plans research and data collection methods, and analyzes pollution sources and their effects. Soil and water samples, mineralogical surveys, and atmospheric monitoring are some of the data that may be studied. Prepares charts, graphs, and other statistics, and analyzes this information to develop pollution control methods. Often specialist in a particular area of environmental study, with title such as pollution analyst, soils analyst, or water quality analyst.

Environmentalist/Ecologist. Studies environmental problems and determines means of preventing or controlling pollution, including air, water, land and land use, noise, and radioactivity. Many are lobbyists with federal, state, and local government agencies and community groups. Others are field workers collecting data or researchers in laboratory settings. May coordinate studies for a group of scientists or specialize in a specific area of environmental study.

Extractive Metallurgist. Designs and supervises extraction and refinement of metals from ore. Decides what processes can be most efficiently used with metals such as gold, silver, copper, and aluminum; and means of producing iron and steel. Specializes in either ferrous (iron and iron alloys) or nonferrous metals. Supervises extraction and refinement processes. Most are employed by iron and steel industry; others by the Atomic Energy Commission, in labs, and in other mining industries. Entering salaries have increased annually by 7 to 8 percent; 1971 average: $888 a month.

Food Chemist. Develops new foods and methods of food preservation. May work as dairy products chemist or cereal chemist, for example, taking nutritional content into account to ensure that government standards are met. Salaries increase rapidly with experience: starting salaries in private industry: with BS, $9,000; with MS, $10,200; and with PhD, $14,000.

Forest Aide. Helps foresters examine and preserve forest resources. Investigates timber thinning or conditions of fire danger, estimates area timber production and supervises use, and helps to inspect for disease, soil erosion, or flood damage. Also trains conservation workers in seasonal projects including planting of seedlings and clearing of roads. Gives instructions about fire prevention and leads fire-fighting crews; maintains forest lands for recreational use by hunters, campers, and other visitors. Both part- and full-time jobs available. Of the approximately 11,000 aides employed year round in 1976, nearly half were in private industries such as logging, lumber, and paper companies. Reforestation projects and tree nurseries also employ forestry aides; federal employment mainly in Forest Service of Department of Agriculture. Physical stamina and enthusiasm for the outdoors are requisite qualifications. Starting salaries in 1976 ranged from $7,500 to $10,000; experienced earned about $12,300.

Geographer. Studies physical properties and characteristics of the earth, also population and cultural tendencies. Related fields—physics, geology, oceanography, meteorology, biology, and ecology—are taken into account. May work for government and international organizations to determine economic development or be specialist in urban geography. More than one-quarter of all geographers specialize in physical and ecological geography: one-third are economic and urban geography specialists. Other branches of geography include political, cultural, and historical geography. Working conditions depend on the specialty: field geographers are affected by area conditions and weather, but many geographers work indoors. The emphasis on market research in business has increased the number of business positions. Salaries vary: in 1973 entering geographers with bachelor's degree averaged $8,000; with master's, $10,000; with PhD, $14,000.

Horticulturist. Uses botany for practical purposes. Plant study and propagation help to determine hardiness, use, and adaptability in various environments for food production, product development, and beautification of parks and communities. Some work in conservation; others in commercial sales, buying contracts with growers, or environmental maintenance. Working conditions vary. Salaries vary according to duties and experience. Many work on their own in private consulting firms or nurseries. Researchers and teachers earned between $10,000 and $30,000 in 1976.

Hydraulic Engineer. Designs and supervises construction of water engineering projects. Designs artificial canals, reservoirs, and conduits, and directs dredging, jetty construction, and other water control projects. Must know how to use equipment such as pumps and pressure valves for accurate water flow and conversion of water power to electricity. Engineers the transport of water for correct water pressure levels and water stabilization; often builds laboratory models to study construction and water flow problems.

Hydrographer. Follows trends in water movement and utilization. Reads meters and gauges in streams, conduits, and pipelines. Measures water levels in lakes, reservoirs, and tanks, and determines water seepage and evaporation in dams and reservoirs. Measures wells to record water depth, and studies snow and its water yield. Data collected are converted to graphs and charts which indicate water patterns, important in planning navigation projects and in constructing dams, bridges, and wells. Also installs and maintains metering instruments for these facilities. Job prospects are expected to be good for hydrographers during the next decade, with starting salaries approximately $500 a month in early 1980s.

Industrial Engineer. Solves organizational problems concerning people, machines, materials in business settings. Designs data processing systems and applies mathematical concepts. Develops management control systems to deal with finances and planning, and designs or improves systems for distribution of goods and services. Does plant location searches and plans salary administration. Because work is related to that of a business manager, many take on management positions. Most work in manufacturing industries, while others might work in a wide range of settings: for insurance companies, public utilities, hospitals, retail organizations, government agencies, and colleges and universities. Starting salaries in 1976 averaged $14,568.

Laboratory Tester. Determines physical and chemical characteristics of materials used in manufacturing to assure quality control and adherence to specifications. May be involved in research and development or in sample testing. Sets up and operates laboratory equipment, tests materials to determine content, and records results in reports or on graphs and charts. Materials tested are those used in manufacture of products such as adhesives, cement, paint, paper, cloth. Qualities tested include purity, viscosity, absorption, and burning rate. Product tested may determine title: gas tester, paint and varnish technician, soils tester.

Land Surveyor. Makes measurements to determine land boundary lines. Often using a team of people and a variety of surveying instruments, measures distances of property tracts, townships, and other land areas. Uses maps, notes, or land title deeds to check accuracy of existing records; findings are used to prepare legal documents such as deeds and leases. Must have an ability to work with numbers and an interest in working outdoors. Most states require licensing or registration. At present about 2,000 women are surveyors, less than 5 percent of all surveyors. Few women employed as part of survey team. Federal surveyors started at salaries of approximately $500 a month in early 1970s; private industry starting salaries were comparable.

Laser Technician. Uses laser engineering and electronics to construct laser devices after reviewing project instructions and specifications with engineers. Specifications are interpreted by technician for workers who produce small laser parts. Laser technicians install sections of laser body and tubing and wiring to connect valves and dials; fill laser body with specified volume and pressure of gases, such as helium and neon; set up test devices for finished instrument. Test data recorded are analyzed and given to engineers.

Marine Engineer. Designs and helps install and repair mechanical and electrical equipment used in ships, docks, and other marine facilities. Power plants, propulsion systems, and heating and ventilating systems must meet complex specifications necessary for the vessel or equipment. May specialize in design of and work solely with equipment such as boilers, electric power systems, heat exchangers.

Marine Surveyor. Examines marine vessels such as boats, ships, tankers, and dredges to assure proper working condition. Evaluates all parts of vessel and determines any repairs needed to meet insurance requirements. Prepares reports on the types of surveys conducted, the recommended repairs, or the conditions that are remedied for submission to the client. Salary/job outlook is the same as for land surveyors.

Mechanical Engineer. Designs and develops power-producing machines such as internal combustion engines and steam and gas turbines, and household or office machinery such as refrigerators, air conditioners, elevators, and printing presses. Working conditions vary, depending on the equipment and industry of specialization. Many do research, test, and design work; others are administrators or managers, or work in maintenance, technical sales, and production. Of nearly 200,000 mechanical engineers employed in 1976, almost three-quarters were in manufacturing; remainder employed by government agencies, educational institutions, consulting engineering firms. Average starting salaries in 1976 relatively high, beginning at $14,964.

Medical Science Careers. See Guide to Health Careers.

Microbiologist. Studies bacteria, viruses, and other organisms to determine their structure, character, and development, and effect on humans, animals, and other living species. Determines how microorganisms function in production of various vitamins and amino acids. Specialists include bacteriologists, dairy bacteriologists, and food bacteriologists. All grow microorganisms for microscopic examination and isolate types among various species. Relatively high salaries comparable to those of other life science professions.

Mining Engineer. Plans and operates mining facilities. Oversees methods and machinery used to extract ore, including safety precautions and location and type of shaft. Most work in direct mine operations; others for mining equipment manufacturers, educational institutions, federal agencies. A small number are private consultants. Average entering salaries in private industry in 1976: with a bachelor's degree, $14,800; with master's but no experience, $16,500; with PhD, over $21,000. Most salaries double after about 20 years of experience.

Nuclear Engineer. Conducts nuclear research to advance nuclear theories; designs and develops nuclear equipment such as reactor cores and radiation shielding. Often a specialist. Work includes nuclear test supervision and monitoring, safety specifications, and modification of nuclear theories. Installation engineers averaged $21,700 in 1976.

Paleontologist. Studies plant and animal fossils in geological formations. Location and classification of fossils help trace plant and animal chronology and evolution. Fossils are arranged according to their biological or zoological family and probable age. Paleontologists work in fossil expeditions and in laboratories; may become museum workers or teachers. Average salary in colleges and universities $13,000 in the early 1970s. Additional earnings from writing for journals and books.

Petroleum Engineer. Works with underground reservoirs of gas or crude oil which are drilled and with refining of gas and oil. Locates sites and determines extraction to be used, perhaps to increase flow of well, and how to run a profitable yet pollution-free oil field. Supervises production and collects data to assure maximum efficiency. Appraises oil-producing property, and acts as consultant to corporations. May be employed by large oil companies or in independent companies as bank advisers, or as researchers and teachers. Many work for government. Salaries among highest of any profession: starting salaries with a bachelor's degree between $16,000 and $17,000 in 1976; federal employees, $9,303 to $11,500. Those with 20 years of experience may earn $20,000.

Physical Metallurgist. Works with metals, ceramics, composite materials, semiconductors, and polymers. Studies their structure and physical properties and means to change these properties. Involved in production processes in metal industry which include melting, forging, casting, and the application of protective surfaces. Most are employed by iron and steel industry in production, supervision, or research and development; others by major contractors of the Atomic Energy Commission, in labs, federal agencies, mining industry, and consulting firms. Salaries have increased annually at a rate of 7 to 8 percent; 1971 average starting salary: $888 a month.

Physicist/Theoretical Physicist. Conducts experiments in physics to formulate theories. Experiments detect and measure physical phenomena, and mathematical concepts are used to express the physical laws. Salaries for entering theoretical physicists at BA level were $8,000 to $10,000 in private industry in early 1970s, increasing $900 to $1,700 with an MA; for PhD physicists, $12,000 to $20,000. Federal salaries were comparable, except for significantly lower PhD salaries.

Pollution Control Technician. Performs field and laboratory tests to obtain data on water, air, and soil pollutants. Field work may include collecting gas samples from smokestacks or water samples from lakes and streams. Samples are tested for chemical composition and other characteristics. Agriculture, meteorology, chemistry, and engineering knowledge used in investigations, and collected information is used by environmental and scientific personnel in finding sources and methods of controlling environmental pollutants. May specialize in a field of environmental pollution and be identified by that field.

Product Design Engineer. Studies engineering proposals to produce designs for equipment such as engines, machines, and other products. Determines project feasibility by using engineering principles, research data, and analysis of proposed specifications. With research personnel, resolves problems and determines design, and then directs building or manufacture of products. Plans and develops experimental programs and analyzes test data to assure the meeting of product specifications. Design engineers are classified according to specialized engineering fields.

Quality Control Technician. Tests and inspects products during production to assure quality and standards. Tests conducted at various stages of production measure performance, content, and durability. Information collected is written up and evaluated, and technician suggests modifications for improvement. May specialize in design, product evaluation, or product reliability. Also involved in research and development and administrative duties.

Research Engineer. Studies specialized field of engineering to discover facts, make evaluations, and apply known engineering theories. Directs engineering personnel in engineering experiments, and evaluates results for development of new concepts, products, equipment, or processes. Prepares technical reports for use by engineering or management personnel in long- and short-term planning. Designated according to the specialized field of work.

Safety Engineer. Helps maintain occupational safety in a working environment. Identifies potential health hazards and suggests preventive measures. May work in a large manufacturing plant, developing a safety program for employees after investigating each job to determine hazards. Analyzes to determine causes and recommends ways of correcting poor design or improper maintenance. Many are also concerned with product safety, working with product designers to develop models that meet safety requirements and then determining safety of finished product. Safety engineers are needed wherever large numbers of people congregate and industrial development occurs. Property and liability insurance companies employ many as consultants. Salaries vary; starting salaries in manufacturing in 1976: with bachelor's degree, between $12,000 and $15,000.

Sales Engineer. Sells equipment and supplies that demand a knowledge of engineering—chemical, mechanical, electrical, and electronic equipment sold to engineers, architects, and other professional and technical persons. Also provides services to the professionals. Reviews blueprints and plans to provide cost estimates of equipment or estimated production increases. Acts as consultant on operation and maintenance of equipment; may draw up a service contract for products or services. Also gives technical instruction to clients or their employees, and usually specializes in sale of particular kind of product. Sales engineering appeals to those persons who enjoy meeting and working with people and who are interested in sales techniques.

Sanitary Engineer. Designs hygiene-related projects and directs their construction—waterworks, sewage, water purification, garbage disposal plants, swamp drainage, and insect spraying. Advises industries on control and disposal of pollutants and chemicals, and inspects sanitary conditions of public areas such as markets, parks, and camps.

Science and Engineering Technician. Works in all aspects of business and government, including research and design, manufacturing, and sales. Although scope more limited than that of engineers and scientists, technicians apply knowledge of science, mathematics, industrial machinery, and technical processes to wide range of jobs. May work in industrial production, aeronautics, and meteorology. Jobs are research oriented; usually assist engineers and scientists in study, design, and testing for production. About two-thirds in 1976 worked in private industry. Also employed by federal and state agencies, universities, and not-for-profit organizations. Average starting salaries in private industry in 1976 after completion of two-year technical school program: $9,000 to $10,800. Experienced averaged $16,000 a year.

Soil Scientist. Studies soil characteristics in various areas and prepares maps of locations to be used by urban and rural planners for building or drainage information. Researches chemical and biological properties of soils to determine productivity in agriculture or response to fertilization. Many states employ soil scientists for antipollution studies and to ensure proper erosion control when highways or buildings are erected. More than half employed in 1976 worked for the Federal Soil Conservation Service; others for colleges of agriculture, fertilizer companies, insurance companies, and real estate firms. Entering federal salaries: with a BS, averaged $9,303 in 1977, with an expected increase of $2,200 after one year; experienced, $17,046 to $28,725.

Specification Writer. Studies architectural plans and prepares specifications to be used as standards by contractors involved in processing, manufacture, or construction. Prepares technical descriptions of processes and may draw rough sketches illustrating specific plans for project or assembly process. Usually specialist and designated according to engineering specialization, product, or process.

Structural Engineer. Involved in construction plans and design of structures requiring stress analysis. Determines load requirements and strength needed in construction parts, and suggests proper size and shape for these parts. Also analyzes plans of construction engineers and inspects buildings and other projects for necessary repairs. May recommend replacement of parts, point out weak areas, or advise on rebuilding of structure.

Tool Designer. Develops tools—drills, cutting tools, dies, and related objects—for production and for experimental use in metal-working machines. Does preliminary sketches and prepares detailed plans of proposed tools of study in conjunction with engineering and shop personnel to resolve design problems. Also experiments in tool improvement or performance. Knowledge of mathematical formulas and standard engineering principles as well as cost, manufacturing procedures, and servicing requirements. Some specialize in specific types of tools. Usually promoted after several years of tool and die making. Experience with tool making necessary. Expansion in manufacturing is expected to increase jobs available. Space and missile industries in particular require new and extremely precise tool design.

Zoologist. Studies animal life and is identified by animals studied (ornithologists study birds, entomologists study insects, and so on). Origins, behavior, and life processes of animal species included in studies. Some take part in experiments with live animals in controlled or natural surroundings: others dissect animals to observe structure. Kind of work determines working conditions—office or scuba-diving. Some work as researchers: others for government agencies or recreational businesses. Salaries depend on training and experience; average federal entering salary $9,303 to $14,000 in 1976. With advanced degrees may earn $20,400 in federal positions; salaries in private industry generally higher.

BETTYE LANE

Guide IV **A Guide to Government and Law Careers**

Funding for part of this Guide was provided by Davis Polk & Wardwell.

BETTYE LANE

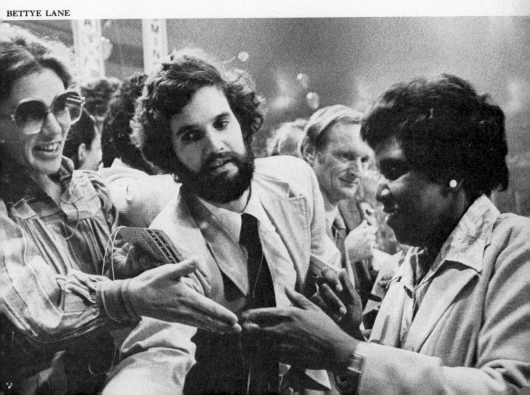

CHAPTER 1

LAW AND GOVERNMENT, GOVERNMENT AND LAW

Law and government are different career fields—but they intersect at many points.

All government careers in this country involve dealing with laws—writing them, administering them, enforcing them. These three functions are performed by the three branches of government: the legislative, the executive and the judicial. Not surprisingly, the many major positions in government are filled by lawyers and those near-lawyers called paralegals.

Even lawyers and paralegals in private practice are involved in government. As they appear in court as advocates, they are a part of the judicial branch of government. Lobbying, they are a part of the legislative branch. In administrative proceedings they are a part of the executive branch. In all their work they have obligations to the government as well as to their clients.

In a very real sense, careers in government include careers in the law; those who are considering the one should also take a look at the other.

In the Public Service

> *I wanted to have an impact on the whole community—change the structure of the system.*
> —Community planner

> *You really know your work means something to people. I couldn't have chosen anything else that would have satisfied me more.*
> —Social worker

> *Some days I'm staggered by the enormity of*
> *the problems I'm dealing with.*
>> —Government administrator

Working for government involves some special things. Where else could your boss say, "Congratulations! You're hired. Now go out and find a job for every unemployed high school dropout in the state!" There's no doubt about it: The highest possible levels of job satisfaction can be reached by working for government. But high levels of frustration are also possible. Red tape is not a myth. To work in government, you have to learn to cope with endless amounts of it.

Power. People in government jobs seek it. Millions, even billions, of dollars are spent on programs, and people in government determine how these funds are spent. There's also power in making and enforcing laws.

Commitment. Many participants in government have it. By definition, government is dealing with public interest. Your whole career will be spent with the public good in mind.

Security. Many of those who look for it in government jobs find it. Civil service and other government jobs (other than elective or appointive positions) have the equivalent of tenure. In the public sector you aren't as personally vulnerable as in the private sector; although government programs and agencies are often reorganized, cut, or eliminated: remember that unlike a business or a corporation, government doesn't fold.

Life-style. Government careers have room for all kinds of people, for those who want worldwide travel and for those who want to stay in their hometowns. You can choose to work in the same job in your community for the rest of your life, or you can become an administrator and find yourself moving from housing to transportation to health systems planning.

Legal Considerations

> *I've had a very rich practice. I've done just*
> *about everything. It's a fantastic experience.*
>> —Government lawyer

> *It's a job where you have a lot of independence—*
> *you can work on your own. It's the right kind of work*
> *for me.*
>> —Legal assistant

> *The work is very hard, very demanding. It's a*
> *tough standard to meet.*
>> —Lawyer in private practice

QUIZ

Women in law and government have been competing with their male colleagues for a long time. Many women have been the first to achieve an important goal for social good. To get off to a good start, here's a quiz.

Do you know . . .

1. What pacifist and children's rights supporter in 1917 was the first woman elected to the United States House of Representatives, and marched on Washington with her own Peace Brigade 51 years later?
2. What government clerk became a foreign service officer in Geneva in 1937?
3. Who was the first woman to be appointed a foreign service officer, despite the efforts of a foreign service personnel officer who called for an Executive Order to prevent women from the post?
4. What woman asserted that "being a woman has only bothered me in climbing trees" and went on to become Secretary of Labor and an organizer of the Social Security Administration?
5. What famous nurse founded a New Jersey public school at the age of 18?
6. Who are some of the women who have run for the presidency?
7. According to a 1975 Gallup Poll, what percentage of American voters would vote for a qualified woman presidential candidate, were she to be nominated by their party?
8. What former slave helped Susan B. Anthony in the fight for women's voting rights?
9. Who was the first black woman to practice law in the United States?
10. What 19th-century women's rights leader was denied the right to practice law as a result of a United States Supreme Court decision after passing the bar examination?

Quiz Answers

1. Three years before national women's suffrage, *Jeannette Rankin* (1880–1973) sat in the House of Representatives lobbying for women's and children's rights. She opposed involvement in World Wars I and II. She also opposed the Vietnam War.
2. *Margaret Hanna* (c.1878–1950) was among many women hired as State Department clerks in the late 1890s. She rose from confidential clerk in the State Department to become a bureau chief and in 1937 a Foreign Service officer in Geneva.
3. *Lucille Atcherson* was appointed the first woman Foreign Service officer in 1922, although Joseph Grew of the Board of Foreign Service Personnel recommended that women be prevented from applying or failed on the exams.

4. *Frances Perkins* (1882–1965) was appointed Secretary of Labor in 1933, the first woman to hold a Cabinet post, and helped organize the Social Security Administration.

5. Better known as founder of the American Red Cross, *Clara Barton* (1821–1912) started one of the first public schools in New Jersey, set up a relief agency for Union troops during the Civil War, and helped to get the Geneva Treaty recognized. A trip to Switzerland in 1870 introduced her to the International Red Cross, and on her return to the United States in 1872 she founded the American Red Cross.

6. In 1872, on the Equal Rights Party slate, *Victoria Woodhull* (1838–1927) became the first woman candidate for President. She was followed in 1884, on the National Equal Rights Party ticket, by *Belva Lockwood* (1830–1917), the first woman lawyer to plead before the Supreme Court. Other candidates have included *Linda Jeness* of the Socialist Worker's Party and *Shirley Chisholm,* a Democrat, in 1972; *Margaret Voight* of the Anti-Abortion People's Party in 1976.

7. Up from 53 percent in 1970, 73 percent of those polled in 1975 said that they would vote for a qualified woman candidate. In addition, 70 percent thought that the country would be better governed if more women held public office.

8. *Sojourner Truth* (1797–1883) joined Susan B. Anthony in seeking both racial equality and women's rights. Both women were to die before the 19th Amendment granted all women voting privileges, but the two were instrumental in awakening Americans to the voting issue.

9. *Charlotte E. Ray* (1850–1911), a graduate of Howard University in 1872, began to practice the same year, the first black woman admitted to the bar in the District of Columbia.

10. *Myra Bradwell* (1831–1894) learned law by working with her husband and brother in their Illinois practice, and established the first weekly law periodical in the West in 1869. Though denied the right to practice law herself, Ms. Bradwell's law periodical paved the way for reforms by the Illinois Supreme Court, and by its own ruling the court admitted her to the bar in 1891.

Our society is based on laws. Getting married or divorced, buying a house, writing a will, starting a business, all require legal documents. People in legal careers help with all these transactions.

As legislators and their aides, people in legal careers write the laws. They sit as judges determining whether laws have been broken or the laws themselves are constitutional. They may prosecute or defend those accused of crimes. They negotiate for labor unions as well as for businesses.

Independence. Those who seek it in legal careers find it. Many lawyers and legal assistants work on their own. Most have their own clients and great responsibility.

Intellectual Challenge. People find it in the law. Legal careers demand the ability to think on your feet, to express yourself well orally and in writing, and to be precise.

Women, Careers, Law, Government

> *I've seen it coming along. There are women who*
> *are in positions where there just weren't any women*
> *five years ago.*
> —Government administrator

In both law and government careers, opportunities for women are undergoing significant change. It *used* to be true that women in government held only the jobs that had contact with the public, or the staff positions, not the administrative ones. It *used* to be that women lawyers worked in obscure research jobs where no client met them or in a government agency where the "client" was the public. This is all changing.

Affirmative Action is one reason. All government contracts and hiring processes now require Affirmative Action procedures.

Also as more women are elected to office and as more women reach higher administrative positions, new women's contact networks are developing. More women are now in positions to help out—serve as "mentors" to women just beginning their careers.

As in any period of transition, the old ways of doing things still persist at the same time new ways are gaining hold. Some law firms and some government agencies continue to discriminate against women, but neither field is monolithic. In both fields jobs are available that are especially conducive to personal growth and professional advancement. If you find yourself in a hostile or negative atmosphere, get out; find another place to work. You have many choices.

Law and Government Careers in General

Pay for Government Workers. It's no longer so low as many people think. Federal personnel up through middle management are generally paid more than their private-sector equivalents and have more generous fringe benefits. State and municipal workers' salaries vary from state to state and city to city. Also, contrary to public opinion, a career in law, except in the most prestigious firms or positions, doesn't necessarily guarantee a life of luxury.

Work Load. In many law and government careers, it can be nearly overwhelming. To advance, young people in law firms, political campaigns, and government offices are often expected to become workahol-

344 A GUIDE TO GOVERNMENT AND LAW CAREERS

ics. Throughout a government career, you may be expected to attend evening meetings. But there's a positive side: you'll be getting tremendous practical experience and, often, considerable responsibility early in your career.

Formal Training and Credentials. These count more in law than in any field other than medicine. Without a law degree you cannot be a lawyer. Many government jobs require training, but experience may often be substituted.

Visibility. It's a significant matter in government careers. For example, if you are in government employment, don't be surprised to see your salary reported in newspapers. Many officeholders are required to disclose their earnings and their assets. A personal problem like a messy divorce case can ruin a political career. Whether you are a lawyer, a bureaucrat, or a politician, your "style" as well as your abilities will be discussed and judged.

Special Restrictions. Government service almost always requires United States citizenship. Political activity is restricted by the Hatch Act or its state equivalent, and lawyers' actions are subject to the judgments of ethics committees of their state bar associations. Elected officials may find their sources of income restricted by conflict-of-interest laws.

Careers in Law and Government—The Future

More and more people are becoming interested in law and government careers. Law schools are now graduating almost 30,000 lawyers a year. The number of inquiries made about federal jobs nearly doubled between 1972 and 1977—to almost 12,000,000. Yet at the same time job openings in both fields have declined, and in both fields the demand for new employees depends in part on government action.

If the federal government or a state or city cuts back on taxes or otherwise suffers an income loss, public employees will be let go, as has happened in California and in New York City. Government reorganizations, which occur as new officials are elected, may shuffle jobs around; for example, Congress is considering reorganizing the federal Civil Service system itself. Also, whole government programs may be cut out or cut back.

At present there are more law school graduates than there are entry-level lawyers' jobs. However, a recent study by the Law Placement Service showed that more than 90 percent of law graduates got law-related jobs.

For women interested in law and government careers, the future may be somewhat different than for men. Although women in government have yet to reach middle- and upper-level jobs in significant numbers, opportunities are increasing. Once past the entry level, women should

THE AMERICAN ATTITUDE TOWARD GOVERNMENT—WHAT HAPPENED?

Widespread public distrust of government is a real problem for the people in government. Many Americans think that anyone who works for government must be stupid, corrupt, or both. These people usually assume:

1. *People who work for government are politicians, and all politicians are corrupt.* Neither assumption is true. A city manager explains: "The public doesn't understand that this is my profession. If I do something wrong no town or state will hire me."
2. *People who work for government don't actually do anything.* False, of course. As one city planner put it, "Working for government is not like manufacturing widgets. We haven't anything to show for our work but plans and maps. Nobody realizes these plans and maps mean controlled growth rates, better public services, and a decrease in the tax rate over the next 20 years."
3. *Government isn't effective anymore.* Also false. The size and complexity of government programs and the problems they face are far beyond that of private enterprise. With such complex issues, it's not surprising government programs aren't 100 percent effective.
4. *Government programs waste taxpayer's money.* Untrue. Government employees are judged by a different set of standards from those in the private sector. Every government expenditure must be justified and scrutinized. What would be considered a personal favor in business is deemed corruption in government.
5. *Government serves minorities, not the majority in the country.* False again. The stakes in some government decisions—offshore oil leases, for example—are so high and the competition so intense that there is usually a vocal group of disappointed losers. All government decisions and all new ideas are suspected of favoring some special interest group. Conservatives accuse government of favoring the poor; liberals accuse government of favoring the rich.

These public attitudes have serious consequences for both the public and its employees. There is a sense of "us versus them" that people both inside and outside government experience: "*They* don't care" or "*They* don't do anything." What has been lost is a sense of common purpose, a sense of community between people in government and the public they work for.

When there's a public attitude against government, government employees feel insecure. Fearing their jobs will be cut indiscriminately, some people who work for government react with an array of "insider symptoms." They try to consolidate their power and position and fight "turf" battles over issues and programs.

Every public employee, no matter what her professional background or experience, can be tarred with the same brush—whether she is the honest police officer in a system with a corrupt district captain or a hard-working welfare department official in a state where child abuse hits the headlines. Such an underserved reputation can make a move to a private-sector job difficult, should such a move become necessary or desirable for personal reasons or because a program has, perhaps, been terminated.

---

have real opportunities for advancement, particularly in nontraditional scientific, technical, and economic areas. In law, much the same thing is true.

Executive Branch

At every level of government, the executive branch is by far the largest. It is headed by an elected chief executive. At the federal level, this is the President; for a state, the governor; and for a town or city, the mayor.

The day-to-day work of the Federal Government is handled within various departments, such as Defense or Agriculture, each with certain responsibilities. (*See* "United States Government Departments" preceding the Compendium of Careers at the end of this Guide.)

WHERE DO YOU FIT IN? UNSCRAMBLING THE GOVERNMENT PUZZLE

For those thinking about a government career, here is a brief overview of how the government functions.

Three Branches: Three Levels

When the thirteen original states ratified the Constitution in 1787, the complete structure and all the functions of the Federal Government were prescribed. State constitutions and municipal articles of incorporation were organized in a parallel fashion.

The three branches of government are the legislative, which makes the laws; the executive, which carries them out; and the judicial, which decides whether the laws are in accordance with the Constitution and punishes infractions of the law.

There are also three levels of government: the Federal (or United States) Government; state government; and local, town, county or city government.

THE MANUAL

The *United States Government Manual,* published annually, is a valuable tool for a woman who wants to know about federal departments and agencies. All departments and agencies are listed and broken down into departmental divisions, with information on organization, activities, publications, resources, and employment. Consult your local library, or order your own copy for $6.50 from the United States Government Printing Office (Superintendent of Documents, Government Printing Office, Washington, D.C. 20402) or from a Federal Government bookstore.

HATCH ACT—WHAT FEDERAL EMPLOYEES CAN AND CAN'T DO POLITICALLY

The Hatch Act protects Federal Government employees from political influence by restricting the kind of activities in which they can engage. They cannot *legally* do certain things—for instance, campaign for their boss (who thus cannot threaten them with the loss of their job if they refuse to campaign). Most states have similar laws covering state employees. State and local government employees who work on a project or in an office financed by federal funds are also subject to the Hatch Act.

Federal employees *may not:*

- Run for state or national office
- Campaign for or against a partisan candidate for public office
- Serve as an officer of a political party
- Take part in managing a political campaign or solicit political contributions

Federal employees *may:*

- Register and vote
- Join a political party and attend meetings
- Sign a petition, express opinions, and write their representatives in Congress
- Take part in nonpartisan or issue-related political activity

At the federal level are also a number of special agencies created by Congress, which report directly to the President, such as the Small Business Administration, the Interstate Commerce Commission, and the Federal Communications Commission.

Other executive branch duties are carried out by the chief executive's personal staff. The President's staff is called the Executive Office of the President and includes the Office of Management and Budget, which oversees the federal budget.

Legislative Branch

The legislative branch of government writes the laws and confirms the chief executive's administrative and judicial appointments. In cities, the legislative branch is usually called the "city council"; in counties, the "county council" or "board of supervisors." Except for Nebraska, all state legislatures are composed of a House of Representatives and a Senate, as is the United States Congress.

The Congress has 100 senators, two from each state who serve for a term of six years, and 435 members of the House of Representatives who serve for two-year terms with the number from each state based on population. State legislators are chosen on the basis of population, with state senators having larger districts and longer terms of office.

Like state legislatures, Congress has a few special agencies reporting

---

A WOMAN PRESIDENT—WHEN?

More women have run for President than most people realize. The first woman candidate was Victoria Woodhull in 1872, followed by Belva Lockwood in 1884, the first woman lawyer to plead before the Supreme Court, who received more than 4,000 votes, mostly from men because women could vote in only a few states at that time. Since then several women have run as minor party candidates.

Although no major political party has yet nominated a woman for President or Vice-President (in 1972 Shirley Chisholm pulled in 5 percent of the delegate votes at the National Democratic Convention), such a nomination may not be far away. According to a 1975 Gallup poll, 73 percent of American voters would vote for a qualified woman nominated by their party. That number is up from 53 percent of those polled in 1970, only five years before. As that trend in voter attitude continues and as more women in lower-level political office gain experience and exposure, our first woman President or Vice-President might well be elected in the next 10 to 15 years.

directly to it. The most important of these is the General Accounting Office, which provides financial data on federal receipts and disbursements to Congress. The Library of Congress and the Government Printing Office are two other important special agencies of Congress.

Judicial Branch

Each level of government has its court system. There are also special courts for special purposes—the customs court and the tax court, for example. State and federal courts have similar organization patterns: at the lowest level are the trial courts (county courts in the state system), then the courts of appeals, and then a highest or supreme court.

The federal courts have the power to hear cases involving the Constitution and acts passed by Congress, cases of maritime law, and cases between citizens of different states. When Foreign Service officials are involved or when one party in a controversy is a state or the United States, the Supreme Court has "original jurisdiction"; that is, it hears the case without any previous trial in an inferior court.

Most federal cases start out at the federal trial or district court level. Each state, depending on population, has four district courts with up to 27 judges. The decisions of these courts may be appealed to higher court, a Circuit Court of Appeals, of which there are 10 for the whole country. Under very rare circumstances, a decision can be appealed in one step to the Supreme Court; the normal procedure is through the Circuit Courts.

CHAPTER 2

WORKING FOR THE GOVERNMENT

By far the greatest number of government jobs are similar to those in the private sector—accounting, administration, ambulance driving, to mention just a few from the beginning of the alphabet. They include jobs you may have held or want to pursue, careers in all fields—from business to skilled trades.

The Federal Government is the largest employer in the United States; in 1976, it employed 2,750,000 civilians. Federal civilian employees, temporary as well as permanent, make up 3.3 percent of the total workforce. With an employer that large, all kinds of jobs are involved. Federal employees walk on the moon; experiment with microcomputers; work as undercover agents; build ships, highways, and buildings; cook; sew —everything. The places of work are as varied—museums, farms, forests, insurance offices, research laboratories, hospitals, publishing companies, offices. Whatever your skills are, it's likely that there are many job opportunities in the Federal Government for you.

Government salaries at starting and middle levels are high. Health and retirement benefits are very good compared to many private sector jobs. And you'll probably be able to work in your own area of the country; only about 12 percent of federal jobs are based in Washington, D.C.

If you decide to work directly for government—at the federal, state, county, or local level—you must "know the ropes" to get your job and to advance, especially in the Federal Government, where your job is likely to be covered by the United States Civil Service system.

Most federal jobs (62 percent of them) are governed by the Civil Service. Only about 2,000 of the top federal positions are political appointments, outside any merit system. Special agencies which have their own merit appointment systems include the Central Intelligence Agency, Federal Bureau of Investigation, Tennessee Valley Authority, and Postal Service. (Some jobs in these agencies and others like them are described in the next chapter.)

350

A Spectrum of Positions

In 1974 about 79 percent of full-time government employees were white-collar workers, nearly half of whom were in professional, technical, and administrative positions.

One group of government jobs termed *clerical and administrative* resembles those in an insurance company: processing forms, handling complaints, making sure claims are not fraudulent, and so forth. Many of these jobs are held by employees of the Social Security Administration, which provides retirement pay and health care benefits for older Americans.

Another category of government work involves *monitoring and overseeing federal expenditures.* The employees of the General Accounting Office (GAO) oversee the expenditures of funds for all nonmilitary government buildings, for example.

Planning and program development is another government function. The President, his advisers, and cabinet members may decide on a new direction for public policy to meet a pressing social or economic issue. The planners and program staff of the appropriate agency measure the extent and nature of the problem. This step is frequently called "needs assessment." After needs assessment, the planning and program development staff determine which programs would best solve the problems they identified.

Congress also initiates *study and action on public issues.* Legislative staff members do research, arrange for public hearings, and draft new legislation affecting the particular issue.

Government jobs are either *staff* or *administrative* (related to *line* jobs in business). An administrator is the manager or supervisor of a group of workers. She may have several "staff" reporting to her. Staff frequently exhibit an area of expertise or professional competence; for example, a staff lawyer for a public agency.

Program administrators run government programs. As more and more federal programs are carried out by local and state governments or private agencies with federal funds, federal program administrators' jobs are more likely to require site evaluations (going out in the field and assuring that the local agency is doing its job) and keeping tabs on the expenditures of program money.

Grade Levels and Salaries

Like many large companies, the Civil Service designates a level or grade for each job. An employee's pay is determined by her grade level.

White-collar workers are covered by the General Schedule (GS) grade levels, which range from GS-1, 2, and 3 for clerical workers through GS-5 for entry-level employees with a college degree to senior level administrative jobs GS-13 and above. GS-18 is the highest level in the rating system. People holding GS-16 through 18 jobs are usually promoted from within the system.

For blue-collar workers the pay scale is called the Wage Grade (WG) system; it ranges from WG-1 for a trainee to WG-9 through 12 for a journeyman. Unlike the General Schedule salaries, WG earnings vary according to geographic areas.

The grade level determines the general pay level; but within each grade, either GS or WG, there may be several "steps" and your specific salary depends on your step. An employee is usually hired at the first step in a grade level. If her work is satisfactory, she may advance automatically to the next step in that grade. Every step increase is an increase in salary. If the employee has exhausted all the step increases in her grade level and if there is no higher grade level for her job, she remains at that salary level and will not get a raise unless she changes to a job with a higher grade level or unless the entire pay scale is raised. If they have the choice, people who hold Civil Service jobs will usually try for

ALPHABET SOUP

Government insiders identify government agencies and departments by their initials. Almost everybody knows some of them—such as the FBI (Federal Bureau of Investigation), but other names can be confusing. Here are a few federal initials:

HUD—(pronounced "hud") Department of Housing and Urban Development
HEW—(pronounced "H-E-W") Department of Health, Education and Welfare
DOL—(pronounced "D-O-L") Department of Labor
EEOC—(pronounced "E-E-O-C") Equal Employment Opportunity Commission
UMTA—(pronounced "um-tah") Urban Mass Transportation Administration
CSC—(pronounced "C-S-C") United States Civil Service Commission
FNMA—(called "Fannie Mae") Federal National Mortgage Association
NASA—(pronounced "nassah") National Aeronautics and Space Administration
OSHA—(pronounced "oh-shah") Occupational Safety and Health Administration

jobs that encompass several grade levels with several steps in each, to put off the day when they must change jobs to merit a raise.

Entry-Level Federal Jobs—How to Get One

A word of caution and of encouragement. The process involved in getting a government job seems discouraging and time-consuming at first, but it's really not so bad. You may even get to know yourself better and value your own accomplishments. In any event it's a necessary process that you must suffer through if you want to do some of the rewarding work government has to offer.

Visit the Federal Job Information Center nearest you (there are more than 100 of them throughout the country). You will find it listed in the phone book under United States Government or call interstate information (800-555-1212) to get the toll-free number for your state. Job Information Centers do not hire people. They can, however, tell you some of the jobs that are available, how you can qualify, and what forms you need to fill out or examinations you need to take.

For entry-level WG jobs, certain scientific and technical jobs, or professional jobs GS-9 or above, you won't need to take a written examination. For these jobs, filling out special forms is all that's necessary.

Applicants are given a rating and placed on a register according to a Civil Service review of their background and qualifications. This is called an "unwritten exam." Since it is your job to supply this information to the Civil Service, make sure that you provide the most complete summary of your education and experience that you can. Don't leave anything out!

For lower-level clerical jobs or for the usual GS-5 through 7 jobs for college graduates without either postgraduate education or work experience, written examinations *are* necessary. The PACE (Professional and

---

BULLETIN: FEDERAL JOB PROSPECTS

Federal Job Prospects Bulletins are issued every 2 months in each region and cover job grades 1 through 12. They list jobs and geographic locations where job openings exist now or will soon; give the grade level of the job, the job code, and any other special forms that need to be filed. They are free for the asking from any Federal Job Information Center.

Administrative Career Exam) is the one given to entry-level college graduates.

The forms you fill out will depend in part on the job you want. The most common forms include the CSC (Civil Service Commission) 226, the government's course transcript form, and the SF (Standard Form) 171, the government's resume. Every applicant for a federal job—no matter what the level—must fill out the SF 171. Your own resume will not be accepted. It is essential to fill out the SF 171 carefully and completely.

Special Factors—They May Affect Your Rating

Armed Services Experience. Veterans have an advantage in applying for a Civil Service position. Usually, 5 points are added to veterans' ratings if they have been honorably discharged, 10 points if they are disabled. Since few women are veterans, women's chances of getting hired tend to be reduced. However, if you are the wife, widow, or mother of a permanently disabled veteran or of someone who died in service, you are eligible for a 10-point bonus.

Your Home State and Geographic Apportionment. The government apportions jobs in Wasnington among people from all 50 states by ranking states in terms of the number of government workers who are from that state. People from states with a low number of federal employees in Washington have an easier time getting a job. If you want to work in the nation's capital, check with the Federal Job Information Center to find out how your state ranks.

A Year of Service. Some vacancy announcements require that an applicant have "status." The use of this term does not mean that the job is restricted to an elite clique! It means that the applicant must be a federal employee with at least a year of satisfactory service.

After the Forms and Exams . . .

Once you've filled out all the forms and taken all the exams, here's how you really get a job. Unless you're experienced in an unusual field of work that the government needs, getting on a government register and receiving a rating is not enough to land a job. The truth is you will have to find the actual job vacancy yourself. Not all job openings go through the Federal Job Information Center; those that do have been known by the program administrator for two months or more. Thus someone already employed by that government agency may have a strong inside edge.

Outsiders have less of a chance, even though the hiring administrator must follow a standard practice. He or she may either promote someone currently in a federal job or ask the area Civil Service office for a "list of

THE SF 171

Standard Form 171 is the most important government form for job hunters. It's what all federal agencies use instead of a personally prepared resume. The SF 171 must be filled out with great care and *always* typewritten. *NO* mistakes, please.

There are two ways to prepare SF 171s. The first way applies when you are responding to a general Civil Service announcement — for a category of jobs, not a specific vacancy. In this case, the SF 171 should include *everything* you have done, *all* your volunteer activities, *all* your extra training courses, *every* award or commendation. Unlike usual resumes in which it's best to be concise and volunteer experience doesn't count for much, the opposite is true for the SF 171. For women returning to the work force after having had children, this factor can be a real plus. Your volunteer work makes a difference.

The second way to fill out the SF 171 applies if you know of a *specific* job vacancy. In this case, you should describe your experience to match as closely as possible the requirements of the job. Information on these requirements can be obtained from four places: the *vacancy announcement,* which outlines what general experience is called for; the *position description,* which will give you more detail; the *Civil Service Commission Handbook X-118,* which describes the experience necessary for each job category and each grade level; and the *Civil Service Commission Classification Standards,* which outlines the duties of jobs at different grade levels.

To fill out an SF 171 with the kind of detail that will help you get the job, you'll need to add pages of information to the form. In each box where you have more to say than room to say it, type "See attachment #_____" and type the complete answer on a separate piece of bond paper.

If you are applying for more than one specific vacancy, complete the first and last pages of the SF 171, fill in "See attached page _____" under Awards, but do not date or sign the last page. Copy the first and last pages for each vacancy, and tailor each statement in your SF 171 to the specific requirements of each job. Date and sign the last page at the time you file an SF 171 for a specific job vacancy.

---

eligibles." This list is compiled from those whose qualifications match those stated in the vacancy announcement. The administrator must then choose from among the top three names on the list of eligibles.

The closer your SF 171 matches the requirements of the job, the closer *your* name will be to the top of the list. And the more you know about the job, the easier it will be to make your SF 171 match its requirements. Since they know more about the actual job available, internal candidates almost always have an edge. For that reason, and to find out where future vacancies will occur, use your networking skills to get to know federal administrators and other employees through family and friends or through temporary work as a student intern. Insiders can help you tailor your SF 171 form to anticipate the job vacancy announcement.

Some More Tactics. Get your name listed on as many registers as possible. Qualify for as many jobs as you can by presenting your experience to fit. Also, you could try for a lower-level job than you are qualified for and bank on advancing from there. In agencies like the Environmental Protection Agency with good internal mobility programs, you can advance fairly rapidly from a clerk typist position to an administrative one. But be careful: Make sure you've picked an agency where this advancement is possible.

A Final Alternative. Take the Junior Federal Assistant examination, which qualifies people for GS-4 positions. This exam is open to you if you've had at least two years of college. If you have had four or more years of college, you should score well and place at the top of the register of eligibles drawn from the exam.

THE PACE EXAM

The Professional and Administrative Career Exam, or PACE, tests the aptitude of college graduates for more than 120 technical, professional, and administrative jobs in the GS-5 through 7 range. PACE evaluates reasoning ability in reading, expression, interpretation, decision making, and numerical ability. The results are in the form of ratings in each of six occupational categories: work with people (management, customs services, public health, etc.); work with money (tax specialist, budget analyst, administration, IRS, etc.); computer specialist; contact representative; writing and editing; and alcohol, tobacco, and firearms inspection. The ratings are used to make a list, or register, of applicants for jobs for which they are qualified and available. As they open, the jobs are filled from these lists.

The PACE is free and is given once or twice a year in more than 700 locations. The Federal Job Information Center will tell you when the test will be given and how to apply and will give you sample questions along with the application forms. You might want to brush up on basic math before taking the exam. Otherwise, there really isn't anything you can study to prepare for it.

One final word of advice: Take the PACE at least 6 to 9 months *before* you start to look for a federal job; it takes from 6 to 12 weeks for you to receive the test results. If you aren't satisfied with your scores, you may be able to take the PACE again if there's time. The highest exam score counts.

No matter how many forms you've filled out, remember that it's still your responsibility to find *yourself* a job.

Types of Federal Appointments

Federal Civil Service appointments are of four types: temporary, term, conditional, and career.

A *temporary* worker is not eligible for retirement benefits and cannot be promoted or transferred. The job usually lasts less than a year but may be renewed for another year.

A *term* appointment is made for a period up to four years for work on a specific project. The employee may be promoted within the project but isn't covered by the retirement systems.

A *career-conditional* appointment leads to a career appointment in three years. The first year is a probationary period. No restrictions are placed on promotions or advancements.

Career appointments are a little like tenure—they cannot be over-turned except for serious, demonstrable reasons, good cause being up-held by a fair hearing. If a layoff occurs, career employees are the last to be let go.

Special Programs to Help Women

The Federal Women's Program works much as an Affirmative Action office in a university or a company. Every federal agency is assigned a Federal Women's Program coordinator who is responsible for helping to provide better opportunities for women.

Federally Employed Women, an independent professional organization with local offices across the country, gives workshops and holds meetings on career subjects to assist women in Civil Service jobs.

Women government employees can also benefit from other types of

---

GOLD FROM THE OOQ

The Winter 1977 issue of *Occupational Outlook Quarterly* is a goldmine of information on the federal hiring system. Look for the issue in your public library or college placement office library.

---

work arrangements. A few federal departments such as HEW and some regional government offices offer a limited number of part-time positions. These jobs offer real advantages to women employees with family responsibilities.

Also, internal training opportunities are very good in most federal agencies. Programs are given at the Federal Executive Institute, the three Executive Seminar Centers, the ten regional training centers, and six other centers in Washington, D.C. In addition, tuition refund opportunities help some employees pursue advanced degrees—a practice that can be very helpful to women seeking to move up. (One drawback: these opportunties are limited in number.)

You've Got a Federal Job, Now How Do You Advance?

Even now barriers to women's advancement in the Civil Service persist. It's still easier for women to get a staff position than an administrative one, and there are still a few areas in government where women have a harder time advancing. On the whole, however, government jobs offer women career opportunities the private sector has yet to match. Some hints on how to advance:

- Join a new, fast-growing agency or government program; your career will advance just as it would in a successful new venture in the private sector.
- Find a mentor, a person who has faith in you and whose own career is moving. As more women are given higher-level jobs, they can make themselves available as mentors to entering women.
- Make your job visible. Then, work like mad for all the notice and appreciation due you.
- Develop a network of contacts at various levels of government. You'll learn where the new government programs and money will be.

GETTING IN, MOVING UP: FEDERAL ADMINISTRATION

College graduates seeking an entry-level Civil Service position in federal service must take the required PACE examination. A special application process and an active job search are also necessary. Federal Job Information Centers throughout the country provide some information about job openings and requirements.

- Another way to learn about new job opportunities and gain visibility: Volunteer for any and all reorganization or personnel policy efforts.
- Don't get locked in to one area of expertise. Be flexible enough to learn about new issues and develop new skills so that if the program you're working under is cut, you'll have some options.
- If you want to make a change and you can't switch your area of expertise, try changing jurisdictions or levels of government. It's likely that there are jobs similar to yours in state, county, and city governments. (The Intergovernmental Personnel Act of 1970 helps people move from Federal Government jobs to state and local government and vice versa. See your Federal Job Information Center for details.)

Even if your reasons for choosing government service are altruistic, be sure to make conscious decisions about your own career. If you are bored or frustrated or cynical about your job, you're not likely to be able to make a real contribution to the people or issues to which you've committed yourself.

State and Local Civil Service Systems

State, county, and municipal civil service systems are generally organized in the same way as the federal Civil Service: exams for entry-level positions, special forms, and a long wait for a job.

Since career ladders in these systems are much shorter than those in the federal system, chances for advancement are fewer, but it's a shorter distance to the top. Also, in these systems it's likely that you will work for an appointed or elected official; this can make your job easier or more difficult, depending on the widely varying professional abilities of these officials.

Personnel laws and merit systems differ extensively from state to state, but they have some things in common. Many jobs in state and local government involve working with the public. Salary scales and benefits tend to be considerably lower than in comparable federal jobs, but the responsibilities are greater. It is much more likely that a person will supervise other people at a younger age in state government than either in the Federal Government or business. In fact, many young people graduating from college seek government employment just to "get a start," planning to transfer to another career or go back to graduate school when they have gained more experience. Civil service jobs, particularly in new and growing agencies, provide that kind of opportunity.

Finally, state and local civil service jobs usually have lower education and work experience requirements than federal jobs do.

To find out about civil service positions in your state, see your state employment agency or look for the civil service listing under your state

BY THE NUMBERS

The numbers that government people are frequently heard spouting are generally numbers of laws or regulations. Some federal laws are known by their names — the Civil Rights Act of 1964, for instance. Others are commonly identified by a number — P.L. 94-142 (pronounced "ninety-four, one forty-two"), for example. A system dictates these numbers. "P.L." stands for "public law," "94" stands for the 94th Congress, and "142" means the 142nd law passed in that Congress. This law, called "94-142" for short, requires public school systems to educate handicapped children.

"Titles" are specific sections of federal laws that may have many different sections in them. For instance, Title VII of the Civil Rights Act of 1964 prohibits job discrimination against women and minorities. It is usually called "Title seven."

If you hear "chapter" followed by a number, it may refer to a state law: for example, Chapter 766 (pronounced "seven-sixty-six") in Massachusetts is the state equivalent of P.L. 94-142. The numbers help distinguish insiders from outsiders. If you are an outsider, using the numbers correctly will make you sound experienced and knowledgeable (even if you aren't). If you write "I am familiar with the programs eligible for Title Twenty funds" on your job application, nobody will believe you. Insiders write title numbers in roman numerals; it's Title XX.

---

government in the phone book. Most large cities, and some counties and towns, also have civil service systems of their own or are part of a statewide system. Call your city hall or county building to find out.

Should You Volunteer?

State, county, and local governments have one entry opportunity that hardly exists at the federal level: state and local boards and citizen participation groups are looking for citizen volunteers. Volunteering is a particularly useful path for a woman who wants to go back to work after having taken time out to raise children. When her children are still young, she can join a community board, and by the time she is ready to go back to work she will have developed a set of contacts, an area of expertise, and some credentials that may make the transition to paid work easier. It's also an excellent way to break in for a woman who is starting a career.

Boards seeking volunteers include town and county recreation commissions, conservation commissions, school boards, and building committees. Investigate how to get on one or more. Some of these board positions are elected; some are appointive by political parties or elected officials. Boards are always looking for volunteer help.

Service on state or regional committees or commissions also is a good preparation for paid work. Investigate opportunities working for such groups as federally supported health service agencies, who plan health facilities and services, or Title XX planning committees, who arrange for social service programs for low-income people. If the members of the commission are elected, as a volunteer you can probably join subcommittees.

Some states maintain listings of these types of positions working for boards and committees. Consult the state citizen participation or citizen volunteer office. Your state or local League of Women Voters may also keep a list.

In many states, intern or volunteer offices also accept part-time help from students and other volunteers. This route is another good way to get visibility and develop contacts—two essentials for getting and moving up in government jobs.

Eileen Wang, Government Administrator

Eileen Wang has a high-level position in the Secretary's office of the Department of Health, Education, and Welfare (HEW). She calls her work environment "very seductive. I don't know how people who have worked on a policy-determining level can ever go back to anything else."

"Some days," Ms. Wang says, "I'm staggered by the enormousness of the problems I'm dealing with. For example, can you imagine what changes will have to be by the year 2000 when 1 out of 4 Americans will be 65 or over? Can you imagine the changes that will be necessary in our health delivery system alone? Or can you imagine trying to reinvent the whole welfare system? Talk about your million-dollar questions!"

Since she joined one of HEW's subordinate agencies about 20 years ago, Ms. Wang has been working with questions like these. In the course of her career she has worked for three agencies within HEW.

Just out of college with a good academic record and no work experience, Ms. Wang used every contact she had to get her first job—"even old boyfriends' fathers." She had grown up in Washington and always knew she wanted to work there.

"My first job," she recalls, "was as a low-level paper pusher, but I knew what I wanted. I got a reputation for being bright and hardworking and good at research. My husband was still in law school and working hard, and so I had plenty of time to spend on my job. When our daughter was born, I knew I was at a crucial point in my career. I managed to negotiate some time off and a part-time position after that."

THE THRILL OF IT ALL: CIVIL SERVICE ADMINISTRATOR

*"I've taken every training opportunity that came my way.
The courses are often really helpful, and they look
good on your SF 171."*

*"At the end of my work life, I want to be able to say
that I helped make the world a better place."*

*"A lot of people like me are in state civil service only
for a few years — for a chance to prove my administrative
abilities at a younger age than I would on the outside.
As a woman, I think I have more chances of advancement
at the state. I'll switch to the private sector later
on."*

Before long Ms. Wang was back full time as an assistant administrator of what should have been a new and exciting research program. "It was in this job," she says, "that I became trapped in the worst working situation of my career. My boss consistently undermined my confidence by such tricks as giving me work to do and then ignoring the product of my work, reassigning parts of my job to people with half my experience or ability, putting me down subtly, forcing me to do make-work. It was awful. I was scared because he was eating me alive. I knew he was wrecking my career, but I didn't know where to turn. I even thought it was time to retire to housework.

"Through my network of contacts I found a job with a woman I knew was bound to rise rapidly, and I became a member of her staff. Many of the women I know working in Washington got their chances the same way, using their contacts and finding a mentor. I'm sure it's the same in business. If you're indispensable to someone who's going to be promoted, you'll get promoted, too. It's just that in the past it's been hard for women to find mentors willing to help them."

Today women face other traps, according to Ms. Wang. "Some women get promoted for Affirmative Action reasons into positions they aren't ready for and then they fail pretty visibly. This is particularly true for management positions. Women often have a difficult time handling the political aspects of these positions. They sometimes think all they need to do is concentrate on substantive issues, the content of their jobs. I would never be where I am today if I hadn't learned the political skills you need to survive and advance in either business or government, and I learned them by imitating my mentor."

The time came when Ms. Wang knew she needed to establish herself on her own, not just as her mentor's right-hand woman. She recalls that it was "very, very hard. She had helped me a lot. I was very valuable to her, and she didn't want to lose me. I had to fight for work that would give me visibility outside my department. I just needed a chance—once people see the kind of work I can do, I'm all right. But she wouldn't give me that chance until I confronted her directly. She had the right to appoint a member of a special interagency committee dealing with policy issues and I begged, threatened, carried on and cajoled until she appointed me.

"I feel I'm in a very important place in government now. In the office of the Secretary of a department like HEW you get to see the political forces of the country in action. Maybe that sounds a little dramatic, but it's true. You're close to presidential policy. You see the Congress at work on legislation, and you see the results of all those programs and evaluations and site visits you did come together to form the basis of new policy. I love it."

THE DAILY GRIND: CIVIL SERVICE ADMINISTRATOR

"I'm at a high enough level in government where the turf problems begin to surface — 'that program should be in our division.' etc. It's a very competitive environment, always trying to outwit the competition."

"No matter where you are, there's always the enormity of the bureaucracy over you, and around you, and under you."

BASIC RESOURCES

For Federal job information, contact:

Federal Job Information Centers
(see your phone book under Federal or under
United States Government or call 800-555-1212)

Federally Employed Women
National Press Building (Room 481)
529 14th Street NW
Washington, D.C. 20045

Internal job training information is available from

Federal Executive Institute
United States Civil Service Commission
1900 E Street NW
Washington, D.C. 20415

For state jobs check with your local state civil service offices, listed in your telephone book under the state name.

CHAPTER 3

PROFESSIONALS IN GOVERNMENT

Government is by far the major employer for certain kinds of jobs. Some of these positions are covered by civil service, others are not. Community service jobs form the largest category of government-only careers. Some of these jobs are blue-collar—firefighter, for example; others are white-collar jobs like city planner. Some are what have been called "pink-collar" jobs, those traditionally held by women, such as teaching or social work.

In pursuing a career, community service workers may keep one role or take on a succession of roles. A teacher may stay in classroom teaching for 20 years or use teaching as a stepping stone to work as an educational consultant or school administrator. Just as in private employment there is flexibility and lateral mobility within and across career lines in government community service jobs.

Some government professionals work for government agencies with no private-sector equivalent, for example, the Foreign Service, Armed Forces, and Postal Service. Of course, certain jobs in these services are equivalent to those "on the outside"—a carpenter in the Army does much the same work as one working for any private employer. However, *most* of the positions in these agencies and the environment in which people work are quite different from private-sector jobs.

Working for an Elected or Appointed Official

Many government professionals work for elected or appointed officials or for commissions—not always an easy thing. Disagreements usually run along the lines of: "I'm the professional, and I'm telling you that you can expect that this is going to happen" from the career professional, versus: "You may call yourself the expert, but I really know what this community (or the governor or the President) wants" from the elected or appointed official.

NOTE FROM THE PAST

Frances Perkins

Frances Perkins once claimed that "being a woman has only bothered me in climbing trees." She began her career fighting for better working conditions for women and children in industry. With the New York State Consumers League and later as chairman of the Industrial Board of the New York Department of Labor, she lobbied successfully for a shorter (48-hour) workweek. She founded the Maternity Center to provide health care to pregnant women. She also developed the New York State Employment Service.

When New York Governor Franklin Roosevelt was elected president, he remembered Francis Perkins, and in 1933 appointed her Secretary of Labor—the first woman to hold a Cabinet post in the United States. In that post, she supported formation of the Works Progress Administration, and the Public Works Administration; developed the Civilian Conservation Corps, and established a federal employment service. Perhaps most importantly, she helped to found the Social Security Administration, providing retirement income and health benefits for older people.

Many community planners, city managers, and other government professionals deal with this problem by making a clear distinction between their role and the roles of elected or appointed officials to whom they report. The elected official is obligated to make decisions; the professional must advise the decision makers of the consequences of proposed action and present them with alternatives.

Sooner or later career government professionals may meet an attempt to influence them to do something either illegal or unethical. The civil service helps protect government employees in cases of this kind. Government professionals advise that the best way to say "no" to something illegal or unethical is by relying on government processes, providing helpful information about the process. For instance: "We'd love to hire your nephew, but you know a complicated civil service process is involved. He should apply to. . . ."

Movement and Career Ladders in Government Professions

All professional government careers require specialized training. Police officers, firefighters, and postal workers all receive such training after

APPOINTED OFFICIALS—WHO ARE THEY? WHAT DO THEY DO?

The jobs of government officials who have been appointed to their positions fall somewhere between those of government professionals and those of elected officials. Whether they are professionals who were given appointive positions because of their professional credibility or campaign supporters who were appointed because of loyalty and effort, they were given their jobs to satisfy a particular constituency.

If you are an appointed official, you must know clearly why you were appointed (aside from your obvious talent, of course) because you will be expected to "deliver" to your constituency. If you were appointed to help satisfy advocates for women, or environmentalists, or people from the western part of the state, then that's part of your job, as well as budget analysis and policy development and all the other things you will be expected to do.

The ambiguity of appointive positions is best explained by a professional woman in an appointive position herself: "I know I'm in a vulnerable job. But I have my own constituency, and frankly the governor needs me. Information is power in government and it works both ways. My staff and my constituency stay loyal to me because I always let them know exactly what new policies or bills are being considered and that gives them the chance to get their act together and take action on issues affecting them. In the same way, I can go to the governor and say, 'You're really going to get creamed if you do such and such.' I've never been wrong; I know she keeps track of that. And I always give her plenty of advance notice and all the chances to take the credit."

---

they are hired. Many other community service careers require a bachelor's or master's degree. As the competition gets tougher for these jobs, a master's degree becomes more important.

Moving up in a government profession usually means moving into administration, which in turn means learning a new set of skills and in effect changing the content of your job. Like the business world, government leaders have begun to think of administration or management as a profession. A master's in public administration or a special training program can be helpful to a government professional.

Career ladders in these professions are short, unless you work for the Federal Government in Washington. The smaller the government entity, generally the shorter the career ladder. A small city may only hire one professional city manager, for example. That city manager may have to move to a large city to get a job with more responsibility or a higher salary.

Recognizing this need for extending job opportunities, the Federal

THE THRILL OF IT ALL: A GOVERNMENT PROFESSIONAL

*"Whenever I go through that city I stop to see if there
are old people sitting in that park or mothers pushing
babies in strollers. I fought for that park when we
did the urban renewal project, and it took years before
it was built. But now it's there forever."*

*"I'll never forget Tony. He was the first kid I placed
in a foster home. Such a great little boy. He
deserved all the work I put in on that case."*

*"Because of work I did,
my city was able to save 30 percent of its energy-
related expenditures. That came to almost $100,000
a year."*

Government has special programs to help professionals in state or local governments change to federal employment. These programs, governed by the Intergovernmental Personnel Act, are administered by the Civil Service Commission. For more information, consult the Federal Job Information Center.

Burnout: A Special Problem in Some Government Professions

Community service professionals, particularly those in the human services, know what "burnout" is. It's what happens when people have worked too long with difficult or unusually disturbing problems and become very depressed or very angry, or both. In this situation you may become either supersensitive to the problem you are dealing with or completely insensitive to it. In either event you may become frustrated and ineffective at what you are doing.

Of course some jobs are more stressful than others and some people have higher tolerance levels than others; but if you are considering a career in community service, be aware of the symptoms of burnout and be prepared to deal with it. Air traffic controllers are considered to have such a highly stressful job, for example, that the Federal Aeronautics Administration makes a special effort to train them for other jobs. Unfortunately, such arrangements have not been made for those with stressful jobs in the human service professions.

Young people in their first two or three years of work are the most susceptible to burnout. After that they have usually adjusted their expectations so that they have a more realistic appraisal of what is possible. Some find that administrative jobs in the same field offer a good way to use their knowledge and skills in less-stressful circumstances.

Those who stick it out must develop ways of staying enthusiastic and committed to their work. One way is to set limits and insist that others respect them; for instance, saying "I will go to only one or two evening meetings a week" or "I won't work more than 50 hours a week." Another way is to develop a strong outside interest. A good supervisor can also help.

Working for a Consulting Firm

Another possible direction for experienced professional government career people is to work for consulting firms that specialize in professional work—in research, law, management, etc.—for government agencies on a contract basis.

THE DAILY GRIND: A GOVERNMENT PROFESSIONAL

*"Reorganizations —they're what I hate most.
Everybody knows they're just a power play.
Reorganizations take so much of our time no real work gets
done. Nobody ever looks at what we were doing or how
well we were doing, or how we could make it better."*

*"Women still aren't accepted as city managers. People
think, 'She can't be hardnosed about the budget; she
won't be able to fire people. What does she know about
sewers, potholes, solid waste?' Once women start to
get elected to more positions in towns and cities,
women in appointed positions in city
government will get more of a chance."*

*"I was going home on the train. I had spent three
16-hour days troubleshooting for
the state, and this
guy sitting next to me had the nerve to say, 'So you're
one of those loafers on the state payroll.'"*

Hiring consultants presents certain advantages for government agencies. A consultant permits an agency to complete a special project without having to hire extra staff; when the project is over, the consultant leaves. If the consultant does an inadequate job, he or she can be fired much more easily than a staff person. Consultants may have special expertise that won't be needed by the agency on a permanent basis. Agencies may also "go outside" to get a recommendation if the subject is a politically sensitive one, such as low-income housing.

Contrary to popular myth, working as a consultant to government doesn't automatically bring fame and riches. A consultant with good business sense and a stable specialty may be able to make more money than in government service; but the competition for government contracts is often intense, sometimes resulting in unprofitable underbidding on a project as a kind of loss leader to get business.

Although working on government contracts can be an insecure business, many consultants enjoy their independence. A consultant can build her own staff of people who thinks the way she does and can usually concentrate on one job at a time. She can undertake discrete, defined tasks—often the most interesting special projects—without having to deal with red tape so much.

Working as a consultant with many clients broadens your knowledge and it is this wider experience that is most valuable to your clients. Often as a consultant your judgment is more valued than that of a staff member simply because it "costs money." On the other hand, you frequently don't have the opportunity to plead for your ideas actually to be realized and carried out in a well-funded program.

Many people in government professions go back and forth between private-sector consulting jobs and government work. For a consultant, a year or two spent in government service is invaluable experience in "what it's like" from the client's standpoint.

Professions Found Only in Government

Community planning, social work, and foreign service are three of the many career opportunities for women in professional government fields.

Community Planning

When they landed in the New World in the 17th and the 18th centuries, European settlers had a marvelous opportunity to plan their new towns and cities instead of just letting them grow haphazardly. Throughout the colonies many settlers took advantage of this opportunity.

American cities and towns, however, were not immune to the Industrial Revolution. As tenements and slums proliferated, only those who

THE PROPOSAL PROCESS: INSIDE INFORMATION

Whether you work for a consultant or a government agency, you have to understand the proposal process. State and federal governments spend money in two ways. In the first, all people or organizations that meet certain "eligibility criteria" or fall into a certain category automatically are entitled to special benefits. For example, if you are over 65 or blind, you get a special exemption on your income taxes. Anyone who qualifies and applies gets the benefit.

Government also spends money in another way, by making grants or by contracting for goods or services. These grants and contracts are usually awarded on a competitive basis. To start this competition among eligible applicants, the government issues an RFP, a Request for Proposal. RFPs may be as much as 50 pages long, outlining what kind of organization is eligible, what it will be asked to do, how it will be required to do it, and roughly how much it should spend.

The consultants, not-for-profit organizations, or government agencies trying for this pot of money send in a proposal that includes all the required information as well as a complete budget and the resumes of the people working on the project. A long time and a lot of work go into writing a proposal, and agencies are not reimbursed for the time and money spent to prepare it.

When the proposals are sent in, they are evaluated by the funding agency. The best among them are given the money to do the work, usually after some negotiation on the budget. There is often a lengthy delay between sending in the proposal and hearing whether it is successful.

Public notice of federal RFPs is given in the *Federal Register* and in the *Commerce Business Daily* (CBD), available on subscription and in large libraries. Both are published every working day.

---

developed the great urban park system, like landscape architect Frederick Law Olmstead, retained the image of a beautiful city. With his friends Daniel Burnham, John Root, and others, Olmstead designed the buildings and park for the great Columbian Exposition of 1893. The dazzling white buildings in a park setting rekindled public interest in urban design and fostered the growth of modern city plans and a new profession of community planners. By 1976, 16,000 community planners were working in the United States.

Where Do Planners Work? Modern planning professionals are concerned with economic and social planning as well as urban design and land use. Planning started as a municipal profession, and today most planners work for towns and cities. But for the past 25 years many more planners have been working for state government or special metropolitan agencies formed for special purposes; transportation authorities or sewer districts, for examples. Approximately 700 councils of government or regional planning agencies exist, falling somewhere between state and municipal jurisdictions. The newest level of planning is neighborhood revitalization.

Some planning professionals work as consultants to the different levels of government. A small number of planners work for large private real estate developers or public utilities.

Much of this planning activity is related to federal requirements. For all its major grant programs, whether in social services, urban revitalization, transportation, or housing, the Federal Government requires that the recipient present a plan for how and when and where the grant money is to be used. Thus the future of planning as a career depends heavily on the availability of federal money for state and local projects.

The Planning Process. Planning for communities involves a process similar to planning by modern business firms, except that it involves public participation. First, an inventory and analysis are made of community resources and needs. Goals and objectives are set by chief executives or planning commissions and the public. Alternatives are developed for reaching the goals, and the outcomes of each alternative are predicted. Feedback from the public is sought in public meetings and through the media, the choice of alternatives is made by the planning commission or elected officials, the alternative is then refined and implemented. Much the same process is used no matter what the content of the plan is—housing, land use, or renewal.

Training in Planning. You can earn both undergraduate and graduate degrees in community planning. Many people who started their careers in another field, such as engineering, landscape architecture, or law, are drawn to the planning field because of the chance to influence public policy. Advanced positions in planning tend to require a master's degree

GETTING IN, MOVING UP: COMMUNITY PLANNING

Community planners earn their credentials working for government or by earning a master's degree in community planning. They can advance on the job to more responsible administrative jobs and to jobs with larger planning agencies. Some planners become consultants to government or work for private developers.

in planning or public administration, or significant work experience. Membership in the American Institute of Planners requires an examination and a combination of education and work experience. To prepare for their careers, planners study law, government programs and policies, sociology, design, and statistics.

Special Advantages for Women. The planning process involves many community boards and committees open to public participation. By staying active in committees like these or in a professional association, women planners can leave the field for a few years to have children and still keep their experience current.

Planning is also a relatively easy area to join for women who are reentering the work force. In the newest areas of planning, such as historic preservation or health services, the body of knowledge is developing so fast that it's possible to become expert quickly because no one has years and years of experience.

Social Work

Social work is a career that women have traditionally pursued. From the time of Jane Addams' work with Chicago's Hull House at the turn of the century, social work has provided some of America's most talented and outspoken women with a fulfilling career. Jane Addams herself was awarded the Nobel Peace Prize in 1931, only four years before her death.

Settlement houses, supported by charitable contributions, provided the location for most early social work. In them, social workers, many of them volunteers, taught English to immigrants and also instructed people in such subjects as sewing, reading, and nutrition. They offered, in addition, a range of cultural and recreational programs to neighborhood residents.

Social work has undergone great changes since then. A body of knowledge and research techniques, a more defined methodology, and standards for professional practice have been developed. Generally speaking, there are two kinds of social workers—"clinical" social workers, who help people with emotional problems, and "community" social workers, who help individuals and groups to use their own and their community's resources to improve their lives.

Social Work Methods. Social workers use three methods: casework, group work, and community organization. Casework may mean working with an individual to help solve an emotional problem, finding a new apartment for a family whose home has been destroyed by fire, arranging for day care for a child whose mother has been hospitalized, or helping an elderly disabled person apply for government support. Group work includes family therapy and working with groups of troubled adolescents. Community organization may involve organizing public housing tenants to develop a residents' security patrol or serving as an advocate for low-income utility users before a state rate-setting commission.

GETTING IN, MOVING UP: SOCIAL WORK

Social workers usually earn college degrees before going to work for government or private social service agencies. Clinical social workers and those interested in administration or program planning should count on getting a master's degree in the field.

Training for Social Work. On the graduate or undergraduate level, training for this field generally includes studying human behavior and development, government and private programs in the social services, and research and therapeutic methods. Although social workers with only bachelor's degrees have been able to find entry-level work, a master's in social work is important if you are considering a clinical, administrative, or teaching career in social work. A listing of accredited programs is available from the Council on Social Work Education.

Where Do Social Workers Work? Of the 330,000 social workers in 1976, two-thirds were working for private human service agencies like nursing homes, rehabilitation centers, and social associations such as YW/YMCAs or for government agencies in welfare departments, housing authorities, and antipoverty programs. Social workers are also employed by hospitals, schools, or companies, usually in the personnel or training departments. Increasingly, clinical social workers are developing part-time and/or full-time private practices.

Like many other government professionals, social workers today work almost entirely on government funds whether they work in a government job or for a private agency reimbursed by government.

Special Advantages for Women. Like women community planners, women social workers have found it relatively easy to take time off to have a family because of the part-time job opportunities in this field. Also, many volunteer opportunities are available to social workers who want to maintain professional contacts and keep up with developments in the field while unemployed.

Foreign Service

The Department of State, which deals with foreign affairs, has a special merit appointment system for its employees who serve overseas and in this country in the Foreign Service and the United States Information Agency (USIA).

Foreign Service officers (FSOs) carry out responsibilities in four main areas: consular, economic, political, and commercial. Consular officers keep in constant contact with foreign citizens and Americans abroad, issuing visas or passports, taking testimony for United States courts, and helping Americans with emergencies. Economic and commercial officers work with foreign governments in matters of trade, investments, or monetary matters. Political officers analyze and report on political matters affecting American interests, specializing in other countries or regions. (In addition, administrative officers manage the support operations in American embassies and consulates abroad or hold administrative jobs in geographic or functional bureaus of the State Department.)

Officers who serve in the USIA (called Foreign Service Information Officers, or FSIOs) handle "public diplomacy," communicating American ideals and culture to the people of other countries. Information officers operate libraries or cultural centers or deal with communications media. Cultural officers arrange for cultural exchanges and help to manage American cultural activities when they are brought to other countries.

Career Information. Although USIA and Foreign Service employees work in 260 American embassies and consulates overseas, many others are employed in Washington, D.C. Every FSO and FSIO must agree to work anywhere she is needed, abroad or at home. About 60 percent of an officer's career is spent abroad, moving frequently from one post to another. The need for frequent relocation may make family life difficult. When both husband and wife are in the Foreign Service, the State Department attempts but does not guarantee to place them in the same location.

Junior officers start at a salary between $11,523 and $16,172, depending on qualifications and experience. The top salary for officers is $47,500. Benefits include housing and cost-of-living allowances, education stipends overseas for children, as well as a retirement program and medical benefits.

How to Apply. Candidates must be American citizens, at least 20 years old, and in good health. Most successful applicants have a bachelor's degree; some have graduate degrees. Good command of spoken and written English is necessary. Knowledge of foreign languages is not necessarily required for entering officers, but the ability to speak a foreign language is necessary for promotion. Every applicant must take a written examination, given once a year at no cost, by the Board of Examiners for the Foreign Service of the State Department.

Along with the application form you will receive a very helpful booklet describing Foreign Service careers in detail and including sample test questions.

Applicants who pass this exam also take an oral exam aimed at determining their ability to think and express themselves clearly and to make decisions. Those who pass the oral exam then undergo a medical exam-

GETTING IN, MOVING UP: FOREIGN SERVICE OFFICER

Foreign Service officers are trained after they have passed both a written and an oral examination and have been accepted by the Foreign Service, an agency of the Department of State. They advance as they gain more experience and training overseas and in Washington. The Foreign Service assigns them a career counselor to help them with career advancement.

ination, as must any dependents who would accompany them abroad. Investigations into the applicants' backgrounds are conducted to determine suitability to represent the United States abroad and to assess possible security risks. A final competitive review process determines which candidates are to be appointed.

Special Program for Women. In 1975 about 9 percent, or 297, of the 3,369 Foreign Service officers were women. A special program has now been devised to encourage women to seek Foreign Service jobs. Applicants for this program must be at least 30 years old, have work experience directly related to that of a Foreign Service officer, and be available to serve worldwide. They do not need to take the written exam but will need to file an SF 171. More information and application forms are available from the Equal Employment Opportunity Office of the Department of State.

Lesley Banks, Foreign Service Officer

Lesley Banks, a Foreign Service Officer at mid-career, is proud that her job is "what I always wanted. I've always learned a lot from the culture I've lived in, and I have been where the action really was. I've helped make arrangements for major diplomatic conferences, even for our Secretary of State, and carried important policy messages. Even when my work is trivial, I feel a closeness to history being made. I feel close to the seat of power, and like everyone else in this business, I want to get in a position where I can really negotiate, really help make foreign policy."

Ms. Banks came to the Foreign Service by chance. She had always wanted to travel and had decided that being a stewardess was out (she gets queasy in airplanes). One day she happened to see a TV interview with a Foreign Service recruiter: "It was like a miracle. I knew that was for me, and they took me!"

There were 25 people in Ms. Banks' junior officer class at the Foreign Service Institute. "All of us who were accepted," she notes, "went through 6 weeks of training before our first assignment. We worked hard and got to know each other well, our first set of Foreign Service connections."

In her first post overseas Ms. Banks worked in a small consulate with only one other FSO, a man who taught her a great deal. In her second post she was a consular officer in a very busy office and dealt with immigrant and tourist problems. She remembers that she "was in an on-the-line job, handling as many as 500 cases a day. In that type of position you must learn all kinds of American laws and regulations about citizenship and passports and visas. I had to make a lot of decisions myself.

"I also had to know some local laws, because I had to help American tourists. Americans are demanding more from their government nowadays and that includes Americans overseas.

"One time when I was on duty some Americans called the consulate about midnight and insisted that we get them admitted to a local bar. I could tell they were drunk; they kept telling me that they paid my salary with their taxes. So I called the bar and found out that it didn't let men in who weren't wearing coats and ties. I called them back, explained the situation, and they cooled down."

Ms. Banks feels that the training you can get in the Foreign Service is fantastic: "If you are assigned a language-designated post, they teach you the language. Very intense and highly respected courses are offered at the Foreign Service Institute. For example, its course in political economics is a six-month version of a master's degree in economics. You even go to graduate school. All these training opportunities are especially available to women these days. The academic training in the Foreign Service helps a lot of officers get academic positions with universities when they retire."

"The Foreign Service is really interested in people's careers," Ms. Banks says. "We all have a career counselor who advises us on career decisions; mine has been particularly helpful. She thinks I should try for an embassy position next time. Embassies represent more and different government functions. There's a lot more going on.

"That's how your career grows in the Foreign Service. You have the opportunity to get training, you have a counselor for general advice, you make contacts with people all over the world, and you try to choose from among the posts offered you the one that will best suit your talents. In the beginning you don't really get much choice of assignments; later on you have more to say."

People always ask Ms. Banks two questions about the Foreign Service: "Isn't it dangerous?" and "What about a woman's family?" "Yes," she answers, "it can be dangerous. My last assignment was in a part of the world that was in conflict, but I faced no more danger than the people who lived there. It didn't bother me. In some places consular officers sit behind bulletproof glass, and you receive training in antiterrorist tactics. You can refuse those assignments if you want to, but a lot of people find them exciting.

"The second question is a little harder to deal with. That old image of the perfect Foreign Service wife fulfilling the social duties of her husband's post has hardly any validity today; so if you are a woman you don't need to do double duty.

"If you marry an FSO, it's harder for both of you to continue your careers outside Washington. The Foreign Service tries its best to give you assignments at the same post, but if it doesn't work out, which one of you takes the choice position? Which one sits around for 2 years? The Foreign Service is working on this problem because it's really interested in advancing its women officers. But it has yet to come up with a good solution for two-career families."

Ms. Banks thinks that there is a type of person who does particularly well in the Foreign Service—someone with inner resourcefulness. "Moving every couple of years is hard. For about a month in the new post you feel a little dazed; you need to be able to figure out how to make yourself comfortable in this new environment and make local contacts to help you with your job. Of course the Foreign Service helps with the basics, information like never blow your nose in public in Afghanistan. (It's considered terribly rude.) Your fellow officers support you, too. But there's something else you need besides the ability to keep your cool and the ability to talk your way out of a paper bag—an independent spirit. I guess that's me."

FEDERAL AGENCIES WITH THEIR OWN MERIT SYSTEMS

These agencies should be contacted directly for jobs in their organizations, rather than through the Civil Service.

Central Intelligence Agency
1820 Fort Myer Drive
Arlington, Virginia 22209

Department of State
Foreign Service of the United States
Employment Division
Washington, D.C. 20520

Federal Bureau of Investigation
J. Edgar Hoover Building (Room 1028)
Washington, D.C. 20535

Federal Reserve System
Board of Governors
20th Street and Constitution Avenue NW
Washington, D.C. 20051

Judicial Branch of the Government (except the Administrative Office of the United States Courts and United States Customs Court)

Clerk
United States Supreme Court Building
1 First Street NE
Washington, D.C. 20543

Legislative Branch of the Government (including the Library of Congress and the Capitol, but not the Government Printing Office nor the General Accounting Office)

Secretary of the Senate
The Capitol
Washington, D.C. 20510
or
Clerk (House of Representatives)
The Capitol
Washington, D.C. 20515

National Science Foundation
1800 G Street NW
Washington, D.C. 20550
(only scientific and engineering positions)

National Security Agency
Fort Meade, Maryland 20775

Tennessee Valley Authority
Division of Personnel
Knoxville, Tennessee 37902

United States Mission to the United Nations
799 United Nations Plaza
New York, New York 10017

United States Nuclear Regulatory Commission
Recruitment Branch
Washington, D.C. 20555

United States Postal Service
(contact: local Postmaster)

Veterans Administration
Department of Medicine and Surgery
Vermont Avenue at H Street NW
Washington, D.C. 20420
(Physicians, dentists, and nurses only)

BASIC RESOURCES

Both United States and state civil services (see your phone book) are information sources, as are the following.

City Management

International City Management Association
1140 Connecticut Avenue NW
Washington, D.C. 20036

Community and Urban Planning

American Institute of Planners
1776 Massachusetts Avenue NW
Washington, D.C. 20036

American Society of Planning Officials
1313 East 60th Street
Chicago, Illinois 60637

Fire Services and Law Enforcement Careers

American Law Enforcement Officers Association
4005 Plaza Tower
New Orleans, Louisiana 70113

American Federation of Police
1100 Northeast 125th Street
North Miami, Florida 33161

International Association of Chiefs of Police
11 Firstfield Road
Gaithersburg, Maryland 20760

International Association of Firefighters
1750 New York Avenue NW
Washington, D.C. 20006

International Association of Fire Chiefs
1725 K Street NW
Washington, D.C. 20006

International Association of Women Police
11017 Jacaranda Drive
Sun City, Arizona 85351

National Police and Firefighters Association
2000 P Street NW (Suite 615)
Washington, D.C. 20036

National Police Officers Association of America
14600 South Tamiami Trail
Venice, Florida 33595

Foreign Service

Department of State
Board of Examiners for the Foreign Service
P.O. Box 9317, Rosslyn Station
Arlington, Virginia 22209
(for test information)

Department of State
Equal Employment Opportunity Office (Room 4421)
Washington, D.C. 20520

Overseas Jobs (other than Foreign Service)

Federal Job Information Center
(addresses under Federal or under United States
Government in telephone directories. Ask for Civil
Service pamphlet BRE-18, "Federal Jobs Overseas.")

Postal Service

American Postal Workers Union
817 14th Street NW
Washington, D.C. 20005

International Mailers Union
3500 Second Avenue (Suite 6)
Des Moines, Iowa 50313

National Alliance of Federal and Postal Employees
1644 11th Street NW
Washington, D. C. 20001

National Association of Letter Carriers of the USA
100 Indiana Avenue NW
Washington, D.C. 20001

Social Work

> Council on Social Work Education
> 345 East 46th Street
> New York, New York 10017

> National Association of Social Workers
> 1425 H Street NW
> Southern Building (Suite 600)
> Washington, D.C. 20005

Teaching

> American Federation of Teachers
> 1012 14th Street NW
> Washington, D.C. 20005

> National Education Association
> 1201 16th Street NW
> Washington, D.C. 20036

CHAPTER 4

CAREERS IN POLITICS

Until the 1970s, it seemed as if the major women's political effort of the 20th century, the passage of the 19th Amendment to the Constitution in 1920, had somehow exhausted women's spirit of political action. The right to vote had brought women the opportunity to participate in party-governing committees at the county, state, and national level, but it did not significantly increase the number of women in public office or in paid campaign positions. In fact, disappointingly few women actually exercised their right to vote.

During the late 1960s and early 70s, however, many more women began to vote and to become active in political campaigns. Some observers attribute this change to the women's movement, others to women's participation in anti-Vietnam War and consumer campaigns. In any event, many politically active women got their start through an issue-oriented campaign of some kind. As women learned to fight for a cause, whether it concerned the environment, the war, or busing, they learned the skills and the excitement of political campaigning. And as they gained training and experience, more women began to win political and elected office.

The year 1972 was significant: 40 percent of the delegates to the 1972 Democratic National Convention were women, compared to 13 percent in 1968; 30 percent of the delegates to the Republican National Convention were women, up from 17 percent in 1968; and the number of women in state legislatures started to grow significantly.

Although still very few women are in state legislatures (only about 9.3 percent), the number in 1974 was double that of 1969! And, also in 1974, Ella Grasso of Connecticut became the first woman to be elected governor who hadn't been preceded in office by her husband. By the elections of 1976 three women lieutenant governors and a second woman governor, Dixie Lee Ray of Washington, had been elected on their own abilities. During the same period, many women were elected mayors of large- and medium-sized cities. In 1972, 10 Connecticut women won elective office as the chief executive of a town or city.

As a result, a whole new range of careers has opened up to women: careers not just in political office holding, but in professional campaign management and in influencing legislation as well. A woman candidate frequently hires women for her campaign staff and for her administration if she wins. Women legislators have encouraged women lobbyists. Women in municipal elected office improve job prospects for women city managers, and so on.

Successful political careers usually span 15 to 20 years. Municipal office and the state legislature are considered "entry-level" elective positions. With more lower-level experience, women should increasingly become candidates for Congress and for higher-level executive office including the Presidency of the United States. And this will mean increased opportunities for the women that have worked with them over the years.

Three Issues of Special Concern to Women

Three issues that seem to be of particular concern to women in politics involve losing, making trade-offs and compromises, and alienating or offending other people.

Losing. Though most people think that politics is one field where coming in second is the same as coming in last, that view isn't completely valid. Politicians who lose well and show a strong base of support are frequently offered political appointments or opportunities to run for office again. Staff members of a losing political campaign who have done a good job will be noticed even by their political opponents. In a big campaign with a famous candidate who is likely to win, opportunities are fewer for staff members to assume major responsibilities. Everybody wants to work for a winner. Working for a lesser-known candidate can give a staff person experience and exposure.

Making Trade-offs or Compromises. Because most women have had more experience in issue-oriented politics than in election campaigns, they generally have little experience with and little tolerance for any form of compromise, especially the political trade-off. Entire networks of relationships among male politicians are built on compromise and favors. Of course, some issues are so important that compromises are not appropriate. The irony, however, is that significant advances in issue politics can be built on the concept of "owing" people something and people "owing" you something. As more women gain political prominence, they are beginning to form similar networks with each other across party lines, in groups like the National Women's Political Caucus or the caucus of women in Congress.

Alienating or Offending Other People. Women have been said to translate differences of opinion on issues into personal differences more often than men. As one woman officer holder puts it:

> Most women cannot deal with the separation of issues from personalities. They may work hard and fight hard on an issue, but when they find that their work didn't buy them what they thought it did—complete agreement with them on the part of the elected official—they cut off the personal relationship with the officeholder. I've found that part of political life particularly hard; I've lost two friends. What they didn't realize of course is that by severing the relationship they lost the opportunity to influence me next time. They've cut off communication on the issues.

This woman, along with many others interviewed, credits her years of experience working with the League of Women Voters for her learned ability to separate people from issues.

A Political Career—How You Begin

Political careers are among the most open and accessible of all careers. All kinds of opportunities are available for people interested in the field, particularly at the entry level. Academic background is not as important as experience and willingness to work. The problem?—most entry positions pay little or nothing and offer very little stability.

Entry options include working for a political party, a candidate, or an advocacy group interested in a particular issue, and working on a community advisory board or in a citizen participation process. In almost every case all you need to do to get started is to volunteer. But there's more to it than that.

If your aim is to use your volunteer experience to gain access to a job, carefully figure out what kind of experience will benefit you most. Do you want to learn more about budgeting and finance? If so, volunteer to work for the campaign treasurer. Do you want to prove your administrative abilities? Then work as director of volunteers or in a campaign scheduling position.

If you do decide to volunteer, you must make clear, not only the *kind* of work you want, but also the *extent* of your participation. In a sense you should negotiate a "contract" along the lines of the following: "I will work as a researcher for 20 hours a week through the month of July or until the profile of ethnic voters is completed." Otherwise, you will find yourself having to say "no" a lot. The more responsibility you have in a political campaign, the harder it will be to limit your participation.

Campaign experience can be invaluable. Not only will you get to learn more about an issue of interest and concern to you, but you also will get hands-on experience *doing* it, experience that counts for you in getting

NOTE FROM THE PAST

Jeannette Rankin

Born in 1883 in Montana, where "men thought of women in the same terms as they thought of themselves," Jeannette Rankin was firmly committed to the issues of pacifism and women's and children's rights. She worked as a social worker in San Francisco and New York City before returning to her home state and lobbying successfully for women's suffrage in Montana. After that victory she ran for Congress as a Republican, basing her campaign on the theme that although there were many men to look after the nation's economic interests, "there isn't a single woman to look after the nation's greatest asset, its children." She was elected to the House of Representatives in 1917, three years before women won the right to vote nationally.

Her very first vote in the House of Representatives came on the proposal to enter World War I, and to follow her conscience she made the unpopular choice. Although 49 other representatives also opposed the war, it was her "no" vote that brought the loud contempt from the press and cost her her seat in the House when she ran for reelection. For the remainder of her term, she fought for women's suffrage and reform of other laws relating to women and children.

After serving in the House, Jeannette Rankin lobbied for many years for labor reform and pacifism. In 1940 she was reelected to the House on a pacifist slogan, "Prepare the limits for defense; keep our men out of Europe." When President Roosevelt asked Congress to declare war, hers was the only negative vote, met by hisses and boos. She explained, "As a woman, I cannot go to war, and I refuse to send anybody else."

In 1968, at age 87, Ms. Rankin was as firm in her beliefs as ever. With the 5,000 women of the Jeannette Rankin Peace Brigade, she marched to Capitol Hill in Washington in opposition to the Vietnam War.

---

a government job, paid or volunteer. You'll get chances to show people what you can do and you'll make valuable contacts.

Political action also can be fun, offering some thrills almost like those of the world of sports: the feeling of working on a team, of giving your all, of suspense and excitement.

Political Careers—Possible Directions

Both the Republican and the Democratic National Committees encourage women to run for political office and to take more responsible roles on campaign staffs. Find out about party jobs by calling your state or local party committee, listed in the phone book. During a campaign parties usually maintain campaign offices in the state capital and in major cities throughout the state.

Although party positions are more stable than positions on a candidate's staff, if you work for a candidate *before* the primary or before he or she receives the party's endorsement, you'll have a better chance for a position with a higher level of responsibility. After the primary, losing candidates and their staff sometimes work for the winning candidate. Women political candidates in the early 70s were often minority party candidates or those who didn't have majority party endorsement early in their campaigns. This situation will change as more women enter the mainstream of American political life.

Special-interest advocacy groups have been organized to express almost every possible point of view. Trade and professional associations usually work with government agencies and elected officials. All these organizations accept committed amateurs as workers. The *Encyclopedia of Associations*, a directory of virtually all associations in the country, is available in most libraries; consult it for the groups near your home that you can work for to gain experience.

Many government programs also have advisory boards. Even those with elected or appointed members may need help on special committees. Ask your city hall, state house, or League of Women Voters for more information.

The League of Women Voters itself has been an important organization in preparing women for the range of political careers. Formed at the time of the passage of the 19th Amendment, it is a nonpartisan organization that takes a stand on public issues, not candidates for public office. A League of Women Voters is located in every state and in many municipalities. (Men were admitted for the first time in 1976.) Members study public issues, arrive at a "consensus" or position that the whole group can support, and take political action. They also run voter information services and candidate forums in election years. Look in your phone book for the League headquarters nearest you.

The League of Women Voters is a good training ground for political careers. According to the Center for American Women and Politics of the Eagleton Institute of Politics at Rutgers University, 40 percent of the women in elected office in 1970 were League members.

Elected Office

In general the two kinds of elected officials are legislators who make laws, and chief executives or administrators who carry them out. In some cases judges are also elected; however, only lawyers are eligible.

Legislators write laws, hold hearings on issues of public concern, and help constituents with particular problems. It is helpful for legislators to be lawyers or to have lawyers on their own staff or on the staffs of their committees. Legislators need real skill at negotiating and forming coalitions to support their point of view. Successful legislators stay in close contact with their constituents through newsletters, speeches, and political dinners. Most state legislators and members of Congress have special staff to help their constituents solve problems like late Social Security checks or information about government regulations. Lawmaking bodies exist at every level of government.

Chief executives, basically administrators, also function at all levels of government, and at each level the office has a different name. In many New England towns the chief executive is called "First Selectman." In most towns and cities the office is that of mayor. Governors are the chief executives at the state level, and the President of course is the chief executive of the United States.

Chief executives administer the law and are responsible for spending the money that legislatures appropriate for their programs. Being a chief executive is like running a large complex business with some significant differences. No job security is one. If you are President or the governor of some states, the number of years you can serve in office is limited by law. Your opponents and the press are always second-guessing your every move and all your actions are up for public scrutiny. Although you may have some latitude in appointing policymakers, if you are working

---

THE THRILL OF IT ALL: BEING AN ELECTED OFFICIAL

"I started out not able to open my mouth before two people; my hands would shake and my mouth would get dry, but the most amazing thing happened to me after a while. I ended up loving it."

"Motherhood is the best training for political office I know. Where else would you have to learn how to listen to one person when two other people are talking to you?"

"I know now that my life has meant something to my children's generation and their children's generation. I know I have helped make this country a better place to live."

THE DAILY GRIND: BEING AN ELECTED OFFICIAL

"People think that because you're running for public office they can say rude things to you."

"What I hate most is the attitude that just because I won I have to be a corrupt politician. I was the good government candidate when I won; why can't I be the good government officeholder?"

"The worst thing is losing. There has been all that hype, all those people crowding around to hear what you say and then —nothing. You're isolated. You're lost."

THE CANDIDATE'S HUSBAND AND FAMILY

All the women officeholders interviewed agreed: If a woman has a husband and/or family, running for office must be a joint decision.

The reason is basic. Being the center of a political campaign—to say nothing of fulfilling the responsibilities of the office once elected—will have a profound effect on all your lives. Both will require sacrifices and adjustments on the part of everyone in the family. It is important to work these out in advance to minimize the inconvenience for everyone.

While family participation is optional, family support is essential. It could be deadly for a candidate to tell people how supportive her husband is—only to find him telling people that her campaign is upsetting his whole life.

Cooperation and support are also essential to family harmony. In the final weeks of a campaign—and often long before—campaigning consumes nearly all the candidate's time and energy. This will inevitably cause some hardship. At the same time, many candidates report that their campaigns added a new dimension to their family life and made their husbands and children extremely proud of them.

— Excerpted from *Consider Yourself for Public Office,*
National Federation of Republican Women.

GETTING IN, MOVING UP: ELECTED OFFICIAL

Theoretically, anyone can be elected to public office regardless of training or experience. All that is necessary is that you have the confidence of a majority of the voters. Getting that confidence, however, is a long and complex process in many cases.

with a civil service system you will often have to work with staff members whose views may or may not be compatible with your own.

A good chief executive is able to act within these limitations and juggle special interests and an array of demands on her time to accomplish her goals.

Campaign Positions

Campaign jobs are many and varied. All campaigns need a campaign manager to orchestrate all campaign activities. All campaigns also should have a legal adviser, a lawyer to make sure the campaigners follow all election laws—from meeting the date for filing to the proper accounting of contributions. In addition, all campaigns need a finance committee,

YOU COULD BE A STATE LEGISLATOR

1. Analyze your legislative districts carefully and look for these vulnerability symptoms:
   - An incumbent who feels "safe" and never bothers to campaign.
   - An incumbent who is colorless or relatively unknown in the district.
   - An incumbent who has taken an unpopular stand on local issues.
   - An incumbent who has remained unchallenged although the political makeup of the population has changed.
   - A district where the voter turnout has been very low.
2. A strong candidate could challenge these incumbents. The best candidate may be a woman who is well known for her political or community activities and who is respected and trusted. Women candidates are often more successful in winning bipartisan support than men.

—Excerpted from *Running for Public Office*,
Women's Division, Democratic National Committee.

GETTING IN, MOVING UP: CAMPAIGN MANAGEMENT

Most campaign managers start out as lower-level volunteers on a campaign staff. They advance to a manager spot as a result of their contacts with candidates and the reputation of their work on earlier campaigns.

finance chairman, or treasurer to raise money and oversee its spending. A press secretary or public relations committee is needed to prepare political advertising or press releases to get media attention.

Scheduling candidate activity is another major campaign function. As the *Campaign Workbook* of the National Women's Education Fund puts it, "The key to effective scheduling is to allocate the candidate's time in direct proportion to the number of influenceable voters she can meet or will contact through media." In large campaigns, "advance" people precede the candidate to an appointment and make sure all the details of such things as seating and loudspeaker systems are in order.

An important campaign need is for research—research into the issues and research on the electorate. Research on the electorate should produce a target group of voters to be persuaded to vote for your candidate. Issue research will help produce position papers, speeches, and responses to opponents' statements.

Increasingly, many of these campaign functions are being offered by political consultants, professional opinion pollsters, and media experts. Thus campaign work can prepare you for jobs with these organizations too. Some professional campaign consultants are public relations firms who specialize in political campaigns; they hire people with some public relations experience. Pollsters look for people with statistical, computer, or mass-marketing backgrounds. Work for a professional political consultant does not usually entail volunteering; you will be paid.

Jobs in Government Relations and Lobbying

A lobbyist is someone who seeks to influence legislation or governmental decisionmaking. Lobbying efforts vary from circulating a student petition or a school board attempt to put a favorite teacher on tenure to the work of highly professional Washington lawyers and lobbyists who can make as much as $750,000 in fees in a year.

Into the range of jobs between these extremes fall the registered lobbyist who must follow strict government guidelines, the government relations expert for a trade association or business firm, the legal expert

MORE INFORMATION ON RUNNING A CAMPAIGN

For more information on how to run a campaign, consult these three excellent sources:

The Campaign Workbook ($15 with special binder, $13 without binder), available from:

> National Women's Education Fund
> 1532 16th Street NW
> Washington, D.C. 20036

Consider Yourself for Public Office ($2) and *Campaign Manual* ($3), available from:

> National Federation of Republican Women
> 310 First Street SE
> Washington, D.C. 20003

"How to" Materials—Running for Public Office and *Democratic Party Organization* (free), available from:

> Democratic National Committee
> Women's Division
> 1625 Massachusetts Avenue NW
> Washington, D.C. 20036

---

on some aspect of government relations, and the advocates of special-interest groups or consumer organizations. Among the latter are the people who work for such groups as those inspired by consumer watchdog Ralph Nader and as the Congress on Racial Equality (CORE), the Children's Legal Defense Fund, Friends of the Earth, etc.

Most government relations and lobbying jobs are located in state cap-

---

GETTING IN, MOVING UP: LOBBYING

Lobbyists start out in a variety of ways—as staff to legislators or legislative committees, as lawyers, as members of a trade or professional association, or in government jobs. They advance by expanding their contacts and increasing their expertise.

itals or in Washington, D.C. Career paths for people in these fields tend to run back and forth between "inside jobs" in government positions and "outside jobs" in government relations.

Salaries vary, depending on the resources of the organization employing you. Business organizations may pay very well for entry-level government relations positions, but they require as much as three years of experience in their area of interest. Public interest groups, on the other hand, are willing to accept people with commitment to the issue but without experience, but they tend to pay much less.

Cathy Rodgers, Mayor

I have met two kinds of women in elected office," Cathy Rodgers, mayor of a medium-sized town says, "the kind that has worked for the party for years and just made it to the front ranks of being nominated and the good-government, League-of-Women-Voter type like me."

Ms. Rodgers has been the mayor of her town for seven years. She tells how she made it: "My story is kind of a funny one. I was a nurse, and good at it. I kept my hand in a little all the time the kids were growing up. Nursing is a good background for politics. If you are a nurse, you learn to get along with everybody, and I mean *everybody*."

Ms. Rodgers joined the League of Women Voters when her children were small, and she became very interested in what the League was doing. She now sees that "it was good training. I learned to speak to small groups, to consider all sides of an issue, to hear people out, to compromise in order to take a public stand. And the League gives you a lot of support."

She became very interested in environmental issues: "I had worked very hard on the League study of what our town could do to help the environmental protection lobby. I started as a resource person at League workshops. Then I ran the workshops. Then I was the person selected to present the results of our study to the Town Council. That was the hardest thing I ever did. I got sick to my stomach both before and after I gave that presentation. I'd heard of stage fright *before*, but stage fright *after*? But I cared so much about the issue that I did it anyway, no matter how hard it was."

That first meeting was reported in the papers, and Ms. Rodgers was invited to speak to community groups around town and in schools. She got better and better at public speaking. She joined a political party and pressed it to take a stand on the issues that concerned her. But as she says, "You have to be careful to separate your League work from your party work, you know. The League doesn't endorse candidates or take political stands.

"It was an important step for me—joining a party and working in it.

By this time there was a real constituency for the League's point of view, and the party knew it. They knew I had lists of people I had worked with, and good lists are crucial in politics. So I was put on a policy committee."

Ms. Rodger's political party was out of power, but her work with the party position on environmental affairs won her an appointment to the town Conservation Commission. "I loved it," she says. "The commission was only an advisory body, but did we advise! We held public hearings and got lots of people involved. When the next election year rolled around my party nominated me to run for the Town Planning and Zoning Commission. I really wanted that—a real chance to make decisions. So I got some of my friends who had helped me do the public relations job on the League study together with the party campaign professionals. We won, believe it or not, and I got the most votes of anyone in the party.

"For the next election four years later," Ms. Rodgers recalls, "the party wanted me to run for mayor. I was kind of a throwaway candidate—my party hadn't won for years. But my opponent had been in office for ages and wasn't doing anything but sitting around with his cronies. I knew my weakness was municipal management, but that was his weakness, too.

"I had some real advantages in that campaign because I'm a woman. I know that sounds funny, but I played them for what they were worth. First, many people around town knew me and knew that I really cared about the town. I wasn't completely identified with my party either, because of my League of Women Voters start. So I had the advantages of being both a party person with the advice, support, and workers that brings and being a good-government candidate, which could win voters who normally voted for the other party. Also, everybody knew I wasn't going to profit from public office. I wouldn't get any business from it. My husband's business was unrelated and located in another town. In the era of Watergate, these things mattered.

"There are also a lot of women voters. Many of them worked for me. In fact, in my first campaign, almost my whole staff were women. The only thing you still need the men for is fund raising. Women don't yet have the same level of fund-raising contacts as men.

"The first time I ran, I was an outsider," Ms. Rodgers says. "That's a lovely position to be in. It's easy to take pot shots at the insider, to sit back and count his flaws. I sure learned that when I ran for reelection. My opponent went after me tooth and nail. He didn't care what he said; he even made things up. I just went on trying to be careful and accurate, but I was shaking with rage inside. Luckily his tactic backfired, and even the town paper endorsed me—the first time it had ever endorsed a candidate of my party.

"The second time I won, not because I was an outsider, but because when I was in office I was accessible to people. I took the time to explain what I was doing and why, and I didn't get hung up on the status and power of the office. Plus I had done something else: When I won the first time, I knew how much I had to learn, and I hired the best professionals I could find for the appointive positions in my administration. They had begun to put new management practices in place and really bring the town into the 20th century without some of the 20th-century problems. In spite of all of that I still nearly lost. But in politics a winner is a winner; there's no second place."

Ms. Rodgers has learned a lot in her time in politics: "Besides learning from the professionals I've hired, I've learned a great deal from the other municipal officials I've met through the National League of Cities and Towns, sort of a professional association of mayors. More women are mayors than many people think. Women serve on or moderate just about every panel or workshop the National League of Cities puts on. There is also a Women in Municipal Government group within the national league, and we're very supportive of each other. It's amazing what we've been able to accomplish together."

Running a town is hard work. As Ms. Rodgers says, "You are always juggling hours and people. Some days it's like having 10 children all screaming at once. I'm sure I work 60 hours a week. And you're campaigning every day you're in office. But you've no idea what a thrill it is to really know you're helping people, solving problems, having an impact. I've done some concrete things, things I can point to—a park, an old people's nutrition program, a new process of hiring town employees, annual energy audits of town buildings. Things like that. They'll be here long after I'm retired."

When she contemplates the future, Ms. Rodgers says, "I don't know where I'm going from here. I'm a manager; I don't like being a part of a legislative body, deliberating and all that. I like to give orders and have them obeyed. So the state legislature is out. Also, I haven't the political base to run for governor. If my party wins the governorship, maybe I'll get an appointive state office—that's a possibility. Or maybe I'll run again. Of course, you never let anyone know you're considering *not* running or you will lose all your clout. What kind of next job is there for a 55-year-old woman who has managed a $35 million business for almost 8 years? Am I unhirable, over the hill? Pretty soon I'm going to have to think about it.

"But I'd miss my job if I left. Sometimes after the last meeting of the day is over and it's only about 10 or 10:30, I go home and pick up my husband. We have a soda or a cup of coffee, and then we just drive around town and look at things. I show him where the roads are being repaired, the new outdoor play equipment, the place where the stop sign will go, the elderly housing site, the curbs, the schools. I look at it all. And I know I belong to it."

CHAPTER 5

MAKING A CASE FOR YOURSELF:
LAW CAREER

Since its beginnings in English common law the American legal system has grown more and more complex. And as it became complex advocates were needed to champion the cause of each adversary in the courts. The advocates took the role of each litigant (party involved in the lawsuit), interpreting the law and marshaling the evidence on each side to persuade the jury that its side was right, and, if necessary, reminding the judge to enforce the roles of the contest.

This is the role of the lawyer today: to interpret the law for her client, to represent the client in court with supporting evidence and legal precedent, and to make sure that the correct procedure ("due process") is used to come to a legal decision. The basic approach also derives from English common law. The case is a contest between opposing lawyers before an impartial judge or jury: the adversary system.

The concept of the common-law system is that a case can always be decided justly, however novel and unique it may be, by reasoning from traditional principles. However, the growing tendency of law in the United States, evident in the immense and growing mass of federal legislation and regulation, is to rely more on specific laws and precise rules of conduct than on the common-law rule of reason.

The modern practice of law does not often involve going to court. Most lawyers spend their time filing official papers. negotiating on behalf of clients, drawing up contracts or other legal documents, and advising clients on how to prevent legal disputes. But all lawyers still anticipate an adversary process and base their actions and advice on reasoning along lines like these: "If we take this action, how can it be contested, and what are our chances of winning?" This work calls for experience and judgment, as well as knowledge of laws and procedures.

Legal Specialization

As the modern legal system has become more and more complex and laws and regulations have proliferated, lawyers have developed specialized skills or areas of knowledge. This specialization usually follows law school and several years of legal practice. Most lawyers have a general practice and an area of specialization as well. For instance, though any lawyer admitted to practice in the United States can appear in court, some, known as trial lawyers, specialize in taking a case to court. Others specialize in a particular body of law, such as constitutional, income tax, real estate, criminal, or labor law. Although it is possible for any lawyer

---

LEGAL TERMS

Litigation (noun). The process of taking a legal controversy to court.

Interrogatory (noun). A set of formal questions used in examining a person involved in a case, such as a witness. Out-of-court written questions posed to one party by the other, they are answered in writing. Intended for getting admissions or discovering evidence. Interrogatories are used in court in limited circumstances only.

Deposition (noun). Testimony, the answers to the questions of an attorney, given outside of court for use during a trial in court or for discovery of evidence. May be oral or written, but must be properly authenticated in either case.

Moot (adjective). An unsettled argument, or one that isn't relevant to the case at hand. An argument without need of adjudication because a controversy no longer exists, because of circumstances outside the litigation. Also a mock or practice hearing, as in the phrase "moot court."

Tort (noun). A private action for personal injury inflicted by one person on another not arising out of a contract. Most tort cases today arise from automobile accidents. Malpractice (medical or legal) is also a tort, as is fraud.

Brief (noun). A written condensation of research prepared for the case, arguments to be used, and relevant points to be made. A "script" for the court presentation.

Real Property (noun). Land and anything growing or built on it.

Title Search (noun). The process of making sure that the buyer for whom the search is being made will have clear legal title to the property.

to do the research in the field and come up with the answers to her clients' needs, specialists often have already studied the possible answers. Some lawyers specialize in appearances before boards or commissions like the Securities and Exchange Commission, which regulates stocks and bonds, or the Federal Communications Commission, which controls television and radio transmission.

A fairly new specialty is public interest law. Public interest lawyers often work for consumer or advocacy organizations such as the Environmental Defense Fund, the Consumer Federation of America, and the American Civil Liberties Union. Public interest lawyers take on "rights" cases that affect a class of people.

Ancillary Legal Professions

An array of special professions has arisen to help lawyers serve clients or make the legal system function. Court stenographers record all the proceedings on a special stenotype machine or repeat exactly what the principals in the case have said into an instrument called a "Stenomask," which records the words for later transcription. Both the machine and the mask are portable so that the court reporter can follow the judge, lawyers, and jury to visit the scene of the crime if necessary. Legal secretaries must understand legal terminology and legal documents. Tax accountants help corporate or tax lawyers in large firms. Law librarians do legal research, classify information, and manage a university or firm's law library.

LEGAL CAREER OPPORTUNITIES IN THE FEDERAL GOVERNMENT

A paperback available from the American Bar Association, *Federal Government Legal Career Opportunities* ($7.50), lists where all the legal functions are located in the Federal Government and how many lawyers are employed in each office. It can usually be found in large public libraries and college placement libraries or can be ordered from:

American Bar Association
Order/Billing Department
1155 East 60th Street
Chicago, Illinois 60637

A new and growing field is that of videotape specialists who record testimony. Witnesses who cannot appear in court are videotaped so that the judge and jury can watch the witness's expression as he or she gives testimony or is cross-examined.

Legal Assistants

A legal specialist who works to help a lawyer, the legal assistant may also be referred to as a paralegal, legal aide, or legal paraprofessional. Legal assistants work in a variety of ways. Only two functions are reserved by law for lawyers that legal assistants may not perform: giving legal advice to clients and arguing a case in court.

Legal assistants may develop special skills in a particular area, such as real estate law, and learn to draw up deeds, research titles, and prepare contracts—all under the supervision of a lawyer, of course. Another fairly common special legal assistant is the legal researcher. Technical paralegal work can vary from filling in standard forms to helping to prepare briefs. Salaries for legal assistants vary with the technical difficulty of the jobs they perform.

Some legal assistants can get a taste of litigation and representing a client. A legal assistant from a legal aid society or legal services office can represent her own client before an administrative judge in Social Security or welfare departments. This legal assistant may be a volunteer or a student intern working for free. At the other end of the spectrum is a legal assistant with specialized understanding of government regulatory provisions who draws a high salary. Entry-level legal assistants can expect to be paid between $7,000 and $10,000 a year.

Legal assistants are part of such a new profession that standards and certification procedures are just being written and accepted; therefore, you can enter this field through several routes. Some legal assistants start as legal secretaries. Legal secretaries learn the value of completely error-free work and become familiar with legal terminology and concepts. As they perform other duties and become more experienced, their secretarial skills are often used less and less and they end up in full-time legal assistant positions.

Another and increasingly more common route is through a formal paralegal training course. Such courses are given either by community colleges, or by universities and may require a college degree. University courses tend to be broadest, introducing students to several aspects of law. The best courses are those accredited by the American Bar Association.

A company or law firm's training program may prepare you to do detailed technical work in the firm's areas of specialty. Learning from a

GETTING IN, MOVING UP: LEGAL ASSISTANCE

Legal assistants or paralegals are trained either in law firms or in special training courses at universities. Most of them have a college degree. Legal assistants advance as they learn more and are able to take on more responsibilities.

firm tends to teach you more about one specific legal area and less about law in general.

Law as a Career

Although our basic legal system is an adversary one, most of what lawyers do for their clients involves preventing conflicts from occurring by spelling out carefully the terms of a contract, lease, trust, or will. Precise wording must be used, and each term carefully defined. Therefore, lawyers and the people working with them know the power of words and learn to be very careful and accurate in using them. Large law firms even employ their own trained proofreaders to guard against mistakes.

For the same reason, lawyers must learn to pay a great deal of attention to detail and to foresee every possible contingency. To protect their clients, they must have the imagination to consider what it would be like to be on the opposing side of a question or to represent another interest.

People in legal careers learn to think by analogy, to look at situations and perceive how they are the same and how they differ. They also must analyze current legal problems in terms of how they correspond to legal precedent. They must be able to reason well.

About two-thirds of all lawyers are in private practice. Almost all the rest work either directly for businesses or for government. In either of these settings, lawyers function like staff members with special technical knowledge. Lawyers in law firms work in much the same way as doctors in private practice. They acquire their own set of clients, usually within a certain geographic area, and develop personal relationships with them. Lawyers tend to work as independent individuals, functioning in teams only in especially complicated situations.

People in ancillary law careers are usually assigned to work with one or two lawyers, but they are expected to be able to work independently. They don't often have direct contact with the client and function in most respects under the lawyer's supervision.

A DIRECTORY OF LAWYERS

The seven-volume *Martindale-Hubbell Law Directory* lists and describes lawyers and law firms in the United States, Canada, and many other countries. The directory, updated annually, is available in most major libraries and law firms.

It includes basic information about individual lawyers, such as where they went to school, when they were admitted to the bar, and where they live and practice. In addition, some lawyers are rated for their legal ability, on the basis of confidential recommendations made by other lawyers and judges.

Law firms and other business groups of lawyers are also listed, with address and phone number, names and titles of the associates, the specialties of the firm, and a representative listing of clients. However, the firms are not rated.

Both lawyers and legal assistants often receive their legal training in the state they intend to work in because of variations in law from state to state. Even in areas where some advertising of legal fees is permitted, law firms remain dependent for their clients on the reputations and personal connections of their partners. For this reason it is particularly difficult for an established lawyer or firm to move to a new state or community.

Within a law firm there is almost no chance to change your job title without getting further education. The only exceptions in a few firms are secretaries who become legal assistants or take on office management responsibilities. But a legal assistant cannot become a lawyer without going to law school. If you are a young lawyer, you are assigned to work for clients or senior lawyers in the firm and eventually develop clients of your own.

THE BAR

There really is a "bar." In almost every courtroom there are spectator seats or benches, and in front of them is a railing about 3 feet high with a gate. That railing is the bar. The lawyers, witnesses, jury, and judge all operate in front of, or "before," the bar, and spectators are not permitted beyond it. "Admitted to the bar," "passed the bar," and similar expressions all refer symbolically to that railing.

Secretaries, legal assistants, and young lawyers earn a straight salary. When lawyers become partners they share in the firm's profits on a percentage usually based on the reputation and expertise of the lawyer and her ability to bring business to the firm and to conduct that business successfully.

From a career in a law firm some legal secretaries and legal assistants go to law school to become lawyers. Lawyers may leave a law firm to work directly for a client as a staff lawyer. Some lawyers become active in politics, succumbing to an understandable desire to help write or implement the laws they've spent their lives interpreting.

Other lawyers may become elected or appointed judges. Candidates for judgeships are usually nominated by a special bar association committee. Judges generally have had 15 or 20 years in the practice of law, have exhibited a high level of professional competence, and have developed a number of friends and contacts and sometimes a reputation for being noncontroversial.

In the federal court system judges are appointed by the President with the consent of the Senate. Most Presidents consider the opinion of the American Bar Association when making appointments. Usually, state court judges are nominated by their political party and elected by the voters. Some progressive states have adopted an appointive system in which merit is considered.

Advancement in Law Careers

Although women have traditionally been the mainstays of the ancillary legal professions, they have only recently begun entering law schools in any great numbers. In the period before the 1970s women lawyers tended to work in staff jobs in business or government or in research jobs in law firms. It was thought that clients, judges, juries, and other lawyers preferred to work with men lawyers.

Women lawyers have tended in the past to seek "safe" specialties in family law, in legal services offices, in partnership with their husbands, or in the more routine field of estates and trusts. Women have also had a hard time gaining access to the highly paid or powerful and prestigious jobs in the profession. For example, only three women were partners in Wall Street law firms in 1965, and in 1977 only 1.1 percent of all judges were women.

Part of the reason for these statistics is that until the 1960s law schools restricted the number of women students. In the decade 1965 to 1976 of expansion of accredited law schools, the student population doubled, but the percentage of women increased 1,200 percent.

A lot of speculating has been done about the effect of the increasing number of women on the legal profession. Will the influx of women

GETTING IN, MOVING UP: LAWYER

Law students go to law school for three years after they earn their BA. Then they must pass the bar examination for the state in which they intend to practice.

Young lawyers go to work for law firms, business, or government. In law firms, lawyers advance to first an associate, then a junior partner, and then a partner sharing in the firm's profits. In business or government, lawyers may advance from a staff to an administrative position.

"humanize" the law, toning down the adversary process? This result doesn't seem likely. One thing is for sure, however: women's careers in the law will be different.

As more and more women take their place in the profession (and prestigious law firms are beginning now to hire women in good proportion, at least as new associates), they will create more pressure for more women to get more prestigious and higher-paying jobs. In the past, business contacts and "old boy" networks of friends operated against women lawyers. With more women in business and other careers, "old girl" (a better expression is "new woman") networks are forming. With many more well-connected and experienced women lawyers, it will even become harder to deny women more judgeships.

Nora Hanson, Lawyer

"It was ten years ago. I was a little late for my first class at law school and most of the other students were already seated. I walked in, and suddenly it occurred to me that there were 10 men for every woman in the room. That realization was a startling revelation. It took me a while to adjust and not to cringe when another woman was called on in class because her answer might reflect on me."

Nora Hanson has learned to thrive on being in the minority. One of six women in a prestigious West Coast law firm with almost 100 lawyers, she says that "I knew if I went into private practice in a firm like this one I would be one of very few women, but it didn't matter to me after three years of law school."

Ms. Hanson states three reasons why she decided to go into private practice: "First, at my law school the rumors were that you could move much more easily from private practice to a government or company job than the other way around. The second reason was related to that too. The big, prestigious law firms had the reputation of giving you the best training. You see, at a law firm, you are their product so to speak; they have to train you to do well. In a government or company there just isn't the same incentive to make you super competent and super efficient.

"The last reason I chose private practice is that it was the easiest thing for me to do. You were more likely to have to seek out a company or government job on your own. The major law firms, even some medium- and small-sized ones, go out and recruit people at law schools. I was recruited.

"My first year of practice was the hardest—I had never done anything but go to school. I had to learn all kinds of things from legal knowledge to how to ask somebody out for lunch. Everyone agrees that law school doesn't really prepare you to practice law. You really do need further training."

In a large firm like Ms. Hanson's, beginning lawyers start off doing mostly legal research and helping one of the partners with their clients. "You watch what the partner does and what questions he asks the client. Slowly you learn how to anticipate what information the partner will need and get it for him or her. You learn to use research tools you didn't know existed. I can't believe how much I learned in my first three years. Slowly, a partner begins to tell the client, 'Why don't you give Nora a ring? She'll find that out for you.' Then you start to get phone calls asking for your help. That's a terrific feeling.

"The best teachers are the lawyers who give you constructive feed- back about your work. The way you are supervised or evaluated changes from firm to firm. In some firms you are assigned a lawyer or group of lawyers to work with, in others you are rotated through each department —six months in litigation, six months in estates, six months in taxation, etc. In our firm a special committee deals with starting lawyers, and a committee member is assigned to each new person. They really knock themselves out trying to help you."

After she had been with her firm for four years, Ms. Hanson began to specialize in tax law. "An area of specialization is very helpful in a firm like this one. Tax law is the kind of field where you must know a lot of detail and keep on learning new things since the body of knowledge is so vast and so changing. I don't know how the small practitioner can possibly keep up. We have a hard time here, and we're highly special- ized. Some days it feels as if we are just inching along, wrapped in a web of government red tape."

Ms. Hanson's daily routine remains very much the same "although my work varies from client to client or from situation to situation. I go to my office and get phone calls from clients with problems. I make phone calls. I review documents and draft some of my own. I keep up with my correspondence. I always leave a part of the day for basic research in my field, although I need it less and less now that I am more experienced. If problems occur, I talk them over with others in the firm. It's easy to bounce ideas off people here. We lead a very independent existence. I function alone mostly, in my office with my secretary and my law books."

She has never felt left out or insulted because she's a woman. "It's easier for the young men in the office to be buddies with each other than it is for me—you can't undo 25 years of socialization. But I never had an inappropriate remark or difficult situation happen with somebody in the firm or with a client. Lawyers, you know, are trapped by their efforts to be intellectually honest. They feel obliged to mouth sentiments of equality—that's the law, after all—then of course they have to practice it. Even the crusty old types who might make a disparaging remark about women lawyers in general will always treat you like a regular lawyer when they meet you in a work situation."

Ms. Hanson would like to see more women stay in private practice in firms like hers. "It's a different kind of business. The work is very hard, very demanding, as in any service industry. I intend to stay with the firm and become a partner if I can. Law firms have a big impact on corporations, and I feel that that's where the power is in this society. And I'd like more women to have access to that power. For me, it's been very rewarding to learn how to make it in this firm, a demanding standard to meet. And I feel proud of myself for having accomplished it."

Janice Fox, Paralegal

Janice Fox has had seven years' experience working as a paralegal in three midatlantic states. And she loves it: "It's the right kind of work for me. It's a job where you have a lot of independence; you can work on your own. You don't have a lot of responsibilities and worries, and so you don't bring the job home with you at night. But it's interesting, and there's a variety of things to do.

"Some people might be concerned that there's not as much money or prestige in being a paralegal as in being a lawyer, but I don't mind. Money and prestige are not what I'm working for. I'm working to enjoy myself and to bring some money home to the family. I don't want to be an attorney, and I don't want to work nights and weekends like the attorneys in my firm."

Ms. Fox entered the paralegal field by chance after graduating from college. "It was a big firm of 60 lawyers, and they had never had a paralegal before. I hadn't had any training, and so we both took chances on each other. In the beginning, nobody was sure what I could do. So usually somebody would say, 'Have you ever done such and such?' and

I'd say I hadn't. Then they'd say, 'Well, here's how you do it.' That's how I learned.

"It would have been easier for me if I had had a training course. Then I would have been a little more familiar with the terminology, but wherever you go you need to be trained again, particularly if you move from state to state as I did. The forms, the way you do things, even the laws —all change from state to state."

The firm she's with now is much smaller than the one she started with; it has only three attorneys. "That means my work is more varied; I take more responsibility and get more credit for my own work. In the big firm I was primarily a real estate paralegal doing title searches and preparing papers for closings. That means I researched the land records in city hall to see if the seller really had the right to sell the house, and prepared all the legal papers for the sale. There can be as many as 20 items you need to have, all ready to go, when a piece of real estate is sold."

In her current firm, Ms. Fox does estate work and tax work as well. This year she handled 70 tax returns, which she likes. "I always enjoyed math. That interest of mine helps in the kind of paralegal work I do. If, for example, you have a background in English, that would help if you were a litigation paralegal, helping prepare briefs. That area of law is much more word oriented than this one."

In a small firm like Ms. Fox's, a paralegal usually has considerable client contact. As Ms. Fox says, "In some big firms like those in large cities, the attorneys don't say, 'This is Ms. Fox, she's going to help prepare your will,' because they don't want the client to know they aren't doing the work themselves. But no clients ever look anything but very happy when my boss introduces me, because he always adds that we charge a lot less per hour for my services than for his own.

"Since I have so much client contact, the line between what I do and what can be done only by lawyers gets kind of fuzzy. For example, if a client who's over 65 is selling his or her house, I'm going to tell him or her what the income tax consequences of the sale are when I'm helping to prepare the closing. Is that 'giving legal advice,' one of the things I'm not supposed to do? I'm not sure.

"What I do know is that I like the work, and I do it well. It's like being a lawyer with a somewhat routine practice, but not having the headaches or the percentage of the profits."

BASIC RESOURCES

Write or phone the following organizations for additional information on:

Careers in law and its specialties

> American Bar Association
> Information Services
> 1155 East 60th Street
> Chicago, Illinois 60637

Paralegal and other law-related professions

> American Association of Law Libraries
> 53 West Jackson
> Chicago, Illinois 60604

> American Bar Association
> Special Committee on Legal Assistants
> 1155 East 60th Street
> Chicago, Illinois 60637

> National Association of Legal Assistants, Inc.
> 3005 East Skelley Drive (Suite 122)
> Tulsa, Oklahoma 74105

> National Association of Legal Secretaries (International)
> 3005 East Skelley Drive
> Tulsa, Oklahoma 74105

> National Federation of Paralegal Associations, Inc.
> Ben Franklin Station P.O. Box 14103
> Washington, D.C. 20044

> National Shorthand Reporters Association
> 2361 Jefferson Davis Highway
> Arlington, Virginia 22202

CHAPTER 6

EDUCATION FOR LAW AND GOVERNMENT CAREERS

Law School

One law student said that law school is like a plane trip between New York and San Francisco, a separate experience in itself—not at all like either the point of departure or the destination. Most students will tell you that law school is not at all like college or graduate school: "It is much more serious." "The students are more competitive." "The professors in school are really out to separate the wheat from the chaff." Also, most lawyers will tell you that law school is not like the actual practice of law either.

Unlike medical school or graduate training in teaching or social work, law school does not require field work. In its place, law schools offer moot court courses in which students play the roles of lawyers on either side of a case and debate points of law. Some students also have the opportunity to work for legal aid offices, but not usually for course credit. Law schools teach general concepts, research techniques, and "thinking like a lawyer." At the end of law school, few students have had the experience of actually doing what a lawyer does or even observing a lawyer in action.

However, unlike that plane trip from New York to San Francisco, law school is the *only* way to get there, the only way to get to be a lawyer. This was not always true. It was once possible for law candidates to "read law," which meant serving as an apprentice in a law office and learning legal skills from a practicing lawyer. After a few years when the apprentice knew enough to become a lawyer, he or she was proposed by a sponsor before the local court. If the sponsor vouched for the student's ethics and knowledge, he or she was admitted to the practice of law on the motion of the sponsor by order of the judge.

In the early 20th century, when the practice of reading law was abolished by statute in favor of formal schooling, many law schools either did not admit women students or restricted them so severely that women were prevented from learning legal skills. Not until 1950, for example, did Harvard Law School admit its first woman. Since the late 1960s many more women have begun to pursue careers in law, and many law schools now enroll 20 to 30 percent women students (some even up to 50 percent). This new climate should make law school a more comfortable experience than it has been for some women in the past.

Law school can be a very grueling experience. Although the traditional kind of law teaching is undergoing changes in some law schools, with some courses being taught in seminars or lectures, most law schools still rely heavily on what they call the "case study" method. In this method, all students prepare for class by reading a set of materials containing particular cases. Each class period the professor questions one or two students in detail about principles in the case before the class.

FOR PROSPECTIVE LAW STUDENTS

One helpful guide for prospective law students is *Looking at Law School: A Student Guide from the Society of American Law Teachers,* edited by Stephen Gillers. The 1977 edition is available either as a paperback (from New American Library, 1301 Avenue of the Americas, New York, New York 10019, for $4.95 plus postage) or as a hardcover book (from Taplinger Publishing Company, Inc., 200 Park Avenue South, New York, New York 10003, for $9.95 plus postage).

Another is *The Pre-Law Handbook,* updated annually by the Law School Admission Service, which includes a sample Law School Admission Test (LSAT) and profiles of law schools. The information enables you to estimate your chances for admission to various schools (make sure you consult the latest edition). The *Handbook* is available from Law School Admission Services, P.O. Box 2000, Newtown, Pennsylvania 18940, for $5 (first-class mail) or for $3 (fourth-class book rate). The bookstore price is $4.

Many law schools have women's groups that publish pamphlets on getting into law school. Write to the group in care of the law school.

(Note: Getting into law school is a lengthy process, and should be explored at least a year in advance of actual application. The LSAT must be taken in July or October a year before your entry.)

In law school, no one "majors" in a speciality. Most law schools have a fairly similar core curriculum, with courses in torts, civil procedure, contracts, property and criminal law in the first year, followed by some choice among courses in the second and third years.

Law school teaches you to "think like a lawyer." What this means is that you are taught to be precise and accurate in your use of words, to back up your opinions with references to substantiating evidence, and to consider a range of alternative—even opposing—points of view.

A word about the study load: Unless you are *exceptionally* bright, you can expect to spend 8 to 12 hours 5 to 6 days a week studying and attending classes—if you want to do well.

Graduation from law school once entitled you to an LLB degree (Legum Baccalauriis, Bachelor of Laws). Now the same degree is called a JD (Juris Doctor, Doctor of Laws). But to become a practicing lawyer you still have to take the "bar exam" after you graduate. This two- or three-day test on the content of law is given generally twice a year. A board of bar examiners in each state is responsible for writing and administering the exam. Most law school graduates prepare for the exam by taking a special six- or eight-week bar exam course. About 75 percent of those who take the bar examination pass the first time, except in some states (California, for one) where the rate is about 50 percent.

Your First Job as a Lawyer

Graduating law students have traditionally been recruited by law firms, corporations, or government agencies who visit the law school to interview students. As the number of graduates increases, most students may find that they will need to take more initiative in looking for a job.

Top students have a chance to become law clerks for prestigious judges while in school, helping them do legal research and write opinions. A clerkship adds immeasurably to your credentials when you look for a job. In these positions, clerks meet other lawyers who appear before the court and can develop valuable contacts for a future job.

Students are often hired by law firms as clerks during the summers before their second and third years in law school. In some cases they are paid very little and worked very hard to see if they will make good candidates for a job with the firm when they graduate. In other cases top students of prestigious schools are paid very well, the firms courting them to accept a position in the future. Summer jobs also give students the chance to look over potential employers.

Government agencies and large corporations have standard salaries for beginning lawyers, as do most large firms.

A Professional Degree for Government Work

Government requires the services of many professionals. Most of them are hired for jobs that have the same requirements as jobs outside of government. (For example, a certified public accountant needs the same qualifications to work for the government as for an insurance company.)

For women interested in careers in community service professions like teaching, social work, library work, or community planning, graduate education can make an important difference.

The trick for those who want to pursue government professions is to pick the master's degree that will do the most good. In each field different degrees are directed at a potential specialty. If you can, work for a while in the field before you make a graduate school commitment. You will then be more likely to know what degree will be most useful to you and whether the career is something you will enjoy. If the government agency you are working for has a tuition refund program, you can study for an advanced degree partly at government expense and may be guaranteed a job at graduation.

Planning and public school administration offer examples of the variety of advanced degrees community service professionals can choose. In the planning field two- and three-year master's degree programs are available in manpower planning, land use planning, ecology, urban design, state planning, etc. In public school administration advanced degrees may be in planning and program design, budgeting, administration, or evaluation.

These professional degrees usually involve both independent research in the form of a thesis and field work or supervised practice doing the job. In planning, for example, graduate students may make a community land-use plan. Field work is very important, not just because of the "hands-on" experience but because of the professional contacts you develop. You should work harder on your field work than anything else in graduate school. Even if the professionals you meet don't have a job for you, they probably have lots of friends. A letter of recommendation from a professional you worked with usually counts much more with other professionals than do letters from professors.

If you can, plan your thesis so that it helps give you contacts and exposure to professionals in the part of the country where you have chosen to work. After all, you're paying for a professional education. It should do as much for you professionally as possible.

A Professional School—How to Pick One

A graduate school is not worth going to if it is not accredited. Write the professional associations listed in the career field Basic Resources for a list of accredited graduate schools.

It's important to find out the reputation among practicing professionals of the graduate schools you are considering. These reputations may change within any five-year period. If a school you are considering has a reputation for being "very academic and not practical," you'll take on that reputation too if you study there. That may be fine if you want an academic career, but it could work against you for other jobs. Consider all the ramifications of the school you choose for your future career.

Another thing to evaluate is the placement office of the school. How successful is it at placing its graduates in professional positions? Does it keep statistics about its graduates' jobs? With the competition for community service jobs keen, an effective placement office is important to any graduating professional.

A Management Degree

A management degree can be helpful to women seeking to advance in an administrative career, particularly in federal service. The three basic management master's degrees for government administrators are: the MBA (Master of Business Administration), the MPA (Master of Public Administration), and the MPP (Master of Public Policy). Each has advantages and disadvantages. As with getting any professional degree, work experience can help you decide which degree would be most useful.

The MBA (fully described in the guide on business careers) takes two years and may help government administrators make a transition to the private sector. Of the three degrees, it gives you the most career options. On the other hand, this degree program can be very rigorous. While an MBA is a useful credential, it may not provide you with much practical knowledge, unless you choose a school that offers some courses in public administration.

The MPA is traditionally the "practical" master's degree for government administrators. The course of study usually emphasizes budgeting, personnel management, work planning, and accounting over more theoretical questions of public policy. Usually graduate students in this program have had some government experience.

The newest and the "softest" of the master's degrees for government administrators is the MPP. Only about a dozen American universities grant this degree, among them Harvard, Michigan, and the University of California at Berkeley. These programs tend to train students in the skills needed for government research or policy and program development positions. Sometimes this degree is granted in combination with a law or planning degree.

As with professional degrees in planning or social work, it is important to take the time to look into the reputation of the graduate school and its placement office before you spend the time and money to get the degree. Pick your course of study carefully so that your degree helps you increase your skills as well as your credentials.

UNITED STATES GOVERNMENT DEPARTMENTS

The business of the Federal Government is handled by the following 12 executive departments, each headed by a member of the Cabinet, for example, the Secretary of Commerce. The top positions in each department are appointive; the rest of the jobs are filled primarily through the United States Civil Service Commission. For more information, write to them at the addresses listed.

Department of Agriculture
14th Street and Independence Avenue SW
Washington, D.C. 20250

Administers legislation affecting loans to farmers, crop insurance, the Agricultural Extension Service, the Agricultural Research Service, marketing and economic research, and the National Forest Service.

Department of Commerce
14th Street between Constitution Avenue
   and E Street NW
Washington, D.C. 20230

Fosters business and economic development activities, researches, and analyzes factual data on American industries, works to help economically depressed parts of the country create new jobs.

Department of Defense
The Pentagon
Washington, D.C. 20301

Provides for American security through the Armed Forces and related research and policy projects.

Department of Energy
12th Street and Pensylvania Avenue NW
Washington, D.C. 20461

Acts to conserve and regulate current energy resources and supports the development of new sources of energy.

Department of Health, Education, and Welfare
330 Independence Avenue SW
Washington, D.C. 20201

Administers government grant programs such as Social Security, research programs such as the National Institutes of Health, and service programs such as the Bureau of Education for the Handicapped.

Department of Housing and Urban Development
451 7th Street SW
Washington, D.C. 20410

Administers funds for urban renewal, design and renovation, historic preservation, state and local planning and management assistance, and mortgage and disaster insurance.

Department of the Interior
C Street between 18th and 19th Streets NW
Washington, D.C. 20240

Is responsible for 500 million acres of federal land including the national parks, all programs for Indians, conservation and recreation, and mine safety and efficiency.

Department of Justice
Constitution Avenue and 10th Street NW
Washington, D.C. 20530

Enforces federal laws, takes legal action on behalf of the government and its agencies, supervises federal prisons, and includes the Federal Bureau of Investigation.

Department of Labor
14th Street and Constitution Avenue NW
Washington, D.C. 20210

Administers and enforces laws relating to wage earners, their working conditions and employment opportunities, including apprenticeship programs, manpower programs, and the Occupational Safety and Health Administration.

Department of State
2201 C Street NW
Washington, D.C. 20520

Formulates foreign policy under the President's direction and supervises foreign relations using the Foreign Service, the United States Information Agency and the Agency for International Development.

Department of Transportation
400 7th Street SW
Washington, D.C. 20590

Plans and administers federally assisted transportation systems including mass transit, railroads, highways, and airports, and includes the Coast Guard.

Department of the Treasury
15th Street and Pennsylvania Avenue NW
Washington, D.C. 20220

Prints or mints money and runs the Customs Service, the Internal Revenue Service, and the Secret Service.

COMPENDIUM OF LAW CAREERS

(The following list of careers is not meant to be exhaustive but rather to give you an idea of the range of career options.)

Court Reporter. Takes stenographic notes of court proceedings, whether trials, hearings, or meetings. Must be able to record about 175 words a minute and to transcribe these notes for the official court record. Reporters work in courts at all judicial levels—local, state and federal— or may be self-employed free-lancers. Average earnings: $15,000 a year. Demand will remain strong through the 1980s owing to rising numbers of court cases. Competition for jobs will also be strong, with certified shorthand reporters most likely to get the jobs.

Judge. Administers judicial system and arbitrates legal disputes brought into court. After hearing evidence from both sides, determines whether complaint in dispute is justified and supported by evidence. Settles in-court disputes between attorneys and instructs jury about applicable law so that it can determine case accordingly. Sentences defendants who are declared guilty. Hears and decides nonjury or "equity" cases. Earns from about $31,000 to, in United States Supreme Court, $65,600 a year. Must be lawyer; appointed or elected to office, frequently as a reward for political work.

Lawyers and Legal Specialists. Although they may have a special knowledge of certain areas of law, most lawyers do not limit practice exclusively to a specialty. A lawyer who does corporate law will need to know tax and real estate law as well as corporation law. Some lawyers serve as court-appointed attorneys for indigent criminal clients or take public interest cases. Specialties describe areas of interest more than job categories. Starting lawyers may earn between $12,000 and about $25,000 a year. (In some very large, prestigious firms starting salaries of up to $30,000 may be offered.)

    Corporate Lawyer. Specializes in giving legal advice to corporations. Advises businesses on corporate legal rights, obligations, and privileges, and on advisability of legal action. Acts on its behalf in dealing with the government, employees, other corporations, and customers. Helps make policy decisions about corporate legal mat-

415

ters; negotiates contracts and lawsuits. May work for law firm, legal
department of corporation, or federal regulating agencies. Well paid
and will be in demand as the business world expands and federal
regulations proliferate.

Criminal Lawyer. Works with people accused of breaking laws.
Interviews client and witnesses; seeks evidence to defend accused.
In court, examines and cross-examines witnesses and summarizes
client's case to convince jury. Wide range of incomes depends on
skill and experience.

Prosecuting and District Attorneys. Work for city, county, state,
and federal court systems representing government's interest in
court. Prepare and present evidence, prosecute criminal cases, and
represent government in other matters. Job is to prove that accused
are guilty.

Patent Lawyer. Provides legal advice about inventions to inventors, investors, and manufacturers. Concerned with patent rights of
inventor, making sure that application for patent involves invention
that is original and unique. May handle copyrights and trademarks.
Many study engineering as a background to working with inventions. (*See also* Guide to Science and Engineering Careers.)

Public Interest Lawyer. Specializes in cases that have implications wider than effect on client alone. Tries to use these cases to
set precedents for social and legal reform in areas such as civil
rights, consumer affairs, and tenants' rights. Because most clients
are poor, does not usually earn as much as other lawyers, but federal
laws permit collection of fee from defendant. Employed by government and special interest groups and consumer agencies. Competition for few jobs is extraordinarily high.

Real Estate Lawyer. Assists in sale and transfer of real property
(land and anything fastened to or growing on it). Does "title search"
to make sure client has only legal claim to ownership of property.
Drafts documents related to property transactions. May also serve as
trustee, taking legal care of property for owner, and represents property owner before municipal zoning commissions.

Tax Lawyer. Advises clients about local, state, federal, and foreign
taxes. Represents client in court or if tax return is contested. Tax law
is growing field with good prospects for employment. Many tax lawyers are self-employed, but they may work directly for corporations.

Trial Lawyer. Specializes in court appearances. Represents
clients in civil and criminal cases at trial after doing necessary pre-
trial preparation research. Range of income depends on talent and
experience.

Legal Assistant (Legal Aide). Assists lawyers, doing whatever employer—individual lawyer, law firm, business, or government agency—
wants accomplished, including researching laws or information, prepar-

ing documents, identifying real estate, getting a case ready for court, managing office employees, interviewing clients and witnesses, accounting, or more. Salaries start at about $7,500. Opportunities for employment are good and getting better as more lawyers understand advantages of hiring legal assistants. Law students and graduates of paralegal training programs are more likely to get these jobs than untrained people.

Legal Librarian. Manages special libraries of material for lawyers and law students. Acquires and catalogs materials such as books, films, tapes, and microfilm; helps people use the library; keeps library in order and up to date. Most librarians have master's degree in library science; sometimes have law degree as well. Employed by universities and large subscription or public law libraries.

Legal Secretary. Handles secretarial duties for lawyers or law firms. May also do some paralegal work, including keeping track of court dockets, completing legal forms, serving and filing notices, locating witnesses, and handling legal correspondence such as summonses and subpoenas. Average earnings: $954 a month. In general, employment outlook good because of projected growth in business and its corresponding paperwork.

COMPENDIUM OF GOVERNMENT CAREERS

(The following list of careers is not meant to be exhaustive but rather to give you an idea of the range of options.)

Air Traffic Controller. Tracks planes in flight and when landing or taking off. Responsible for preventing collisions and for maintaining safe, efficient operation of runways. Each handles a specific section of the air and gives directions and information to planes there. Job is highly stressful. Only employer is Federal Aeronautics Administration, which provides necessary training. Applicants must have three years of work experience or four years of college. Starting pay is about $11,500; average pay, $22,300. Competition for these jobs is strong and should remain so, since there are more applicants than openings, and also since more automatic equipment is being used to handle air traffic.

City Manager. Coordinates day-to-day operations of city, relieving elected officials of some duties. Often handles such tasks as tax collection and disbursement, law enforcement management, overseeing public works, hiring, budget planning, and problem solving in areas like traffic control, pollution, etc. Many have master's degree in public administration or related fields. Most are hired or appointed by elected city officials. Competition is strong in this expanding field. Average starting salaries for assistant city managers are $11,000 to $14,000.

Community and Urban Planner. Develops plans and programs for growth and revitalization of cities, towns, regions, and states. Planning focuses on transportation, housing, land use, etc. Researches and studies community land-use patterns and economic base, and predicts trends that will affect community. Many have master's degree in city planning or related fields. Are hired by city, county, state, regional, and federal governments. With continued federal support for planning, employment outlook will remain good. Starting planners earn about $11,000 to $14,000.

Firefighter. Trained to respond to emergency situations, especially fires. Works under supervisor, who directs performance of duties such as

connecting hoses, operating pumps, handling ladders, giving fir:
etc. Inspects buildings for fire hazards, educates public about fire prevention, investigates possible arson, and maintains firefighting equipment. Employed by cities and towns, federal installations, factories.
High school diploma is usually required. As volunteer firefighters are
replaced by professionals, new jobs will open. Competition is easier in
small towns than in cities. Starting pay is generally $9,900 to $12,200.

Foreign Service Officer. Representative of United States in its relations with foreign countries and international organizations, responsible
for protecting and advancing American interests. Manages American
consulates abroad and reports on the nation in which located. Provides
services to Americans abroad and to foreigners planning trips to the
States. Handles questions on passports, visas, and citizenship eligibility.
Employed by State Department at starting salary of $11,500 to $16,000,
may advance to $47,500.

Military Jobs. Armed Forces offer wide range of job training and employment opportunities. Many enlist (two- or three-year minimum tour
of duty) to take advantage of benefits (medical care, housing, education,
travel) while learning trade. Experience gained in service often helps
veterans to get good jobs when they get out; also, veterans are given
preference on Civil Service ratings. Anyone between the ages of 17 and
27 with a high school diploma or its equivalent may take written and
physical exams necessary for acceptance into Armed Forces. Enlisted
personnel make between $6,346 and $7,566; officers, between $10,553
and $13,973.

Police Officer. Jobs for community include traffic control; crime investigation; emergency and first aid services; patrol duty by car, boat, horse,
motorcycle and foot; scientific analysis of evidence; and public education. State police enforce automobile and other highway safety laws.
Strong competition for jobs; training in law enforcement techniques improves employment outlook. Usually a high school diploma is required.
State police start at annual salary of about $10,500; municipal police are
paid slightly more. Average salary for all types of police work is $13,600.

Postal Worker. Performs variety of tasks related to mail collection,
processing, and delivery. Some load, unload, and move mail, while others separate and distribute it. Some operate postal machinery, do maintenance and inspection in post offices, or supervise other employees.
Jobs include clerks, carriers, mail handlers, supervisors, postmasters,
inspectors, guards, drivers, administrators, and secretaries. Many jobs do
not require formal training. Increasing use of telephone telex and telejax
service and automated postal processing machinery makes employment
prospects poor. Postal Service employees earn starting salary of $12,000.

Social Worker. Works with individuals and families to help solve financial, educational, and other problems. Provides information on and
referrals to government programs or private service agencies. May work

for state's department of public assistance or for another government agency. Many schools and hospitals hire social workers, and so do some business firms. Most have bachelor's degree; many employers require master's. Starting pay is about $9,500 a year; average salary, $12,100. With the expansion of social services, employment outlook is good but competition is fairly high.

Teacher. Presents information and ideas to students. Plans and carries out lessons. Much administrative paperwork, plus dealing with parents and planning special trips, speakers, films, etc. Most work for public school systems, some in private schools. Public school teachers must be certified by state and must have a bachelor's degree, in some cases a master's. Average salaries: secondary school, $12,395; elementary level, $11,870. Since birth rate has declined and there are fewer students, job outlook is poor. Layoffs, rather than hirings, may be trend.

MARTHA TABOR

Guide V A Guide to Skilled Trades Careers

Funding for this Guide was provided by American Telephone and Telegraph Company.

BETTYE LANE

FOCUS ON THE CONSTRUCTION OUTLOOK

Many women—probably more than you think—work in the skilled trades: as carpenters, electricians, welders, plumbers, painters, and even bulldozer operators. A short time ago this wasn't true. In 1960 most of these trades had no women workers, and only 1 in 50 people working in skilled trades jobs was a woman. By 1970, just 10 years later, the number had more than doubled, and it's still growing.

There are excellent reasons to consider a career in the skilled trades. A craft worker has skills rewarded by respect, high pay, and in many cases good job benefits. Perhaps even more important is the tradition of real pride in being a craft worker. And for *women*, some special reasons to consider a career in this field are:

- *Good Job Prospects.* New government regulations require companies, trade unions, and contractors to hire women. Not only is it illegal for employers to discriminate against women, but employers and unions must take positive steps to find women for their skilled trades jobs.
- *Money.* Jobs in the skilled trades pay far more than most jobs traditionally held by women. Starting salaries in most trades jobs are usually above the minimum wage, even while you are still learning. After only four or five years, many craft workers may earn double their hourly starting salary, and cost of living clauses in their contracts ensure that they are somewhat protected against inflation. (The Compendium section of this Guide has more details.) A job in the trades makes it possible for a woman to support herself as well as her children if she is widowed or divorced.
- *On-the-job Training.* Skilled trades jobs have few formal education requirements. Although it helps to have a high school diploma or its equivalent, it's not always necessary. Training programs are usually on an earn-while-you-learn basis. Very few traditional jobs for women have this advantage.

- *Skill Power.* Wherever you go, you'll have a skill that will get you a job. Work in the trades can be part-time. It's the kind of work you can leave for a few years and return to later. (These advantages are all a bonus for the woman who wants to raise a family.)
- *Physical Activity.* Craft work is great for women who enjoy physical work or who like to work outside.
- *Growth.* The job outlook in the skilled trades is good. Although construction jobs have been hard to get in some parts of the country, the prediction is such jobs will open and increase faster than other kinds of jobs in the 1980s. The number of skilled trades jobs in business and industry is also expected to grow. Trades jobs in industry offer good job security: skilled industrial workers are usually among the last laid off in hard times.

In addition, there's another very special motivation. In the skilled trades at the end of a day, you can actually see the results of your work— the pipes you installed; the wiring you put in; the wall you built; the dam, the bridge, the highway that your skills and effort helped make possible. You will know that what you've done has had a real effect on other people's lives.

All kinds of skilled "blue-collar" jobs are included in the category called "skilled trades"—not only jobs in construction. Jobs like that of machinist, making parts for machines, are not construction jobs, since machinists work mainly in shops or factories. You'll find this guide most helpful in thinking about careers in construction, highlighted here because of their good prospects for women.

Getting There. The two usual stages in a skilled trades career are apprentice and journeyman. An apprentice is someone who is learning

---

NOTE FROM THE PAST

Early American Craftswomen

During the post-Revolutionary period some women managed to run very successful workshops, producing articles not associated with later stereotypes of "womanly" skills.

In an issue of the *Maryland Journal* in 1788, Mrs. Mary Rawlins informs "her friends and the Public in general that she carries on the composition work in all its Branches (such as moulding and ornaments for Doors, Windows, and for Wood Cornices, and particularly chimney Pieces in the newest Fashion) which was carried on by her late Husband. ..."

---

a trade in a formal training program that includes both on-the-job training and related classroom instruction. A journeyman is a professional who has completed the necessary apprenticeship training. In some states and for some trades a third category is craft worker. For example, to be a private plumbing or electrical contractor in Massachusetts and many other states, you must have a master's license.

Independence, Teamwork. In the skilled trades, especially the construction trades, these are key concepts. Independence: you are relied on to know your job and to do it well on your own. Teamwork: you know how your job fits into the project, when you'll be needed, and how you can help out. Many of the traditional jobs for women don't require this kind of teamwork; teachers or secretaries, for instance, work mostly on their own.

Skilled trades construction workers are part of a team that includes architects, drafters, engineers, contractors, and building inspectors.

Architects design the structures to be built and draw up detailed plans or blueprints (so called because they were originally printed on blue paper). *Drafting people,* specialists in precise detailed technical drawing, help draw up these plans.

Engineers study the blueprints to make sure that no structural problems exist. Engineers also draw up the specifications, or "specs," for a building—the details about what materials are to be used and how. The engineer also writes up what kind of wood or steel is to be bought and what particular construction process used for each part of the building.

Contractors, like football coaches or orchestra conductors, decide what needs to be done and who will do it; for example, how many electricians or pipefitters are needed and when they should report to work. The contractor orders the supplies, supervises the work, keeps the project on schedule, and so forth.

Building inspectors examine construction sites to see that all the laws about construction are followed.

All these members of the building team need to know they can count on the skill of the craft workers who are doing the building construction. An incompetent electrician, for example, can damage a building and endanger the lives of the other people working there. So government, industry, and unions have outlined exactly what a skilled worker in each trade should know.

Since the Middle Ages the skill of a craft worker has been recognized and respected. Unlike peasants or serfs, a craft worker was a "free man" —free to journey from place to place. (This is the derivation of our word *journeyman.*) A master craftsman could travel across Europe to the major construction jobs of those days, building the great cathedrals.

As populous towns became cities, there was an ever-increasing need for resident craftsmen in every specialty. To maintain the quality of their work and protect their reputation, they formed guilds—the forerunners

QUIZ

How knowledgeable are you about the skilled trades? Not sure? Take our true-or-false quiz, and you'll soon find out.

1. Hourly wage rates for experienced skilled trades jobs may be as much as three to five times higher than those of most jobs traditionally held by women.
2. Stationary engineers are the people who design cute writing paper.
3. Less than 1 percent of carpenters, truckdrivers, brickmasons, mechanics, plumbers, and firefighters are women.
4. A major barrier to women's participation in the skilled trades has been a lack of exposure to vocational-type classes in high-school.
5. A plumber's helper is a little gnome who helps plumbers get to those hard-to-reach places.
6. There are laws to protect your rights as a woman worker and places to complain if they are being violated.
7. Form builders make mannequins for store windows.
8. Women often lack the physical readiness necessary for many skilled trades jobs.

Quiz Answers

1. *True.* As an apprentice or trainee, you earn while you learn, and your wages may start at about $3 or $4 per hour. After four or five years of experience, you could be making $9 or more per hour.
2. *False.* Stationary engineers operate power machines that stay in one place (hence stationary), such as boilers and generators.
3. *True,* unfortunately. But the numbers are growing. Women also make up less than 5 percent of all craft workers, while 99 percent of all secretarial workers are women.
4. *True.* Most women were never offered shop courses in high school and may be completely unaware of what the trades are about. As more women continue to enter the trades, girls will begin to consider these jobs at an earlier age.
5. *False.* Plumber's helpers are those large rubber suction cups with handles that unclog drains and toilets.
6. *True.* These laws include the Equal Pay Act, Executive Order 11246, etc.
7. *False.* Form builders make prefabricated forms into which concrete is poured.
8. *True.* However, it's not because women don't have the necessary physical abilities, but rather that they often just aren't physically fit. A program of physical fitness should be followed by all women, but especially by those contemplating a job in the skilled trades.

of our present-day unions. Committees of guild members assigned apprentices to master craftsmen for training, then promoted them to journeymen, and finally to master status. (Our word *masterpiece* comes from that approval process.)

Women were admitted to guild membership during the Middle Ages and recognized as master craftswomen. In fact, the notion of a "man's job" is fairly new—in ancient Rome plumbing was considered a woman's job, and in American Indian and some African cultures women were the builders. They stripped trees and cured animal skins, sewing them to make tepees. They wove sticks and applied mud wattle to make hogans and form the adobe walls of the Indian villages of the Southwest.

In our own country the real exclusion of women from the craft trades occurred in the 19th century; before that they worked alongside their craftsmen husbands. The shop was part of the house. Mrs. Paul Revere worked with her husband in his silver shop and was responsible for running it when he was out politicking. The daughters of craftsmen were considered a good catch by journeymen in the same trade because they understood the work.

In the 19th century factories producing large amounts of goods began to replace shops in the home. As a result, a woman couldn't continue to work in the shop and keep track of her children or break for a short while to perform household duties.

Women and children held some of the first factory jobs. When men began to do factory work, their wives had to stay home and take care of the children.

By the early 20th century things had changed enough so that some jobs came to be thought of as men's and others as women's, and the women's jobs were only for the unmarried. Some of these old distinctions no longer hold. For instance, the job of secretary was once considered a strictly male profession; after the invention of the typewriter, secretarial work became women's work.

Twice during the 20th century women took over men's jobs—during the two World Wars. When asked what he was using for manpower since many men were engaged in combat, President Franklin D. Roosevelt replied, "We have no manpower problem. We have *woman* power." Women went to work building guns, ships, and airplanes for the war effort. They learned fast, and they did their job well. After the war, people seemed to forget that women had done skilled trades work reliably and efficiently. When the returning veterans went back to work, women who wanted to stay in such occupations were discouraged.

Now in the last quarter of the 20th century things are changing again. More and more women are working, and more and more women are choosing nontraditional careers in the skilled trades.

Women in the Skilled Trades Today

Women wishing to work in nontraditional jobs realize very soon that "the system" still presents some barriers. Some, such as height and weight requirements or age limits for apprentices, are slowly disappearing. Others are harder to deal with, veterans' preference arrangements, for instance.

Another tough institutional barrier is the seniority system. In many industrial settings, training programs for skilled trades jobs are open to employees with seniority in the maintenance department. Since few women have had a chance for those maintenance jobs, choice training opportunities frequently go only to men. In other companies, craft workers are laid off according to their seniority; as newcomers, women are more vulnerable to layoffs.

Also, in the past, women haven't been made aware of job or training opportunities in the trades. Guidance counselors didn't suggest them to female high school students. Training opportunities or job openings

---

GETTING/BEING IN SHAPE FOR THE JOB

Many jobs in construction don't require unusual strength, but almost all construction jobs *do* require a good overall physical condition. By learning to use your body properly, you will make the most efficient use of your strength and conserve your energy. To increase your stamina as well as your strength, develop a routine that includes the following activities:

Cardiovascular warmup/workout: easy jogging in place followed by running.

Spine flexibility and back strength: neck rolls, spine rolls, toe touching, torso stretching, side stretching, torso twists.

Leg/hip flexibility and abdominal strength: a series of stretches, situps, leg lifts.

Leg strength: knee bends pressing up to toes, jumps, hops, running in place, side and back lunges.

And especially relaxation: body awareness exercises.

—Vivian Guilfoy, director of the Boston
YWCA program on Nontraditional
Occupations for Women

were posted in men's rooms of factories. Obviously, women didn't have much of a chance.

If you face such institutional barriers, you need to know your rights. One possible course of action is to discuss your problem with the Affirmative Action officer of your company or union, or the job counselor at your training program. (See the *Know Your Rights* section of this Guide.)

Hassles

One thing most women want to know *before* they decide on a career in the skilled trades is: What can a woman really expect in terms of interpersonal relations? Are women hassled? Treated badly? The answer is a qualified *yes*.

First, a certain type of harassment is normal in the construction trades —for men and women. Some of it takes the form of constant teasing and reflects the competition between trades: "Here come the electricians; maybe they'll do some work," or "All you plumbers need to know is that payday is on Friday and shit don't run up hill." (Swearing is a normal part of conversation at a construction site. So is off-color language—some mechanical tools are called by what may be considered vulgar names.)

Male or female, apprentices and new people on a construction site are always hassled to some degree. Practical jokes are continually played on new people: tool boxes are nailed to the floor, apprentices are sent for tools that don't exist, someone shakes the ladder you're standing on— that kind of thing.

Now that women are entering the trades, they're faced both with this normal hassling and with a special hostility reserved for women. Many

---

HOW TO BUY TOOLS

All you'll need for a start is a small number of basic tools. Ask your instructor, your friends at work, your boss what to buy.

Don't buy cheap tools at a discount center. Cheap tools break more easily, can cause accidents, and can make any job much tougher. Check out the tools before you buy them. Do they look well made? Are the straight parts really straight, the sharp parts really sharp?

You will need a special place to store your tools where your kids (or your friends) won't tamper with them and something to carry them in. Check and see what the other workers are using.

---

men actually do resent the fact that women are entering the trades. For a woman new to the field, it's hard to distinguish between what's being directed at her because she's a woman and what's "just normal" harassment. It's even harder for her to know how to react.

None of the women interviewed for this book has ever been put in physical danger. The real harassment is verbal intimidation or obscenity, which can be very irritating. But most women soon learn to ignore it.

Another problem women face is being overprotected. They may end up in desk jobs; or they may have to fight to get opportunities to learn and to not be given the "dumb" jobs to do all the time.

One of the most serious problems women face in the building trades is isolation. They frequently aren't given any feedback about their work, good or bad, and often they are made to feel that their work isn't important to the team. Consequently their self-respect and confidence in their own skills may be constantly undercut.

If you're faced with this type of discrimination in any job, don't give up. Find other women in construction to talk to, or a job counselor, or family and friends, or join an assertiveness training group; but, above all, don't lose faith in your ability or your right to belong. By being there you are helping to change the situation for yourself and for other women.

Although the new regulations under Executive Order 11246 require the employer to make sure women employees aren't harassed, no law can regulate widespread ingrained behavior. Each woman has to decide for herself how to react. Of course, physical violence or threats of physical violence require immediate legal action. But swearing, teasing, and hassling must be handled when they occur, according to your own sense of what's right, and with knowledge of how much you personally can

---

THE WEAKER SEX?

Medical research is casting doubt on the idea that women are much weaker than men. It has been proved that to the age of 12 there isn't much difference between girls and boys in either strength or endurance. After 12, women's body strength declines in relation to men's. Many doctors think this is because women in our country don't get enough exercise. In one study, nonathletic young women were given a 10-week training program and their strength improved by a dramatic 30 percent! Studies of college athletes show that men and women are similar in terms of overall endurance and strength, although men are still stronger in their upper bodies. These new studies indicate that when women receive physical fitness training there is almost no difference between their strength and the strength of men of about the same size.

---

take. Women who are now working in the building trades offer this advice.

- You've got to let some of it run off your back. Don't go out there looking for trouble or you'll find lots of it. If you get yourself into that attitude, you might see it even if it's not there.

MYTH AND REALITY

The Women's Bureau of the Department of Labor has studied some myths about women and work. Women looking for jobs in skilled trades have to deal with these fictions more often than in other fields. Some of the misconceptions and the truth about them (excerpted from the Women's Bureau publication "The Myth and the Reality"):

The Myth	The Reality
Women aren't seriously attached to the labor force; they work only for extra pocket money.	Of the nearly 34 million women in the labor force in March 1973, nearly half were working because of pressing economic need. They were either single, widowed, divorced or separated, or had husbands whose incomes were less than $3,000 a year. Another 4.7 million had husbands with incomes between $3,000 and $7,000.
Women are out ill more than male workers.	A recent Public Health Service study shows little difference in the absentee rate due to illness or injury: 5.6 days per year for women; 5.2 days for men.
Women don't work as long or as regularly as their male co-workers; their training is costly —and largely wasted.	Even with a break in employment, the average woman worker has a worklife expectancy of 25 years compared to 43 years for the average male worker. The *single* woman averages 45 years in the labor force.
Married women take jobs away from men; in fact, they ought to quit those jobs they now hold.	In March 1973, 19.8 million married women (husbands present) were in the labor force; the number of unemployed men was 2.5 million. If all the married women stayed home and were replaced by unemployed men, there would be 17.3 million unfilled jobs.

- You have to be prepared to be assertive. There are ways of standing up for yourself that won't make enemies.
- There's a lot of stress on the job. The guys who work with me let off steam by swearing or taking a swing at each other. When it builds up for me, I cry. We just do things differently, that's all. Never stay home because you cried the day before.
- You're there to learn and to do a job. That's all you need to remember. Sooner or later they'll respect you for it.

What Will Family and Friends Think?

Naturally, the attitudes of your family and friends are important. Some families have a very definite idea of what is "woman's work." Parents, for example, might be concerned about their daughter being part of otherwise all-male work crews.

However you choose to handle people's reactions, be prepared for some expressions of surprise or disbelief. One editor who recently left the publishing business after 10 years to take a job as a mechanic in a shipyard described her strategy this way: "When some people asked me why, I just smiled and said I felt more like tinkering with machines than manuscripts these days."

If someone close to you seems particularly uneasy about your decision, it might be helpful to have a third person (perhaps another woman in a nontraditional job or a placement counselor) meet and talk with you both informally. Usually though, if you are able to persuade a training program to take you or a contractor to hire you, you won't find it hard to persuade your family and friends, too. One initially resistant father we spoke to said, "My girl's a welder. She's the best. They laid off three guys, but not Martha. I'm really proud of her."

Choosing the Trade

Once you have decided that you want a career in the skilled trades, the next decision is: *Which* trade?

Take a look at yourself. Examine your abilities. What is it you *really* like to do? What is it that you can do that makes you feel proud of yourself? When you have answered these questions, you'll have a pretty good idea of what direction to take.

Next, get more information about different trades to know which fits your interests and abilities. Study the Compendium in the back of this Guide and consult the Apprenticeship Information Centers. Talk to people you know who have chosen skilled trades careers. Different trades require different abilities and training, from the delicate craftsmanship of cabinetmaking to the physical strength and courage of ironwork.

Naturally your decision also depends on what's readily available. You need to know what the chances are of actually getting paid work. The Apprenticeship Information Centers have information on the job outlook for each trade in your area. If you're looking for an apprenticeship in an area in which 60 percent of the journeymen are unemployed, even if you do get a job, you're likely to face a lot more hostility.

Finally, look for good opportunities. In this career field a chance for a good training or job opportunity may not come up very often. If you get a chance through a friend or another contact, even it it's not *exactly* the trade you want, consider it.

BASIC RESOURCES: KNOW YOUR RIGHTS

Equal Pay Act — You have a right to equal pay for equal work, including equal fringe benefits, vacation time, and incentive payments. The exceptions are wages based on a seniority or merit system. The place for you or your union to make a complaint is the Wage and Hour and Public Contracts Division of your regional United States Department of Labor Office. For the office nearest you, consult the phone book for United States Government listings or write:

> Department of Labor
> Wage and Hour and Public Contracts
> Washington, D.C. 20210

Civil Rights Act of 1964, Title VII — You have a right not to be discriminated against because you are a woman — in hiring, layoffs, promotions or training. Because of this law, it is illegal save for a very few exceptions for your employer to categorize some jobs as "for women" or "for men," or to fire you because you are pregnant or refuse to hire you because you are married. To file a complaint, you or your union should get in touch with your nearest regional Equal Employment Opportunity Commission office. For the one nearest you, consult the phone book for the United States Government listings or write:

> Equal Employment Opportunity Commission
> 1800 G Street NW
> Washington, D.C. 20506

Executive Order 11246 — All companies which have government contracts over $10,000 must take "affirmative action" to recruit women for all jobs and training programs. On every construction job using federal dollars, the contractor has to take special steps to let women know jobs are available and to set goals for hiring a significant percentage of women for each construction site. Formal complaints should go to the nearest Office of Federal Contract Compliance. For that address, consult the phone book for the United States Government listings or write:

Department of Labor
Office of Federal Contract Compliance
14th Street and Constitution Avenue NW
Washington, D.C. 20210

Equal Employment in Apprenticeship Programs — New regulations require that apprenticeship training programs seek out women and admit a significant percentage of them in each program. To find out about apprenticeship opportunities, you should contact the nearest Bureau of Apprenticeship Training. A list of their regional offices is given immediately preceding the Compendium of Construction Trades at the end of this Guide.

Two tips . . . when you don't know where to complain, complain everywhere. Also, even though these governmental processes are often slow and frustrating, threatening to use them can be very effective with both unions and employers.

CHAPTER 2

DOING THE GROUNDWORK

Naturally, all construction starts from the ground up—with a "site," the land on which the building or structure will be built. If a building already stands on the site, it must of course be demolished first. Valuable parts of the old building, like stained glass windows or wood paneling, will be salvaged before cranes and bulldozers tear down the old structure. Operating engineers (construction machinery operators) run the heavy equipment. Haulers drive the trucks that cart away the rubble.

Even if there is no preexisting building, operating engineers are needed to clear the site of trees and grade it. Hills may be leveled or contours changed to provide better drainage or a rolling lawn. Next, the location of the outer walls of the building is marked at the corners and outlined by twine, and the foundation dug out by a front loader or bulldozer. Topsoil is separated from the subsoil, which is set aside, to be put back eventually around the building's foundation when it has been completed.

Then the foundation is built. The foundation of a house frequently is made from concrete blocks stacked by cement masons to form walls, or else wooden forms are built to the foundation shape by carpenters and concrete poured into them by masons. When the concrete is hard, the forms are removed. Bricklayers may be employed to face the outside wall with brick.

When the foundation is in place, the floor framing is added. This framing is both the ceiling for the basement and the floor of the ground floor. The wall framing comes next; windows and doors are "roughed out," followed by ceiling and roof framing. Framing is fairly hard carpentry work, and crews must work together to help each other as walls or sections of walls are commonly built on the ground and then tilted up and nailed in place.

In commercial buildings the framework is not wood but steel. Ironworkers or riggers assemble the frame of the building. The foundation

435

work for these structures is more complicated and more specialized than that for a house. The foundations of tall buildings, bridges, and other weight-supporting structures must be stabilized by pilings or piers driven deep to anchor the structure against the force of the wind and the pressure of the weight of the structure. Iron or sheet piling is hauled up by the leads hanging off the boom of a crane and then driven into the ground by pile drivers. The steel beams of the frame are held in place by cranes while crews of welders join them.

Two of the most important craft workers needed for this phase of construction, the structural phase, are carpenters and operating engineers.

Carpenters and Their Work

One of the oldest and most varied of the skilled trades (and now one of the trades employing the most women), carpentry is necessary to all types and phases of construction, both residential and commercial. Carpenters are the most important members of the construction team when building a wood frame building, but they are indispensable to all other kinds of buildings, too, for concrete foundations, framing and sheathing walls, and finishing work like hanging doors or windows, or building and installing kitchen cabinets. Carpenters work in industry also. Almost all factories and industrial plants employ carpenters—as workers on maintenance crews or as wood machinists. Carpenters may specialize in laying hardwood floors or building forms, in making cabinets or furniture, or in renovating old buildings. It is not surprising that more than 1 million carpenters work in America, more craft workers than in any other trade.

Carpenters' Tools. The basic hand tools of a carpenter are the hammer and handsaw. Hammers are available in many weights and styles for particular purposes. The same is true of saws, chisels, planes, levels, and screwdrivers. Handsaws differ, for example, according to the type of cut and the material to be cut—hacksaws cut metal, coping saws cut curves in thin wood or plastic, crosscut saws cut *across* the grain of a piece of wood, and ripping saws have coarser teeth shaped to cut *with* the grain. Increasingly in the past 20 or 30 years, power tools have come into use.

Carpenters are using many new kinds of building materials today, including new varieties of glues, plastics, wood finishes, floor coverings, and insulation materials. However, wood is still basic to carpentry.

Another development that will continue to change carpentry work is the use of factory-built houses and housing components. Carpenters will be needed to build them in the factory and to assemble the components at the site.

Training to Be a Carpenter. The formal apprenticeship program in carpentry entails four years of on-the-job training, with 144 hours of

GETTING IN, AND MOVING UP: CARPENTRY

Formal apprenticeship training is the most thorough way to get carpentry training. However, you may have many other options. Vocational schools, trade schools, and community colleges offer basic courses, and local contractors and self-employed journeymen will often take on carpenters' helpers and train them.

General carpenters, because they work with all other crafts from the start to the finish of a construction project, have good opportunities to advance to the position of supervisor.

Carpenters frequently become contractors and go into business for themselves. They may be subcontractor specialists or home builders or maintenance and repair workers for homes and businesses.

related classroom instruction each year. However, you can also learn what is taught in an apprenticeship program in other ways. Trade schools, vocational–technical schools, and some community colleges have courses in drafting, basic woodworking, blueprint reading, etc. Experienced self-employed workers frequently take on a "carpenter's helper" to train in the craft.

Local contractors sometimes offer shorter on-the-job training programs. If the contractor is a specialist, for example, as a subcontractor who does rough framing or Formica installation, the training program may be only in that specialty. Larger contractors may offer better all-round training involving more skills. Since the job market fluctuates, the more skills you have, the more chances you have to survive employment downs.

Carpentry Quirks. Carpentry is less seasonal than many of the construction trades. When winter shuts down outside work in the North, as summer does in the hottest parts of the South, you can work inside on finishing work or "bench work" in a shop. You can also use your skill to build things, like bookcases or children's furniture, and sell them.

To reiterate: Carpentry is one of the construction trades with the most women workers.

Operating Engineers

The people who run the heavy machinery at construction sites are the operating engineers. A Department of Labor survey for 1974 reports that

500,000 skilled trades workers in the United States were employed as operating engineers, almost a third of them as bulldozer operators. Other kinds of machines that require this skill are earthmoving or roadbuilding equipment, such as graders, backhoes, scrapers, front end loaders, and Gradalls; hoists; cranes; air compressors; and dredges. Almost all operating engineers work on major construction projects—highways, sewer and water systems, airports, factories, etc. Only about one-tenth of them are self-employed. Some work on power-driven machinery in factories and mines.

Operating construction machinery may look easy to handle, but it's not. The tremendous power of the machines and, frequently, the pressure of getting the job done on time demand a great deal of responsibility. If you're doing excavation work in a city, you must be extremely careful not to cut through gas or water mains. Crane operators are among the most skilled and highest paid members of this trade. Various auxiliary equipment can be attached to cranes for specific tasks—wrecking balls to demolish old buildings, booms to raise steel I-beams into place for framework. There are many controls on a crane for moving a boom or bucket around, and a serious mistake could kill or injure other workers. Roadbuilders, who contour the land according to engineering drawings, take a great deal of pride in their ability to grade earth precisely.

Stationary engineers are somewhat similar to operating engineers. These craft workers operate and maintain boilers, diesel engines, turbines, generators, compressors, pumps, and other power machines that stay in one spot. Stationary engineers also work for cities and towns, operating sewage treatment plants, power stations, or hospitals.

Operating Engineers' Tools. Some operating engineers are licensed to

GETTING IN, MOVING UP: OPERATING ENGINEERING

It's almost impossible to become an operating engineer without going through a formal three-year apprenticeship training program; the machines you use are so valuable that their owners want to be very sure you are skilled before you run them. You can also learn how to operate certain kinds of heavy equipment at private trade schools throughout the country. Before you enroll, check out the school's reputation with construction employers in your area.

In the well-paid and fast-growing field of operating engineering, workers have employment opportunities in factories and mass transit systems in repair, maintenance, and moving materials, as well as on construction sites.

THE DAILY GRIND: OPERATING ENGINEERS

*"You've got no idea how hot 'hot' is until
you've been on top of one of those big machines
in July."*

*"There is an awful lot of dust in demolition
work. It gets in your nose, your hair, your
eyes; it sticks to your skin."*

*"When you make a mistake with one of these
machines, you make a big mistake. A broken
water main or a gouge out of a wrong place
isn't something you can hide — everyone can see it."*

run many kinds of machines; others specialize. Operating engineers
don't often own their own tools or machines; a complicated piece of
earthmoving equipment may cost as much as $250,000. Contractors and
subcontractors may rent heavy equipment from specialized trade
dealers.

Training. The apprenticeship training program for operating engineers is three years. Apprentices start off as "oilers" or helpers, cleaning,
greasing, and starting the machines. In classes after work, apprentices
learn about soil and the principles of drainage and seepage; first-aid and
safety; maintenance and minor repairs for heavy equipment. Welding is
a skill machine operators are taught; they also need to learn basic math
to set and check grades or build slopes in accordance with engineering
plans.

The formal training period for stationary engineers is four years. In
many states stationary engineers are licensed; classes of licenses are
based on the horsepower or steam pressure of the equipment used. Apprentice programs prepare workers for these licenses. Apprentices are
also taught practical chemistry, blueprint reading, applied electricity,
and other technical subjects. (Experience running farm machinery is
valuable to someone starting a career in this field.)

Operating Engineering Quirks. Although operating engineers are
among the highest-paid construction workers, employment is seasonal
in most parts of the country. Also, the job can be tiring; operators are
shaken by the constant movement of such machines as scrapers or bulldozers.

THE THRILL OF IT ALL: OPERATING ENGINEERS

> *"I found that I'm really fascinated by those big machines. And they're really big."*
>
> *"It's the power I like about it. The power! It's like having huge bionic arms, ripping and digging and lifting."*
>
> *"When I was a kid on a farm, my Dad always let my brothers drive the farm machines. It was the sight of one of those huge combines with the driver way up near the sky, it seemed, that gave me the desire to run a great big machine."*

Sandy Norris, Carpenter

Sandy Norris, 35, grew up in a small city in Pennsylvania. "I always worked after school. When I finished high school, I went to the local community college to study art. To support myself, I took a production job in a factory, where I worked with power tools."

Ms. Norris' best friend, Anne Bryant, was nearby studying to be an architect. To make a little extra money, they got together and decided to set up a small business doing odd jobs for people. To start, they put signs up in supermarkets and drugstores and advertised in the community newspaper.

The first person who called wanted them to remove an old toilet seat and put on a new one. Still finding it hard to believe even now, Ms. Norris remembers what occurred: "The woman showed me the old toilet seat, and I just couldn't figure it out. There was really nothing to do; nothing at all. Just unscrew two plastic nuts and take off the old toilet seat and put the new one on. She asked me how much would I charge, and I just didn't know what to say. I mean, it would take me about two minutes to do it, but after all I had driven over there and brought along my tools. So I said I'd charge her $5. The woman was very grateful. And that's the story of my first big break in this industry."

Sandy Norris and Anne Bryant found that they really enjoyed their business, particularly working with wood. They were lucky in finding others to help them learn, including a young contractor who hired them when he was shorthanded.

"The first year or two we made hardly any money. Everything we made we spent on tools. We became so involved that we both quit school and decided we wanted to be full-time carpenters."

At a friend's suggestion, they decided to apply for a formal apprentice-ship training program. First they had to wait until the application period opened; then there was an interim of six months while the applications were processed, followed by another year-long waiting period. By then Ms. Norris was three months over the age limit for apprentices in that area. "If we had known about apprenticeship sooner, or if we had fig-ured out sooner that carpentry was what we wanted to do, apprentice-ship would have made a lot of sense. As it turned out, formal apprenticeship training wasn't necessary for either of us."

The partners got a chance for that indispensable work experience when their contractor friend employed them to help renovate and win-terize an old resort complex in the Pocono Mountains. They lived there for over a year, working directly with an engineer the whole time. "You only learn things in this business by asking questions and then trying yourself. Common sense is your best friend in carpentry. If I don't un-derstand what to do, I draw a plan of what's there already, and when I've finished it, I can generally figure out what the problem is. Anne and I were lucky; our boss had faith in us. When people have faith in you, you can take the risks you need to take to learn."

Relocating to a small city in Massachusetts after Ms. Bryant moved to Texas, Ms. Norris started a business on her own again, advertising in local papers and putting up notices in supermarkets this time also. "It was easier to get started the second time. If you're serious about your work, people will respect you for it. Of course, you have to let people know who you are and what you want. I went to a lumberyard once to pick up some materials, and they gave me junk, just junk—boards that were all warped with knotholes all over them. So I told them I was going up into the loft there to pick out my own materials, and I did. A lot of men I know would have had a problem being that assertive."

With her business established, Ms Norris hired women apprentices. "I think women make excellent carpenters. We have the capability to be extremely careful in our work, even painfully so, to the point of really wanting everything to come out *perfect*."

Many of Ms. Norris' clients are women. "Some women prefer to have other women working in their homes. I remember an old lady in Penn-sylvania who waited until her husband and the men on the work team had left and came up to Anne and me. We were packing up our tools. 'Can I just ask you what's going on,' she said. 'I'm afraid to ask in front of those men, and I know you'll tell me!'

"It's different being a woman carpenter," Ms. Norris states. "For ex-ample, I know there are jobs I haven't gotten because I'm a woman. One time, I was doing a small job for a friend in Boston. I had to go get a special permit for something from the city. I was entitled to it but the clerk kept delaying and delaying. If I had been a man, he probably would have stopped hemming around and asked me right out for five or ten bucks, a bribe, you know, but because I was a woman, he was afraid I'd turn him in."

BASIC RESOURCES

Among the trade and professional organizations which you can contact for career information include:

Associated General Contractors of America, Inc.
1957 E Street NW
Washington, D.C. 20006

Brick Institute of America
1750 Old Meadow Road
McLean, Virginia 22101

International Union of Bricklayers and
    Allied Craftsmen
International Masonry Apprenticeship Trust
815 15th Street NW
Washington, D.C. 20006

International Union of Elevator Constructors
Clark Building (Suite 332)
5565 Sterrett Place
Columbia, Maryland 21044

International Union of Operating Engineers
1125 17th Street NW
Washington, D.C. 20036

Laborers' International Union of North America
905 16th Street NW
Washington, D.C. 20006

National Roofing Contractors Association
1515 North Harlem Avenue
Oak Park, Illinois 60302

United Brotherhood of Carpenters and Joiners
    of America
101 Constitution Avenue NW
Washington, D.C. 20001

CHAPTER 3

MORE MECHANICAL ASPECTS

After the framework of a building has been constructed, the mechanical systems are installed. In commercial or residential buildings these are the plumbing, electrical, and heating and air-conditioning systems.

Two stages are involved. First, the systems are "roughed in," that is, the parts of the systems that go inside the walls are installed. The second stage involves installing the things that we see: light switches and outlets, sinks and toilets, radiators and air conditioners.

All mechanical systems bring something in or carry something out of a building. In the electrical system, electrical power is brought in from the power company's outlets to a central "buss duct" to which the meter is attached. From there it is relayed throughout the building by wires or cables to appliances, fixtures, and electrical outlets.

Water is piped into the building by the plumbing system from water mains under the street. Some of it passes through a hot-water heater, and then hot and cold water are circulated to the sinks and bathrooms in the building. Wastewater is carried out of the building in larger pipes called soil or wastewater pipes. Usually, the plumbing in a building is designed to be part of a "plumbing core," one central location on each floor, to save the expense of extra piping.

Heating or air-conditioning systems utilize a variety of power sources. Most air-conditioning systems are powered by electricity and installed by electricians. Gas or steam heating systems are usually installed by pipefitters. Plumbers or pipefitters also install radiators and the piping for hot-water heating systems whether they burn gas or oil. In some parts of the country, oil-fired hot-air systems are common. Air is heated as it passes through the furnace and blown by a fan throughout the building. In large buildings a special ventilating system draws in air from outside the building, mixes it with the recirculating air, and feeds it back through the furnace. Sheet-metal workers build all the duct work for this hot air/ventilation system.

NOTE FROM THE PAST

A Long History

Women in hardhats seem like a fairly recent phenomenon, but actually women have long been involved in construction. Among the many Indian tribes of America, architecture and construction were the domain solely of the women. Plains Indian women are credited with one of the most innovative and creative dwellings—the tepee, an architectural innovation which could be erected quickly and dismantled and moved easily.

Sheet-Metal Work and Workers

Sheet-metal workers make, install, and repair ventilation systems and air ducts. They work with sheets of metal, cutting, hammering, soldering, and welding them into the needed shapes. About 65,000 sheet-metal workers were employed in 1976, most of them by heating and air-conditioning contractors. Some work for large companies or government agencies that do their own construction work.

Sheet-metal workers do their work in two places, in the shop and at the construction site. In the shop they read blueprints, make patterns of the finished pieces, and construct the pieces of the system that will later be installed at the site. Some sheet-metal workers become specialists in

GETTING IN, MOVING UP: SHEET-METAL WORK

Many sheet-metal workers start as helpers in a sheet-metal shop, cleaning up scraps and fetching tools or pieces of metal. The formal apprenticeship training program is usually three or four years of on-the-job training and 144 hours a year of related classroom instruction.

Sheet-metal work is one of the highest-paid trades. Skilled craft workers in this field may advance to pattern-making a designing specialty, assume a supervisory role, or start their own contracting business.

shop work; some, specialists at installation. Many do both with equal ease.

Many other skilled specialists work in this field. Installing, repairing, and maintaining heating and air-conditioning systems call for a variety of trades. Plumbers and pipefitters cut, bend, and join metal pipes that carry water, steam, or the gas to run a boiler. Electricians wire the building for electrical air-conditioning and heating units. Stationary engineers and building mechanics maintain and repair boilers and air-conditioning units. All the specialties in this field are growing, as new homes and buildings are built and the heating and air-conditioning systems in older buildings are upgraded to be more energy efficient.

Training to Be a Sheet-Metal Worker. Most sheet-metal workers go through an apprenticeship training program lasting three to four years that includes classroom instruction in related subjects such as blueprint reading, drafting, and pattern making. Some sheet-metal workers start as helpers in sheet-metal shops.

GETTING PHYSICAL: HOW TO CARRY HEAVY OBJECTS THE RIGHT WAY

When the male interviewer at the warehouse asked, "What the hell are you going to do when you have to lift that 500-pound box over there?" the perceptive young woman replied, "Call that Russian Olympic weightlifter; he's the only one I know who would be able to do it." Situations like that verge on the absurd. Nobody expects anyone to carry 500 pounds. It's even illegal. In fact, the first things you should learn about a trade are its safety rules and "standard operating practices." You'll never have to carry some heavy things without the help of a partner, and that goes for everyone — male or female.

On the other hand, you'll have to be ready to lift a jackhammer; to pick up a 20-pound, 6-inch block as often as 150 times a day and position it properly; to carry 50 pounds of sheet rock or maneuver a 20-foot ladder; to carry electrical cable on your shoulders up and down staircases and through narrow passages.

Your legs, your arms, your shoulders, your abdominal muscles, your back — all these parts of your body are involved in carrying things, and they must become strong. How? Through exercise. And, of course, you must breathe properly. Keep your heart and lungs in shape through some sort of aerobic exercise and proper diet — and by avoiding cigarettes.

—Vivian Guilfoy, director of the Boston
YWCA program on Nontraditional
Occupations for Women

Sheet-Metal Work Quirks. Sheet-metal work pays very well, but it is exhausting and heavy work. In the shop, workers are expected to lift 50 pounds of metal many times a day. When duct work, roof flashing, or gutters are installed, sheet-metal workers must work high above the ground.

Electrical Work and Workers

Electrical work is one of the youngest of the building trades. It is also, owing to stringent training and safety codes, one of the safest skilled crafts.

In 1976, 300,000 maintenance electricians and 260,000 construction electricians were employed in the United States. Many other skilled jobs for people with electrical training are available. All the machines in this country that run on electricity—from electric can openers to printing presses—need trained people to build and often to operate them. Electric and telephone companies also employ electricians.

Maintenance electricians require a special problem-solving talent. They are the ones who inspect and maintain equipment to prevent breakdowns; if a breakdown occurs, they locate the trouble and make the necessary repairs. Maintenance electricians work in large manufacturing plants, and in hospitals, mines, and office buildings. Wherever it is, their job is to keep the lighting system and the generators and other equipment going.

THE THRILL OF IT ALL: ELECTRICAL WORKERS

"I enjoy explaining what I'm doing to my customers —like what I mean by 'grounded' and things like that."

"People think working with electricity is something mysterious, so they really respect you."

"The master electrician talks all the time he's teaching me. 'Score the thread so it doesn't back up on you. Hold it tight there. Hit it, now. Right.' When he says 'right,' I feel so proud."

THE DAILY GRIND: ELECTRICAL WORKERS

*"We spent two days putting in 8-foot-long fluorescent
lights with reflector shields all over this
renovated building and the architect thought they
looked awful. We had to take them all down and do
the job again."*

*"It's misplaced tools that get me. 'Where's my
ruler?' 'Where's my screwdriver?' 'Where's this
or that?' all day long."*

*"Sometimes I'm so tired at the end of the day those
little colored wires can get confusing
and all look the same color!"*

Construction electricians install the electrical system in a building.
The heating and air-conditioning, lighting, power and refrigeration, and
ventilation in a building can all be run by electricity.

Because mistakes in electrical wiring can cause injuries and fires, governments regulate electrical work very heavily. Almost always electricians must pass a state or city examination and get a license before they

GETTING IN, MOVING UP: ELECTRICAL WORK

Electrical work is highly regulated for some very practical reasons; for example, poor wiring jobs can kill people by electric shock or start fires. A lot of training is necessary to prepare you for the journeyman's license exam. Apprenticeship training programs in this field involve four years of on-the-job training and 144 hours of classroom instruction. Courses in electrical work are also available at private trade schools, vocational-technical schools, and community colleges.

Some electricians can move up through jobs in business and industry, working in plants that make automobiles, machinery, and chemicals or by working for public utilities like electric companies or the phone company. Most construction electricians work for electrical contractors.

can work as journeymen. Part of the examination tests the applicant's knowledge of national, state, and local building codes.

Training to Be an Electrician. Courses in electrical work are offered at many vocational and technical schools, private trade schools, and community colleges. Experienced electricians also frequently take on helpers and teach them the trade.

More electricians obtain training through apprenticeship training programs than do construction craft workers in the other trades. Apprenticeship usually lasts four years and includes 144 hours of classroom instruction a year. The program prepares you to pass the licensing exams for both construction and maintenance work.

Electrical Work Quirks. Electricians must be very good with their hands. Color blindness is prohibitive since many wires are color-coded. The only really strenuous work is carrying heavy cable. In some jobs, though, electricians may need to stand for a long time or work in uncomfortable positions. Electrical workers are better paid and their work less seasonal than most construction jobs.

Some women electricians say there is an advantage to being a woman in the field. Since women are generally smaller, they can work fairly easily in tight places. Their smaller hands often make it easier to do complex wiring jobs in tight places.

Plumbing and Pipefitting Work and Workers

About 385,000 plumbers and pipefitters were working in construction in 1976. Although many people consider plumbing and pipefitting a single

---

SOLAR POWER—IMPLICATIONS FOR CONSTRUCTION JOBS

Using solar power means transforming the heat and light of the sun into a usable energy source. How can you collect, transfer, and store solar energy? That question is a big problem for government, architects, builders, home owners.

Two main approaches have been developed. The first uses the sun to heat water, and then stores the hot water or pumps it throughout a building. In the other way, called a "passive solar system," the sun warms rocks, which store heat, and then air is blown across the rocks to transfer it through conduction.

A lot of time and money has been spent trying to invent better solar energy systems. New systems that are developed will benefit skilled crafts workers for they will be needed to install these systems in stores, homes, factories, and offices.

---

trade, a craft worker can specialize in either. Plumbers generally install and maintain the water systems in buildings—the hot and cold running water, the plumbing fixtures, the wastewater and sprinkler systems. Pipefitters generally work with high- or low-pressure pipes carrying hot water, steam, or industrial gases for heating systems or industrial processes.

Plumbers generally work for plumbing contractors, whereas pipefitters may work for heating contractors or in industries that use piped-in gases for their industrial processes. Such industries include chemical processing, food processing, and oil refineries. Many pipefitters are also employed by gas companies.

Like electrical work, plumbing and pipefitting are highly regulated. Journeymen plumbers and pipefitters must pass a state or local exam and obtain a license. They must also follow state and local building codes that specify what kind of pipes and what kind of construction processes should be used for each job. To qualify to be a private contractor, in most parts of the country you must have a master's license.

Training to Be Plumbers and Pipefitters. Most people in plumbing and pipefitting start as a helper to an experienced craft worker, carrying pipes and equipment and cleaning up after the work is done. Since you must know building code specifications to get a plumber's license, many helpers also take courses at local trade schools or vocational and technical schools. Those who sign up for apprenticeship training in this field can expect to spend from three to five years as an apprentice and take as many as 216 hours a year of related classroom instruction in chemistry, blueprint reading, and drafting, among other subjects.

Plumbing and Pipefitting Quirks. Plumbers and pipefitters are among the highest-paid construction craft workers. Although they may be re-

---

GETTING IN, MOVING UP: PLUMBING

A formal apprenticeship in plumbing usually consists of three to five years of on-the-job training with about 200 hours a year of related classroom instruction. Another way to learn plumbing is to work as a plumber's helper for a plumbing contractor. To qualify as a journeyman plumber, you must pass a special state examination.

Some plumbers and pipefitters move up by working in industrial settings doing installation and maintenance. Others work for public utilities. Some plumbers or pipefitters become supervisors for contractors. Many others become small private contractors.

THE DAILY GRIND: PLUMBERS

> *"This man said after he stopped laughing, 'You*
> *want to go down in the sewer with a lot of rats?'*
> *And then he started laughing again."*
>
> *"Some people look down on plumbers. That shouldn't*
> *be, you have to work hard to get a plumber's*
> *license."*
>
> *"When I started out, I didn't even know how to*
> *hold tools. I didn't know anything, and there*
> *was so much I had to learn."*

quired to work outside and the work can be strenuous, craft workers in these trades are less subject to seasonal layoffs and the cyclical ups and downs of the construction industry than other trades. Plumbing work is sometimes dirty and unpleasant, including a lot of standing or working in uncomfortable positions. On the other hand, plumbing work can be exciting, challenging both your muscles and your mind.

Gina Han, Apprentice Sheet-Metal Worker

In the last year of her sheet-metal apprenticeship, Gina Han is looking forward to being a journeyman: "When I have my journeyman's card I'll have a lot of alternatives. I could work part time and open a small art studio on the side. I might even remarry. Not many men work with sheet metal for 30 years straight; it's too demanding a job. Maybe I won't either, but not because I don't like the work—I *do* like it—but when I have my card, my little boy and I can live anywhere we want to, and I will be able to make enough money to be independent and support us."

Before selecting a building trades career, Ms. Han had been a waitress, a seamstress, and a department store clerk—and she had hated every job. She knew a few things about the skilled trades because her father was a contractor.

"One day I was in the office of a special program for women interested in construction careers, and I saw the notice of openings for sheet-metal apprentices. I thought, why not?" Ironically, if she had known that a skilled trades career could be a possibility for her, Ms. Han might have

THE THRILL OF IT ALL: PLUMBERS

*"First time I learned how to use the machine
that makes threads on pipes I could have done
it all day, I liked it so much."*

*"No, I told them, I know that's not my work —I
would have used only copper pipe on that kind
of job. I'm a real professional, and I know my
job."*

*"I know now that I am strong. And I'm proud of
it."*

made the decision a lot sooner. As she remembers, she "was a real tomboy as a kid and I had the highest mechanical aptitude scores in my whole high school. I wanted to take both wood shop and metal shop, but they wouldn't let me."

The counselors in the office of the women's program suggested that Ms. Han get some physical training before she started sheet-metal work. "You really have to be in shape for this kind of work. You have to be able to lift 50 pounds again and again all day long. I worked out with weights, and it really helped a lot. But I was still exhausted when I came home the first week."

Ms. Han now works for a sheet-metal contractor who works on large commercial buildings. "Some days I work in the shop making heating ducts. Other days I'm working on the construction site installing the ducting. I really prefer the outside work."

About a third of the time, Ms. Han does straight production work, bending sheet metal and soldering it together into standard duct work. She says that "some sheet-metal work is a lot like sewing except that you work with a blueprint. First you take this flat material and, using a pattern, you cut it out and form it into the shape the engineer wants.

"If you're really good at patterns you can make a lot of money in sheet-metal work. I have met layout guys working in aircraft industries who make $30,000 a year building hyperbolic curves and things like that."

Gina Han cautions that sheet-metal work can be dangerous. "You simply cannot go to work tired, or you'll make dumb mistakes and hurt yourself. Last week I hit myself on the head with a hammer. Just one of those dumb things. But the guys with experience always help the new people with safety. There are government regulations, too, about how to do things—like you can't wear gloves or have long hair on the job.

"The hair rule was a real bummer for me. I had hair down to my waist when I started. They made me cut it." But Ms. Han thinks these rules may change as more women go into sheet-metal work, and the industry adapts.

Ms. Han has a very good relationship with the men she works with. "In this trade, you have to help each other or someone'll get hurt. I've never had any trouble of any kind. I really like the guys I work with, and they really like me. I remember only one out-of-place remark, but the guy didn't really mean anything by it.

"This one time, I was on a construction site and I stepped off the elevator. There was this work crew from another sheet-metal contractor looking at me. The man on the ladder said, 'Well, look what we have here, a lady construction worker. What trade are you in, honey?' 'I'm a sheet-metal worker,' I said. The guy on the ladder took off his tool belt, and climbed down the ladder. 'I'm quitting,' he said. 'I always said I'd quit if this happened.' So I just answered him, 'Shoot, here's a man quitting after just *talking* to a woman. He hasn't even worked with one yet.' Everybody laughed. And he climbed back up the ladder."

Ms. Han once met a woman carpenter who complained a lot about working with men, and her reaction was that "if you don't like working with men or you don't like being outside, what in the world are you doing being a carpenter?

"I think the reason I get along so well with the men I work with is because I'm a very traditional woman. The fellows have really treated me like a lady and that's because I act like one. I'm not into women's movement things although I can respect women who are. But, on the job, I'm not waving any signs. I'm not here to prove anything—just to do my job. If you're antagonistic to men, they'll pick up on it and make life rough for you.

"Another reason I get along is that I am very good at what I do. I'm a specialist in stainless steel. People respect that. If you try hard, if you try to learn, they'll respect you for that too."

Ms. Han is proud because "I'm pretty sure I'm the only woman in California in sheet-metal work. That's going to change soon though, and things'll be different then. I met a woman once who was an oral historian at a California university. 'You really ought to be tape-recording people like me,' I told her. 'There are a lot of women in other trades, like me— the first in our trade. We're the pioneers. It's going to be a whole other thing for the women who follow us.' "

BASIC RESOURCES

Write or phone the organizations listed for career information.

Electrical Work

International Brotherhood of Electrical Workers
1125 15th Street NW
Washington, D.C. 20005

National Electrical Contractors Association
7315 Wisconsin Avenue NW
Washington, D.C. 20014

National Joint Apprenticeship and Training
Committee for the Electrical Industry
9700 East George Palmer Highway
Lanham, Maryland 20801

Sheet-metal, Plumbing and Pipefitting, and Allied Trades

Air Conditioning and Refrigeration Contractors of America
20 North Wacker Drive (Suite 2232)
Chicago, Illinois 60606

American Society of Heating, Refrigeration and Air
Conditioning Engineers
1016 20th Street NW
Washington, D.C. 20036

Mechanical Contractors Association of America
666 3d Avenue (Suite 1464)
New York, New York 10017

National Association of Plumbing-Heating-Cooling Contractors
1016 20th Street NW
Washington, D.C. 20036

National Automatic Sprinkler and Fire Control Association
P.O. Box 719
Mt. Kisco, New York 10549

Plumbing-Heating-Cooling Information Center
35 East Wacker Drive
Chicago, Illinois 60601

Sheet-Metal and Air Conditioning Contractors'
National Association, Inc.
8224 Old Courthouse Road
Tyson's Corner, Vienna, Virginia 22180

Sheet-Metal Workers' International Association
100 Connecticut Avenue NW
Washington, D.C. 20036

United Association of Journeymen and Apprentices of the
Plumbing and Pipe Fitting Industry of the United States and Canada
901 Massachusetts Avenue NW
Washington, D.C. 20001

CHAPTER 4

THE FINISHING STAGE—
Getting the Job Done

When the framework of the building has been sheathed (covered with wooden siding or shingles, glass or aluminum panels, bricks or masonry), and the mechanical systems installed, the finishing work can begin. Finishing work involves plastering or sheetrocking the walls, preparing and painting them, installing all the cabinets and built-in furniture, hanging the doors, plastering the ceilings, and laying hardwood floors or installing vinyl flooring or carpeting. Since this is the part of a building that everybody sees, finishing work is done with careful attention to detail. Finishing work requires the greatest variety of craft workers.

A great deal of finishing work is done by carpenters and related specialists. This work includes building and installing cabinets, closets, and counters; putting in sound insulation; and applying baseboard and ceiling molding. Carpenters build stairs, frame them, and install handrails. Sometimes carpentry finishing on large construction jobs is done by specialists. One person installs the doors; another, the hardwood floors; another, the Formica counters; and so forth.

In some cases, particularly on small projects, carpenters also install the tape sheetrock. Sheetrock or gypsum wallboard is a rigid wall covering which looks like a plaster wall when it is finished. It is nailed to the framework of a room in large pieces. Where the pieces meet and where there are indentations from the nails, a special joint compound cement is used to fill in the cracks. Perforated paper tape is applied over the seams, and covered with the joint cement. When it dries, the wall is sanded or sponged smooth. This type of wall construction is known as drywall construction, and on large jobs sheetrock installers and tapers do the work instead of general carpenters.

The old way to finish walls is by using lath and plaster. Since plaster

WELDING AND WELDERS

Welding is a skill used by many craft workers, such as carpenters, plumbers, pipefitters, sheet-metal workers, and ironworkers, as well as a construction trade in itself.

Welding involves fusing two materials, usually both metal, using heat. All heavy equipment — cars, bridges, ships, building frameworks, anything built with metal — once had welders working on it. In gas welding, a welder holds a rod of metal in one hand and a gas-fired blowtorch in the other. The blowtorch melts the metal rod, and the liquid metal from the rod joins the pieces of metal together. In arc welding an electric power supply is attached to the metal rod, and another power supply to the piece of metal to be welded. When the rod is held at the right distance from the piece of metal, a spark jumps across between them. This spark (the electrical arc) melts the end of the rod. In factories, welders operate welding machines, which requires far less skill.

Welders must know the characteristics of different metals and the welding processes. Construction welders who work on bridges or other jobs where the strength of the weld is critical may be required to pass a welding examination.

Welding is taught in many vocational schools, some community colleges, and at some large companies. It is one of the easiest construction trades to get training in and one of the trades in which women have been most successful. Women have a reputation as good welders, perhaps because they are usually considered patient, persistent, and detail oriented.

is wet when it is applied, it must be put on a supporting surface, called lath, which may be made of wood, gypsum, fiberboard, or metal (for bathtub enclosures) and is nailed to the framework of the room by *lathers*. *Plasterers* cover the lath with plaster, a powdered material made from ground limestone mixed with water to a thick consistency. Several coats are necessary. For the finish coat, the plaster is mixed either with sand to give it a textured finish or with lime to give it a smooth finish. Plaster walls provide good sound insulation and an attractive appearance, but are much more expensive than sheetrock in time, labor, and materials.

Ceilings are finished the same ways that walls are, with lath and plaster or with wallboard. Ceilings are sometimes covered with acoustical tile to deaden noise. "Hung ceilings" are made of tiles set into a metal framework hung from the true ceiling. This technique is frequently used to hide exposed pipes or ducts.

Floor-covering installers put in vinyl flooring (tiles or sheets) and glue

GETTING PHYSICAL: HOW TO PUSH AND PULL THE RIGHT WAY

Your hands are full, and there's a 20-pound bag of plaster on the ground You decide to push it with your foot. Suddenly there's a sharp pain in your knee—you've twisted it. But instead of taking the pain as a warning, you just switch legs and continue to push the bag across the floor. Now your knee hurts even more. Without realizing it, you have set various muscles and bones against one another.

If you're pushing, learn to position your body to take full advantage of your body strength. If your technique isn't working, don't keep pushing. Reposition yourself and start again.

Don't forget to use your head too: Why push or pull something if a dolly is available? Learn the tricks of the trade.

—Vivian Guilfoy, director of the Boston
YWCA program on Nontraditional
Occupations for Women

it to wooden subflooring. Carpeting may be installed, glued on or taped with wide double-sided tape.

Ceramic tile and marble or terrazzo (marble chip) floors are installed by specialists known as tile setters. They lay square ceramic tiles glued to a mesh base onto a cement or mastic setting bed that has not yet hardened. Grouting material or mortar is used to fill in between the tiles and the excess is wiped off.

When the walls have been put up, the ceilings finished, and the floor covering put on, the rooms are painted or covered with wallpaper. Painters treat unfinished surfaces with a primer (first coat of paint), then cover it with a finish coat. Paperhangers use a special paste to apply the wallpaper. When the interior surfaces of the building have been painted or papered, the building is given a final cleaning by construction laborers and then turned over to its owner.

Two of the most important trades in this phase of construction are cabinetmaking and painting.

Cabinetmaking and Cabinetmakers

Woodworking craftsmen who specialize in making furniture, kitchen cabinets, and built-to-order woodwork of all kinds, cabinetmakers are skilled in the most detailed and exacting kind of carpentry. Unlike gen-

ENERGY CONSERVATION AND BUILDING RETROFIT

Altering buildings to conserve energy is called "building retrofit"—a fast-growing field with a real future for craft workers.

Workers will be needed to install insulation to save on heating and air-conditioning bills. Heating and air-conditioning specialists will be called on to fine-tune heating and air-conditioning systems. There will be a demand for glaziers and carpenters to make and install storm doors and windows. Electricians will be needed to install energy-efficient lighting systems.

eral or house carpenters, cabinetmakers almost always work in factories or in woodworking shops. Those in factories tend to make or finish only a part of the completed product. Those who work in shops or are self-employed tend to do a greater variety of things, from custom-made built-in furniture to special millwork used in the restoration of old buildings.

Cabinetmakers must know the special characteristics of different kinds of wood and wood finishes. Unlike general carpenters, cabinetmakers must be concerned with the finish of their work. This means that cabinetmakers often may use glue and dowels instead of nails if a nail

THE THRILL OF IT ALL: CABINETMAKERS

"I love making something beautiful, something special—a piece of furniture, a good-looking doorway, a porch railing."

"The feel of the wood when I've sanded it really smooth, the smell of the wood when I'm working on it—those are both real thrills."

"Various kinds of wood are completely different. They behave differently in your hands. I've kept a little piece of every kind of wood I've worked with."

would show on the finished piece. Most cabinetmakers also prefer to work with hardwoods, such as maple, oak, rosewood, or teak, that have a natural grain, and to use a clear finish so the beauty of the wood shows through. They may sometimes cover a finished piece of work with veneer, a thin layer of a piece of hardwood, or a laminated plastic veneer such as Formica.

Training to Be a Cabinetmaker. Nearly all cabinetmakers learn their trade from other cabinetmakers, not in formal training programs. Many start as a helper to a master craft worker. Woodworking and wood sculpture courses are sometimes the first entry to a cabinetmaking career. General carpenters may develop their skills in cabinetmaking and open their own shop.

There are also formal apprenticeship training programs, usually available only in the larger cabinetmaking manufacturing plants, that include four years of on-the-job training and after-hours classroom instruction.

Cabinetmaking Quirks. Cabinetmakers must be patient, careful, and precise. They need a good sense of design and excellent skill in using their hands. Practically all cabinetmaking is inside work using both power and hand tools.

Painting and Paperhanging and Painters and Paperers

Painters and paperers are employed by painting contractors or building maintenance companies; they may also work directly for large construction firms. Hotels, hospitals, shipyards, schools, government, and industry employ painters for building maintenance. Approximately 410,000

THE DAILY GRIND: CABINETMAKERS

"Too many people think that if you hire a woman you don't have to pay as much."

"I find I'm taking in the same hourly money, but the cost of materials is going up and up and up."

"Some days when all I've done in the shop is sanding, I think my arms are going to fall off, and my mouth feels like it's filled with gravel."

---

painters and 15,000 paperhangers were employed in construction and maintenance jobs in 1976.

Production painters work in factories painting finished products like cars, furniture, or toys. There were about 104,000 production painters in 1976. Unlike construction or maintenance painters who tend to use rollers and brushes, production painters use machinery like spray machines and dipping tanks. As production painting has become increasingly mechanized, production painters have begun to be involved in more preparation work, such as taping or masking parts that should not be exposed to paint, and in more machine maintenance and repair.

Construction and maintenance painters must also know how to erect scaffolding or staging and prepare surfaces for painting. New wood surfaces that have never been painted need a primer coat before a finishing coat can be applied. New plaster walls must "cure" or stand a while before oil-based paint can be applied. New drywall needs a latex-base prime coat.

Old surfaces take more time to prepare: chipped and cracked paint must be sanded smooth; holes or cracks must be patched with plaster and sanded smooth; old glossy or semigloss paint must be roughed up with sandpaper to make new paint adhere; greasy wall surfaces must be cleaned with a strong detergent.

Training to Be a Painter or Paperer. Most painters and paperhangers start out as helpers to more experienced craft workers. A high school diploma is not necessary. Very few apprenticeship training programs exist for this craft. The few available programs usually require three years of on-the-job training and 144 hours of related classroom instruction a year.

Painting and Papering Quirks. Painters and paperhangers must stand for long periods of time. They are required to do a lot of bending, reaching, and stooping. Painting and papering are among the least dangerous of the skilled trades, but the workers are paid a little less than those in

---

GETTING IN, MOVING UP: PAINTING

Painting is one of the easiest trades in which to get a job. Many people start painting as a way to make money while going to school, others start out working for paint and wallpaper stores. Some apprenticeship training opportunities are available in construction painting and some industries.

Painters may advance to being estimators, foremen, or painting contractors. Industrial painting usually pays much better than house painting.

---

other crafts. Painters are never required to work outside when it's hot, cold, or wet because paint won't adhere well in that kind of weather; when the weather is bad, however, most painters can find indoor work. Painters must have good color perception, and paperers must be able to line things up correctly vertically and horizontally.

Juana Johnson, Painter

"My friends ask me what I'm doing now. And I tell them I'm a painter. 'Painting what?' they ask me. I say, 'Houses.' I paint houses and I love it.'"

Juana Johnson is 19 and had been unable to find work until she joined a special program for women at the YWCA. "The program turned out good for me. I got a chance to try out carpentry and electrical work, painting, and other things. Mostly, I liked painting."

Within a week after the program finished, Ms. Johnson had a job with a large building maintenance corporation as a painter's helper. "There's only one other woman in the company; that's Annie. She's a carpenter. We're pretty good friends.

"I work for a guy who gets along with me all right. But he believes that women can't do anything they want, that a man has to be there to help women out. I like working with the men there, but sometimes I think they're too bossy.

"But worse than that are the people where I paint. Some of them come right over to me while I'm standing there painting their walls and say to me, 'Are you really a painter?' So I just tell them, 'Look, I went to a special training program and learned painting and lots of other things, and I've been painting for nine or ten months now. I'm really good at it.'

"The first time you go into a place, people are very worried. They've got good rugs or new furniture, they don't want paint spots on their stuff. It's almost like an insult to me, because I'm really careful. But they don't know that yet.

"In the last two months we've been working in this big housing project, painting the apartments. There, the people have gotten to know me, and they ask for me because they like my work. Other people choose me because they're women by themselves, and they feel more secure with another woman around the house.

"Most of last year, we painted outside. During the winter, we've been painting apartments inside. In the morning, I start at 8. The first thing I do is go into the room to see what I need. Then I go down to the basement and bring up my things—drop cloths, rollers, brushes, and ladders. The man I work with brings up the paint for me. It comes in 5-gallon paint cans, and it's pretty heavy for me—I'm only 105 pounds and not even 5 feet tall. But I can carry paint cans around an apartment when I need to.

"It takes me about an hour to prepare the room for painting; I sand the walls and putty the holes. Then I do the ceiling as fast as I can without rushing. I've learned to time myself, and my speed has really been improving. It's important not to get rushed. If you rush, you tense up, and your shoulders really ache. The guy I work with and I are usually ahead of our schedule, but we never rush.

"Painting is a good job for a woman. It doesn't have much heavy work. You may have to move the ladder a little more often if you're short like me.

"I really enjoy my work. When you think about it, I'm really lucky. I don't have a high school diploma, I'd never even had another job, and here I am working a job that pays good money and getting better at it all the time.

"I'm real pleased with my life. I love seeing clean things. In this job, you go into a house that looks awful, and after three or four days, you've made it a completely different place."

BASIC RESOURCES

For information on careers contact the organizations listed.

Floor, Ceiling, and Wall Installers and Finishers

Bricklayers, Masons and Plasterers' International Union of America
815 15th Street NW
Washington, D.C. 20005

Carpet and Rug Institute
P.O. Box 2048
Dalton, Georgia 30720

International Association of Marble, Slate, and Stone Polishers, Rubbers and
    Sawyers, Tile and Marble Setters' Helpers and Marble Mosaic and Terrazzo
    Workers' Helpers
821 15th Street Street NW
Washington, D.C. 20005

International Association of Wall and Ceiling Contractors/Gypsum Drywall
    Contractors International
1711 Connecticut Avenue NW
Washington, D.C. 20009

International Council for Lathing and Plastering
221 North LaSalle Street
Chicago, Illinois 60601

International Brotherhood of Painters and Allied Trades
1750 New York Avenue NW
Washington, D.C. 20006

International Union of Bricklayers and Allied Craftsmen
815 15th Street NW
Washington, D.C. 20005

National Joint Painting, Decorating and Drywall Finishing Apprenticeship and
    Training Committee
1709 New York Avenue NW (Suite 110)
Washington, D.C. 20006

National Lathing Industries Joint Apprenticeship Program
815 16th Street NW
Washington, D.C. 20006

Operative Plasterers' and Cement Masons' International Association of the
    United States and Canada
1125 17th Street NW
Washington, D.C. 20036

Painting and Decorating Contractors Association of America
7223 Lee Highway
Falls Church, Virginia 22046

Resilient Floor Covering Institute
1030 15th Street NW (Suite 350)
Washington, D.C. 20005

Tile Contractors Association of America, Inc.
112 North Alfred Street
Alexandria, Virginia 22314

Wood, Wire, and Metal Lathers International Union
815 16th Street NW
Washington, D.C. 20006

Welders

American Welding Society
2501 Northwest 7th Street
Miami, Florida 33125

International Union, United Automobile, Aerospace and Agricultural Implement
    Workers of America
8000 East Jefferson Avenue
Detroit, Michigan, 48214

CHAPTER 5

COLLECTIVELY OR ON YOUR OWN?

A skilled craft worker has the choice of working in a union, for a non-union employer, or for herself.

In a Construction Union

Construction unions are organized into locals, town- or area-based groups of craft workers. The business agent of the local negotiates with contractors to get jobs. When the union has a contract to do a certain job for a construction company, it assigns the required number of journeymen and apprentices to do the work.

Union members receive the highest wages and benefits. If a union local is successful in getting work, you don't have to go out and look for jobs. You are not, however, prohibited from seeking unionized jobs on your own.

However, in a construction union the work may be seasonal. When the weather is bad, union members who must work outside can't always work. Work is also cyclical; when the construction business is booming, there are lots of jobs and overtime pay. But in a business downturn, union construction jobs are the first ones to go.

For a Private Employer

If you work for a private employer, such as a company, a factory, a hospital, or a university, you will have a steady job, usually inside, with good benefits but at a lower wage and with fewer fringe benefits than in construction unions. Skilled craft workers are usually among the last people laid off when business is bad. Company jobs are usually easier for women to get than union jobs, and once you are employed, there are often opportunities for advancement.

CONSTRUCTION UNION HALLS—HOW THEY WORK

Congratulations! You're a union journeyman. You've just received your union card—your "book." You've got a union hall (a "local").

Now, what about the job? How do you get your assignments? You go down to the hall, usually very early in the morning, and try to see the BA (business agent). Let him know you're ready, willing, and able. The BA may have orders for only a limited number of journeymen that day. If you're lucky, he'll send you out to a job. It's hard to say how a BA selects the people who are sent. It probably helps if you know the BA, have a good track record, are "one of the boys" or one of a required minority for the job.

It definitely helps if the super (the union foreman on a specific job) wants you. If you learn about a job from him, all you have to do is show up at the job site and he can sign you on immediately.

You also have the option of "pounding the pavement," follow-up on any "leads" you have read about or a friend has mentioned. In that case, you just walk up to the union foreman there and ask for a job.

Now you're working, maybe for a couple of days, or if it's a major construction job, maybe a year. You show up each morning. If the weather is bad or something else holds up a contractor, you must stay there until about 10:00 AM. If there's no work, there's no pay either. Jobs may be interrupted for months at a time, particularly in the winter months in the North.

—Vivian Guilfoy, director of the Boston
YWCA program on Nontraditional
Occupations for Women

The disadvantages are that the work will mostly be repair and maintenance and the working conditions vary a great deal from company to company. It's worth checking with employees to find out what a particular company is like. Also, it can be difficult to change from one type of employment to the other unless the company is affiliated with a construction union.

On Your Own

Most construction work in this country is done by small private contractors. The 1972 Census of Construction found that over half of the more than 900,000 contractors had *no* employees and that 62 percent had four or fewer employees.

Most of these small contractors worked as subcontractors. On large construction jobs, a "general contractor" agrees to do the work and hires smaller or specialized contractors to do specific kinds of work—concrete, finishing carpentry, laying hardwood floors, etc. Most small contractors work in residential construction.

Many skilled craftsmen who work in industry or for large contractors "moonlight" working as a small private contractor after work hours. Unemployed union craft workers also moonlight, at lower pay than they usually receive, when they can't get union employment.

Being a private contractor has some real advantages. The first one is the obvious sense of independence and flexibility. Also, it's usually fairly easy to get started. If you don't have apprentices or other people working for you, you probably don't have any licensing concerns. To find out what your state requires, call the nearest office of the United States Small Business Administration.

SMALL BUSINESS ADMINISTRATION

An agency of the Federal Government, the Small Business Administration (SBA) is something you should know about if you want to be a contractor.

The SBA can help you get a bank loan or guarantee a loan for you. You can also get basic advice on starting a small business through SBA-sponsored courses, workshops, publications, and counseling. Their one-day prebusiness workshop can help you think through the major steps in starting your own business.

Also, a special "SBA 8a Procurement Program" helps small businesses that are "socially or economically disadvantaged" get government contracts. To qualify, you need to prove you have had trouble getting loans or making other business arrangements. Even though few women's companies have been helped by this program, the benefits are so good you should ask anyway.

For more information, visit or contact your nearest SBA field office and ask for its list of free publications. You can also write the Washington office (1441 L Street NW, Washington, D.C. 20416) to request the list. Be sure to get the business plan for the kind of business you want to start. If you want to see a counselor, it's a good idea to fill out the business plan ahead of time, so that he or she can get together the necessary background information to help you.

SBA publications that will give you valuable information include:

—*SBA —What It Does*
—*Women and the Small Business Administration*
—*Business Plan for Small Construction Firms, No. 221*
—*Business Plan for Small Service Firms, No. 153*

The risks involved in going into business for yourself can be great. It's expensive to buy medical insurance or the equivalent of workman's compensation for yourself. If you don't get many customers, you may lose any money you have invested in your business. Your expenses add up —advertising, phone, answering service, business cards, tools, transportation—surprisingly fast.

Contractors do have an advantage in starting a small business: the initial investment is not so great as that for other types of small businesses.

There are risks in success as well. If you get a great many contracts and you can't complete them all by the time you said you would, you can lose customers. You will have to prepare for success by figuring out who can help you get your work done if you are backed up. If you have been working in the trade for a while, you probably know people whose work you respect. If they'll agree to help out if you need them, you'll be prepared. You also might get jobs on their recommendation.

Getting Those First Customers. You probably get your first customers through relatives or friends. Advertising in local papers and putting up notices on supermarket bulletin boards are good ways of seeking business.

Some women contractors specialize in working for women customers. Women in small businesses, from "handywomen" to electricians, report that many women prefer to have women craft workers come into their homes. Some women tell of barter arrangements with their customers when they are starting out. For example, one woman did a minor plumbing repair for a printer in exchange for business cards.

Getting/Staying Insured. Insurance is such a complex subject, you will want to talk to the Small Business Administration, your lawyer, or an insurance agent to find out what's best for you. The most important kinds of insurance for a small contractor just starting out are:

Disability Insurance. It pays for the time you are away from your work because of illness or injury.

Health Insurance. It pays a major proportion of your medical bills if you are injured in an accident or hospitalized.

Liability Insurance. This covers accidents in which you damage other people's property.

Workmen's Compensation. This covers on-the-job injuries for your employees. You *must* buy it. (Most people, when they start out, pay people who work with them as subcontractors not as employees, thereby avoiding some of the expenses of having employees, such as Social Security, workmen's compensation, and unemployment insurance.)

Unemployment Insurance. It provides for your employees in case of layoff and is paid to the state in which you work.

Government Regulations. All sorts of rules and regulations influence private contractors and builders. Zoning laws regulate where buildings are built and how big and what they can be. Building codes specify materials or construction standards and the procedures to be followed during construction, such as the strength of scaffolding. Building or renovation plans in some cities must be submitted in advance to the city building department and then to the fire department. Occupational Safety and Health Administration (OSHA) regulations are federal work safety regulations administered by the Department of Labor, governing working conditions including the exposure to hazardous materials. A license to be a private contractor is necessary in some states; in some

WHO'S WHO ON A CONSTRUCTION SITE

Apprentice. A person in a formal skilled craft training program that includes on-the-job training and related classroom instruction.

Registered Trainee. A person who doesn't meet apprentice program requirements but works on a construction site like an apprentice, getting apprentice wages and being entitled to training.

Union Apprentice Coordinator. The person responsible for seeing that apprentices get the training they need. Coordinators also serve as advisers and help find jobs for apprentices.

Union Business Agent. The full-time union official managing the day-to-day relationship between union members and the place they work. For example, a business agent hears grievances and enforces labor agreements.

Journeyman. A skilled craft worker who has completed the apprenticeship in a trade. Journeymen supervise work crews on construction sites.

Foreman. The person in charge of all the journeymen in his or her trade on the construction site. The foreman makes sure the work crews meet their work schedules.

Job Superintendent. The person who directs foremen. On a big construction job, he or she may be responsible for a particular phase of construction.

General Superintendent. The one in charge of all the work on a major construction job.

Project Manager. The individual who sets up all work schedules, policies, and procedures and oversees the flow of supplies. The project manager is the boss.

large cities you may need a city license as well. Journeymen plumbers and electricians are always licensed.

Estimating a Job. One of the hardest things to do in contracting is estimating. If you make too high an estimate, you may not get the job. If your estimate is too low, the job can cost you money. Material costs are generally easy to estimate; it is the labor costs that are difficult.

In estimating, experience really helps. Collect your own experience. If you write down how much time you spent and the specific job you did, you will soon be able to estimate how long certain types of work take.

Good courses in estimating construction work are usually offered at community or junior colleges. Standard estimating books can be very helpful too. These books have tables that are easy to use once you get the hang of them. The *National Repair and Remodeling Estimator* (Craftsman Books, 543 Stevens Avenue, Solano Beach, California 92075) is one of these books.

Ways of Organizing Your Business. Of the three main ways to organize your business, the simplest is an individual proprietorship, a form in which the business has one owner and a low overhead or cost of operation, and has few, if any, employees. About a third of the builder contractors in this country fall into this category.

A partnership is a business owned by two or more people who work together as equals. Sometimes partners will specialize in different aspects of the business: one partner may do the books, and another may do all the estimating. Partners share both the profits and the losses of their business.

When a business gets big it should be incorporated. Corporations do not need to be huge and wealthy, however. There are legal and tax advantages to incorporating; if your corporation goes bankrupt, your savings and your house will be safe from the corporation's creditors.

Getting Good Advice. To advise you on how to organize your business, comply with government regulations, collect from customers who don't pay, and to protect you if you are sued, you need a lawyer. Choose and contact one *before* you need his or her services; it will save you time and effort. Call your state or city bar association to get a listing of lawyers or to find out about available free legal services, or ask a friend who's in business for herself to recommend a lawyer.

A bookkeeper can help you set up a way to keep records of all your business financial transactions, how much you spent on lumber or tools, the repair of your truck or van as well as how much you made on each job.

Accountants can advise you on the ins and outs of taxes, budgets, and investment, and can help you save or make more money.

WHO'S WHO IN THE OFFICE IN CONSTRUCTION WORK

Estimator. The person who works with blueprints and engineering specifications to estimate the amount of and cost of the materials, the kinds of machines, and the number of hours of each kind of labor that will be necessary to complete a job.

Purchasing Agent. The one who buys the supplies and arranges for the purchase or rental of equipment.

Expeditor. The individual who schedules the delivery of material and equipment and arranges for the arrival of work teams.

For more information about white-collar construction-related jobs, write or phone:

Women in Construction
2800 West Lancaster Avenue
Fort Worth, Texas 76107

or check your library for or order from the publisher (Contemporary Books, Inc., 180 North Michigan Avenue, Chicago, Illinois 60601) the 1977 hardcover edition ($8.95) or the 1978 paperback edition ($5.95):

A Woman's Guide to New Careers in Real Estate, by Ruth Rejinis.

Amy Rodaikis, Construction Firm Administrator

After she started working 10 years ago as a teacher, Amy Rodaikis discovered that "it was just not the right kind of work for me. When I quit, my brother, who is a contractor, got me a job as a clerk at a construction site. You've seen those trailers on big construction sites; inside them is pretty much a whole office to run all the paperwork connected with the job—payroll, estimates, orders, everything. I typed letters and did bookkeeping at first.

"The first six months were pure hell. The men just didn't want me around. I think I know some of the attitudes of the men on the work site. They sometimes think women come there to catch a husband. Or, if they think the woman is a woman's libber, then they conclude that she's just out to prove something, not to work. They don't realize that women like me *have* to work; the younger men are more likely to understand that."

Ms. Rodaikis advises that "it's important to find a place to work where there are people willing to teach you. After the men got to know me and to know that I was eager to learn, they helped me. They taught me to read blueprints, for example. The surveyor taught me a little about his job, too. Working in that trailer was a great opportunity for me."

Part of the work Ms. Rodaikis did was helping the estimator. She became so interested in estimating that she went to night school to learn more about it. In time, her estimating work became more and more important to her company, and another woman, whom Ms. Rodaikis hired and trained, replaced her as clerk. "I was doing simple cost projections based on my estimates and then cost reports on the jobs for which I had done the projections. This work was very helpful to my construction company."

What she had done at that site was so valuable that Ms. Rodaikis was asked to set up similar jobs at six of the company's other construction sites.

In the course of her new work she began to deal with government inspectors. She started helping her company with requisitions, the formal requests for payment. She feels that this was her big break.

"I did so well with the government people that the company realized I could be very important to them. The government group would give me more on the requisitions than they had given the men who had made the requests. I started branching out. Now I am working in the financial end of the business, working directly with several project managers to put deals together, estimate costs, hire on-site superintendents, contract with subcontractors, etc. I do everything now."

Ms. Rodaikis belongs to a local chapter of Women in Construction, a national organization of women working in office jobs in construction companies. They have monthly meetings. "It's mostly a social and an educational organization, but you meet women it's important to know. For example, one project got in a bind because one of our suppliers didn't have enough of the door hardware we had ordered. I knew a woman in the supplier's company, and I called her. She went out to their warehouses and nosed around until she actually found enough hardware for us. Everybody in my company was amazed.

"There are beginning to be enough of us so that it will make a difference. I know I'm one of a very few women in this business. In some of the boards and committees I'm on, I'm the token woman, and I know it. But since I'm there, I'm going to use my position to help other women."

CHAPTER 6

BECOMING A PRO

In the skilled trades ultimately it's experience, not education, that counts. To learn a trade, you must have hands-on work experience. Getting access to that experience can be as hard as getting your first job in other fields. There are some real advantages to on-the-job learning. For one thing, it means you can earn while you learn. It also means that when you finish your training, you are not a beginner, but a professional who knows her job. This is particularly true if you choose apprenticeship as your way of entering the trades.

"Elite" Trades

Plumbing and electrical work are called the "elite trades." In these trades you must take state exams and obtain a state license to get journeyman status. To take the exams, you must have both job experience and course work. In some states licenses are needed by carpenters, pipefitters, and other craft workers, but plumbing and electrical work are generally considered the fields with the toughest requirements.

The license exams are difficult, and sometimes people take them several times before they pass. Even George Meany, former president of the AFL-CIO, was not ashamed to say it took him two tries to become a journeyman plumber!

Getting Training, a Problem for Women

Women face special problems in getting training for the skilled trades. Although it's easy for women to take some basic courses in their chosen field, it's very difficult for women to get work experience. The best work experience positions are hard for anyone to obtain, man or woman, but women have an especially hard time.

472

Informal Chances to Learn. Most women haven't had enough informal chances to learn basic skills or find out about the kinds of jobs available in the skilled trades. Girls usually haven't been taught by their fathers how to use hammers and other hand tools whereas many boys end their school years with a good understanding of what the skilled trades are like. To catch up, women need to find special chances to learn from books or other people.

Low Age Limits. By the time many women decide on a career in the skilled trades, they may be over the age limits for the usual training programs. Many women don't decide on a nontraditional career until after they have already tried such traditional fields as teaching or waitressing or secretarial work. A girl must decide to go to a vocational-technical school at the end of eighth grade; by the early teens, she must decide on a craft. Most girls that age aren't ready to settle on a nontraditional career.

In formal apprenticeship training the same age barrier exists. Although age limits have been outlawed in California and Washington, upper age limits for many programs are around 25. Most women returning to the work force after having children are older than that and simply ineligible to apply.

As more women become carpenters, plumbers, electricians, and painters, girls will consider the skilled trades at an earlier age. Until then women will find they have to work a little harder to get around the age barriers to get work experience.

Counselors and Teachers. Job counselors in employment centers, guidance counselors in schools, and personnel staff in industry are sometimes reluctant to give help to women who want to go into the trades. Some don't believe women are able to do construction work; others can't be bothered taking the extra time to find a woman the work experience she needs in the trades. You may find that some counselors may try to talk you into another kind of job.

If you meet such counselors, you will have to know which job you want and be sure of your right to have it.

Even some of the teachers in training programs, whether in a course or at the job site, may give you a false idea of what is expected by giving you all the hard work or all the dirty work. On the other hand, the opportunities may be equally limited if you are given all the easy work. If this happens to you, ask a friend or counselor to help you talk to your teacher about your needs and concerns.

Unemployment. In the skilled trades unemployment has been a very serious problem in some parts of the country, running as high as 40 percent for carpenters, for example. In these areas the resistance to training or hiring women is strong. Why should the carpenters union or a contractor accept a woman trainee when 40 percent of union journeymen are out of work? And these are "men supporting a family"! What people forget, of course, is that almost all women looking for full-time work are supporting themselves or helping support a family, too. You might need to remind them.

Women Have to Prove Seriousness. To get work experience in the construction trades, women have to prove they are seriously committed to a career. If a woman can show in some way that she has committed herself to a construction trades career, it will help her get work experience. Adult education courses, correspondence courses, and related work experience (even if it's only working on a relative's house) really help people believe you are committed.

If you want to be a professional, you will need to try every way you can to get work experience. Waiting for your name to come up on an apprenticeship list is not enough. While you're waiting, try trade schools, company training programs, government-sponsored special training programs. The more things you try for, the more chances you will have to become a skilled craft worker. What's more, experience gained in such courses and programs may count toward becoming a journeyman. The important thing to remember is to try *everything* until you find a way to get the skills you need.

Formal Apprenticeship Programs—a Job Plus

In formal apprenticeship programs you get on-the-job training and classroom instruction *free* and earn money at the same time.

When you enter an apprenticeship program you make a formal written agreement with an employer stating how much you will earn, how long you will be in training, and what you will be taught. Generally, there is a probationary period of six months during which the employer may end the program; after that the employer *must* allow you to finish the program if *you* want to and there's work for you to do. As an apprentice, on the other hand, you are free to leave the program at any time. If you complete the training, you will become a certified journeyman, a skilled craft worker whose qualifications are recognized and respected in every state.

Apprenticeship varies from trade to trade, but usually takes from two to five years and includes from 144 to over 200 hours of classroom instruction a year. An apprentice is paid about half the wages of a journeyman in the same trade, with an increase every six months. At the end, an apprentice may be making 90 percent of a journeyman's pay. Apprentices receive fringe benefits and sometimes free tools.

Apprenticeship programs are not easy to get into for either men or women.

How Formal Apprenticeship Programs Began. Apprenticeship is the centuries-old way of learning a craft. The National Apprenticeship Act, signed into law by President Roosevelt in 1937, set national standards

ONE COMPANY'S JOB TITLES AND WHAT THEY MEAN

Women entering the telephone company can choose to be trained for these four skilled craft jobs all in the electrical field.

Outside Plant Technician (lineman). Works with heavy-duty power equipment and hand tools to connect wires and cables. Drives a company truck, climbs poles and works in manholes. Works on shifts outside in all kinds of weather.

Installation Technician. Installs, changes, and removes phones in homes and businesses. Climbs poles, drives a company truck, plans how to bring wire from pole to building, and installs inside wiring and connects it. Works in shifts, with hand tools, both inside and outside.

Repair Technician. Solves telephone trouble problems. Tests equipment, repairs and rearranges equipment, climbs poles and works with hand tools. Drives a company truck, works in shifts, and works inside and outside in all kinds of weather.

Frame Attendant. Works inside phone company central offices, connecting and disconnecting wires. Uses small hand tools, climbs ladders, and uses test equipment.

After you have been in the telephone company for a while, you can apply for a higher-level training program. Here are four titles of the many higher-level jobs you can apply for.

Switching Equipment Technician. Analyzes defects in, tests, repairs, and maintains telephone switching circuits and equipment. Works inside, in shifts.

Transmission Testing Technician. Adjusts, maintains, tests, and repairs circuit and other communications equipment such as telephones, microwave radio, telegraph, and data processing. Drives a company truck, works in shifts, and may be required to work outside in all kinds of weather.

Test Desk Technician. Provides centralized testing service for installation and repair work and cable and circuit transfers, including work with radio and foreign exchange lines. Works inside, seated at a test board and wearing a headset; works in shifts.

Cable Splicing Technician. Works with hot metal, small hand tools and mechanical equipment, splicing wires and installing cables and conductors inside and outside. Also operates hydraulic aerial lifts (buckets) and ladders mounted on trucks.

For more information about these jobs, see the employment office of your local telephone company.

for apprenticeship training. Through a federal agency now known as the Bureau of Apprenticeship Training, unions and employers came together and decided for each trade what kind of training apprentices should get and how much they should be paid. National standards exist today for all trades.

Bureau of Apprenticeship Training. The federal Bureau of Apprenticeship Training has 10 regional offices. These offices can give you information about the training for each craft and where to find a training program. State apprenticeship offices can refer you to state-supported apprenticeship programs. (Addresses of regional offices of the Bureau of Apprenticeship Training and Apprenticeship Information Centers are listed shortly before the Compendium of Construction Trades at the end of this Guide.)

Apprenticeship Program Requirements. To get into a formal apprenticeship training program, you almost always need a high school diploma or a GED (General Educational Development) certificate. Even if high school is not required, it is always preferred. High-school-level courses in general math are important. Algebra and geometry are required for apprentice electricians and are helpful for apprentice carpenters and plumbers. Mechanical drawing is also desirable. You will be expected to have a driver's license and be in good physical condition with a physician's certificate indicating that you are in good health required for most trades.

Union Apprenticeship Programs. Trade unions also sponsor apprenticeship programs. At stated times during the year applications are accepted for openings in these programs. If you meet the basic requirements, you will be given an aptitude test. Your grade on the test will be considered together with your high school grades and your score on a personal interview. At the interview, apprenticeship applicants are rated on their interest in the trade. It also is a plus if the applicant has already had some trade experience or training.

On the basis of their records, tests, and interviews, applicants are ranked and put on a list. As openings occur in the apprenticeship programs, people are taken from the top of the list. In parts of the country with comparatively few job openings in the skilled trades, you may have to wait a very long time.

To find out how and where to apply to an apprenticeship program, you can call a union local, a local state employment office, or an Apprenticeship Information Center.

Another Solution—Be a Registered Trainee

You can also obtain some paid work experience by becoming a registered trainee. A registered trainee is someone who does not meet the requirements for formal apprenticeship training; normally, a registered trainee does not have a high school diploma or is too old to apply for regular apprenticeship programs.

To become a registered trainee, you must first get on a list of "approved trainees"—a contractor, construction company, or the local office of the Bureau of Apprenticeship Training can tell you how. Unions and contractors have formal mechanisms for employing trainees, interviewing applicants, and picking from the approved list. Employers are usually looking for people with some work experience in construction, and you'll probably have to make a lot of calls before you find a company that is hiring trainees.

In many ways being a registered trainee is like being an apprentice. You are entitled to training and to be paid the same wages as apprentices. (The Davis-Bacon Act requires that all workers on a federal construction project be paid the "prevailing wage" of a skilled craft worker unless they are apprentices or registered trainees.) Some trainees have a hard time making the transition to journeyman status because they did not get proper on-the-job training and they may end up working as unskilled laborers. Employers and unions don't always like to credit trainee experience, and trainees can get stuck in the trainee position.

However, if you don't fulfill the requirements for apprenticeship, becoming a trainee is a good way to get into construction. Construction companies should be hiring women trainees during the late 70s and 80s to comply with new government regulations.

Apprenticeship and Training Opportunities in the Armed Forces

The Armed Forces train people to be skilled craft workers, and Army or Navy training and experience count toward apprenticeship training.

In the Armed Forces you can get on-the-job experience and classroom training without worrying about job insecurity or seasonal layoffs. There are other advantages, too: free housing, medical care, and additional education opportunities, for example. When you get out, you'll find that many unions and some civil service systems give preference to veterans when making up their apprentice lists.

The basic requirements are that you must be 17 to 27 years old to join the Army and 17 to 31 for the Navy. You must also have a high school diploma or its equivalent. You will have to sign up for at least three years. It's all right if you're married or have children, but someone else must be available to take care of the children.

Interested in investigating this way of getting training and experience? See your Army or Navy recruiter. In the Navy construction work is done by the Sea Bees or CBs (Construction Battalion). In the Army construction work is done by General Engineering and Combat Engineering battalions. By law, women cannot now be assigned to Combat Engineering battalions or any other "hazardous" duty, but this prohibition may change in the future.

For both services you must take a standard written test and a physical. The test will determine what jobs you are qualified for. Be careful to answer positively all questions that show an interest in the construction trades, even if they start "When you were a boy, did you. . . ."

After the test you will talk to a counselor about possible job assignments. The counselor may try to interest you in another work area; *be sure you know what you want* and don't hesitate to be adamant. Finally, there will be a contract to sign. Make sure the contract says what you want it to, and don't sign it without having a friend or counselor read it too.

Other Ways to Get Started

You can get work experience in the construction trades in some other ways also. Men often start as a laborer or helper. In 1977 construction laborers earned from about $3.50 to about $8.00 an hour, depending on the part of the country. In some areas there are brief training programs. Working as a laborer can be exhausting and heavy work, but combined with some night school courses, it's one way to start out.

Men often work as helpers to skilled craft workers to learn a trade. Nonunion contractors sometimes advertise for "carpenter's helpers," for example. Small subcontractors may also take on one or two helpers and teach them a craft. News of these training opportunities usually travels by word of mouth within the family or among friends. Few women have yet had the necessary contacts to take advantage of this informal training system.

Other ways for women to get training in the construction trades are through schools, special programs, and in companies.

Craft Training in Schools

Although school learning is not a substitute for work experience, schools can help you prepare for a trade career. Some vocational-technical schools, trade schools, and community colleges have "cooperative programs" with employers, which include both school courses and work experience and may even guarantee a job with the cooperating employer on graduation.

Public Vocational–Technical High Schools. Public school systems frequently have vocational–technical high schools or courses that prepare students for skilled trades jobs. Graduates of these "voc-tech" schools may go directly into apprenticeship programs, and some of their courses will count toward fulfillment of apprenticeship requirements.

LOOKING FOR WORK—AT THE JOB SITE

If you are trying to find your first job by asking for work at the jobsite:

1. Try to get a list of union jobsites from the local.
2. Go to the jobsite ready to work and looking like it (wearing work clothes, boots, etc.).
3. You will not be able to go onto the site without a hard hat. If you can, borrow one and take it with you. If not, ask for one in the general contractor's trailer.
4. Ask where you can find the foreman of your trade. Besides the foreman for the general contractor, there may be foremen for subcontractors on the site as well; be sure to ask for them. Check with the shop steward, too. In general, the more people you talk with and the more information you get, the better off you'll be.
5. If they say they are not hiring, ask when they will be putting people on again. Try to get a definite date.
6. If the job is almost finished, ask where the same company has other jobs where they might be hiring.
7. Ask other workers at the site if they know of jobsites where they might be hiring.
8. Keep a record of where you tried to get in, the date, and the names of the contractor and the foremen to whom you spoke.
9. If you have tried a particular site a number of times and feel that you have not been hired because of sex or age, you can file a complaint with the local union and at the apprenticeship school or relevant government agency. [See "Know Your Rights" in the first chapter of this Guidebook.]

> —excerpted from *Blue Collar Trades
> Handbook for Women,* published by
> Women Working in Construction,
> Washington, D.C.

Even if you don't attend a vocational-technical school, you can use their guidance or placement libraries to learn about different trades and their requirements.

Many women are enrolled in these schools across the country but almost all of them are preparing to go into traditional fields, such as hairdressing, cosmetology, and secretarial training. Very, very few are concentrating in construction. Counselors tend to discourage girls from going into nontraditional career fields; and in their early teens, not many girls will have the assertiveness to disagree. Other girls, even if they already know they want to be carpenters or plumbers, are afraid of being ridiculed in all-male classes with all-male instructors. These girls may not know that they have a right to take any course for which they qualify.

Many vocational–technical schools are now beginning to encourage their women students to look into nontraditional careers. At some schools the entire freshman class, boys *and* girls, spends some time in every career area.

Private Vocational Schools. Throughout the country private vocational schools can help prepare you for a job in the construction trades. You can find them in the yellow pages under "Schools, Technical" or "Schools, Trade."

Courses at private vocational schools tend to cost more than courses at community colleges, and course quality can vary a great deal. Although most private schools don't offer on-the-job work experience, many do offer very practical courses such as blueprint reading, electrical circuits, and estimating.

Good private vocational schools are *accredited,* approved by an independent organization, the National Association of Trade and Technical Schools. Your State Department of Education probably has a list of recommended vocational schools.

Before you sign anything, go to the school and look it over. Talk to other students and meet the teachers. If it's a good school, it will refer you to people you can talk to who know the school—former students or employers who have hired graduates.

Before you sign a contract, ask a friend or adviser to read it. Make sure you understand it. Make sure you have signed up for *only* the courses you need.

Adult Education Courses. Most high schools and community colleges offer adult education courses free or at low cost. Among them are often some basic skills courses in home appliance repair, carpentry, and auto mechanics. These courses can help you learn how to use simple tools and, more important, get a better idea of whether you really want to go into a skilled trades career.

GETTING FINANCED

Almost any school or program in which you have to pay for training has a financial assistance or student loan program.

Many CETA (government-sponsored) programs have day-care allowances. Transportation to the work site and cost of tools may be included in some programs. If you don't ask for it, you may not get this kind of help.

The high school courses are often given in the high school shop, where you can learn a little about power tools. Community colleges also offer useful courses in blueprint reading or electrical circuitry and some have special courses for women interested in skilled trades careers. More than 30 community colleges offer degrees in construction. For information on such colleges near you, write:

National Association of Home Builders
Manpower Department
15th and M Streets NW
Washington, D.C. 20005

Craft Training in Special Programs for Women

Special programs to help women become skilled craft workers are springing up all over the country. Some will help you get into an apprenticeship program or find other training opportunities; some will help you find jobs; and others offer training, day care, part-time work experience, or help in getting a GED.

To find out if there is a special program for women near you, write:

TWO RECRUITMENT PROGRAMS

Recruitment and Training Programs (RTP). At first recruiting and training minority men for skilled trades jobs, RTP has now expanded its program to include women. You do not necessarily need to be a low-income or minority person to apply. To find out if RTP has an office near you, look in the phone book or write:

Recruitment and Training Program
162 Fifth Avenue
New York, New York 10011

LEAP. The National Urban League also has a special program, called LEAP, to train women for nontraditional jobs. Like RTP, it was started to train minority people for skilled jobs. Both white and minority women can apply. To find the program nearest you, look in the phone book for the Urban League, or write:

National Urban League
500 East 62d Street
New York, New York 10021

Wider Opportunities for Women
1649 K Street NW
Washington, D.C. 20006

Many inner-city or metropolitan YWCAs offer training or placement in nontraditional jobs for women. Some YWCAs also offer women information about construction jobs or training available through local public works projects. Almost all YWCAs offer career counseling or career decision-making workshops that can help you. Call the YWCA nearest you to learn if they have such a program.

Another place to go to find a special program for women is your local state employment office or CETA (Comprehensive Employment Training Act) office.

Craft Training in Companies

Many companies have in-house training programs for craft workers. Sometimes these programs are available only to people who have been employees of the company for a minimum length of time, usually at least six months. If you are an assembly-line worker or a clerk in a company, there may be chances for you to get training in one of the trades at your company's expense.

One reason more women have not applied for craft training in companies is that they didn't know that the jobs or the training were available. A job in the maintenance department sounds like being a janitor to some women, but maintenance work also involves plumbing repair and maintenance, electrical work, carpentry, and many other skills. Women are also frequently not familiar with what company job titles mean. The skilled craft jobs in a company sometimes have elaborate or misleading names, including terms like *technician*. If you hear of an opportunity for training in the company maintenance department or for a job with an unfamiliar title, don't pass it up—ask somebody about it.

Some companies, like American Telephone and Telegraph Company, are actively recruiting women inside and outside the organization for craft training slots. Talk to the company training or personnel department to find out about such a program.

Many companies also have job posting systems, a real help to women employees interested in switching to the skilled trades. If there is a job opening or an on-the-job training opportunity, the job and its requirements are listed on a special bulletin board or in the company newsletter.

Women outside a company often seem to have trouble finding company on-the-job training positions. For one thing, concerns prefer to invest in people they already know as reliable workers. A few women have taken unskilled custodian jobs to get into a firm that has a good skills training program. They signed up with the understanding that at the end of a year, if they did good work, they would automatically enter a skills training program.

Some companies, especially ones that work on government contracts, are under pressure to hire women for nontraditional jobs. These employers include hospitals, universities, and industries related to space or military technology. Colleges and universities are particularly good places to look for a job like that of carpenter's helper.

A few companies are under court order to take positive steps to move women into nontraditional jobs, and naturally they are good places to try, too. But it's hard to find out which they are, since they don't advertise their troubles. Keep up with the newspapers to find out.

The Affirmative Action officer of a company, the one responsible for seeing that employment opportunities are made available to women and minorities, is a good person to ask about nontraditional job training opportunities. Affirmative Action officers are not usually in the personnel department, and don't ask in personnel for his or her name—the two offices aren't always on the best of terms. Make a separate phone call to the Affirmative Action office.

There are some real advantages to company training programs. For one thing, you are trained for jobs that are needed, so there's generally a job waiting for you. The training programs are usually good. Finally, firms that have training programs tend to be growing and expanding, good places to work because of the advancement opportunities.

Stacy Erdeski, Company-Trained Electrician

When Stacy Erdeski was 28, she was working in the billing department of a large manufacturer. One day, someone from personnel came around to the billing department and tried to interest the women there in craft jobs within the company. "I jumped at the chance. The high point of my day in the billing department had been walking to the file cabinets. But now I'd get to do new things. It also meant a $100 pay raise a week. Besides, I had always enjoyed fixing things."

Ms. Erdeski and another woman, Colleen Cockerell, were chosen for electrician training. "For the first two years, we were in what they called on-the-job training. Mostly we did menial kinds of work and weren't learning much. Then they sent us to school.

"What I can really say for big companies is that they really offer you a lot of training. You can get whatever you need to do the job. They even offer to help toward getting a college degree.

"I really love my work. I really enjoy electrical work. It's fun for me.

Wiring is like a puzzle—the more complicated the better. The pay is good, too.

"But I also really feel isolated. Part of the problem is the way we work. We are all dispatched from a central location to do troubleshooting in the plants in the area. These plants use some pretty complicated electrical machinery. That means there's a lot of variety in what I do, but I'm really on my own all the time. I am always worried that I'm not pulling my own weight, doing the job as well as the men technicians. I feel I'm playing catch-up all the time. It's hard to learn if you're nervous and it takes more energy to learn under pressure.

"When one of the men gets into trouble on the job, he doesn't have any problem calling up another man and asking for help. But I agonize over calling. I feel so inadequate. I'm going to have to learn how to ask for help and not feel bad about it.

"Colleen really helps me. We support each other if we have problems. One or two fellows are very nice here when you talk to them on the phone or by themselves; but when they're in a group, it's hard.

"Before Colleen and I came, they were like a fraternity. When we came back from our training, they just couldn't accept us. They mostly tend to leave us out and leave us alone. Only a few make sexual comments like 'I'd sure like to be in that inner office with you, honey,'—things like that.

"When I get a little more confidence in myself I'm going to take some more courses and look for a promotion. It's not hard to do in this company. You can use the job posting system and nominate yourself for a better job.

"I know there are lots of women who could do the kind of work I do. You don't need to be especially big or strong to do electrical work. A lot of women have technical talent. Talents are human, not male or female."

BASIC RESOURCES

Special Programs for Women

These programs help women who live in their area of the country. Write or phone the one(s) in your area for more information.

> All-Craft Foundation
> 19–23 St. Marks Place
> New York, New York 10003

Better Jobs for Women
1038 Bannock Street
Denver, Colorado 80204

Mechanica
4224 University Way NW
Seattle, Washington 98105

YWCA
Nontraditional Jobs for Women
140 Clarendon Street
Boston, Massachusetts 02166

Wider Opportunities for Women (WOW)
1649 K Street NW
Washington, D.C. 20008

Wisconsin Division of Apprenticeship
  and Training
201 East Washington Avenue
Madison, Wisconsin 53707

Women in Apprenticeship
25 Taylor Street
San Francisco, California 94102

Women's Enterprises of Boston
755 Boylston Street
Boston, Massachusetts 02116

Apprenticeship Information Centers

Write to the center nearest you for more information.

In Alabama

Alabama State Employment Service
1818 8th Avenue North
Birmingham, Alabama 35203

In Arizona

207 East McDowell
Phoenix, Arizona 85004

In California

> 161 West Venice Boulevard
> Los Angeles, California 90015

> 235 12th Street
> Oakland, California 94607

In Washington, D.C.

> 555 Pennsylvania Avenue NW
> Washington, D.C. 20212

In Illinois

> 150 North Clinton Street
> Chicago, Illinois 60606

In Indiana

> 745 Washington Street
> Gary, Indiana 47402

> 141 West Georgia Street
> Indianapolis, Indiana 46225

In Kansas

> 512 West 6th Street
> Topeka, Kansas 66604

> 402 East 2d Street
> Wichita, Kansas 67202

In Massachusetts

> 255 Huntington Avenue
> Boston, Massachusetts 02115

In Maryland

> 1100 North Eutaw Street (Room 205)
> Baltimore, Maryland 21201

In Michigan

> 7310 Woodward Avenue
> Detroit, Michigan 48202

In Minnesota

> 390 North Robert Street
> St. Paul, Minnesota 55101

In Missouri

> 1411 Main Street
> Kansas City, Missouri 64105
>
> 505 Washington Avenue
> St. Louis, Missouri 63101

In New Jersey

> 143 Bacharach Boulevard
> Atlantic City, New Jersey 08401
>
> 32– 40 North Van Brunt Street
> Englewood, New Jersey 07631
>
> 517 Federal Street
> Camden, New Jersey 08101
>
> 1004 Broad Street
> Newark, New Jersey 07102
>
> 65 Morris Street
> New Brunswick, New Jersey 08903
>
> 370 Broadway
> Paterson, New Jersey 07501

In New York

> 488 Broadway
> Albany, New York 12207
>
> 730 Fillmore Avenue
> Buffalo, New York 14202
>
> 344 Fulton Avenue
> Hempstead, New York 11550
>
> 255 West 54th Street
> New York, New York 10019
>
> 155 West Main Street
> Rochester, New York 14614

In Oregon

> 432 West 11th Avenue
> Eugene, Oregon 97424

> 1427 SW 4th Avenue
> Portland, Oregon 97201

In Pennsylvania

> 2048 Arch Street
> Philadelphia, Pennsylvania 19122

> 915 Penn Avenue
> Pittsburgh, Pennsylvania 15222

In Rhode Island

> 40 Fountain Street
> Providence, Rhode Island 02903

In Tennessee

> 1295 Poplar Avenue
> Memphis, Tennessee 38104

> 1802 Hayes Street
> Nashville, Tennessee 37203

In Virginia

> 904 Granby Street
> Norfolk, Virginia 23510

> 318 East Cary Street
> Richmond, Virginia 23219

In Washington

> 233 6th Avenue North
> Seattle, Washington 98109

Bureau of Apprenticeship and Training — Regional Offices

Write or visit the office nearest you.

Region I

> JFK Federal Building (Room 1001)
> Government Center
> Boston, Massachusetts 02203

Region II

> 1515 Broadway (Room 3731)
> New York, New York 10036

Region III

> P.O. Box 8796
> Philadelphia, Pennsylvania 19101

Region IV

> 1371 Peachtree Street NE (Room 700)
> Atlanta, Georgia 30309

Region V

> Federal Building (Room 1, 4th Floor)
> 230 South Dearborn Street
> Chicago, Illinois 60604

Region VI

> 555 Griffin Square Building (Room 858)
> Griffin & Young Streets
> Dallas, Texas 75202

Region VII

> Federal Office Building (Room 1100)
> 911 Walnut Street
> Kansas City, Missouri 64106

Region VIII

> Federal Building (Room 16440)
> 1961 Stout Street
> Denver, Colorado 80294

Region IX

> 450 Golden Gate Avenue (Room 9008)
> P.O. Box 36017
> San Francisco, California 94102

Region X

> Federal Office Building (Room 8014)
> 909 1st Avenue
> Seattle, Washington 98174

COMPENDIUM OF SKILLED TRADES

(The following list of careers is not meant to be exhaustive but rather to give you an idea of the range of career options.)

Asbestos and Insulation Worker. Insulates hot or cold surfaces such as pipes, boilers, and heating and coiling systems. Most employed by insulation contractors or in large firms such as chemical factories and petroleum refineries with big heating and cooling plants. Union average: $9.75 an hour in 1976. Job openings will increase much faster than average for all occupations through mid-1980s.

Bricklayer. Builds walls, fireplaces, other masonry structures; installs firebrick linings in industrial furnaces. Most employed by building or general contractors. Union average: $9.90 an hour in 1976, but time lost because of poor weather and unemployment between jobs make annual earnings less than the hourly rates would suggest. Job openings will increase about as fast as average for all occupations through mid-1980s.

Carpenter. In almost every kind of construction activity. Builds wood framework in buildings; installs windows, doors and cabinets; builds stairs; lays floors, installs heavy timbers in docks and railroad trestles; builds forms for pouring concrete; erects scaffolding. Some specialize. Most work for builders and contractors who build new buildings or alter, remodel, and repair old ones. About one of five carpenters is self-employed. Some alternate between working for contractors and self-employment on small jobs. Union average: $9.85 an hour in 1976, but annual earnings are lower than this would suggest because of lost time due to poor weather and unemployment between jobs. Job openings will grow about as fast as average for all occupations through mid-1980s.

Cement Mason. Finishes concrete surfaces on construction projects ranging from floors to dams to highways. Often works with one to several helpers. Most work for general contractors who construct entire projects or for concrete contractors. One of 10 is self-employed. Union average: $9.35 an hour in 1976, but annual earnings lower than this would suggest because of time lost due to bad weather and unemployment between jobs. Often works overtime with extra pay. Job openings should grow faster than average for all occupations through mid-1980s.

490

Construction Laborer. Works on construction projects, prepares site for a building or a highway; does most of the wrecking and salvage work in tearing down buildings, pours and spreads concrete, puts up and takes down scaffolding, braces sides of excavations, cleans up rubble and debris, and unloads and delivers materials and equipment to other construction workers. Most work for construction contractors, state and city public works and highway departments, and public utilities. Union average: $7.50 an hour in 1976, but annual earnings may be lower than hourly rates suggest because of time lost during bad weather and unemployment between jobs. Job openings will probably grow more slowly than average for all occupations through mid-1980s.

Drywall Installer and Finisher. Puts up drywall panels used as walls and ceilings of houses and other buildings and prepares panels for painting. Some specialize in hanging drywall panels on metal frameworks. Usually has helper to help handle large panels. Most work in cities (carpenters do this kind of work in small towns). Most work for contractors specializing in drywall construction, but some work for general contractors. Earned about $6.50 to $9.00 an hour in 1976: finishers, about $6 to $8. Many contractors pay installers and finishers according to the number of panels they complete. Job openings should grow faster than average for all occupations through mid-1980s.

Electrician. Assembles, installs and wires electrical systems that provide heat, light, power, air conditioning, and refrigeration in buildings. Also installs and tests electrical machinery, electronic equipment, controls, and communications systems. Generally furnishes own tools. Most work for electrical contractors; many self-employed. In most cities, contractor must have master electrician's license. Average earnings: $10.33 an hour in 1976; annual earnings tend to be higher than in most building trades because they can work year-round. Job openings should grow faster than average for all occupations through mid-1980s.

Elevator Constructor. Assembles, installs, maintains, and repairs elevators and escalators. Most employed by elevator manufacturers, but some by small local contractors specializing in elevator maintenance and repair. Hourly wage rates and annual earnings among highest in skilled building trades. Average earnings: $10.30 an hour in 1976. Job openings should grow faster than average for all occupations through mid-1980s.

Floor Covering Installer. Installs and replaces carpeting, tile, linoleum, and vinyl floor coverings over wood, concrete, and other floors. About three-fourths specialize in putting down carpets. Most work for flooring contractors; some for sellers of floor coverings and for home alteration and repair contractors; about one out of four is self-employed. Experienced earned approximately $6.25 to $9 an hour in 1976. Most are paid by the hour, but some may get bonuses or monthly salaries or be paid according to the amount of work done. Job openings will grow at about same rate as average for all occupations through mid-1980s.

Floor Sander and Finisher. Sands floors with sanding machines, works for building contractors who build or renovate houses. In demand in residential housing construction, and demand should grow.

Glazier. Installs plate glass, window glass, and special items such as leaded glass panels. Also installs structural glass such as shower doors, mirrors, and automatic glass doors. Most work for glazing contractors in new construction or in alteration and repair. Union earnings: about $9.25 an hour in 1976. Job openings should grow faster than average for all occupations through the mid-1980s.

Hauler. Drives trucks to haul fill or to remove debris from construction site. Usually works as truck driver for independent hauling contractor. Earned about $6.59 an hour in 1974.

Heating and Air Conditioning Installer. Installs heating and air-conditioning equipment in houses, factories, and commercial buildings. Furnace installers often trained to handle specific brands of furnaces. Most work for contractors; many self-employed. Hourly wages vary greatly, but mechanics earn about $10.50 an hour. Job opportunities should continue to grow, particularly in solar heating.

Ironworker. Erects steel framework in buildings, bridges, other structures. Makes alterations such as installing stairs and ornamental facades, does repair work such as replacing metal bridge parts. **Riggers** get heavy construction machinery ready for moving and move it to a new site. Ironworkers often specialize as structural ironworkers, riggers, ornamental ironworkers, and reinforcing ironworkers (who set steel rods to make reinforced concrete). Most ironworkers and riggers work for general contractors on large building projects, for steel erection contractors, or for ornamental iron contractors. Very few are self-employed. Union earnings: about $10 an hour in 1976, slightly higher than average for union building trades workers, but annual earnings may be lower than hourly wage suggests because of time lost in bad weather or unemployment between jobs. Job openings for ironworkers should grow faster than average for all occupations through mid-1980s.

Landscaper. Uses a tractor to grade the land around a building to prepare it for seeding or sodding; also plants shrubs and trees. Usually works for landscape contractors. Usually very low paid, earning minimum wage.

Lather. Fastens wood, wire, metal, or rockboard laths to building framework so that plaster, stucco, or concrete can be applied to ceilings or walls. Most work for contractors building new residential, commercial, or industrial buildings. Union average: about $9.80 an hour in 1976. Probably not much change in job openings through mid-1980s.

Marble Setter. Sets marble or structural glass into buildings for structural support or decoration. **Tilesetters** fasten tiles to walls, floors, and ceilings. **Terrazzo workers** lay ornamental concrete flooring. All work mainly in nonresidential construction projects, such as schools, hospitals, and public and commercial buildings. About one out of five tilesetters is self-employed. In 1974, union marble setters earned average of $8.45 an hour; tilesetters, $8.05; terrazzo workers, $8.20. Job openings will probably grow more slowly than average for all occupations through mid-1980s.

Millwright. Prepares site for and installs heavy machinery. May build platforms for heavy machinery, dismantle and move machinery, and assemble new machinery in manufacturing plants. Most work for manufacturing companies, but some for construction contractors. Employment concentrated in heavily industrialized cities. Average earnings: $7.25 an hour in 1976. Job openings should grow about as fast as for all occupations through mid-1980s.

Operating Engineer. Runs bulldozers, cranes, trench excavators, paving machines, heavy construction machinery. Most work for contractors building highways, dams, airports, and other large projects. Some work for firms that do own construction work for state and local highway and public works departments. Fewer self-employed than in most building trades. Wages vary depending on the machine operated; in 1976, union crane operators averaged $9.90 an hour; bulldozer operators, $9.55; air-compressor operators, $8.65. Annual earnings may be lower than hourly average wages suggest due to time lost in bad weather and from unemployment between jobs. Job openings should grow much faster than average for all occupations through mid-1980s.

Painter. Cleans and prepares surfaces for painting by scraping and sanding. Applies paint, varnish, or other finishes to buildings. Also puts up scaffolding to work on. Many work for contractors in new construction, repair, alteration and modernization work. Some organizations that manage own buildings hire painters for maintenance. About one-fourth are self-employed. Union average: about $9.25 an hour in 1976. Job openings for painters will probably grow more slowly than average for all occupations through mid-1980s.

Paperhanger. Prepares surfaces to be papered by removing old paper, putting on sizing, doing minor plaster patching. Covers walls and ceilings with wallpaper of various materials. More than half are self-employed, others work for contractors in new construction, alteration, or modernization. Union average: $9.25 an hour in 1976. Job opportunities will probably increase about as fast as average for all occupations through mid-1980s.

Piledriver. Does steelwork on buildings, bridges, and subways which go below ground surface. Drives pilings, welds, cuts with acetylene torch, rigs and places steel, loads and unloads truckloads of steel. Works for large contractors on big projects such as bridges and subway systems. Job opportunities depend on growth of heavy construction industry.

Pipefitter. Installs high- and low-pressure piping systems for hot water, steam, and other liquids and gases such as those in oil refineries and chemical processing plants. Sometimes specializes in gas, steam, or sprinkler fitting. Most work for plumbing and pipefitting contractors in new construction. Average earnings: $10.40 an hour in 1976, among highest in building trades. Demand should grow faster than average for all occupations through mid-1980s.

Plasterer. Plasters interior walls and ceilings, puts cement plaster or stucco on exterior walls, sometimes casts ornamental designs in plaster. One of every five is self-employed. Most work on new construction. Union average: $9.48 an hour in 1976. Job openings will probably not change much through mid-1980s.

Plumber. Installs, changes, and repairs pipe systems carrying water, steam, air, or other gases. Also installs plumbing fixtures, appliances, and heating and refrigeration systems. Some specialize in gas, steam, or sprinkler fitting. Most work for contractors in new construction at site. Many are self-employed or work for plumbing contractors who do repair, alteration, and modernization jobs. Union average: $10.40 an hour in 1976, making annual earnings among highest in building trades. Job openings for plumbers should grow faster than average for all occupations through mid-1980s.

Roofer. Covers roofs with materials such as wooden shingles, composition roofing, tile, slate, and metal roofing to make them waterproof. Also waterproofs masonry and concrete floors and walls. Most work for roofing contractors on construction or repair jobs; a few self-employed. Union average: $9.30 an hour in 1976, but annual earnings may not be as high as hourly pay rates would suggest because of time lost due to bad weather or unemployment between jobs. Jobs should grow faster than average for all occupations through mid-1980s.

Sewer and Water Installer. Lays and makes joints in sewer or water pipes and fire hydrants. May cover sewer pipes with concrete. Most work for contractors or local public works departments. Works with a crew of other workers including backhoe operator, crane operator, and/or bulldozer operator. Usually earns less than average skilled crafts worker but more than average common laborer.

Sheet-Metal Worker. Makes and installs metal ducts for heating, ventilating, air-conditioning systems. May also make metal roofing or siding or other finished products like kitchen cabinets or gutters. Most are employed by heating and air-conditioning contractors or by large building contractors. Union average: $10.10 an hour in 1976. Job openings will increase approximately as fast as average for all occupations through mid-1980s.

Weatherstripper. Usually a carpenter specializing in putting metal, rubber, or synthetic weatherstripping on exterior doors and windows and in refitting doors or windows properly. May also install storm doors and windows. Usually works for supply companies or is self-employed.

Welder. Joins pieces of metal together by heating the pieces that are to be joined. The many kinds of welding processes require different skills and equipment. Often specializes in a particular kind of welding, such as ship welding or maintenance welding. About two-thirds work in manufacturing plants; most of rest for construction firms on bridges, pipelines, and large buildings, or in repair of metal products. Earnings range widely: welding machine operators earned $3.93 to $5.10 an hour in 1976; welders in the construction industry, $6 to $12. Job opportunities should increase faster than average for all occupations through mid-1980s.

Guide VI **A Guide to Business Careers**

Funding for this Guide was provided by Xerox Corporation;
General Motors Corporation; Philip Morris, Inc.; John Hancock
Mutual Life Insurance Company; Citibank, N.A.; Western
Electric Fund; and Continental Illinois National Bank and Trust.

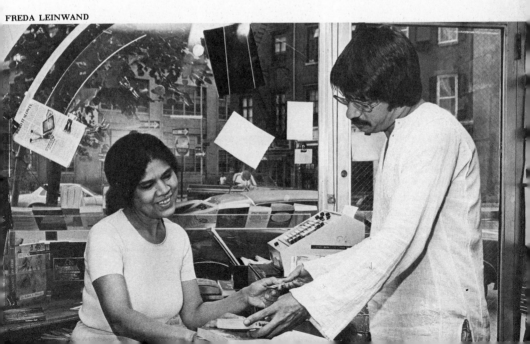

CHAPTER 1

BUSINESS AS USUAL

Calvin Coolidge's famous assertion that "the business of America is business" is not far off the mark. As far back as 1607, when Virginia's Jamestown Colony was founded by a corporation, the London Company, shareholders were seeking a good growth stock and employees were hoping for fame and fortune through the new opportunities the company gave them. Although the London Company failed in its first venture, other American businesses followed, providing the capital and the impetus behind the phenomenal growth and expansion of our country.

The American Dream—that anybody who is clever and works hard can become rich and successful—is an idea closely identified with business enterprise. To be part of that dream 40 million immigrants came to this country, and for millions of them business was the way they made it happen.

Women are just beginning to participate fully in American economic life and to recognize the opportunities for personal growth that exist in business careers. The variety of possible business careers is staggering. People in business own restaurants and shoe stores, design production systems, invent computer processes, analyze balance sheets, and sell everything from insurance to peanut butter. Companies employ social workers, psychologists, teachers, doctors, lawyers, artists, writers, and designers. In business you can go to work for someone else or go into business for yourself in the field of your choice. The career opportunities are endless.

In a single business field you'll find many workplace options. For example, if you want to sell insurance, you can work directly for an insurance company in its home office or in one of its field offices, be in business for yourself as an insurance broker selling several companies' insurance programs, or be a risk manager advising a large manufacturing

Funding for this chapter was provided by Xerox Corporation.

499

concern which insurance to buy. If you decide on a business career, you have the opportunity to make a conscious choice about your work atmosphere and working conditions not only in your first job but throughout your career.

Women and Business Enterprise

Before the Industrial Revolution of the 19th century, women and men worked at home. Whether they were shop owners, farmers, or craft workers, home and workplace were the same. Husbands and wives worked together in the family business, and the older children helped or cared for younger children. The family was the economic unit.

The first factories changed that picture. For the first time in civilian life, people worked away from their homes. The earliest factory workers in the United States were children and women.

By the end of the 19th century, factory work had become a recognized lifelong occupation. Industrially employed families no longer worked together as an economic unit; women stayed home to raise the children while their husbands went to work in the factory. When the children were old enough, the women sometimes left the home to work in the factories too.

Although women had early opportunities to work at factory jobs, few had the chance to become capitalists during this unprecedented period of industrial expansion. According to the tradition of English law inherited by the United States, only single adult women had the right to own property.

This issue of property ownership was an important one for such 19th-century women's rights activists as Susan B. Anthony. In 1880, Belva Lockwood, a woman attorney in a time when few women practiced law, brought a landmark case before the United States Supreme Court, involving women's rights to their own earnings. This case was also the first one argued by a woman lawyer before the Supreme Court. It involved a woman worker whose husband took her earnings and spent it on liquor, leaving the family with no money for food. Ms. Lockwood won the case, securing the right for married women to their wages.

During the first part of the 20th century, working women were concentrated in a small number of relatively low-paying occupations. Women became secretaries not managers, bookkeepers not accountants, retail saleswomen not sales managers, tellers not bank officers, insurance claim representatives not actuaries or underwriters. Except for a small number of extraordinary individuals, many of them entrepreneurs, few women advanced to important positions in the business world.

Ironically, the greatest advance in equal rights in employment came about by accident. In 1964 a major civil rights bill was introduced to

QUIZ

Women in business are not new. In fact, many of them have been leaders throughout history. Here's a quiz on "firsts" and famous women in business history—you may find out a lot you didn't know.

Do you know . . .

1. What female entrepreneur made a fortune selling a "remedy," first concocted in her kitchen and bearing her countenance on all labels and advertisements?
2. What woman doll designer helped catapult her toy company into the largest in the world by 1970?
3. What millionaire speculator was reportedly so miserly she wouldn't "waste" fuel to heat her porridge?
4. What "Florence Nightingale" made a considerable fortune by establishing a cosmetics empire?
5. What businesswoman made a name for herself in gelatin?
6. What department store president began her career by making dolls with her sister?
7. What Negro woman founded a bank and established a newspaper?
8. What woman acquired a large fortune from the sale of a doll that became the rage in 1913?

Quiz Answers

1. At the time of her death, *Lydia Pinkham* (1819– 83) was earning $300,000 from sales of her Vegetable Compound. She stoutly believed in the efficacy of her product which claimed to cure everything from uterine tumors to spinal weakness.
2. Designed by *Ruth Handler* in 1959, Barbie Doll boosted the fortunes of the Mattel Toy Company, which she had founded in 1945.
3. A speculator in government bonds, railroad stock and real estate, *Henrietta Green* was worth $100 million by 1916. Reputedly the richest woman in the United States and the greatest miser, she wore old clothes and lived in run-down boarding houses.
4. *Florence Nightingale Graham*—Elizabeth Arden—was a pioneer in scientific beauty programs. In addition to creating luxurious health resorts in Maine and Arizona, she was founder, president, and chairman of the board of Elizabeth Arden until her death in 1966.
5. In 1890 *Rose Knox* and her husband invested $5,000 in a gelatin business. After his death, Mrs. Knox's shrewd use of advertising and marketing techniques tripled the value of the company by 1915 and helped make gelatin a common part of the American diet.
6. When Lord & Taylor purchased some dolls she and her sister designed and made, *Dorothy Shaver* had no idea that by 1946 she would be elected president of the

store, making her the first woman in mercantile history to head an organization doing an annual business of $30 million.

7. In 1903 *Maggie Walker,* an insurance and banking executive, founded the St. Luke Penny Savings Bank and became its first president. She also published a newspaper called the *St. Luke Herald.*

8. In 1913 *Rose O'Neill* designed a little doll that would make her a rich woman. Her Kewpie Doll, which originally came in various sizes and positions and was made of porcelain, added to her fortune for nearly 20 years and is now a collector's item.

---

prevent discrimination against black Americans. All strategies for blocking passage of the bill had failed, when Congressman Howard Smith from Virginia added an amendment to include discrimination against women in the section of the legislation about employment (Title VII). His strategy was to rally the anti-civil-rights forces by adding something to the bill that was so unpopular that even pro-civil-rights congressmen would vote against it. Congressman Smith was wrong. The bill became law, and it became illegal to discriminate against women in hiring, promotion, and training.

Although Congress had passed the Equal Pay Act the year before, in 1963, to guarantee "equal pay for equal work," women remained for the most part in the lowest-level jobs until Title VII of the Civil Rights Act of 1964 was passed, and discrimination in hiring and promotion became illegal, thus opening better-paying positions to women. Title VII is enforced by the Equal Employment Opportunity Commission (EEOC), and although the EEOC has a reputation for being backlogged in processing complaints, the lawsuits that have been won against major corporations have been so expensive for them that most employers have become eager to find a way to avoid complaints. Women employees have also made sophisticated use of the law by forming women's groups within companies and hiring lawyers to negotiate for better employment opportunities.

Since the 60s the employment picture for women in business has changed dramatically in all areas. Between 1960 and 1973 the number of women accountants grew from 80,000 to 180,000, four times the growth rate for men accountants. The number of women stockbrokers more than quadrupled. Women sales managers increased from 100 to 8,700, while the number of women bank officers and financial managers grew from 2,100 in 1960 to 54,500 in 1970. By 1973 nearly 1.6 million women were working in managerial or administrative positions. And today these numbers continue to grow.

However, these great changes haven't yet guaranteed that women won't still be passed over for promotion because they are women or be

"CORPORATE" DRESSING: DO'S AND DON'TS

Women have been bombarded by books, articles, and pamphlets containing helpful advice on how to dress and look successful. These publications are filled with a variety of do's and dont's —the premise being that if you want to be upwardly mobile, you have to dress the part.

In *The Woman's Dress for Success Book* (New York: Warner Books, 1978, $3.95), one of the more popular of these publications, John T. Molloy advises women to wear plain pumps, skirted suits, and generally to dress "upper middle class." As Molloy says, "Dress for the job you want, not for the job you have."

Every company has its own range of acceptable styles of dress. What you wear will greatly depend on the nature of the job and on what your colleagues are wearing. For some women, this may mean a change in dressing habits. As one research associate put it, "I would have felt pretty silly sitting in meetings in slacks or a sundress with corporate executives in pin-striped suits."

How can you tell what's "executively" acceptable? Observe everyone else. In *Games Mother Never Taught You* (New York: Warner Books, 1978, $2.50), Betty Lehan Harragan advises women to keep an eye on what her superiors are wearing. This will give her a clue as to the "tone" or "look" adopted by the upwardly mobile.

The best advice is to use your instincts and common sense. Aim for comfort and don't go overboard on anything—makeup, jewelry, or clothing. Adapt yourself to a company's style. Conformity is the rule if you want an "upwardly mobile" image.

---

discriminated against in other ways. The median income of women workers with college degrees in 1973 was still only about 60 percent of the median income of men with a college degree and about $4,000 less than the median income of men with only high school diplomas. The earnings gap between men and women has continued to widen. But as women enter the labor force in greater numbers and more and more advance from entry-level positions, this situation should begin to change.

Something else is changing for women in business—people's attitudes. The stereotypes of the rigid or incapable or emotional woman boss are changing as more men and women have experience working with women superiors. Advance training opportunities for women have increased both as graduate schools admit a larger proportion of women and as employers offer seminars and workshops in different career areas, some of them especially for women. Your chances as a woman for a rewarding career in business have never been greater.

Some Misconceptions About the Business World

Many people, including many women, have developed stereotyped views of what the business world is like. These assumptions can cut them off from opportunities, from areas of work that are financially rewarding and personally satisfying. Many people make these four common, mistaken assumptions:

Myth 1. Business only accepts women in clerical or entry-level positions.

This statement was true once. Women who owned businesses had often inherited them from husbands or fathers. Only the exceptional woman was promoted, and to advance she often had to sacrifice her personal life. Businessmen held stereotyped views of women and of jobs; "women's jobs" were the only openings for which a woman would be hired.

Although some in the business world (and the professions too) may still be reluctant to give women a chance, many businessmen have learned from their women associates what women can really accomplish.

Myth 2. Business careers aren't intellectually stimulating or don't require you to exercise your creativity. Stimulated by competition, businesses support significant research and development efforts in almost every field. Management jobs in planning, analysis, or troubleshooting require creativity and intelligence. Even a routine business job presents an intellectual challenge: how to make the job more interesting and profitable for the company—and for yourself.

Myth 3. Business degrades the people working for it, fouls the water and air, exploits the poor.

Businesses are stereotyped just as people are. Some companies are exploitive, but many others have a real interest in public service. Companies have revitalized urban neighborhoods and trained and guaranteed jobs for the "hard-core" unemployed. They have lent executives to community projects, given release time to employees for community service, contributed money to advocacy groups, and donated land to conservation agencies. Some businesses have experimented with new and more satisfying working conditions for both production and management employees. Find out which companies have an interest in public service and which ones treat their employees well; it's research well worth doing if you're planning a business career.

Myth 4. Even ethical businesses work for the profit motive, not the public good.

Working for an organization with a high public purpose, for example, a university, a hospital, or a government agency, doesn't mean that you don't still have to consider money, using it well, and being "business-like." If you are the kind of person who wants her work life to have meaning for other people, you can choose from lots of business jobs, especially in the management and human resources field.

Business Functions and Business Jobs

All businesses, from giant international corporations to the corner store, have the same functions to perform: management, marketing, selling, financial analysis and record keeping, production, and personnel or human resources management. To be successful, businesses also need the help and advice of professionals in accounting, information systems, and law. The next seven chapters of this Guide describe in detail these functions and the job areas related to them. For each function there are specialized jobs, and although the job titles may vary from company to company, the functions remain the same.

People in all functional areas work together to keep the company successful, "running in the black." In a firm manufacturing pencils, for instance, people in *production* buy the raw material, design the production lines, maintain machines, and see that the pencils are packed and delivered in good condition. Production managers make decisions about such questions as, "Is it cheaper to manufacture our own erasers or buy them from another company?" and "If we buy this machine will it pay for itself in efficiency or productivity?"

People in *marketing* study who is buying the pencils and why, and what alterations in the pencils or what new products would be profitable. They are also responsible for designing the pencil advertising to reach and appeal to people to buy the company's product.

The *sales* division sells pencils to wholesale office supply companies and stores. Sales managers set goals and provide support for salesworkers, plan sales campaigns, and consult with both production ("My customer hasn't received his last order") and marketing ("My customers wish we'd offer red pencils").

The *personnel* department screens job applicants for company positions, handles employee grievances, and often deals with labor disputes, training needs, and benefit and compensation plans. *Financial analysts* work with financial data and record keeping from throughout the company. *Accountants* keep track of the firm's expenses and receipts and manage the billing process. *Computer specialists* will be used as more and more data on inventory, expenses, and invoices are handled with computers.

There are also *managers* whose job it is to oversee departments within

WHAT THEY'RE READING

Reading business periodicals and newspapers is an excellent way to keep up with current employment, business, and economic trends, as well as to keep informed about what the "competition" is doing and how they're doing it. Here are several publications that no self-respecting business person would be caught without:

- The bible of the business world is *The Wall Street Journal,* a weekday daily that runs news stories and feature articles on business and economic affairs, as well as stock market information. Thursday is the traditional day for carrying job listings.
- Two of the more popular magazines are *Business Week* (weekly) and *Fortune* (monthly). *Business Week* reports on business and economic news and offers its own statistical analysis of economic activity. *Fortune* (of Fortune 500 fame) focuses on the people and news of the corporate world.
- In addition, the business "elite" (or would-be "elites") will often be found reading publications such as *Harvard Business Review, Dun's Review, Business and Society Review,* and *Boardroom Reports.* There are also publications offered by professional organizations, including *MBA* (MBA Communications), and *The Executive Female Digest* (National Association for Female Executives). Of special interest to business-women, *The Woman MBA* is published annually by Corporate Woman Communications, Inc.
- Finally, three basic books expound modern management practices: *The Professional Manager* by Douglas McGregor (New York: McGraw-Hill, 1967, $14.95), *The Practice of Management* by Peter F. Drucker (Scranton, Pennsylvania: Harper and Row, 1954, $11.95), and *The Exceptional Executive* by Harry Levinson (New York: New American Library, 1971, $1.75).

---

functional areas, and managers in corporate headquarters or the company's general offices whose job it is to make major corporate decisions.

In different kinds of companies the jobs within each function may vary. In a bank, for example, the equivalent of the production function is providing services to customers, such as arranging for loans, cashing checks, and making deposits to customer accounts. In a retail business or in insurance or real estate, the sales function hires the most people. (You will find a description of various industries and their special job needs in the boxed sections entitled "Industry Profile.")

CHAPTER 2

MANAGING IT ALL

Management in a company represents the interests of those who own the company. Company management is interested in producing salable products or services, earning the greatest possible profit, and helping the firm and its business grow.

Essentially, a manager's job is to make decisions for the firm, decisions such as what products or services to sell, where to market them, how to capitalize new equipment—every kind of business decision. Professional management techniques all focus on the traditional management functions of planning, organizing, and controlling, and on reducing the risk of making poor decisions.

Being a manager has some rather powerful rewards, and not only financial ones. As a manager, to a large extent you can control your own work, what you do and when you do it. You can determine to a great degree your own work environment. In addition, you can have a crack at trying out your pet theories about how people are motivated, how they are *really* led. As a manager you have real responsibility to the company and the people for whom you work.

As a manager, your position is one of power and prestige. A manager experiences some of the same sense of control and independence as the person who starts a small business. In spite of the days you may struggle with delays and red tape, as a manager you can find what one production manager called "that feeling of being a functioning part of that great machine, the American economy . . . actually making a contribution to improving America's standard of living."

You can make the move to a management career in a large corporation primarily in two ways. One route is to be hired as a management trainee. Generally college or business school graduates who spend one to two years rotating from one company department to another, management trainees learn about the firm (and vice versa) and are hired by one of its

---

Funding for this chapter was provided by General Motors Corporation.

departments at the end of the training period. The second and more common way to become a manager is to start off as a functional specialist and then move up to become a supervisor of specialists, the first step in a management career.

The Profession of Management

Since the late 19th and early 20th century, the concept of professional management has evolved into a whole body of thought—the science of management. Pioneer management theorists like Frederick W. Taylor and Frank and Lillian Gilbreth promoted new concepts of industrial engineering, designing workers' tasks and environments to make production more efficient. They introduced some ideas basic to management theory today—that a manager's job involves special skills that can be learned, that a manager is responsible for designing subordinates' tasks for most efficient production, and that study and research in management problems can produce results that have an impact on the profit margin.

Today many early theories seem out of date, depicting workers too much like parts of a machine and not human beings. Americans, now better educated and more financially secure, seek something more from their work lives, a sense of purpose, of personal growth, of satisfaction. Along with the changes in the labor force have come accelerating technological changes, the growth of larger, more complex organizations, and a much more complicated and dynamic business world.

In response to these changes a new generation of management theorists began to gain acceptance in the 1960s and 70s. Their ideas are firmly grounded in the behavioral sciences. These theorists include Douglas McGregor, Peter Drucker, and Harry Levinson, who present a view of employees as people who work harder and are more loyal when given more responsibility, more challenging work, and more credit for their efforts.

Among the new management techniques that have been developed is management by objectives, or MBO. MBO is a business planning and implementation process by which decision makers set measurable objectives for fulfilling company goals and a timetable for reaching them. As progress is evaluated (the level of sales of the company's products, for instance), it may be necessary to modify the goals and objectives to reflect such realities of doing business as the emergence of a new competitor, an increase in the cost of raw materials, or market saturation.

Management in Large Corporations

Management is a way of describing not just a group of corporate jobs but also a set of skills people need throughout the business world. In all business functions, including marketing, sales, finance, and personnel, anyone in a supervisory position must know management techniques as well as the basics of her functional area. Top corporate management has the even more difficult job of integrating these separate functions so that all company activity works toward company goals.

Generally speaking, there are three levels of management in large companies. Top or corporate management sets corporate goals and makes plans and policies for achieving those goals. Middle management carries out top management's plans. Operating managers supervise the day-to-day tasks of the concern's production employees. Management in small organizations often combines several functional areas and levels of management. The manager of a small retail store or restaurant combines them all. She's the purchasing manager, personnel manager, controller, and sales manager.

Large companies are organized in many very different ways. Some of the largest, like General Electric, for example, are highly decentralized. These concerns are almost a consortium of smaller companies. Firms with only one or two plants or locations, or those with a corporate headquarters and many field offices, tend to be more highly controlled and tightly structured. Within this range companies are generally organized in either of two ways: "line and staff" or "functional." In a "line and staff" organization each employee (whether a manager with administrative duties or a staff specialist) reports to one manager in a clear chain of command. In a functionally organized company each employee may report to one manager for some aspects of her job and to another manager for others. For instance, a personnel manager in a company division may report to the division chief for employment and staffing matters and also to the corporate personnel office for guidelines on company policies or programs.

What managers are expected to do varies a great deal from company to company, but all modern management jobs have some things in common. All managers report to somebody higher and supervise other people lower in the hierarchy. A manager is always in the middle between two sets of expectations, those of the people above her and those of the people below her in the organizational structure. To be successful, managers must be able to communicate well with both groups, plan and organize their own work time and that of others, and motivate those who work with them.

With time and experience managers develop their own personal "management style," but as with any other style in a company—style of dress, for example—their personal style must fall within the boundaries of an acceptable *company* style of management. Some firms have certain management processes that they expect their management employees to follow, like special formulas for evaluating subordinates. Other firms believe that managers are born and not made, and test their employees for certain traits before promoting them to management positions. Yet

INDUSTRY PROFILE: DRUG INDUSTRY

About 165,000 Americans worked in the drug industry in 1976. This industry produces both pharmaceutical preparations and biological products like vaccines and the chemicals used in making pharmaceutical preparations. Many companies also make diagnostic instruments and machines such as x-ray equipment or heart pacemakers.

A great deal of money and effort is spent researching and developing new products. The industry may test as many as 150,000 substances a year and end up with only 10 new medicines to market. This research emphasis is part of the reason why one out of every six people employed is a scientist, engineer, or technician.

Emphasis on quality control is another trait of this highly regulated industry. All aspects of the production process must be carefully monitored, so there are a lot of quality control jobs, many of which require a highly technical education or an advanced degree. Even drug salespeople are involved in quality control when they check drugstores for outdated products.

The industry places a premium on education, even for its management employees. A college or technical school degree is increasingly a necessity for entry-level technical or administrative positions and advanced degrees for research. Administrative positions tend to be filled by people with scientific or technical backgrounds. Most companies offer advanced education for their scientific, technical, and administrative employees.

The drug industry growth rate is expected to slow somewhat and settle down to the average rate of growth for American industry during the 1980s.

---

other companies value real "hands-on" experience so much that they prefer to promote people from the ranks and train them in management techniques when they get to the supervisory level.

What this means to you as a potential employee is that if you have already developed a management style, you would do well to look for a job in a company with which your style of management is compatible. If you haven't yet developed a style of your own, then you should carefully observe what management style your company expects and rewards.

Staff Professionals in Management

Managers use an array of professionals to supply the information to help them make the best decisions. Usually these professionals are in staff or advisory positions, although they may also be managers of their own staff. For example, the top company lawyer advising top management may also be the head of the legal staff. Many companies have specialists in their area of business, either in staff positions or as consultants to top management. These specialists may be scientists, economists, psychologists, physicians, or any number of other professionals with special skills. One professional that all companies must have is a lawyer. Another profession becoming universal in companies is that of computer specialist in electronic data processing.

Corporate Legal Staff

Virtually every large corporation has a legal staff with regular employees working full time on the company payroll. Corporations also hire law firms to do legal work. They tend to hire the law firms for special situations (to negotiate a particular contract, for instance, or to represent the corporation in a trial), although a firm may also be hired on a retainer basis to provide the corporation with all its legal services.

Computers in Business Firms

Electronic data processing (EDP) refers to the computer processing of information. A relatively new tool of business management, computers were first used by business for financial, production, and personnel functions, for keeping track of customer billing, invoices, sales orders, payroll, shipping, and inventory. They are increasingly used for marketing and corporate planning purposes. Modern computers can, for example, simulate all the conditions of the market that market researchers can predict, and they can help researchers foresee what will happen if a new product is introduced.

GETTING IN, MOVING UP: MANAGEMENT

You can enter a management career in two traditional ways. The first is to get a Master in Business Administration degree and/or be hired as a management trainee. The second is to start in a technical job, move to a supervisory position overseeing other technical workers, and advance to management from there. In some companies the line between supervisory and management jobs is a tough one to cross and may require additional training.

Because management jobs are fewer and fewer as you move up, competition for managerial positions can be very intense; long hours and hard work may be necessary if you want to advance. Managers frequently transfer to other companies or functions to improve their chances for advancement.

Business use of computers has grown so fast that the number of people trained to run them has fallen behind the demand. Moreover, jobs also change as new "generations" of computers are built. Researchers are now designing computers that respond to voice instructions and written instruction in English which will make some data processing skills unnecessary and some jobs obsolete.

Computers work by taking in information (input), processing it, and spewing it out again (output). Input is achieved by a variety of devices —punch/cards, magnetic tape, typewriters, paper tape. One set of computer-related jobs is that of feeding information into the computer through these input devices. A *keypunch operator* transcribes the data from its original form onto punched cards. A *data inputer* types information into a computer through a console with a typewriter keyboard. *Tape librarians* maintain the tapes, set up computer operating schedules, and keep operating logs. *Repair technicians* keep the machines in operating condition.

Regardless of what input device a computer has, a *programmer* is necessary. Programmers tell the computer what to do and how to do it through combinations of symbols or "languages" to which computers are designed to respond. The two most common languages are COBOL (Common Business-Oriented Language), used in business applications, and FORTRAN (Formula Translation), used for scientific and mathematical research. Using a computer language, the programmer will convert a problem of a business or scientific nature into a detailed flow chart for entry into the machine, mapping out the processing path the computer will use, deciding what information is necessary and the form that will present that information. Programmers often work as a team, depending on the project; job levels of the team may include programming manager, staff programmers, junior programmers, and trainees.

Systems analysts are the industrial engineers of the computer world. They figure out how computers can be used to solve particular problems, and interpret the results to management or to clients. Programmers carry out the plans of systems analysts.

Sales representatives and *systems engineers* work for computer manufacturers. The people who find new uses and users for computers, they also frequently help systems analysts and the company data processing manager determine what EDP services the company needs.

Historians have long characterized cultures by the tools they used, hence the names given to the Stone Age and the Iron Age. The tools people use do in fact have an impact on how we think. And this is true of the "age of computers." "The systems approach" to management is both a philosophy of management and a pattern of thought directly related to the widespread use of EDP. It represents a further evolution of the concept of scientific management toward management information and decision-making systems. Modern corporate managers must learn

A NOT-FOR-PROFIT CORPORATION—WHAT IS IT?

A not-for-profit (formerly referred to as nonprofit) corporation is a special kind of legal entity with no stockholders or investors that must spend what money it earns. A bank or an individual may lend the not-for-profit corporation money and get interest on that loan as it is repaid, but may not have a financial interest in the corporation.

In other respects not-for-profit corporations are similar to "for-profit" corporations. Both can have boards of directors, executive officers, financial officers, salaried employees, articles of incorporation, bylaws, etc. Salaries in some not-for-profit corporations are as high as in profit-making corporations of the same size.

Most not-for-profit corporations seek tax-exempt status, meaning that their earnings are not taxed and also that a contribution to the corporation can be taken as an income tax deduction by the donor. This status can be very important since most individuals and all foundations will contribute only to organizations that are tax exempt. The Internal Revenue Service of the Treasury Department awards tax-exempt status (and a tax-exemption number) to not-for-profit corporations that conform to certain regulations and are organized for educational, charitable, or scientific purposes.

There are two major differences between working for a not-for-profit corporation and working for a profit-making corporation. If you are a higher-level manager in a not-for-profit corporation, you will be expected to be able to bring money to the corporation either through direct fund-raising efforts or through grant applications to government or foundations. You will also be expected to work well with a board of directors. In not-for-profit corporations these boards can be stronger and more interested in making management decisions than in profit-making corporations. Members of the board can come from widely differing backgrounds, but they all represent sources of support (usually financial) for the not-for-profit corporation. When looking for a job, be sure to analyze the pros and cons of for-profit and not-for-profit employers to determine which is better for you.

about EDP, not just to understand their options when buying computer "hardware" (the machines themselves) or to help design and use "software" (computer programs), but to understand new directions in the profession of corporate management.

No matter how technical the decision to be made or how significant the computer information to be analyzed, only a human being, a professional manager, has the authority and responsibility to integrate information and company resources and to make the final decisions that will achieve company goals.

Arlene Sterling, General Manager

When Arlene Sterling graduated from the Harvard Business School with an MBA in marketing, she had the same qualifications as but less ambition than her male counterparts. It's a testament to her innate talent for business management that she has risen to the coveted position of president and general manager of the book clubs division of a huge publishing conglomerate. Today she manages an operating unit that employs roughly 700 people and has sales of over $100 million.

"Although I always advise people starting their careers to have a game plan, I frankly didn't have one myself," she recalls. "I have a number of women friends—all now in their late 30s—who got MBAs around the same time I did. Looking back, we see how we stumbled into business careers almost by accident. In undergraduate school we banished the thought that we might have to work for the rest of our lives. I think we all had vague aspirations to do something interesting if not downright challenging; but the idea of running a business or making a lot of money was not high in our consciousness.

"After we got our first jobs and found we were good at them, were promoted, and brought home a good-sized paycheck, we got a taste of power and recognition. Eventually, you're addicted to these things. I was out of business school five years before I developed any career goals."

Ms. Sterling's first two jobs were anything but ego-satisfying. As a market researcher for a large consumer products company, she set up computer codes, coded questionnaires, and supervised other coders. At her next job in the Chicago office of a New York advertising agency, she made all the media buying decisions for a lawnmower account.

Pregnancy and motherhood were partially responsible for the lowliness of these jobs, she concedes. Married right after her graduation from Harvard, for the six months she held her first job she was pregnant. After nine months at home caring for her baby son, she landed her second job and has been working full time at progressively better jobs ever since.

Her husband's transfer to New York opened up a new world of career opportunities for Ms. Sterling. Originally, her plan was to take an account executive's job with her agency's New York headquarters, but fate intervened. A college friend was secretary to the chairman of a large, respected book publisher. Ms. Sterling was dubious about working in a publishing house because "I knew such places were filled with bright young women who make $70 a week." But she agreed to an interview with the chairman and came away very impressed.

"The chairman seemed genuinely interested in developing promising individuals for management slots even though the company had no formal training program. Also, I liked the fact that there was a deficiency of MBA-types like myself in the middle-management ranks. It would be a ground-floor opportunity for internal promotion."

Ms. Sterling joined the firm as a research analyst, a corporate staff function. It was an ideal entry-level job for someone with an MBA and ambition. Analysts were exposed to all the company's operating units; in turn, division managers had a chance to assess the analysts' capabilities. Research analysts did sophisticated financial and market information gathering for any executive who needed assistance. A typical project might be to evaluate the trade book division's sales territories in terms of the volume of business each generated.

This was the mid-60s, a go-go period for the publishing industry and for Ms. Sterling's employer in particular. Every day another independent publishing house was acquired by some industrial giant or to expand and diversify a publishing company bought firms in related industries. Ms. Sterling's employer took the latter route, affording her the opportunity to do mergers and acquisitions research. She analyzed the profit-and-loss statements and overall management health of acquisitions candidates in industries ranging from broadcasting to educational audio-visuals.

After two years, she was tapped to become manager of the research department, which consisted of three analysts. She almost refused the promotion fearing it might type her as a staff person when a line marketing spot was her real goal. Her boss convinced her that a turndown would be an insult to the higher-ups who had faith in her ability. She accepted. "I learned something from that decision: never be too proud. If you're offered the chance to get a new kind of experience, grab it."

Ms. Sterling's fears did not materialize; one year later she was advertising manager in the book clubs division. "I knew I wanted to work in the clubs because it was the company's most sophisticated marketing operation."

Ms. Sterling was in charge of all direct-response advertising for 20-odd book clubs. She had one assistant, a secretary, a budget of $5 million that grew to $9 million, and five outside advertising agencies doing her bidding.

"What I remember most about that period was being tired all the time. The ad agency people lined up outside my door and filed through my office and about all I had time to do was say, 'Yes . . . No . . . Run that . . . Shelve that.' It was an incredibly fatiguing job."

After two years, the division was reorganized, and a product manager system was instituted. Where once one hard-working manager was in charge of advertising for all 20 clubs, now seven product managers had overall responsibility for three or four clubs each. The company's flagship book club and three others fell to Ms. Sterling.

Ms. Sterling's star began to shine in this job, although she claims her tenure there seemed interminable. "I thought I would live and die a product manager." However, she admits she learned a number of lessons in that spot. The biggest? " . . . to take responsibility for my mistakes as well as my triumphs. Many people, particularly fast-track MBAs, move up so fast that they never get saddled with the consequences of any bad, long-term decisions they make. The people who succeed them get stuck cleaning up the mess. I cleaned up my own messes."

She also learned about risk-taking: "I introduced some new clubs, an expensive proposition, and a few didn't work out. But this is a fair place and if the logic leading you to make the decision is sensible and the project well executed, you won't be crucified for the attempt."

She learned another political lesson: never launch a new idea without enlisting the support of your boss. "Sure, you should take chances and try out your ideas, but let your superiors know what you're doing every step of the way so the end result, good or bad, doesn't come as a surprise. Of course, the other side of that coin is the problem of theft—bosses and peers who try to take credit for your successful innovations. Fortunately, I'm a prolific writer and I learned early to document all my moves in memos and marketing plans. If you do that in this business, then you're home free because direct-mail advertising is one field where your results are quantifiable. If you create good ads, you get a good coupon response. It's a good business for women in that respect. It's quite evident if you are doing well."

Ms. Sterling's decisions as product manager added up to explosive sales and increased profits, feats her superiors could hardly ignore. She was made group marketing director, supervising three product managers —her first *bona fide* management position.

From this point on, promotions came fast. In less than a year, she became the director of marketing, the springboard to her present position as president and general manager of the division, a job which she's held for the last four years. Two group marketing directors, two creative directors, one editorial director, one business manager, and one director of services report to her. She, in turn, reports to a corporate group vice-president. Within the corporate hierarchy, she has risen to the lower senior management level.

Her job is extremely people oriented, although she continues to fulfill a number of "hands-on, task-oriented functions," such as the evaluation of financial reports, marketing plans, and editorial memos. While she delegates a lot of responsibility, she continues to act as a sounding board for new ideas and has gotten the message across that she's the ultimate decision maker on important, big-ticket projects. She also mediates major "squabbles" be they internal or concern outside suppliers or regulatory bodies.

As a general rule, she tries to assume the role of "nudger and prodder" and let subordinates work out their own problems. "As a manager, I've had to learn to live with the things I no longer do myself that I may consider suboptimal. It's the old problem, 'If you want something done right, do it yourself.' If I have to fire the person responsible, I never do it without giving him or her ample opportunity to shape up."

Such confrontations are still the aspect of the job Ms. Sterling likes least. "I think women have difficulty dealing with confrontations on the job, although I see plenty of men who don't relish them either. Gradually, I've learned I can't please everybody and that's helped me take unpopular stands."

The personnel aspects of Ms. Sterling's job continue to pose the greatest challenge. "Developing an ideal managerial body is very difficult ... minimizing people's weaknesses and trying to get the most out of their strengths, trying to get people to improve. You don't learn this in business school. This is where I think maturity and experience pay off. Often I see young managers in their late 20s or early 30s who are technically superior and have good ideas, but they're an abomination when it comes to managing people because they are very insensitive to others' feelings."

What advice does Ms. Sterling have for those aspiring to a job like her own? "Get the best education you can—preferably an MBA from one of the big-name schools. Work for a good company, one that's technically sophisticated and demands excellence. Get a variety of experience— line experience is essential. And don't expect to start out as a general manager. Fewer and fewer companies hire 'generalists' for their management training programs. A 'general manager' is something a specialist becomes as she is promoted up the corporate ladder."

BASIC RESOURCES

The American Management Association (AMA) is a professional association for managers offering periodicals, survey reports, meetings, conferences, courses, and hardcover books. A basic resource for business people, the AMA operates through 12 divisions, including finance, general management, marketing, and human resources. For more information contact:

American Management Association
American Management Association Building
135 West 50th Street
New York, New York 10020

Programmers and systems analysts seeking information should contact the following professional organizations:

American Federation of Information
   Processing Societies
210 Summit Avenue
Montvale, New Jersey 07645

Association for Computing Machinery
1133 Avenue of the Americas
New York, New York 10036

Association for Systems Management
24587 Bagley Road
Cleveland, Ohio 44138

CHAPTER 3

IN THE MARKETPLACE

Marketing means different things to different people and to different companies. In some companies the marketing department is a product-related research wing of the sales department. But in those companies which place a major emphasis on the marketing concept, the director or vice-president of marketing plays a major part in business planning and decision making, with the departments of research, advertising, public relations, and distribution subordinate.

Marketing—What Is It?

The marketing concept is that a company can make more money by tailoring its products or services to the needs of its customers than it can by just making a standard product that may be easier for the company to design and manufacture.

Only since the Second World War has this relatively new concept really taken hold. But taken hold it has; look at the Ford Motor Company, for instance. Henry Ford started with only one model car, the Model T. The car was offered in only one color (black) and was manufactured in the same form for 10 years. In the period since World War II, the company has built all types of cars for all kinds of customers in all price ranges— station wagons, pickups, vans, luxury cars, sports cars, sedans, subcompacts, and everything in between. Available in a range of colors and with many options, each model changes every year.

For just about every product—from candy bars to continuing education courses—the choices confronting the modern consumer are more numerous than ever before, thanks largely to the marketing concept.

Funding for this chapter was provided by Philip Morris, Inc.

NOTE FROM THE PAST

Sarah Breedlove Walker, Inventor, Marketer, and Businesswoman

Sarah Breedlove Walker (1867–1919), or Madame Co Jo Walker, as she became known, was a black born in rural Louisiana who invented and became the ingenious marketer of the Walker Method of straightening hair. To support herself and her daughter, Madame Walker worked as a washerwoman in St. Louis. She mixed her first ointments and soaps in her washtubs. The Walker System consisted of a shampooing followed by applying a hair-grower pomade accompanied by vigorous brushing. Afterward the hair was straightened with hot iron combs. At one point Madame Walker's factory and distribution network consisted of 3,000 employees. Walker Agents, or "hair culturists" as she called them, went from door to door to demonstrate and sell her beauty products. Most of the agents were women, identifiable by their white shirts, long black skirts, and black satchels. The agents were trained to promote "cleanliness and loveliness" among their clients. This direct and personal selling system was so successful that by 1920 many European firms were imitating it. Madame Walker used her wealth to support educational and philanthropic projects for blacks.

This concept has been expanded to include creating the need for the product in consumers' minds.

The success of the marketing concept has created a whole new job specialty and added new elements to old jobs. Marketing professionals work for corporations and consulting firms to identify consumers for products and services and to get the company's message across to those consumers. Within the general framework of marketing are three kinds of marketing positions: marketing research, advertising, and public relations.

Marketing Research

Marketing research is a technique used to help make company decisions. Marketing personnel study what motivates consumers to buy company products, how and when the products are used, who might use them, and how much people are willing to pay for them. A firm's public relations department can use market research techniques to discover the public's attitude toward the company and later retest it to determine how effective a public relations campaign has been. Advertising agen-

CHECKLIST OF PERSONALITY TRAITS

Would-be marketing majors, see if you can affirmatively answer the following questions:

- Am I capable of seeing the big picture in terms of shifting economic and social trends, political realities, and changing lifestyles?
- Am I temperamentally equipped to cope with uncertainty, high pressure, and constant change on a daily basis?
- Do I enjoy besting a competitor?
- Am I willing to work long hours if necessary?
- Do I have a good memory for facts and figures, and am I able to see the relationships between them?
- Am I good at following up on details?
- Am I an extrovert?

---

cies routinely do market research to track how their ads are received by the public, how effective they are.

The basic method of market research is survey research in which a sample group of people is identified and either interviewed by phone or in person or given questionnaires to complete. If the sample is a good one, the company learns what it can expect from the group as a whole.

Another way marketing managers compile information about their products and markets is by keeping careful records of *what* is purchased and *where*. You've probably filled out a guarantee card for a small appliance and wondered why they asked all those questions like, "Where did you buy this item?" and "Is this item a gift?" The information on that card helps the company make marketing decisions. Companies also interview their sales force and distributors for information about the product. All this information goes into a marketing decision.

At the entry level, careers in marketing include interviewing and tabulating statistical information as a research assistant or a junior analyst. (Without a statistical background or computer training, however, it is hard to advance to the point where you are designing as well as carrying out research projects.) Another way into marketing is from a position as a sales representative in the field. Sales reps really know company products, sales concepts, and consumer response to them. People with company advertising or promotional experience can also make the move to market research, but they will need to work hard to learn research techniques and how to evaluate research data. As one brand manager put it, "There are always more technical things to learn. I'm learning all the time."

How you move up in marketing depends on how your company views the marketing function. If marketing is a heavily research-oriented formal business planning process in your firm, you may need an advanced degree like an MBA with a concentration in marketing to make it to middle management. If in your company brand managers are responsible for all promotion and advertising decisions as well as marketing research for their brands, then an advertising, promotion, or sales background can help you become a marketing manager.

Although the fashion in these things changes, many top corporate managers have come up through marketing. Thus marketing management jobs are highly desirable if you want to make it to the top.

Advertising

Advertising is part of a firm's marketing and sales strategy. Its purpose is to convey information about the characteristics of company products and services to induce people to buy them. Advertising generally uses the print and broadcast media—newspapers and magazines, radio, and television. But modern advertising campaigns extend across an extraordinary range of media, including direct mailings, billboards, handouts, posters, tee shirts, and skywriting.

As competition for the consumer dollar increases and the number of new products proliferates, so do the job opportunities in advertising.

GETTING IN, MOVING UP: MARKET RESEARCH

It is possible to enter this field as an interviewer and move into a supervisory position, but you will not usually be able to advance beyond that level without at least a college degree. Marketing research is a highly technical field; training in statistics and electronic data processing is particularly helpful. Marketing research departments may hire management trainees, some of whom may have advanced degrees. Sales specialists in company products may also qualify for some marketing positions.

Moving up in marketing research begins with being the director of a small research project or the assistant director of a larger one and continuing to direct larger and larger projects. Director of marketing research is the top position in a company department.

The dollars spent for advertising increase also: in 1976 more than $10 billion was spent on advertising, and about 180,000 people worked in jobs related to advertising.

Advertising budgets vary a great deal from industry to industry. For example, industrial manufacturers spend less than 1 percent of their net sales revenue on advertising, whereas makers of toiletry products spend as much as 30 percent. Most advertising jobs involve consumer goods.

Advertising has the reputation of being a glamorous field because of its emphasis on talent and creative abilities. Advertising agencies hire artists, filmmakers, musicians, writers, actors, and models. And talented people can make a fortune in advertising with little or no formal education.

However, advertising is a field that is very sensitive to the economic climate. In a recession, advertising budgets are often the first to be cut. Despite exciting opportunities for rapid advancement, advertising jobs, in agencies particularly, are often not very stable. After heading a large successful national ad campaign, an account executive may instantly become a new vice-president of her firm. But if the campaign fails, not only the account manager but her top creative staff may find themselves jobless. (This can also occur with many jobs in the public relations field.)

Women have been a part of the advertising industry for some time. They have achieved some measure of success in just about every area of the business, and they play a decision-making role in many agencies. There have been female "stars" in advertising too, women who broke the job barrier and went on to become real success stories. Mary Wells Lawrence, chief executive officer and chairman of Wells, Rich, Greene, Inc., is a highly respected industry figure. She is reputedly one of the highest-paid women in the nation, earning more than $250,000 a year.

Advertising jobs can be found in both corporations and advertising agencies. Generally speaking, most company, or in-house, advertising departments handle sales promotions, produce the materials their sales representatives use, and do mail-order advertisements, leaving other advertising to a hired private agency. Retail stores, however, are a common exception. They often handle *all* their advertising in house: preparing the copy, photographs, and artwork and then placing the ads in local newspapers and magazines.

Corporation advertising departments may employ entry-level personnel such as copywriters for writing ads and graphic artists for handling artwork and layout. An advertising manager runs the department and also hires outside agencies. She works along with the ad agency representatives, outlining the company's objectives and budget and helping to plan campaigns.

The power centers of advertising are the independent advertising agencies. They account for most of the money spent on advertising and are the most visible symbols of the industry. More and more businesses

THE CASE OF VIRGINIA SLIMS

In advertising the name of the game is generating sales. Agencies use a wide variety of approaches and sales techniques to make their products attractive and to induce people to buy.

Women form a large percentage of the total number of consumers; many ad campaigns are specifically geared toward the very profitable female market. In the past, women featured in advertisements conformed to the stereotypes of wife, housewife, mother. More recently, women in advertisements have been featured in roles such as busdrivers, doctors, and lawyers.

Here is the story of how one ad agency built a highly successful campaign by identifying the product, in this case Virginia Slims, specifically with the woman consumer. If you're interested in the field of marketing, you'll find this account, taken from "How an Agency Builds a Brand—The Virginia Slims Story," by Hal Weinstein, vice-president and creative director of Leo Burnett Company of Chicago, full of tips on how to market a product well.

This story is about Virginia Slims—and how it happened at the agency, as seen from the creative side.

In the cigarette world, as you know, if you don't have a strong personality—an identity—you don't have a brand. The smoker's motivation and loyalty to a brand comes from identifying with the personality of that brand.

So the creative task in cigarette advertising is very simply to establish and maintain a clear and attractive personality for your brand. The more attractive—and the broader the appeal—the better.

The story starts in the fall of 1967 when American Tobacco Company brought out Silva Thins—and the question came to us from Philip Morris—"What would you do with a thin cigarette like Silva Thins if Philip Morris were to make one?"

... "The first cigarette for women only." This selling idea which had been kicking around between agency and client for so many years without going anywhere now suddenly had at hand the perfect product difference needed to bring it to life—the slimmer cigarette. In fact, it was the key. With that our creative horizons suddenly opened up. . . .

We had two of the three key ingredients in cigarette success—an appreciable product difference, that fit with an important market segment. What remained was to develop a great personality for the brand—as attractive as possible—with the right kind of advertising. . . .

It was at 11 AM on the day before our creative review committee meeting—at the eleventh hour, you might say—that lightning finally struck. One great brain came up with the concept of women's rights, and a strong line that expressed it:

"You've come a long way, baby." The story was simple, and went like so: "It used to be that women had no rights. Now they have the rights. Now they have everything. You've COME A LONG WAY, Baby. And now you even have a cigarette brand for your very own." It was fun, it was simple, and it was fresh. And like all good ideas, it was easy to write. Between 11 AM and 10 PM our group put together a dozen ads for the next day's meeting.

It takes three right ingredients to create a cigarette brand. First, enough of a product difference to be interesting. Second, a market segment that that product difference can appeal to. And third, the appeal has to be right. Which means the personality has to be strong and in the right mood for the people you're talking to. When we got these rough layouts on paper, we knew we were home. We felt we had all the ingredients. . . .

Everything new that has been done for the brand, i.e., promotions, outdoor, in-store material, spread ads, even new test market products, has been built off of the same base. Which all goes to prove one thing: the right product with the right positioning and the right execution can be an unbeatable combination in marketing.

---

are relying on outside agencies, or else are combining forces with them to sell their products and services through the media.

About one-third of the jobs in advertising are found in the approximately 6,000 agencies. Agencies work on a commission basis and usually receive 15 percent of the value of the newspaper or magazine space and television or radio time they buy for their clients. The client company also pays the agency's direct expenses, such as the costs of artwork, printing, and talent.

Advertising agencies are generally used to conduct national advertising campaigns. Large agencies maintain market research staff to appraise the "pull" or appeal of their ads and changes in market. For each corporate client the agency assigns an account executive whose job includes determining the best marketing strategy, planning the campaign, producing the ads or commercials, and placing them in the broadcasting or print media.

Ad agencies hire copywriters and graphic artists just as corporate advertising departments do, but these positions are so sought after that sometimes applicants must take clerical or "go-fer" jobs to break into the business. One good access route to advertising is working in the advertising department of a retail store. Any work that you can do that will help you build up a portfolio to show potential employers will help you prove your abilities and talents when looking for an advertising job.

Middle management in ad agencies includes art directors, who oversee the creation of the advertising campaign; production managers, who produce radio and television ads or arrange to have ads printed; space buyers, who secure space in magazines and newspapers; and time buyers, who purchase air time for radio and television commercials. (Media buyers must be able to make crucial choices. One minute on national prime-time television or one full-page four-color ad in a national magazine can cost over $50,000.)

Ad agency employees often work as a team on accounts, combining areas of special expertise. A characteristic of the careers of the most successful account executives is that at a certain point they start their own agencies, often taking both their accounts and their team with them. Although advertising managers in corporations have the option of moving into sales or management careers within the company, or even into outside ad agencies, ad agency staff is usually considered too creative or not sufficiently skilled or disciplined in business techniques to be able to move into corporate management positions. So if you are interested in an advertising career but would like to reserve the option of moving into corporate management, it would be best to find work within a company advertising department rather than in a private agency.

Public Relations

Public relations (PR) people require many of the same skills as people in advertising and marketing, but the *goals* of a public relations campaign (and therefore of those who conduct it) are different from the goals of an advertising or marketing campaign. As a PR person you may need to research public attitudes and have writing or graphic arts skills, just as in marketing and advertising. But in public relations you are seeking public exposure and awareness for a company project or a company name, not a company product. Although a company PR effort may be part of a large marketing plan and may also heavily influence the firm's sales picture, its focus is not on any particular market segment or on the nature of any product that will be sold.

GETTING IN, MOVING UP: ADVERTISING

Advertising is a creative and highly competitive field. To break into it, people sometimes take clerical jobs. Entry positions include copy writers, who produce the words, copy text, and headlines for ads; artists, layout workers, and photographers, who illustrate and design the ads; and space and time buyers, who place the ads in the media.

Advancement is to a supervisory position in one of these specialties: copy chief, art director, or media director. In advertising agencies, account executive is the management position that deals directly with clients. Your ability to advance in the field depends on the effectiveness of the ads you help produce, according to market research data and the satisfaction of the client. Some talented people in advertising start firms of their own.

INDUSTRY PROFILE: THE MEDIA

Printing and publishing firms employed 1.1 million Americans in 1976; radio and television, another 160,000. Most people in printing and publishing worked for newspapers—more than 380,000 of them; in broadcasting, most were employed by the three major national networks.

All media hire specialized technicians, and in both printing and broadcasting, technological advances have caused labor problems and led to unemployment. For example, the increasing use of videotape in television news broadcasts is putting film technicians' and film editors' jobs on the line. In printing, "hot type" linotype operators have been replaced by "cold type" printing processes such as phototypesetting and computerized typesetting.

Publishing and radio and TV are industries with a glamorous image. Very talented people—artists, writers, performers—work for these companies. Popular theory has it that media employees succeed or fail on the basis of creative abilities only, earn fabulous salaries, and attain fame. But, as one communications executive put it, "People forget we're basically a business like any other."

This glamour image influences jobs. For one thing, at the entry level a great deal of competition exists. Often people with good training accept lower-level jobs as secretaries or "go-fers" in broadcasting or as editorial assistants in publishing just to "break into the field." In broadcasting or journalism, it's easier to get that first job in a small local station or newspaper than in a large metropolitan area. In communications the upper-level jobs are highly paid but not as stable as equivalent jobs in other industries. Because of the emphasis on talent, rigid academic or experience qualifications are not always required, and companies haven't often offered their employees significant training opportunities except for on-the-job training in technical areas.

Jobs in the broadcasting media are expected to grow as fast as most occupations during the 1980s, but in publishing the growth rate is expected to slow.

In public relations the concern is with the broad public perception of the company you represent. This endeavor may include creating a new public image through the use of a new logo or a company-sponsored public event such as a professional golf tournament or trade conference. It may mean placing information in the news media about everything from hiring and promotions to the news of products. Public relations may involve acting as a company spokesperson or arranging interviews with corporate executives for newspaper reporters.

In a PR career you will be called on to do a variety of writing assignments beyond that of crafting the ubiquitous press release. You may have to write reports, pamphlets, newsletters, radio and TV copy,

GETTING IN, MOVING UP: PUBLIC RELATIONS

Public relations is one of those fields where talent and experience count more than training or degrees. The traditional way to get into PR is as a writer or organizer of promotional events. A college degree is required, and journalism is a good background to have.

To advance in the field, experience is very important. You can become a candidate for a PR management position by taking on progressively more and more difficult and complex assignments involving supervisory duties. Once they have had significant experience, many people in this field form consulting firms of their own.

---

speeches, trade paper and magazine articles, and perhaps even technical materials. In some corporations the public relations staff edit and publish employee publications, brochures, internal newsletters, and the corporate annual report. The PR department usually handles the theme, layout, photos, and artwork for these publications.

PR is a field that is constantly expanding to meet the demand for its services. One index of this boom is that the number of people employed has risen from less than 1,000 only 30 years ago to more than 250,000 today. Three new PR specialties have evolved during this period: PR for not-for-profit organizations, community and consumer relations, and government relations.

Fund raising for not-for-profit organizations is a relatively new field, using direct-mail marketing campaigns or staging events or benefits. For most major not-for-profit corporations a professional public relations campaign has taken the place of volunteer, door-to-door, or phone solicitation for funds and support.

Community and consumer relations is another new specialty in the PR field, handling customer complaints and special customer/company projects. One example of a community relations PR effort is that of the staff of a large Northeastern utility who give free energy-conservation talks and cooking demonstrations to community groups across the state.

Another PR specialty is government relations. Jobs in this field are usually located in state capitals or in Washington, D.C., and include not only lobbying efforts on behalf of a company but also keeping track of regulations affecting the firm and its industry and helping to prepare company testimony before government regulatory bodies.

Entry-level jobs generally involve writing, editing, or graphic design. A business, journalism, or graphic design background is generally a good

THE THRILL OF IT ALL: PUBLIC RELATIONS

"I know my job. And that means a lot of detail. I know printing processes, typefaces, inks, papers, plus hundreds of little tricks to make things look good."

"I like this kind of concrete, specific work. I've got something to show for myself at the end of the day. And I've got a portfolio to show what I've accomplished over the last three years."

"The most fun is getting something back from the printer when it's been done right."

one for getting into the field. PR jobs that involve creative work rather than policy making have been among the business careers traditionally most accessible to women. About one-fourth of all public relations workers are women.

To advance from an entry-level job you must move to an administrative position. A first step in this move up might involve supervising the graphic arts department and participating in PR campaign planning sessions. In that case, whether your background is in writing or graphics, you will need to learn enough about all the fields and skills used in PR work so that you will be able to plan and evaluate other people's work.

PR jobs in companies are not usually considered stepping stones to the higher-level management positions. In some firms PR people are considered "creative and not businesslike." Many experienced PR professionals who have the necessary extensive contacts form independent consulting firms.

Public relations is a well-paying field, especially in the upper ranks of the consulting business. An account executive in a high-powered firm in a large city can make from $75,000 to $100,000. A good PR person in a large firm, with at least five years' experience, can probably make $25,000. There may be little job security, however, particularly in the larger consulting firms, where an important client defection can result in firings. In this respect, as in others, public relations is similar to advertising.

THE DAILY GRIND: PUBLIC RELATIONS

*"Everybody thinks they can do your job if you're
in public relations. They don't know the knowledge
and experience it takes to make certain kinds
of judgments."*

*"In PR you have to produce on time, accurately,
and within certain specifications —whether
you're inspired or not."*

*"I'm doing too much ghost writing. I'm beginning
to feel like a ghost. Oh, for something with my
name on it, so people would say to me, 'That was
a great article.' "*

Applying Marketing Concepts to a Marketing Career

Many of the most lucrative and creative careers in marketing are the
least secure. Lower-level or highly technical research jobs are usually
the most secure. However, the person responsible for the important
marketing decisions is likely to get either the blame or the credit for the
results. At the decision-making level in marketing careers, you can expect a "what have you done for me lately" attitude; so past successes
won't always cover for present failures.

People in marketing may find that their careers, like the consumer
attitudes they try to predict, will go through a lot of changes. As one
marketing manager whose specialty is media advertising said,

> In parts of our business you aren't considered to be any good if you
> haven't been fired at least once. If you haven't been fired, you haven't
> had the guts to take the risks you need to take to be successful in this
> racket.

What this kind of atmosphere means is that for talented, energetic, and
creative women the chances for rapid promotions are good. Your talent
is your most important product, so apply your understanding of marketing techniques to your own career. Here are some examples:

> *Product life cycle* is the idea that a new product has a slow period of
> initial growth after it has been introduced, followed by a rapid period of

growth to a peak of popularity, which then falls off slowly to a low constant level. If your career has peaked and started to slow down, maybe you should consider an expansion of your product line—a new set of skills perhaps or developing a new use for an old product—for example, applying your skills and experience to a new area.

Marketing mix refers to the right blend of product, promotion (advertising), price, and distribution or place. If you are having trouble selling yourself, assess whether you have the right abilities, priced at the right salary level, with the right resume in the right part of the company to reach your "consumers," your potential employers. You may need to do some research, for example, on the salary levels for people with your skills.

Market segmentation is the practice of identifying what portion of the market is the most likely to buy the product and then of gearing all promotional efforts to that segment. When you are looking for a job, you might want to consider your most likely potential employers and focus all your efforts on selling yourself to them.

Ellen Finestein, Marketing Manager

Perhaps the essence of marketing is timing and teamwork—the coordination of consumer research with product introduction, advertising with product distribution.

"It takes a certain kind of person to be good at marketing," says 31-year-old Ellen Finestein, a brand manager for a huge cosmetics company with over $1 billion in sales annually. "You have to be both creative and detail oriented. And above all, you have to be extroverted and amiable, or you'll never get your colleagues to work with you rather than against you."

Ms. Finestein may be a minor expert on the subject of teamwork gone awry. Her first marketing job was in another cosmetics firm world-renowned for its internecine political wars. She recalls being extremely unhappy there because co-workers were seldom cooperative.

"As an assistant marketing manager, I was always being sent off to get something accomplished, and I'd constantly be blocked by people who didn't like my boss and wouldn't budge or who purposely missed the agreed-on deadlines. It was a very frustrating and brutal atmosphere. When I left that company, no one was surprised. If I left my present employer, I'd almost have to apologize for it. Everyone is so helpful and supportive here."

The contrasting political climate is not the only difference between her former and present employers. Her old company distributed its line of beauty products through regular retail channels, maintaining counters in all the large department stores and stocking drug and variety chain stores throughout the country. Her current employer eschews those outlets and sells its products through a vast network of independent sales representatives in the United States and abroad.

Ms. Finestein holds the title of campaign planner (comparable to a brand manager elsewhere) in the company's Costa Rican division. She is responsible for formulating 5 of the division's 20 yearly sales campaigns. She plans each campaign, comprising a sales period of approximately 3 weeks, in a highly disciplined and organized fashion.

First, Ms. Finestein analyzes the results from previous campaigns and notes which offers and promotional gimmicks resulted in the highest sales. Next, she decides what pricing, space allotment, and product mix to feature in the slick, four-color sales brochure that accompanies each campaign. Then, she indulges her imagination in choosing a theme for the brochure that will tie all the products and offers together and make an impact on the customer.

At this point, Ms. Finestein must present her rough ideas to the eight other marketing professionals in the Costa Rican division. These informal brainstorming sessions are a true test of teamwork in action and the reason why the Costa Rican subsidiary is considered one of the most innovative in the company. "Unlike other divisions, we always try to work out each campaign in theory and concept before we get involved in the numbers and statistics. We find that separating the purely creative aspects from the purely technical aspects of marketing helps us to formulate more effective plans."

The campaigns, in polished form, are then presented to a cross section of people from other company divisions during one of the four formal sales conferences held each year. Each planner explains his or her campaign, knowing that at least one top corporate officer is listening to every word.

"There is a lot of pressure on us to put on a good show," she says. "The flashiness and organization of your presentation and your ability as a public speaker all count heavily for or against you. I wasn't in this company long before I realized how essential it was that I learn to think on my feet and speak off the cuff. Fortunately, the company holds in-house workshops in speech communications and they helped me a lot. The course was a confidence-builder besides teaching me some useful presentation techniques."

Ms. Finestein returns home from each sales planning conference armed with further suggestions to improve her campaign and an OK from superiors to proceed. During this final wrap-up stage, she writes up the raw data for the brochure and turns it over to a copywriter and art director, who turn out the finished booklet. They will confer with her and get her approval every step of the way. In the meantime, she must inform the packaging group of the special offers being made in her campaign so they can design appropriate packages and labels.

Finally, Ms. Finestein alerts the liaison office in Costa Rica of the forthcoming campaign so that the staff can drum up interest among the sales representatives in the field. Since the products are manufactured in Costa Rica, campaign plans must be forwarded to the production staff well ahead of time to ensure an adequate inventory of each product when the campaign commences.

What Ms. Finestein likes best about her job is the challenge. "There is a reason for every offer included in one of my campaigns. Either it's based on my instincts about a developing trend in the beauty or fashion field, or it supports the theme of the brochure, or it's an experiment to test a new marketing strategy, or it's a proven winner, a product or offer that has sold spectacularly well in the past."

Ms. Finestein also enjoys analyzing the final results of each of her campaigns. "I learn a lot by carefully reviewing the sales figures for each item offered during a campaign and trying to speculate why it did well or poorly. Usually, nothing is inherently wrong with the product. The failure, if it lies anywhere, is in the presentation. Fortunately, the cosmetics industry is very lucrative, and money is built into the budget for market experimentation and the failures that sometimes result."

What she likes least about her job, and marketing in general, is the "tedium" of working with numbers. "I happen to enjoy the conceptual side of marketing the best, but I'd be pretty lousy at my job if I couldn't work with figures as well. Working with a calculator is not my idea of a good time and I admit I do it because I have to. I recognize it's a necessary aspect of marketing and, in a way, I'm thankful this job requires a lot of it. You can have all the wild, way-out marketing ideas in the world but without numerical documentation, few companies will let you proceed with them. Statistics give you the ammunition to get your creative ideas implemented."

Ms. Finestein took a circuitous route to arrive in her current occupation. She graduated from the University of Wisconsin in 1969 with a degree in history and aspirations to become a teacher. She immediately landed a job teaching second-graders in a private school on Long Island and entered night school at Columbia Teachers' College to work toward an MA in education. By the time she earned that MA, she'd decided an MBA was the degree she really coveted. To achieve that goal she attended New York University's graduate business school program at night.

The first business job was that of a sales representative for a well-known cosmetics company. Her teaching experience was invaluable here, for a large part of her job involved the training of the sales clerks who sold the company's products in department and specialty stores. She also conferred with the stores' managements on such matters as the hiring of qualified cosmetic-counter saleswomen, in-store product merchandising, promotion and advertising, and general public relations. On special promotions, she occasionally turned demonstrator herself and gave lectures to customers about effective make-up application and other tricks of the beauty trade.

It wasn't long before Ms. Finestein began to see that she was just another spoke emanating from the central hub of decision-making power and prestige back in the headquarters office. "The minute I focused on the fact that I was just implementing policies and decisions made by the marketing staff in the home office," she says, "a marketing job became my goal. It took me two years to make the transition because marketing people tend to see themselves as a cut above sales. As an interim step, I moved into the home office as a promotional events coordinator, in essence the liaison between the marketing decision makers and sales reps in the field. Six months later I accomplished my goal and became an assistant marketing manager, a good entry-level job for someone straight out of school with a background in marketing."

For reasons already mentioned, Ms. Finestein found that the job's headaches cancelled out its virtues; she left to spend six months devoting herself full time to the completion of her MBA. She does not discount the valuable introduction she got to the disciplines of sales and marketing in that company, however, nor the insight she gained about her own strengths and weaknesses. As she recalls, "While I was assistant marketing manager, I had two bosses who were always countermanding each other's orders. I'd be caught in the middle. I found the only way to deal with the problem from my end was to disregard their step-by-step instructions and get them to tell me what they wanted accomplished, the end result rather than the interim steps. Once I knew that, I could use my own initiative to get the job done."

Ms. Finestein had been told that the way to get on a fast track in her present company is to: (1) do a superior job planning campaigns and (2) undertake special marketing research projects. She spent her first year learning everything she could about the company, its market, and its operations, and how to formulate sales campaigns that brought results. Now, she feels she's ready to move on to Phase 2. Recently, she was given her first special assignment: analyze the effectiveness of the company's demonstration kit as a sales aid and compare it with those used by competitors.

Ideally, Ms. Finestein would like to be promoted to senior campaign planner within six months and become a marketing manager six months after that. By that time she would be making at least $30,000. In her company, marketing manager is a plateau job that people usually hold for a minimum of 10 years. Marketing managers retain that title as they are rotated through various divisions, getting exposure to all the important functional areas. While the moves marketing managers make may appear to be lateral, the best managers are given progressively more and more responsibility in larger and larger divisions. Those who prove themselves are eventually rewarded with a directorship, comparable to a vice-presidency elsewhere.

If Ms. Finestein had her career to plan over again, she'd make some changes. Although she feels an undergraduate major in liberal arts is excellent preparation for marketing, she regrets her detour into teaching, "which hasn't actually hurt me except in terms of time." She wishes she had gone straight on to a graduate business school for her MBA, which she feels is crucial for the ambitious marketing pro: "In lieu of an MBA in marketing, you usually have to enter the field through sales. And as I learned the hard way, making the transition from sales into marketing isn't always easy. Most of my peers have MBAs, and the few who don't get away with it only because they have a superior, almost instinctive, marketing sense or speak exceptionally well.

"As in sales, glib talkers occasionally go far. I must confess that is one thing I dislike about the field. It has its share of charlatans. But they are getting ahead less and less frequently as consumer research and statistical techniques gain a foothold. Pretty soon the Babbitts of the profession are going to need MBAs too."

BASIC RESOURCE: MARKETING RESEARCH

Marketing research workers seeking career information should write or phone:

American Marketing Association
222 South Riverside Plaza
Chicago, Illinois 60606

BASIC RESOURCES: ADVERTISING AND PUBLIC RELATIONS

If you are in advertising or public relations or would like to be, you should understand the technical side of printing processes. An excellent handbook is *Pocket Pal,* published by the International Paper Company. It clearly explains type and typesetting, copy and art preparation, and the qualities of different papers and inks. It also has a good glossary of graphic arts terms. *Pocket Pal* is available for $1.58 a copy only by writing to:

International Paper Company
220 East 42d Street
New York, New York 10017

Good sources for news and current developments in the field of public relations are:

PR Reporter
Dudley House
P.O. Box 600
Exeter, New Hampshire 03833

Public Relations News
127 East 80th Street
New York, New York 10021

Professional organizations and information sources for both fields include:

American Advertising Federation
1225 Connecticut Avenue NW
Washington, D.C. 20036

American Association of Advertising Agencies
200 Park Avenue
New York, New York 10017

Public Relations Society of America, Inc.
Career Information
845 3d Avenue
New York, New York 10022

CHAPTER 4

SALES CAREERS

Almost 5.5 million Americans, or about 7 percent of the total American labor force, worked in sales occupations in 1976, and the number of sales workers is growing steadily. Every company, whether in manufacturing or in services, is in the business of selling something to somebody. Retail sales workers account for the largest number—2.7 million people in 1976—and the most annual job openings. Real estate, wholesale, and insurance account for most of the other sales categories.

Jobs in sales are different from most other business jobs. Salespeople may be paid only a salary, as are the lower-level retail sales workers, or earn on a straight commission basis. Those who are on commission earn a certain percentage of the total income from sales they have made. For example, if your commission is 10 percent and you sell $200,000 worth of products and services, you earn $20,000. Some companies provide a small base salary in addition to a commission. Working on commission can be important to some people. As one sales manager put it,

> In sales, you're paid what you're worth, no more, no less. If you sluff off, your earnings fall. If you work a little extra, you're paid a little extra. In other fields if you work like crazy for someone, you might get a raise or a promotion—next year. But in sales you get a direct, usually imme- diate, financial return for your effort.

Another characteristic of many sales positions is that you can usually continue to advance and make more money without having to change your job. For instance, though you can advance to the position of sales manager, you can also remain a salesperson and make as much, if your company isn't too restrictive about sales territories. According to one

Funding for this chapter was provided by John Hancock Mutual Life Insurance Company.

537

saleswoman, "You can continue to build on what you have learned for the rest of your life, if you like."

People enter sales from a variety of backgrounds. you can become a retail sales clerk without a high school diploma, but you may find that you need a four-year college degree to become a buyer or to advance to better-paid jobs in retailing. Sales managers in companies with highly technical products tend to seek salespeople with related technical backgrounds. As one medical technician in a large Midwestern hospital who moved to a job in sales said:

> I wanted to move out of the hospital atmosphere, and frankly I wanted to make more money. I knew who made the best equipment I was using and I got to know their salesmen. I told them I understood the needs of medical technicians, and the company gave me a job.

Most jobs in sales have many things in common with being the owner-manager of a business. Salespeople are expected to maintain their

---

THE "SALES PERSONALITY"—DOES IT EXIST?

Many women in sales would say that there is no such thing as a "sales personality." The stereotype of the loud-mouthed, overly aggressive salesperson riddled with insecurities doesn't seem to be accurate in today's sales careers.

As one woman sales manager says, "Women are usually more 'soft-sell' than men. But the days of the high-pressure salesman are over. Women tend to build up a certain confidence that encourages people to tell them their needs and problems. That's the best possible first step toward making a sale."

"High-pressure sales tactics just aren't as successful as they once were," claims one woman in insurance sales. "Besides, most of our clients are calm, quiet, knowledgeable people, and calm, quiet, knowledgeable salespeople are the ones who do the best with them." "The best saleswoman in my office is almost what you might call the shy type," said one real estate broker. "A lot of people feel more comfortable with her." A woman in computer sales put it best: "There isn't really a sales personality, but there sure is something else you need as a salesperson—a sense of self-confidence or the feeling you really have something important to offer your client." As she says, "Maybe that confidence comes from taking a close look at your own personal style and working out a sales strategy that builds on your strengths as a person; a strategy you feel personally comfortable with will be the result." Her advice is: "Develop your own strategy and you'll be successful in sales."

own financial records, work independently, and have both drive and self-confidence.

Choosing What You Sell

If you are considering a career in sales, you owe it to yourself to choose to sell something you believe in. People who believe in their product or service make the best sales workers. If you love the latest fashions, a career in retail clothing sales or as a clothing manufacturer's sales representative would be a better choice for you than selling, say, lawnmowers or office equipment.

People with experience in sales careers say that there is a great deal of difference between selling tangibles, such as cars, houses, or cameras, and selling intangibles, such as insurance, stock and bonds, or computer services. When selling intangibles you must first sell a person on his or her need for the product or service before you can sell the thing itself.

How much you make in sales depends in part on what you're selling. Generally, the "big ticket" (higher priced) items carry the largest commission or the highest salary. For example, in the same department store the people selling children's clothes on the second floor may be making only two-thirds of what the personnel on the fourth floor selling refrigerators or sewing machines are making. A person selling one life insurance policy to the head of a family may not make nearly as much as someone selling a complete insurance "package" to a small business.

Many women have not been aware of the pay and benefit differences among sales jobs. In some cases you can earn commissions not just when a sale is made but also on the basis of long-term contracts or on sales contracts that are automatically renewed each year. In real estate, for instance, a woman who sells commercial real estate might make a lot more money than one who sells homes—not only because the "deals" are often bigger, but because, when a lease arrangement is made in commercial real estate, the agent gets a commission on more than simply the first year's rent. She also gets a percentage for every year of the term of the lease. For example, 10,000 square feet rented at $8 a square foot for 5 years is a $400,000 "sale."

In all insurance companies agents receive commissions for every year policies are renewed. So, if an agent made $30,000 in commissions on her sales in the first year, she would be entitled to renewal commissions the second year as the anniversary dates are reached. The first-year commission is generally higher, and renewal commissions smaller.

Choosing a Company

Choosing a company to sell for can be as important as choosing a product or service to sell. Working for a company with a high commission rate but with a low rate of success is not going to earn you as much money as being a successful salesperson in a company whose commission rate is lower but whose products are better known. Of course, successful sales-people are working for every company, but picking the right company can enhance your chances for success. Here are some suggestions from experienced sales workers:

1. *Choose a well-known, well-respected company.* With a well-known company you won't need to sell the company as well as the product to your customer.
2. *Pick a company with a good training program for their salespeo-ple.* Especially in your first sales job, training can make the difference in your ability to succeed. Ask to see training program materials or have the program explained to you.
3. *Select a sales manager or general agent who you feel really wants to help.* New salespeople need the help of others to be successful.
4. *Make sure your sales job is near your source of supply.* If you are dealing with tangibles (raincoats, screwdrivers, coffee), it can be quite a problem to deal with a home office in San Diego if you're based in Baltimore.
5. *Follow the company's guidelines indicating what successful sales-people must do to succeed.* Usually companies have spent time and money testing techniques that really work. You may have to change your own personal methods, work hours, and even your entire sales approach.

General Characteristics of Various Sales Jobs

Retail Sales

Retailing is the second largest industry in the United States, with sales totaling more than $350 billion annually. Women make up 60 percent of the retail sales force in this country, and, interestingly, women also do most of the retail purchasing.

Jobs in retailing can be divided into five major categories: merchandising, sales promotion, personnel, financial control, and store operation.

Of these five categories, merchandising, with its two main functions of buying and selling, is the area that has traditionally offered women the greatest advancement opportunities. *Retail clerks* help customers locate the merchandise they want and then write up the sales; they are also expected to assist with inventory tallies and balance the daily cash drawers. *Department managers* supervise areas of the store, directing the sales and stock personnel within their specific divisions. *Buyers* are responsible for planning the store's merchandise offerings and for ordering the merchandise. They often have assistants who maintain liaisons with the sales department. *Merchandise managers* coordinate the activities of related departments, supervise buyers, and implement the store's overall sales policies.

Retail sales jobs have traditionally been women's jobs except in those departments selling items such as automobiles and appliances. Part-time jobs at Christmastime or during summer vacations offer young women an opportunity to test their interest in retailing. Entry-level jobs in retail sales, which may not require a high school diploma, do not pay very well, but they can supply the needed experience to move up in sales and to find out what area you want to pursue. And background in sales can be very useful for many career fields.

Manufacturer and Wholesale Sales

All companies that make products need salespeople to sell them. These salespeople sell either directly to company customers or to wholesalers, who then sell the products for the company. A manufacturer of power tools might sell directly to hardware stores and also to a wholesaler that distributes all kinds of products to hardware stores.

A salesperson who works for a manufacturer is called a manufacturer's representative. There were 360,000 people employed in these sales jobs in 1976. A manufacturer's representative works on salary and commission to sell the products of one manufacturer throughout a territory exclusively assigned to her. Manufacturers' sales personnel will sell one or more products to all kinds of buyers, including factories, railroads, banks, schools, hospitals, wholesalers, and retailers. Manufacturers that

---

GETTING IN, MOVING UP: RETAIL SALES

You can get into retail sales either by working as a sales clerk, which may require only a high school diploma, or by getting a position as a management trainee, in which case you may be required to have a junior college or four-year college degree. Retail sales is one of the few areas in which you don't necessarily have to have a college degree to advance. Exceptional salespeople as well as management trainees may move to assistant buyer and buyer positions and from there into jobs as branch store managers, department managers, or merchandising managers. In large stores it is possible to advance to other kinds of work, in personnel or advertising, for example. In smaller stores with owner/managers the chances for advancement are not so great.

INDUSTRY PROFILE: WHOLESALE AND RETAIL TRADE

In 1976, 22 percent of the people working in all jobs worked in wholesale and retail trade. Retail businesses sell products directly to consumers in stores, through the mail, and door to door. Retail businesses include specialty, department, and discount stores. Wholesalers distribute manufacturers' products and goods to retail outlets.

Jobs in these two fields include store managers and owners, managers in special sales areas of stores, and wholesale sales workers who sell to store representatives or buyers. In 1976, one out of every five trade workers was in sales; managers and proprietors were another fifth. Jobs in trade include everything from a part-time sales job at the local drugstore to the presidency of a large corporation owning hundreds of stores or restaurants. The outlook in trade is good for all jobs except clerical, and the industry is expected to grow at least as much as the rest of the economy throughout the 1980s.

maintain branch offices are generally those which handle large sales volumes and promotional efforts. A sales office does not usually maintain an inventory of products but rather is a local contact point where customers (stores, local businesses, etc.) can discuss products and place orders with company representatives.

Some highly technical products, such as prescription drugs and complex or advanced machinery, require sales representatives with advanced technical training (a degree from a college of pharmacy or a degree in engineering, for example). The salesperson must be comfortable with and knowledgeable about the technical details of the product, and the customer's particular needs and problems must be carefully analyzed before a sale can be made. For instance, sales representatives for highly technical products like electronic equipment are frequently called sales engineers. They inventory their customers' needs and help them select the right pieces of equipment. Sales engineers will also help install the equipment and train the buyer's workers in its use and maintenance. These salespeople play an important role in installing industrial equipment such as computers, aircraft, conveyor belts, air-conditioning, and pollution control devices.

Wholesalers employ salespeople to sell to retailers, to other wholesalers, or to industrial users. Occasionally they will sell in small amounts directly to the consumer. Wholesalers usually serve one type of retailer. Wholesale drug companies serve drugstores, for example, and wholesale produce or meat companies supply grocery stores. Buyers depend on wholesalers' representatives to call on them at regular intervals, judge the needs of the store, and even help keep inventory records. In addition, wholesale salespeople may suggest new products or offer marketing and advertising advice.

Both salespeople who work for manufacturers and those who work for wholesalers do a lot of traveling from customer to customer, most of it by car and some of it on evenings and weekends. They are expected to keep their own records of sales, expenses, and customer contacts, but their schedule is usually their own to arrange. In this field of sales women are said to have an advantage over men; as one wholesaler put it, "They're still so new in the field that businesses will grant them appointments just to meet them."

Sales workers in these two fields most often earn base salaries, with commissions or bonuses as extras. They also receive the company's benefit package of insurance, vacations, and pensions. A career in this kind of sales can lead to administrative positions like sales manager or branch office manager as well as to "super salesperson" status, making over $30,000 a year. People in sales often can climb their company's management ladder. They often make good corporate leaders because they know the company's products very well, and they also have the communications skills and the power to persuade that are needed by an administrator.

Real Estate Sales

In 1976, 1.5 million people were licensed as real estate brokers or salespeople, but only 450,000 worked selling or renting real estate on a full-time basis. Part-time real estate sales workers include lawyers and other property owners. All states require that real estate sales workers have a high school diploma and pass a special exam to become a real estate agent.

GETTING IN, MOVING UP: MANUFACTURERS' SALES

Manufacturers generally hire sales trainees or people with other sales experience and train them to sell company products. Sales representatives can advance by making more sales, getting a more lucrative sales territory, or moving to a sales position with another company. Usually the more expensive the product, the higher the commission.

Sales representatives may become sales managers or move into marketing jobs as a first rung in moving up in a corporation.

A real estate agent represents the property owner; she helps locate prospective buyers or renters, shows the property, and helps negotiate a sale or lease between the owner and a buyer or renter. Agents usually work entirely on a commission basis under contract to a real estate broker for a specified proportion of the commission of any sales they make. Like any sales job paid entirely on a commission basis, there is a lot of money to be made if you are successful, and a lot of frustration if you are working hard but not making sales.

A real estate agency is usually run and owned by one or more real estate brokers. A broker is licensed to take a more active role in real estate transactions than an agent. For example, she can handle the "closing," when buyers and sellers meet and the property legally changes hands. To become a broker, an agent must have from one to three years' experience working in a real estate firm, about 90 hours of additional course work, and pass a brokerage examination. Brokers also receive a commission for work they do.

A broker may also appraise real estate, that is, estimate the value of a property for a fee. Real estate appraisal is an important specialty. Appraisers may work for county or town governments to set the value of land and building for property tax purposes; for owners, so that they will know how much to ask for a property they want to sell; or for banks, to help determine how much of a mortgage to grant to a building owner.

Another area of specialization is real estate management; for instance, management of an apartment house or office building. Many real estate agencies are prepared to collect the rents, arrange contracts with fuel oil companies, hire and fire the building superintendent, see that the building is in good repair, and handle thousands of day-to-day problems for the owner of the building. The fee for managing a building is usually a percentage of the annual rents. A company that manages property well is likely to have the opportunity to become the broker if the owner decides to sell.

Real estate brokers and agents need a steady stream of both buyers (or renters) and properties to be successful. For this reason, good social and business contacts are important. Many agents and brokers spend a lot of time on the telephone contacting property owners and investors; they also keep in touch with other brokers who have clients or properties that could complete a transaction and who may want to "co-broke." Real estate agencies usually attract buyers with newspaper ads; some agencies offer videotapes of homes on the market, while others offer to help with office or store design to attract companies to purchase or lease new stores or office space.

Although it is customary for brokers to represent sellers, they represent buyers when they "assemble" property. A broker may assemble all the properties in a city block so that a new office building can be built or coordinate transactions for adjacent farm and residential properties needed for an industrial site or corporate headquarters in the country. Real estate assembly is usually done with "cloak and dagger" secrecy and may appeal to your sense of intrigue.

Real estate agencies usually specialize in one kind of property—either farmland, homes and apartments (residential real estate), stores and offices (commercial real estate), or factory space (industrial real estate). Agencies also may specialize in a certain area of a city or town.

Women in real estate have traditionally sold houses or rented apartments, residential real estate. But renting or selling commercial real estate can be a great deal more lucrative.

In addition to independent real estate firms, there are real estate departments in many large corporations. A chain such as MacDonald's or a manufacturer with many retail outlets (Exxon, for instance) will have its own real estate stall, and will use local brokers and lawyers to assist them in making specific transactions.

Insurance Sales

Three kinds of insurance are sold: life insurance, casualty insurance, and health insurance. Approximately half of those in insurance sales sell life insurance. Life insurance pays benefits to the policyholder's survivors or the policyholder and may also be designed to help pay for children's college expenses or provide retirement income. Casualty insurance is also called property and liability insurance. It protects against damage or loss of property from accidents, fire, and theft. It also guards against loss resulting from a lawsuit, such as for a defective product or a malpractice claim. Health insurance covers medical bills in the case of serious illness or hospitalization. It may also include "disability" payments, which partially compensate for loss of earnings while the policyholder is recuperating.

In 1976 there were about 465,000 full-time insurance agents and bro-

GETTING IN, MOVING UP: REAL ESTATE SALES

To get a job as a real estate agent, you must first pass a state licensing examination. Real estate agents make more money by making more sales or arranging for more rentals, which usually means handling more listings. Work as an agent on a part-time basis is possible. After working as an agent and passing the state's real estate broker's exam, you may want to become a broker and open your own office.

WOMEN IN INSURANCE — THEY'RE A NATURAL

Women who want to do well in this business must have a fantastic desire to succeed. If a woman leaves herself an out with other options, if she is thinking, "There's something else I can do, if this doesn't work out," it probably *won't* work out. If a woman doesn't have the dedication when she first begins, she isn't going to make it.

I tell managers to look for aggressive women who like money and want it. I don't mean just extroverts, because all kinds of personalities, introverted and extroverted, can succeed in this business. If you ask a woman how much money she wants to make and she says $10,000, she's not the kind of person we're looking for. She doesn't have high enough expectations to be successful in this business.

The income potential of life insurance sales is only one thing that attracts women to this field. There's no question that they'll earn equal pay for equal effort, but I think the attraction is much bigger than that. The independence, the excitement of every day being different, the lack of routine, and the contact with people are all magnets. But I think one big element of the business that draws women to it is the opportunity to be of service to people.

> —From an interview with Jane Howell, director of Women's Market Plans at John Hancock Mutual Life Insurance Company. The interview appeared in the John Hancock newspaper, "News Weekly."

kers of all kinds. As in real estate, agents and brokers are licensed by the state in which they operate. An insurance *agent* works directly for an insurance company or is an independent under contract with one or two companies to sell their insurance. A *broker* has no formal relationship with any one company but places business with different companies to suit her client's needs, frequently, for example, to place high risks.

The basic principle of insurance is that an individual or company policyholder can guard against a large possible loss (fire, theft, or personal injury, for example) or the definite loss of death by making small periodic payments called premiums. By pooling the premiums and investing them itself, the insurance company can afford to pay those policyholders who die or suffer losses at any time. In effect, the insurance company assumes the risk of the policyholder. To stay in business, an insurance company must calculate very carefully the probability of loss and determine whether the applicant should be insured, under what conditions, and at what premium rate.

INDUSTRY PROFILE: INSURANCE INDUSTRY

About 4,600 insurance companies of all kinds employed approximately 1 6 million workers in 1976. Of these roughly one-third were in sales as *agents,* who represent one company, or *brokers,* who sell more than one company's insurance policies. Insurance companies and insurance brokers have thousands of sales offices across the country. Half of all insurance industry workers are clerical workers, including *claims adjusters* and *claims examiners* who investigate insurance claims and decide whether they are covered by policies.

The three basic types of insurance are life, property— liability, and health. Insurance companies tend to specialize in only one type, although most life companies sell health insurance as well. Life insurance provides policy holders with benefits for their survivors in case of death and many other benefits like retirement or disability income as well. Property and liability insurance covers damage to property either caused or sustained by the policyholder. It protects against accidents, fire, and theft. Health and accident insurance helps policyholders pay medical expenses.

One out of 15 insurance company employees works at home offices (corporate headquarters). Among these are lawyers, accountants, and investment analysts. Two special insurance professionals are *actuaries* and *underwriters.* Actuaries are specially trained statisticians who study the probability of certain risks actually occurring; underwriters evaluate applications for insurance policies and determine the degree of risk. For these and other professional and management employees within the industry, insurance companies often offer special training sessions or tuition refund programs. Most insurance companies tend to promote from within.

Insurance company employment is expected to rise as fast as other occupations throughout the 1980s, and while insurance pay rates in jobs outside of sales are certainly a little less than for the rest of business, the job benefits such as vacation time, health insurance, and pension plans are usually especially good.

Insurance is sold to individuals, companies, and groups. Group insurance is sold at special rates to specific groups of people such as the employees of a company.

Both companies and families need all three kinds of insurance. Recognizing that fact, more and more insurance agents, brokers, and some of the larger companies are offering both casualty and life protection and sometimes health insurance as well. These agents are called multi-line agents. With the increased complexity of the insurance world, many businesses employ risk managers who act as insurance buyers and try to reduce insurance costs by lowering the firm's accident rate.

Although selling all kinds of insurance can make you a lot of money, it is hard work. At the beginning few interviews may result in sales, and after the contract is written it must be followed up by continuing contact with the client to encourage policy renewals and monitor changes in circumstances, reporting of losses, and the settlement of claims. A good agent keeps up with pension and tax law revisions that affect her clients. Lots of energy and communications skills are needed. As an insurance company recruiter put it:

> We're looking for people who want to succeed, who want the things that money can buy and are willing to work for them. We're looking for someone who can handle rejection and can take pride in her own accomplishments. We're looking for people who want the independence of being on their own, and we'll give them all the training and support they need to make it.

Underwriting

The term "underwriter" can be confusing to people outside the field of insurance. Life insurance agents can earn the title chartered life underwriter (CLU) by taking advanced training and a series of qualifying examinations. A CLU after your name means you have a high level of professional competence and usually leads to higher income. It also means that you sell insurance.

But "underwriter" is usually used to refer to the people who review and make decisions on applications for insurance. These underwriters *do not sell* insurance. In a life insurance company, underwriters work in the firm's home office. They review applications sent in by agents in the field and other pertinent information like medical reports. Underwriters in life insurance companies receive training in human anatomy, disease, and medical treatment so they can evaluate complex policy applications.

GETTING IN, MOVING UP: INSURANCE SALES

Insurance companies have traditionally been employers of liberal arts graduates and are known for their internal training programs. Of the several insurance specialties to choose from, the major emphasis has been on sales. It's sometimes possible to get entry-level jobs without college degrees, but a degree and advanced study are necessary to move ahead. People with strong records in sales management, underwriting, and actuarial work have good opportunities to advance to corporate management programs.

With training and passage of a series of examinations an underwriter may become a Fellow of the Academy of Life Underwriting.

Underwriters who work for property and liability insurance companies have a slightly different role. They also analyze insurance applications, but they may be found in a company field office as well as the home office, working closely with company agents on complex policies. In some cases, these underwriters may go into the field with an insurance agent to review a client's potential for loss. Underwriters in property and liability companies become experts in fire, theft, accidents, and personal injury. With special training and passage of a series of examinations, they may earn the designation chartered property casualty underwriter (CPCU).

Linda Sterling, Insurance Agent

"Sell insurance? You've got to be kidding!" That's what Linda Sterling told the man at the employment agency who suggested she pursue a career in insurance sales. "Since then, however," she says, "I haven't met anyone in the insurance sales business who actually intended from the start to end up in an insurance career."

Linda Sterling, a successful insurance agent in her early 30s, works in a Western field office of a major national insurance company. In spite of her initial reaction to a career selling insurance, Ms. Sterling was persuaded by her employment counselor to go for an interview at an insurance company "just to get some experience interviewing." And as she says, "I was hooked 15 minutes into the interview. Insurance sales turned out to be just the job I wanted. I've been at it seven years, and I still love it.

"My first few months in this business were hard, and sometimes I doubted my own credibility. It bothered me, too, to work from 8 in the morning to 11 at night. I even went to Ray, my general agent, and said maybe I wasn't cut out for an insurance career. I guess I was really saying I needed some encouragement to get me through those first few weeks and months. I got a tremendous amount of advice and support from Ray, and he's been an outstanding example for me. He taught me that things didn't have to be the way I had been envisioning them. After our talk, I realized that I didn't have to work all those nights, and if I wanted more daytime business all I had to do was go out and look for it. Now, when I line up an interview, instead of asking a prospect what night is most convenient, I say, 'Would you prefer to see me in the morning or afternoon?'

"Rejection was hard for me to handle in the beginning," Ms. Sterling says, "but the training and support I received from the people I work with got me through that period. They taught me that it's not you they're rejecting but what you're trying to sell them. Still it's hard for a woman. Women are brought up to need the approval of men. For women whose manager and clients are all men there's a special pain in disapproval from that source."

As Ms. Sterling says, "People think that insurance agents are a bunch of vultures. But it's not so. My company terminates agents who sell clients too much insurance; I've seen it happen. Sooner or later the client will realize what's happened and he'll get mad. He'll cancel his policy and tell all his friends to stay away from us. We can't afford that. If anything, I'll sell less than a person needs. I intend to be in this business for a long time, and I can always go back and sell more. No one can ever blame me for selling him more than he can afford to pay for.

"To sell life insurance you need to be able to talk about two subjects which are taboo for Americans—death and money. That makes it hard to boast about the insurance plan you wrote that made it possible for someone's kids to finish college after the policyholder's death.

"The other day a company plane crashed killing four key executives. The bank was about to withdraw its line of credit, and the business would have folded except that the company had life insurance on its top executives and that saved the day. The story was in the paper, and everyone in our office was making copies of that article to show that what we do can really pay off. Of course, people call our office every day with stories like that, but the public doesn't know.

"I would classify insurance as a helping profession," Ms. Sterling says. "The people I know in this field tend to be helpers; they can really empathize with their clients. If you don't have the attitude that you're here to understand your client's needs and help him or her do what's best, you won't make very many sales."

Most of Ms. Sterling's leads to new clients come from referrals from her old clients. "A really solid referral is very important to me. A good referral gets you an appointment; you're taken seriously. I prospect all the time. Exposure is the most important thing in the insurance business. The more exposure you have to people, the greater your chances of getting appointments and being successful."

Barring any early appointments, Ms. Sterling typically begins her working day by methodically crisscrossing several widely scattered communities by car, calling on policyholders.

"I'll stop by whenever I'm in an area just to say hello to a policyholder without any specific idea of selling additional insurance," she says. "But I get a number of referrals as a result of this random combing. In fact, I've even had policyholders pick up the phone and make appointments for me. It's not something I try to make happen. I just love people, and it's natural to form close relationships with them."

Ms. Sterling thinks there are some real advantages to being a woman agent. "First of all, women are generally better on the telephone than men. They tend to be smoother about getting appointments. Second, women tend to be better listeners than men. By listening to a prospect's or client's problems, they can sell insurance more easily.

"Most of my clients are in the middle-management group, making anywhere from $15,000 to $25,000 a year. And they're often reluctant about telling a man, particularly one who is extremely successful, that they're having a hard time sending their kids to college or meeting the mortgage payments. But they'll open up to me, probably because they assume I'm having the same kind of problems. Of course, I don't know whether this attitude will continue as women become more and more successful. Then there's the simple angle of novelty. People are all too used to talking with salesmen, and there's a certain refreshing novelty about a saleswoman.

"In sales, there is often what I call the football school of management. The team comes in at half time and they haven't been doing so well. The coach gets them all together and screams at them, 'You lazy good-for-nothings, get out there on that field' and so forth—you know what I mean. Well, most men respond with anger - 'I'm going to go out there and show him' . . . while women don't respond well to threats and intimidation. They think, 'Daddy's scolding me.' Women are going to have to learn how to get along in that kind of world, too.

"We women have to own up to our own competitiveness. We know what competition is—anybody who's made halfway decent grades in college does. Selling insurance is highly competitive. Every month the company publishes sales reports showing where every agent stands, how much each one sold and to whom. There are all kinds of contests and awards, commemorative plaques, trips, clubs, etc., for making a certain number of sales. In the beginning, I thought, 'This is *so* silly and undignified!' But after a while you find yourself really appreciating the stimulus to work harder (and the acknowledgment of your hard work). Even though you may think it's silly and undignified, you still say to yourself, 'This is fun!' Those wooden plaques may not look good to anyone else, but they mean something very special to me."

BASIC RESOURCES: RETAIL SALES

For further information on retail sales occupations, write or phone:

National Retail Merchants Association
100 West 31st Street
New York, New York 10001

Manufacturers' agents will find the following sources very useful:

Manufacturers' Agents National Association
P.O. Box 16878
Irvine, California 92713

Sales and Marketing Executives International
Career Education Division
380 Lexington Avenue
New York, New York 10017

BASIC RESOURCES: INSURANCE SALES

For additional information on careers in the various insurance areas, write or phone:

American Council of Life Insurance
1850 K Street NW
Washington, D.C. 20006

American Society of Pension Actuaries
1700 K Street NW
Washington, D.C. 20006

Casualty Actuarial Society
200 East 42d Street
New York, New York 10017

Insurance Information Institute
110 William Street
New York, New York 10038
(particularly for property-liability insurance careers)

Life Insurance Management and Research Association
170 Sigourney Street
Hartford, Connecticut 06105

National Association of Independent Insurers
Public Relations Department
2600 River Road
Des Plaines, Illinois 60018

Society of Actuaries
208 South La Salle Street
Chicago, Illinois 60604

BASIC RESOURCE: REAL ESTATE SALES

For information about real estate licenses and examinations, write your state's real estate board or commission on real estate at your state capital. Ask a real estate agency near you for the address or check with your local library.

The National Association of Realtors distributes career information and a list of colleges and universities offering courses in real estate. Write or phone:

National Association of Realtors
430 North Michigan Avenue
Chicago, Illinois 60611

CHAPTER 5

MONEY IN BUSINESS
Banking and Finance

The business of business is to make money. The financial wing of a company keeps track of daily operations, analyzes its current position, and makes financial plans for the future. Outside of companies an entire community of financial organizations serves corporate needs for capital, expert advice, and audits.

The world of "high finance" may seem forbidding to many people. At first glance it appears to be a world that requires special mathematical ability to understand, but it's simply not true that "ordinary" people cannot make sense of the world of finance. What *is* true is that finance, as it is handled both inside and outside corporations, has its own special language for expressing ideas; it also involves special analytical techniques and standard ways of presenting information. If you learn these terms and practices, you can understand finance.

If you are considering a career in business, you must learn the language of finance and the techniques of financial analysis whether you need to secure a bank loan for the business you are starting or to manage a market research project. For top management positions experience in finance and knowledge of financial analysis is essential and finance has traditionally been the route to corporate management.

Accounting—Inside Companies

Accounting is the basic tool of financial analysis. Even in ancient Babylon businesses kept accounting records. In the Middle Ages and Renais-

Funding for this chapter was provided by Citibank, N.A.

sance the accounting profession was like a guild, admitting only members who had served an apprenticeship and passed an examination. In 1887 the first professional organization for public accountants, the American Association of Public Accountants, was formed.

The growth of modern business into the complex, government-regulated, computer-assisted corporations of today has both changed the jobs accountants do and greatly increased the need for them. Accounting jobs are expected to continue to increase faster than openings in other fields.

A degree in accounting or an MBA with an accounting concentration is a common requirement for an entry-level job in corporate financial management. And a career in financial management is one of the traditional ways to gain access to jobs in top corporate management. Many top industrial executives are also CPAs. Although it is not necessary to be a CPA to advance in the world of financial management, it certainly helps.

In "private accounting," or management accounting as it is sometimes called, you work directly for a company. Jobs differ depending on the size of the company and the degree of specialization in its accounting functions. Beginning accountants are usually hired to work in a section of the firm that administers one part of the record-keeping process—in the tax department, in accounts payable, or in the internal audit department. Some companies hire fiscal management trainees and rotate them through corporate financial departments.

Bookkeeping is the clerical job that involves keeping records of financial transactions. Once bookkeeping was the only way women got into the accounting field. Most modern accounting jobs are now so sophisti-

GETTING IN, MOVING UP: ACCOUNTING WITHIN A COMPANY

To get into corporate accounting, you can either move from a public accounting firm after you have had some experience or take a lower-level accounting position in the company and work your way up. Usually bookkeepers need more training or a college degree to advance. To move toward top corporate accounting positions, most people in the field seem to think it's important to get exposure to various accounting departments, particularly the cost accounting department and the production or operations division. As you advance in this field, you need to become more of a generalist and less of a technician. Experience in an office with an overview of company operations, such as that of the controller or treasurer, can be very helpful.

cated and so specialized that the route from bookkeeping to accounting is not an easy one.

The top accountant in a company is usually called the controller or comptroller. Her office oversees all record-keeping, auditing, and budgeting procedures. The word *controller* suggests a main emphasis of the function—controlling costs, controlling expenditures, controlling payment and billing processes.

Under the controller are the heads of each financial department and the chief plant accountant for each company facility. The financial departments include *internal auditing*, generally headed by a general auditor; a *tax department* and a *credit and collections* department with their managers; a *budget department*, whose director prepares estimates of income and expenses for the company and its production units; and a *cost accounting department*. The chief cost accountant oversees company expenses for material, labor, and management, and keeps records of all these expenses. Jobs in any one of these areas are usually very stable, but to advance to middle management you generally need experience in more than one department.

Accounting—Outside Companies

Outside public accounting firms are hired by businesses to set up financial record-keeping processes, give tax and money management advice, and perform audits of a company's finances. Public accountants are certified by the state in which they practice after taking a rigorous set of

---

WHERE THE JOBS ARE: ACCOUNTING FIRMS

The "big eight" public accounting firms are, in alphabetical order:

- —Arthur Andersen and Company
- —Coopers and Lybrand
- —Ernst and Ernst
- —Haskins and Sells
- —Peat, Marwick, Mitchell and Company
- —Price Waterhouse and Company
- —Touche Ross and Company
- —Arthur Young and Company

All have offices in major cities across the United States.

---

examinations, and in some states, working for a public accounting firm for a minimum number of years as well. After fulfilling these requirements, they take on the respected title of certified public accountant (CPA).

About half of all accounting graduates go to work for CPA firms. Public accounting firms are much like law firms in that they work for many clients who hire them on either a retainer or a fee basis. The firm's partners own the business and share in its profits. Assistants or junior partners or managers may share in corporate profits, and staff members work on a salary basis. Staff members are classified as "juniors," who are accounting graduates; "semiseniors," who have had about two years of experience; and "seniors," who supervise projects.

Like large law firms, large public accounting firms train very carefully the people they have hired for entry-level jobs. The "big eight" public accounting firms (see the listing in the box entitled "Where the Jobs Are: Accounting Firms") even have special training schools and make a practice of rotating new employees to different divisions.

A young accountant can expect to start work as a member of a company audit team under the supervision of a senior staff member. An audit team not only reviews a company's figures and accounting processes but also checks on the facts behind the information. That means going to ware-

---

CPA: HOW TO BECOME ONE

About 20 percent of the 865,000 people working in accounting jobs in 1976 were CPAs. To become a CPA or certified public accountant, you must pass a 2½-day examination (if taken all at once) given by the Board of Examiners of the American Institute of Certified Public Accountants, but fortunately you usually don't take all parts of the examination at once. The parts of the exam are Theory of Accounts, Commercial Law, Theory of Auditing, and Practical Accounting (Problems).

All states require the examination, but education and experience requirements differ from state to state. In most states you must have a college degree and have worked in a public accounting firm for two to three years to qualify.

For information on your state's requirements, write or phone the Board of Accountancy in your state capital or your state or local branch of the American Institute of Certified Public Accountants, or the national office:

American Institute of Certified Public Accountants
1211 Avenue of the Americas
New York, New York 10036

---

houses and checking on inventory in addition to visiting plants and offices.

Working for a public accounting firm has other advantages besides training: a chance to learn all about the financial operations of several companies, to examine internal corporate financial positions in person, and to make contact with potential employers. It's not uncommon for young accountants to be hired by the firm they have worked with.

Public accounting is a career that requires a continuing effort to stay on top of new technical developments in the field. This area of accounting work is often more technically demanding than working in a company. Although deadlines exist in corporate financial jobs, January through income tax time in April is always a time of long hours and high pressure for public accountants. As one Chicago-based CPA put it, "If you see anybody on the streets of this city with a suntan any time between January 1 and April 15, you know he or she is not an accountant."

Financial Management Jobs in Companies

The line between financial management and accounting often blurs in modern business. Once accountants were involved only in record-keeping and controlling operations. Accountants would devise accounting systems and procedures, record financial data, and interpret it for management. Projecting economic trends, handling corporate investments, and dealing with the financial community to arrange for corporate capital needs used to be considered financial management functions under the authority of the company treasurer. Management trainees in the controller's office had accounting degrees, but management trainees in the treasurer's office had MBAs.

In many companies, particularly small- and medium-sized ones, employees can move easily from internal financial management jobs to ones dealing with the outside financial community. Just as public accounting firms have increasingly begun to market management consulting services, internal financial analysts have become part of the top management team planning capital requirements, corporate investments, and audit policies.

Like jobs in production, jobs in corporate finance have traditionally not been open to women. Now that more women have had advanced training in financial analysis and are working at high-level jobs within the financial community outside of corporations, this situation is changing.

Some financial executives manage and make decisions about company investments. Firms with pension funds to administer or undistributed corporate profits invest money to earn money for the corporation. Many corporate giants, for example, have an acquisitions department whose job is to research and advise top management on buying smaller companies. And companies with large sums of money to invest, such as insurance companies, often maintain large investment divisions—frequently prestigious departments within a corporation.

You can get into corporate investment from other parts of the investment field, such as banking, or from a specialty in an area of investment. For example, a real estate investment trust hires people with real estate background. Pension investment is an area subject to a great many government regulations, and so someone with a training in these regulations would also be eligible for a position in a corporate investment department.

Many firms employ economic analysts to project future trends for the company and for the industry. Economists, statisticians, and business analysts work for this department or are hired for special research projects from outside consulting companies. People in these jobs provide a base of information that helps in corporate planning.

Corporate financial personnel help the company raise the capital needed for operations. Capital, the money needed to start, expand, or run a business, can be raised through borrowing money from a bank, offering shares of stock for sale and broadening the ownership base of the corporation, and borrowing money directly from private investors through bonds. All these transactions require the involvement of the financial community outside the corporation as well as financial analysts within it to advise top corporate managers on the advantages of alternatives.

Jobs in the Financial Community

The financial community is made up of businesses that provide financial services to both individuals and corporations. These institutions generally lend money and arrange investments, and people who work in it need many of the same skills as those in corporate financial positions: to be able to analyze financial information presented to them and make judgments about the economy and the financial health of corporations and industries.

As with jobs in the sales field, "big ticket" transactions earn the most money. People in the financial community who work on corporate accounts generally make more money than those who work with individual accounts. The major institutions in the financial community are banks, investment banks, and stockbrokerage firms.

Banking

Banks are the central arteries of capitalism; they keep money pumping through the system, circulating in an uninterrupted stream from the lender to the borrower. As money moves through a bank, payment (in-

MORE HELP . . . NATIONAL ASSOCIATION OF BANK WOMEN

A professional organization of women bank officers, the National Association of Bank Women (NABW) was founded in 1921 and is dedicated solely to the professional interests and advancement of women bankers. Through its Educational Foundation established in 1973, NABW provides educational programs to help women gain management skills needed to move ahead in the industry. NABW programs help women break down the barriers that separate them from upper management levels and positions of power.

NABW is affiliated with Simmons College in Boston, Mundelein College in Illinois, and Pitzer College in California to offer both a bachelor's degree program and intensive, two-week Management Institutes. For more information write or phone:

National Association of Bank Women, Inc.
111 East Wacker Drive
Chicago, Illinois 60601

---

terest) is made to the lender or depositor and charged to the borrower. The bank in turn charges the borrower more than it pays the depositor; the difference is the bank's profit.

Commercial banks offer a wide spectrum of financial services to individuals and corporations, and they employ the largest percentage of bank employees. Sometimes described as "financial department stores," commercial banks provide not only loans to both consumers and corporations but checking and savings accounts, credit cards, safe-deposit boxes, collection of payments, trust assistance, administration of estates, and supervision of endowments such as pension funds and investments. Savings and loan associations offer analogous but fewer services, specializing mainly in home mortgage financing.

Banking is changing as the market for banking services changes. Most banks are based on a standard model of organization, but a few of the larger national banks are now developing new models. In banking the equivalent of production jobs is in "operations." Operations accounts for the largest single group of employees in many banks organized along traditional patterns including customer service (or tellers), clerks, and managing supervisors. Processing of daily transactions, bookkeeping, check handling, and data processing are all covered by this department. Such supportive functions as accounting, systems management, personnel, security, and distribution services may or may not be part of operations also, depending again on the model of organization. Managing the

INDUSTRY PROFILE: BANKING INDUSTRY

Though the banking industry has long provoked the image of stuffiness, conservativism, and restrictedness, it no longer deserves that reputation. The banking industry has been growing and changing. New services have been added—bank-based charge cards, new credit systems, money management counseling, accounting and billing services, and new marketing, advertising, and data processing functions to back up the expanded services. Banking is expected to grow faster than most industries thoughout the 1980s.

Banks, savings and loan associations, and credit agencies of various kinds employed almost 2 million workers in 1976. A large proportion of these—25 percent—were bank officers, including treasurers, branch managers, vice-presidents, and other management personnel. Banks are relying more and more on electronic data processing and have an increased need for statisticians, computer programmers, and systems analysts.

Working conditions in the banking industry are good. The fringe benefits are excellent. The salaries in smaller banks may sometimes be a little lower than in nonbanking companies, but they may be more stable in a recession. The salaries in larger banks, however, are competitive with those in nonbanking companies.

Banks often provide excellent training opportunities for their employees, usually through banking associations like the American Bankers Association, for officers; the American Institute of Banking, for support personnel; and the National Association of Bank Women (see the box in this chapter entitled "More Help . . . The National Association of Bank Women" on the services of the NABW). Banks also are frequently active in the communities they serve, with investment in inner-city neighborhoods or economic development programs.

Everest of paperwork that accumulates daily in banks is no easy matter. For instance, one major bank processes 1 million checks each day as well as 5,600 security transfers and $1.5 billion in money transfers.

Trust departments in banks are responsible for handling individual trusts and estates, and these departments may also provide administration and investment help to corporate pension and profit-sharing funds. A bank's corporate trust department works closely with corporations to handle loans and to supervise stock transfers, the registration of stocks, and the payment of dividends on stock. Corporate trust departments often issue shares of stock in new companies or recently merged companies. When shares are sold, corporate trust officers sometimes serve as stock transfer agents, keeping track of the owners of record of each share or block of stock.

THE THRILL OF IT ALL: BANKING AND FINANCE

"Numbers are sometimes presented as a barrier to people. But I can look right through the figures on the page and see what's going on in a company."
—Public accountant

"Companies can't afford poor financial decisions in this economic climate; so jobs like mine are becoming more and more important."
—Company financial analyst

"The climate right now in banking for women is excellent, and we are getting to the stage where it will be truly neutral with regard to sexism. And all the new developments in banking make it a very exciting field."
—Banker

THE DAILY GRIND: BANKING AND FINANCE

"The first big account my boss gave me to manage was a $1,500,000 trust fund for a woman in her 70s. I went to call on her and explain I was taking over her account, and she got furious and called my boss: 'I don't want some young woman *managing my account. I want a man who knows what he's doing.'"*
—Stockbroker

"It's hard being away from home in a smelly hotel room eating cold, take-out food, and with deadlines that sometimes seem impossible to meet."
—Public accountant

"Finance sometimes really still seems so much of an 'old-school, old-boy' world that I get discouraged."
—Investment banker

GETTING IN, MOVING UP: BANKING

Banks hire management trainees with college or graduate school background; sometimes tellers are promoted to supervisory or lower-level management positions. The skills and knowledge usually acquired through a college degree and an MBA program are useful for advancement. The National Association of Bank Women helps women in banking become more qualified through education programs.

Banks offer good training programs to help you advance, and most moderate- to large-sized banks have many officer and manager positions to move into once you are qualified.

Loan and credit departments in banks lend money to individuals and companies. Jobs in this part of banking require good business skills and the ability to make solid business judgments. In smaller banks and in local small towns loan officer positions are considered prestigious. "Maybe that's because loans are where most banks make the most money," suggests a commercial bank's personnel director. Promotions to higher-level management come frequently from loan and credit department positions, but now they also come increasingly from other departments. Especially in larger banks, promotions now can come from operations, systems, marketing, staff, auditing, and consumer services.

Banks are good employers. They tend to promote to the extent possible from within and will provide continued training programs for employees who demonstrate the ability to perform effectively and take on more responsibility. As a rule, bank jobs in general pay less than other jobs in the financial community but offer more stability and better benefits. However, larger banks are now setting their salary policies along the lines and standards of other major nonbanking corporations.

Investment Banking

In the business of providing business and government with capital, the primary function of investment banking firms is lending, just as the primary function of stockbrokerage houses is selling. Acting as go-betweens, investment bankers put together a group of investors to meet capital needs. For example, a group, or "syndicate," of investment bankers may get together and buy all or part of a corporate bond issue in a transaction called underwriting a bond issue. They then sell the bonds to private investors or stockbrokers to sell to their clients. Investment bankers also underwrite the sale of government bonds.

Sometimes investment bankers "originate" a capital issue—they advise business or government on the best way to arrange for financing, given current market conditions, and how to do it.

Investment banking is considered the glamorous upper reaches of the financial community. Because an enormous amount of capital is often at risk, investment banking is truly one of the most challenging—and therefore prestigious—fields in the financial community. Investment bankers, their financial analysts, and accountants work directly with corporations to raise money for new business or business expansion, and they often play the role of investment midwives to corporate mergers and acquisitions.

Stocks and Bonds—Brokerage

Stockbrokerage houses serve as wholesalers and retailers of corporate stocks and bonds. Just as the investment banking community offers corporations the opportunity to borrow capital, stockbrokerage houses offer the opportunity to invest to both individuals and corporations (which are called institutional investors).

Most brokerage firms have three main divisions: a sales department, which trades securities; a research department, which studies market conditions and companies; and a department that records trades, bills customers, and handles other accounting chores.

Brokerage houses are classified by the type of business they do. A *retail or "wire house"* deals mainly in large numbers of individual accounts and has a sizable sales staff. An *institutional house* handles large portfolios for pension funds, churches, universities, and other institutions. A large brokerage firm may offer both retail and institutional services as well as other forms of financial management, including supervision of private trusts and estates.

Most jobs in the securities field are sales positions. Like real estate brokers, stockbrokers must be registered and they earn commissions on their work. As a broker, you provide customers with information about the quality of different investments, quote prices, and handle orders. Brokers rely heavily on the firm's research reports on various securities a customer owns or intends to buy.

In institutional investing, sales positions are invariably specialized. Registered representatives concentrate on equities (stocks), corporate bonds, municipal bonds, government/agency bonds, stock options, commodity futures, mutual funds, or annuities.

Other common careers in the securities field include securities analysts, investment counselors, portfolio managers, and traders. Securities analysts are researchers who specialize in specific industries or in companies within an industry, but they must be intimately familiar with the broad picture as well. They evaluate investments to provide the information on which brokers make recommendations to their clients.

Investment counselors work on a fee basis, advising clients on the management of their portfolio (investment holdings), suggesting appropriate investments, guided in part by the research backup provided by security analysts and economists.

Portfolio managers have the autonomy actually to run an account, to make the buying and selling decisions for a client; they may manage a small trust for a bank or a multimillion-dollar mutual or pension fund.

Traders barter securities with other firms or at the stock exchanges. Major securities firms have specialized trading desks devoted to different types of issues, either municipal bonds, government or agency bonds, corporate bonds, or equities. Traders are the high-paid high-wire artists of the industry, making split-second decisions that involve thousands and hundreds of thousands of dollars—and ready to stand or fall on their judgments. They generally make a commission on the firm's profit.

The Changing World of Finance

The financial world both inside and outside corporations is changing. In corporations, new management and accounting processes and new tools such as computers have changed the jobs of both accounting and financial management. In the financial community the same types of changes are occurring. The financial community's old reputation for rigidity and conservatism is no longer deserved. With the influx of new ideas and new technology, there has also been an influx of new people. Banks and security brokerages particularly are opening up middle- and upper-level jobs to women.

The boundaries between investment finance, corporate finance, and banking are blurring. *Business Week* has predicted that banks of the future will provide nonbanking financing and services expanding into areas of mergers and acquisitions and even into stockbrokerage.

Perhaps the most far-reaching and visible change will stem from technology. Many financial observers foresee a paper-free credit world where electronic funds transfer will become common. Using special computer terminals, individuals and corporations are actually already able to make deposits, transfer funds, buy stock, and even pay bills by simply pushing buttons.

Marsella McHugh, Banker

What could rattle a woman who is the top manager of a unique banking division of five departments, a corporate vice-president who is directly responsible for the operations of more than 120 people, and someone who must keep constant watch on the movements of billions of dollars every day? She's going back to school. Again.

Jumping into situations with self-assurance has become a career skill for Marsella McHugh, one that she learned early. She notes that in banking, and in top management in general, "you have to have a certain flexibility. Some of it's luck—being in the right place at the right time. But it's up to you to make sure that you're in the right place at the right time. It's a matter of constantly adjusting your perspectives and broadening your skills."

For example, after little more than a year in her present job, she's moving on again—the bank is paying her to attend a special management program at Harvard. She muses ironically that "the hardest thing about going back to school is having to study and concentrate, take tests, learn advanced mathematics, calculus, and statistics, on which I need a bit of brushing up; it's just the basic discipline of school as opposed to the discipline of running a bank—they're quite different."

But then banking itself is diverse. As Ms. McHugh points out, "The most important thing for people considering a career in banking to realize is that banking offers every kind of experience, not just lending money. You can be a specialist in marketing, in operations, or in branch banking. Managing a bank very early in your career offers you a broad range of experience. Just like other large corporations, banks have needs for accounting, personnel, marketing, and other business services. Recently I've been interviewing new MBAs whom we're considering hiring, and it's incredible how many can graduate and really know only that banking involves lending money."

Ms. McHugh's own career in banking certainly demonstrates the diversity that she stresses. "My career has not been a typical one in today's environment because I'm older—I'm 40. For a long time, I was kept way back. Anything that's ever been said about discrimination against women, well, I've lived through it. You know, like being told at first that I couldn't travel because I'm a woman, although of course later I did travel."

Ms. McHugh emphasizes that she really doesn't like to stress her negative experiences, because they're "a thing of the past," but unfortunately "noncooperation from a man when he first realizes he's working for a woman" is a too-prevalent reaction women encounter. "It's very hard for some men, and maybe also for some women, to take women seriously. In sales I would go into a customer's office, and for the first 15 minutes in every case I had to prove that I knew what I was talking about. A man is considered competent until proven otherwise, but I don't think that's true for women."

Ms. McHugh's early experience in sales involved a lot of contact with corporate banking, and she was the logical choice to set up and manage a training program for business services representatives. During this time she was completing work for her MBA degree at night. As she stresses, one can't expect to continue to be successful by letting skills fall behind. "It helps to have all the credentials you can. Otherwise it's a sure dead end."

With MBA in hand, Ms. McHugh opted to leave sales and enter a training program in corporate finance. "There is a centralized training program now, and the training is identical no matter what department you are going to wind up in. Generally, trainees are recruited by a specific department, and after training, they're given their first assignment within that department. For example, I started as a junior lending officer, sometimes called a relationship manager. Candidates for the program can be MBAs or bachelor degree students recruited on campus, mid-career hires within the bank (as I was) or from outside the bank. But there is a direct effort to recruit specific personnel."

Getting into corporate lending further broadened her perspectives in banking and increased her chances for upward mobility, since corporate lending's a basic line function of the bank. It also brought a further surprise: "Because of my undergraduate studies in French, I was sent to Paris to work with subsidiaries in France and with French multinationals for our international corporate lending department. France has an extremely complicated banking system with probably a hundred types of loans whereas in the United States there are only six or seven. France also has very complicated foreign-exchange regulations, and primarily I counseled American subsidiaries on foreign-exchange issues, helping them structure their finances to comply with regulations. I also dealt with French multinational corporations on their foreign financing."

Working in a strange culture away from family and friends was balanced by the opportunity to travel widely, observe foreign banks and businesses, and freshen her mental perspective. But when Ms. McHugh returned to the States to assume the position of senior relations manager, she found another surprise in store for her. One day her boss asked her, "How would you like to do a stint in marketing, Ms. McHugh? Now that you've been developing your involvement with our international mining and chemical operation for a year, you know we could use a new point of view in our marketing operation. And with your sales background, you'd be perfect."

"So that set me in a very unusual position for someone at that point in a career," she remarks. "It was a classic situation of being involved with a job that called on one type of skills primarily and then being asked to take on a job with a completely new dimension, to make a stretch— which gives you greater visibility. For many people in banking who are marketing managers specifically, this job is in their line of career development. For me, it was a new learning experience."

Ms. McHugh went back to school to get an advanced professional certificate in marketing—the equivalent of changing the major on her

MBA—even though she saw it as more of an interruption in her career than an advancement.

Experience in the marketing side of operations eventually led Ms. McHugh back to doing what she had been originally trained to do. As she now realizes, it was "a question of broadening my background and my approach to staff functions. To expand my base in still other areas of banking, for the last year I have been in operations. My department is funds management—we are the bank's cash manager, responsible for monitoring billions of dollars every day. We handle transfers of money from all over the world and maintain the bank's cash position at the 'Fed' [Federal Reserve Bank], keeping track of how much money we have in terms of buying and selling Fed funds and exactly what our fiscal position is. It's a tremendous job for my managers, who are the ones who really do it because we're such a large bank. Tracking 500 different computer terminals around the state means that a lot of transactions are occurring simultaneously."

Ms. McHugh describes her present position as "just a typical straight management job, one in which a portion of your time is devoted to planning the activities of the department, and the direction in which you're going; part of your time is spent holding meetings to discuss the various projects, and then you work out a plan to actualize them; a certain amount of your time goes to dealing with personnel, the problems that people have, you know; and then there's the time spent on filling out all the forms for everything. And time must be found for various classes and staff development meetings."

She spends a great deal of time talking with people in her department: "I just wander around. I feel that this is a production environment for the most part, and it all needs to be managed." As an example of a manager's duties, she cites this situation: "One of my unit managers in a training program in a particular department was having a communications problem with two or three otherwise potentially successful trainees. Her job is to get these people through the program successfully to fill existing positions, and she had not understood the changes in the direction of the overall strategy the bank was implementing." So Ms. McHugh was required to step in quickly to relieve the problem—one of the things she likes to do best. As she says, "This is one of the things that I like most about my job, seeing people that you have confidence in come about."

Other situations she handles involve personnel interactions as in this example: "One of my account executives may be spending too much time paper shuffling—you know, people think of banking as being a purely reactive, paperwork type of job: trying to dig yourself out of the paper on your desk every morning and to move as much as possible from one basket to the other. But that is not what banking is all about. We have an overall strategy for developing our business. My managers study their accounts, determine what our position is and devise ways to improve it. My job is to make sure that this plan fits into the bank's overall funds management operations strategy."

Her job has turned out, according to Ms. McHugh, "to be much more in many ways than I expected it to be before I moved into it, especially in terms of challenge and involvement. It's turned out to be a lot more fun, too. I just like managing. My cardinal rule is that you spend three-quarters of your waking hours at work, and it ought to be fun." Until now, the bank had not had the type of department that Ms. McHugh manages. "We took five existing departments and reformed them into a group called funds management. I'd never heard of another bank doing this, and because it was so new I didn't really know what to expect. But I am more than pleased with the way it's turned out and the way that the department has jelled." Thriving on new things, she appreciates the fact that "it worked—things that exist as separate functions in other banks we put together as one department.

"So you could say that finally I found my thing, and it's managing money," Ms. McHugh explains. "It took me a while because I thought I enjoyed selling when I first started, and marketing is interesting also, but I get more involved in managing than in anything else. I guess it's as simple as that."

She finds, too, that she thrives on change: "I wish there were training programs just to teach change, adaptability; hard work and experience do that, of course, but I'm not so sure most people do like changing." This is one of the things that she really tries to get across to her managers. As she says, "One of the things that I found the most interesting when I first moved into this job—and which certainly benefited me but I think it has also benefited the bank equally—was the fact that someone like me who had no experience in what I was getting ready to do had of necessity to ask a lot of seemingly elementary questions. The fact that I was questioning everything produced a very stimulating situation." And this initial experience is one she has tried to carry with her through her jobs, to help others in her department. She says that "I like to almost force that kind of change whenever I'm in something long enough to exert that kind of control. I think 'musical chairs' stimulates progress and growth."

With regard to widening opportunities for women in banking, Ms. McHugh thinks that "the climate right now in banking for women is excellent. Despite the initial flurry following enactment of Equal Employment Opportunity legislation, we're not quite past the stage where it's an entry-level advantage to be a woman. But we are getting to where the percentages will begin to level out in middle-level positions right across the board. Progress is being made in these higher positions, but it will take a long time." Her advice to women is to "get on those career paths and work their way up."

BASIC RESOURCES: BANKING AND FINANCE

Merrill Lynch, Pierce, Fenner and Smith publishes an excellent pamphlet called "How to Read a Financial Report." Available free from their local offices, it defines financial terms clearly and explains how financial information is presented. Read it — it's a great tool for anyone, even if you're more interested in selling socks than stocks. Call your local Merrill Lynch office or write:

> Merrill Lynch, Pierce, Fenner and Smith
> 1 Liberty Plaza
> New York, New York 10038

For information on stockbrokerage and securities sales careers, write or phone:

> Security Industry Association
> 20 Broad Street
> New York, New York 10005

Those interested in banking careers should write or phone:

> American Bankers Association
> 1120 Connecticut Avenue NW
> Washington, D.C. 20036

BASIC RESOURCES: ACCOUNTING

For information on accounting careers, write or phone:

> American Institute of Certified Public Accountants
> 1211 Avenue of the Americas
> New York, New York 10036

> Institute of Internal Auditors
> 249 Maitland Avenue
> Altamonte Springs, Florida 32701

> National Association of Accountants
> 919 3d Avenue
> New York, New York 10022

National Society of Public Accountants
1717 Pennsylvania Avenue NW
Washington, D.C. 20006

CHAPTER 6

PEOPLE MANAGEMENT —
Human Resources Development/Personnel

The concept of personnel management has changed during the 20th century. Personnel jobs were once primarily considered to involve record keeping and hiring, and not to be so important or intellectually demanding as, for example, finance. But since the purpose of a personnel department is to help company management in its relationship to company employees and since management has been looking for ways to make more effective use of its human resources, personnel departments have begun to offer new services. Among them are career development, personal counseling, planning future workforce needs, and redesigning work settings.

Personnel management has also changed dramatically in response to government regulations. In 1935 the Wagner Act established collective bargaining, and company personnel departments took on the new task of labor relations. More recently, Affirmative Action and Equal Employment Opportunity regulations have caused companies to examine and alter their hiring and promoting processes. Occupational health and safety regulations have forced a reexamination of working conditions by personnel staff.

Management theorist Peter Drucker once described personnel management as being "partly a file clerk's job, partly a housekeeping job, partly a social worker's job, and partly 'fire fighting,' heading off union trouble or settling it." The fact is that what personnel departments do varies a great deal from one firm to another.

In small companies personnel management is done by the chief executive officer or business owner, who hires and fires employees with the help of the accountant or bookkeeper, who writes out the paychecks and

Funding for this chapter was provided by the Western Electric Fund.

keeps track of fringe benefits and business. As firms grow larger, personnel tasks become more complex and more differentiated and require more specialists.

Although about 250,000 people held personnel jobs in 1976, personnel departments have no standard set of jobs and no standard forms of organization. But all people in personnel jobs have the difficult task of balancing the needs of the individual and the needs of the company. Doing this task well requires a solid knowledge of the firm and its managers. Almost all personnel jobs require working with managers as well as employees, whether the job involves instituting new safety practices, designing a training program, or writing a job description.

In large companies personnel departments are among the most highly structured of departments. Various systems and processes have been devised for treating employees fairly and for complying with the increasing number of government regulations, and personnel jobs generally relate to a particular system. Although each firm's system may be different, all personnel departments perform most of the following functions.

(1) *Hiring.* Hiring is a function of every personnel department. In some companies standard tests are given to employees applying for certain jobs. Personnel department employees administer the tests and often a professional psychologist or guidance counselor helps evaluate the results.

Many companies use job-posting systems. Descriptions of job vacancies, including duties, pay range, and supervisor, are posted on a bulletin board or listed in an employee newsletter. Job-posting systems require job analysts who collect information from supervisors and employees and write position descriptions for each job.

Wage and salary administrators evaluate the position description and compare it with other jobs in the company and assign it a pay rate. Since pay discrepancies are a major source of employee discontent, wage and salary administrators must do very careful work to assure that the pay rates are equitable.

The job of the employment interviewer is to determine if an applicant has the basic qualifications for a job. The manager who will supervise the position is the one who has the power to hire.

All interviewers know that besides the formal application process, an informal hiring process is at work, too. People tell their friends about job vacancies, or newly appointed managers hire people they have worked with elsewhere. Most personnel staffs make the informal system work for them.

Generally speaking, most middle- and top-management positions are filled directly by upper-level management with little or no personnel department involvement. This is sometimes true of another form of hiring—recruitment. Recruiters for management or technical jobs, whether they are recruiting college or business school graduates or trying to attract people from other companies, can come from the personnel department, the division doing the hiring, or a special executive recruitment department. A recruiter in some firms might even be a recent graduate of the university he is canvassing.

(2) *Employee Services.* Business firms can offer quite a range of employee services. Some concerns have employee cafeterias, employee stores, credit unions, employee recreation programs, or special events —all generally administered by personnel department employees with appropriate skills in retailing, banking, or promotion.

Some companies' medical services hire physicians and nurses to staff clinics or health centers. People with social work or counseling training are employed to help employees remain productive while they are going through a period of personal difficulty.

More and more companies are offering career counseling, and not just to special groups like minorities, women, people who have been laid off, or people whose career has hit a plateau, but to all employees. Corporations such as Polaroid, for example, have developed career workshops to help individuals evaluate their abilities and interests and learn about various career possibilities within the firm.

A most important employee service is training and education. Training and education departments hire former teachers and psychologists from outside the company, sometimes on a part-time or consultant basis, or train people from within the company to give courses or workshops.

(3) *Record Keeping.* All businesses must keep track of their employees once they have been hired. Files are maintained, detailing test re-

---

GETTING IN, MOVING UP: PERSONNEL

Personnel was once an area in which college degrees were not required for entry-level jobs, but this situation is changing rapidly, particularly in large companies in major metropolitan areas. Specialist jobs in labor relations and benefits administration often require advanced training as well.

In a small company a personnel position may encompass the duties of an interviewer, recruiter, job analyst, or other personnel specialists. In large companies positions are more differentiated, and you may need to move from one kind of position to another to get a good general background. People in supervisory positions in large- or medium-sized corporations sometimes move to smaller companies to get a job as a top administrator.

Personnel departments tend to promote from within for many jobs. Transferring from personnel management to other kinds of management positions can be difficult.

sults, work records, supervisors' evaluations, transfers, promotions, extra training, and so forth. Companies also keep records of fringe benefits, bonuses, health insurance, Social Security, vacation time, unemployment compensation, and workmen's compensation. Separate "Compensation and Benefits" departments in some companies hire job analysts and wage and salary administrators. Accountants, insurance specialists, and computer specialists also work for the record-keeping part of a personnel department. This personnel department data base is crucial to labor relations and to internal workforce planning.

(4) *Labor Relations.* Companies that employ unionized workers are bound by special government regulations when handling strikes, contract negotiations, employee grievances, or any prolonged labor and management disagreement. Labor relations staff work directly with top corporate management and legal staff to represent the company. In some firms labor relations is a part of personnel staff and the vice-president for personnel is the chief negotiator. In others it is primarily a function of the firm's legal staff, with data support from the personnel department. Labor relations work is both well paying and prestigious; it requires specialized knowledge and, at upper levels, legal training or a master's degree.

Higher-Level Personnel Jobs

If you pursue a career in personnel, your job will gradually involve more research, policy setting, and system design. For instance, higher-level personnel work may involve studying employee motivation or morale problems and proposing solutions. It may include instituting a series of courses to keep technical personnel up to date on new developments in their field, arranging workshops for new managers in personnel practices, or instituting a standard company-wide employee evaluation process called a "performance appraisal." At its most sophisticated, personnel management means "replacement planning" for top management posts, making sure the company has two or three executives who could take over if the people in key executive positions were lost, and "manpower planning," making sure the company has enough workers with the right skills to meet its workforce needs.

For some high-level personnel jobs it is often helpful to have an MBA or an advanced degree in organizational development or industrial psychology. But personnel management, or human resources management as it is increasingly called, offers you unique satisfactions no matter what level you're in. One personnel executive explains:

> Human resources management is the last frontier. We're using up all our oil and natural resources. If it's greater productivity we're after,

we've got to learn how to use our people better so they are more productive and more satisfied in their work. Besides, people spend such a huge part of their life working, they ought to be happy at it. I've been working on that all my working life. I know I would have advanced further in this company if I had moved into sales or marketing instead of staying in personnel. In my company, personnel is not a glamour field. I know I've done something really important for people.

Two Special Personnel Jobs

Two special personnel jobs require you to serve as an internal representative of federal legislation—OSHA (Occupational Safety and Health) officer and Affirmative Action or Equal Employment Opportunity (EEO) officer. Safety and health have long been a part of personnel management in some firms. This area may have included safety inspections, training employees in safe practices, and risk management (evaluating company accident insurance). Now it also includes making sure a company's labor practices and workplaces meet federal standards. Federal OSHA inspectors have the right to inspect business premises at any time without advance notice. Although there are so many businesses and regulations and so few federal inspectors that noncompliant companies aren't always vulnerable, complaints on the behalf of disgruntled employees can be very expensive to a company.

The same thing is true of Affirmative Action or Equal Employment Opportunity complaints. These cases don't often come to court, but when they do a company can be in big trouble. In small companies Affirmative Action may be one of a number of functions a manager performs; in larger firms there may be a separate Affirmative Action office. An Affirmative Action or EEO office tries to make sure the company is protected from lawsuits by seeing to it that women (Affirmative Action) and minority group members (EEO) are not discriminated against in hiring and promotion practices. This requires both knowledge of the law and real negotiating skill; the job is a tough one.

Lorraine Hughes, Executive Recruiter

Ask Lorraine Hughes, a 37-year-old executive recruiter for a small but respected search firm, to outline the character traits necessary to succeed in her field, and her description sounds like a self-profile: "It's a caveat that personnel professionals must enjoy working with people. Obviously that's true. But beyond that, they must be sensitive to people's need for emotional as well as intellectual fulfillment in their jobs. Also, I think the best personnel workers have to be bright, with inquiring minds.

They have to be willing to learn an awful lot of things about the company for which they are working."

Ms. Hughes concedes that, historically, a low level of intelligence too often characterized people employed in personnel jobs. "Enthusiasm and a clerical mentality used to be the only requirements. Personnel departments were considered the corporate backwater, the place where all the other departments could dump their mediocre workers. But the advent of discrimination suits, pension laws, and delicate labor problems has changed all that. Now ambitious personnel professionals can aspire to the lofty and high-paying post of vice-president in charge of human resources. To get there, it helps if you have an undergraduate or graduate degree in personnel administration, business administration or, possibly, psychology; or, at least, have taken courses in those subjects."

Ms. Hughes' own career, however, proves there are other routes to top-drawer personnel jobs and other undergraduate degrees that are acceptable.

At the University of Massachusetts, Ms. Hughes was a premed student on scholarship and made the Dean's List every semester. About halfway through a master's in biochemistry she decided that "I wasn't going to be the next Madame Curie and dropped out of school for a while." Although she couldn't type, she captured a spot as administrative assistant to the chief engineer of an engineering consulting firm that specialized in aerospace research and development.

"I really hated that job. So after three months, I marched into the president's office and announced I was quitting, which didn't upset him terribly since he didn't even know who I was. After I told him, he asked what I ideally wanted to do. I told him I thought the firm needed a personnel department—I had been doing all the preliminary screening of engineers for my boss. Of course, I had no formal personnel training, but the president thought I was smart and admired my pluck. His exact words were: 'OK, big mouth, start a personnel department!' "

Ms. Hughes admits she learned personnel administration "by the seat of my pants," although she did take courses, paid for by her employer, in wage and salary administration, personnel management, and labor relations at Northeastern University and audited some engineering courses at MIT. "When you are recruiting technical people it is absolutely essential to have some understanding of their discipline."

She held her post as personnel director for five years and watched the company triple in size to 225 employees. She recruited everyone from clerical workers to engineers with advanced degrees, advised new employees of their benefits, and interviewed the personnel directors of competing companies in order to design detailed job descriptions and salary guidelines for her own firm.

A childhood friend offered Ms. Hughes the perfect opportunity to move onward and upward. A year earlier he had opened a phenomenally successful employment agency in San Diego. It was the height of the Vietnam War, and the agency specialized in placing ex-military junior officers in industry. "My friend made me a financial offer I couldn't refuse and promised me I'd have to live in San Diego for only six to eight months. Six months later to the day, I arrived in New York City to open and run the branch office there."

Ms. Hughes and the agency's other recruiters pioneered "career weekends." A "career weekend" brings together hundreds of applicants and potential employers in one place—usually a hotel ballroom—for two days of mass recruiting. The employment agency sponsoring the weekend gets a fee for every placement made.

Administration of the New York office and its five employees and the supervision of one "career weekend" a month did not constitute a full-time job for Ms. Hughes. Therefore she did something that has become the hallmark of her career: talked her boss into letting her undertake a new venture. In this case, it was the direct placement of engineers, particularly nuclear engineers, with client companies. "In retrospect, I see that every place I've worked, I've carved out my own niche," she muses.

After four years, salary considerations again beckoned her elsewhere. Although her compensation had risen to $18,000 a year based on a salary plus bonus, Ms. Hughes knew the only way to get paid equivalent to her productivity was to affiliate with an agency that paid a low salary but high commission on each placement.

"I didn't pretend that money isn't very important to me," she says. "In this country, particularly, it is a measure of your worth. In my first two jobs, I was making less than my male peers and I screamed bloody murder. Fortunately for me, I was valuable enough that I got a modicum of what I asked for and didn't get fired for insubordination."

Her next employer was also an employment agency making high-level placements, a competitor of her former employer. She joined this firm in 1972, shortly after Revised Order 4 was signed by the President. It had the force of law and promised to increase opportunities for women and minorities to move into jobs previously considered "for white males only" and to be admitted into training programs that would accelerate their advancement into management-level jobs.

Again, Ms. Hughes saw the main chance and capitalized on what she saw as the wave of the future. "My new employers were not enthusiastic about letting me specialize in the placement of degreed women and minorities in well-paying jobs, mainly because they didn't think it would work. My comeback was, 'You may be right, but give me six months to experiment.' They did, and I was extremely successful, partially because of my own passionate belief in the justness of the equal opportunity cause. I also made a lot of money in the process. My commissions were 40 percent of the fee to the agency."

Why did Ms. Hughes eventually leave such a lucrative job? For prestige reasons: "I'd worked for agencies for 10 years and I wanted to take the next step up and work for an executive search firm. Search firms, which are paid by their clients whether or not they find the right candidate to fill a vacancy, are generally held in more esteem than employment agencies. And the candidates you deal with are the cream of the crop."

On a typical workday Ms. Hughes arrives in her midtown Manhattan office at about 8:30 AM. On the average, she sees three candidates a day, by appointment only, and tries to schedule them either early in the day, at lunchtime, or after 5. The rest of her time is spent revising resumes ("most people just describe their duties on a job rather than listing their accomplishments"), talking on the phone to potential candidates ("in contrast to the way employment agents work, executive recruiters often seek out candidates who are already happily employed"), and visiting clients. She finds one-on-one meetings with her contacts at client companies a vital part of her job. "Industries have personalities but so do the individual companies within an industry."

Ms. Hughes spends a great deal of time preparing candidates for interviews—she may see a candidate as many as seven times. Her objective is to train candidates to ask the right questions to determine whether they'll feel comfortable in a company. "I also try to give candidates insights about the corporate people who will be interviewing them. I might point out that the person a candidate is to see is always a cold fish so don't take it personally. These are the things that can make or break an interview."

Her biggest daily challenge is "trying to find the person who fits precisely into a job slot . . . and being able to help the candidate who probably couldn't have found the spot without my intervention. Don't get me wrong. The people I place are excellently qualified—Harvard, Wharton, Stanford MBAs and the like. None of them would pound the pavement if I weren't around to help them. But because of my inside information about my client companies, I really know where they are going to feel most comfortable and prosper."

Ms. Hughes agrees that women make excellent recruiters because they tend to be more intuitive and sensitive to emotional requirements. Unfortunately, few have infiltrated the ranks of the large, well-known search firms—the Boydens, Heidrick & Struggles, and Ward Howells. However, many women are in employment agencies and some are working for the lower-echelon executive recruiting firms. Furthermore, National Personnel Associates reports that more women managers are being hired to work in corporate personnel departments than in any other area. The field is definitely opening up to women.

What Ms. Hughes likes most about her current job is the freedom—"the fact that I don't really have a boss. Even though the two owners of the firm are technically my bosses, as long as I generate X-amount of business, they don't care how I do it or who I deal with."

That taste of freedom is prompting her to start her own recruiting firm in the near future to specialize in the placement and outplacement of women and minorities. "Outplacement counselors—they're also called dehiring firms—are retained by corporations to help released executives find good jobs elsewhere," Ms. Hughes explains. Once again, Ms. Hughes has found a vacuum that she is uniquely qualified to fill.

Harriet McCord and Kathleen Joselow, Two Different Human Resources Careers

Harriet McCord: "If I had been born a boy in the 1940s, I would probably have become a machinist like my dad or an industrial engineer like my brother. I always loved playing around in the workshop with my dad, watching him take things apart and make things, but instead I became a teacher in a technical high school.

"About 15 years ago this plant realized that more and more of their production line workers were poor inner-city people, some of them Spanish-speaking, and they couldn't read company notices or understand their supervisors too well. Efficiency was down, and the accident rate was up. The company decided to hire someone to teach basic reading skills; my brother told me about the opening, and I got it.

"The program was very successful. The people were dying to learn; they knew they were trapped in the lowest-level jobs if they couldn't read and write. Once they found out it wasn't going to be like school— that they weren't going to be graded or compared or put down in any way—they worked hard. We ended up offering basic math as well. Some of those employees have gone on to night school at the community college after passing the high school equivalency exam. I can't tell you how proud I am of my students.

"And the program has paid off for the company too. The statistics prove it in greater productivity and a lower accident rate. It's given me a new career. I got to know the production supervisors and would suggest ways to explain changes in production processes to people on the line. Now I work directly with the industrial engineering staff whenever they need me to design training programs for production line workers to go with new machinery or new processes. I am a very happy person."

Kathleen Joselow: "I was a psychology major as an undergraduate, but I knew I wanted to end up in the business world, not sitting behind a desk as a therapist, talking to one person at a time. I worked for a couple years in a bank before I went back to school to get a PhD in organizational behavior. I love the field. I love the people in it. It's exciting, dynamic, fun, crazy—all those things and more—once you learn the special language.

"My first real job in the field was while I was still in graduate school. There were four of us and our professor. It could hardly have been more frustrating. We were supposed to help implement an Affirmative Action plan for women and minorities in 10 plants of a company that had been run pretty much as autonomous units. We dealt with every possible problem—union problems, terrified employees, jealousies. But it was a great learning experience.

"I learned enough to pick my company as well as my job when I graduated, and here I am in a small but growing company with a progressive top management team. I'm doing human resources planning, teaching newly promoted managers how to manage their employees effectively, and developing training programs for first-line supervisors. I now have a small staff. And I'm bound to be made a manager within two years. How do you like that!"

BASIC RESOURCES

For information on careers in personnel contact:

American Society for Training and Development
P.O. Box 5307
Madison, Wisconsin 53705

American Society of Personnel Administration
19 Church Street
Berea, Ohio 44017

National Labor Relations Board
Director of Personnel
1717 Pennsylvania Avenue NW
Washington, D.C. 20570

CHAPTER 7

PRODUCING THE GOODS

The goods produced by manufacturing companies are largely responsible for what Americans have come to call "the good life." Factories churn out everything from typewriters and paper products to computers, cake mixes, microwave ovens, storm windows, pillow cases, alarm clocks, and fire engines. Another group of manufacturers produces the "primary" materials—the steel, glass, plastic, and paper—needed to make these finished goods.

Of the nine major segments comprising the American economy (agriculture, mining, construction, transportation/public utilities, wholesale/retail trade, finance/insurance/real estate, services, government, and manufacturing), manufacturing probably has the biggest influence on our daily lives. Certainly, it is the largest economic subdivision. Manufacturing companies employed almost 20 million workers in 1976—that's 23 percent of the total employment in all industries—and they accounted for 24 percent of our gross national product.

Some real satisfactions can be gained from careers in production management. The sense of power that comes from working with large machines is one. Seeing the results of your work is another. A production supervisor explains, "I like what I do because it's tangible. I'm not just pushing papers or designing systems. My work is measurable. Everybody can see what I've done."

And meeting the demands of the work can give you a real sense of accomplishment. As one operations manager says, "I'm absolutely compulsive about not missing production deadlines. You may think that's an awful way to live, but the sense of achievement I feel when we finish on time makes it all worthwhile."

Production management, like financial management, is a traditional way to make it into top corporate jobs. Manufacturing companies, espe-

Funding for this chapter was provided by General Motors Corporation.

cially, respect people who have had real "hands-on," "nuts and bolts" experience.

Production Jobs

Production is the process by which natural resources are transformed into the goods we use either directly as consumers or indirectly in the manufacture of other, more complex products. Roughly two-thirds of all production employees are "blue-collar" workers—craft workers, factory foremen, operatives, and laborers. The remaining third are clerical, professional/technical, and managerial workers, often referred to as "white-collar" workers.

Before the Industrial Revolution this distinction between workers and managers didn't really exist. Production was a one-person operation. A master shoemaker bought his own supplies and made the complete shoe himself to his own set of standards. Today the complexity of the modern manufacturing process requires management specialists with sophisticated knowledge and often special training in each phase of the production process; purchasing, operations, and quality control.

Purchasing

The purchasing department of a manufacturing firm buys the materials needed for production to take place. Originally, raw materials were the primary goods procured by industrial buyers, or *purchasing agents*. But as companies began to produce more sophisticated products, such as computers and turbojet engines, purchasing agents needed some knowledge of engineering, production, finance, and marketing to make intelligent decisions about the purchase of such complex items as component parts and subassembly units.

Today even industrial buyers looking for raw materials (commodities) require more training to deal with the imbalances, shortages, and price fluctuations of the current commodities market. Consequently, purchasing departments are recruiting better-educated and higher-caliber trainees.

A purchasing agent's job is to buy goods of acceptable quality, in the right quantity, at the best time, for the lowest price, from the most reliable source, with delivery guaranteed for a specified date and location. Therefore the ideal purchasing professional must have a thorough grasp of her company's needs (a buyer for Du Pont's chemical division should have a degree in chemistry, for instance). She will also need the determination to shop around for the best value; and the forcefulness to drive a hard, yet tactful bargain involving large amounts of money. Today's buyer needs a knowledge of computerized buying and inventory control systems, a mastery of traffic management techniques, and an understanding of how procurement decisions affect the bottom line of the company's financial statement.

In a manufacturing firm the purchasing department can make a big difference in profitability. The National Association of Purchasing Management (NAPM) claims that approximately 50 percent of every dollar received in sales by a company is expended on the purchase of goods and services. In short, a dollar saved through careful purchasing is worth as much as one made through effective selling.

Traditionally, the top purchasing person in a manufacturing company holds the title *purchasing manager* or purchasing director. However, the trend is toward enlarging the purchasing executive's responsibility within the corporation, resulting in the creation of the new position of materials manager. A *materials manager* supervises anyone remotely involved in the procurement or processing of the materials used by a firm in the course of production. Such seemingly disparate departments as purchasing, receiving, inspection, inventory control and scheduling, storing, invoice auditing, scrap disposal, and shipping may report to a materials manager.

Surveys done by NAPM indicate that about 70 percent of the purchasing departments in larger American corporations report directly to the president or vice-president. In some instances a vice-president for purchasing or for materials management is part of the senior management team, especially if the company relies heavily on the purchase of a commodity, as a flour milling concern does. The outmoded practice of assigning purchasing a subordinate role to production has largely disappeared.

A 1971 *Purchasing Magazine* survey showed that 77 percent of all purchasing managers had attended college and 38 percent had received degrees. Today a much higher proportion of purchasing executives holds degrees, although there continue to be no universally accepted educational credentials for entry-level purchasing spots. If anything, the size and industry of the hiring firm dictate the amount and type of education required. But if a purchasing executive seeks to move up the corporate ladder, a college degree is very important.

The Bureau of Labor Statistics estimates that more than half of all purchasing professionals now work for manufacturers and that the job category as a whole will grow by 35 percent by 1985 to 259,000 purchasing agents nationwide.

In large manufacturing organizations the responsibility for the shipment of raw materials and finished goods is assigned to an industrial *traffic manager*. In smaller companies traffic falls within the domain of the purchasing department, for in a sense it is a highly specialized form of purchasing—the purchase of transportation.

Traffic managers analyze the various transportation alternatives (rail, air, road, water, pipeline, or some combination of them) and select the best carrier, carefully weighing such factors as freight classifications and regulations, charges, time schedules, volume and weight of shipments, and loss and damage ratios.

The Bureau of Labor Statistics classified 21,000 persons as industrial traffic managers in 1976, and found that most of them worked for manufacturers. Because high-level traffic managers frequently represent their firms before rate-making and regulatory bodies such as the Interstate Commerce Commission, state commissions, and local traffic bureaus, a college education is increasingly important in this field. Specialized training is available at selected colleges and universities and a number of trade and technical schools. Training seminars are sponsored by such professional associations as the American Society of Traffic and Transportation in Chicago.

Production

In a manufacturing firm the production work, often referred to as operations, is directed by engineers, scientists, and technicians holding such titles as production supervisor (or manager), plant manager, or vice-president of operations. To qualify for these white-collar jobs, an engineering (whether industrial or some other type) degree is a good door opener, although physical science or data processing degrees may also be acceptable.

Operations personnel determine the most efficient way for a company to use the three basic factors of production—labor, machines, and materials. People trained as *industrial engineers* are generally more concerned with designing methods and systems that will make the best use of these production factors, whereas mechanical and other kinds of engineers involve themselves more with the purely practical mechanical aspects of carrying out the production processes. The scientists and spe-

---

GETTING IN, MOVING UP: PRODUCTION MANAGEMENT

Women have not traditionally had careers in production management, partly because few women have had the engineering or scientific background to qualify. Plant management positions rarely go to people without some technical skills. The traditional job move is from that of a technical specialist to that of a generalist. You may first supervise other technical specialists, and then advance to higher and higher management positions. To advance you will need to learn something about other technical specialties important to your company, about accounting and financial analysis, and how to communicate your ideas in person and on paper.

---

cialty engineers focus on the details; the industrial engineers survey the big picture.

Mechanical engineering is perhaps the most general of all the engineering disciplines. In 1976 three-fourths of all mechanical engineers were employed in manufacturing, mainly in primary and fabricated metals, machinery, transportation equipment, and electrical equipment firms. Mechanical engineers employed in production jobs are involved in the design, development, use, and repair of the assembly-line machinery that produces the goods.

Until recently, Purdue University was one of the few schools in the country that offered courses in operations theory and practice leading to an MBA degree. However, many colleges now offer two- or four-year programs leading to degrees in engineering technology. These programs prepare students for practical design and production work rather than for higher-level operations jobs requiring a more theoretical science and math background.

About 250 colleges and universities currently offer a bachelor's degree in engineering, and more than 50 schools award a bachelor's degree in the new discipline of engineering technology. Unfortunately, the acceptance of this degree among employers is still unclear, with many companies assigning engineering technology graduates a status closer to that of a technician than a full-fledged engineer.

But regardless of the academic training a new recruit brings to a production job, one fact remains the same: production is learned on the job, since all manufacturers employ their own unique modes of operation. This is one reason operations personnel rarely move from one industry to another and tend to advance through internal promotion rather than through industry job-hopping.

Technological obsolescence is a real problem for many highly specialized engineers. One company official estimates that one-tenth of all his engineers' technical knowledge becomes obsolete every year and that therefore "our people must either spend a lot of time keeping up to date in their specialty, or they have to develop the skills to make a move to sales or advance to a higher management position."

Another problem facing some engineers in the past 15 years has been that the demand for their specialty can change dramatically. For instance, the space program created a great need for aerospace engineers, and the big cutbacks in that program in the 70s put thousands of aerospace engineers out of work at mid-career.

Engineering professional associations such as the Institute of Electrical and Electronics Engineers are now helping their members find ways to update or transfer their skills. They are also seeking changes in the engineering curriculum in colleges and universities so that the course of study emphasizes general engineering principles that are applicable to a variety of special fields.

Inventory and production control managers are also a part of the operations function. In essence, production and inventory control is a scheduling job and "supply and demand" are the watchwords. The object is to keep warehouses stocked at an optimum level, ensuring a continuous supply of goods as needed without committing too much of the company's capital to excess inventory. Today these tasks involve sophisticated, computerized forecasting and monitoring systems.

Production planning personnel requisition the materials and parts needed for production, allowing sufficient time for buyers to find an appropriate supplier, negotiate the purchase, secure delivery, and see that the goods are properly tested. At the other end of the production process inventory control specialists direct the movement of the finished products from the factory into warehouses. They make sure there is a smooth flow of materials and parts through all stages of the fabrication process.

Since production and inventory control is an emerging profession,

---

INDUSTRY PROFILE: ELECTRONICS INDUSTRY

The burgeoning electronics industry is responsible for televisions, radios, calculators, electronic testing equipment, production control equipment, and space stations, among other things. In 1976, 1.4 million people worked to produce and sell electronic devices and their components.

Like other high-technology industries, electronics employs a large number of scientists and engineers to research and develop new products. Many of this industry's employees hold administrative jobs, and many middle- and high-level management employees have scientific or technical backgrounds. Technicians and sales personnel often have received specialized training as well.

In the past 20 years several small electronic firms, started in inventors' garages, have gone on to become large companies. In concerns with real growth potential, employees have a chance for significant career advancement. Electronics is a highly competitive field, and the competition is based not just on price and quality but also on the flexibility to incorporate the latest technology into electronic devices. Although consumer electronics products require the capital and marketing techniques of a large corporation, smaller companies also thrive if they have the ability to respond quickly to a demand for the latest and most sophisticated components and instruments.

Although the demand for consumer goods such as televisions and radios will continue to rise as incomes and populations grow, increasing reliance on imports may slow down production, and employment in this industry may decline during the 1980s. However, government, business, and medical use of electronic equipment is expected to increase rapidly during that period.

there is still no recommended education program or clear-cut job or career progression. In 1957 the American Production and Inventory Control Society (APICS) was founded to promote the occupation and provide continuing education programs to train new recruits. Today APICS has over 24,000 members and sponsors a certification program to help upgrade the job category.

Quality Control

Quality control, the inspection of goods to make sure they meet predetermined standards of quality, is an important part of the production process. In some industries it is required by government regulatory agencies.

Quality control inspectors work closely with both the purchasing and the production divisions in a plant. Inspectors are on hand as the raw materials and goods purchased by the buyers arrive at the factory. Before the shipment is given final approval, inspectors run tests, often in a special quality assurance laboratory, documenting the materials' suitability for use in production. Quality control personnel also accompany buyers on visits to inspect vendors' facilities or test a sample of a supplier's product before the purchasing agent begins negotiations.

When the finished product comes off the production line, quality control personnel again administer a series of tests. A variety of methods may be employed to make certain products meet company specifications and government regulations. An inspector may smell and examine a good product for any telltale signs of spoilage or study a pill capsule under a magnifying glass for flaws or defects. For checks on durable goods an inspector may use sophisticated instruments such as micrometers, protractors, and gauges. Inspectors frequently make simple calculations to measure parts against the original work orders or blueprints to verify that the finished products conform to company standards. When the number of rejected items reaches a specified level, inspectors sound the alarm and notify their superiors.

In 1976 about 692,000 American workers were classified as inspectors, two-thirds of them working in factories that produced durable goods. The extent and type of education required for a quality control job vary widely, depending on the complexity of the products that need testing and the degree to which they are government regulated. In drug companies, for example, quality control inspectors may need advanced degrees.

However, the average quality control job is in the blue-collar category. Inspectors are usually trained on the job and their work is often repetitive and routine. However, a young engineer might be given a supervisory quality control position initially and then be promoted into middle management relatively fast. An experienced production manager might

CONTROVERSIAL ISSUE: OSHA—WHAT IS IT? IS IT NEEDED?

For years the proverbial monkey on the back of American industry was organized labor. Now manufacturers have a new enemy—the Federal Government in the guise of the Occupational Safety and Health Administration (OSHA).

With the possible exception of the Environmental Protection Agency, OSHA and its research arm, the National Institute for Occupational Safety and Health (NIOSH), have done more to stir the ire of manufacturers than any other recent federal legislation. With heavy labor union support, OSHA was established in 1971. It is empowered to study the problems of workplace safety, make recommendations for worker health standards, and enforce those standards through periodic inspections of production facilities.

The majority of the nation's manufacturers are adamant in their stop-OSHA efforts. One Portland, Oregon, factory owner summed up the feeling of many of his peers in a letter published in *The Wall Street Journal*. He characterized OSHA as "a Gestapo federal agency . . . . power hungry, morally corrupt and generally unneeded." Why unneeded? The factory owner maintains workplace safety, and health regulations have for years been enforced adequately by local, county, and state agencies. So why have federal interference?

OSHA proponents answer that question by citing a battery of statistics:

- A quarter of all working Americans are exposed to one or more of the approximately 400 disease-causing agents covered by the more stringent federal health regulations. One million people are exposed to one or more of these agents for more than 4 hours each day.
- Almost 3 million workers are exposed to 17 carcinogens; 80,000 are exposed for more than 4 hours a day—and these figures exclude the hundreds of other workers exposed to chemicals *suspected* of causing cancer.

OSHA also claims many manufacturers put new technologies and chemicals into use before they have been thoroughly tested for potential worker health risks, and that they expose an estimated 7½ million workers to industrial chemicals whose composition is unknown because the ingredients are a "trade secret."

OSHA spokespeople point out that occupational injuries are relatively easy to quantify and prevent, but occupational illnesses are another matter. Here, any statistics are often based on scientific guesswork, since OSHA claims many company physicians refuse to level with public health authorities about any signs of disease problems among workers. One 1976 survey estimated that as many as 100,000 "excess deaths" occur each year as a consequence of unhealthful working conditions. Furthermore, work-related factors play a significant role in all cancer deaths that can be broadly classified as environmentally caused, and in such chronic respiratory diseases as silicosis, asbestosis, and pneumoconiosis.

While the debate rages, OSHA continues to grow in strength and influence, and at the same time manufacturers continue to evade the expense of instituting comprehensive medical monitoring and prevention programs to protect workers.

---

also be moved over into quality assurance to direct the company's program.

Because of the growing influence of the federal Occupational Safety and Health Administration (OSHA), a booming job category is that of *safety engineer.* Although all safety engineers have one primary function, to prevent accidents, their specific tasks depend on where they work. In a large manufacturing facility, where most of these specialists are employed, their job would be both preventive (identifying potential hazards and eliminating them before a mishap takes place) and investigatory (determining the cause of an accident after it occurs).

Many safety engineers consult with design engineers concerning the safety of their company's product. They advise on the development of prototypes, making sure they meet all safety standards. Later they monitor the manufacturing process to ensure the safety of the finished product.

Designing and maintaining a healthy work environment is the job of the industrial hygienist. A pre-med or life sciences background is necessary here. Some type of engineering degree would be more appropriate for fire protection engineers who safeguard workers and industrial property against loss from fire, explosion, and related hazards. In industrial firms occupational safety and health workers can advance to plant safety and health manager or a corporate managerial post, overseeing several facilities.

The Outlook for Women in Production

Manufacturing companies are clamoring for qualified women to fill middle-management production slots. The problem has been that few women have had production experience or even engineering degrees until recently. Production positions in manufacturing have been traditionally a male preserve.

Although any woman with a solid technical education ought to have no trouble landing an entry-level job in production, purchasing, or any other related function, she should expect to be "the only" or "the first" woman in her field in most companies. A woman purchasing agent recalls, "More than one salesman's mouth has literally dropped open when

I was introduced as the company's LNG [liquefied natural gas] buyer. It's kind of funny."

She may also experience some resistance from her male superiors when she attempts to advance into more senior-level positions. This situation will change, however, as more women move into other corporate management positions and more women qualify for production jobs. Right now women in production are certainly noticed, and this can be a real advantage. In the words of one production executive, "I'm very ambitious, and I think this job gives me the kind of visibility I need to get ahead."

Evelyn Anderson, Production Manager

"The biggest problem women production managers face is that male factory workers don't know what to expect from them," says Evelyn Anderson, 28-year-old production supervisor in a large pharmaceutical plant in Indiana. "They wonder how a woman will react when a piece of machinery breaks down. Is she going to sit in her office and give orders? Or is she going to go out on the floor and become part of the operation and actually get grease on her hands?"

Ms. Anderson does the latter. As section supervisor/packaging inspector in the quality control division of a multinational chemical and pharmaceutical corporation, she oversees 13 employees, most of them men, and interacts daily with an all-male crew of machinists and mechanics who are responsible for repairing plant equipment.

According to Ms. Anderson, production is one discipline you don't learn in a classroom, although she admits her BS in mechanical engineering has stood her well.

For example, Ms. Anderson still remembers the time an expletive taught her a valuable lesson. Because of her mechanical aptitude, Ms. Anderson often finds herself crouched on all fours helping the mechanical crew repair faulty machinery in the plant, a frustrating job under the best of circumstances.

"One time, I was just as stymied as they were so I inadvertently let go with a bit of profanity when my monkey wrench refused to catch. There was a deafening silence. First, the men looked at each other, then they looked at me, and slowly smiles broke out on all their faces as if to say, 'You're human, after all.' My slip of the tongue did not lead to excessive swearing on the job or any other evils. What it did was make the mechanics feel less self-conscious around me."

Ms. Anderson maintains this was a case of men not knowing what to expect from a woman boss. "Before that incident, I never realized how uncomfortable the mechanics felt around me. Apparently, they thought I was a very proper young lady in white gloves who was easily shocked.

Since then, I've made it a point to talk to any new group of workers informally and outline what I expect of them, and most important, what they can anticipate from me. My message is that women are the same as men when it comes to wanting to get the job done."

Ms. Anderson's ability to handle people has paid off. Since she joined the company as a pharmaceutical engineering supervisor in early 1976, she's been singled out as an unusually competent manager with a bright future. In that entry-level job, she supervised 3 foremen and 24 mechanics, and was responsible for setting up and maintaining a steady production flow on 19 oral products assembly lines. She also assumed the role of a project engineer and designed some new equipment for two of the company's other plants and held the title of department safety officer responsible for on-site OSHA compliance.

In record time, Ms. Anderson was promoted into her present job in the quality control division. The position requires a unique cluster of skills. Half of the job is pure troubleshooting, and since the cause of the problem is often human error, the job requires a sensitive manager who knows the workers well. A brilliant mechanic with no people sense would fail miserably.

The other half of the job focuses on quality control, the testing of materials and products to make sure they meet predetermined standards of excellence. Ms. Anderson supervises 13 samplers and inspectors who pretest all packaging materials (syringes, capsules, bottles, etc.) in the lab before they are okayed for use, check out new packaging designs, and inspect package labels.

Ms. Anderson also interacts with every other aspect of operations and production—outside suppliers and in-house purchasing agents, materials management, package design and development, manufacturing, long-range planning, and the Federal Food and Drug Administration concerning labeling control or any consumer complaints involving packaging.

Ms. Anderson admits she got her present job because a mentor brought her capabilities to the attention of the right people. She thinks such a sponsor is an indispensable aid to advancement in a large company. Her patron is a microbiologist several hierarchal levels above her. With a few other friends, they began meeting for lunch "and immediately recognized in each other the desire to maintain high ethical standards while we were getting the job done."

In addition to championing her cause in the executive suite, Ms. Anderson's mentor has made her aware of company politics—"something many competent people forget and then wonder why they aren't moving ahead faster."

Ms. Anderson may have found the perfect occupation for a person who dislikes routine tasks and thrives on challenge and responsibility. Furthermore, she dislikes sitting behind a desk and enjoys moving around the factory, talking to workers, and trying to solve problems. "Being able to think on your feet is extremely important. In this job, my decisions can affect hundreds of thousands of dollars worth of production. And my decisions hold. They aren't easily appealed."

Ms. Anderson's ability to come up with instant solutions to tough problems has, on occasion, turned enemies into allies. Once a lead man had to bring a highly technical problem to Ms. Anderson because his boss was out sick. The lead man had broadcast his displeasure when Ms. Anderson was hired, so the sour look on his face as he awaited an answer came as no surprise. After a moment's reflection, Ms. Anderson delivered her verdict. The man was dumbfounded. It was precisely the decision he would have made—but it was coming from a woman! "He was my pal from then on. It's amazing how competence can win people over."

But not everyone. Periodically, Ms. Anderson contends with discriminatory remarks, but she's learned to turn the other cheek. "The best way to deal with such comments is not to take them personally. I may respond by saying, 'I acknowledge we have a personal difference, but this is work so let's ignore that for now.' If the person persists, I diplomatically turn him aside. I've noticed that the people who witness such scenes find it extremely embarrassing and I know the embarrassment is in my favor, which is one reason I don't overreact. If you don't become frenzied and don't run off complaining to everybody about the behavior of the individual, I find you earn greater respect. And as a result, the barbs are cast less frequently."

Ms. Anderson's career goals were formulated at an early age. "I went into engineering because I liked practical applications of physics and math. I picked mechanical engineering because it's the most general of the engineering disciplines. I wasn't certain what I wanted to do after graduation, but I knew I'd have several choices. I'd learned that whenever there were teams of engineers, a mechanical engineer was usually in charge. That appealed to me because I've always liked to direct things. Even then, a managerial position was a hazy goal. I guess I expected I'd end up out in the field, either as a project manager who travels frequently or in a factory directing a production crew."

Ms. Anderson refined these goals once she was out in the working world. For three years she labored as a theater operations consultant and taught a course in stagecraft at a large Midwestern university. Although she loved the creative latitude of the theater, she found it no substitute for the higher salary and advancement potential a production job in a large corporation could provide.

Ms. Anderson's move into the corporate world was surprisingly effortless. An employment agency got her four interviews—and four job offers. She chose her present employer because of its size, stature, and the quality of its products.

Today, her immediate aims are more money (she's reached a $25,000 plateau) and more responsibility (she'd like to have the quality control inspectors who check products coming off the production line reassigned to her). Her long-range target? . . ."a corporate vice-presidency, of course. I've made no secret of it, and since nobody has made a disparaging remark as yet, I will continue to maintain that as my goal."

Except for her theatrical detour, Ms. Anderson's background and entry into the production field are fairly typical. Her next logical step up would be to department production manager, then to assistant plant manager, plant manager, and production vice-president. If she chose to leave her present employer, she could make an easy transition into several related industries: cosmetics, foods, chemicals, and consumer products in general. She would have to start from near ground zero at each new company, however, because "every manufacturing company has its own production methods."

Ms. Anderson attributes her success to "my engineering background because it's helped me understand the machinery and to my ability to get along with people. Maybe my gender helped a little bit. But I doubt it will help much in the future as more and more women enter the field. And I'm glad to see that because I don't want to get ahead because I'm a woman. I want to get ahead because I'm an exceptionally qualified manager."

BASIC RESOURCES

The following organizations are good sources for additional career information:

For purchasing agents:

National Association of Purchasing Management, Inc.
11 Park Place
New York, New York 10007

For traffic managers:

American Society of Traffic and Transportation, Inc.
547 W. Jackson Boulevard
Chicago, Illinois 60606

For some engineering careers:

American Institute of Industrial Engineers, Inc.
25 Technology Park/Atlanta
Norcross, Georgia 30092

American Society of Mechanical Engineers
345 East 47th Street
New York, New York 10017

American Society of Safety Engineers
850 Busse Highway
Park Ridge, Illinois 60068

CHAPTER 8

WORKING FOR YOURSELF —
In Your Own Business or as a Consultant

It's part of the American Dream: the idea that you too can think up a new kind of product (who would have dreamed of the success of such items as a pet rock or mood ring?) and become a millionaire. But there are other reasons why people go into business for themselves—perhaps to exploit an untapped talent or indulge in a favorite hobby. Or, as one freelancer put it, "It's not just that I don't have to deal with a boss anymore, it's that I have more control over my time and my work. Even though I work longer hours, *I* decide what I do and when I do it."

But no matter how attractive it may seem, working for yourself can also be very risky. No one who hasn't thought about it and planned *very* carefully should go into business for herself. Half of all new small businesses fail, and business failure can be devastating not just financially but personally as well. People who start new businesses always feel very closely tied to them, and when the business fails the feelings of loss as well as of guilt and incompetence can be overwhelming.

People who go into business for themselves must be prepared to manage all the business functions discussed in this Guide—finances, marketing, sales, production, and personnel. They must analyze their resources carefully and plan every aspect of the business, including hiring business professionals when necessary, or turning to the free help available today to women who are starting or running small businesses.

Analyzing Your Resources

A businesswoman must have a number of real resources to go into business for herself successfully. She must have enough *income* to support

Funding for this chapter was provided by Continental Illinois National Bank and Trust.

596

herself with while her business is getting started. She must have the *time* to shop around for the best deal and location and enough *knowledge* of the value of supplies and equipment to know when she is getting a good deal. In terms of marketing, she must know her community well and the type of business that will succeed, and she must have had some *experience* in the area. But most of all she must have the *energy* and *patience* to make it succeed.

Many women have found ways to capitalize on their skills and contacts to get started. Some have tested the market, even gotten initial orders or contracts before setting up. One woman became a free-lance graphic designer on an inspiration:

> I had always thought maybe someday I'd work for myself, but I was new in town and didn't have the contacts to do it. I went around to about ten places that advertised for graphics help, but none of them could afford to pay me what I had been getting. Just on inspiration, I called them all back and asked them if they would like to hire me on a free-lance basis. Six of them said 'yes,' and I was off and running.

The kinds of resources you will need depend partly on the type of business you are opening. The graphics designer, for instance, had to make practically no financial investment in her business. She had an initial set of clients and started in her home by herself. A retail store owner, on the other hand, would need to buy an inventory of things to sell, sign a lease, hire a lawyer to incorporate, buy advertising, and hire sales help all before she opened the doors.

Whatever kind of business you are interested in starting, ask yourself these kinds of questions:

Management

—Have you decided on the form of ownership you will need?
—Do you have management skills or experience?
—Do you know the lawyer you will use?
—Have you set up a bookkeeping system?
—Do you need an accountant?
—What is the best kind of location for your type of business?

Financing

—Do you have a credit record? (Have you ever taken out a loan and paid it back on time?)
—Have you estimated your initial costs, for example, rent, electricity, telephone, stationery, business cards, inventory, etc.?
—Do you know what your operating expenses will be?

—What kind of insurance do you need?

—Can you support yourself while your business is getting started?

Production

—Do you know where you'll buy your supplies?

—Who is going to make the product or perform the service you will offer?

—What kinds of equipment do you need to buy or lease?

—If you get a big order or contract, whom can you call on to help you fulfill it?

Marketing

—What information do you have that there is a need for your product or service? Who is going to buy it?

—How are your customers going to find out about you?

—What kind of advertising or public relations activity do you need?

—Who's going to do your advertising and how much will it cost?

—Do you know how to price your product or service so you'll be making a living after your expenses are paid?

Sales

—Who is going to sell your service or product?

—If you are running the business, will you have time to sell too?

—What kinds of sales techniques sell products like yours?

Human Resources

—Will you need to hire someone to help you? What tasks will they perform?

—What's the going rate for jobs in your area?

—How will you find the right person?

—What are the government requirements dealing with the hiring and working conditions of employees in your type of business?

Choosing Your Business

You can become a business owner in three ways: start your own business, buy a business from its present owner, and buy a franchise. If you start your own business, you'll be starting from scratch. You will need to analyze all your options carefully.

If you buy an existing business, you can use the same process of analyzing resources to evaluate the business that you are buying. For example, instead of asking yourself what the best location would be for your business, ask yourself, "Is *this* business in the right location?"

Business sellers will usually present interested buyers with information about their business. It's very important, however, for you to do your own research and discover the facts you need, on your own, before you make the decision to buy. You will also need a lawyer and accountant to help you assess the information supplied about the business being sold and to help you find out for yourself *why* it is being sold. The lawyer will also help negotiate a fair price. It would be a good idea to go to your local bank first. Banks provide many services for small businesses and give valuable advice to those starting their own businesses.

One way to reduce the risks of owning your own business is to buy a franchise, essentially a contract with a company to be the local distributor or retail outlet for its goods and services. Fast-food companies like McDonald's, Kentucky Fried Chicken, and Carvel's are franchises. But services such as the relatively new real estate franchises, like Century 21, can be franchised, too.

Franchise agreements vary a great deal, but all franchises have their own standard way of doing business. National franchisor companies offer management training, marketing advice, national advertising and promotion campaigns, and a proven product. The investor or franchisee pays an initial fee, arranges for financing (often with the help of the franchisor), buys equipment and supplies from the franchisor, and pays the national franchisor a percentage of the profits.

You can find out about franchises from the local offices or outlets in

---

THE THRILL OF IT ALL: ENTREPRENEUR

> "The fun of working for yourself is watching something grow."

> "When you work for yourself, you can order the best supplies and do it right. You're not accountable to anyone."

> "I'd never go back to working for somebody else. I don't know how to explain it, but it's a real thrill working for yourself, no matter how many hassles there are. If this business fails, I'll start another one."

THE DAILY GRIND: ENTREPRENEUR

*"Oh, do I hate doing the books. The only
thing worse is doing the taxes."*

*"I think about the business all the time —
driving home, eating dinner. I even dream
about it. You can't get away from your work
when you're in business for yourself."*

*"Cash flow is what's killing me. I've got
bills, but my biggest customer is delaying
and delaying. Plus I've got a payroll to meet, and rent too."*

your area, the "Business Opportunities" section of your local newspaper, the national headquarters of the company, or in your public library. Large metropolitan areas often attract annual franchise fairs or expositions where franchisors set up booths to attract investors.

Again, you will need the services of a lawyer to look over the franchise agreement and help you negotiate favorable terms. Another important thing you must do when considering a franchise is to talk to other franchisees in the same business. Find out all you can about the company and how it follows through on its agreements before you invest your money and your time.

Help for Small Businesses

The Small Business Administration (SBA) is a federal agency that gives many kinds of help and advice to small businesses. The SBA is now making a special effort to help women who want to go into business for themselves get started. More than 100 SBA field offices are located in large- and medium-sized cities throughout the country. You can find their phone numbers and addresses in the telephone book under United States Government. (Your local bank can help direct you to SBA services and get you through any red tape that may confront you.)

You can get various kinds of management assistance from the SBA. Its field offices run day-long Pre-Business Workshops a couple of times a month for people who are considering starting a business. These workshops cover the basics of financing, business organization, taxes, insurance, and site selection. SBA field offices also offer individual counseling sessions to help you with your business plan or any of its details. All this advice is free; so be sure to take advantage of it. You can also get more than 300 helpful free publications from the SBA.

And if you need funds (and who doesn't when starting a business?), the SBA can help you get loans or in some cases it will lend you money itself. The SBA offers loan programs—from startup or expansion loans to disaster loans given to businesses damaged as a result of natural disaster to loans that help small businesses comply with government safety or pollution regulations. The SBA also helps small businesses get their share of federal contracts.

Two other places to look for help when starting a business are the Internal Revenue Service (IRS) and your local Chamber of Commerce. The IRS will give you advice on how to keep records for tax purposes, and it also offers some good free booklets. The Chambers of Commerce in large cities often offer programs to help small businesses; look them up in the phone book and call to request information on what your local chamber can do for you. The National Association of Women Business Owners, a relatively new organization, has programs that help women business owners and women considering business ownership in some large cities.

Working for a Consulting Firm

Working for a consulting firm may have many of the characteristics of going into business for yourself. Unless you are not a member of the professional staff or unless you are a lower-level research assistant in a large firm, you can expect to be responsible for some of the functions of a business firm. In effect, you will not just be using your skills in the "production work" of the projects you're involved in but you'll be doing marketing, management, and sales work as well. Your abilities and skills must be sold both to your associates and to potential clients to bring work into the firm. This process is an ongoing one, with the constant need to bring new projects to the firm. You will also be expected to keep up with your special field, seek out new markets for your services and new services for your firm. Finally, you will have to be able to manage your own projects, taking responsibility for the project staff and project budget.

Consulting work involves almost as much variety as business in general. Consulting firms are usually small- to medium-sized businesses that sell services to businesses, industry, institutions, and sometimes to government as well. These services may range from product testing to market research to strategic planning to chemical analysis. Consulting firms abound in all the functional areas of business and in technical and research areas as well. For that reason consulting firms hire people with all kinds of business and technical backgrounds.

Consulting firms, like other businesses, may be individual proprietor-ships, partnerships, or corporations. But even those that have become corporations have something of the flavor of a law office, with senior staff who own or have the greatest interest in the business and junior staff who work closely with senior staff. Research assistants and sup-port staff complete the organization.

Senior staff are expected to bring projects into the firm and make business contacts. They may assign junior staff to their projects and introduce them to the firm's clients. In time, junior staff are expected to be able to make client contacts on their own. In other words, junior and senior staff take on the responsibility for the sales function of the firm: making the initial contact, developing a proposal for the project the client has in mind, negotiating a contract. But unlike other sales people, consulting staff actually carry out the terms of the contract themselves.

Research assistants, although they may do work similar to that of entry-level junior staff, have much less contact with the firm's clients and are usually paid less. The line between research assistant and junior staffer may be as hard to cross as the one between support staff and research assistant. Research assistants usually have few if any adminis-trative responsibilities on a project.

Credentials are important to consulting firms, and those who work for such firms must have good ones if the firm is to be successful. Companies seek out consulting firms because they are looking for experts, people whose technical knowledge or experience is greater than that of the company's own staff, and advanced degrees and years of experience are impressive on the resumes that accompany the consulting firm's project proposals. "Quite frankly, we're looking for all the degrees we can get in a new person," states the recruitment manager of a medium-sized consulting firm. "A Harvard or Stanford MBA with an undergraduate or better yet a master's degree in statistics or chemical engineering can help us make a lot of money and therefore can herself usually do well working for us."

If you want to do consulting work but don't have advanced degrees, experience is a good substitute. Consulting is the one area of business where age counts *for* you not *against* you. "I could really use a few gray hairs and wrinkles," one senior staffer complained. "I look too young now that I've lost some weight. Companies know that you can't go out and get wisdom injections, not even at universities. They know it takes years and years of experience and they want that kind of experienced senior person working on their project. So they look for the gray hair—even if there's nothing underneath it."

Advantages of Consulting Jobs

Women in business may seek out jobs in consulting at different stages of their careers. Some retire from other jobs to work in a consulting firm,

GETTING IN, MOVING UP: CONSULTING

Entry-level jobs in consulting go to people with advanced degrees or people with an established reputation. To advance in consulting you need to be able to bring in business to the firm and manage your own project well. The traditional path is to work as a research associate (a higher-level position than research assistant), then become an assistant project director, and then the project director. Consulting is one way of going into business for yourself. (But you have to make it pretty clear that you *have* business, because "consultant" is something many people put on their resumes when they are out of work looking for a job.)

where their experience and business contacts make them valuable. Part-time work is much more likely to be available in consulting firms than in most businesses. The one disadvantage part-timers face is that they are rarely given administrative responsibilities, and this means their opportunities for advancement are somewhat limited. For women who want to stay home with young children or work while they are earning an advanced degree, part-time consulting jobs are a good way to stay current in their field. In addition, graduate school or business school professors often serve as consultants to business part-time and may hire students to help them on some projects.

Besides offering the possibility for part-time work, consulting is a

THE THRILL OF IT ALL: CONSULTANT

"The thrill for me is in the selling part of consulting —walking in and showing what our firm can do, hooking the client."

"I think the best part of consulting is conceptualizing the project, figuring out what you're going to do and how to do it."

"I like working on a team. There's a lot of cooperation, and not that much competition among people once you're working on a project."

built-in way to look for a new job. If your consulting work includes dealing with clients, you will get a chance to look at many potential employers and to find out what jobs may become available. One financial analyst had her job terminated as a result of a company reorganization. In place of severance pay, she astutely negotiated an independent consulting contract for the firm she had been working for. The contract gave her a reason to visit other companies to study how they handled a particular problem she had worked on. It gave her the chance to learn more, to keep earning money, and (most importantly) to look for a new job as she worked on the contract. It was a perfect tie-in all the way around, and by the time her project report was written, she had a new job.

Disadvantages of Consulting Jobs

In consulting work you work entirely on a project basis, so your salary is paid only when you're working on a project. If you haven't got a project to work on, essentially you haven't got a job. This condition naturally places you under a great deal of pressure to bring in new projects all the time. The work load may also be uneven in consulting firms. It's not uncommon to work 25 hours one week and 60 hours the next as a deadline approaches. And the job insecurity in consulting is accompanied by a lack of a clear hierarchy of authority. On one project you may be project

---

THE DAILY GRIND: CONSULTANT

"You don't always get good feedback from your clients. They don't often say, 'Gee, you did a really great job.' Usually you just drop your report in the mail and wait."

"You have to psych out the client—what they really want or expect. Sometimes you have to draw them out and force them to figure out what they want."

"Managing the workload can be very rough. If you get a lot of short-term projects, you may either have to 'kill' your staff or 'staff up' and then lay them off."

---

director and on another an adviser and on still another a research person, depending in part on which projects you helped attract to the firm.

Martha Tomlinson
Small Business Owner/Manager

Talk to Ms. Tomlinson about starting a business, and the words you hear most frequently are "common sense"; "activity" and "energy" run close seconds. For example, if you ask her about borrowing money and going into debt to start up her rustic roadside inn, she'll say, "Common sense tells me that a business like this must operate for about three years before you realize a profit from it. It takes time to get known—you take a few bad breaks, you learn a lot you never knew before, you strive for a quality product or service—and then maybe after a few years you can make out on it OK, but common sense says there's no 'pie-in-the-sky-get-rich-quick' way to do it."

As for activity, at the age of 49 and widowed with a very limited income, Ms. Tomlinson had, as she puts it, "a talk with myself, and I decided I had to do it because I'm a very active person, always on the go, with a lot of energy, and I want to remain that way—mentally and physically."

Ms. Tomlinson, or "Ms. T.," as her staff and regular customers know her, says that the idea of having her own business came when her husband was still alive, but at that time the plan was to own and operate a lobster boat. She even worked on one for a year, learning the business.

"We had a friend, an old man who'd been on the sea for over 50 years. Fishing and building boats were his livelihood, and I found it fascinating going out with him dragging the nets in the winter at 3 o'clock in the morning, the boat rolling back and forth. Then you brought the catch back and gutted it and iced it up and shipped it to the fish market in New York."

While not everybody's cup of tea, this robust approach to life clearly characterizes Ms. Tomlinson's entrepreneurial spirit. She is skeptical that anyone can make a go of a new business without loving it, being devoted to making it a success every day.

"I love dealing with the public," she says. "My restaurant is very informal; people feel comfortable. 'Repeat' business is so important and we're having more and more regulars. I really felt a need existed for this type of place in this area; there are so many fine dining places, you know, expensive, but there was no place where you could go and get a half-pint of clams to go or a good fresh haddock plate for $2.69."

Needing to be active and actively filling a need resulted in the Local

Yokel, Ms. T.'s unique eatery in rural New England, about 30 miles inland from the coast. But between the need and the fulfillment came the questions and the planning. As Ms. T. puts it, "I filled notebook after notebook—big notebooks—with everything I could find out or might possibly want to know about what I wanted to do. I have a big mouth, and I wasn't afraid to ask questions. I maintain that you should just dig in and get all the information you can and sort it out afterward. Go to places similar to the type you have in mind—I haven't found anybody who isn't delighted to be helpful. And listen, always listen. Get all types of people's opinions on everything, and then make your own decisions.

"I found this place in April of '76, and it was just a shell of a building with a cement floor. I took it from there and battled the state to put in a septic system and. . . ." From there the story is off and running—a story of meticulous planning, complete confidence in what she was doing, and a shrewd nose for business, or what she calls "common sense."

Her stress on detailed planning to the nth degree puzzled some restaurateurs with whom Ms. T. talked. "They said, 'When are you going to open?' I said, 'When I'm ready.' It took me five months to actually get the whole thing together before I opened, which was fine by me. They said, 'You ought to at least get your grill started; you'll miss the holidays.' And I said, 'Oh sure, with the workmen still sawing up on the roof?' They said, 'You'll miss Labor Day.' 'So there's not going to be one next year?' I asked. I told them, 'I'll open when I'm ready.' I opened September 20, and things have run smoothly without a major hitch ever since. Good planning."

Mrs. T. relates that the very first thing she did was to have a thorough physical checkup before undertaking a project so demanding of time and energy. "I'm a widow and I have married children; but I don't think anyone ought to be dependent on someone else and what I was about to tackle is a lot of plain hard work. I think it's a good idea for a person of any age to have a medical exam before taking a job working a minimum of 60, anywhere up to 80, hours a week."

Next came the matter of permits and licensing. "I went to the statehouse, and I checked out with the board of health exactly what you have to have for this type of place. I went to the local fire department, the fire chief, and found out all the rules and regulations—what they want in the building and the way they want it built. Want it set up proper in the first place so I don't have to tear it down later. Really," she insists, "it's all just common sense."

Common sense not to overlook the obvious, which can be the downfall of many a neophyte entrepreneur.

"Of course, our major item is seafood. We're quite a ways into the country out here, and it has to be fresh every day. And what with steamed clams and so forth, I wanted to serve draught beer. So that's another license, and I had the local liquor commissioner come in, and I myself verified the rules and regulations to determine how many square feet I had to have to determine seating capacity. I found this phase of looking into legalities fascinating; I just dug and dug, and it was so interesting that I actually lost 40 pounds during this period, which was great. I was too tired to eat, but happy tired."

After the first year things look promising, but Ms. T. looks forward to the crucial second year. "I have a limited income on which to live that I think everyone starting a business venture ought to have before they plunge in, but my needs are minimal. I know what I want," she says determinedly; "I want my restaurant.

"People come in and tell me that there's something unique and different about this place; they'll say it's cozy. I have 6-foot tables with benches in there—and outside in the summer—and I serve fresh seafood platters, hamburgers ground fresh in the little village every day, frankfurters, and so on. It's great for people on limited incomes. Elderly people come in and meet and stay to chat. And young families with children. I've tried to position myself very carefully in the market that exists here. I'm not depending on the tourists—campers in summer or skiers in winter. They haven't yet discovered we're here, but the local people have been great."

"Find out everything" seems to be Ms. T.'s rule of thumb. And stay abreast of the laws because city, county, and state requirements and codes for businesses are always changing, and that usually involves an expense for the small businessperson.

"Right now," she relates, "my insurance policy is up for renewal, and insurance is very expensive. And also insurers can require you by law to meet certain requirements or they will not issue a policy. Before I opened, I asked the local fire chief to check with the state fire marshal about fire codes, and he checked my place—I had a 5-foot hood over my grill then, and it was all okay to go ahead as it was. But the insurance people didn't want to insure me because I did not have a CO_2 sprinkler system. Other existing restaurants do not have them, and the fire marshal did not know of any law requiring me to have one, and so I got the insurance. But since then they *have* passed such a law, and I have put in more equipment and gone to a 12-foot hood, but I'm going to have to put in the CO_2 system at great expense to keep the insurance."

Trying to gauge food costs can also be something of an art because wholesalers change their prices every week as the market fluctuates, but the food retailer has to advertise food prices in advance, and, as Ms. T. notes, "You cannot pull your menu board and your menu up and down like a yo-yo. So if I don't do my research well ahead and get up on next season's food prices, I'll wind up selling certain items at a loss. So I'm learning to look at that side of things very carefully."

The proprietor of the Local Yokel is aware of the precarious nature of the restaurant business, but not a bit intimidated. "Now I do not have a family to support; if I were younger, the risk would be much, much greater. If it fails, I go down the tube alone; but if it succeeds," she says with a thrill in her voice, "that will be great!"

BASIC RESOURCES

Your library will have a number of books that can help a woman going into business for herself. Two that are especially helpful are:

The Woman's Guide to Starting a Business. Claudia Jessup and Genie Chips. (Holt, Rinehart and Winston)

How to Organize and Operate a Small Business. Clifford M. Baumback, Kenneth Lawyer, and Pearce C. Kelley. (Prentice-Hall)

Write to the Small Business Administration (1441 L Street NW, Washington, D.C. 20416) or call its toll-free number (800– 433– 7212) (Texas only, call 800– 729– 8901) for information on its more than 300 free publications, including

— "Checklist for Going into Business"
— "Measuring the Performance of Salesmen"
— "Advertising Guidelines for Small Retail Firms"

The Internal Revenue Service (Department of the Treasury, 15th Street and Pennsylvania Avenue NW, Washington, D.C. 20220) will advise you on record keeping for tax purposes. Local offices are listed in the phone book under United States Government. Its free booklets include

— "Tax Guide for Small Business"
— "Recordkeeping for a Small Business"

The National Association of Women Business Owners (2000 P Street NW, Washington, D.C. 20036) is a good source of information for women business owners or would-be owners.

QUALIFYING FOR A CAREER IN BUSINESS

Qualifying for a career in the business world means taking an active approach. It's not so clear cut as qualifying for a career in a professional field like law where academic credentials are essentially all you need; rather, both experience and training count. Whether you are looking for your first job or for advancement, it's up to you to manage your own career so that you can get the right combination of training and experience to help you qualify for the job you want.

Taking an active approach toward your career in business means (1) setting goals for yourself, (2) analyzing the strengths of your training and your experience, and (3) planning how to overcome any shortcomings. You will need to take this approach not just when you leave college or business school but several times throughout your career to make sure your credentials and experience enable you to compete successfully.

In the past women in business have not had as many opportunities to make the investment in academic credentials and advanced or specialized courses in their fields as their male counterparts. This situation has sometimes made it easier for the companies women work for to pass them over for promotion. The story of the woman who ran a department on a temporary basis but didn't get the job permanently is not as uncommon as you might think. She may have proved she could do the job, but without a BA or MBA or a professional degree, she didn't have a chance. Women must have academic credentials at least as good as those of their male co-workers if they expect to be successful.

Another reason to take advantage of training opportunities is that it shows high motivation, the desire to get ahead so much admired in the business world. Even if there isn't an in-house seminar or workshop or a company tuition-refund program available to you, consider taking a course on your own at a local university or community college if that would help bolster your career by filling in gaps in your education and experience.

Throughout your business career, company personnel departments and potential managers will review your experience as well as your training before considering you for a job. Even business recruiters interviewing college graduates are not necessarily looking only for courses in business math or economics, good grades, and professor's recommendations. They are looking to see what your work record is, whether they can count on you to come in on time, take deadlines seriously, really "produce."

They will also look to see if your work or college experience prepares you for a particular area of business. For example, did you sell advertising for the yearbook? If so, maybe you'd be good for a job in sales. Recruiters may also look to see what kinds of responsibilities you have had managing either people or money. Were you the president or treasurer of a club at college? That kind of experience can be valuable for launching a business career.

Graduate Degrees

For some business careers, graduate degrees are *very* important. Professional jobs in the business world—as lawyers, social workers, psychologists, nurses—require the same special training they would anywhere else. And advanced engineering degrees in a technical area of importance to the firm, such as industrial engineering in a manufacturing company, can lead to more interesting and technically sophisticated jobs. A move from an engineering to a supervisory and then to a management job is a career path many men engineers have followed.

Why You Should Consider an MBA

For some kinds of business careers, a Master in Business Administration (MBA) is a big help, and in some management careers in many national corporations, it's a necessity. Before the employment crunch of the 70s, an MBA was almost a guarantee of a good entry-level job several rungs above a new employee with only a BA. Today the competition for entering business school has grown (although not to the cutthroat extent it has for law school) and the number of graduates of MBA programs on the job market is growing steadily.

In 1964, 6,000 people were graduated with MBA degrees from the 15 schools that offered them. In 1977 approximately 32,000 students received an MBA from an estimated 550 colleges and universities. Women are making up a substantially larger proportion of this influx. At the

University of Pennsylvania's Wharton School of Business, for example, women averaged less than 4 percent of the students between 1968 and 1970. In 1976 they made up roughly one-quarter of the class—a pattern that is roughly duplicated in business schools throughout the country.

Most graduate schools of management or business administration prefer applicants with some work experience (Columbia University and the University of Chicago are exceptions). This requirement provides you the opportunity to work in the business world and see what area you might like to specialize in, or if an MBA would really help your career, before you commit yourself to the two years and approximately $8,000 to $18,000 that getting an MBA as a full-time student requires.

There's a special advantage to an MBA beyond the knowledge and skills your courses will teach you. At business school you'll have a chance to meet and get to know a group of people like you who plan to have careers in business management. This first network of contacts can be important to you throughout your career.

FINANCIAL AID FOR AN MBA

All graduate schools offering MBA degrees also have financial aid sources. They are your best bet for information on how to get financial support for a degree program. Most graduate schools of business or management tend to offer loans, not grants, to incoming students. They feel that after you've taken their course of study, you should be able to pay them back easily!

Some business schools have joined with businesses and foundations to offer fellowships for gifted minority students. COGME (Council of Opportunity in Graduate Management Education) serves 10 universities: California at Berkeley, Carnegie–Mellon, Chicago, Columbia, Cornell, Harvard, MIT, Stanford, Tuck (Dartmouth), and Wharton (Pennsylvania). Project ABLE (Accelerated Business Leadership) includes Arizona, Atlanta, Howard, Massachusetts, New York University, and Syracuse. The Consortium for Graduate Study in Management: Fellowships for Minorities works with Indiana, North Carolina at Chapel Hill, Rochester, Southern California, Washington at St. Louis, Missouri, and Wisconsin at Madison.

Specific information on financial aid for each graduate school is available in *Graduate Study in Management,* published by Educational Testing Service, $3.95 (Box 2614, Princeton, New Jersey 08540). This book is also available in most college placement libraries.

How to Apply to Business School

Graduate schools of business administration require that applicants take the Graduate Management Admission Test (GMAT). It is given four times a year at locations all across the country. The "GMAT Bulletin of Information," including sample test questions, is available from:

> Graduate Management Admission Test
> Educational Testing Service
> Box 966
> Princeton, New Jersey 08541

An undergraduate background in business is not necessary for admission to an MBA program, but some undergraduate training in economics and enough background in math, particularly calculus or statistics, is essential for working with charts and graphs and handling numbers easily.

Graduate schools of management or business differ widely in what they are looking for in a student. Some, such as Wharton and the Massachusetts Institute of Technology, are looking for a student with a strong quantitative background. Some require a special competency exam for applicants who haven't had much math. Others, Yale and Harvard, for instance, accept very few who haven't had work experience. Other schools, such as Stanford, offer some work/study jobs to students who need them; yet others, such as Harvard, discourage students from working at all during the first year.

In spite of these differences among schools, your application will always be judged on the basis of your GMAT scores, your academic record, your work experience, and your "leadership potential." Like employers, business schools look for applicants who have been an officer or business manager of a campus club or a community organization.

Read business school bulletins or course catalogues carefully. Various business schools have different approaches and somewhat different curricula. If you look for what distinguishes one school from another, you'll be able to pick the schools that best suit your interests. You'll also be able to write a better application form, one that shows you understand and appreciate the special attributes of the school.

What Business School Is Really Like

Graduate schools of management or business were designed to give the student in two years of graduate study the equivalent of five or more years working for a company. Students in many schools now learn the analytical techniques of the business world by the case method, in which students are given materials describing actual business problems to prepare for class. In class these problems are analyzed intensely by both students and professor. Students are expected to be able to dissect the case on their feet in front of the class. Full-time graduate work in the best graduate schools of management demands such hard work that part-time jobs on the side are just not usually possible.

Most graduate business schools have a set curriculum for the first year of study, which often includes courses in economics for managers, financial analysis, production and operations, marketing, and organizational behavior or managing people. The second year is generally more flexible, with fewer required courses and a chance to specialize in one area, such as marketing or health care administration. Many universities also offer the opportunity of taking courses in other schools of the university, for example, the law school.

Many graduate schools of management or business teach their students to work in teams by assigning group projects. Students coming directly from college may find it hard at first to work in a group, particularly working for a group grade. The experience is a really valuable one, however, not just because it simulates "real world" working conditions in business but because it also helps you develop a network of contacts among your classmates.

Company Training Opportunities

Most large firms offer training opportunities for their employees. Take advantage of them. For one thing, they are usually free; for another, it's a feather in your cap to have been selected for the training program. Also, companies usually choose fairly carefully from among area universities, teachers, and training programs to make sure they're the most relevant to company needs.

Even if you are presently working, neither you nor your manager or supervisor may be aware of what your company can offer you. It may be up to you to find it out. If you are interviewing for a job, it's important to find out about the firm's training opportunities. Companies can offer five kinds of training opportunities: cooperative, tuition refund, in-house training, special training for certain jobs, and special programs for women. Some companies offer all five types; others may offer only one or two.

Cooperative Programs

Many universities and community colleges have teamed up with businesses in their areas to offer cooperative programs. Usually a form of work/study program, they pay the student for the hours she works and are usually geared to the special needs of the business. For example, Polaroid Corporation has a cooperative program with Northeastern University in Boston to train specially selected employees in chemistry, electrical engineering, and physics, among other fields.

Some cooperative programs are designed for students who are not company employees. The students work in business jobs on a part-time basis and earn academic credit. Participation in this type of program is a good way to get to know what a company is like and to let management see what you can do.

Tuition Refund

Tuition refund is a common type of educational opportunity for a company to offer its employees. In a tuition-refund program the firm pays all or part of your education at a local university or community college if you maintain a certain grade point average and if your education is relevant to your work. Usually you must be in a degree program to qualify. Sometimes a company will offer "release time," or time off from work, at no reduction in pay for employees in tuition-refund programs. One of the most elaborate programs of the tuition-refund type is that offered by the Kimberly-Clark Corporation, which has a system of educational credits based on the number of years an employee has worked with the company. These credits can be saved up and used to pay for further education for an employee or any member of her immediate family.

In-House Training

Many companies have their own training programs, some of which may be designed to meet special needs within the company. Equitable Life Insurance Company, for instance, will train employees from all parts of the company to be life insurance salespeople. Some firms, like the Chemicals and Plastics Division of Union Carbide, even have separate sales training facilities where sales trainees spend a few weeks getting to know company products and the techniques that sell them. Sales is an area in which many companies offer training.

Management or supervisory training is another such area. For new managers there may be company workshops in company personnel and management techniques. Sometimes management training is offered to new employees or lower-level employees who the company feels have the potential for a career in management. In many large corporations, all kinds of seminars, courses, and workshops are available to middle- and upper-level managers, often as perquisites or special bonuses; these courses and workshops can be on almost any topic, from transcendental meditation to new methods of financial planning.

If you get a chance to take advantage of in-house training workshops or courses in your career field, by all means do so. These courses are often good and very well taught. But company courses also have the added advantage of introducing you to people in other parts of the firm. In-house courses can give you, not only a chance to make valuable contacts and gain some visibility, but also a chance to learn important information, for instance, where the growth areas in the company are or what departments may be cut back.

THREE TRADITIONAL CAREER TRAPS FOR WOMEN

Some traditional traps for women may lead to career dead ends, although some can be used as stepping stones if they are handled the right way. Learn to recognize the traps and avoid them.

The Token Woman. Some women have been appointed to positions with great titles, fairly good salaries, and no power. There usually aren't any women in positions above them or around them. The work of the corporation goes on around these women, but they don't participate in the decision-making process. Opportunities for women in a token position are few unless another token position is created higher up the ranks of management.

Some token women have used their good title, high visibility, and lack of heavy workload as an opportunity to look for a position in another firm, one in which women have an opportunity to do serious work. Another way women have gotten out of this trap is by devising projects beyond the normal scope of their offices, and then using that project as a stepping stone to find a job with substance inside or outside the company.

Affirmative Action Officer. This job has a built-in trap. If a woman does her job as Affirmative Action officer well, she is likely to anger supervisors throughout the firm or at least to make them resentful of the "interference" in their hiring process. If she doesn't do her job well, she'll be known as that nice person who isn't doing her job well. In other words, it's very hard to win.

If you are faced with this sort of dilemma, the only way out is to talk the problem over with the person offering you the job *before* you accept. Ask quite frankly what other jobs in the company this one will prepare you for. One advantage for those holding Affirmative Action positions is that they are frequently not in the regular personnel hierarchy; they often report to top corporate officers. This factor gives you a chance to show top management what you can do, if you can solve the dilemma of the nature of the job.

Family Traps. The most difficult trap for women to deal with is the tendency for you and the men you work with to fall into patterns of behavior that are based on family roles: "mommy," "daddy's little girl," and "the patient wife." Women who have fallen into these traps may not realize it until they want to advance to another job. That's when the reaction is something like "My precious child will get hurt going out into the bad world," or "Mommy's abandoning us, and we can't make it without her," or "How could you leave me after all we've been through together?" The people you work with may try almost anything to keep you a member of "the family."

These family traps can be personally very difficult for women who haven't seen the problem coming. Most women have a sense of loyalty to the place they work or the people for whom they work. The trick is to stay loyal to yourself by putting your own career first. Eric Berne's *Games People Play* (Westminster, Maryland: Ballantine Books, 1978, $2.25) may give you some perspectives on how to deal with patterns of behavior you may see developing. Transactional analysis, a theory about how people behave, to which Berne has been a major contributor, is frequently taught to managers in company management training programs.

Special Programs for Women

As a part of their effort to move women into more responsible positions, some concerns offer special programs for their women employees, ranging from an afternoon workshop run by outside experts to a comprehensive management development plan for promising individuals. But before you rush over and sign up, ask yourself some questions:

(1) *Will participation in the program stigmatize me?* Is the program

---

HAS YOUR CAREER HIT A DEAD END?

Today there is such an emphasis on advancement in the business world that some people feel they should be seeking advancement even if they like the job they have. As a manager for a large insurance company said wistfully:

> I know I should have really gotten a broader background or a variety of experience. I'll never be able to move past the job I have now or its equivalent. But, you know, while I'd really like to have a better job with a better title, I'd much rather be doing what I'm doing.

So the first thing to ask yourself if your career has hit a dead end is, "Do I mind?"

If the answer is yes and you really *are* unhappy, bored, used, trapped, or miserable, how can you get unstuck? The only way is to set yourself new goals and arrange for the training or experience that will help you accomplish them. The hard part is working up the energy and self-confidence to get *un*stuck. These books can help:

> *What Color Is Your Parachute?* Richard Bolles. (Berkeley, California: Ten Speed Press, 1978, $4.95)
> *Self-Assessment and Career Development,* John P. Kotter, Victor A. Faux and Charles McArthur. (Englewood Cliffs, New Jersey: Prentice-Hall, 1978, $15.95)

The basic process described in both books is the same: assess your current abilities, figure out where you want to go, and plan how to get there. You've probably used the same process in your work for your company. Professional career counselors can help you with this analysis, but unless you have talked to people they have helped, be cautious about whom you sign up with because some are very expensive while others are not at all helpful.

The best person to talk to about your career objectives is your boss. You may not want to divulge your immediate career objectives, especially if they involve leaving your present job. But if you approach the topic the right way, your boss can give you valuable information about how others perceive you and your abilities and job performance. Others you should consult about your career issues are your family, your co-workers, and the personnel office of your company.

Find out what kinds of training opportunities are available where you work. What kinds of experience might be helpful to you? Don't be afraid to volunteer for it. One woman in a staff position in corporate headquarters asked her boss if she could help him with the part of his job that involved troubleshooting at company field offices, saying that she needed to understand the problems in the field to do her own job better. She ended up where she wanted to be, managing a field office.

Remember, in the dynamic world of business, there are many, many chances and choices for you. New opportunities knock on your door every business day. Take full advantage of them.

---

considered merely remedial? Who will know I've taken it? Who else is taking it and what do I think of them?

(2) *What is the followup on the program?* Will my manager be involved? Will the program give me a chance for a promotion or a new job? Will it qualify me for a training program open to both men and women?

One old-line company felt that if its women employees had some workshops in assertiveness training they would have more chances to get ahead. But when the women who took the workshops went back to their jobs and acted assertively, their managers were furious with them.

The best special programs for women involve not just the woman but her manager as well.

(3) *Will the special program give me something I need?* Will it help me learn special skills or earn credit toward a certificate or degree? Will it help fill a gap in my experience or education?

Some companies have offered seminars for their women employees so that they would appear to be doing something, without thoroughly evaluating or backing what they were offering. "What will it do for my career?" is a good question to ask.

ADDITIONAL RESOURCES

Additional references to consult about careers in business:

Advertising: Its Role in Modern Marketing, S. Watson Dunn and Arnold M. Barba. 3d ed. New York: Dryden Press, 1974.

The Bankers, Martin Mayer. New York: Weybright and Talley, 1974.

Book Publishing: What It Is; What It Does. John Dessauer. New York: R. R. Bowker, 1974.

Consultants and Consulting Organizations, Paul Wasserman and W. R. Greer, Jr. Ithaca, New York: Graduate School of Business and Public Administration, Cornell University, 1976.

Creative Salesmanship: Understanding Essentials, Kenneth B. Haas and John W. Ernest. 2d ed. Riverside, New Jersey: Glencoe Press, 1974.

An Introduction to Computer Systems, Richard A. Bassler and Edward O. Joslin. 2d ed. Arlington, Virginia: College Readings, Inc., 1972.

Modern Retailing Management: Basic Concepts and Practices, Delbert J. Duncan and C. Phillips. 8th ed. Homewood, Illinois: Richard D. Irwin, 1972.

Professional Guide to Public Relations, Richard Weiner. Englewood Cliffs, New Jersey: Prentice-Hall, Inc.

Up Your Own Organization. A Handbook for the Employed, the Underemployed, and the Self-Employed on How to Start and Finance a New Business, Donald M. Dible. Santa Clara, California: The Entrepreneur Press, 1971.

What Advertising Agencies Are: What They Do and How They Do It, Frederic R. Gamble. New York: American Association of Advertising Agencies, 1963. This is a free pamphlet.

COMPENDIUM OF BUSINESS CAREERS

(The following list of careers is not meant to be exhaustive but rather to give an idea of the range of career options.)

Accountant. Designs financial record-keeping systems and analyzes and prepares financial statements. Prepares tax returns, audits company records, analyzes investments, and prepares budgets. Specialized training necessary. Bachelor's or master's in accounting and some training in computer technology desirable for positions. Beginning accountants earned $11,500 in 1976; chief accountants, between $20,500 and $33,900.

Accounting positions in a company include:

Budget Department Auditor. Prepares estimates of income and expenses.

Controller. Top corporate accountant overseeing all accounting departments.

Cost Accountant. Keeps records of company expenses for labor and materials and advises on pricing company products.

Credit and Collection Department Auditor. Manages billing process.

Internal Auditor. Analyzes company financial records.

Tax Department Accountant. Prepares company income tax forms.

Certified Public Accountant. Works for public accounting firms. Provides companies with audits, income tax advice and preparation, and financial management advice and analysis. Trainees in major firms increasingly expected to have graduate degrees; also trained by the company that hires. Certification requires passage of examinations and, in almost every state, two years' public accounting experience. Entry-level salaries generally higher than average accounting salaries; partners in major accounting firms may earn more than $50,000.

Administrative Assistant. Helps executives organize correspondence, forms, record-keeping systems, office services, work flow, and budgets. Often a transition job from clerical work; many do some clerical work.

Some positions may require college degree. Salaries vary with level of responsibility.

Advertising Workers. Help businesses persuade people to buy products and services through advertisements in magazines, newspapers, on TV and radio programs, and on billboards. Work directly for businesses or for advertising agencies. Advanced education and training not as important as talent and experience, especially in creative jobs like artist and copywriter.

Account Executive. Responsible for overseeing all of advertising agency's work for particular client. In 1975 average salary: $18,500.

Artist. Layout artists design and illustrate advertisements. May also sketch sample scenes for TV. In 1975 average earnings: junior layout artists, $9,300; senior layout artist, $12,900; art director, $17,100 and up.

Copywriter. Writes text for ads. May work closely with account executives, specializing in copy for a particular market, group of consumers, or product. In 1975 average earnings: junior copywriters, $10,500; senior copywriter, $16,500; copy chief (supervisor of copywriters), $22,300.

Director/Manager. Manages firm's advertising. Salaries higher in companies producing consumer goods than in industrial products firms. In 1975 median salary range: $8,000 to $34,000, depending on annual sales volume of firm.

Media Director. Decides which TV, radio stations, newspapers, or magazines most effective for selling company product or service and what combination of media to use. May also act as space and time buyer. In 1975 average salary: $16,800.

Production Manager. Handles details of ad production—printed for publications, filmed for TV, and recorded for radio. In 1975 average salary: $14,400.

Space/Time Buyer. Generally has business or sales background. Negotiates contracts for advertising space in newspapers and magazines or air time on radio and TV. Entry-level buyers averaged $9,500 in 1975.

Bookkeeper. Maintains business financial records such as orders and bills, operates complex bookkeeping machines, types vouchers and invoices, and prepares income statements. High school diploma with courses in business mathematics minimum requirement. On average, bookkeepers earn more than other clerical workers: with experience, $805 a month in 1976.

Bank Occupations

Bank Clerk. Handles paperwork in banks. High school diploma with courses in bookkeeping, typing, office machine operation, and business mathematics frequently expected. Salaries lower than those for other industries.

Office/Manager. Often starts as management trainee in a one- or two-year bank-run training program. Degree expected; increasingly MBA. In 1976 earned $800 to $900 a month without graduate degree, $1,000 to $1,400 with graduate degree. Senior bank officers earn several times these salaries, although salaries vary with size of bank. Employees in large banks tend to earn more.

Bank officers include:

Branch Manager. Runs branch banks.

Correspondent Bank Officer. Responsible for relations with other banks.

International Officer. Advises on overseas financial dealings.

Loan Officer. Has authority to lend money to individuals and businesses.

Operations Officer. Does internal administrative work.

Trust Officer. In charge of investing money for individuals and corporations.

Teller. Handles customer financial transactions in commercial banks; cashing checks, selling traveler's checks, computing interest on accounts, entering deposits, and making withdrawals on accounts. Also responsible for keeping track of transactions handled and balancing cash drawer. High school diploma necessary. In 1976 most earned betwen $125 and $175 a week.

Controller. *See* Accountant.

Corporate Treasurer. Is responsible for managing company investments and capital needs, projecting economic trends, and setting company financial policy. Top corporate officer may earn over $100,000 in large corporations.

Electronic Data Processing

Console Operator. Makes sure computer is properly loaded, starts machine and monitors it while operating. In 1976 average salaries: $150 week for beginners, $210 for experienced operators, and $230 to $260 for a lead operator.

Keypuncher, Data Typist, Etc. Feed data into machine. May have high school diploma and some clerical skills. Earnings on par with other clerical jobs in 1976: from $120 week average for trainees to $180 for experienced.

Programmer. Writes detailed problem-solving instructions for computers, altering program if it doesn't produce desired results. Training at technical schools, universities, community colleges; plus company training on new job. Most have college education: in high-technology companies, advanced degrees may be required. In 1976 average salaries: $200 a week for trainees, for programmers $375.

Systems Analyst. Plans how to process data and derive needed information. Discuss with company management problem to be solved or analysis to be made; prepares plans for programmers to follow. Degree in computer science, accounting, and business management important. Most start out as programmers. In 1976, average salaries: for beginning analysts, $250 week, for lead analysts $400.

Financial Analyst. Interprets investment data, and research; analyzes financial trends, investment risks, and economic influences. College and often an advanced degree required. May be economist or statistician. Salaries vary with education and responsibility.

Industrial Engineer. Determines how to use people, machines, and materials most efficiently. Designs production and control systems and distribution systems for products. Two-thirds work for manufacturers. Degree or advanced specialized training necessary. Average starting salary in 1976: $14,568.

Insurance Workers

Actuary. Specialized statistician able to estimate likelihood that a certain insurable risk, such as death, accident, fire, and theft, will occur during a given period of time. Calculates price (premium) insurance company should charge for assuming that risk. Increased use of insurance and recent government regulations concerning union and company pension funds have created high demand for actuaries. A particular sequence of training and examination is necessary; strong background in mathematics is essential. In 1976 college graduates who had not yet passed any of required actuarial exams averaged $10,000; full-fledged actuary earned average of $43,000 in life insurance companies.

Agent/Broker. Sells insurance policies. Agent either insurance company employee or independent authorized to represent one or more companies. Broker is independent and not under contract with any single company, may place clients' policies with different companies. Both agents and brokers must be state licensed. Degree preferred for most insurance sales jobs, but high school graduate with proven sales ability may be hired. Large companies may spend six months or more training new agents, paying them as much as $1,000 a month during training period; after that on commission basis. No limit to earnings: thousands earn over $30,000; most successful make more than $100,000.

Claim Representative. Settles policyholders' claims for insured loss. *Claim adjuster* in property–liability insurance companies determines whether policy covers loss and estimates actual loss. *Insurance investigator* or *claim examiner* works for life insurance agencies to straighten out policyholders' problems, find lost beneficiaries, etc. Degrees not always required. Special professional training programs available. Most states require licensing of adjusters. In 1976 claim adjusters averaged $13,000; claim supervisors, $17,300.

Underwriter. Appraises and selects risks insurance company will insure. Works in life insurance company home office and assesses medical risks. In property/liability companies may also work in field offices with company agents and appraise risks of damage, loss, or personal injury for potential client. Degree preferred, but small companies may hire without. Continued training, usually at company expense, necessary to advance to senior positions. Salaries tend to be higher in larger companies. In 1976 average earnings: with two to four years' experience in life insurance, $12,600; supervisors, $17,500 to $23,000.

Manager. Oversees supervisors and other managers. Generally, top corporate management sets company policy and long-range plans, which middle management carries out. College degree is required, advanced degree helpful. Salaries vary with industry, geographic location, and level of management. Among the highest-paid workers in America; entry-level salaries with an MBA between $16,000 and $23,000.

Manufacturer's Representative/Manufacturer's Sales Representative. Sells mainly to other businesses. Specialists in certain industries or products. May require specialized training usually provided by manufacturer. Degree increasingly desirable; necessary for selling complex products. Considerable traveling may be required. Usually works on salary plus commission. In 1976 starting salaries for inexperienced, from $6,000 to over $24,000; highest-paid earned $40,000 and up.

Marketing Research Workers. Conduct marketing surveys by mail, telephone, and in person. Analyze data gathered on products and sales, make recommendations to company officials on product design and promotion. May make sales forecasts and analyze company data as well. Most employed in manufacturing companies, advertising agencies, independent marketing research firms.

Analyst. Interprets research data and runs research projects. Experienced may earn over $19,000 a year.

Assistant/Junior Analyst. Management trainee in market research. May start with tasks similar to those of field supervisors; writes reports on survey findings. Degree usually required; master's in business administration, statistics, or related fields may be necessary to advance. Knowledge of data processing increasingly important. In 1976 salary about $11,000; with graduate degrees, $15,000 in entry-level positions.

Brand Manager. Directs and coordinates research and promotion for a particular brand company manufactures. Undergraduate or master's degree required. Salaries vary from company to company; many earn $22,000 and up.

Director. Manages marketing research department. May come from technical marketing specialty or research analysis position. Advanced degrees important. Salaries well over $25,000.

Field Supervisor. Oversees work of interviewers and directs office workers who tabulate data. Some college work may be required. Pay somewhat higher than that of workers they supervise.

Interviewer. Generally has high school diploma and earns just above minimum wage. May have to own car.

Miscellaneous: Statistician, Computer Expert, Psychologist. Do motivational research for marketing. Tend to have advanced degrees or specialized training and earn salaries commensurate with training.

Mechanical Engineer. Researches, designs, and tests power-producing and power-using machines. Work varies by industry. Three-quarters work for manufacturers. Degree or advanced specialized training necessary. In 1976 average starting salary, $14,964.

Personnel Occupations

Administrator. Oversees corporate personnel functions. May have advanced training in administration or psychology as well as undergraduate degree. In unionized companies may need background in labor relations, collective bargaining, or labor economics. Can earn $30,000 or more.

Employee Benefits Supervisor. Responsible for company benefits, such as health insurance, life insurance, disability insurance, and pension plans. May have highly technical background (accountant or actuary, for instance). Salaries comparable to other industry positions for people with same background. Degree needed. Entry-level earnings on par with recruiters or interviewers.

Job Analyst. Analyzes job descriptions and worker qualifications to determine job requirements. Degree usually required. In 1976 average earnings: $11,200; with experience, $19,200.

Labor Relations Specialist. Advises management on union-management relations. May enter field as trainee with graduate training in law or industrial relations, or move from other personnel positions and seek special training. Earns more than other personnel workers.

Recruiter/Employment Interviewer. Screens current or perspective employees for company jobs. Expected to travel. May administer tests and discuss pay and working conditions. Degree is usually required. Salaries from $11,000 to $16,000.

Salary and Wage Administrator. Establishes pay systems equitable to company employees and in compliance with law and labor contracts. Degree is required. Averaged $19,800 in 1976.

Training Specialist. Devises and conducts training sessions for employees. May counsel employees with work-related problems or planning retirement. Background and compensation vary with training programs and companies.

Purchasing Agent. Buys raw materials, parts, finished goods, or services needed for company operations. Selects suppliers, meets with manufacturer's representatives, and maintains inventory of supplies. Over half of agents work for manufacturers. Degree required by most large companies. In 1976 average earnings: entry-level junior agents, $11,700; department managers, $24,000.

Public Relations Workers. Keep public aware of company activities and accomplishments and inform company management on public attitudes. Write speeches and arrange conferences for company officials, produce company publications, make arrangements for media stories on the company. Make all company publicity arrangements. Employed by corporations, universities, government, and public relations consulting firms. *Entry-level positions* include writers, researchers, graphic designers, photographer. College education required. In 1976 starting salaries from $7,000 to $10,000.

Account Executive. Works for consulting firms and handles one client's public relations program. Degree and public relations experience required. Averaged $15,000 in 1975.

Director. In charge of corporate public relations department. In 1975 average earnings: $20,100 in small companies; of large departments, $21,000 to $31,000, depending on annual sales volume of firm. Executives of major consulting firms earn significantly more.

Quality Control Personnel. Inspects finished product for compliance with specifications and legal requirements. May come from production-line jobs, and may have technical school background. Many belong to unions. This level earned between $2.70 and $7.02 an hour in 1976. In high-technology companies, specialists may have engineering or graduate degrees in variety of fields. Salary reflects training and experience.

Real Estate.

Agent. Shows real estate to prospective buyers or renters, arranges for sale or lease, searches for new properties to list. Must be licensed by state; many states require formal training program as well as special exam to qualify for licensing. Almost all work strictly on commission which varies with value and type of property sold or rented. In 1965 average earnings: $13,000.

Broker. Independent business person who may oversee the work of agents; manages sales or rental transaction and own offices. Appraises real estate, manages property, and develops new building projects. Licensed by state; many states require one to three years of experience as an agent before broker's examination taken. In 1976 average earnings: $27,000.

Retail Trades

Buyer. Orders merchandise for stores. To advance, degree from trade school, junior college, or college increasingly necessary. Some stores have training programs. Frequently required to travel. In 1976 most earned between $15,000 and $25,000.

Department Manager. Supervises areas of store and their sales and stock personnel. *Merchandise manager* coordinates activities of related departments. Usually positions require college education;

further training often provided by large employers. Merchandise managers often expected to travel. Many retail managers earned over $25,000 in 1976.

Sales Clerk/Retail Clerk. Helps customers find what they want, writes up sales, assists with inventory. High school diploma usually required. Inexperienced usually paid minimum wage. Experienced earned $4.37 hour on average in 1977.

Safety Engineer. Designs and manages safety programs to prevent accidents on company premises and ensure safety standards for company products. Must know government safety regulations and take seminars or continuing education courses to keep up with changing technologies. Bachelor's degree in science or engineering required; graduate degree helpful in some high-technology industries. In 1976 average salaries: started at $12,000 to $15,000; experienced averaged $18,000 to $22,000.

Sales Manager. Oversees work of sales representatives. Establishes sales territories and goals, arranges for training of sales staff, reports to management on sales volume. Frequently promoted from sales representative. Salaries generally above sales staff supervised. Incentive bonuses sometimes given.

Selling Positions. *See* specific subjects as Insurance, Manufacturer, Real Estate, Retail Sales.

Stockbroker/Securities Salesperson. Often called *Account Executive.* Sells stocks and bonds or shares in mutual funds to individuals or large institutions; for example, to universities, corporations, mutual funds, and insurance companies. Almost every state requires passage of special licensure examination and posting of personal bond. Usually must be registered as representative of firm with stock exchange where firm does business. Registration requires special training (usually offered by employer), a character investigation, and another examination. Trainees usually salaried until licensed and registered; then commission basis. In 1976 average earnings: stockbroker serving individual investors, $25,000; those on institutional accounts, $44,000.

Supervisor. Oversees production employees, manages production schedules, estimates worker hours, interprets company policy to employees, maintains some employee and production records. First-level management job. Some college work may be required. Salaries vary depending on production salaries in industry.

Traffic Manager, Industrial. Arranges for transportation of materials and finished products. Analyzes modes of transportation, selects appropriate carrier and route. Degree becoming important for entry-level jobs. In 1976 starting salaries began at $11,000, ranged to over $50,000 for traffic executive.